THE
FAMILY READER
OF
AMERICAN
MASTERPIECES

RALPH L. WOODS

AUTHOR OF

AMERICA REBORN: A PLAN FOR THE DECENTRALIZATION
OF INDUSTRY
PILGRIM PLACES IN NORTH AMERICA, *A Guide to
Catholic Shrines* (with Henry F. Woods)

EDITOR OF

A TREASURY OF THE FAMILIAR
BEHOLD THE MAN, *An Anthology of Jesus Christ*
THE WORLD OF DREAMS, *The Literature of Dreaming
from the Pharaohs to Freud*
A SECOND TREASURY OF THE FAMILIAR
A TREASURY OF INSPIRATION
THE BUSINESSMAN'S BOOK OF QUOTATIONS
A TREASURY OF CATHOLIC THINKING
THE CONSOLATIONS OF CATHOLICISM
THE CATHOLIC COMPANION TO THE BIBLE
A TREASURY OF THE DOG
A TREASURY OF FRIENDSHIP
THE CATHOLIC CONCEPT OF LOVE AND MARRIAGE
THE FAMILY READER OF AMERICAN MASTERPIECES

THE
FAMILY READER
OF
AMERICAN
MASTERPIECES

Compiled and Edited by RALPH L. WOODS

THOMAS Y. CROWELL COMPANY

New York · *Established 1834*

ACKNOWLEDGMENTS

The editor and the publisher are grateful to the following publishers, authors, copyright owners, and agents for granting permission to use the material indicated below:

CHICAGO DAILY NEWS: George Weller's dispatch from the Pacific, December 14, 1942.

BOB CONSIDINE: his International News Service story on the Lewis-Schmeling fight, June 22, 1938.

JOHN DOS PASSOS: from *U.S.A.*, by John Dos Passos, published by Houghton Mifflin Company, copyright, 1930, 1958, John Dos Passos.

DOUBLEDAY & COMPANY, INC.: *Adventures in Contentment*, by David Grayson, copyright, 1906, 1907, by The Phillips Publishing Co. copyright 1907 by Doubleday & Company, Inc.

HARCOURT, BRACE AND COMPANY, INC.: From *The People, Yes*, by Carl Sandburg, copyright, 1936, by Harcourt, Brace and Company, Inc.; from *Babbitt* by Sinclair Lewis, copyright, 1922, by Harcourt, Brace and Company, Inc.; renewed, 1950, by Sinclair Lewis; from *Collected Edition of Heywood Broun*, copyright, 1941, by Heywood Hale Broun; from *A Curtain of Green and Other Stories* by Eudora Welty, copyright, 1938, by Eudora Welty.

LOUIS A. TOEPFER: from address by Justice Oliver Wendell Holmes, New York, N. Y., February 15, 1913.

THE VIKING PRESS, INC.: from *The Grapes of Wrath* by John Steinbeck, copyright, 1939, by John Steinbeck; from *Philosopher's Holiday*, by Irwin Edman, copyright, 1938, by Irwin Edman.

W. W. WHITE: pieces by William Allen White from *Emporia Gazette*, July 27, 1922, December 23, 1925.

WIDE WORLD PHOTOS, INC.: from Associated Press dispatches by Kirk L. Simpson, November 9–11, 1921, and Hal Boyle, May 12, 1956.

I am grateful to Jean Meeker for superb typing, to the editorial department of the Thomas Y. Crowell Company for good suggestions, and particularly thankful to Josephine Rogers who cheerfully gave so generously of her time and skill to this project.

Ramsey, N. J.   R.L.W.

PREFACE

Barely two hundred years have passed since men like Thomas Paine were moved by the tensions of pre-Revolutionary times to write their masterful essays. Yet within that short period, every aspect of a growing and expanding country has been recorded in every form of writing from fiction and poetry to essays and news reporting. In compiling this anthology, I have chosen from this vast heritage those selections that seem most readable today.

To many people, any writing of an earlier age seems dated and stylized. I have here tried to dispel this notion by including writings from every period in order to show how often masterly writers have created works that transcend particular events in specific times to become universal and timeless. Considered together, these selections reveal the distinct flavor of American writing; they also prove that much of what was readable, entertaining and informative in the eighteenth and nineteenth centuries is equally so in this age of the atom. And, when a work fits this definition, I feel justified in calling it a masterpiece.

Good short stories abound: from Edgar Allan Poe and Bret Harte to William Saroyan and William Faulkner; from the world of the essay there is frivolous Benchley and austere Emerson; excerpts from the novel go back to Herman Melville's *Moby Dick* and continue to John Steinbeck's *The Grapes of Wrath*; poetry ranges from Walt Whitman to Robert Frost; journalism is represented by Ernie Pyle, among others, with his graphic reporting of World War II. And, of course, there is adventure, history, travel, speeches, satire and humor.

Many of these works are truly literary masterpieces and would always be quoted as examples of literary trends and the best of American writing.

Others show the variety of American life; and for this reason I have organized the book along regional lines, heading the four sections North, South, Midwest and West. Consequently, the placement of each piece has been determined by its locale, rather than by the author's home base. Sometimes, of course, both are the same. Nathaniel Hawthorne lived in New England and wrote about it. But Francis Parkman, also a New Englander, did his best work about the West. For the most part, the selections are arranged chronologically within each geographical section, except where a deviation would add to the effectiveness of that particular extract. Thus, E. B. White's essay on Walden is more meaningful when placed next to Thoreau's writing, though a strict chronological order would place it much later.

Above all, I have tried very hard to compile a book of *masterpieces*, American writings that will appeal to every mood of the modern American family and illuminate the infinite richness of our literary heritage.

RALPH L. WOODS

CONTENTS

ix

THE SOUTH

THE MIDWEST

THE WEST

THE
FAMILY READER
OF
AMERICAN
MASTERPIECES

THOMAS WOLFE

"Go, Seeker, If You Will"

Go, seeker, if you will, throughout the land and you will find us burning in the night.

There where the hackles of the Rocky Mountains blaze in the blank and naked radiance of the moon, go make your resting stool upon the highest peak. Can you not see us now? The continental wall juts sheer and flat, its huge black shadow on the plain, and the plain sweeps out against the East, two thousand miles away. The great snake that you see there is the Mississippi River.

Behold the gem-strung towns and cities of the good, green East, flung like star-dust through the field of night. That spreading constellation to the north is called Chicago, and that giant wink that blazes in the moon is the pendant lake that it is built upon. Beyond, close-set and dense as a clenched fist, are all the jeweled cities of the eastern seaboard. There's Boston, ringed with the bracelet of its shining little towns, and all the lights that sparkle on the rocky indentations of New England. Here, southward and a little to the west, and yet still coasted to the sea, is our intensest ray, the splintered firmament of the towered island of Manhattan. Round about her, sown thick as grain, is the glitter of a hundred towns and cities. The long chain of lights there is the necklace of Long Island and the Jersey shore. Southward and inland, by a foot or two, behold the duller glare of Philadelphia. Southward further still, the twin constellations— Baltimore and Washington. Westward, but still within the borders of the good, green East, that nighttime glow and smolder of hell-fire is Pittsburgh. Here, St. Louis, hot and humid in the cornfield belly of the land, and bedded on the mid-length coil and fringes of the snake. There at the snake's mouth, southward six hundred miles or so, you see the jeweled

1

crescent of old New Orleans. Here, west and south again, you see the gemmy glitter of the cities on the Texas border.

Turn now, seeker, on your resting stool atop the Rocky Mountains, and look another thousand miles or so across moon-blazing fiend-worlds of the Painted Desert and beyond Sierras' ridge. That magic congeries of lights there to the west, ringed like a studded belt around the magic setting of its lovely harbor, is the fabled town of San Francisco. Below it, Los Angeles and all the cities of the California shore. A thousand miles to north and west, the sparkling towns of Oregon and Washington.

Observe the whole of it, survey it as you might survey a field. Make it your garden, seeker, or your backyard patch. Be at ease in it. It's your oyster—yours to open if you will.

You Can't Go Home Again, 1940

THE NORTH

THOMAS PAINE

"These Are the Times That Try Men's Souls"

Paine's brilliant pamphleteering during the Revolutionary War inspired the hesitant and persuaded the doubting to take up arms. His writing was an invaluable service that Washington acknowledged.

These are the times that try men's souls: The summer soldier and the sunshine patriot will in this crisis, shrink from the service of his country; but he that stands it NOW, deserves the love and thanks of man and woman. Tyranny, like hell, is not easily conquered; yet we have this consolation with us, that the harder the conflict, the more glorious the triumph. What we obtain too cheap, we esteem too lightly:—'Tis dearness only that gives everything its value. Heaven knows how to put a proper price upon its goods; and it would be strange indeed, if so celestial an article as FREEDOM should not be highly rated. Britain, with an army to enforce her tyranny, has declared that she has a right (*not only to*) TAX but "to BIND *us in* ALL CASES WHATSOEVER," and if being *bound in that manner*, is not slavery, then is there not such a thing as slavery upon earth. Even the expression is impious, for so unlimited a power can belong only to GOD.

Whether the Independence of the Continent was declared too soon, or delayed too long, I will not now enter into as an argument; my own simple opinion is, that had it been eight months earlier, it would have been much better. We did not make a proper use of last winter, neither could we, while we were in a dependent state. However, the fault, if it were one, was all our own; we have none to blame but ourselves. But no great deal is lost yet; all that Howe has been doing for this month past, is rather a ravage than a conquest, which the spirit of the Jersies a year ago would have

5

quickly repulsed, and which time and a little resolution will soon recover.

I have as little superstition in me as any man living, but my secret opinion has ever been, and still is, that God Almighty will not give up a people to military destruction, or leave them unsupportedly to perish, who have so earnestly and so repeatedly sought to avoid the calamities of war, by every decent method which wisdom could invent. Neither have I so much of the infidel in me, as to suppose that he has relinquished the government of the world, and given us up to the care of devils; and as I do not, I cannot see on what grounds the king of Britain can look up to Heaven for help against us: a common murderer, a highwayman, or a house-breaker, has as good a pretence as he.

'Tis surprising to see how rapidly a panic will sometimes run through a country. All nations and ages have been subject to them: Britain has trembled like an ague at the report of a French fleet of flat-bottomed boats; and in the fourteenth century the whole English army, after ravaging the kingdom of France, was driven back like men petrified with fear; and this brave exploit was performed by a few broken forces collected and headed by a woman, Joan of Arc. Would that heaven might inspire some Jersey maid to spirit up her countrymen, and save her fair fellow sufferers from ravage and ravishment! Yet panics, in some cases, have their uses; they produce as much good as hurt. Their duration is always short; the mind soon grows through them, and acquires a firmer habit than before. But their peculiar advantage is, that they are the touchstones of sincerity and hypocrisy, and bring things and men to light, which might otherwise have lain forever undiscovered. In fact, they have the same effect on secret traitors which an imaginary apparition would have upon a private murderer. They sift out the hidden thoughts of man, and hold them up in public to the world. Many a disguised Tory has lately shown his head, that shall penitentially solemnize with curses the day on which Howe arrived upon the Delaware. . . .

I shall not attempt to give all the particulars of our retreat to the Delaware; suffice it for the present to say, that both officers and men, though greatly harassed and fatigued, frequently without rest, covering, or provision, the inevitable consequences of a long retreat, bore it with a manly and martial spirit. All their wishes centred in one, which was, that the country would turn out and help them to drive the enemy back. *Voltaire* has remarked that King William never appeared to full advantage but in difficulties and in action; the same remark may be made on General Washington, for the character fits him. There is a natural firmness in some minds which cannot be unlocked by trifles, but which, when unlocked, discovers a cabinet of fortitude; and I reckon it among those kind of public blessings, which we do not immediately see, that GOD hath blessed him with uninterrupted health, and given him a mind that can even flourish upon care.

I shall conclude this paper with some miscellaneous remarks on the

6

state of our affairs; and shall begin with asking the following question: Why is it that the enemy have left the New-England provinces, and made these middle ones the seat of war? The answer is easy: New England is not infested with Tories, and we are. I have been tender in raising the cry against these men, and used numberless arguments to show them their danger, but it will not do to sacrifice a world either to their folly or their baseness. The period is now arrived, in which either they or we must change our sentiments, or one or both must fall. And what is a Tory? GOOD GOD! what is he? I should not be afraid to go with a hundred Whigs against a thousand Tories, were they to attempt to get into arms. Every Tory is a coward; for servile, slavish, self-interested fear is the foundation of Toryism; and a man under such influence, though he may be cruel, never can be brave.

But before the line of irrecoverable separation be drawn between us, let us reason the matter together: Your conduct is an invitation to the enemy, yet not one in a thousand of you has heart enough to join him. Howe is as much deceived by you as the American cause is injured by you. He expects you will all take up arms, and flock to his standard, with muskets on your shoulders. Your opinions are of no use to him, unless you support him personally, for 'tis soldiers, and not Tories, that he wants.

I once felt all that kind of anger, which a man ought to feel against the mean principles that are held by the Tories: A noted one, who kept a tavern at Amboy, was standing at his door, with as pretty a child in his hand, about eight or nine years old, as I ever saw, and after speaking his mind as freely as he thought was prudent, finished with this unfatherly expression, *"Well! give me peace in my day."* Not a man lives on the continent but fully believes that a separation must some time or other finally take place, and a generous parent should have said, *"If there must be trouble, let it be in my day, that my child may have peace:"* and this single reflection, well applied, is sufficient to awaken every man to duty. Not a place upon earth might be so happy as America. Her situation is remote from all the wrangling world, and she has nothing to do but to trade with them. A man can distinguish himself between temper and principle, and I am as confident, as I am that GOD governs the world, that America will never be happy till she gets clear of foreign dominion. Wars, without ceasing, will break out till that period arrives, and the continent must in the end be conqueror; for though the flame of liberty may sometimes cease to shine, the coal can never expire.

America did not, nor does not want force; but she wanted a proper application of that force. Wisdom is not the purchase of a day, and it is no wonder that we should err at the first setting off. From an excess of tenderness, we were unwilling to raise an army, and trusted our cause to the temporary defence of a well-meaning militia. A summer's experience has now taught us better; yet with those troops, while they were collected, we were able to set bounds to the progress of the enemy, and, thank God!

they are again assembling. I always considered militia as the best troops in the world for a sudden exertion, but they will not do for a long campaign. Howe, it is probable, will make an attempt on this city [Philadelphia]; should he fail on this side the Delaware, he is ruined. If he succeeds, our cause is not ruined. He stakes all on his side against a part on ours; admitting he succeeds, the consequences will be, that armies from both ends of the continent will march to assist their suffering friends in the middle states; for he cannot go everywhere, it is impossible. I consider Howe as the greatest enemy the Tories have; he is bringing war into their country, which, had it not been for him and partly for themselves, they had been clear of. Should he now be expelled, I wish with all the devotion of a Christian, that the names of Whig and Tory may never more be mentioned; but should the Tories give him encouragement to come, or assistance if he come, I as sincerely wish that our next year's arms may expel them from the continent, and the Congress appropriate their possessions to the relief of those who have suffered in well-doing. A single successful battle next year will settle the whole. America could carry on a two years' war by the confiscation of the property of disaffected persons, and be made happy by their expulsion. Say not that this is revenge, call it rather the soft resentment of a suffering people, who, having no object in view but the GOOD of ALL, have staked their OWN ALL upon a seemingly doubtful event. Yet it is folly to argue against determined hardness; eloquence may strike the ear, and the language of sorrow draw forth the tear of compassion, but nothing can reach the heart that is steeled with prejudice.

Quitting this class of men, I turn with the warm ardor of a friend to those who have nobly stood, and are yet determined to stand the matter out: I call not upon a few, but upon all: not in THIS state or THAT state, but on EVERY state: up and help us; lay your shoulders to the wheel; better have too much force than too little, when so great an object is at stake. Let it be told to the future world, that in the depth of winter, when nothing but hope and virtue could survive, that the city and country, alarmed at one common danger, came forth to meet and to repulse it. Say not that thousands are gone, turn out your tens of thousands; throw not the burden of the day upon Providence, but *"shew your faith by your works,"* that God may bless you. It matters not where you live, or what rank of life you hold, the evil or the blessing will reach you all. The far and the near, the home counties and the back, the rich and the poor, will suffer or rejoice alike. The heart that feels not now is dead; the blood of his children will curse his cowardice, who shrinks back at a time when a little might have saved the whole, and made *them* happy. I love the man that can smile in trouble, that can gather strength from distress, and grow brave by reflection. 'Tis the business of little minds to shrink; but he whose heart is firm, and whose conscience approves his conduct, will pursue his principles unto death. My own line of reasoning is to my-

8

self as straight and clear as a ray of light. Not all the treasures of the world, so far as I believe, could have induced me to support an offensive war, for I think it murder; but if a thief breaks into my house, burns and destroys my property, and kills or threatens to kill me, or those that are in it, and to *"bind me in all cases whatsoever"* to his absolute will, am I to suffer it? What signifies it to me, whether he who does it is a king or a common man; my countryman or not my countryman; whether it be done by an individual villain, or an army of them? If we reason to the root of things we shall find no difference; neither can any just cause be assigned why we should punish in the one case and pardon in the other. Let them call me rebel and welcome, I feel no concern from it; but I shall suffer the misery of devils, were I to make a whore of my soul by swearing allegiance to one whose character is that of a sottish, stupid, stubborn, worthless, brutish man. I conceive likewise a horrid idea in receiving mercy from a being, who at the last day shall be shrieking to the rocks and mountains to cover him, and fleeing with terror from the orphan, the widow, and the slain in America.

There are cases which cannot be overdone by language, and this is one. There are persons, too, who see not the full extent of the evil which threatens them; they solace themselves with hopes that the enemy, if he succeed, will be merciful. It is the madness of folly, to expect mercy from those who have refused to do justice; and even mercy, where conquest is the object, is only a trick of war: The cunning of the fox is as murderous as the violence of the wolf, and we ought to guard equally against both. . . . Ye men of Pennsylvania, do reason upon these things! Were the back counties to give up their arms, they would fall an easy prey to the Indians, who are all armed; this perhaps is what some Tories would not be sorry for. Were the home counties to deliver up their arms, they would be exposed to the resentment of the back counties, who would then have it in their power to chastise their defection at pleasure. And were any one state to give up its arms, THAT state must be garrisoned by all Howe's army of Britons and Hessians to preserve it from the anger of the rest. Mutual fear is the principal link in the chain of mutual love, and woe be to that state that breaks the compact. . . .

I thank God that I fear not. I see no real cause for fear. I know our situation well, and can see the way out of it. While our army was collected, Howe dared not risk a battle; and it is no credit to him that he decamped from the White Plains, and waited a mean opportunity to ravage the defenseless Jersies; but it is great credit to us, that, with a handful of men, we sustained an orderly retreat for near an hundred miles, brought off our ammunition, all our field-pieces, the greatest part of our stores, and had four rivers to pass. None can say that our retreat was precipitate, for we were near three weeks in performing it, that the country might have time to come in. Twice we marched back to meet the enemy, and remained out till dark. The sign of fear was not seen in our camp, and had not some of the cowardly and disaffected inhabitants spread false alarms through the country, the Jersies had never been ravaged. Once more we are again collected and collecting, our new army at both ends of the continent is recruiting fast, and we shall be able to open the next campaign with sixty thousand men, well armed and clothed. This is our situation, and who will may know it. By perseverance and fortitude we have the prospect of a glorious issue; by cowardice and submission, the sad choice of a variety of evils—a ravaged country—a depopulated city—habitations without safety, and slavery without hope—our homes turned into barracks and bawdy-houses for Hessians, and a future race to provide for, whose fathers we shall doubt of. Look on this picture and weep over it! and if there yet remains one thoughtless wretch who believes it not, let him suffer it unlamented.

The American Crisis, December 1776

BENJAMIN FRANKLIN

Some Episodes from His Autobiography

Franklin's Autobiography, written when he was an old man, was the first American "rags-to-riches" story. Its style is an admirable illustration of the simplicity and sincerity of the man often called a "universal genius."

At Newport we took in a number of passengers for New York, among which were two young women, companions, and a grave, sensible, matron-like Quaker woman, with her attendants. I had shown an obliging readiness to do her some little services, which impress'd her I suppose with a degree of good will toward me; therefore, when she saw a daily growing familiarity between me and the two young women, which they appear'd to encourage, she took me aside, and said, "Young man, I am concern'd for thee, as thou has no friend with thee, and seems not to know much of the world, or of the snares youth is expos'd to; depend upon it, those are very bad women; I can see it in all their actions; and if thee art not upon thy guard, they will draw thee into some danger; they are strangers to thee, and I advise thee, in a friendly concern for thy welfare, to have no acquaintance with them." As I seem'd at first not to think so ill of them as she did, she mentioned some things she had observ'd and heard that had escap'd my notice, but now convinc'd me she was right. I thank'd her for her kind advice, and promis'd to follow it. When we arriv'd at New York, they told me where they liv'd, and invited me to come and see them; but I avoided it, and it was well I did; for the next day the captain miss'd a silver spoon and some other things, that had been taken out of his cabbin, and, knowing that these were a couple of strumpets, he got a warrant to search their lodgings, found the stolen goods, and had the thieves punish'd. So, tho' we had escap'd a sunken rock, which we scrap'd upon in the passage, I thought this escape of rather more importance to me.

At New York I found my friend Collins, who had arriv'd there some time before me. We had been intimate from children, and had read the same books together; but he had the advantage of more time for reading and studying, and a wonderful genius for mathematical learning, in which he far outstript me. While I liv'd in Boston, most of my hours of leisure for conversation were spent with him, and he continu'd a sober as well as an industrious lad; was much respected for his learning by several of the clergy and other gentlemen, and seemed to promise making a good figure in life. But, during my absence, he had acquir'd a habit of sotting with brandy; and I found by his own account, and what I heard from others, that he had been drunk every day since his arrival at New York, and behav'd very oddly. He had gam'd, too, and lost his money, so that I was oblig'd to discharge his lodgings, and defray his expenses to and at Philadelphia, which prov'd extremely inconvenient to me.

The then governor of New York, Burnet (son of Bishop Burnet), hearing from the captain that a young man, one of his passengers, had a great many books, desir'd he would bring me to see him. I waited upon him accordingly, and should have taken Collins with me but that he was not sober. The gov'r treated me with great civility, show'd me his library, which was a very large one, and we had a good deal of conversation about books and authors. This was the second governor who had done me the honor to take notice of me; which, to a poor boy like me, was very pleasing.

We proceeded to Philadelphia. I received on the way Vernon's money, without which we could hardly have finish'd our journey. Collins wished to be employ'd in some counting-house; but, whether they discover'd his dramming by his breath, or by his behaviour, tho' he had some recommendations, he met with no success in any application, and continu'd lodging and boarding at the same house with me, and at my expense. Knowing I had that money of Vernon's, he was continually borrowing of me, still promising repayment as soon as he should be in business. At length he had got so much of it that I was distress'd to think what I should do in case of being call'd on to remit it.

His drinking continu'd, about which we sometimes quarrell'd; for, when a little intoxicated, he was very fractious. Once, in a boat on the Delaware with some other young men, he refused to row in his turn. "I will be row'd home," says he. "We will not row you," says I. "You must, or stay all night on the water," says he, "just as you please." The others said, "Let us row; what signifies it?" But, my mind being soured with his other conduct, I continu'd to refuse. So he swore he would make me row, or throw me overboard; and coming along, stepping on the thwarts, toward me, when he came up and struck at me, I clapped my hand under his crutch, and, rising, pitched him head-foremost into the river. I knew he was a good swimmer, and so was under little concern about him; but before he could get round to lay hold of the boat, we had with a few strokes pull'd her out of his reach; and ever when he drew near the boat, we ask'd if he would row, striking a few strokes to slide her away from him. He was ready to die with vexation, and obstinately would not promise to row. However, seeing him at last beginning to tire, we lifted him in and brought him home dripping wet in the evening. We hardly exchang'd a civil word afterwards, and a West India captain, who had a commission to procure a tutor for the sons of a gentlemen at Barbadoes, happening to meet with him, agreed to carry him thither. He left me then, promising to remit me the first money he should receive in order to discharge the debt; but I never heard of him after. . . .

There are croakers in every country, always boding its ruin. Such a one then lived in Philadelphia; a person of note, an elderly man, with a wise look and a very grave manner of speaking; his name was Samuel Mickle. This gentleman, a stranger to me, stopt one day at my door, and asked me if I was the young man who had lately opened a new printing-house. Being answered in the affirmative, he said he was sorry for me, because it was an expensive undertaking, and the expense would be lost; for Philadelphia was a sinking place, the people already half-bankrupts, or near being so; all appearances to the contrary, such as new buildings and the rise of rents, being to his certain knowledge fallacious; for they were, in fact, among the things that would soon ruin us. And he gave me such a detail of misfortunes now existing, or that were soon to exist, that he left me half melancholy. Had I known him before I engaged in this business, probably I never should have done it. This man continued to live in this decaying place, and to declaim in the same strain, refusing for many years to buy a house there, because all was going to destruction; and at last I had the pleasure of seeing him give five times as much for one as he might have bought it for when he first began his croaking. . . .

I had hitherto continu'd to board with Godfrey, who lived in part of my house with his wife and children, and had one side of the shop for his glazier's business, tho' he worked little, being always absorbed in his mathematics. Mrs. Godfrey projected a match for me with a relation's daughter, took opportunities of bringing us often together, till a serious courtship on my part ensu'd, the girl being in herself very deserving. The old folks encourag'd me by continual invitations to supper, and by leaving us together, till at length it was time to explain. Mrs. Godfrey manag'd our little treaty. I let her know that I expected as much money with their daughter as would pay off my remaining debt for the printing-house, which I believe was not then above a hundred pounds. She brought me word they had no such sum to spare; I said they might mortgage their house in the loan-office. The answer to this, after some days, was, that they did not approve the match; that, on inquiry of Bradford, they had been informed the printing business was not a profitable one; the types would soon be worn out, and more wanted; that S. Keimer and D. Harry had failed one after the other, and I should probably soon follow them; and, therefore, I was forbidden the house, and the daughter shut up.

Whether this was a real change of sentiment or only artifice, on a supposition of our being too far engaged in affection to retract, and therefore that we should steal a marriage, which would leave them at liberty to give or withhold what they pleas'd, I know not; but I suspected the latter, resented it, and went no more. Mrs. Godfrey brought me afterward some more favorable accounts of their disposition, and would have drawn me on again; but I declared absolutely my resolution to have nothing more to do with that family. This was resented by the Godfreys; we differ'd, and they removed, leaving me the whole house, and I resolved to take no more inmates.

But this affair having turned my thoughts to marriage, I look'd around me and made overtures of acquaintance in other places; but soon found that, the business of a printer being generally thought a poor one, I was not to expect money with a wife, unless with such a one as I should not otherwise think agreeable. In the mean time, that hard-to-be-governed passion of youth hurried me frequently into intrigues with low women that fell in my way, which were attended with some expense and great inconvenience, besides a continual risque to my health by a distemper which of all things I dreaded, though by great good luck I escaped it. A friendly correspondence as neighbors and old acquaintances had continued between me and Mrs. Read's family, who all had a regard for me from the time of my first lodging in their house. I was often invited there and consulted in their affairs, wherein I sometimes was of service. I piti'd poor Miss Read's unfortunate situation, who was generally dejected, seldom cheerful, and avoided company. I considered my giddiness and inconstancy when in London as in a great degree the cause of her unhappiness, tho' the mother was good enough to think the fault more her own than mine, as she had prevented our marrying before I went thither, and persuaded the other match in my absence. Our mutual affection was revived, but there were now great objections to our union. . . . We ventured, however, over all these difficulties, and I took her to wife, September 1st, 1730. None of the inconveniences happened that we had apprehended; she proved a good and faithful helpmate, assisted me much by attending the shop; we throve together, and have ever mutually endeavor'd to make each other happy. Thus I corrected that great *erratum* as well as I could. . . .

At the time I established myself in Pennsylvania, there was not a good bookseller's shop in any of the colonies to the southward of Boston. In New York and Philadelphia the printers were indeed stationers; they sold only paper, etc., almanacs, ballads, and a few common school-books. Those who lov'd reading were oblig'd to send for their books from England; the members of the Junto had each a few. We had left the alehouse, where we first met, and hired a room to hold our club in. I propos'd that we should all of us bring our books to that room, where they would not only be ready to consult in our conferences, but become a common benefit, each of us being at liberty to borrow such as he wish'd to read at home. This was accordingly done, and for some time contented us.

Finding the advantage of this little collection, I propos'd to render the benefit from books more common, by commencing a public subscription library. I drew a sketch of the plan and rules that would be necessary, and got a skilful conveyancer, Mr. Charles Brockden, to put the whole in form of articles of agreement to be subscribed, by which each subscriber engag'd to pay a certain sum down for the first purchase of books, and an annual contribution for increasing them. So few were the readers at that time in Philadelphia, and the majority of us so poor, that I was not able, with great industry, to find more than fifty persons, mostly young tradesmen, willing to pay down for this purpose forty shillings each, and ten shillings per annum. On this little fund we began. The books were imported; the library was opened one day in the week for lending to the subscribers, on their promissory notes to pay double the value if not duly returned. The institution soon manifested its utility, was imitated by other towns, and in other provinces. The libraries were augmented by donations; reading became fashionable; and our people, having no publick amusements to divert their attention from study, became better acquainted with books, and in a few years were observ'd by strangers to be better instructed and more intelligent than people of the same rank generally are in other countries.

When we were about to sign the above-mentioned articles, which were to be binding on us, our heirs, etc., for fifty years, Mr. Brockden, the scrivener, said to us, "You are young men, but it is scarcely probable that any of you will live to see the expiration of the term fix'd in the instrument." A number of us, however, are yet living; but the instrument was after a few years rendered null by a charter that incorporated and gave perpetuity to the company.

The objections and reluctances I met with in soliciting the subscriptions, made me soon feel the impropriety of presenting one's self as the proposer of any useful project, that might be suppos'd to raise one's reputation in the smallest degree above that of one's neighbors, when one has need of their assistance to accomplish that project. I therefore put myself as much as I could out of sight, and stated it as a scheme of a *number of friends,* who had requested me to go about and propose it to such as they thought lovers of reading. In this way my affair went on more smoothly, and I ever after practis'd it on such occasions; and, from my frequent successes, can heartily recommend it. The present little sacrifice of your vanity will afterwards be amply repaid. If it remains a while uncertain to whom the merit belongs, some one more vain than yourself will be encouraged to claim it, and then even envy will be disposed to do you justice by plucking those assumed feathers, and restoring them to their right owner.

This library afforded me the means of improvement by constant study, for which I set apart an hour or two each day, and thus repair'd in some degree the loss of the learned education my father once intended for me. Reading was the only amusement I allow'd myself. I spent no time in taverns, games, or frolicks of any kind; and my industry in my business continu'd as indefatigable as it was necessary. I was indebted for my printing-house; I had a young family coming on to be educated, and I had to contend with for business two printers, who were established in the place before me. My circumstances, however, grew daily easier. My original habits of frugality continuing, and my father having, among his instructions to me when a boy, frequently repeated a proverb of Solomon, "Seest thou a man diligent in his calling, he shall stand before kings, he shall not stand before mean men," I from thence considered industry as a means of obtaining wealth and distinction, which encourag'd me, tho' I did not think that I should ever literally *stand before kings*, which, however, has since happened; for I have stood before *five*, and even had the honour of sitting down with one, the King of Denmark, to dinner.

We have an English proverb that says, "He that would thrive, must ask his wife." It was lucky for me that I had one as much dispos'd to industry and frugality as myself. She assisted me cheerfully in my business, folding and stitching pamphlets, tending shop, purchasing old linen rags for the paper-makers, etc, etc. We kept no idle servants, our table was plain and simple, our furniture of the cheapest. For instance, my breakfast was a long time bread and milk (no tea), and I ate out of a twopenny earthen porringer, with a pewter spoon. But mark how luxury will enter families, and make a progress, in spite of principle: being call'd one morning to breakfast, I found it in a China bowl, with a spoon of silver! They had been bought for me without my knowledge by my wife, and had cost her the enormous sum of three-and-twenty shillings, for which she had no other excuse or apology to make, but that she thought *her* husband deserv'd a silver spoon and China bowl as well any any of his neighbors. This was the first appearance of plate and China in our house, which afterward, in a course of years, as our wealth increas'd, augmented gradually to several hundred pounds in value. . . .

In 1732 I first publish'd my Almanack, under the name of *Richard Saunders*; it was continu'd by me about twenty-five years, commonly call'd *Poor Richard's Almanack*. I endeavor'd to make it both entertaining and useful, and it accordingly came to be in such demand, that I reap'd considerable profit from it, vending annually near ten thousand. And observing that it was generally read, scarce any neighborhood in the province being without it, I consider'd it as a proper vehicle for conveying instruction among the common people, who bought scarcely any other books; I therefore filled all the little spaces that occurr'd between the remarkable days in the calendar with proverbial sentences, chiefly such as inculcated industry and frugality, as the means of procuring wealth, and thereby securing virtue; it being more difficult for a man in want, to act always honestly, as, to use here one of those proverbs, *it is hard for an empty sack to stand upright*.

These proverbs, which contained the wisdom of many ages and nations, I assembled and form'd into a connected discourse prefix'd to the Almanack of 1757, as the harangue of a wise old man to the people attending an auction. The bringing all these scatter'd counsels thus into a focus enabled them to make greater impression. The piece, being universally approved, was copied in all the newspapers of the Continent; reprinted in Britain on a broad side, to be stuck up in houses; two translations were made of it in French, and great numbers bought by the clergy and gentry, to distribute gratis among their poor parishioners and tenants. In Pennsylvania, as it discouraged useless expense in foreign superfluities, some thought it had its share of influence in producing that growing plenty of money which was observable for several years after its publication.

I considered my newspaper, also, as another means of communicating instruction, and in that view frequently reprinted in it extracts from the Spectator, and other moral writers; and sometimes publish'd little pieces of my own, which had been first compos'd for reading in our Junto. Of these are a Socratic dialogue, tending to prove that, whatever might be his parts and abilities, a vicious man could not properly be called a man of sense; and a discourse on self-denial, showing that virtue was not secure till its practice became a habitude, and was free from the opposition of contrary inclinations. These may be found in the papers about the beginning of 1735.

In the conduct of my newspaper, I carefully excluded all libelling and personal abuse, which is of late years become so disgraceful to our country. Whenever I was solicited to insert any thing of that kind, and the writers pleaded, as they generally did, the liberty of the press, and that a newspaper was like a stage-coach, in which any one who would pay had a right to a place, my answer was, that I would print the piece separately if desired, and the author might have as many copies as he pleased to distribute himself, but that I would not take upon me to spread his detraction; and that, having contracted with my subscribers to furnish them with what might be either useful or entertaining, I could not fill their papers with private altercation, in which they had no concern, without doing them manifest injustice. Now, many of our printers make no scruple of gratifying the malice of individuals by false accusations of the fairest characters among ourselves, augmenting animosity even to the producing of duels; and are, moreover, so indiscreet as to print scurrilous reflections on the government of neighboring states, and even on the conduct of our best national allies, which may be attended with the most pernicious consequences. These things I mention as a caution to young printers, and that they may be encouraged not to pollute their presses and disgrace their profession by such infamous practices, but refuse steadily, as they may see by my example that such a course of conduct will not, on the whole, be injurious to their interests.

Autobiography, 1771–1790

WASHINGTON IRVING

Rip Van Winkle

A POSTHUMOUS WRITING OF DIEDRICH KNICKERBOCKER

> *By Woden, God of Saxons,*
> *From whence comes Wensday, that is Wodensday.*
> *Truth is a thing that ever I will keep*
> *Unto thylke day in which I creep into*
> *My sepulchre.*—Cartwright.

[The following Tale was found among the papers of the late Diedrich Knickerbocker, an old gentleman of New York, who was very curious in the Dutch history of the province, and the manners of the descendants from its primitive settlers. His historical researches, however, did not lie so much among books as among men; for the former are lamentably scanty on his favorite topics; whereas he found the old burghers, and still more their wives, rich in that legendary lore, so invaluable to true history. Whenever, therefore, he happened upon a genuine Dutch family, snugly shut up in its low-roofed farmhouse, under a spreading sycamore, he looked upon it as a little clasped volume of black-letter, and studied it with the zeal of a book-worm.

The result of all these researches was a history of the province during the reign of the Dutch governors, which he published some years since. There have been various opinions as to the literary character of his work, and, to tell the truth, it is not a whit better than it should be. Its chief merit is its scrupulous accuracy, which indeed was a little questioned on its first appearance, but has since been completely established; and it is now admitted into all historical collections, as a book of unquestionable authority.

The old gentleman died shortly after the publication of his work, and now that he is dead and gone, it cannot do much harm to his memory to say that his time might have been much better employed in weightier labors. He, however, was apt to ride his hobby his own way; and though it did now and then kick up the dust a little in the eyes of his neighbors, and grieve the spirit of some friends, for whom he felt the truest deference and affection; yet his errors and follies are remembered "more in sorrow than in anger," and it begins to be suspected, that he never intended to injure or offend. But however his memory may be appreciated by critics, it is still held dear by many folk, whose good opinion is well worth having; particularly by certain biscuit-bakers, who have gone so far as to imprint his likeness on their new-year cakes; and have thus given him a chance for immortality, almost equal to the being stamped on a Waterloo Medal, or a Queen Anne's Farthing.]

Whoever has made a voyage up the Hudson must remember the Kaatskill mountains. They are a dismembered branch of the great Appalachian family, and are seen away to the west of the river, swelling up to a noble height, and lording it over the surrounding country. Every change of season, every change of weather, indeed, every hour of the day, produces some change in the magical hues and shapes of these mountains, and they are regarded by all the good wives, far and near, as perfect barometers. When the weather is fair and settled, they are clothed in blue and purple, and print their bold outlines on the clear evening sky; but, sometimes, when the rest of the landscape is cloudless, they will gather a hood of gray vapors about their summits, which, in the last rays of the setting sun, will glow and light up like a crown of glory.

At the foot of these fairy mountains, the voyager may have descried the light smoke curling up from a village, whose shingle-roofs gleam among the trees, just where the blue tints of the upland melt away into the fresh green of the nearer landscape. It is a little village, of great antiquity, having been founded by some of the Dutch colonists, in the early times of the province, just about the beginning of the government of the good Peter Stuyvesant (may he rest in peace!) and there were some of the houses of the original settlers standing within a few years, built of small yellow bricks brought from Holland, having latticed windows and gabled fronts, surmounted with weather-cocks.

In that same village, and in one of these very houses (which, to tell the precise truth, was sadly time-worn and weather-beaten), there lived many years since, while the country was yet a province of Great Britain, a simple good-natured fellow, of the name of Rip Van Winkle. He was a descendant of the Van Winkles who figured so gallantly in the chivalrous days of Peter Stuyvesant, and accompanied him to the siege of Fort Christina. He inherited, however, but little of the martial character of his ancestors. I have observed that he was a simple good-natured man; he was, moreover, a kind neighbor, and an obedient henpecked husband. Indeed, to the latter circumstance might be owing that meekness of spirit which gained him such universal popularity; for those men are most apt to be obsequious and conciliating abroad, who are under the discipline of shrews at home. Their tempers, doubtless, are rendered pliant and malleable in the fiery furnace of domestic tribulation; and a curtain lecture is worth all the sermons in the world for teaching the virtues of patience and long-suffering. A termagant wife may, therefore, in some respects, be considered a tolerable blessing; and if so, Rip Van Winkle was thrice blessed.

Certain it is, that he was a great favorite among all the good wives of the village, who, as usual, with the amiable sex, took his part in all family squabbles; and never failed, whenever they talked those matters over in their evening gossipings, to lay all the blame on Dame Van Winkle. The children of the village, too, would shout with joy whenever he approached. He assisted at their sports, made their playthings, taught them to fly kites and shoot marbles, and told them long stories of ghosts, witches, and Indians. Whenever he went dodging about the village, he was surrounded by a troop of them, hanging on his skirts, clambering on his back, and playing a thousand tricks on him with impunity; and not a dog would bark at him throughout the neighborhood.

The great error in Rip's composition was an insuperable aversion to all kinds of profitable labor. It could not be from the want of assiduity or perseverance; for he would sit on a wet rock, with a rod as long and heavy as a Tartar's lance, and fish all day without a murmur, even though he should not be encouraged by a single nibble. He would carry a fowling-piece on his shoulder for hours together, trudging through woods and swamps, and up hill and down dale, to shoot a few squirrels or wild pigeons. He would never refuse to assist a neighbor even in the roughest toil, and was a foremost man at all country frolics for husking Indian corn, or building stone-fences; the women of the village, too, used to employ him to run their errands, and to do such little odd jobs as their less obliging husbands would not do for them. In a word Rip was ready to attend to anybody's business but his own; but as to doing family duty, and keeping his farm in order, he found it impossible.

In fact, he declared it was of no use to work on his farm; it was the most pestilent little piece of ground in the whole country; every thing about it went wrong, and would go wrong, in spite of him. His fences were continually falling to pieces; his cow would either go astray, or get among the cabbages; weeds were sure to grow quicker in his fields than anywhere else; the rain always made a point of setting in just as he had some out-door work to do; so that though his patrimonial estate had dwindled away under his management, acre by acre, until there was little more left than a mere patch of Indian corn and potatoes, yet it was the worst conditioned farm in the neighborhood.

His children, too, were as ragged and wild as if they belonged to nobody. His son Rip, an urchin begotten in his own likeness, promised to inherit the habits, with the old clothes of his father. He was generally seen trooping like a colt at his mother's heels, equipped in a pair of his father's cast-off galligaskins, which he had much ado to hold up with one hand, as a fine lady does her train in bad weather.

Rip Van Winkle, however, was one of those happy mortals, of foolish, well-oiled dispositions, who take the world easy, eat white bread or brown, whichever can be got with least thought and trouble, and would rather starve on a penny than work for a pound. If left to himself, he would have whistled life away in perfect contentment; but his wife kept continually dinning in his ears about his idleness, his carelessness, and the ruin he was bringing on his family. Morning, noon, and night, her tongue was incessantly going, and every thing he said or did was sure to produce a torrent of household eloquence. Rip had but one way of replying to all lectures of the kind, and that, by frequent use, had grown into a habit. He shrugged his shoulders, shook his head, cast up his eyes, but said nothing. This, however, always provoked a fresh volley from his wife; so that he was fain to draw off his forces, and take to the outside of the house—the only side which, in truth, belongs to a henpecked husband.

Rip's sole domestic adherent was his dog Wolf, who was as much henpecked as his master; for Dame Van Winkle regarded them as companions in idleness, and even looked upon Wolf with an evil eye, as the cause of his master's going so often astray. True it is, in all points of spirit befitting an honorable dog, he was as courageous an animal as ever scoured the woods—but what courage can withstand the ever-during and all-besetting terrors of a woman's tongue? The moment Wolf entered the house his crest fell, his tail drooped to the ground, or curled between his legs, he sneaked about with a gallows air, casting many a sidelong glance at Dame Van Winkle, and at the least flourish of a broomstick or ladle, he would fly to the door with yelping precipitation.

Times grew worse and worse with Rip Van Winkle as years of matrimony rolled on; a tart temper never mellows with age, and a sharp tongue is the only edged tool that grows keener with constant use. For a long time he used to console himself, when driven from home, by frequenting a kind of perpetual club of the sages, philosophers, and other idle personages of the village; which held its sessions on a bench before a small inn, designated by a rubicund portrait of His Majesty George the Third. Here they used to sit in the shade through a long lazy summer's day, talking listlessly over village gossip, or telling endless sleepy stories about nothing. But it would have been worth any statesman's money to have heard the profound discussions that sometimes took place, when by chance an old newspaper fell into their hands from some passing traveller. How solemnly they would listen to the contents, as drawled out by Derrick Van Bummel, the schoolmaster, a dapper learned little man, who was not to be daunted by the most gigantic word in the dictionary; and how sagely they would deliberate upon public events some months after they had taken place.

The opinions of this junto were completely controlled by Nicholas Vedder, a patriarch of the village, and landlord of the inn, at the door of which he took his seat from morning till night, just moving sufficiently to avoid the sun and keep in the shade of a large tree; so that the neighbors could tell the hour by his movements as accurately as by a sun-dial. It is true he was rarely heard to speak, but smoked his pipe incessantly. His adherents, however (for every great man has his adherents), perfectly understood him, and knew how to gather his opinions. When any thing that was read or related displeased him, he was observed to smoke his pipe vehemently, and to send forth short, frequent and angry puffs; but when pleased, he would inhale the smoke slowly and tranquilly, and emit it in light and placid clouds; and sometimes, taking the pipe from his mouth, and letting the fragrant vapor curl about his nose, would gravely nod his head in token of perfect approbation.

From even this stronghold the unlucky Rip was at length routed by his termagant wife, who would suddenly break in upon the tranquillity of the assemblage and call the members all to naught; nor was that august personage, Nicholas Vedder himself, sacred from the daring tongue of this terrible virago, who charged him outright with encouraging her husband in habits of idleness.

Poor Rip was at last reduced almost to despair; and his only alternative, to escape from the labor of the farm and clamor of his wife, was to take gun in hand and stroll away into the woods. Here he would sometimes seat himself at the foot of a tree, and share the contents of his wallet with Wolf, with whom he sympathized as a fellow-sufferer in persecution. "Poor Wolf," he would say, "thy mistress leads thee a dog's life of it; but never mind, my lad, whilst I live thou shalt never want a friend to stand by thee!" Wolf would wag his tail, look wistfully in his master's face, and if dogs can feel pity I verily believe he reciprocated the sentiment with all his heart.

In a long ramble of the kind on a fine autumnal day, Rip had unconsciously scrambled to one of the highest parts of the Kaatskill mountains. He was after his favorite sport of squirrel shooting, and the still solitudes had echoed and re-echoed with the reports of his gun. Panting and fatigued, he threw himself, late in the afternoon, on a green knoll, covered with mountain herbage, that crowned the brow of a precipice. From an opening between the trees he could overlook all the lower country for many a mile of rich woodland. He saw at a distance the lordly Hudson, far, far below him, moving on its silent but majestic course, with the reflection of a purple cloud, or the sail of a lagging bark, here and there sleeping on its glassy bosom, and at last losing itself in the blue highlands.

On the other side he looked down into a deep mountain glen, wild, lonely, and shagged, the bottom filled with fragments from the impending cliffs, and scarcely lighted by the reflected rays of the setting sun. For some time Rip lay musing on this scene; evening was gradually advancing; the mountains began to throw their long blue shadows over the valleys; he saw that it would be dark long before he could reach the village, and he heaved a heavy sigh when he thought of encountering the terrors of Dame Van Winkle.

As he was about to descend, he heard a voice from a distance, hallooing, "Rip Van Winkle! Rip Van Winkle!" He looked around, but could see nothing but a crow winging its solitary flight across the mountain. He thought his fancy must have deceived him, and turned again to descend, when he heard the same cry ring through the still evening air: "Rip Van Winkle! Rip Van Winkle!"—at the same time Wolf bristled up his back, and giving a low growl, skulked to his master's side, looking fearfully down into the glen. Rip now felt a vague apprehension stealing over him; he looked anxiously in the same direction, and perceived a strange figure slowly toiling up the rocks, and bending under the weight of something he carried on his back. He was surprised to see any human being in this lonely and unfrequented place, but supposing it to be some one of the neighborhood in need of his assistance, he hastened down to yield it.

On nearer approach he was still more surprised at the singularity of the stranger's appearance. He was a short square-built old fellow, with thick bushy hair, and a grizzled beard. His dress was of the antique Dutch fashion—a cloth jerkin strapped round the waist—several pair of breeches, the outer one of ample volume, decorated with rows of buttons down the sides, and bunches at the knees. He bore on his shoulder a stout keg, that seemed full of liquor, and made signs for Rip to approach and assist him with the load. Though rather shy and distrustful of this new acquaintance, Rip complied with his usual alacrity; and mutually relieving one another, they clambered up a narrow gully, apparently the dry bed of a mountain torrent. As they ascended, Rip every now and then heard long rolling peals, like distant thunder, that seemed to issue out of a deep ravine, or rather cleft, between lofty rocks toward which their rugged path conducted. He paused for an instant, but supposing it to be the muttering of one of those transient thunder-showers which often take place in mountain heights, he proceeded. Passing through the ravine, they came to a hollow, like a small amphitheatre, surrounded by perpendicular precipices, over the brinks of which impending trees shot their branches, so that you only caught glimpses of the azure sky and the bright evening-cloud. During the whole time Rip and his companion had labored on in silence; for though the former marvelled greatly what could be the object of carrying a keg of liquor up this wild mountain, yet there was something strange and incomprehensible about the unknown, that inspired awe and checked familiarity.

On entering the amphitheatre, new objects of wonder presented themselves. On a level spot in the centre was a company of odd-looking personages playing at nine-pins. They were dressed in a quaint outlandish fashion; some wore short doublets, others jerkins, with long knives in their belts, and most of them had enormous breeches, of similar style with that of the guide's. Their visages, too, were peculiar: one had a large beard, broad face, and small piggish eyes: the face of another seemed to consist entirely of nose, and was surmounted by a white sugar-loaf hat, set off with a little red cock's tail. They all had beards, of various shapes and colors. There was one who seemed to be the commander. He was a stout old gentleman, with a weather-beaten countenance; he wore a laced doublet, broad belt and hanger, high crowned hat and feather, red stockings, and high-heeled shoes, with roses in them. The whole group reminded Rip of the figures in an old Flemish painting, in the parlor of Dominie Van Schaick, the village parson, and which had been brought over from Holland at the time of the settlement.

What seemed particularly odd to Rip was, that though these folks were evidently amusing themselves, yet they maintained the gravest faces, the most mysterious silence, and were, withal, the most melancholy party of pleasure he had ever witnessed. Nothing interrupted the stillness of the scene but the noise of the balls, which, whenever they were rolled, echoed along the mountains like rumbling peals of thunder.

As Rip and his companion approached them, they suddenly desisted from their play, and stared at him with such fixed statue-like gaze, and such strange, uncouth, lack-lustre countenances, that his heart turned within him, and his knees smote together. His companion now emptied the contents of the keg into large flagons, and made signs to him to wait upon the company. He obeyed with fear and trembling; they quaffed the liquor in profound silence, and then returned to their game.

By degrees Rip's awe and apprehension subsided. He even ventured, when no eye was fixed upon him, to taste the beverage, which he found had much of the flavor of excellent Hollands. He was naturally a thirsty soul, and was soon tempted to repeat the draught. One taste provoked another; and he reiterated his visits to the flagon so often that at length his senses were overpowered, his eyes swam in his head, his head gradually declined, and he fell into a deep sleep.

On waking, he found himself on the green knoll whence he had first seen the old man of the glen. He rubbed his eyes—it was a bright sunny morning. The birds were hopping and twittering among the bushes, and the eagle was wheeling aloft, and breasting the pure mountain breeze. "Surely," thought Rip, "I have not slept here all night." He recalled the occurrences before he fell asleep. The strange man with a keg of liquor— the mountain ravine—the wild retreat among the rocks—the wobegone party at nine-pins—the flagon—"Oh! that flagon! that wicked flagon!" thought Rip—"what excuse shall I make to Dame Van Winkle!"

He looked round for his gun, but in place of the clean, well-oiled fowling-piece, he found an old firelock lying by him, the barrel incrusted with rust, the lock falling off, and the stock worm-eaten. He now suspected that the grave roysters of the mountain had put a trick upon him, and, having dosed him with liquor had robbed him of his gun. Wolf, too, had disappeared, but he might have strayed away after a squirrel or partridge. He whistled after him and shouted his name, but all in vain; the echoes repeated his whistle and shout, but no dog was to be seen.

He determined to revisit the scene of the last evening's gambol, and if he met with any of the party, to demand his dog and gun. As he rose to walk, he found himself stiff in the joints, and wanting in his usual activity. "These mountain beds do not agree with me," thought Rip, "and if this frolic should lay me up with a fit of the rheumatism, I shall have a blessed time with Dame Van Winkle." With some difficulty he got down into the glen: he found the gully up which he and his companion had ascended the preceding evening; but to his astonishment a mountain stream was now foaming down it, leaping from rock to rock, and filling the glen with babbling murmurs. He, however, made shift to scramble up its sides, working his toilsome way through thickets of birch, sassafras, and witch-hazel, and sometimes tripped up or entangled by the wild grapevines that twisted their coils or tendrils from tree to tree, and spread a kind of network in his path.

At length he reached to where the ravine had opened through the cliffs to the amphitheatre; but no traces of such opening remained. The rocks presented a high impenetrable wall over which the torrent came tumbling in a sheet of feathery foam, and fell into a broad deep basin, black from the shadows of the surrounding forest. Here, then, poor Rip was brought to a stand. He again called and whistled after his dog; he was only answered by the cawing of a flock of idle crows, sporting high in air about a dry tree that overhung a sunny precipice; and who, secure in their elevation, seemed to look down and scoff at the poor man's perplexities. What was to be done? the morning was passing away, and Rip felt famished for want of his breakfast. He grieved to give up his dog and gun; he dreaded to meet his wife; but it would not do to starve among the mountains. He shook his head, shouldered the rusty firelock, and, with a heart full of trouble and anxiety, turned his steps homeward.

As he approached the village he met a number of people, but none whom he knew, which somewhat surprised him, for he had thought himself acquainted with every one in the country round. Their dress, too, was of a different fashion from that to which he was accustomed. They all stared at him with equal marks of surprise, and whenever they cast their eyes upon him, invariably stroked their chins. The constant recurrence of

24

this gesture induced Rip, involuntarily, to do the same, when, to his astonishment, he found his beard had grown a foot long!

He had now entered the skirts of the village. A troop of strange children ran at his heels, hooting after him, and pointing at his gray beard. The dogs, too, not one of which he recognized for an old acquaintance, barked at him as he passed. The very village was altered; it was larger and more populous. There were rows of houses which he had never seen before, and those which had been his familiar haunts had disappeared. Strange names were over the doors—strange faces at the windows—every thing was strange. His mind now misgave him; he began to doubt whether both he and the world around him were not bewitched. Surely this was his native village, which he had left but the day before. There stood the Kaatskill mountains—there ran the silvery Hudson at a distance—there was every hill and dale precisely as it had always been—Rip was sorely perplexed —"That flagon last night," thought he, "has addled my poor head sadly."

It was with some difficulty that he found the way to his own house, which he approached with silent awe, expecting every moment to hear the shrill voice of Dame Van Winkle. He found the house gone to decay —the roof fallen in, the windows shattered, and the doors off the hinges. A half-starved dog that looked like Wolf was skulking about it. Rip called him by name, but the cur snarled, showed his teeth, and passed on. This was an unkind cut indeed—"My very dog," sighed poor Rip, "has forgotten me!"

He entered the house, which, to tell the truth, Dame Van Winkle had always kept in neat order. It was empty, forlorn, and apparently abandoned. This desolateness overcame all his connubial fears—he called loudly for his wife and children—the lonely chambers rang for a moment with his voice, and then all again was silence.

He now hurried forth, and hastened to his old resort, the village inn— but it too was gone. A large rickety wooden building stood in its place, with great gaping windows, some of them broken and mended with old hats and petticoats, and over the door was painted, "the Union Hotel, by Jonathan Doolittle." Instead of the great tree that used to shelter the quiet little Dutch inn of yore, there was now reared a tall naked pole, with something on the top that looked like a red night-cap, and from it was fluttering a flag, on which was a singular assemblage of stars and stripes— all this was strange and incomprehensible. He recognized on the sign, however, the ruby face of King George, under which he had smoked so many a peaceful pipe; but even this was singularly metamorphosed. The red coat was changed for one of blue and buff, a sword was held in the hand instead of a sceptre, the head was decorated with a cocked hat, and underneath was painted in large characters, GENERAL WASHINGTON.

There was, as usual, a crowd of folk about the door, but none that Rip recollected. The very character of the people seemed changed. There was a busy, bustling, disputatious tone about it, instead of the accustomed phlegm and drowsy tranquillity. He looked in vain for the sage Nicholas Vedder, with his broad face, double chin, and fair long pipe, uttering clouds of tobacco-smoke instead of idle speeches; or Van Bummel, the schoolmaster, doling forth the contents of an ancient newspaper. In place of these, a lean, bilious-looking fellow, with his pockets full of handbills, was haranguing vehemently about rights of citizens—elections—members of congress—liberty—Bunker's Hill—heroes of seventy-six—and other words, which were a perfect Babylonish jargon to the bewildered Van Winkle.

The appearance of Rip, with his long grizzled beard, his rusty fowling-piece, his uncouth dress, and an army of women and children at his heels, soon attracted the attention of the tavern politicians. They crowded round him, eyeing him from head to foot with great curiosity. The orator bustled up to him, and, drawing him partly aside, inquired "on which side he voted?" Rip stared in vacant stupidity. Another short but busy little fellow pulled him by the arm, and, rising on tiptoe, inquired in his ear, "Whether he was Federal or Democrat?" Rip was equally at a loss to comprehend the question; when a knowing, self-important old gentleman, in a sharp cocked hat, made his way through the crowd, putting them to the right and left with his elbows as he passed, and planting himself before Van Winkle, with one arm akimbo, the other resting on his cane, his keen eyes and sharp hat penetrating, as it were, into his very soul, demanded in an austere tone, "what brought him to the election with a gun on his shoulder, and a mob at his heels, and whether he meant to breed a riot in the village?"— "Alas! gentlemen," cried Rip, somewhat dismayed, "I am a poor quiet man, a native of the place, and a loyal subject of the king, God bless him!"

Here a general shout burst from the by-standers—"A tory! a tory! a spy! a refugee! hustle him! away with him!" It was with great difficulty that the self-important man in the cocked hat restored order; and, having assumed a tenfold austerity of brow, demanded again of the unknown culprit, what he came there for, and whom he was seeking? The poor man humbly assured him that he meant no harm, but merely came there in search of some of his neighbors, who used to keep about the tavern.

"Well—who are they?—name them."

Rip bethought himself a moment, and inquired, "Where's Nicholas Vedder?"

There was a silence for a little while, then an old man replied, in a thin piping voice, "Nicholas Vedder! why, he is dead and gone these eighteen years! There was a wooden tombstone in the church-yard that used to tell all about him, but that's rotten and gone too."

"Where's Brom Dutcher?"

"Oh, he went off to the army in the beginning of the war; some say he was killed at the storming of Stony Point—others say he was drowned in

26

a squall at the foot of Anthony's Nose. I don't know—he never came back again."

"Where's Van Bummel, the schoolmaster?"

"He went off to the wars too, was a great militia general, and is now in congress."

Rip's heart died away at hearing of these sad changes in his home and friends, and finding himself thus alone in the world. Every answer puzzled him, too, by treating of such enormous lapses of time, and of matters which he could not understand: war—congress—Stony Point;—he had no courage to ask after any more friends, but cried out in despair, "Does nobody here know Rip Van Winkle?"

"Oh, Rip Van Winkle!" exclaimed two or three, "Oh, to be sure! that's Rip Van Winkle yonder, leaning against the tree."

Rip looked, and beheld a precise counterpart of himself, as he went up the mountain: apparently as lazy, and certainly as ragged. The poor fellow was now completely confounded. He doubted his own identity, and whether he was himself or another man. In the midst of his bewilderment, the man in the cocked hat demanded who he was, and what was his name?

"God knows," exclaimed he, at his wit's end; "I'm not myself—I'm somebody else—that's me yonder—no—that's somebody else got into my shoes—I was myself last night, but I fell asleep on the mountain, and they've changed my gun, and every thing's changed, and I'm changed, and I can't tell what's my name, or who I am."

The by-standers began now to look at each other, nod, wink significantly, and tap their fingers against their foreheads. There was a whisper, also, about securing the gun, and keeping the old fellow from doing mischief, at the very suggestion of which the self-important man in the cocked hat retired with some precipitation. At this critical moment a fresh comely woman pressed through the throng to get a peep at the gray-bearded man. She had a chubby child in her arms, which, frightened at his looks, began to cry. "Hush, Rip," cried she, "hush, you little fool; the old man won't hurt you." The name of the child, the air of the mother, the tone of her voice, all awakened a train of recollections in his mind. "What is your name, my good woman?" asked he.

"Judith Gardenier."

"And your father's name?"

"Ah, poor man, Rip Van Winkle was his name, but it's twenty years since he went away from home with his gun, and never has been heard of since—his dog came home without him; but whether he shot himself, or was carried away by the Indians, nobody can tell. I was then but a little girl."

Rip had but one more question to ask; but he put in with a faltering voice:

"Where's your mother?"

"Oh, she too had died but a short time since; she broke a blood-vessel in a fit of passion at a New-England peddler."

There was a drop of comfort, at least, in this intelligence. The honest man could contain himself no longer. He caught his daughter and her child in his arms. "I am your father!" cried he—"Young Rip Van Winkle once—old Rip Van Winkle now!—Does nobody know poor Rip Van Winkle?"

All stood amazed, until an old woman, tottering out from among the crowd, put her hand to her brow, and peering under it in his face for a moment, exclaimed, "Sure enough! it is Rip Van Winkle—it is himself!—Welcome home again, old neighbor—Why, where have you been these twenty long years?"

Rip's story was soon told, for the whole twenty years had been to him but as one night. The neighbors stared when they heard it; some were seen to wink at each other, and put their tongues in their cheeks: and the self-important man in the cocked hat, who, when the alarm was over, had returned to the field, screwed down the corners of his mouth, and shook his head—upon which there was a general shaking of the head throughout the assemblage.

It was determined, however, to take the opinion of old Peter Vander-donk, who was seen slowly advancing up the road. He was a descendant of the historian of that name, who wrote one of the earliest accounts of the province. Peter was the most ancient inhabitant of the village, and well versed in all the wonderful events and traditions of the neighborhood. He recollected Rip at once, and corroborated his story in the most satisfactory manner. He assured the company that it was a fact, handed down from his ancestor the historian, that the Kaatskill mountains had always been haunted by strange beings. That it was affirmed that the great Hendrick Hudson, the first discoverer of the river and country, kept a kind of vigil there every twenty years, with his crew of the Half-moon; being permitted in this way to revisit the scenes of his enterprise, and keep a guardian eye upon the river, and the great city called by his name. That his father had once seen them in their old Dutch dresses playing at nine-pins in a hollow of the mountain; and that he himself had heard, one summer afternoon, the sound of their balls, like distant peals of thunder.

To make a long story short, the company broke up, and returned to the more important concerns of the election. Rip's daughter took him home to live with her; she had a snug, well-furnished house, and a stout cheery farmer for a husband, whom Rip recollected for one of the urchins that used to climb upon his back. As to Rip's son and heir, who was the ditto of himself, seen leaning against the tree, he was employed to work on the farm; but evinced an hereditary disposition to attend to any thing else but his business.

Rip now resumed his old walks and habits; he soon found many of his former cronies, though all rather the worse for the wear and tear of time;

and preferred making friends among the rising generation, with whom he soon grew into great favor.

Having nothing to do at home, and being arrived at that happy age when a man can be idle with impunity, he took his place once more on the bench at the inn door, and was reverenced as one of the patriarchs of the village, and a chronicle of the old times "before the war." It was some time before he could get into the regular track of gossip, or could be made to comprehend the strange events that had taken place during his torpor. How that there had been a revolutionary war—that the country had thrown off the yoke of old England—and that, instead of being a subject of His Majesty George the Third, he was now a free citizen of the United States. Rip, in fact, was no politician; the changes of states and empires made but little impression on him; but there was one species of despotism under which he had long groaned, and that was—petticoat government. Happily that was at an end; he had got his neck out of the yoke of matrimony, and could go in and out whenever he pleased, without dreading the tyranny of Dame Van Winkle. Whenever her name was mentioned, however, he shook his head, shrugged his shoulders, and cast up his eyes; which might pass either for an expression of resignation to his fate, or joy at his deliverance.

He used to tell his story to every stranger that arrived at Mr. Doolittle's hotel. He was observed, at first, to vary on some points every time he told it, which was, doubtless, owing to his having so recently awaked. It at last settled down precisely to the tale I have related, and not a man, woman, or child in the neighborhood, but knew it by heart. Some always pretended to doubt the reality of it, and insisted that Rip had been out of his head, and that this was one point on which he always remained flighty. The old Dutch inhabitants, however, almost universally gave it full credit. Even to this day they never hear a thunderstorm of a summer afternoon about the Kaatskill, but they say Hendrick Hudson and his crew are at their game of nine-pins; and it is a common wish of all henpecked husbands in the neighborhood, when life hangs heavy on their hands, that they might have a quieting draught out of Rip Van Winkle's flagon.

NOTE

The foregoing Tale, one would suspect, had been suggested to Mr. Knickerbocker by a little German superstition about the Emperor Frederick *der Rothbart*, and the Kypphauser mountain: the subjoined note, however, which he had appended to the tale, shows that it is an absolute fact, narrated with his usual fidelity:

"The story of Rip Van Winkle may seem incredible to many, but nevertheless I give it my full belief, for I know the vicinity of our old Dutch settlements to have been very subject to marvellous events and appearances. Indeed, I have heard many stranger stories than this, in the villages along the Hudson; all of which were too well authenticated to admit of a doubt. I have even talked with Rip Van Winkle myself, who, when last I saw him, was a very venerable old man, and so perfectly rational and consistent on every other point, that I think no conscientious person could refuse to take this into the bargain; nay, I have seen a certificate on the subject taken before a country justice and signed with a cross, in the justice's own handwriting. The story, therefore, is beyond the possibility of doubt.

D.K."

POSTSCRIPT

The following are travelling notes from a memorandum-book of Mr. Knickerbocker:

The Kaatsberg, or Catskill Mountains, have always been a region full of fable. The Indians considered them the abode of spirits, who influenced the weather, spreading sunshine or clouds over the landscape, and sending good or bad hunting seasons. They were ruled by an old squaw spirit, said to be their mother. She dwelt on the highest peak of the Catskills, and had charge of the doors of day and night to open and shut them at the proper hour. She hung up the new moons in the skies, and cut up the old ones into stars. In times of drought, if properly propitiated, she would spin light summer clouds out of cobwebs and morning dew, and send them off from the crest of the mountain, flake after flake, like flakes of carded cotton, to float in the air; until, dissolved by the heat of the sun, they would fall in gentle showers, causing the grass to spring, the fruits to ripen, and the corn to grow an inch an hour. If displeased, however, she would brew up clouds black as ink, sitting in the midst of them like a bottle-bellied spider in the midst of its web; and when these clouds broke, wo betide the valleys!

In old times, say the Indian traditions, there was a kind of Manitou or Spirit, who kept about the wildest recesses of the Catskill Mountains, and took a mischievous pleasure in wreaking all kinds of evils and vexations upon the red men. Sometimes he would assume the form of a bear, a panther, or a deer, lead the bewildered hunter a weary chase through tangled forests and among ragged rocks; and then spring off with a loud ho! ho! leaving him aghast on the brink of a beetling precipice or raging torrent.

The favorite abode of this Manitou is still shown. It is a great rock or cliff on the loneliest part of the mountains, and, from the flowering vines which clamber about it, and the wild flowers which abound in its neighborhood, is known by the name of the Garden Rock. Near the foot of it is a small lake, the haunt of the solitary bittern, with water-snakes basking in the sun on the leaves of the pond-lilies which lie on the surface. This place was held in great awe by the Indians, insomuch that the boldest hunter would not pursue his game within its precincts. Once upon a time, however, a hunter who had lost his way, penetrated to the garden rock, where he beheld a number of gourds placed in the crotches of trees. One of these he seized and made off with it, but in the hurry of his retreat he let it fall among the rocks, when a great stream gushed forth, which washed him away and swept him down precipices, where he was dashed to pieces, and the stream made its way to the Hudson, and continues to flow to the present day; being the identical stream known by the name of the Kaaterskill.

The Sketch Book, 1818–1819

NATHANIEL HAWTHORNE

The Minister's Black Veil

A PARABLE *

The origin and nature of evil and sin were recurring themes in Hawthorne's work. In this symbolic tale, both themes are suggested rather than treated directly or broadly.

The sexton stood in the porch of Milford meeting-house, pulling busily at the bell-rope. The old people of the village came stooping along the street. Children, with bright faces, tripped merrily beside their parents, or mimicked a graver gait, in the conscious dignity of their Sunday clothes. Spruce bachelors looked sidelong at the pretty maidens, and fancied that the Sabbath sunshine made them prettier than on week days. When the throng had mostly streamed into the porch, the sexton began to toll the bell, keeping his eye on the Reverend Mr. Hooper's door. The first glimpse of the clergyman's figure was the signal for the bell to cease its summons.

"But what has the good parson got upon his face?" cried the sexton in astonishment.

All within hearing immediately turned about, and beheld the semblance of Mr. Hooper, pacing slowly his meditative way towards the meeting-house. With one accord they started, expressing more wonder than if some strange minister were coming to dust the cushions of Mr. Hooper's pulpit.

"Are you sure it is our parson?" inquired Goodman Gray of the sexton.

* Another clergyman in New England, Mr. Joseph Moody, of York, Maine, who died about eighty years since, made himself remarkable by the same eccentricity that is here related of the Reverend Mr. Hooper. In this case, however, the symbol has a different import. In early life he had accidentally killed a beloved friend; and from that day till the hour of his own death, he hid his face from men. (Hawthorne's note)

31

"Of a certainty it is good Mr. Hooper," replied the sexton. "He was to have exchanged pulpits with Parson Shute, of Westbury; but Parson Shute sent to excuse himself yesterday, being to preach a funeral sermon."

The cause of so much amazement may appear sufficiently slight. Mr. Hooper, a gentlemanly person, of about thirty, though still a bachelor, was dressed with due clerical neatness, as if a careful wife had starched his band, and brushed the weekly dust from his Sunday's garb. There was but one thing remarkable in his appearance. Swathed about his forehead, and hanging down over his face, so low as to be shaken by his breath, Mr. Hooper had on a black veil. On a nearer view it seemed to consist of two folds of crape, which entirely concealed his features, except the mouth and chin, but probably did not intercept his sight, further than to give a darkened aspect to all living and inanimate things. With this gloomy shade before him, good Mr. Hooper walked onward, at a slow and quiet pace, stooping somewhat, and looking on the ground, as is customary with abstracted men, yet nodding kindly to those of his parishioners who still waited on the meeting-house steps. But so wonder-struck were they that his greeting hardly met with a return.

"I can't really feel as if good Mr. Hooper's face was behind that piece of crape," said the sexton.

"I don't like it," muttered an old woman, as she hobbled into the meeting-house. "He has changed himself into something awful, only by hiding his face."

"Our parson has gone mad!" cried Goodman Gray, following him across the threshold.

A rumor of some unaccountable phenomenon had preceded Mr. Hooper into the meeting-house, and set all the congregation astir. Few could refrain from twisting their heads towards the door; many stood upright, and turned directly about; while several little boys clambered upon the seats, and came down again with a terrible racket. There was a general bustle, a rustling of the women's gowns and shuffling of the men's feet, greatly at variance with that hushed repose which should attend the entrance of the minister. But Mr. Hooper appeared not to notice the perturbation of his people. He entered with an almost noiseless step, bent his head mildly to the pews on each side, and bowed as he passed his oldest parishioner, a white-haired great-grandsire, who occupied an arm-chair in the centre of the aisle. It was strange to observe how slowly this venerable man became conscious of something singular in the appearance of his pastor. He seemed not fully to partake of the prevailing wonder, till Mr. Hooper had ascended the stairs, and showed himself in the pulpit, face to face with his congregation, except for the black veil. That mysterious emblem was never once withdrawn. It shook with his measured breath, as he gave out the psalm; it threw its obscurity between him and the holy page, as he read the Scriptures; and while he prayed, the veil lay heavily on his uplifted countenance. Did he seek to hide it from the dread Being whom he was addressing?

Such was the effect of this simple piece of crape, that more than one woman of delicate nerves was forced to leave the meeting-house. Yet perhaps the pale-faced congregation was almost as fearful a sight to the minister, as his black veil to them.

Mr. Hooper had the reputation of a good preacher, but not an energetic one: he strove to win his people heavenward by mild, persuasive influences, rather than to drive them thither by the thunders of the Word. The sermon which he now delivered was marked by the same characteristics of style and manner as the general series of his pulpit oratory. But there was something, either in the sentiment of the discourse itself, or in the imagination of the auditors, which made it greatly the most powerful effort that they had ever heard from their pastor's lips. It was tinged, rather more darkly than usual, with the gentle gloom of Mr. Hooper's temperament. The subject had reference to secret sin, and those sad mysteries which we hide from our nearest and dearest, and would fain conceal from our own consciousness, even forgetting that the Omniscient can detect them. A subtle power was breathed into his words. Each member of the congregation, the most innocent girl, and the man of hardened breast, felt as if the preacher had crept upon them, behind his awful veil, and discovered their hoarded iniquity of deed or thought. Many spread their clasped hands on their bosoms. There was nothing terrible in what Mr. Hooper said, at least, no violence; and yet, with every tremor of his melancholy voice, the hearers quaked. An unsought pathos came hand in hand with awe. So sensible were the audience of some unwonted attribute in their minister, that they longed for a breath of wind to blow aside the veil, almost believing that a stranger's visage would be discovered, though the form, gesture, and voice were those of Mr. Hooper.

At the close of the services, the people hurried out with indecorous confusion, eager to communicate their pent-up amazement, and conscious of lighter spirits the moment they lost sight of the black veil. Some gathered in little circles, huddled closely together, with their mouths all whispering in the centre; some went homeward alone, wrapt in silent meditation; some talked loudly, and profaned the Sabbath day with ostentatious laughter. A few shook their sagacious heads, intimating that they could penetrate the mystery; while one or two affirmed that there was no mystery at all, but only that Mr. Hooper's eyes were so weakened by the midnight lamp, as to require a shade. After a brief interval, forth came good Mr. Hooper also, in the rear of his flock. Turning his veiled face from one group to another, he paid due reverence to the hoary heads, saluted the middle-aged with kind dignity as their friend and spiritual guide, greeted the young with mingled authority and love, and laid his hands on the little children's heads to bless them. Such was always his custom on the Sabbath day. Strange and bewildered looks repaid him for his courtesy. None, as on former occasions, aspired to the honor of walking by their pastor's side. Old Squire Saunders, doubtless by an accidental lapse of memory, neglected to invite Mr. Hooper to his table, where the good clergyman had been wont to bless the food, almost every Sunday since his settlement. He returned, therefore, to the parsonage, and, at the moment of closing the door, was observed to look back upon the people, all of whom had their eyes fixed upon the minister. A sad smile gleamed faintly from beneath the black veil, and flickered about his mouth, glimmering as he disappeared.

"How strange," said a lady, "that a simple black veil, such as any woman might wear on her bonnet, should become such a terrible thing on Mr. Hooper's face!"

"Something must surely be amiss with Mr. Hooper's intellects," observed her husband, the physician of the village. "But the strangest part of the affair is the effect of this vagary, even on a sober-minded man like myself. The black veil, though it covers only our pastor's face, throws its influence over his whole person, and makes him ghost-like from head to foot. Do you not feel it so?"

"Truly do I," replied the lady; "and I would not be alone with him for the world. I wonder he is not afraid to be alone with himself!"

"Men sometimes are so," said her husband.

The afternoon service was attended with similar circumstances. At its conclusion, the bell tolled for the funeral of a young lady. The relatives and friends were assembled in the house, and the more distant acquaintances stood about the door, speaking of the good qualities of the deceased, when their talk was interrupted by the appearance of Mr. Hooper, still covered with his black veil. It was now an appropriate emblem. The clergyman stepped into the room where the corpse was laid, and bent over the coffin, to take a last farewell of his deceased parishioner. As he stooped, the veil hung straight down from his forehead, so that, if her eyelids had not been closed forever, the dead maiden might have seen his face. Could Mr. Hooper be fearful of her glance, that he so hastily caught back the black veil? A person who watched the interview between the dead and living, scrupled not to affirm, that, at the instant when the clergyman's features were disclosed, the corpse had slightly shuddered, rustling the shroud and muslin cap, though the countenance retained the composure of death. A superstitious old woman was the only witness of this prodigy. From the coffin Mr. Hooper passed into the chamber of the mourners, and thence to the head of the staircase, to make the funeral prayer. It was a tender and heart-dissolving prayer, full of sorrow, yet so imbued with celestial hopes, that the music of a heavenly harp, swept by the fingers of the dead, seemed faintly to be heard among the saddest accents of the minister. The people trembled, though they but darkly understood him when he prayed that they, and himself, and all of mortal race, might be ready, as he trusted this young maiden had been, for the dreadful hour that should snatch the veil from their faces. The bearers went heavily forth, and the mourners followed, saddening all the street, with the dead before them, and Mr. Hooper in his black veil behind.

"Why do you look back?" said one in the procession to his partner.

"I had a fancy," replied she, "that the minister and the maiden's spirit were walking hand in hand."

"And so had I, at the same moment," said the other.

That night, the handsomest couple in Milford village were to be joined in wedlock. Though reckoned a melancholy man, Mr. Hooper had a placid cheerfulness for such occasions, which often excited a sympathetic smile where livelier merriment would have been thrown away. There was no quality of his disposition which made him more beloved than this. The company at the wedding awaited his arrival with impatience, trusting that the strange awe, which had gathered over him throughout the day, would now be dispelled. But such was not the result. When Mr. Hooper came, the first thing that their eyes rested on was the same horrible black veil, which had added deeper gloom to the funeral, and could portend nothing but evil to the wedding. Such was its immediate effect on the guests that a cloud seemed to have rolled duskily from beneath the black crape, and dimmed the light of the candles. The bridal pair stood up before the minister. But the bride's cold fingers quivered in the tremulous hand of the bridegroom, and her deathlike paleness caused a whisper that the maiden who had been buried a few hours before was come from her grave to be married. If ever another wedding were so dismal, it was that famous one where they tolled the wedding knell. After performing the ceremony, Mr. Hooper raised a glass of wine to his lips, wishing happiness to the new-married couple in a strain of mild pleasantry that ought to have brightened the features of the guests, like a cheerful gleam from the hearth. At that instant, catching a glimpse of his figure in the looking-glass, the black veil involved his own spirit in the horror with which it overwhelmed all others. His frame shuddered, his lips grew white, he spilt the untasted wine upon the carpet, and rushed forth into the darkness. For the Earth, too, had on her Black Veil.

The next day, the whole village of Milford talked of little else than Parson Hooper's black veil. That, and the mystery concealed behind it, supplied a topic for discussion between acquaintances meeting in the street, and good women gossiping at their open windows. It was the first item of news that the tavernkeeper told to his guests. The children babbled of it on their way to school. One imitative little imp covered his face with an old black handkerchief, thereby so affrighting his playmates that the panic seized himself, and he well-nigh lost his wits by his own waggery.

It was remarkable that of all the busybodies and impertinent people in the parish, not one ventured to put the plain question to Mr. Hooper, wherefore he did this thing. Hitherto, whenever there appeared the slightest call for such interference, he had never lacked advisers, nor shown himself averse to be guided by their judgment. If he erred at all, it was by so painful a degree of self-distrust, that even the mildest censure would lead him to consider an indifferent action as a crime. Yet, though so well acquainted with this amiable weakness, no individual among his parishioners chose to make the black veil a subject of friendly remonstrance. There was a feeling of dread, neither plainly confessed nor carefully concealed, which caused each to shift the responsibility upon another, till at length it was found expedient to send a deputation of the church, in order to deal with Mr. Hooper about the mystery, before it should grow into a scandal. Never did an embassy so ill discharge its duties. The minister received them with friendly courtesy, but became silent, after they were seated, leaving to his visitors the whole burden of introducing their important business. The topic, it might be supposed, was obvious enough. There was the black veil swathed around Mr. Hooper's forehead, and concealing every feature above his placid mouth, on which, at times, they could perceive the glimmering of a melancholy smile. But that piece of crape, to their imagination, seemed to hang down before his heart, the symbol of a fearful secret between him and them. Were the evil but cast aside, they might speak freely of it, but not till then. Thus they sat a considerable time, speechless, confused, and shrinking uneasily from Mr. Hooper's eye, which they felt to be fixed upon them with an invisible glance. Finally, the deputies returned abashed to their constituents, pronouncing the matter too weighty to be handled, except by a council of the churches, if, indeed, it might not require a general synod.

But there was one person in the village unappalled by the awe with which the black veil had impressed all beside herself. When the deputies returned without an explanation, or even venturing to demand one, she, with the calm energy of her character, determined to chase away the strange cloud that appeared to be settling round Mr. Hooper every moment more darkly than before. As his plighted wife, it should be her privilege to know what the black veil concealed. At the minister's first visit, therefore, she entered upon the subject with a direct simplicity, which made the task easier both for him and for her. After he had seated himself, she fixed her eyes steadfastly upon the veil, but could discern nothing of the dreadful gloom that had so overawed the multitude; it was but a double fold of crape, hanging down from his forehead to his mouth, and slightly stirring with his breath.

"No," she said aloud, and smiling, "there is nothing terrible in this piece of crape, except that it hides a face which I am always glad to look upon. Come, good sir, let the sun shine from behind the cloud. First lay aside your black veil: then tell me why you put it on."

Mr. Hooper's smile glimmered faintly.

"There is an hour to come," said he, "when all of us shall cast aside our veils. Take it not amiss, beloved friend, if I wear this piece of crape till then."

"Your words are a mystery, too," returned the young lady. "Take away the veil from them, at least."

"Elizabeth, I will," said he, "so far as my vow may suffer me. Know, then, this veil is a type and a symbol, and I am bound to wear it ever, both in light and darkness, in solitude and before the gaze of multitudes, and as with strangers, so with my familiar friends. No mortal eye will see it withdrawn. This dismal shade must separate me from the world; even you, Elizabeth, can never come behind it!"

"What grievous affliction hath befallen you," she earnestly inquired, "that you should thus darken your eyes forever?"

"If it be a sign of mourning," replied Mr. Hooper, "I, perhaps, like most other mortals, have sorrows dark enough to be typified by a black veil."

"But what if the world will not believe that it is the type of an innocent sorrow?" urged Elizabeth. "Beloved and respected as you are, there may be whispers that you hide your face under the consciousness of secret sin. For the sake of your holy office, do away with this scandal!"

The color rose in her cheeks as she intimated the nature of the rumors that were already abroad in the village. But Mr. Hooper's mildness did not forsake him. He even smiled again—that same sad smile, which always appeared like a faint glimmering of light, proceeding from the same obscurity beneath the veil.

"If I hide my face for sorrow, there is cause enough," he merely replied; "and if I cover it for secret sin, what mortal might not do the same?"

And with this gentle, but unconquerable obstinacy did he resist all her entreaties. At length Elizabeth sat silent. For a few moments she appeared lost in thought, considering, probably, what new methods might be tried to withdraw her lover from so dark a fantasy, which, if it had no other meaning, was perhaps a symptom of mental disease. Though of a firmer character than his own, tears rolled down her cheeks. But, in an instant, as it were, a new feeling took the place of sorrow: her eyes were fixed insensibly on the black veil, when, like a sudden twilight in the air, its terrors fell around her. She arose, and stood trembling before him.

"And do you feel it then, at last?" said he mournfully.

She made no reply, but covered her eyes with her hand, and turned to leave the room. He rushed forward and caught her arm.

"Have patience with me, Elizabeth!" cried he passionately. "Do not desert me, though this veil must be between us here on earth. Be mine, and hereafter there shall be no veil over my face, no darkness between our souls! It is but a mortal veil—it is not for eternity! O! you know not how lonely I am, and how frightened, to be alone behind my black veil. Do not leave me in this miserable obscurity forever!"

37

"Lift the veil but once, and look me in the face," said she.

"Never! It cannot be!" replied Mr. Hooper.

"Then farewell!" said Elizabeth.

She withdrew her arm from his grasp, and slowly departed, pausing at the door, to give one long shuddering gaze, that seemed almost to penetrate the mystery of the black veil. But, even amid his grief, Mr. Hooper smiled to think that only a material emblem had separated him from happiness, though the horrors, which it had shadowed forth, must be drawn darkly between the fondest of lovers.

From that time no attempts were made to remove Mr. Hooper's black veil, or, by a direct appeal, to discover the secret which it was supposed to hide. By persons who claimed a superiority to popular prejudice, it was reckoned merely an eccentric whim, such as often mingles with the sober actions of men otherwise rational, and tinges them all with its own semblance of insanity. But with the multitude, good Mr. Hooper was irreparably a bugbear. He could not walk the street with any peace of mind, so conscious was he that the gentle and timid would turn aside to avoid him, and that others would make it a point of hardihood to throw themselves in his way. The impertinence of the latter class compelled him to give up his customary walk at sunset to the burial grounds; for when he leaned pensively over the gate, there would always be faces behind the gravestones, peeping at his black veil. A fable went the rounds that the stare of the dead people drove him thence. It grieved him, to the very depths of his kind heart, to observe how the children fled from his approach, breaking up their merriest sports, while his melancholy figure was yet afar off. Their instinctive dread caused him to feel more strongly than aught else, that a preternatural horror was interwoven with the threads of the black crape. In truth, his own antipathy to the veil was known to be so great, that he never willingly passed before a mirror, nor stooped to drink at a still fountain, lest, in its peaceful bosom, he should be affrighted by himself. This was what gave plausibility to the whispers, that Mr. Hooper's conscience tortured him for some great crime too horrible to be entirely concealed, or otherwise than so obscurely intimated. Thus, from beneath the black veil, there rolled a cloud into the sunshine, an ambiguity of sin or sorrow, which enveloped the poor minister, so that love or sympathy could never reach him. It was said that ghost or fiend consorted with him there. With self-shudderings and outward terrors, he walked continually in its shadow, groping darkly within his own soul, or gazing through a medium that saddened the whole world. Even the lawless mind, it was believed, respected his dreadful secret, and never blew aside the veil. But still good Mr. Hooper sadly smiled at the pale visages of the worldly throng as he passed by.

Among all its bad influences, the black veil had the one desirable effect, of making its wearer a very efficient clergyman. By the aid of his mysterious emblem—for there was no other apparent cause—he became a man of awful power over souls that were in agony for sin. His converts always regarded him with a dread peculiar to themselves, affirming, though but figuratively, that, before he brought them to celestial light, they had been with him behind the black veil. Its gloom, indeed, enabled him to sympathize with all dark affections. Dying sinners cried aloud for Mr. Hooper, and would not yield their breath till he appeared; though ever, as he stooped to whisper consolation, they shuddered at the veiled face so near their own. Such were the terrors of the black veil, even when Death had bared his visage! Strangers came long distances to attend service at his church, with the mere idle purpose of gazing at his figure, because it was forbidden them to behold his face. But many were made to quake ere they departed! Once, during Governor Belcher's administration, Mr. Hooper was appointed to preach the election sermon. Covered with his black veil, he stood before the chief magistrate, the council, and the representatives, and wrought so deep an impression, that the legislative measures of that year were characterized by all the gloom and piety of our earliest ancestral sway.

In this manner Mr. Hooper spent a long life, irreproachable in outward act, yet shrouded in dismal suspicions; kind and loving, though unloved, and dimly feared; a man apart from men, shunned in their health and joy, but ever summoned to their aid in mortal anguish. As years wore on, shedding their snows above his sable veil, he acquired a name throughout the New England churches, and they called him Father Hooper. Nearly all his parishioners, who were of mature age when he was settled, had been borne away by many a funeral: he had one congregation in the church, and a more crowded one in the churchyard; and having wrought so late into the evening, and done his work so well, it was now good Father Hooper's turn to rest.

Several persons were visible by the shaded candle-light, in the death chamber of the old clergyman. Natural connections he had none. But there was the decorously grave, though unmoved physician, seeking only to mitigate the last pangs of the patient whom he could not save. There were the deacons, and other eminently pious members of his church. There, also, was the Reverend Mr. Clark, of Westbury, a young and zealous divine, who had ridden in haste to pray by the bedside of the expiring minister. There was the nurse, no hired handmaiden of death, but one whose calm affection had endured thus long in secrecy, in solitude, amid the chill of age, and would not perish, even at the dying hour. Who, but Elizabeth! And there lay the hoary head of good Father Hooper upon the death pillow, with the black veil still swathed about his brow, and reaching down over his face, so that each more difficult gasp of his faint breath caused it to stir. All through life that piece of crape had hung between him and the world: it had separated him from cheerful brotherhood and woman's love, and kept him in that saddest of all prisons, his own heart; and still it lay upon his face, as if to deepen the gloom of his darksome chamber, and shade him from the sunshine of eternity.

For some time previous, his mind had been confused, wavering doubtfully between the past and the present, and hovering forward, as it were, at intervals, into the indistinctness of the world to come. There had been feverish turns, which tossed him from side to side, and wore away what little strength he had. But in his most convulsive struggles, and in the wildest vagaries of his intellect, when no other thought retained its sober influence, he still showed an awful solicitude lest the black veil should slip aside. Even if his bewildered soul could have forgotten, there was a faithful woman at his pillow, who, with averted eyes, would have covered that aged face, which she had last beheld in the comeliness of manhood. At length the death-stricken old man lay quietly in the torpor of mental and bodily exhaustion, with an imperceptible pulse, and breath that grew fainter and fainter, except when a long, deep, and irregular inspiration seemed to prelude the flight of his spirit.

The minister of Westbury approached the bedside.

"Venerable Father Hooper," said he, "the moment of your release is at hand. Are you ready for the lifting of the veil that shuts in time from eternity?"

Father Hooper at first replied merely by a feeble motion of his head; then, apprehensive, perhaps, that his meaning might be doubtful, he exerted himself to speak.

"Yea," said he, in faint accents, "my soul hath a patient weariness until that veil be lifted."

"And is it fitting," resumed the Reverend Mr. Clark, "that a man so given to prayer, of such a blameless example, holy in deed and thought, so far as mortal judgment may pronounce; is it fitting that a father in the church should leave a shadow on his memory, that may seem to blacken a life so pure? I pray you, my venerable brother, let not this thing be! Suffer us to be gladdened by your triumphant aspect as you go to your reward. Before the veil of eternity be lifted, let me cast aside this black veil from your face!"

And thus speaking, the Reverend Mr. Clark bent forward to reveal the mystery of so many years. But, exerting a sudden energy, that made all the beholders stand aghast, Father Hooper snatched both his hands from beneath the bedclothes, and pressed them strongly on the black veil, resolute to struggle, if the minister of Westbury would contend with a dying man.

"Never!" cried the veiled clergyman. "On earth, never!"

"Dark old man!" exclaimed the affrighted minister, "with what horrible crime upon your soul are you now passing to the judgment?"

Father Hooper's breath heaved; it rattled in his throat; but, with a mighty effort, grasping forward with his hands, he caught hold of life,

40

and held it back till he should speak. He even raised himself in bed; and there he sat, shivering with the arms of death around him, while the black veil hung down, awful, at that last moment, in the gathered terrors of a lifetime. And yet the faint, sad smile, so often there, now seemed to glimmer from its obscurity, and linger on Father Hooper's lips.

"Why do you tremble at me alone?" cried he, turning his veiled face round the circle of pale spectators. "Tremble also at each other! Have men avoided me, and women shown no pity, and children screamed and fled, only for my black veil? What, but the mystery which it obscurely typifies, has made this piece of crape so awful? When the friend shows his inmost heart to his friend; the lover to his best beloved; when man does not vainly shrink from the eye of his Creator, loathsomely treasuring up the secret of his sin; then deem me a monster, for the symbol beneath which I have lived, and die! I look around me, and lo! on every visage a Black Veil!"

While his auditors shrank from one another, in mutual affright, Father Hooper fell back upon his pillow, a veiled corpse, with a faint smile lingering on the lips. Still veiled, they laid him in his coffin, and a veiled corpse they bore him to the grave. The grass of many years has sprung up and withered on that grave, the burial stone is moss-grown, and good Mr. Hooper's face is dust; but awful is still the thought that it mouldered beneath the Black Veil!

Twice-Told Tales, 1835

HENRY WADSWORTH LONGFELLOW

Hymn to the Night

'Ασπασίη, τρίλλιστος

I heard the trailing garments of the Night
    Sweep through her marble halls!
I saw her sable skirts all fringed with light
    From the celestial walls!

I felt her presence, by its spell of might,
    Stoop o'er me from above;
The calm, majestic presence of the Night,
    As of the one I love.

I heard the sounds of sorrow and delight,
    The manifold, soft chimes,

That fill the haunted chambers of the Night,
  Like some old poet's rhymes.

From the cool cisterns of the midnight air
  My spirit drank repose;
The fountain of perpetual peace flows there,—
  From those deep cisterns flows.

O holy Night! from thee I learn to bear
  What man has borne before!
Thou layest thy fingers on the lips of Care,
  And they complain no more.

Peace! Peace! Orestes-like I breathe this prayer!
  Descend with broad-winged flight,
The welcome, the thrice-prayed-for, the most fair,
  The best-beloved Night!

Poems, 1839

Hiawatha's Ghostly Guests

  Through the forest, wide and wailing,
Roamed the hunter on his snow-shoes;
In the village worked the women,
Pounded maize, or dressed the deer-skin;
And the young men played together
On the ice the noisy ball-play,
On the plain the dance of snow-shoes.
  One dark evening, after sundown,
In her wigwam Laughing Water
Sat with old Nokomis, waiting
For the steps of Hiawatha
Homeward from the hunt returning.
  On their faces gleamed the firelight,
Painting them with streaks of crimson,
In the eyes of old Nokomis
Glimmered like the watery moonlight,
In the eyes of Laughing Water
Glistened like the sun in water;
And behind them crouched their shadows
In the corners of the wigwam,
And the smoke in wreaths above them
Climbed and crowded through the smoke-flue.
  Then the curtain of the doorway
From without was slowly lifted;

Brighter glowed the fire a moment,
And a moment swerved the smoke-wreath,
As two women entered softly,
Passed the doorway uninvited,
Without word of salutation,
Without sign of recognition,
Sat down in the farthest corner,
Crouching low among the shadows.

From their aspect and their garments,
Strangers seemed they in the village;
Very pale and haggard were they,
As they sat there sad and silent,
Trembling, cowering with the shadows.

Was it the wind above the smoke-flue,
Muttering down into the wigwam?
Was it the owl, the Koko-koho,
Hooting from the dismal forest?
Sure a voice said in the silence:
"These are corpses clad in garments,
These are ghosts that come to haunt you,
From the kingdom of Ponemah,
From the land of the Hereafter!"

Homeward now came Hiawatha
From his hunting in the forest,
With the snow upon his tresses,
And the red deer on his shoulders.
At the feet of Laughing Water
Down he threw his lifeless burden;
Nobler, handsomer she thought him,
Than when first he came to woo her,
First threw down the deer before her,
As a token of his wishes,
As a promise of the future.

Then he turned and saw the strangers,
Cowering, crouching with the shadows;
Said within himself, "Who are they?
What strange guests has Minnehaha?"
But he questioned not the strangers,
Only spake to bid them welcome
To his lodge, his food, his fireside.

When the evening meal was ready,
And the deer had been divided,
Both the pallid guests, the strangers,
Springing from among the shadows,
Seized upon the choicest portions,

Seized the white fat of the roebuck,
Set apart for Laughing Water,
For the wife of Hiawatha;
Without asking, without thanking,
Eagerly devoured the morsels,
Flitted back among the shadows
In the corner of the wigwam.

Not a word spake Hiawatha,
Not a motion made Nokomis,
Not a gesture Laughing Water;
Not a change came o'er their features;
Only Minnehaha softly
Whispered, saying, "They are famished;
Let them do what best delights them;
Let them eat, for they are famished."

Many a daylight dawned and darkened,
Many a night shook off the daylight
As the pine shakes off the snow-flakes
From the midnight of its branches;
Day by day the guests unmoving
Sat there silent in the wigwam;
But by night, in storm or starlight,
Forth they went into the forest,
Bringing fire-wood to the wigwam,
Bringing pine-cones for the burning,
Always sad and always silent.

And whenever Hiawatha
Came from fishing or from hunting,
When the evening meal was ready,
And the food had been divided,
Gliding from their darksome corner,
Came the pallid guests, the strangers,
Seized upon the choicest portions
Set aside for Laughing Water,
And without rebuke or question
Flitted back among the shadows.

Never once had Hiawatha
By a word or look reproved them;
Never once had old Nokomis
Made a gesture of impatience;
Never once had Laughing Water
Shown resentment at the outrage.
All had they endured in silence,
That the rights of guest and stranger,
That the virtue of free-giving,

By a look might not be lessened,
By a word might not be broken.
　　Once at midnight Hiawatha,
Ever wakeful, ever watchful,
In the wigwam, dimly lighted
By the brands that still were burning,
By the glimmering, flickering firelight,
Heard a sighing, oft repeated,
Heard a sobbing, as of sorrow.
　　From his couch rose Hiawatha,
From his shaggy hides of bison,
Pushed aside the deer-skin curtain,
Saw the pallid guests, the shadows,
Sitting upright on their couches,
Weeping in the silent midnight.
　　And he said: "O guests! why is it
That your hearts are so afflicted,
That you sob so in the midnight?
Has perchance the old Nokomis,
Has my wife, my Minnehaha,
Wronged or grieved you by unkindness,
Failed in hospitable duties?"
　　Then the shadows ceased from weeping,
Ceased from sobbing and lamenting,
And they said, with gentle voices:
"We are ghosts of the departed,
Souls of those who once were with you.
From the realms of Chibiabos
Hither have we come to try you,
Hither have we come to warn you.
　　"Cries of grief and lamentation
Reach us in the Blessed Islands;
Cries of anguish from the living,
Calling back their friends departed,
Sadden us with useless sorrow.
Therefore have we come to try you;
No one knows us, no one heeds us.
We are but a burden to you,
And we see that the departed
Have no place among the living.
　　"Think of this, O Hiawatha!
Speak of it to all the people,
That henceforward and forever
They no more with lamentations
Sadden the souls of the departed

In the Islands of the Blessed.
    "Do not lay such heavy burdens
In the graves of those you bury,
Not such weight of furs and wampum,
Not such weight of pots and kettles,
For the spirits faint beneath them.
Only give them food to carry,
Only give them fire to light them.
    "Four days is the spirit's journey
To the land of ghosts and shadows,
Four its lonely night encampments;
Four times must their fires be lighted.
Therefore, when the dead are buried,
Let a fire, as night approaches,
Four times on the grave be kindled,
That the soul upon its journey
May not lack the cheerful firelight,
May not grope about in darkness.
    "Farewell, noble Hiawatha!
We have put you to the trial,
To the proof have put your patience,
By the insult of our presence,
By the outrage of our actions.
We have found you great and noble.
Fail not in the greater trial,
Faint not in the harder struggle."
    When they ceased, a sudden darkness
Fell and filled the silent wigwam.
Hiawatha heard a rustle
As of garments trailing by him,
Heard the curtain of the doorway
Lifted by a hand he saw not,
Felt the cold breath of the night air,
For a moment saw the starlight;
But he saw the ghosts no longer,
Saw no more the wandering spirits
From the kingdom of Ponemah,
From the land of the Hereafter.
From "The Song of Hiawatha" in *Poems*, 1855

HENRY ADAMS

Boyhood in Quincy, Massachusetts [1838–1848]

Although Adams wrote one of the truly great American autobiog-raphies, it is far from a free-wheeling confession. He revealed only what he desired, but always with a brilliant yet quiet urbanity.

Under the shadow of Boston State House, turning its back on the house of John Hancock, the little passage called Hancock Avenue runs, or ran, from Beacon Street, skirting the State House grounds, to Mount Vernon Street, on the summit of Beacon Hill; and there, in the third house below Mount Vernon Place, February 16, 1838, a child was born, and christened later by his uncle, the minister of the First Church after the tenets of Boston Unitarianism, as Henry Brooks Adams.

Had he been born in Jerusalem under the shadow of the Temple and circumcised in the Synagogue by his uncle the high priest, under the name of Israel Cohen, he would scarcely have been more distinctly branded, and not much more heavily handicapped in the races of the coming century, in running for such stakes as the century was to offer; but, on the other hand, the ordinary traveller, who does not enter the field of racing, finds advantage in being, so to speak, ticketed through life, with the safeguards of an old, established traffic. Safeguards are often irksome, but sometimes convenient, and if one needs them at all, one is apt to need them badly. A hundred years earlier, such safeguards as his would have secured any young man's success; and although in 1838 their value was not very great compared with what they would have had in 1738, yet the mere accident of starting a twentieth-century career from a nest of associations so colonial —so troglodytic—as the First Church, the Boston State House, Beacon Hill, John Hancock and John Adams, Mount Vernon Street and Quincy, all crowding on ten pounds of unconscious babyhood, was so queer as to offer a subject of curious speculation to the baby long after he had witnessed the solution. What could become of such a child of the seventeenth and eighteenth centuries, when he should wake up to find himself required to play the game of the twentieth? Had he been consulted, would he have cared to play the game at all, holding such cards as he held, and suspecting that the game was to be one of which neither he nor any one else back to the beginning of time knew the rules or the risks or the stakes? He was not consulted and was not responsible, but had he been taken into the confidence of his parents, he would certainly have told them to change nothing as far as concerned him. He would have been astounded by his own luck. Probably no child, born in the year, held better cards than he.

Whether life was an honest game of chance, or whether the cards were marked and forced, he could not refuse to play his excellent hand. He could never make the usual plea of irresponsibility. He accepted the situation as though he had been a party to it, and under the same circumstances would do it again, the more readily for knowing the exact values. To his life as a whole he was a consenting, contracting party and partner from the moment he was born to the moment he died. Only with that understanding—as a consciously assenting member in full partnership with the society of his age—had his education an interest to himself or to others.

As it happened, he never got to the point of playing the game at all; he lost himself in the study of it, watching the errors of the players; but this is the only interest in the story, which otherwise has no moral and little incident. A story of education—seventy years of it—the practical value remains to the end in doubt, like other values about which men have disputed since the birth of Cain and Abel; but the practical value of the universe has never been stated in dollars. Although every one cannot be a Gargantua-Napoleon-Bismarck and walk off with the great bells of Notre Dame, every one must bear his own universe, and most persons are moderately interested in learning how their neighbors have managed to carry theirs.

This problem of education, started in 1838, went on for three years, while the baby grew, like other babies, unconsciously, as a vegetable, the outside world working as it never had worked before, to get his new universe ready for him. Often in old age he puzzled over the question whether, on the doctrine of chances, he was at liberty to accept himself or his world as an accident. No such accident had ever happened before in human experience. For him, alone, the old universe was thrown into the ash-heap and a new one created. He and his eighteenth-century, troglodytic Boston were suddenly cut apart—separated forever—in act if not in sentiment, by the opening of the Boston and Albany Railroad; the appearance of the first Cunard steamers in the bay; and the telegraphic messages which carried from Baltimore to Washington the news that Henry Clay and James K. Polk were nominated for the Presidency. This was in May, 1844; he was six years old; his new world was ready for use, and only fragments of the old met his eyes.

Of all this that was being done to complicate his education, he knew only the color of yellow. He first found himself sitting on a yellow kitchen floor in strong sunlight. He was three years old when he took this earliest step in education; a lesson of color. The second followed soon; a lesson of taste. On December 3, 1841, he developed scarlet fever. For several days he was as good as dead, reviving only under the careful nursing of his family. When he began to recover strength, about January 1, 1842, his hunger must have been stronger than any other pleasure or pain, for while in after life he retained not the faintest recollection of his illness, he

48

remembered quite clearly his aunt entering the sick-room bearing in her hand a saucer with a baked apple.

The order of impressions retained by memory might naturally be that of color and taste, although one would rather suppose that the sense of pain would be first to educate. In fact, the third recollection of the child was that of discomfort. The moment he could be removed, he was bundled up in blankets and carried from the little house in Hancock Avenue to a larger one which his parents were to occupy for the rest of their lives in the neighboring Mount Vernon Street. The season was midwinter, January 10, 1842, and he never forgot his acute distress for want of air under his blankets, or the noises of moving furniture.

As a means of variation from a normal type, sickness in childhood ought to have a certain value not to be classed under any fitness or unfitness of natural selection; and especially scarlet fever affected boys seriously, both physically and in character, though they might through life puzzle themselves to decide whether it had fitted or unfitted them for success; but this fever of Henry Adams took greater and greater importance in his eyes, from the point of view of education, the longer he lived. At first, the effect was physical. He fell behind his brothers two or three inches, and proportionally in bone and weight. His character and processes of mind seemed to share in this fining-down process of scale. He was not good in a fight, and his nerves were more delicate than boys' nerves ought to be. He exaggerated these weaknesses as he grew older. The habit of doubt; of distrusting his own judgment and of totally rejecting the judgment of the world; the tendency to regard every question as open; the hesitation to act except as a choice of evils; the shirking of responsibility; the love of line, form, quality; the horror of ennui; the passion for companionship and antipathy to society—all these are well-known qualities of New England character in no way peculiar to individuals but in this instance seemed to be stimulated by the fever, and Henry Adams could never make up his mind whether, on the whole, the change of character was morbid or healthy, good or bad for his purpose. His brothers were the type; he was the variation.

As far as the boy knew, the sickness did not affect him at all, and he grew up in excellent health, bodily and mental, taking life as it was given; accepting its local standards without a difficulty, and enjoying much of it as keenly as any other boy of his age. He seemed to himself quite normal, and his companions seemed always to think him so. Whatever was peculiar about him was education, not character, and came to him, directly and indirectly, as the result of that eighteenth century inheritance which he took with his name.

The atmosphere of education in which he lived was colonial, revolutionary, almost Cromwellian, as though he were steeped, from his greatest grandmother's birth, in the odor of political crime. Resistance to something was the law of New England nature; the boy looked out on the world with the instinct of resistance; for numberless generations his predecessors had viewed the world chiefly as a thing to be reformed, filled with evil forces to be abolished, and they saw no reason to suppose that they had wholly succeeded in the abolition; the duty was unchanged. That duty implied not only resistance to evil, but hatred of it. Boys naturally look on all force as an enemy, and generally find it so, but the New Englander, whether boy or man, in his long struggle with a stingy and hostile universe, had learned also to love the pleasure of hating; his joys were few. . . .

Boys are wild animals, rich in the treasures of sense, but the New England boy had a wider range of emotions than boys of more equable climates. He felt his nature crudely, as it was meant. To the boy Henry Adams, summer was drunken. Among senses, smell was the strongest—smell of hot pine-woods and sweet-fern in the scorching summer noon; of new-mown hay; of ploughed earth; of box hedges; of peaches, lilacs, syringas; of stables, barns, cow-yards; of salt water and low tide on the marshes; nothing came amiss. Next to smell came taste, and the children knew the taste of everything they saw or touched, from pennyroyal and flagroot to the shell of a pignut and the letters of a spelling book—the taste of A–B, AB, suddenly revived on the boy's tongue sixty years afterwards. Light, line, and color as sensual pleasures, came later and were as crude as the rest. The New England light is glare, and the atmosphere harshens color. The boy was a full man before he ever knew what was meant by atmosphere; his idea of pleasure in light was the blaze of a New England sun. His idea of color was a peony, with the dew of early morning on its petals. The intense blue of the sea, as he saw it a mile or two away, from the Quincy hills; the cumuli in a June afternoon sky; the strong reds and greens and purples of colored prints and children's picture-books, as the American colors then ran; these were ideals. The opposites or antipathies, were the cold grays of November evenings, and the thick, muddy thaws of Boston winter. With such standards, the Bostonian could not but develop a double nature. Life was a double thing. After a January blizzard, the boy who could look with pleasure into the violent snow-glare of the cold white sunshine, with its intense light and shade, scarcely knew what was meant by tone. He could reach it only by education.

Winter and summer, then, were two hostile lives, and bred two separate natures. Winter was always the effort to live; summer was tropical license. Whether the children rolled in the grass, or waded in the brook, or swam in the salt ocean, or sailed in the bay, or fished for smelts in the creeks, or netted minnows in the salt-marshes, or took to the pine-woods and the granite quarries, or chased muskrats and hunted snapping-turtles in the swamps, or mushrooms or nuts on the autumn hills, summer and country were always sensual living, while winter was always compulsory learning. Summer was the multiplicity of nature; winter was school.

The bearing of the two seasons on the education of Henry Adams was no fancy; it was the most decisive force he ever knew; it ran through life, and made the division between its perplexing, warring, irreconcilable problems, irreducible opposites, with growing emphasis to the last year of study. From earliest childhood the boy was accustomed to feel that, for him, life was double. Winter and summer, town and country, law and liberty, were hostile, and the man who pretended they were not, was in his eyes a schoolmaster—that is, a man employed to tell lies to little boys. Though Quincy was but two hours' walk from Beacon Hill, it belonged in a different world. For two hundred years, every Adams, from father to son, had lived within sight of State Street, and sometimes had lived in it, yet none had ever taken kindly to the town, or been taken kindly by it. The boy inherited his double nature. He knew as yet nothing about his great-grandfather, who had died a dozen years before his own birth: he took for granted that any great-grandfather of his must have always been good, and his enemies wicked; but he divined his great-grandfather's character from his own. Never for a moment did he connect the two ideas of Boston and John Adams; they were separate and antagonistic; the idea of John Adams went with Quincy. He knew his grandfather John Quincy Adams only as an old man of seventy-five or eighty who was friendly and gentle with him, but except that he heard his grandfather always called "the President," and his grandmother "the Madam," he had no reason to suppose that his Adams grandfather differed in character from his Brooks grandfather who was equally kind and benevolent. He liked the Adams side best, but for no other reason than that it reminded him of the country, the summer, and the absence of restraint. Yet he felt also that Quincy was in a way inferior to Boston, and that socially Boston looked down on Quincy. The reason was clear enough even to a five-year-old child. Quincy had no Boston style. Little enough style had either; a simpler manner of life and thought could hardly exist, short of cave-dwelling. The flint-and-steel with which his grandfather Adams used to light his own fires in the early morning was still on the mantelpiece of his study. The idea of a livery or even a dress for servants, or of an evening toilette, was next to blasphemy. Bathrooms, water-supplies, lighting, heating, and the whole array of domestic comforts were unknown at Quincy. Boston had already a bathroom, a water-supply, a furnace, and gas. The superiority of Boston was evident, but a child liked it no better for that. . . .

The attachment to Quincy was not altogether sentimental or wholly sympathetic. Quincy was not a bed of thornless roses. Even there the curse of Cain set its mark. There as elsewhere a cruel universe combined to crush a child. As though three or four vigorous brothers and sisters, with the best will, were not enough to crush any child, every one else conspired towards an education which he hated. From the cradle to the grave this problem of running order through chaos, through space, discipline through freedom, unity through multiplicity, has always been, and must always be, the task of education, as it is the moral of religion, philosophy, science, art, politics, and economy; but a boy's will is his life, and he dies when it is broken, as the colt dies in harness, taking a new nature in becoming tame. Rarely has the boy felt kindly towards his tamers. Between him and his master has always been war. Henry Adams never knew a boy of his generation to like a master, and the task of remaining on friendly terms with one's own family, in such a relation, was never easy.

All the more singular it seemed afterwards to him that his first serious contact with the President should have been a struggle of will, in which the old man almost necessarily defeated the boy, but instead of leaving, as usual in such defeats, a lifelong sting, left rather an impression of as fair treatment as could be expected from a natural enemy. The boy met seldom with such restraint. He could not have been much more than six years old at the time—seven at the utmost—and his mother had taken him to Quincy for a long stay with the President during the summer. What became of the rest of the family he quite forgot; but he distinctly remembered standing at the house door one summer morning in a passionate outburst of rebellion against going to school. Naturally his mother was the immediate victim of his rage; that is what mothers are for, and boys also; but in this case the boy had his mother at unfair disadvantage, for she was a guest, and had no means of enforcing obedience. Henry showed a certain tactical ability by refusing to start, and he met all efforts at compulsion by successful, though too vehement protest. He was in a fair way to win, and was holding his own, with sufficient energy, at the bottom of the long staircase which led up to the door of the President's library, when the door opened, and the old man slowly came down. Putting on his hat, he took the boy's hand without a word, and walked with him, paralyzed by awe, up the road to the town. After the first moments of consternation at this interference in a domestic dispute, the boy reflected that an old gentleman close on to eighty would never trouble himself to walk near a mile on a hot summer morning over a shadeless road to take a boy to school, and that it would be strange if a lad imbued with the passion of freedom could not find a corner to dodge around, somewhere before reaching the school door. Then and always, the boy insisted that this reasoning justified his apparent submission; but the old man did not stop, and the boy saw all his strategical points turned, one after another, until he found himself seated inside the school, and obviously the centre of curious if not malevolent criticism. Not till then did the President release his hand and depart.

The point was that this act, contrary to the inalienable rights of boys, and nullifying the social compact, ought to have made him dislike his grandfather for life. He could not recall that it had this effect even for a moment. With a certain maturity of mind, the child must have recognized that the President, though a tool of tyranny, had done his disreputable work with a certain intelligence. He had shown no temper, no irritation, no personal feeling, and had made no display of force. Above all, he had held his tongue. During their long walk he had said nothing; he had uttered no syllable of revolting cant about the duty of obedience and the wickedness of resistance to law; he had shown no concern in the matter; hardly even a consciousness of the boy's existence. Probably his mind at that moment was actually troubling itself little about his grandson's iniquities, and much about the iniquities of President Polk, but the boy could scarcely at that age feel the whole satisfaction of thinking that President Polk was to be the vicarious victim of his own sins, and he gave his grandfather credit for intelligent silence. For this forbearance he felt instinctive respect. He admitted force as a form of right; he admitted even temper, under protest; but the seeds of a moral education would at that moment have fallen on the stoniest soil in Quincy, which is, as every one knows, the stoniest glacial and tidal drift known in any Puritan land.

Neither party to this momentary disagreement can have felt rancor, for during these three or four summers the old President's relations with the boy were friendly and almost intimate. Whether his older brothers and sisters were still more favored he failed to remember, but he was himself admitted to a sort of familiarity which, when in his turn he had reached old age, rather shocked him, for it must have sometimes tried the President's patience. He hung about the library; handled the books; deranged the papers; ransacked the drawers; searched the old purses and pocketbooks for foreign coins; drew the sword-cane, snapped the travelling-pistols; upset everything in the corners, and penetrated the President's dressing-closet where a row of tumblers, inverted on the shelf, covered caterpillars which were supposed to become moths or butterflies, but never did. . . .

As for his grandfather, it is even possible he may have felt a certain self-reproach for his temporary role of schoolmaster—seeing that his own career did not offer proof of the worldly advantages of docile obedience—for there still exists somewhere a little volume of critically edited Nursery Rhymes with the boy's name in full written in the President's trembling hand on the flyleaf. Of course there was also the Bible, given to each child at birth, with the proper inscription in the President's hand on the flyleaf; while their grandfather Brooks supplied the silver mugs.

So many Bibles and silver mugs had to be supplied, that a new house, or cottage, was built to hold them. It was "on the hill," five minutes walk above "old house," with a far view eastward over Quincy Bay, and northward over Boston. Till his twelfth year, the child passed his summers there, and his pleasures of childhood mostly centered in it. Of education he had as yet little to complain. Country schools were not very serious. Nothing stuck to the mind except home impressions, and the sharpest were those of kindred children; but as influences that warped a mind, none compared with the mere effect of the back of the President's bald head, as he sat in his pew on Sundays, in line with that of President Quincy, who, though some ten years younger, seemed to children about the same age. Before railways entered the New England town, every parish church showed half-a-dozen of these leading citizens, with gray hair, who sat on the main aisle in the best pews, and had sat there, or in some equivalent dignity, since the time of St. Augustine, if not since the glacial epoch. It was unusual for boys to sit behind a President grandfather, and to read over his head the tablet in memory of a President great-grandfather, who had "pledged his life, his fortune, and his sacred honor" to secure the independence of his country and so forth; but boys naturally supposed, without much reasoning, that other boys had the equivalent of President grandfathers, and that churches would always go on, with the bald-headed leading citizens on the main aisle, and Presidents or their equivalents on the walls. The Irish gardener once said to the child: "You'll be thinkin' you'll be President too!" The casualty of the remark made so strong an impression on his mind that he never forgot it. He could not remember ever to have thought on the subject; to him, that there should be a doubt of his being President was a new idea. What had been would continue to be. He doubted neither about Presidents nor about Churches, and no one suggested at that time a doubt whether a system of society which had lasted since Adam would outlast one Adams more.

The Madam was a little more remote than the President, but more decorative. She stayed much in her own room with the Dutch tiles, looking out on her garden with the box walks, and seemed a fragile creature to a boy who sometimes brought her a note or a message, and took distinct pleasure in looking at her delicate face under what seemed to him very becoming caps. He liked her refined figure; her gentle voice and manner; her vague effect of not belonging there, but to Washington or to Europe, like her furniture, and writing-desk with little glass doors above and little eighteenth-century volumes in old binding, labelled "Peregrine Pickle" or "Tom Jones" or "Hannah More." Try as she might, the Madam could never be Bostonian, and it was her cross in life, but to the boy it was her charm. . . .

By that time she was seventy years old or more, and thoroughly weary of being beaten about a stormy world. To the boy she seemed singularly peaceful, a vision of silver gray, presiding over her old President and her Queen Anne mahogany; an exotic, like her Sèvres china; an object of deference to every one, and of great affection to her son Charles; but hardly more Bostonian than she had been fifty years before, on her wedding-day, in the shadow of the Tower of London.

Such a figure was even less fitted than that of her old husband, the President, to impress on a boy's mind, the standards of the coming century. She was Louis Seize, like the furniture. The boy knew nothing of her interior life, which had been, as the venerable Abigail, long since at peace, foresaw, one of severe stress and little pure satisfaction. He never dreamed that from her might come some of those doubts and self-questionings, those hesitations, those rebellions against law and discipline, which marked more than one of her descendants; but he might even then have felt some vague instinctive suspicion that he was to inherit from her the seeds of the primal sin, the fall from grace, the curse of Abel, that he was not of pure New England stock, but half exotic. As a child of Quincy he was not a true Bostonian, but even as a child of Quincy he inherited a quarter taint of Maryland blood. . . .

A boy who began his education in these surroundings, with physical strength inferior to that of his brothers, and with a certain delicacy of mind and bone, ought rightly to have felt at home in the eighteenth century and should, in proper self-respect, have rebelled against the standards of the nineteenth. The atmosphere of his first ten years must have been very like that of his grandfather at the same age, from 1767 till 1776, barring the battle of Bunker Hill, and even as late as 1846, the battle of Bunker Hill remained actual. The tone of Boston society was colonial. The true Bostonian always knelt in self-abasement before the majesty of English standards; far from concealing it as a weakness, he was proud of it as his strength. The eighteenth century ruled society long after 1850. Perhaps the boy began to shake it off rather earlier than most of his mates.

Indeed this prehistoric stage of education ended rather abruptly with his tenth year. One winter morning he was conscious of a certain confusion in the house in Mount Vernon Street, and gathered, from such words as he could catch, that the President, who happened to be then staying there, on his way to Washington, had fallen and hurt himself. Then he heard the word paralysis. After that day he came to associate the word with the figure of his grandfather, in a tall-backed, invalid chair, on one side of the spare bedroom fireplace, and one of his old friends, Dr. Parkman or P. P. F. Degrand on the other side, both dozing.

The end of this first, or ancestral and Revolutionary, chapter came on February 21, 1848—and the month of February brought life and death as a family habit—when the eighteenth century, as an actual and living companion, vanished. If the scene on the floor of the House, when the old President fell, struck the still simple-minded American public with a sensation unusually dramatic, its effect on a ten-year-old boy, whose boy-life was fading away with the life of his grandfather, could not be slight. One had to pay for Revolutionary patriots; grandfathers and grandmothers; Presidents; diplomats; Queen Anne mahogany and Louis Seize chairs, as well as for Stuart portraits. Such things warp young life. Americans commonly believed that they ruined it, and perhaps the practical common-sense of the American mind judged right. Many a boy might be ruined by much less than the emotions of the funeral service in the Quincy church, with its surroundings of national respect and family pride. By another dramatic chance it happened that the clergyman of the parish, Dr. Lunt, was an unusual pulpit orator, the ideal of a somewhat austere intellectual type, such as the school of Buckminster and Channing inherited from the old Congregational clergy. His extraordinarily refined appearance, his dignity of manner, his deeply cadenced voice, his remarkable English and his fine appreciation, gave to the funeral service a character that left an overwhelming impression on the boy's mind. He was to see many great functions—funerals and festivals—in after-life, till his only thought was to see no more, but he never again witnessed anything nearly so impressive to him as the last services at Quincy over the body of one President and the ashes of another.

The Education of Henry Adams, 1907

RALPH WALDO EMERSON

Self-Reliance

Although written over a hundred years ago, the enduring wisdom from one of Emerson's more famous essays will be recognized by its astonishing relevance to our own tense times.

To believe your own thought, to believe that what is true for you in your private heart is true for all men,—that is genius. Speak your latent conviction, and it shall be the universal sense; for the inmost in due time becomes the outmost, and our first thought is rendered back to us by the trumpets of the Last Judgment. Familiar as the voice of the mind is to each, the highest merit we ascribe to Moses, Plato and Milton is that they set at naught books and traditions, and spoke not what men, but what *they* thought. A man should learn to detect and watch that gleam of light which flashes across his mind from within, more than the lustre of the firmament of bards and sages. Yet he dismisses without notice his thought, because it is his. In every work of genius we recognize our own rejected thoughts; they come back to us with a certain alienated majesty. Great works of art have no more affecting lesson for us than this. They teach us to abide by our spontaneous impression with good-humored inflexibility then most when the whole cry of voices is on the other side. Else tomorrow a stranger will say with masterly good sense precisely what we have thought and felt all the time, and we shall be forced to take with shame our own opinion from another.

There is a time in every man's education when he arrives at the conviction that envy is ignorance; that imitation is suicide; that he must take himself for better for worse as his portion; that though the wide universe is full of good, no kernel of nourishing corn can come to him but

56

through his toil bestowed on that plot of ground which is given him to till. The power which resides in him is new in nature, and none but he knows what that is which he can do, nor does he know until he has tried. . . . We but half express ourselves, and are ashamed of that divine idea which each of us represents. It may be safely trusted as proportionate and of good issues, so it be faithfully imparted, but God will not have his work made manifest by cowards. A man is relieved and gay when he has put his heart into his work and done his best; but what he has said or done otherwise shall give him no peace. It is a deliverance which does not deliver. In the attempt his genius deserts him; no muse befriends; no invention, no hope.

Trust thyself: every heart vibrates to that iron string. Accept the place the divine providence has found for you, the society of your contemporaries, the connection of events. Great men have always done so, and confided themselves childlike to the genius of their age, betraying their perception that the absolutely trustworthy was seated at their heart, working through their hands, predominating in all their being. And we are now men, and must accept in the highest mind the same transcendent destiny; and not minors and invalids in a protected corner nor cowards fleeing before a revolution, but guides, redeemers and benefactors, obeying the Almighty effort and advancing on Chaos and the Dark. . . .

Society everywhere is in conspiracy against the manhood of every one of its members. Society is a joint-stock company, in which the members agree, for the better securing of his bread to each shareholder, to surrender the liberty and culture of the eater. The virtue in most request is conformity. Self-reliance is its aversion. It loves not realities and creators, but names and customs.

Whoso would be a man, must be a nonconformist. He who would gather immortal palms must not be hindered by the name of goodness, but must explore if it be goodness. Nothing is at last sacred but the integrity of your own mind. . . . No law can be sacred to me but that of my nature. Good and bad are but names very readily transferable to that or this; the only right is what is after my constitution; the only wrong what is against it. A man is to carry himself in the presence of all opposition as if every thing were titular and ephemeral but he. I am ashamed to think how easily we capitulate to badges and names, to large societies and dead institutions. . . .

Men do what is called a good action, as some piece of courage or charity, much as they would pay a fine in expiation of daily non-appearance on parade. Their works are done as an apology or extenuation of their living in the world—as invalids and the insane pay a high board. Their virtues are penances. I do not wish to expiate, but to live. My life is for itself and not for a spectacle. I much prefer that it should be of a lower strain, so it be genuine and equal, than that it should be glittering and unsteady. I wish it to be sound and sweet, and not to need diet and bleeding. I ask primary evidence that you are a man, and refuse this appeal from the man to his actions. I know that for myself it makes no difference whether I do or forbear those actions which are reckoned excellent. I cannot consent to pay for a privilege where I have intrinsic right. Few and mean as my gifts may be, I actually am, and do not need for my own assurance or the assurance of my fellows any secondary testimony.

What I must do is all that concerns me, not what the people think. This rule, equally arduous in actual and in intellectual life, may serve for the whole distinction between greatness and meanness. It is the harder because you will always find those who think they know what is your duty better than you know it. It is easy in the world to live after the world's opinion; it is easy in solitude to live after your own; but the great man is he who in the midst of the crowd keeps with perfect sweetness the independence of solitude. . . .

For nonconformity the world whips you with its displeasure. And therefore a man must know how to estimate a sour face. The by-standers look askance on him in the public street or in the friend's parlor. If this aversion had its origin in contempt and resistance like his own he might well go home with a sad countenance; but the sour faces of the multitude, like their sweet faces, have no deep cause, but are put on and off as the wind blows and a newspaper directs. Yet is the discontent of the multitude more formidable than that of the senate and the college. It is easy enough for a firm man who knows the world to brook the rage of the cultivated classes. Their rage is decorous and prudent, for they are timid, as being very vulnerable themselves. But when to their feminine rage the indignation of the people is added, when the ignorant and the poor are aroused, when the unintelligent brute force that lies at the bottom of society is made to growl and mow, it needs the habit of magnanimity and religion to treat it godlike as a trifle of no concernment. . . .

A foolish consistency is the hobgoblin of little minds, adored by little statesmen and philosophers and divines. With consistency a great soul has simply nothing to do. He may as well concern himself with his shadow on the wall. Speak what you think now in hard words and to-morrow speak what to-morrow thinks in hard words again, though it contradict every thing you said to-day.—"Ah, so you shall be sure to be misunderstood." —Is it so bad then to be misunderstood? Pythagoras was misunderstood, and Socrates, and Jesus, and Luther, and Copernicus, and Galileo, and Newton, and every pure and wise spirit that ever took flesh. To be great is to be misunderstood. . . .

Act singly, and what you have already done singly will justify you now. Greatness appeals to the future. If I can be firm enough to-day to do right and scorn eyes, I must have done so much right before as to defend me now. Be it how it will, do right now. Always scorn appearances and you always may. The force of character is cumulative. All the foregone days of virtue work their health into this. . . .

I hope in these days we have heard the last of conformity and consistency. Let the words be gazetted and ridiculous henceforward. Instead of the gong for dinner, let us hear a whistle from the Spartan fife. Let us never bow and apologize more. A great man is coming to eat at my house. I do not wish to please him; I wish that he should wish to please me. I will stand here for humanity, and though I would make it kind, I would make it true. Let us affront and reprimand the smooth mediocrity and squalid contentment of the times, and hurl in the face of custom and trade and office, the fact which is the upshot of all history, that there is a great responsible Thinker and Actor working wherever a man works; that a true man belongs to no other time or place, but is the centre of things. Where he is, there is nature. He measures you and all men and all events. . . .

Let a man then know his worth, and keep things under his feet. Let him not peep or steal, or skulk up and down with the air of a charity-boy, a bastard, or an interloper in the world which exists for him. But the man in the street, finding no worth in himself which corresponds to the force which built a tower or sculptured a marble god, feels poor when he looks on these. To him a palace, a statue, or a costly book have an alien and forbidding air, much like a gay equipage, and seem to say like that, "Who are you, Sir?" Yet they all are his, suitors for his notice, petitioners to his faculties that they will come out and take possession. The picture waits for my verdict; it is not to command me, but I am to settle its claims to praise. That popular fable of the sot who was picked up dead-drunk in the street, carried to the duke's house, washed and dressed and laid in the duke's bed, and, on his waking, treated with all obsequious ceremony like the duke, and assured that he had been insane, owes its popularity to the fact that it symbolizes so well the state of man, who is in the world a sort of sot, but now and then wakes up, exercises his reason and finds himself a true prince. . . .

If any man consider the present aspects of what is called by distinction *society*, he will see the need of these ethics. The sinew and heart of man seem to be drawn out, and we are become timorous, desponding whimperers. We are afraid of truth, afraid of fortune, afraid of death, and afraid of each other. Our age yields no great and perfect persons. We want men and women who shall renovate life and our social state, but we see that most natures are insolvent, cannot satisfy their own wants, have an ambition out of all proportion to their practical force and do lean and beg day and night continually. . . .

If our young men miscarry in their first enterprises they lose all heart. If the young merchant fails, men say he is *ruined*. If the finest genius studies at one of our colleges and is not installed in an office within one year afterwards in the cities or suburbs of Boston or New York, it seems to his friends and to himself that he is right in being disheartened and in complaining the rest of his life. A sturdy lad from New Hampshire or Vermont, who in turn tries all the professions, who *teams it, farms it, peddles*, keeps a school, preaches, edits a newspaper, goes to Congress, buys a township, and so forth, in successive years, and always like a cat falls on his feet, is worth a hundred of these city dolls. He walks abreast with his days and feels no shame in not "studying a profession," for he does not postpone his life, but lives already. He has not one chance, but a hundred chances. Let a Stoic open the resources of man and tell men they are not leaning willows, but can and must detach themselves; that with the exercise of self-trust, new powers shall appear; that a man is the word made flesh, born to shed healing to the nations; that he should be ashamed of our compassion, and that the moment he acts from himself, tossing the laws, the books, idolatries and customs out of the window, we pity him no more but thank and revere him;—and that teacher shall restore the life of man to splendor and make his name dear to all history.

It is easy to see that a greater self-reliance must work a revolution in all the offices and relations of men; in their religion; in their education; in their pursuits; their modes of living; their association; in their property; in their speculative views. . . .

Insist on yourself; never imitate. Your own gift you can present every moment with the cumulative force of a whole life's cultivation; but of the adopted talent of another you have only an extemporaneous half possession. That which each can do best, none but his Maker can teach him. No man yet knows what it is, nor can, till that person has exhibited it. Where is the master who could have taught Shakespeare? Where is the master who could have instructed Franklin, or Washington, or Bacon, or Newton? Every great man is a unique. . . . Do that which is assigned you, and you cannot hope too much or dare too much. . . .

So use all that is called Fortune. Most men gamble with her, and gain all, and lose all, as her wheel rolls. But do thou leave as unlawful these winnings, and deal with Cause and Effect, the chancellors of God. In the Will work and acquire, and thou hast chained the wheel of Chance, and shall sit hereafter out of fear from her rotations. A political victory, a rise of rents, the recovery of your sick or the return of your absent friend, or some other favorable event raises your spirits, and you think good days are preparing for you. Do not believe it. Nothing can bring you peace but yourself. Nothing can bring you peace but the triumph of principles.

From "Self-Reliance" in *Essays*, 1841

Terminus

It is time to be old,
To take in sail:—
The god of bounds,
Who sets to seas a shore,

Came to me in his fatal rounds,
And said: "No more!
No farther shoot
Thy broad ambitious branches, and thy root.
Fancy departs; no more invent;
Contract thy firmament
To compass of a tent.
There's not enough for this and that,
Make thy option which of two;
Economize the failing river,
Not the less revere the Giver,
Leave the many and hold the few.
Timely wise accept the terms,
Soften the fall with wary foot;
A little while
Still plan and smile,
And,—fault of novel germs,—
Mature the unfallen fruit.
Curse, if thou wilt, thy sires,
Bad husbands of their fires,
Who, when they gave thee breath,
Failed to bequeath
The needful sinew stark as once,
The Baresark marrow to thy bones,
But left a legacy of ebbing veins,
Inconstant heat and nerveless reins,—
Amid the Muses, left thee deaf and dumb,
Amid the gladiators, halt and numb."

    As the bird trims her to the gale,
I trim myself to the storm of time,
I man the rudder, reef the sail,
Obey the voice at eve obeyed at prime:
"Lowly faithful, banish fear,
Right onward drive unharmed;
The port, well worth the cruise, is near,
And every wave is charmed."

Poems, 1866

JAMES RUSSELL LOWELL

Emerson

There are persons, mole-blind to the soul's make and style,
Who insist on a likeness, 'twixt him and Carlyle;
To compare him with Plato would be vastly fairer,
Carlyle's the more burly, but E. is the rarer;
He sees fewer objects, but clearlier, trulier,
If C.'s as original, E.'s more peculiar;
That he's more of a man you might say of the one,
Of the other he's more of an Emerson;
C.'s the Titan, as shaggy of mind as of limb,—
E. the clear-eyed Olympian, rapid and slim;
The one's two-thirds Norseman, the other half Greek,
Where the one's most abounding, the other's to seek;
C.'s generals require to be seen in the mass,—
E.'s specialties gain if enlarged by the glass;
C. gives nature and God his own fits of the blues,
And rims common-sense things with mystical hues,—
E. sits in a mystery calm and intense,
And looks coolly around him with sharp common sense;
C. shows you how every-day matters unite
With the dim transdiurnal recesses of night,—
While E., in a plain, preternatural way,
Makes mysteries matters of mere every day;
C. draws all his characters quite à la Fuseli,—
Not sketching their bundles of muscles and thews illy,
He paints with a brush so untamed and profuse,
They seem nothing but bundles of muscles and thews;
E. is rather like Flaxman, lines strait and severe,
And a colorless outline, but full, round, and clear;—
To the men he thinks worthy he frankly accords
The design of a white marble statue in words.
C. labors to get at the centre, and then
Take a reckoning from there of his actions and men;
E. calmly assumes the said centre as granted,
And, given himself, has whatever is wanted.

A Fable for Critics, 1848

HERMAN MELVILLE

Ahab and the Whale

I, Ishmael, was one of that crew; my shouts had gone up with the rest; my oath had been welded with theirs; and stronger I shouted, and more did I hammer and clinch my oath, because of the dread in my soul. A wild, mystical, sympathetical feeling was in me; Ahab's quenchless feud seemed mine. With greedy ears I learned the history of that murderous monster against whom I and all the others had taken our oaths of violence and revenge.

For some time past, though at intervals only, the unaccompanied, secluded White Whale had haunted those uncivilized seas most frequented by the Sperm Whale fishermen. But not all of them knew of his existence; only a few of them, comparatively, had knowingly seen him; while the number who as yet had actually and knowingly given battle to him, was small indeed. For, owing to the large number of whale cruisers; the disorderly way they were sprinkled over the entire watery circumference, many of them adventurously pushing their quest along solitary latitudes, so as to be seldom or never for a whole twelvemonth or more on a stretch, to encounter a single news-telling sail of any sort; the inordinate length of each separate voyage; the irregularity of the times of sailing from home; all these, with other circumstances, direct and indirect, long obstructed the spread through the whole world-wide whaling-fleet of the special individualized tidings concerning Moby Dick. . . . Yet as of late the Sperm Whale fishery had been marked by various and not infrequent instances of great ferocity, cunning, and malice in the monster attacked; therefore it was, that those who by accident ignorantly gave battle to Moby Dick; such hunters, perhaps, for the most part, were content to ascribe the peculiar terror he bred, more, as it were, to the perils of the Sperm Whale fishery at large, than to the individual cause. In that way, mostly, the disastrous encounter between Ahab and the whale had hitherto been popularly regarded.

And as for those who, previously hearing of the White Whale, by chance caught sight of him; in the beginning of the thing they had every one of them, almost, as boldly and fearlessly lowered for him, as for any other whale of that species. But at length, such calamities did ensue in these assaults—not restricted to sprained wrists and ankles, broken limbs, or devouring amputations—but fatal to the last degree of fatality; those repeated disastrous repulses, all accumulating and piling their terrors upon Moby Dick; those things had gone far to shake the fortitude of many brave hunters, to whom the story of the White Whale had eventually come.

Nor did wild rumors of all sorts fail to exaggerate, and still the more horrify the true histories of these deadly encounters. For not only do fabulous rumors naturally grow out of the very body of all surprising terrible events,—as the smitten tree gives birth to its fungi; but, in maritime life, far more than in that of terra firma, wild rumors abound, wherever there is any adequate reality for them to cling to. And as the sea surpasses the land in this matter, so the whale fishery surpasses every other sort of maritime life, in the wonderfulness and fearfulness of the rumors which sometimes circulate there. . . .

No wonder, then, that ever gathering volume from the mere transit over the wildest watery spaces, the outblown rumors of the White Whale did in the end incorporate with themselves all manner of morbid hints, and half-formed foetal suggestions of supernatural agencies, which eventually invested Moby Dick with new terrors unborrowed from anything that visibly appears. So that in many cases such a panic did he finally strike, that few who by those rumors, at least, had heard of the White Whale, few of those hunters were willing to encounter the perils of his jaw. . . .

So that overawed by the rumors and portents concerning him, not a few of the fishermen recalled, in reference to Moby Dick, the earlier days of the Sperm Whale fishery, when it was oftentimes hard to induce long-practised Right Whalemen to embark in the perils of this new and daring warfare; such men protesting that although other Leviathans might be hopefully pursued, yet to chase and point lances at such an apparition as the Sperm Whale was not for mortal man. That to attempt it, would be inevitably to be torn into a quick eternity. On this head, there are some remarkable documents that may be consulted.

Nevertheless, some there were, who even in the face of these things were ready to give chase to Moby Dick; and a still greater number who, chancing only to hear of him distantly and vaguely, without the specific details of any certain calamity, and without superstitious accompaniments, were sufficiently hardy not to flee from the battle if offered.

One of the wild suggestings referred to, as at last coming to be linked with the White Whale in the minds of the superstitiously inclined, was the unearthly conceit that Moby Dick was ubiquitous; that he had actually been encountered in opposite latitudes at one and the same instant of time.

Nor, credulous as such minds must have been, was this conceit altogether without some faint show of superstitious probability. For as the secrets of the currents in the seas have never yet been divulged, even to the most erudite research; so the hidden ways of the Sperm Whale when beneath the surface remain, in great part, unaccountable to his pursuers; and from time to time have originated the most curious and contradictory speculations regarding them, especially concerning the mystic modes whereby, after sounding to a great depth, he transports himself with such vast swiftness to the most widely distant points. . . .

Forced into familiarity, then, with such prodigies as these; and knowing that after repeated, intrepid assaults, the White Whale had escaped alive; it cannot be much matter of surprise that some whalemen should go still further in their superstitions; declaring Moby Dick not only ubiquitous, but immortal (for immortality is but ubiquity in time; that though groves of spears should be planted in his flanks, he would still swim away unharmed; or if indeed he should ever be made to spout thick blood, such a sight would be but a ghastly deception; for again in unensanguined billows hundreds of leagues away, his unsullied jet would once more be seen.

But even stripped of these supernatural surmisings, there was enough in the earthly make and incontestable character of the monster to strike the imagination with unwonted power. For, it was not so much his uncommon bulk that so much distinguished him from other Sperm Whales, but, as was elsewhere thrown out—a peculiar snow-white wrinkled forehead, and a high, pyramidical white hump. These were his prominent features; the tokens whereby, even in the limitless, uncharted seas, he revealed his identity, at a long distance, to those who knew him.

The rest of his body was so streaked, and spotted, and marbled with the same shrouded hue, that, in the end, he had gained his distinctive appellation of the White Whale; a name, indeed, literally justified by his vivid aspect, when seen gliding at high noon through a dark blue sea, leaving a milky-way wake of creamy foam, all spangled with golden gleamings.

Nor was it his unwonted magnitude, nor his remarkable hue, nor yet his deformed lower jaw, that so much invested the whale with natural terror, as that unexampled, intelligent malignity which, according to specific accounts, he had over and over again evinced in his assaults. More than all, his treacherous retreats struck more of dismay than perhaps aught else. For, when swimming before his exulting pursuers, with every apparent symptom of alarm, he had several times been known to turn round suddenly, and, bearing down upon them, either stave their boats to splinters, or drive them back in consternation to their ship.

Already several fatalities had attended his chase. But though similar disasters, however little bruited ashore, were by no means unusual in the fishery; yet, in most instances, such seemed the White Whale's infernal aforethought of ferocity, that every dismembering or death that he caused, was not wholly regarded as having been inflicted by an unintelligent agent.

Judge, then, to what pitches of inflamed, distracted fury the minds of his more desperate hunters were impelled, when amid the chips of chewed boats, and the sinking limbs of torn comrades, they swam out of the white curds of the whale's direful wrath into the serene, exasperating sunlight, that smiled on, as if at a birth or a bridal.

His three boats stove around him, and oars and men both whirling in the eddies; one captain, seizing the line-knife from his broken prow, had dashed at the whale, as an Arkansas duellist at his foe, blindly seeking with a six-inch blade to reach the fathom-deep life of the whale. That captain was Ahab. And then it was, that suddenly sweeping his sickle-shaped lower jaw beneath him, Moby Dick had reaped away Ahab's leg, as a mower a blade of grass in the field. No turbaned Turk, no hired Venetian or Malay, could have smote him with more seeming malice. Small reason was there to doubt, then, that ever since that almost fatal encounter, Ahab had cherished a wild vindictiveness against the whale, all the more fell for that in his frantic morbidness he at last came to identify with him, not only all his bodily woes, but all his intellectual and spiritual exasperations. The White Whale swam before him as the monomaniac incarnation of all those malicious agencies which some deep men feel eating in them, till they are left living on with half a heart and half a lung. That intangible malignity which has been from the beginning; to whose dominion even the modern Christians ascribe one-half of the worlds; which the ancient Ophites of the east reverenced in their statue devil;—Ahab did not fall down and worship it like them; but deliriously transferring its idea to the abhorred White Whale, he pitted himself, all mutilated, against it. All that most maddens and torments; all that stirs up the lees of things; all truth with malice in it; all that cracks the sinews and cakes the brain; all the subtle demonisms of life and thought; all evil, to crazy Ahab, were visibly personified, and made practically assailable in Moby Dick. He piled upon the whale's white hump the sum of all the general rage and hate felt by his whole race from Adam down; and then, as if his chest had been a mortar, he burst his hot heart's shell upon it.

It is not probable that this monomania in him took its instant rise at the precise time of his bodily dismemberment. Then, in darting at the monster, knife in hand, he had but given loose to a sudden, passionate, corporal animosity; and when he received the stroke that tore him, he probably but felt the agonizing bodily laceration, but nothing more. Yet, when by this collision forced to turn towards home, and for long months of days and weeks, Ahab and anguish lay stretched together in one hammock, rounding in mid winter that dreary, howling Patagonian Cape; then it was, that his torn body and gashed soul bled into one another; and so interfusing, made him mad. That it was only then, on the homeward voyage, after the encounter, that the final monomania seized him, seems all but certain from the fact that, at intervals during the passage, he was a raving lunatic; and, though unlimbed of a leg, yet such vital strength yet lurked in his Egyptian chest, and was moreover intensified by his delirium, that his mates were forced to lace him fast, even there, as he sailed, raving in his hammock. In a strait-jacket, he swung to the mad rockings of the gales. And, when running into more sufferable latitudes, the ship, with mild stun'sails spread, floated across the tranquil tropics, and, to all appearances, the old man's delirium seemed left behind him with the Cape Horn swells, and he came forth from his dark den into the blessed light and air; even then, when he bore that firm, collected front, however pale, and issued his calm orders once again; and his mates thanked God the direful madness was now gone; even then, Ahab, in his hidden self, raved on. Human madness is oftentimes a cunning and most feline thing. When you think it fled, it may have but become transfigured into some still subtler form. Ahab's full lunacy subsided not, but deepeningly contracted; like the unabated Hudson, when that noble Northman flows narrowly, but unfathomably through the Highland gorge. But, as in his narrow-flowing monomania, not one jot of Ahab's broad madness had been left behind; so in that broad madness, not one jot of his great natural intellect had perished. That before living agent, now became the living instrument. If such a furious trope may stand, his special lunacy stormed his general sanity, and carried it, and turned all its concentrated cannon upon its own mad mark; so that far from having lost his strength, Ahab, to that one end, did now possess a thousand fold more potency than ever he had sanely brought to bear upon any one reasonable object.

This is much; yet Ahab's larger, darker, deeper part remains unhinted. But vain to popularize profundities, and all truth is profound. Winding far down from within the very heart of this spiked Hotel de Cluny where we here stand—however grand and wonderful, now quit it;—and take your way, ye nobler, sadder souls, to those vast Roman halls of Thermes; where far beneath the fantastic towers of man's upper earth, his root of grandeur, his whole awful essence sits in bearded state; an antique buried beneath antiquities, and throned on torsoes! So with a broken throne, the great gods mock that captive king; so like a Caryatid, he patient sits, upholding on his frozen brow the piled entablatures of ages. Wind ye down there, ye prouder, sadder souls! question that proud, sad king! A family likeness! aye, he did beget ye, ye young exiled royalties; and from your grim sire only will the old State-secret come.

Now, in his heart, Ahab had some glimpses of this, namely: all my means are sane, my motive and object mad. Yet without power to kill, or change, or shun the fact; he likewise knew that to mankind he did not long dissemble; in some sort, did still. But that thing of his dissembling was only subject to his perceptibility, not to his will determinate. Nevertheless, so well did he succeed in that dissembling, that when with ivory leg he stepped ashore at last, no Nantucketer thought him otherwise than but naturally grieved, and that to the quick, with the terrible casualty which had overtaken him.

The report of his undeniable delirium at sea was likewise popularly ascribed to a kindred cause. And so too, all the added moodiness which always afterwards, to the very day of sailing in the Pequod on the present voyage, sat brooding on his brow. Nor is it so very unlikely, that far from distrusting his fitness for another whaling voyage, on account of such dark symptoms, the calculating people of that prudent isle were inclined to harbor the conceit, that for those very reasons he was all the better qualified and set on edge, for a pursuit so full of rage and wildness as the bloody hunt of whales. Gnawed within and scorched without, with the infixed, unrelenting fangs of some incurable idea; such an one, could he

67

be found, would seem the very man to dart his iron and lift his lance against the most appalling of all brutes. Or, if for any reason thought to be corporeally incapacitated for that, yet such an one would seem superlatively competent to cheer and howl on his underlings to the attack. But be all this as it may, certain it is, that with the mad secret of his unabated rage bolted up and keyed in him, Ahab had purposely sailed upon the present voyage with the one only and all-engrossing purpose of hunting the White Whale. Had any one of his old acquaintances on shore but half dreamed of what was lurking in him then, how soon would their aghast and righteous souls have wrenched the ship from such a fiendish man! They were bent on profitable cruises, the profit to be counted down in dollars from the mint. He was intent on an audacious, immitigable, and supernatural revenge.

Here, then, was this grey-headed, ungodly old man, chasing with curses a Job's whale round the world, at the head of a crew, too, chiefly made up of mongrel renegades, and castaways, and cannibals—morally enfeebled also, by the incompetence of mere unaided virtue or right-mindedness in Starbuck, the invulnerable jollity of indifference and recklessness in Stubb, and the pervading mediocrity in Flask. Such a crew, so officered, seemed specially picked and packed by some infernal fatality to help him to his monomaniac revenge. How it was that they so aboundingly responded to the old man's ire—by what evil magic their souls were possessed, that at times his hate seemed almost theirs; the White Whale as much their insufferable foe as his; how all this came to be—what the White Whale was to them, or how to their unconscious understandings, also, in some dim, unsuspected way, he might have seemed the gliding great demon of the seas of life,—all this to explain, would be to dive deeper than Ishmael can go.

Moby Dick, 1851

WALT WHITMAN

"The United States . . . the Greatest Poem"

The Americans of all nations at any time upon the earth have probably the fullest poetical nature. The United States themselves are essentially the greatest poem. In the history of the earth hitherto the largest and most stirring appear tame and orderly to their ampler largeness and stir. Here at last is something in the doings of man that corresponds with the broadcast doings of the day and night. Here is not merely a nation but a teeming nation of nations. Here is action untied from strings necessarily blind to particulars and details magnificently moving in vast masses. Here is the hospitality which forever indicates heroes. . . . Here are the roughs and beards and space and ruggedness and nonchalance that the soul loves. Here the performance disdaining the trivial unapproached in the tremendous audacity of its crowds and groupings and the push of its perspective spreads with crampless and flowing breadth and showers its prolific and splendid extravagance. One sees it must indeed own the riches of the summer and winter, and need never be bankrupt while corn grows from the ground or the orchards drop apples or the bays contain fish or men beget children upon women.

Other states indicate themselves in their deputies . . . but the genius of the United States is not best or most in its executives or legislatures, nor in its ambassadors or authors or colleges or churches or parlors, nor even in its newspapers or inventors . . . but always most in the common people. Their manners speech dress friendships—the freshness and candor of their physiognomy—the picturesque looseness of their carriage . . . their deathless attachment to freedom—their aversion to anything indecorous or soft or mean—the practical acknowledgment of the citizens of one state by the citizens of all other states—the fierceness of their roused resentment—their curiosity and welcome of novelty—their self-esteem and wonderful sympathy—their susceptibility to a slight—the air they have of persons who never knew how it felt to stand in the presence of superiors—the fluency of their speech—their delight in music, the sure symptom of manly tenderness and native elegance of soul . . . their good temper and openhandedness—the terrible significance of their elections—the President's taking off his hat to them not they to him—these too are unrhymed poetry. It awaits the gigantic and generous treatment worthy of it.

The largeness of nature or the nation were monstrous without a corresponding largeness and generosity of the spirit of the citizen. Not nature nor swarming states nor streets and steamships nor prosperous business nor farms nor capital nor learning may suffice for the ideal of man . . . nor suffice the poet. No reminiscences may suffice either. A live nation can always cut a deep mark and can have the best authority the cheapest . . . namely from its own soul. This is the sum of the profitable uses of individuals or states and of present action and grandeur and of the subjects of poets. . . .

The American poets are to enclose old and new for America is the race of races. Of them a bard is to be commensurate with a people. . . . To him the hereditary countenance descends both mother's and father's. To him enter the essences of the real things and past and present events—of the enormous diversity of temperature and agriculture and mines—the tribes of red aborigines—the weather-beaten vessels entering new ports or making landings on rocky coasts—the first settlements north or south— the rapid stature and muscle—the haughty defiance of '76, and the war and peace and formation of the constitution . . . the union always surrounded by blatherers and always calm and impregnable—the perpetual coming of immigrants—the wharf-hem'd cities and superior marine—the unsurveyed interior—the loghouses and clearings and wild animals and hunters and trappers . . . the free commerce—the fisheries and whaling and gold-digging—the endless gestation of new states—the convening of Congress every December, the members duly coming up from all climates and the uttermost parts . . . the noble character of the young mechanics and of all free American workmen and workwomen . . . the general ardor and friendliness and enterprise—the perfect equality of the female with the male . . . the large amativeness—the fluid movement of the population— the factories and mercantile life and laborsaving machinery—the Yankee swap—the New-York firemen and the target excursion—the southern plantation life—the character of the northeast and of the northwest and southwest—slavery and the tremulous spreading of hands to protect it, and the stern opposition to it which shall never cease till it ceases or the speaking of tongues and the moving of lips cease. For such the expression of the American poet is to be transcendent and new. It is to be indirect and not direct or descriptive or epic. Its quality goes through these to much more. Let the age and wars of other nations be chanted and their eras and characters be illustrated and that finish the verse. Not so the great psalms of the republic. Here the theme is creative and has vista. Here comes one among the well-beloved stonecutters and plans with decision and science and sees the solid and beautiful forms of the future where there are now no solid forms.

Of all nations the United States with veins full of poetical stuff most need poets and will doubtless have the greatest and use them the greatest.

From the Preface to the 1855 edition of *Leaves of Grass*

There Was a Child Went Forth

There was a child went forth every day,
And the first object he look'd upon, that object he became,
And that object became part of him for the day or a certain part of the day,
Or for many years or stretching cycles of years.

The early lilacs became part of this child,
And grass and white and red morning-glories, and white and red clover,
        and the song of the phoebe-bird,
And the Third-month lambs and the sow's pink-faint litter, and the mare's
        foal and the cow's calf,
And the noisy brood of the barnyard or by the mire of the pond-side,
And the fish suspending themselves so curiously below there, and the beau-
        tiful curious liquid,
And the water-plants with their graceful flat heads, all became part of him.

The field-sprouts of Fourth-month and Fifth-month became part of him,
Winter-grain sprouts and those of the light-yellow corn, and the esculent
    roots of the garden,
And the apple-trees cover'd with blossoms and the fruit afterward, and
    wood-berries, and the commonest weeds by the road,
And the old drunkard staggering home from the outhouse of the tavern
    whence he had lately risen,
And the schoolmistress that pass'd on her way to the school,
And the friendly boys that pass'd, and the quarrelsome boys,
And the tidy and fresh-cheek'd girls, and the barefoot Negro boy and girl,
And all the changes of city and country wherever he went.

His own parents, he that had father'd him and she that had conceiv'd him
    in her womb and birth'd him,
They gave this child more of themselves than that,
They gave him afterward every day, they became part of him.

The mother at home quietly placing the dishes on the supper-table,
The mother with mild words, clean her cap and gown, a wholesome odor
    falling off her person and clothes as she walks by,
The father, strong, self-sufficient, manly, mean, anger'd, unjust,
The blow, the quick loud word, the tight bargain, the crafty lure,
The family usages, the language, the company, the furniture, the yearning
    and swelling heart,
Affection that will not be gainsay'd, the sense of what is real, the thought
    if after all it should prove unreal,
The doubts of day-time and the doubts of night-time, the curious whether
    and how,
Whether that which appears so is so, or is it all flashes and specks?
Men and women crowding fast in the streets, if they are not flashes and
    specks what are they?
The streets themselves and the façade of houses, and goods in the windows,
Vehicles, teams, the heavy-plank'd wharves, the huge crossing at the ferries,
The village on the highland seen from afar at sunset, the river between,
Shadows, aureola and mist, the light falling on roofs and gables of white
    or brown two miles off,
The schooner near by sleepily dropping down the tide, the little boat slack-
    tow'd astern,
The hurrying tumbling waves, quick-broken crests, slapping,
The strata of color'd clouds, the long bar of maroon-tint away solitary by
    itself, the spread of purity it lies motionless in,
The horizon's edge, the flying sea-crow, the fragrance of salt marsh and
    shore mud,
These became part of that child who went forth every day, and who now
    goes, and will always go forth every day.

Leaves of Grass, 1855

"Come Lovely and Soothing Death"

Come lovely and soothing death,
Undulate round the world, serenely arriving, arriving,
In the day, in the night, to all, to each,
Sooner or later delicate death.

Prais'd be the fathomless universe,
For life and joy, and for objects and knowledge curious,
And for love, sweet love—but praise! praise! praise!
For the sure-enwinding arms of cool-enfolding death.

Dark mother always gliding near with soft feet,
Have none chanted for thee a chant of fullest welcome?
Then I chant it for thee, I glorify thee above all,
I bring thee a song that when thou must indeed come, come, unfalteringly.

Approach strong deliveress,
When it is so, when thou hast taken them I joyously sing the dead,
Lost in the loving floating ocean of thee,
Laved in the flood of thy bliss O death.

From me to thee glad serenades,
Dances for thee I propose saluting thee, adornments and feastings for thee,
And the sights of the open landscape and the high-spread sky are fitting,
And life and the fields, and the huge and thoughtful night.

The night in silence under many a star,
The ocean shore and the husky whispering wave whose voice I know,
And the soul turning to thee O vast and well-veil'd death,
And the body gratefully nestling close to thee.

Over the tree-tops I float thee a song,
Over the rising and sinking waves, over the myriad fields and the prairies
        wide,
Over the dense-pack'd cities all and the teeming wharves and ways,
I float this carol with joy, with joy to thee O death.

From When Lilacs Last in the Dooryard Bloomed, 1865

L. E. CHITTENDEN

Lincoln Pardons a Sleeping Sentinel

> *Chittenden was a Vermont lawyer and politician who served as registrar of the United States Treasury during Lincoln's administrations. This passage may lack literary polish, but it shows Lincoln in a most human and understanding light.*

On a dark September morning in 1861, when I reached my office, I found waiting there a party of soldiers, none of whom I personally knew. They were greatly excited, all speaking at the same time, and consequently unintelligible. One of them wore the bars of a captain. I said to them pleasantly: "Boys, I cannot understand you. Pray let your captain say what you want and what I can do for you." They complied, and the captain put me in possession of the following facts.

They belonged to the Third Vermont Regiment, raised, with the exception of one company, on the eastern slope of the Green Mountains, and mustered into service while the battle of Bull Run was progressing. . . .

The story which I extracted from the boys was, in substance, this: William Scott, one of these mountain boys, just of age, had enlisted in Company K. Accustomed to his regular sound and healthy sleep, not yet inured to the life of the camp, he had volunteered to take the place of a sick comrade who had been detailed for picket duty, and had passed the night as a sentinel on guard. The next day he was himself detailed for the same duty and undertook its performance. But he found it impossible to keep awake for two nights in succession and had been found by the relief sound asleep on his post. For this offense he had been tried by a court-martial, found guilty, and sentenced to be shot within twenty-four hours after his trial and on the second morning after his offense was committed.

Scott's comrades had set about saving him in a characteristic way. They had called a meeting [and] appointed a committee with power to use all the resources of the regiment in his behalf. Strangers in Washington, the committee had resolved to call on me for advice because I was a Vermonter, and they had already marched from the camp to my office since daylight that morning.

The captain took all the blame from Scott upon himself. Scott's mother opposed his enlistment on the ground of his inexperience and had only consented on the captain's promise to look after him as if he were his own son. This he had wholly failed to do. He must have been asleep or stupid himself, he said, when he paid no attention to the boy's statement that he had fallen asleep during the day and feared he could not keep awake on the second night on picket. Instead of sending some one or going himself in Scott's place, as he should, he had let him go to his death. He alone was guilty—"if anyone ought to be shot, I am the fellow, and everybody at home would have the right to say so." "There must be some way to save him, Judge!" "He is as good a boy as there is in the army, and he ain't to blame. You will help us, now, won't you?" he said, almost with tears.

The other members of the committee had a definite if not a practicable plan. They insisted that Scott had not been tried and gave this account of the proceeding. He was asked what he had to say to the charge and said he would tell them just how it all happened. He had never been up all night that he remembered. He was "all beat out" by the night before and knew he should have a hard fight to keep awake; he thought of hiring one of the boys to go in his place, but they might think he was afraid to do his duty, and he decided to chance it. Twice he went to sleep and woke himself while he was marching, and then—he could not tell anything about it—all he knew was that he was sound asleep when the guard came. It was very wrong, he knew. He wanted to be a good soldier and do his duty. What else did he enlist for? They could shoot him, and perhaps they ought to, but he could not have tried harder; and if he was in the same place again, he could no more help going to sleep than he could fly.

One must have been made of sterner stuff than I was not to be touched by the earnest manner with which these men offered to devote even their farms to the aid of their comrade. The captain and the others had no words to express their emotions. I saw that the situation was surrounded by difficulties of which they knew nothing.

The more I reflected upon what I was to do, the more hopeless the case appeared. Thought was useless. I must act upon impulse, or I should not act at all.

"Come," I said, "there is only one man on earth who can save your comrade. Fortunately, he is the best man on the continent. We will go to President Lincoln."

I went swiftly out of the Treasury over to the White House and up the stairway to the little office where the President was writing. The boys followed in a procession. I did not give the thought any time to get a hold on me that I, an officer of the government, was committing an impropriety in thus rushing a matter upon the President's attention. The President was the first to speak.

"What is this?" he asked. "An expedition to kidnap somebody or to get another brigadier appointed or furlough to go home to vote? I cannot do it, gentlemen. Brigadiers are thicker than drum majors, and I couldn't get a furlough for myself if I asked it from the War Department."

There was hope in the tone in which he spoke. I went straight to my point. "Mr. President," I said, "these men want nothing for themselves. They are Green Mountain boys of the Third Vermont, who have come to stay as long as you need good soldiers. They don't want promotion until they earn it. But they do want something that you alone can give them— the life of a comrade."

"What has he done?" asked the President. "You Vermonters are not a bad lot, generally. Has he committed murder or mutiny, or what other felony?"

"Tell him," I whispered to the captain.

"I cannot! I cannot! I should stammer like a fool! You can do it better!"

"Captain," I said, pushing him forward, "Scott's life depends on you. You must tell the President the story. I only know it from hearsay."

He commenced like the man by the Sea of Galilee who had an impediment in his speech, but very soon the string of his tongue was loosened, and he spoke plain. He began to word-paint a picture with the hand of a master. As the words burst from his lips they stirred my own blood. He gave a graphic account of the whole story and ended by saying: "He is as brave a boy as there is in your army, sir. Scott is no coward. Our mountains breed no cowards. They are the homes of thirty thousand men who voted for Abraham Lincoln. They will not be able to see that the best thing to be done with William Scott will be to shoot him like a traitor and bury him like a dog! Oh, Mr. Lincoln, can you?"

"No, I can't!" exclaimed the President. It was one of the moments when his countenance became such a remarkable study. It had become very earnest as the captain rose with his subject; then it took on that melancholy expression which, later in his life, became so infinitely touching. I thought I could detect a mist in the deep cavities of his eyes. Then in a flash there was a total change. He smiled and finally broke into a hearty laugh as he asked me: "Do your Green Mountain boys fight as well as they talk? If they do, I don't wonder at the legends about Ethan Allen." Then his face softened as he said: "But what can I do? What do you expect me to do? As you know, I have not much influence with the departments."

"I have not thought the matter out," I said, "I feel a deep interest in saving young Scott's life. I think I knew the boy's father. It is useless to apply to General Smith. An application to Secretary Stanton would only be referred to General Smith. The only thing to be done was to apply to you. It seems to me that, if you would sign an order suspending Scott's execution until his friends can have his case examined, I might carry it to the War Department and so insure the delivery of the order to General Smith today, through the regular channels of the War Office."

"No! I do not think that course would be safe. You do not know these officers of the regular army. They are a law unto themselves. They sincerely think that it is a good policy occasionally to shoot a soldier. I can see it, where a soldier deserts or commits a crime, but I cannot in such a case as Scott's. They say that I am always interfering with the discipline of the army and being cruel to the soldiers. Well, I can't help it; so I shall have to go right on doing wrong. I do not think an honest, brave soldier, conscious of no crime but sleeping when he was weary, ought to be shot or hung. The country has better uses for him.

"Captain," continued the President, "your boy shall not be shot—that is, not tomorrow, nor until I know more about his case." To me he said: "I will have to attend to this matter myself. I have for some time intended to go up to the [camp]. I will do so today. I shall know then that there is no mistake in suspending the execution."

I remarked that he was undertaking a burden that we had no right to impose, that it was asking too much of the President in behalf of a private soldier.

"Scott's life is as valuable to him as that of any person in the land," he said. "You remember the remark of a Scotchman about the head of a nobleman who was decapitated. 'It was a small matter of the head, but it was valuable to him, poor fellow, for it was the only one he had.' "

Later in the day the President started in the direction of the camp. . . .

Within a day or two the newspapers reported that a soldier sentenced to be shot for sleeping on his post had been pardoned by the President and returned to his regiment.

It was a long time before Scott would speak of his interview with Mr. Lincoln. One night, when he had received a long letter from home, he opened his heart and told Evans the story.

Scott said: "The President was the kindest man I had ever seen; I knew him at once, by a Lincoln medal I had worn. I was scared at first, for I had never before talked with a great man. But Mr. Lincoln was so easy with me, so gentle, that I soon forgot my fright. He asked me all about the people at home, the neighbors, the farm, and where I went to school, and who my schoolmates were. Then he asked me about mother and how she looked, and I was glad I could take her photograph from my bosom and show it to him. He said how thankful I ought to be that my mother still lived and how, if he was in my place, he would try to make her a proud mother and never cause her a sorrow or a tear. I cannot remember it all, but every word was so kind.

"He said nothing yet about that dreadful next morning. I thought it must be that he was so kindhearted that he didn't like to speak of it. But why did he say so much about my mother and my not causing her a sorrow or a tear when I knew that I must die the next morning. But I suppose that was something that would have to go unexplained, and so I determined to brace up and tell him that I did not feel a bit guilty and ask him wouldn't he fix it so that the firing party would not be from our regiment! That was going to be the hardest of all—to die by the hands of my comrades. Just as I was going to ask him this favor, he stood up, and he says to me, 'My boy, stand up here, and look me in the face.' I did as he bade me. 'My boy,' he said, 'you are not going to be shot tomorrow. I believe you when you tell me that you could not keep awake. I am going to trust you and send you back to your regiment. But I have been put to a good deal of trouble on your account. I have had to come up here from Washington when I have a great deal to do; and what I want to know is, how are you going to pay my bill?' There was a big lump in my throat; I could scarcely speak. I had expected to die, you see, and had kind of got used to thinking that way. To have it all changed in a minute! But I got it crowded down, and managed to say: 'I am grateful, Mr. Lincoln! I hope I am as grateful as ever a man can be to you for saving my life. But it comes upon me sudden and unexpected-like. I didn't lay out for it at all. But there is some way to pay you, and I will find it after a little. There is the bounty in the savings bank. I guess we could borrow some money on the mortgage of the farm.' There was my pay was something, and if he would wait until payday, I was sure the boys would help; so I thought we could make it up, if it wasn't more than five or six hundred dollars. 'But it is a great deal more than that,' he said. Then I said I didn't just see how, but I was sure I would find some way out—if I lived.

"Then Mr. Lincoln put his hands on my shoulders and looked into my face as if he was sorry and said: 'My boy, my bill is a very large one. Your friends cannot pay it, nor your bounty, nor the farm, nor all your comrades! There is only one man in all the world who can pay it, and his name is William Scott! If from this day William Scott does his duty, so that, if I was there when he comes to die, he can look me in the face as he does now, and say, "I have kept my promise, and I have done my duty as a soldier," then my debt will be paid. Will you make that promise and try to keep it?'

"I said I would make the promise and with God's help I would keep it. I could not say any more. I wanted to tell him how hard I would try to do all he wanted, but the words would not come; so I had to let it all go unsaid. He went away, out of my sight forever."

Recollections of President Lincoln and His Administration, 1891

T. V. SMITH

This Man Lincoln

There is, appropriately, a Lincolnesque quality in the brevity and eloquence of this notable tribute. Smith's career was a divided one. In academic life he was a professor at Texas Christian, the University of Texas, the University of Chicago and Syracuse University. His political interests took him to the Illinois legislature and the United States Congress. After World War II he served on several government missions abroad.

No man made great by death offers more hope to lowly pride than does Abraham Lincoln; for while living he was himself so simple as often to be dubbed a fool. Foolish he was, they said, in losing his youthful heart to a grave and living his life on married patience; foolish in pitting his homely ignorance against Douglas, brilliant, courtly, and urbane; foolish in setting himself to do the right in a world where the day goes mostly to the strong; foolish in dreaming of freedom for a long-suffering folk whom the North was as anxious to keep out as the South was to keep down; foolish in choosing the silent Grant to lead to victory the hesitant armies of the North; foolish, finally, in presuming that government for the people must be government of and by the people.

Foolish many said; foolish, many, many believed.

This Lincoln whom so many living friends and foes alike deemed foolish, hid his bitterness in laughter; fed his sympathy on solitude; and met recurring disaster with whimsicality to muffle the murmur of a bleeding heart. Out of the tragic sense of life he pitied where others blamed; bowed his own shoulders with the woes of the weak; endured humanely his little day of chance power; and won through death what life disdains to bestow upon such simple souls—lasting peace and everlasting glory.

How prudently we proud men compete for nameless graves, while now and then some starveling of Fate forgets himself into immortality.

Speech, Lincoln Day, Springfield, Illinois, 1936

GEORGE ALFRED TOWNSEND

The Capture and Killing of John Wilkes Booth

Reporter Townsend had joined Federal troopers pursuing Booth after Lincoln's assassination. La Fayette Baker, chief of the United States Secret Service, was in charge of the pursuit. The captain referred to in the opening sentence was a Confederate officer who had aided Booth in crossing the Potomac.

Townsend covered the Civil War for both the New York WORLD and the HERALD and during the forty years following the war he contributed to some hundred newspapers, besides writing several books.

Taking the captain along for a guide, the worn-out horsemen retraced, although some of the men were so haggard and wasted with travel that they had to be kicked into intelligence before they could climb to their saddles. The objects of the chase thus at hand, the detectives, full of sanguine purpose, hurried the cortege so well along that by two o'clock early morning, all halted at Garrett's gate.

In the dead stillness, Baker dismounted and forced the outer gate;

78

Conger kept close behind him, and the horsemen followed cautiously. They made no noise in the soft clay, nor broke the all-foreboding silence anywhere, till the second gate swung open gratingly; yet even then no hoarse nor shrill response came back, save the distant croakings, as of frogs or owls, and the whiz of some passing night hawk. So they surrounded the pleasant old homestead, each horseman carbine in poise, adjusted under the grove of locusts, so as to enclose the dwelling with a circle of fire. After a pause, Baker rode to the kitchen door on the side and, dismounting, rapped and hallooed lustily. An old man, in drawers and nightshirt, hastily undrew the bolts and stood on the threshold, peering into the darkness.

The old man told La Fayette Baker that Booth and Herold had gone, but his young son confessed that they were in the barn. The troopers, with cocked pistols at the informer's head, approached the barn.

The troops, dismounted, were stationed at regular intervals around it and, ten yards distant at every point, four special guards placed to command the door and all with weapons in supple preparation, while Baker and Conger went directly to the door. It had a padlock on it, and the key of this Baker secured at once. In the interval of silence that ensued, the rustling of planks and straw was heard inside, as of persons rising from sleep.

At the same moment, Baker hailed: "To the persons in this barn. I have a proposal to make; we are about to send into you the son of the man in whose custody you are found. Either surrender him your arms and then give yourselves up, or we'll set fire to the place. We mean to take you both, or have a bonfire and a shooting match."

No answer came to this of any kind. The lad, John M. Garrett, who was in deadly fear, was here pushed through the door by a sudden opening of it, and immediately Lieutenant Baker locked the door on the outside. The boy was heard to state his appeal in an undertone. Booth replied:

"Damn you! Get out of here. You have betrayed me."

At the same time he placed his hand in his pocket as for a pistol. A remonstrance followed, but the boy slipped out and over the reopened portal, reporting that his errand had failed and that he dared not to enter again. The boy was placed at a remote point and the summons repeated by Baker.

A bold, clarion call came from within, so strong as to be heard at the house door:

"Who are you and what do you want with us?"

Baker again urged: "We want you to give up your arms and become our prisoners."

"But who are you?" hallooed the same strong voice.

Baker—That makes no difference. We know who you are and we want you. We have here fifty men, armed with carbines and pistols. You cannot escape.

There was a long pause, and then Booth said: "Captain, this is a very bad case, I swear. Perhaps I am being taken by my own friends." No reply from the detectives.

Booth—Well, give us a little time to consider.

Baker—Very well. Take time.

Here ensued a long and eventful pause. What thronging memories it brought to Booth we can only guess. In this little interval he made the resolve to die; but he was cool and steady to the end. Baker, after a lapse, hailed for the last time:

"Well, we have waited long enough. Surrender your arms and come out, or we'll fire the barn."

Booth answered thus: "I am but a cripple, a one-legged man. Withdraw your forces one hundred yards from the door and I will come. Give me a chance for my life, Captain. I will never be taken alive."

Baker—We did not come here to fight, but to capture you. I say again, appear, or we fire the barn.

Then, with a long breath, which could be heard outside, Booth cried, in sudden calmness, still invisible as we were to him:

"Well, then, my brave boys, prepare a stretcher for me."

There was a pause, repeated, broken by low discussions within between Booth and his associate, the former saying, as if in answer to some remonstrance or appeal, "Get away from me. You are a damned coward, and mean to leave me in my distress, but go, go. I don't want you to stay. I won't have you stay." Then he shouted aloud:

"There's a man inside who wants to surrender."

Baker—Let him come, if he will bring his arms.

Here Herold, rattling at the door, said, "Let me out. Open the door. I want to surrender."

Baker—Hand out your arms, then.

Herold—I have not got any.

This was said in a whining tone and with an almost visible shiver. Booth cried aloud at this hesitation. "He hasn't got any arms. They are mine, and I have kept them."

Baker—Well, he carried the carbine, and he must bring it out.

Booth—On the word and honor of a gentleman, he has no arms with him. They are mine, and I have got them.

At this time Herold was quite up to the door, within whispering distance of Baker. The latter told him to put out his hands to be handcuffed, at the same time drawing open the door a little distance. Herold thrust forward his hands, when Baker, seizing him, jerked him into the night and straightway delivered him over to a deputation of cavalrymen. The fellow began to talk of his innocence and plead so noisily that Conger threatened to gag him unless he ceased. Then Booth made his last appeal, in the same clear, unbroken voice:

"Captain, give me a chance. Draw off your men, and I will fight them singly. I could have killed you six times tonight, but I believe you to be a brave man and would not murder you. Give a lame man a show."

Ere he ceased speaking, Colonel Conger, slipping around to the rear, drew some loose straws through a crack, and lit a match upon them. They were dry and blazed up in an instant, carrying a sheet of smoke and flame through the parted planks and heaving in a twinkling a world of light and heat upon the magazine within. The blaze lit up the black recesses of the great barn until every wasp's nest and cobweb in the roof was luminous, flinging streaks of red and violet across the tumbled farm gear in the corner, plows, harrows, hoes, rakes, sugar mills, and making every separate grain in the high bin adjacent gleam like a mote of precious gold. They tinged the beams, the upright columns, the barricades, where clover and timothy, piled high, held toward the hot incendiary their separate straws for the funeral pile. They bathed the murderer's retreat in a beautiful illumination, and while in bold outline his figure stood revealed, they rose like an impenetrable wall to guard from sight the hated enemy who lit them. Behind the blaze, with his eye to a crack, Conger saw Wilkes Booth standing upright on a crutch. He likens him in this instant to his brother, Edwin, whom he says he so much resembled that he half believed, for the moment, the whole pursuit to have been a mistake. At the gleam of the fire Wilkes dropped his crutch and his carbine, and on both hands crept up to the spot to espy the incendiary and shoot him dead. His eyes were lustrous like fever, and swelled and rolled in terrible beauty, while his teeth were fixed and he peered with vengeance in his look. The fire that made him visible concealed his enemy. A second he turned glaring at the fire, as if to leap upon it and extinguish it, but it had made such headway that this was a futile impulse and he dismissed it. As calmly as upon a battlefield a veteran stands amidst a hail of ball and shell and plunging iron, Booth turned at a man's stride and pushed for the door, carbine in poise, and the last resolve of death, which we name despair, set on his high bloodless forehead.

As so he dashed, intent to expire not unaccompanied, a disobedient sergeant, at an eyehole, drew upon him the fatal bead. The barn was all glorious with conflagration, and in the beautiful ruin this outlawed man strode like all we know of wicked valor, stern in the face of death. A shock, a shout, a gathering up of his splendid figure as if to overtip the stature God gave him, and John Wilkes Booth fell headlong to the floor, lying there in a heap, a little life remaining.

"He has shot himself," cried Baker, unaware of the source of the report, and rushing in, he grasped his arms to guard against any feint or strategy. A moment convinced him that further struggle against prone flesh was useless. Booth did not move, nor breathe nor gasp. Conger and two sergeants now entered and, taking up the body, they bore it in haste from the advancing flames and laid it without upon the grass, all fresh with heavenly dew.

"Water," cried Conger, "bring water."

When this was dashed into his face, he revived a little and stirred his lips. Baker put his ear close down and heard him say:

"Tell Mother—I die—for my country."

New York *World*, April 29, 1865

HENRY DAVID THOREAU

The Moose Hunt

Although Thoreau is most closely associated with Walden Pond in Concord, Massachusetts, he also traveled through the White Mountains of New Hampshire, to Cape Cod and Canada, as far west as Minneapolis, and made three trips to the Maine woods. Vigorously opposed to hunting as a sport, Thoreau was a spectator rather than a participant at this moose hunt.

Though I had not come a-hunting, and felt some compunctions about accompanying the hunters, I wished to see a moose near at hand, and was not sorry to learn how the Indian managed to kill one. I went as reporter or chaplain to the hunters,—and the chaplain has been known to carry a gun himself. After clearing a small space amid the dense spruce and fir trees, we covered the damp ground with a shingling of fir-twigs, and, while Joe was preparing his birch-horn and pitching his canoe,—for this had to be done whenever we stopped long enough to build a fire, and was the principal labor which he took upon himself at such times,—we collected fuel for the night, large, wet, and rotting logs, which had lodged at the head of the island, for our hatchet was too small for effective chopping; but we did not kindle a fire, lest the moose should smell it.

At starlight we dropped down the stream, which was a dead-water for three miles, or as far as the Moosehorn; Joe telling us that we must be very silent, and he himself making no noise with his paddle, while he urged the canoe along with effective impulses. It was a still night, and suitable for this purpose,—for if there is wind, the moose will smell you,—and Joe was very confident that he should get some. The harvest moon had just risen, and its level rays began to light up the forest on our right, while we glided downward in the shade on the same side, against the little breeze that was stirring. The lofty, spiring tops of the spruce and fir were very black against the sky, and more distinct than by day, close bordering this broad avenue on each side; and the beauty of the scene, as the moon rose above the forest, it would not be easy to describe.

A bat flew over our heads, and we heard a few faint notes of birds from time to time, perhaps the myrtle-bird for one, or the sudden plunge of a musquash, or saw one crossing the stream before us, or heard the sound of a rill emptying in, swollen by the recent rain.

At length . . . Joe laid down his paddle, drew forth his birch-horn,—a straight one, about fifteen inches long and three or four wide at the mouth, tied round with strips of the same bark,—and standing up, imitated the call of the moose,—*ugh-ugh-ugh*, or *oo-oo-oo-oo*, and then a prolonged *oo-o-o-o-o-o-o-o*, and listened attentively for several minutes. We asked him what kind of noise he expected to hear. He said that if a moose heard it, he guessed we should find out; we should hear him coming half a mile off; he would come close up, perhaps into, the water, and my companion must wait till he got fair sight, and then aim just behind the shoulder.

The moose venture out to the river-side to feed and drink at night. Earlier in the season the hunters do not use a horn to call them out, but steal upon them as they are feeding along the sides of the stream, and often the first notice they have of one is the sound of the water dropping from its muzzle. An Indian whom I heard imitate the voice of the moose, and also that of the caribou and the deer, using a much longer horn than Joe's, told me that the first could be heard eight or ten miles, sometimes; it was a loud sort of bellowing sound, clearer and more sonorous than the lowing of cattle,—the caribou's a sort of snort,—and the small deer's like that of a lamb.

At length we turned up the Moosehorn, where the Indians at the carry had told us that they killed a moose the night before. This is a very meandering stream, only a rod or two in width, but comparatively deep, coming in on the right, fitly enough named Moosehorn, whether from its windings or its inhabitants. It was bordered here and there by narrow meadows between the stream and the endless forest, affording favorable places for the moose to feed, and to call them out on. We proceeded half a mile up this, as through a narrow, winding canal, where the tall, dark spruce and firs and arborvitae towered on both sides in the moonlight, forming a perpendicular forest-edge of great height, like the spires of a Venice in the forest. In two places stood a small stack of hay on the bank, ready for the lumberer's use in the winter, looking strange enough there. We thought of the day when this might be a brook winding through smooth-shaven meadows on some gentleman's grounds; and seen by moonlight then, excepting the forest that now hems it in, how little changed it would appear!

Again and again Joe called the moose, placing the canoe by some favorable point of meadow for them to come out on, but listened in vain to hear one come rushing through the woods, and concluded that they had been hunted too much thereabouts. We saw, many times, what to our imaginations looked like a gigantic moose, with his horns peering from out the forest edge; but we saw the forest only, and not its inhabitants, that night. So at last we turned about. There was now a little fog on the water, though it was a fine, clear night above. There were very few sounds to break the stillness of the forest. Several times we heard the hooting of a great horned-owl, as at home, and told Joe that he would call out the moose for him, for he made a sound considerably like the horn,— but Joe answered, that the moose had heard that sound a thousand times, and knew better; and oftener still we were startled by the plunge of a musquash.

Once, when Joe had called again, and we were listening for moose, we heard, come faintly echoing, or creeping from far, through the moss-clad aisles, a dull, dry, rushing sound, with a solid core to it, yet as if half smothered under the grasp of the luxuriant and fungus-like forest, like the shutting of a door in some distant entry of the damp and shaggy wilderness. If we had not been there, no mortal had heard it. When we asked Joe in a whisper what it was, he answered, "Tree fall."

There is something singularly grand and impressive in the sound of a tree falling in a perfectly calm night like this, as if the agencies which overthrow it did not need to be excited, but worked with a subtle, deliberate, and conscious force, like a boa-constrictor, and more effectively then than even in a windy day. If there is any such difference, perhaps it is because trees with the dews of the night on them are heavier than by day.

Having reached the camp, about ten o'clock, we kindled our fire and went to bed. Each of us had a blanket, in which he lay on the fir-twigs, with his extremities toward the fire, but nothing over his head. It was worth the while to lie down in a country where you could afford such great fires; that was one whole side, and the bright side, of our world. We had first rolled up a large log some eighteen inches through and ten feet long, for a backlog, to last all night, and then piled on the trees to the height of three or four feet, no matter how green or damp. In fact, we burned as much wood that night as would, with economy and an airtight stove, last a poor family in one of our cities all winter.

It was very agreeable, as well as independent, thus lying in the open air, and the fire kept our uncovered extremities warm enough. The Jesuit missionaries used to say, that, in their journeys with the Indians in Canada, they lay on a bed which had never been shaken up since the creation, unless by earthquakes. It is surprising with what impunity and comfort one who has always lain in a warm bed in a close apartment, and studiously avoided drafts of air, can lie down on the ground without a shelter, roll himself in a blanket, and sleep before a fire, in a frosty, autumn night just after a long rainstorm, and even come soon to enjoy and value the fresh air.

I lay awake awhile, watching the ascent of the sparks through the firs, and sometimes their descent in half-extinguished cinders on my blanket. They were as interesting as fireworks, going up in endless, successive

84

crowds, each after an explosion, in an eager, serpentine course, some to five or six rods above the treetops before they went out. We do not suspect how much our chimneys have concealed; and now air-tight stoves have come to conceal all the rest. In the course of the night, I got up once or twice and put fresh logs on the fire, making my companions curl up their legs.

When we awoke in the morning (Saturday, September 17), there was considerable frost whitening the leaves. We heard the sound of the chickadee, and a few faintly lisping birds, and also of ducks in the water about the island. I took a botanical account of stock of our domains before the dew was off, and found that the ground hemlock, or American yew, was the prevailing under-shrub. We breakfasted on tea, hard bread, and ducks.

Before the fog had fairly cleared away we paddled down the stream again, and were soon past the mouth of the Moosehorn. These twenty miles of the Penobscot, between Moosehead and Chesuncook lakes, are comparatively smooth, and a great part dead-water; but from time to time it is shallow and rapid, with rocks or gravel beds, where you can wade across. There is no expanse of water, and no break in the forest, and the meadow is a mere edging here and there. There are no hills near the river nor within sight, except one or two distant mountains seen in a few places. The banks are from six to ten feet high, but once or twice rise gently to higher ground. In many places the forest on the bank was but a thin strip, letting the light through from some alder swamp or meadow behind.

After passing through some long rips, and by a large island, we reached an interesting part of the river called the Pine Stream Dead-Water, about six miles below Ragmuff, where the river expanded to thirty rods in width and had many islands in it, with elms and canoe-birches, now yellowing, along the shore, and we got our first sight of Ktaadn.

Here, about two o'clock, we turned up a small branch three or four rods wide, which comes in on the right from the south, called Pine Stream, to look for moose signs. We had gone but a few rods before we saw very recent signs along the water's edge, the mud lifted up by their feet being quite fresh, and Joe declared that they had gone along there but a short time before. We soon reached a small meadow on the east side, at an angle in the stream, which was, for the most part, densely covered with alders. As we were advancing along the edge of this, rather more quietly than usual, perhaps, on account of the freshness of the signs,—the design being to camp up this stream, if it promised well,—I heard a slight crackling of twigs deep in the alders, and turned Joe's attention to it; whereupon he began to push the canoe back rapidly; and we had receded thus half a dozen rods, when we suddenly spied two moose standing just on the edge of the open part of the meadow which we had passed, not more than six or seven rods distant, looking round the alders at us.

They made me think of great frightened rabbits, with their long ears and half-inquisitive, half-frightened looks; the true denizens of the forest (I saw at once), filling a vacuum which now first I discovered had not been filled for me,—moose-men, wood-eaters, the word is said to mean,—clad in a sort of Vermont gray, or homespun. Our Nimrod, owing to the retrograde movement, was now farthest from the game; but being warned of its neighborhood, he hastily stood up, and, while we ducked, fired over our heads one barrel at the foremost, which alone he saw, though he did not know what kind of creature it was; whereupon this one dashed across the meadow and up a high bank on the northeast, so rapidly as to leave but an indistinct impression of its outlines on my mind.

At the same instant, the other, a young one, but as tall as a horse, leaped out into the stream, in full sight, and there stood cowering for a moment, or rather its disproportionate lowness behind gave it that appearance, and uttering two or three trumpeting squeaks. I have an indistinct recollection of seeing the old one pause an instant on the top of the bank in the woods, look toward its shivering young, and then dash away again. The second barrel was leveled at the calf, and when we expected to see it drop in the water, after a little hesitation, it, too, got out of the water, and dashed up the hill, though in a somewhat different direction.

All this was the work of a few seconds, and our hunter, having never seen a moose before, did not know but they were deer, for they stood partly in the water, nor whether he had fired at the same one twice or not. From the style in which they went off, and the fact that he was not used to standing up and firing from a canoe, I judged that we should not see anything more of them. The Indian said that they were a cow and her calf,—a yearling, or perhaps two years old, for they accompany their dams so long; but, for my part, I had not noticed much difference in their size. It was but two or three rods across the meadow to the foot of the bank, which, like all the world thereabouts, was densely wooded; but I was surprised to notice, that, as soon as the moose had passed behind the veil of the woods, there was no sound of footsteps to be heard from the soft, damp moss which carpets that forest, and long before we landed, perfect silence reigned. Joe said, "If you wound 'em moose, me sure get 'em."

We all landed at once. My companion reloaded; the Indian fastened his birch, threw off his hat, adjusted his waistband, seized the hatchet, and set out. He told me afterward, casually, that before we landed he had seen a drop of blood on the bank, when it was two or three rods off. He proceeded rapidly up the bank and through the woods, with a peculiar, elastic, noiseless, and stealthy tread, looking to right and left on the ground, and stepping in the faint tracks of the wounded moose, now and then pointing in silence to a single drop of blood on the handsome, shining leaves of the Clintonia borealis, which, on every side, covered the ground, or to a dry fern-stem freshly broken, all the while chewing some leaf or else the spruce gum. I followed, watching his motions more than the trail of the moose. After following the trail about forty rods in a pretty direct course, stepping over fallen trees and winding between standing ones, he at length lost it, for there were many other moose tracks there, and, returning once more to the last blood-stain, traced it a little way and lost it again, and, too soon, I thought, for a good hunter, gave it up entirely. He traced a few steps, also, the tracks of the calf; but, seeing no blood, soon relinquished the search.

I observed, while he was tracking the moose, a certain reticence or moderation in him. He did not communicate several observations of interest which he made, as a white man would have done, though they may have leaked out afterward. At another time, when we heard a slight crackling of twigs and he landed to reconnoitre, he stepped lightly and gracefully, stealing through the bushes with the least possible noise, in a way in which no white man does,—as it were, finding a place for his foot each time.

About half an hour after seeing the moose, we pursued our voyage up Pine Stream, and soon, coming to a part which was very shoal and also rapid, we took out the baggage, and proceeded to carry it round, while Joe got up with the canoe alone. We were just completing our portage and I was absorbed in the plants, admiring the leaves of the Aster macrophyllus, ten inches wide, and plucking the seeds of the great round-leaved orchis, when Joe exclaimed from the stream that he had killed a moose. He had found the cow-moose lying dead, but quite warm, in the middle of the stream, which was so shallow that it rested on the bottom, with hardly a third of its body above water. It was about an hour after it was shot, and it was swollen with water. It had run about a hundred rods and sought the stream again, cutting off a slight bend. No doubt a better hunter would have tracked it to this spot at once.

I was surprised at its great size, horse-like, but Joe said it was not a large cow-moose. My companion went in search of the calf again. I took hold of the ears of the moose, while Joe pushed his canoe downstream toward a favorable shore, and so we made out, though with some difficulty, its long nose frequently sticking in the bottom, to drag it into still shallower water. It was a brownish black, or perhaps a dark iron-gray, on the back and sides, but lighter beneath and in front. I took the cord which served for the canoe's painter, and with Joe's assistance measured it carefully, the greatest distances first, making a knot each time. The painter being wanted, I reduced these measures that night with equal care to lengths and fractions of my umbrella, beginning with the smallest measures, and untying the knots as I proceeded; and when we arrived at Chesuncook the next day, finding a two-foot rule there, I reduced the last to feet and inches; and, moreover, I made myself a two-foot rule of a thin and narrow strip of black ash, which would fold up conveniently to six inches.

All this pains I took because I did not wish to be obliged to say merely that the moose was very large. Of the various dimensions which I obtained I will mention only two. The distance from the tips of the hoofs of the fore-feet, stretched out, to the top of the back between the shoulders, was seven feet and five inches. I can hardly believe my own measure, for this is about two feet greater than the height of a tall horse. (Indeed, I am now satisfied that this measurement was incorrect, but the other measures given here I can warrant to be correct, having proved them in a more recent visit to those woods.) The extreme length was eight feet and two inches. Another cow-moose, which I have since measured in those woods with a tape, was just six feet from the tip of the hoof to the shoulders, and eight feet long as she lay.

Here, just at the head of the murmuring rapids, Joe now proceeded to skin the moose with a pocket-knife, while I looked on; and a tragical business it was,—to see that still warm and palpitating body pierced with a knife, to see the warm milk stream from the rent udder, and the ghastly naked red carcass appearing from within its seemly robe, which was made to hide it. The ball had passed through the shoulder-blade diagonally and lodged under the skin on the opposite side, and was partially flattened. My companion keeps it to show to his grandchildren. He has the shanks of another moose which he has since shot, skinned and stuffed, ready to be made into boots by putting in a thick leather sole. Joe said, if a moose stood fronting you, you must not fire, but advance toward him, for he will turn slowly and give you a fair shot.

In the bed of this narrow, wild, and rocky stream, between two lofty walls of spruce and firs, a mere cleft in the forest which the stream had made, this work went on. At length Joe had stripped off the hide and dragged it trailing to the shore, declaring that it weighed a hundred pounds, though probably fifty would have been nearer the truth. He cut off a large mass of the meat to carry along, and another, together with the tongue and nose, he put with the hide on the shore to lie there all night, or till we returned. I was surprised that he thought of leaving this meat thus exposed by the side of the carcass, as the simplest course, not fearing that any creature would touch it; but nothing did. This could hardly have happened on the bank of one of our rivers in the eastern part of Massachusetts; but I suspect that fewer small wild animals are prowling there than with us. Twice, however, in this excursion, I had a glimpse of a species of large mouse.

This stream was so withdrawn, and the moose tracks were so fresh, that my companions, still bent on hunting, concluded to go farther up it and camp, and then hunt up or down at night. Half a mile above this, at a place where I saw the Aster puniceus and the beaked hazel, as we paddled along, Joe, hearing a slight rustling amid the alders, and seeing something black about two rods off, jumped up and whispered, "Bear!" but before the hunter had discharged his piece, he corrected himself to

88

"Beaver!"—"Hedgehog!" The bullet killed a large hedgehog more than two feet and eight inches long. The quills were rayed out and flattened on the hinder part of its back, even as if it had lain on that part, but were erect and long between this and the tail. Their points, closely examined, were seen to be finely bearded or barbed, and shaped like an awl, that is, a little concave, to give the barbs effect. After about a mile of still water, we prepared our camp on the right side, just at the foot of a considerable fall. Little chopping was done that night, for fear of scaring the moose. We had moose meat fried for supper. It tasted like tender beef, with perhaps more flavor,—sometimes like veal.

After supper, the moon having risen, we proceeded to hunt a mile up this stream, first "carrying" about the falls. We made a picturesque sight, wending single file along the shore, climbing over rocks and logs,—Joe, who brought up the rear, twirling his canoe in his hands as if it were a feather, in places where it was difficult to get along without a burden. We launched the canoe again from the ledge over which the stream fell, but after half a mile of still water, suitable for hunting, it became rapid again, and we were compelled to make our way along the shore, while Joe endeavored to get up in the birch alone, though it was still very difficult for him to pick his way amid the rocks in the night.

We on the shore found the worst of walking, a perfect chaos of fallen and drifted trees, and of bushes projecting far over the water, and now and then we made our way across the mouth of a small tributary on a kind of network of alders. So we went tumbling on in the dark, being on the shady side, effectually scaring all the moose and bears that might be thereabouts. At length we came to a standstill, and Joe went forward to reconnoiter; but he reported that it was still a continuous rapid as far as he went, for half a mile, with no prospect of improvement, as if it were coming down from a mountain. So we turned about, hunting back to the camp through the still water.

It was a splendid moonlight night, and I, getting sleepy as it grew late, —for I had nothing to do,—found it difficult to realize where I was. This stream was much more unfrequented than the main one, lumbering operations being no longer carried on in this quarter. It was only three or four rods wide, but the firs and spruce through which it trickled seemed yet taller by contrast. Being in this dreamy state, which the moonlight enhanced, I did not clearly discern the shore, but seemed, most of the time, to be floating through ornamental grounds,—for I associated the fir-tops with such scenes;—very high up some Broadway, and beneath or between their tops, I thought I saw an endless succession of porticoes and columns, cornices and facades, verandas and churches. I did not merely fancy this, but in my drowsy state such was the illusion. I fairly lost myself in sleep several times, still dreaming of that architecture and the nobility that dwelt behind and might issue from it; but all at once I would be aroused and brought back to a sense of my actual position by the sound of Joe's

birch-horn in the midst of all this silence calling the moose, *ugh, ugh,
oo,-oo-oo-oo-oo-oo*, and I prepared to hear a furious moose come rushing
and crashing through the forest, and see him burst out on to the little
strip of meadow by our side.

But, on more accounts than one, I had had enough of moose-hunting.
I had not come to the woods for this purpose, nor had I foreseen it, though
I had been willing to learn how the Indian maneuvered; but one moose
killed was as good, if not as bad, as a dozen. That afternoon's tragedy, and
my share in it, as it affected the innocence, destroyed the pleasure of my
adventure. It is true, I came as near as possible to come to being a hunter
and miss it, myself; and as it is, I think that I could spend a year in the
woods, fishing and hunting just enough to sustain myself, with satisfaction. This would be next to living like a philosopher on the fruits of the
earth which you had raised, which also attracts me.

But this hunting of the moose merely for the satisfaction of killing him,
—not even for the sake of his hide,—without making any extraordinary
exertion or running any risk yourself, is too much like going out by night
to some wood-side pasture and shooting your neighbor's horses. These are
God's own horses, poor, timid creatures, that will run fast enough as
soon as they smell you, though they *are* nine feet high. Joe told us of some
hunters who a year or two before had shot down several oxen by night,
somewhere in the Maine woods, mistaking them for moose. And so
might any of the hunters; and what is the difference in the sport, but
the name? In the former case, having killed one of God's and *your own*
oxen, you strip off its hide,—because that is the common trophy, and,
moreover, you have heard that it may be sold for moccasins,—cut a steak
from its haunches, and leave the huge carcass to smell to heaven for you.
It is no better, at least, than to assist at a slaughterhouse.

This afternoon's experience suggested to me how base or coarse are
the motives which commonly carry men into the wilderness. The ex-
plorers and lumberers generally are all hirelings, paid so much a day for
their labor, and as such they have no more love for wild nature than
wood-sawyers have for forests. Other white men and Indians who come
here are for the most part hunters, whose object is to slay as many
moose and other wild animals as possible. But, pray, could not one spend
some weeks or years in the solitude of this vast wilderness with other employments than these—employments perfectly sweet and innocent and
ennobling? For one that comes with a pencil to sketch or sing, a thousand
come with an axe or rifle. What a coarse and imperfect use Indians and
hunters make of Nature! No wonder that their race is so soon exterminated. I already, and for weeks afterward, felt my nature the coarser for
this part of my wood-land experience, and was reminded that our life
should be lived as tenderly and daintily as one would pluck a flower.

With these thoughts, when we reached our camping-ground, I decided to leave my companions to continue moose-hunting down the stream, while I prepared the camp, though they requested me not to chop much nor make a large fire, for fear I should scare their game. In the midst of the damp fir-wood, high on the mossy bank, about nine o'clock of this bright moonlight night, I kindled a fire, when they were gone, and sitting on the fir-twigs, within sound of the falls, examined by its light the botanical specimens which I had collected that afternoon, and wrote down some of the reflections which I have here expanded; or I walked along the shore and gazed up the stream, where the whole space above the falls was filled with mellow light. As I sat before the fire on my fir-twig seat, without walls above or around me, I remembered how far on every hand that wilderness stretched, before you came to cleared or cultivated fields, and wondered if any bear or moose was watching the light of my fire; for Nature looked sternly upon me on account of the murder of the moose.

Strange that so few ever came to the woods to see how the pine lives and grows and spires, lifting its evergreen arms to the light,—to see its perfect success; but most are content to behold it in the shape of many broad boards brought to market, and deem *that* its true success! But the pine is no more lumber than man is, and to be made into boards and houses is no more its true and highest use than the truest use of a man is to be cut down and made into manure. There is a higher law affecting our relation to pines as well as to men.

A pine cut down, a dead pine, is no more a pine than a dead human carcass is a man. Can he who has discovered only some of the values of whalebone and whale oil be said to have discovered the true use of the whale? Can he who slays the elephant for his ivory be said to have "seen the elephant"? These are petty and accidental uses; just as if a stronger race were to kill us in order to make buttons and flageolets of our bones; for everything may serve a lower as well as a higher use. Every creature is better alive than dead, men and moose and pine-trees, and he who understands it aright will rather preserve its life than destroy it.

Is it the lumberman, then, who is the friend and lover of the pine, stands nearest to it, and understands its nature best? Is it the tanner who has barked it, or he who has boxed it for turpentine, whom posterity will fable to have been changed into a pine at last? No! no! it is the poet; he it is who makes the truest use of the pine,—who does not fondle it with an axe, nor tickle it with a saw, nor stroke it with a plane,—who knows whether its heart is false without cutting into it,—who has not bought the stumpage of the township on which it stands. All the pines shudder and heave a sigh when *that* man steps on the forest floor. No, it is the poet, who loves them as his own shadow in the air, and lets them stand.

I have been into the lumber-yard, and the carpenter's shop, and the tannery, and the lampblack factory, and the turpentine clearing; but when at length I saw the tops of the pines waving and reflecting the light at a distance high over all the rest of the forest, I realized that the former were not the highest uses of the pine. It is not their bones or hide or tallow that I love most. It is the living spirit of the tree, not its spirit of turpentine, with which I sympathize, and which heals my cuts. It is as immortal as I am, and perchance will go to as high a heaven, there to tower above me still.

The Maine Woods, 1864

E. B. WHITE

Walden

> *It is interesting to observe that Mr. White occasionally and adroitly paraphrases Thoreau's* Walden, *a touch Thoreau himself might well have enjoyed.*

Miss Nims, take a letter to Henry David Thoreau. Dear Henry: I thought of you the other afternoon as I was approaching Concord doing fifty on Route 62. That is a high speed at which to hold a philosopher in one's mind, but in this century we are a nimble bunch.

On one of the lawns in the outskirts of the village a woman was cutting the grass with a motorized lawn mower. What made me think of you was that the machine had rather got away from her, although she was game enough, and in the brief glimpse I had of the scene it appeared to me that the lawn was mowing the lady. She kept a tight grip on the handles, which throbbed violently with every explosion of the one-cylinder motor, and as she sheered around bushes and lurched along at a reluctant trot behind her impetuous servant, she looked like a puppy who had grabbed something that was too much for him. Concord hasn't changed much, Henry; the farm implements and the animals still have the upper hand.

I may as well admit that I was journeying to Concord with the deliberate intention of visiting your woods; for although I have never knelt at the grave of a philosopher nor placed wreaths on moldy poets, and have often gone a mile out of my way to avoid some place of historical interest, I have always wanted to see Walden Pond. The account which you left of your sojourn there is, you will be amused to learn, a document of increasing pertinence; each year it gains a little headway, as the world loses ground. We may all be transcendental yet, whether we like it or not. As our common complexities increase, any tale of individual simplicity (and yours is the best written and the cockiest) acquires a new fascination; as our goods accumulate, but not our well-being, your report of an existence without material adornment takes on a certain awkward credibility.

My purpose in going to Walden Pond, like yours, was not to live cheaply or to live dearly there, but to transact some private business with the fewest obstacles. Approaching Concord, doing forty, doing forty-five, doing fifty, the steering wheel held snug in my palms, the highway held grimly in my vision, the crown of the road now serving me (on the righthand curves), now defeating me (on the lefthand curves), I began to rouse myself from the stupefaction which a day's motor journey induces. It was a delicious evening, Henry, when the whole body is one sense, and imbibes delight through every pore, if I may coin a phrase. Fields were richly brown where the harrow, drawn by the stripped Ford, had lately sunk its teeth; pastures were green; and overhead the sky had the same everlasting great look which you will find on page 144 of the Oxford pocket edition. I could feel the road entering me through tire, wheel, spring, and cushion; shall I not have intelligence with earth, too? Am I not partly leaves and vegetable mold myself?—a man of infinite horsepower, yet partly leaves.

Stay with me on 62 and it will take you into Concord. As I say, it was a delicious evening. The snake had come forth to die in a bloody S on the highway, the wheel upon its head, its bowels flat now and exposed. The turtle had come up too to cross the road and die in the attempt, its hard shell smashed under the rubber blow, its intestinal yearning (for the other side of the road) forever squashed. There was a sign by the wayside which announced that the road had a "cotton surface." You wouldn't know what that is, but neither, for that matter, did I. There is a cryptic ingredient in many of our modern improvements—we are awed and pleased without knowing quite what we are enjoying. It is something to be traveling on a road with a cotton surface.

The civilization round Concord to-day is an odd distillation of city, village, farm, and manor. The houses, yards, fields look not quite suburban, not quite rural. Under the bronze beech and the blue spruce of the departed baron grazes the milch goat of the heirs. Under the porte-cochère stands the reconditioned station wagon. Under the grape arbor sit the puppies for sale. (But why do men degenerate ever? What makes families run out?)

It was June and everywhere June was publishing her immemorial stanza; in the lilacs, in the syringa, in the freshly edged paths and the sweetness of moist beloved gardens, and the little wire wickets that preserve the tulips' front. Farmers were already moving the fruits of their toil into their yards, arranging the rhubarb, the asparagus, the strictly fresh eggs on the painted stands under the little shed roofs with the patent shingles. And though it was almost a hundred years since you had taken your ax and started cutting out your home on Walden Pond, I was interested to observe that the philosophical spirit was still alive in Massachusetts; in the center of a vacant lot some boys were assembling the framework of a rude shelter, their whole mind and skill concentrated in the rather inauspicious helter-skeleton of studs and rafters. They too were escaping from town, to live naturally, in a rich blend of savagery and philosophy.

That evening, after supper at the inn, I strolled out into the twilight to dream my shapeless transcendental dreams and see that the car was locked up for the night (first open the right front door, then reach over, straining, and pull up the handles of the left rear and the left front till you hear the click, then the handle of the right rear, then shut the right front but open it again, remembering that the key is still in the ignition switch, remove the key, shut the right front again with a bang, push the tiny keyhole cover to one side, insert key, turn, and withdraw). It is what we all do, Henry. It is called locking the car. It is said to confuse thieves and keep them from making off with the laprobe. Four doors to lock behind one robe. The driver himself never uses a laprobe, the free movement of his legs being vital to the operation of the vehicle; so that when he locks the car it is a pure and unselfish act. I have in my life gained very little essential heat from laprobes, yet I have ever been at pains to lock them up.

The evening was full of sounds, some of which would have stirred your memory. The robins still love the elms of New England villages at sundown. There is enough of the thrush in them to make song inevitable at the end of day, and enough of the tramp to make them hang round the dwellings of men. A robin, like many another American, dearly loves a white house with green blinds. Concord is still full of them.

Your fellow-townsmen were stirring abroad—not many afoot, most of them in their cars; and the sound which they made in Concord at evening was a rustling and a whispering. The sound lacks steadfastness and is wholly unlike that of a train. A train, as you know who lived so near the Fitchburg line, whistles once or twice sadly and is gone, trailing a memory in smoke, soothing to ear and mind. Automobiles, skirting a village green, are like flies that have gained the inner ear—they buzz, cease, pause, start, shift, stop, halt, brake, and the whole effect is a nervous polytone curiously disturbing.

As I wandered along, the toc toc of ping pong balls drifted from an attic window. In front of the Reuben Brown house a Buick was drawn up. At the wheel, motionless, his hat upon his head, a man sat, listening to Amos and Andy on the radio (it is a drama of many scenes and without an end). The deep voice of Andrew Brown, emerging from the car, although it originated more than two hundred miles away, was unstrained by distance. When you used to sit on the shore of your pond on Sunday morning, listening to the church bells of Acton and Concord, you were aware of the excellent filter of the intervening atmosphere. Science has attended to that, and sound now maintains its intensity without regard for distance. Properly sponsored, it goes on forever.

A fire engine, out for a trial spin, roared past Emerson's house, hot with readiness for public duty. Over the barn roofs the martins dipped and chittered. A swarthy daughter of an asparagus grower, in culottes, shirt, and bandanna, pedalled past on her bicycle. It was indeed a delicious evening, and I returned to the inn (I believe it was your house once) to rock with the old ladies on the concrete veranda.

Next morning early I started afoot for Walden, out Main Street and down Thoreau, past the depot and the Minuteman Chevrolet Company. The morning was fresh, and in a bean field along the way I flushed an agriculturalist, quietly studying his beans. Thoreau Street soon joined Number 126, an artery of the State. We number our highways nowadays, our speed being so great we can remember little of their quality or character and are lucky to remember their number. (Men have an indistinct notion that if they keep up this activity long enough all will at length ride somewhere, in next to no time.) Your pond is on 126.

I knew I must be nearing your woodland retreat when the Golden Pheasant lunchroom came into view—Sealtest ice cream, toasted sandwiches, hot frankfurters, waffles, tonics, and lunches. Were I the proprietor, I should add rice, Indian meal, and molasses—just for old time's sake. The Pheasant, incidentally, is for sale: a chance for some nature lover who wishes to set himself up beside a pond in the Concord atmosphere and live deliberately, fronting only the essential facts of life on Number 126. Beyond the Pheasant was a place called Walden Breezes, an oasis whose porch pillars were made of old green shutters sawed into lengths. On the porch was a distorting mirror, to give the traveler a comical image of himself, who had miraculously learned to gaze in an ordinary glass without smiling. Behind the Breezes, in a sun-parched clearing, dwelt your philosophical descendants in their trailers, each trailer the size of your hut, but all grouped together for the sake of congeniality. Trailer people leave the city, as you did, to discover solitude and in any weather, at any hour of the day or night, to improve the nick of time; but they soon collect in villages and get bogged deeper in the mud than ever. The camp behind Walden Breezes was just rousing itself to the morning. The ground was packed hard under the heel, and the sun came through the clearing to bake the soil and enlarge the wry smell of cramped housekeeping. Cushman's bakery truck had stopped to deliver an early basket of rolls. A camp dog, seeing me in the road, barked petulantly. A man emerged from one of the trailers and set forth with a bucket to draw water from some forest tap.

Leaving the highway I turned off into the woods toward the pond, which was apparent through the foliage. The floor of the forest was strewn with dried old oak leaves and *Transcripts*. From beneath the flattened popcorn wrapper (*granum explosum*) peeped the frail violet. I followed a footpath and descended to the water's edge. The pond lay clear and blue in the morning light, as you have seen it so many times. In the shallows a man's waterlogged shirt undulated gently. A few flies came out to greet me and convoy me to your cove, past the No Bathing signs on which the fellows and the girls had scrawled their names. I felt strangely excited suddenly to be snooping around your premises, tiptoeing along watchfully, as though not to tread by mistake upon the intervening century. Before I got to the cove I heard something which seemed to me quite wonderful: I heard your frog, a full, clear *troonk*, guiding me, still hoarse and solemn, bridging the years as the robins had bridged them in the sweetness of the village evening. But he soon quit, and I came on a couple of young boys throwing stones at him.

Your front yard is marked by a bronze tablet set in a stone. Four small granite posts, a few feet away, show where the house was. On top of the tablet was a pair of faded blue bathing trunks with a white stripe. Back of it is a pile of stones, a sort of cairn, left by your visitors as a tribute I suppose. It is a rather ugly little heap of stones, Henry. In fact the hillside itself seems faded, browbeaten; a few tall skinny pines, bare of lower limbs, a smattering of young maples in suitable green, some birches and oaks, and a number of trees felled by the last big wind. It was from the bole of one of these fallen pines, torn up by the roots, that I extracted the stone which I added to the cairn—a sentimental act in which I was interrupted by a small terrier from a nearby picnic group, who confronted me and wanted to know about the stone.

I sat down for a while on one of the posts of your house to listen to the bluebottles and the dragonflies. The invaded glade sprawled shabby and mean at my feet, but the flies were tuned to the old vibration. There were the remains of a fire in your ruins, but I doubt that it was yours; also two beer bottles trodden into the soil and become part of earth. A young oak had taken root in your house, and two or three ferns, unrolling like the ticklers at a banquet. The only other furnishings were a DuBarry pattern sheet, a page torn from a picture magazine, and some crusts in wax paper.

Before I quit I walked clear round the pond and found the place where you used to sit on the northeast side to get the sun in the fall, and the beach where you got sand for scrubbing your floor. On the eastern side of the pond, where the highway borders it, the State has built dressing rooms for swimmers, a float with diving towers, drinking fountains of porcelain, and rowboats for hire. The pond is in fact a State Preserve, and carries a twenty-dollar fine for picking wild flowers, a decree signed in all solemnity by your fellow-citizens Walter C. Wardwell, Erson B. Barlow, and Nathaniel I. Bowditch. There was a smell of creosote where they had been building a wide wooden stairway to the road and the parking area. Swimmers and boaters were arriving; bodies plunged vigorously into the water and emerged wet and beautiful in the bright air. As I left, a boatload of town boys were splashing about in mid-pond, kidding and fooling, the young fellows singing at the tops of their lungs in a wild chorus:

> *Amer-ica, Amer-ica, God shed his grace on thee,*
> *And crown thy good with brotherhood*
> *From sea to shi-ning sea!*

I walked back to town along the railroad, following your custom. The rails were expanding noisily in the hot sun, and on the slope of the road-bed the wild grape and the blackberry sent up their creepers to the track.

The expense of my brief sojourn in Concord was:

Canvas shoes	$1.95	
Baseball bat	.25	gifts to take
Left-handed fielder's glove	1.25	back to a boy
Hotel and meals	4.25	
In all	$7.70	

As you see, this amount was almost what you spent for food for eight months. I cannot defend the shoes or the expenditure for shelter and food: they reveal a meanness and grossness in my nature which you would find contemptible. The baseball equipment, however, is the kind of impedi-ment with which you were never on even terms. You must remember that the house where you practiced the sort of economy which I respect was haunted only by mice and squirrels. You never had to cope with a short-stop.

One Man's Meat, 1939

OLIVER WENDELL HOLMES, JR.

"The Secret Isolated Joy of the Thinker"

No man has earned the right to intellectual ambition until he has learned to lay his course by a star which he has never seen,—to dig by the divin-ing rod for springs which he may never reach. In saying this, I point to that which will make your study heroic. For I say to you in all sadness of conviction, that to think great thoughts you must be heroes as well as idealists. Only when you have worked alone,—when you have felt around you a black gulf of solitude more isolating than that which surrounds the dying man, and in hope and in despair have trusted to your own unshaken will,—then only can you gain the secret isolated joy of the thinker, who knows that, a hundred years after he is dead and forgotten, men, who have never heard of him will be moving to the measure of his thought,—

the subtle rapture of a postponed power, which the world knows not because it has no external trappings, but which to his prophetic vision is more real than that which commands an army. And if this joy should not be yours, still it is only thus that you can know that you have done what it lay in you to do,—can say that you have lived, and be ready for the end.

From "The Profession of the Law," Harvard Lecture, 1886

MARY E. WILKINS FREEMAN

The Revolt of "Mother"

Forced to support herself at the age of thirty-six, Mrs. Freeman turned to writing. Her short stories, stanchly New England in flavor, are enlivened by characters she must have known.

"Father!"

"What is it?"

"What are them men diggin' over there in the field for?"

There was a sudden dropping and enlarging of the lower part of the old man's face, as if some heavy weight had settled therein; he shut his mouth tight, and went on harnessing the great bay mare. He hustled the collar on to her neck with a jerk.

"Father!"

The old man slapped the saddle upon the mare's back.

"Look here, father, I want to know what them men are diggin' over in the field for, an' I'm goin' to know."

"I wish you'd go into the house, mother, an' 'tend to your own affairs," the old man said then. He ran his words together, and his speech was almost as inarticulate as a growl.

But the woman understood; it was her most native tongue. "I ain't goin' into the house till you tell me what them men are doin' over there in the field," said she.

Then she stood waiting. She was a small woman, short and straight-waisted like a child in her brown cotton gown. Her forehead was mild and benevolent between the smooth curves of gray hair; there were meek downward lines about her nose and mouth; but her eyes, fixed upon the old man, looked as if the meekness had been the result of her own will, never of the will of another.

They were in the barn, standing before the wide open doors. The spring air, full of the smell of growing grass and unseen blossoms, came in their faces. The deep yard in front was littered with farm wagons and piles of wood; on the edges, close to the fence and the house, the grass was a vivid green, and there were some dandelions.

The old man glanced doggedly at his wife as he tightened the last buckles on the harness. She looked as immovable to him as one of the rocks in his pastureland, bound to the earth with generations of blackberry vines. He slapped the reins over the horse, and started forth from the barn.

"*Father!*" said she.

The old man pulled up. "What is it?"

"I want to know what them men are diggin' over there in that field for."

"They're diggin' a cellar, I s'pose, if you've got to know."

"A cellar for what?"

"A barn."

"A barn? You ain't goin' to build a barn over there where we was goin' to have a house, father?"

The old man said not another word. He hurried the horse into the farm wagon, and clattered out of the yard, jouncing as sturdily on his seat as a boy.

The woman stood a moment looking after him, then she went out of the barn across a corner of the yard to the house. The house, standing at right angles with the great barn and a long reach of sheds and out-buildings, was infinitesimal compared with them. It was scarcely as commodious for people as the little boxes under the barn eaves were for doves.

A pretty girl's face, pink and delicate as a flower, was looking out of one of the house windows. She was watching three men who were digging over in the field which bounded the yard near the road line. She turned quietly when the woman entered.

"What are they digging for, mother?" said she. "Did he tell you?"

"They're diggin' for—a cellar for a new barn."

"Oh, mother, he ain't going to build another barn?"

"That's what he says."

A boy stood before the kitchen glass combing his hair. He combed slowly and painstakingly, arranging his brown hair in a smooth hillock over his forehead. He did not seem to pay any attention to the conversation.

"Sammy, did you know father was going to build a new barn?" asked the girl.

The boy combed assiduously.

"Sammy!"

He turned, and showed a face like his father's under his smooth crest of hair. "Yes, I s'pose I did," he said, reluctantly.

"How long have you known it?" asked his mother.

" 'bout three months, I guess."

"Why didn't you tell of it?"

"Didn't think 'twould do no good."

"I don't see what father wants another barn for," said the girl, in her

99

sweet, slow voice. She turned again to the window, and stared out at the digging men in the field. Her tender, sweet face was full of a gentle distress. Her forehead was as bald and innocent as a baby's with the light hair strained back from it in a row of curlpapers. She was quite large, but her soft curves did not look as if they covered muscles.

Her mother looked sternly at the boy. "Is he goin' to buy more cows?"

The boy did not reply; he was tying his shoes.

"Sammy, I want you to tell me if he's goin' to buy more cows."

"I s'pose he is."

"How many?"

"Four, I guess."

His mother said nothing more. She went into the pantry, and there was a clatter of dishes. The boy got his cap from a nail behind the door, took an old arithmetic from the shelf, and started for school. He was lightly built, but clumsy. He went out of the yard with a curious spring in the hips, that made his loose home-made jacket tilt up in the rear.

The girl went to the sink, and began to wash the dishes that were piled up there. Her mother came promptly out of the pantry, and shoved her aside. "You wipe 'em," said she, "I'll wash. There's a good many this mornin'."

The mother plunged her hands vigorously into the water, the girl wiped the plates slowly and dreamily. "Mother," said she, "don't you think it's too bad father's going to build that new barn, much as we need a decent house to live in?"

Her mother scrubbed a dish fiercely. "You ain't found out yet we're women-folks, Nanny-Penn," said she. "You ain't seen enough of men-folks yet to. One of these days you'll find it out, and then you'll know that we know only what men-folks think we do, so far as any use of it goes, an' how we'd ought to reckon men-folks in with Providence, an' not complain of what they do any more than we do of the weather."

"I don't care; I don't believe George Eastman is anything like that, any-how," said Nanny. Her delicate face flushed pink, her lips pouted softly, as if she were going to cry.

"You wait an' see. I guess George Eastman ain't no better than other men. You hadn't ought to judge father, though. He can't help it, 'cause he don't look at things jest the way we do. An' we've been pretty comfortable here, after all. The roof don't leak—ain't never but once—that's one thing. Father's kept it shingled right up."

"I do wish we had a parlor."

"I guess it won't hurt George Eastman any to come to see you in a nice clean kitchen. I guess a good many girls don't have as good a place as this. Nobody's ever heard me complain."

"I ain't complained either, mother."

"Well, I don't think you'd better, a good father an' a good home as you've got. S'pose your father made you go out an' work for your livin'?

Lots of girls have to that ain't no stronger an' better able to than you be."

Sarah Penn washed the frying-pan with a conclusive air. She scrubbed the outside of it as faithfully as the inside. She was a masterly keeper of her box of a house. Her one living-room never seemed to have in it any of the dust which the friction of life with inanimate matter produces. She swept, and there seemed to be no dirt to go before the broom; she cleaned, and one could see no difference. She was like an artist so perfect that he has apparently no art. To-day she got out a mixing bowl and a board, and rolled some pies, and there was no more flour upon her than upon her daughter who was doing finer work. Nanny was to be married in the fall, and she was sewing on some white cambric and embroidery. She sewed industriously while her mother cooked; her soft milk-white hands and wrists showed whiter than her delicate work.

"We must have the stove moved out in the shed before long," said Mrs. Penn. "Talk about not havin' things, it's been a real blessin' to be able to put a stove up in that shed in hot weather. Father did one good thing when he fixed that stove-pipe out there."

Sarah Penn's face as she rolled her pies had that expression of meek vigor which might have characterized one of the New Testament saints. She was making mince-pies. Her husband, Adoniram Penn, liked them better than any other kind. She baked twice a week. Adoniram often liked a piece of pie between meals. She hurried this morning. It had been later than usual when she began, and she wanted to have a pie baked for dinner. However deep a resentment she might be forced to hold against her husband, she would never fail in sedulous attention to his wants.

Nobility of character manifests itself at loop-holes when it is not provided with large doors. Sarah Penn's showed itself to-day in flaky dishes of pastry. So she made the pies faithfully, while across the table she could see, when she glanced up from her work, the sight that rankled in her patient and steadfast soul—the digging of the cellar of the new barn in the place where Adoniram forty years ago had promised her their new house should stand.

The pies were done for dinner. Adoniram and Sammy were home a few minutes after twelve o'clock. The dinner was eaten with serious haste. There was never much conversation at the table in the Penn family. Adoniram asked a blessing, and they ate promptly, then rose up and went about their work.

Sammy went back to school, taking soft sly lopes out of the yard like a rabbit. He wanted a game of marbles before school, and feared his father would give him some chores to do. Adoniram hastened to the door and called after him, but he was out of sight.

"I don't see what you let him go for, mother," said he. "I wanted him to help me unload that wood."

Adoniram went to work out in the yard unloading wood from the wagon. Sarah put away the dinner dishes, while Nanny took down her curl papers and changed her dress. She was going down to the store to buy some more embroidery and thread.

When Nanny was gone, Mrs. Penn went to the door. "Father!" she called.

"Well, what is it!"

"I want to see you jest a minute, father."

"I can't leave this wood nohow. I've got to git it unloaded an' go for a load of gravel afore two o'clock. Sammy had ought to helped me. You hadn't ought to let him go to school so early."

"I want to see you jest a minute."

"I tell ye I can't, nohow, mother."

"Father, you come here." Sarah Penn stood in the door like a queen; she held her head as if it bore a crown; there was that patience which makes authority royal in her voice. Adoniram went.

Mrs. Penn led the way into the kitchen, and pointed to a chair. "Sit down, father," said she; "I've got somethin' I want to say to you."

He sat down heavily; his face was quite stolid, but he looked at her with restive eyes. "Well, what is it, mother?"

"I want to know what you're buildin' that new barn for, father?"

"I ain't got nothin' to say about it."

"It can't be you think you need another barn?"

"I tell ye I ain't got nothin' to say about it, mother; an' I ain't goin' to say nothin'."

"Be you goin' to buy more cows?"

Adoniram did not reply; he shut his mouth tight.

"I know you be, as well as I want to. Now, father, look here"—Sarah Penn had not sat down; she stood before her husband in the humble fashion of a Scripture woman—"I'm goin' to talk real plain to you; I never have sence I married you, but I'm goin' to now. I ain't never complained, an' I ain't goin' to complain now, but I'm goin' to talk plain. You see this room here, father; you look at it well. You see there ain't no carpet on the floor, an' you see the paper is all dirty, an' droppin' off the wall. We ain't had no new paper on it for ten year, an' then I put it on myself, an' it didn't cost but ninepence a roll. You see this room, father; it's all the one I've had to work in an' eat in an' sit in since we was married. There ain't another woman in the whole town whose husband ain't got half the means you have but what's got better. It's all the room Nanny's got to have her company in; an' there ain't one of her mates but what's got better, an' their fathers not so able as hers is. It's all the room she'll have to be married in. What would you have thought, father, if we had had our weddin' in a room no better than this? I was married in my mother's parlor, with a carpet on the floor, an' stuffed furniture, an' a mahogany card-table. An' this is all the room my daughter will have to be married in. Look here, father!"

Sarah Penn went across the room as though it were a tragic stage. She flung open a door and disclosed a tiny bedroom, only large enough for a bed and bureau, with a path between. "There, father," said she—"there's all the room I've had to sleep in forty year. All my children were born there—the two that died, an' the two that's livin'. I was sick with a fever there."

She stepped to another door and opened it. It led into the small, ill-lighted pantry. "Here," said she, "is all the buttery I've got—every place I've got for my dishes, to set away my victuals in, an' to keep my milkpans in. Father, I've been takin' care of the milk of six cows in this place, an' now you're goin' to build a new barn, an' keep more cows, an' give me more to do in it."

She threw open another door. A narrow crooked flight of stairs wound upward from it. "There, father," said she, "I want you to look at the stairs that go up to them two unfinished chambers that are all the places our son an' daughter have had to sleep in all their lives. There ain't a prettier girl in town nor a more ladylike one than Nanny, an' that's the place she has had to sleep in. It ain't so good as your horse's stall; it ain't so warm an' tight."

Sarah Penn went back and stood before her husband. "Now, father," said she, "I want to know if you think you're doin' right an' accordin' to what you profess. Here, when we was married, forty year ago, you promised me faithful that we should have a new house built in that lot over in the field before the year was out. You said you had money enough, an' you wouldn't ask me to live in no such place as this. It is forty year now, an' you've been makin' more money, an' I've been savin' of it for you ever since, an' you ain't built no house yet. You've built sheds an' cow-houses an' one new barn, an' now you're goin' to build another. Father, I want to know if you think it's right. You're lodgin' your dumb beasts better than you are your own flesh an' blood. I want to know if you think it's right."

"I ain't got nothin' to say."

"You can't say nothin' without ownin' it ain't right, father. An' there's another thing—I ain't complained; I've got along forty year, an' I s'pose I should forty more, if it wasn't for that—if we don't have another house, Nanny she can't live with us after she's married. She'll have to go some-where else to live away from us, an' it don't seem as if I could have it so, noways, father. She wasn't ever strong. She's got considerable color, but there wasn't never any backbone to her. I've always took the heft of every-thing off her, an' she ain't fit to keep house an' do everything herself. She'll be all worn out inside of a year. Think of her doin' all the washin' an' ironin' an' bakin' with them soft white hands an' arms, an' sweepin'! I can't have it so, noways, father."

Mrs. Penn's face was burning; her mild eyes gleamed. She had pleaded her little cause like a Webster; she had ranged from severity to pathos; but her opponent employed that obstinate silence which makes eloquence futile with mocking echoes. Adoniram arose clumsily.

"Father, ain't you got nothin' to say?" said Mrs. Penn.

"I've got to go off after that load of gravel. I can't stan' here talkin' all day."

"Father, won't you think it over, an' have a house built there instead of a barn?"

"I ain't got nothin' to say."

Adoniram shuffled out. Mrs. Penn went into her bedroom. When she came out, her eyes were red. She had a roll of unbleached cotton cloth. She spread it out on the kitchen table, and began cutting out some shirts for her husband. The men over in the field had a team to help them this afternoon; she could hear their haloos. She had a scanty pattern for the shirts; she had to plan and piece the sleeves.

Nanny came home with her embroidery, and sat down with her needle-work. She had taken down her curl-papers, and there was a soft roll of hair like an aureole over her forehead; her face was as delicately fine and clear as porcelain. Suddenly she looked up, and the tender red flamed all over face and neck. "Mother," said she.

"What say?"

"I've been thinkin'—and I don't see how we're goin' to have any—wedding in this room. I'd be ashamed to have his folks come if we didn't have anybody else."

"Mebbe we can have some new paper before then; I can put it on. I guess you won't have no call to be ashamed of your belongin's."

"We might have the wedding in the new barn," said Nanny, with gentle pettishness. "Why, mother, what makes you look so?"

Mrs. Penn had started, and was staring at her with a curious expression. She turned again to her work, and spread out a pattern carefully on the cloth. "Nothin'," said she.

Presently Adoniram clattered out of the yard in his two-wheeled dump cart, standing as proudly upright as a Roman charioteer. Mrs. Penn opened the door and stood there a minute looking out; the haloos of the men sounded louder.

It seemed to her all through the spring months that she heard nothing but the haloos and the noises of saws and hammers. The new barn grew fast. It was a fine edifice for this little village. Men came on pleasant Sundays, in their meeting suits and clean shirt bosoms, and stood around it admiringly. Mrs. Penn did not speak of it, and Adoniram did not mention it to her, although sometimes, upon a return from inspecting it, he bore himself with injured dignity.

"It's a strange thing how your mother feels about the new barn," he said, confidentially, to Sammy one day.

Sammy only grunted after an odd fashion for a boy; he had learned it from his father.

The barn was all completed ready for use by the third week in July. Adoniram had planned to move his stock in on Wednesday; on Tuesday he received a letter which changed his plans. He came in with it early in the morning. "Sammy's been to the post-office," said he, "an' I've got a letter from Hiram." Hiram was Mrs. Penn's brother, who lived in Vermont.

"Well," said Mrs. Penn, "what does he say about the folks?"

"I guess they're all right. He says he thinks if I come up country right off there's a chance to buy jest the kind of horse I want." He stared reflectively out of the window at the new barn.

Mrs. Penn was making pies. She went on clapping the rolling-pin into the crust; although she was very pale, and her heart beat loudly.

"I dun know but what I'd better go," said Adoniram. "I hate to go off jest now, right in the midst of hayin', but the ten-acre lot's cut, an' I guess Rufus an' the others can git along without me three or four days. I can't get a horse round here to suit me, nohow, an' I've got to have another for all that wood-haulin' in the fall. I told Hiram to watch out, an' if he got wind of a good horse to let me know. I guess I'd better go."

"I'll get out your clean shirt an' collar," said Mrs. Penn calmly.

She laid out Adoniram's Sunday suit and his clean clothes on the bed in the little bedroom. She got his shaving water and razor ready. At last she buttoned on his collar and fastened his black cravat.

Adoniram never wore his collar and cravat except on extra occasions. He held his head high, with a rasped dignity. When he was all ready, with his coat and hat brushed, and a lunch of pie and cheese in a paper bag, he hesitated on the threshold of the door. He looked at his wife, and his manner was definitely apologetic. "If them cows come to-day, Sammy can drive 'em into the new barn," said he; "an' when they bring the hay up, they can pitch it in there."

"Well," replied Mrs. Penn.

Adoniram set his shaven face ahead and started. When he had cleared the door-step, he turned and looked back with a kind of nervous solemnity. "I shall be back by Saturday if nothin' happens," said he.

"Do be careful, father," returned his wife.

She stood in the door with Nanny at her elbow and watched him out of sight. Her eyes had a strange, doubtful expression in them; her peaceful forehead was contracted. She went in, and about her baking again. Nanny sat sewing. Her wedding-day was drawing nearer, and she was getting pale and thin with her steady sewing. Her mother kept glancing at her.

"Have you got that pain in your side this mornin'?" she asked.

"A little."

Mrs. Penn's face, as she worked, changed, her perplexed forehead smoothed, her eyes were steady, her lips firmly set. She formed a maxim for herself, although incoherently with her unlettered thoughts. "Unsolicited opportunities are the guide-posts of the Lord to the new roads of life," she repeated in effect, and she made up her mind to her course of action.

"S'posin' I *had* wrote Hiram," she muttered once, when she was in the pantry—"s'posin' I had wrote, an' asked him if he knew of any horse? But I didn't, an' father's goin' wa'n't none of my doin'. It looks like a providence." Her voice rang out quite loud at the last.

"What you talkin' about, mother?" called Nanny.

"Nothin'."

Mrs. Penn hurried her baking; at eleven o'clock it was all done. The load of hay from the west field came slowly down the cart track, and drew up at the new barn. Mrs. Penn ran out. "Stop!" she screamed. "Stop!"

The men stopped and looked; Sammy upreared from the top of the load, and stared at his mother.

"Stop!" she cried again. "Don't you put the hay in that barn; put it in the old one."

"Why, he said to put it in here," returned one of the haymakers, wonderingly. He was a young man, a neighbor's son, whom Adoniram hired by the year to help on the farm.

"Don't you put the hay in the new barn; there's room enough in the old one, ain't there?" said Mrs. Penn.

"Room enough," returned the hired man, in his thick, rustic tones. "Didn't need the new barn, nohow, far as room's concerned. Well, I s'pose he changed his mind." He took hold of the horse's bridle.

Mrs. Penn went back to the house. Soon the kitchen windows were darkened, and a fragrance like warm honey came into the room.

Nanny laid down her work. "I thought father wanted them to put the hay into the new barn?" she said, wonderingly.

"It's all right," replied her mother.

Sammy slid down from the load of hay, and came in to see if dinner was ready.

"I ain't goin' to get a regular dinner to-day, as long as father's gone," said his mother. "I've let the fire go out. You can have some bread an' milk an' pie. I thought we could get along." She set out some bowls of milk, some bread, and a pie on the kitchen table. "You'd better eat your dinner now," said she. "You might jest as well get through with it. I want you to help me afterwards."

Nanny and Sammy stared at each other. There was something strange in their mother's manner. Mrs. Penn did not eat anything herself. She went into the pantry, and they heard her moving dishes while they ate. Presently she came out with a pile of plates. She got the clothes-basket out of the shed, and packed them in it. Nanny and Sammy watched. She brought out cups and saucers, and put them in with the plates.

"What you goin' to do, mother?" inquired Nanny, in a timid voice. A sense of something unusual made her tremble, as if it were a ghost. Sammy rolled his eyes over his pie.

"You'll see what I'm goin' to do," replied Mrs. Penn. "If you're through, Nanny, I want you to go upstairs an' pack up your things, an' I want you, Sammy, to help me take down the bed in the bedroom."

"Oh, mother, what for?"

106

"You'll see."

During the next few hours a feat was performed by this simple, pious New England mother which was equal in its way to Wolfe's storming the heights of Abraham. It took no more genius and audacity of bravery for Wolfe to cheer his wondering soldiers up those steep precipices, under the sleeping eyes of the enemy, than for Sarah Penn, at the head of her children, to move all their household goods into the new barn while her husband was away.

Nanny and Sammy followed their mother's instructions without a murmur; indeed, they were overawed. There is a certain uncanny and superhuman quality about all such purely original undertakings as their mother's was to them. Nanny went back and forth with her light load, and Sammy tugged with sober energy.

At five o'clock in the afternoon the little house in which the Penns had lived for forty years had emptied itself into the new barn.

Every builder builds somewhat for unknown purposes, and is in a measure a prophet. The architect of Adoniram Penn's barn, while he designed it for the comfort of four-footed animals, had planned better than he knew for the comfort of humans. Sarah Penn saw at a glance its possibilities. Those great box-stalls, with quilts hung before them, would make better bedrooms than the one she had occupied for forty years, and there was a tight carriage-room. The harness-room, with its chimney and shelves, would make a kitchen of her dreams. The great middle space would make a parlor, by-and-by, fit for a palace. Up-stairs there was as much room as down. With partitions and windows, what a house would there be! Sarah looked at the row of stanchions before the allotted space for cows, and reflected that she would have her front entry there.

At six o'clock the stove was up in the harness room, the kettle was boiling, and the table set for tea. It looked almost as home-like as the abandoned house across the yard had ever done. The young hired man milked, and Sarah directed him calmly to bring the milk to the new barn. He came gaping, dropping little blots of foam from the brimming pails on the grass. Before the next morning he had spread the story of Adoniram Penn's wife moving into the new barn all over the little village. Men assembled in the store and talked it over, women with shawls over their heads scuttled into each other's houses before their work was done. Any deviation from the ordinary course of life in this quiet town was enough to stop all progress in it. Everybody paused to look at the staid, independent figure on the side track. There was a difference of opinion with regard to her. Some held her to be insane; some, of a lawless and rebellious spirit.

Friday the minister went to see her. It was in the forenoon, and she was at the barn door shelling peas for dinner. She looked up and returned his salutation with dignity, then she went on with her work. She did not invite him in. The saintly expression of her face remained fixed, but there was an angry flush over it.

The minister stood awkwardly before her, and talked. She handled the peas as if they were bullets. At last she looked up, and her eyes showed the spirit that her meek front had covered for a lifetime.

"There ain't no use talkin', Mr. Hersey," said she. "I've thought it all over an' over, an' I believe I'm doin' what's right. I've made it the subject of prayer, an' it's betwixt me an' the Lord an' Adoniram. There ain't no call for nobody else to worry about it."

"Well, of course, if you have brought it to the Lord in prayer, and feel satisfied that you are doing right, Mrs. Penn," said the minister, helplessly. His thin gray-bearded face was pathetic. He was a sickly man; his youthful confidence had cooled; he had to scourge himself up to some of his pastoral duties as relentlessly as a Catholic ascetic, and then he was prostrated by the smart.

"I think it's right jest as much as I think it was right for our forefathers to come over here from the old country 'cause they didn't have what belonged to 'em," said Mrs. Penn. She arose. The barn threshold might have been Plymouth Rock from her bearing. "I don't doubt you mean well, Mr. Hersey," said she, "but there are things people hadn't ought to interfere with. I've been a member of the church for over forty years. I've got my own mind an' my own feet, an' I'm goin' to think my own thoughts an' go my own way, an' nobody but the Lord is goin' to dictate to me unless I've a mind to have him. Won't you come in an' set down? How is Mis' Hersey?"

"She is well, I thank you," replied the minister. He added some more perplexed apologetic remarks; then he retreated.

He could expound the intricacies of every character study in the Scriptures, he was competent to grasp the Pilgrim Fathers and all historical innovators, but Sarah Penn was beyond him. He could deal with primal cases, but parallel ones worsted him. But, after all, although it was aside from his province, he wondered more how Adoniram Penn would deal with his wife than how the Lord would. Everybody shared the wonder. When Adoniram's four new cows arrived, Sarah ordered three to be put in the old barn, the other in the house shed where the cooking-stove had stood. That added to the excitement. It was whispered that all four cows were domiciled in the house.

Towards sunset on Saturday, when Adoniram was expected home, there was a knot of men in the road near the new barn. The hired man had milked, but he still hung around the premises. Sarah Penn had supper all ready. There were brown-bread and baked beans and a custard pie; it was the supper that Adoniram loved on a Saturday night. She had on a clean calico, and she bore herself imperturbably. Nanny and Sammy kept close at her heels. Their eyes were large, and Nanny was full of nervous tremors. Still there was to them more pleasant excitement than anything else. An inborn confidence in their mother over their father asserted itself.

Sammy looked out of the harness-room window. "There he is," he announced, in an awed whisper. He and Nanny peeped around the casing.

Mrs. Penn kept on about her work. The children watched Adoniram leave the new horse standing in the drive while he went to the house door. It was fastened. Then he went around to the shed. That door was seldom locked, even when the family was away. The thought how her father would be confronted by the cow flashed upon Nanny. There was a hysterical sob in her throat. Adoniram emerged from the shed and stood looking about in a dazed fashion. His lips moved; he was saying something, but they could not hear what it was. The hired man was peeping around a corner of the old barn, but nobody saw him.

Adoniram took the new horse by the bridle and led him across the yard to the new barn. Nanny and Sammy slunk close to their mother. The barn doors rolled back, and there stood Adoniram, with the long mild face of the great Canadian farm horse looking over his shoulder.

Nanny kept behind her mother, but Sammy stepped suddenly forward, and stood in front of her.

Adoniram stared at the group. "What on airth you all down here for?" said he. "What's the matter over to the house?"

"We've come here to live, father," said Sammy. His shrill voice quavered out bravely.

"What"—Adoniram sniffed—"what is it smells like cookin'?" said he. He stepped forward and looked in the open door of the harness-room. Then he turned to his wife. His old bristling face was pale and frightened. "What on airth does this mean, mother?" he gasped.

"You come in here, father," said Sarah. She led the way into the harness-room and shut the door. "Now, father," said she, "you needn't be scared. I ain't crazy. There ain't nothin' to be upset over. But we've come here to live, an' we're goin' to live here. We've got jest as good a right here as new horses an' cows. The house wasn't fit for us to live in any longer, an' I made up my mind I wa'n't goin' to stay there. I've done my duty by you forty year, an' I'm goin' to do it now; but I'm goin' to live here. You've got to put in some windows and partitions; an' you'll have to buy some furniture."

"Why, mother!" the old man gasped.

"You'd better take your coat off an' get washed—there's the wash basin —an' then we'll have supper."

"Why, mother!"

Sammy went past the window, leading the new horse to the old barn. The old man saw him, and shook his head speechlessly. He tried to take off his coat, but his arms seemed to lack the power. His wife helped him. She poured some water into the tin basin, and put in a piece of soap. She got the comb and brush, and smoothed his thin gray hair after he had washed. Then she put the beans, hot bread, and tea on the table. Sammy came in, and the family drew up. Adoniram sat looking dazedly at his plate, and they waited.

"Ain't you goin' to ask a blessin', father?" said Sarah.

And the old man bent his head and mumbled.

All through the meal he stopped eating at intervals, and stared furtively at his wife; but he ate well. The home food tasted good to him, and his old frame was too sturdily healthy to be affected by his mind. But after supper he went out, and sat down on the step of the smaller door at the right of the barn, through which he had meant his Jerseys to pass in stately file, but which Sarah designed for her front house door, and he leaned his head on his hands.

After the supper dishes were cleared away and the milk-pans washed, Sarah went out to him. The twilight was deepening. There was a clear green glow in the sky. Before them stretched the smooth level of field; in the distance was a cluster of hay-stacks like the huts of a village; the air was very cool and calm and sweet. The landscape might have been an ideal one of peace.

Sarah bent over and touched her husband on one of his thin, sinewy shoulders. "Father!"

The old man's shoulders heaved: he was weeping.

"Why, don't do so, father," said Sarah.

"I'll—put up the—partitions, an'—everything you—want, mother."

Sarah put her apron up to her face; she was overcome by her own triumph.

Adoniram was like fortress whose walls had no active resistance, and went down the instant the right besieging tools were used. "Why, mother," he said, hoarsely, "I hadn't no idee you was so set on't as all this comes to."

A New England Nun and Other Stories, 1891

EMILY DICKINSON

This Is My Letter to the World

> This is my letter to the world,
>   That never wrote to me.—
> The simple news that Nature told,
>   With tender majesty.
>
> Her message is committed
>   To hands I cannot see;
> For love of her, sweet countrymen,
>   Judge tenderly of me!

The Railroad Train

I like to see it lap the miles,
And lick the valleys up,
And stop to feed itself at tanks;
And then, prodigious, step

Around a pile of mountains,
And, supercilious, peer
In shanties by the sides of roads;
And then a quarry pare

To fit its sides, and crawl between,
Complaining all the while
In horrid, hooting stanza;
Then chase itself down hill

And neigh like Boanerges;
Then, punctual as a star,
Stop,—docile and omnipotent—
At its own stable door.

Success

Success is counted sweetest
By those who ne'er succeed.
To comprehend a nectar
Requires sorest need.

Not one of all the purple host
Who took the flag to-day
Can tell the definition,
So clear, of victory,

As he defeated, dying,
On whose forbidden ear
The distant strains of triumph
Break, agonized and clear.

Poems, 1890 and 1891

EDWIN ARLINGTON ROBINSON

Cliff Klingenhagen

Cliff Klingenhagen had me in to dine
With him one day; and after soup and meat,
And all the other things there were to eat,
Cliff took two glasses and filled one with wine
And one with wormwood. Then, without a sign
For me to choose at all, he took the draught
Of bitterness himself, and lightly quaffed
It off, and said the other one was mine.

And when I asked him what the deuce he meant
By doing that, he only looked at me
And smiled, and said it was a way of his.
And though I know the fellow, I have spent
Long time a-wondering when I shall be
As happy as Cliff Klingenhagen is.

Richard Cory

Whenever Richard Cory went down town,
We people on the pavement looked at him:
He was a gentleman from sole to crown,
Clean favored, and imperially slim.

And he was always quietly arrayed,
And he was always human when he talked;
But still he fluttered pulses when he said,
"Good morning," and he glittered when he walked.

And he was rich—yes, richer than a king—
And admirably schooled in every grace:
In fine, we thought that he was everything
To make us wish that we were in his place.

So on we worked, and waited for the light,
And went without the meat, and cursed the bread;
And Richard Cory, one calm summer night,
Went home and put a bullet through his head.

Poems, 1897

SARAH ORNE JEWETT

The Hiltons' Holiday

> *Willa Cather noted that Miss Jewett, "by instinctive preference,"*
> *wrote "of the people who grew out of the soil and the life of the*
> *country near her heart"—that is, Maine. She claimed that time*
> *and change would not disturb the eminence of Miss Jewett's finest*
> *work.*

There was a bright, full moon in the clear sky, and the sunset was still shining faintly in the west. Dark woods stood all about the old Hilton farmhouse, save down the hill, westward, where lay the shadowy fields which John Hilton, and his father before him, had cleared and tilled with much toil,—the small fields to which they had given the industry and even affection of their honest lives.

John Hilton was sitting on the doorstep of his house. As he moved his head in and out of the shadows, turning now and then to speak to his wife, who sat just within the doorway, one could see his good face, rough and somewhat unkempt, as if he were indeed a creature of the shady woods and brown earth, instead of the noisy town. It was late in the long spring evening, and he had just come from the lower field, as cheerful as a boy, proud of having finished the planting of his potatoes.

"I had to do my last row mostly by feelin'," he said to his wife. "I'm proper glad I pushed through, an' went back an' ended off after supper. 'T would have taken me a good part o' to-morrow mornin' an' broke my day."

"'T ain't no use for ye to work yourself all to pieces, John," answered the woman quickly. "I declare it does seem harder than ever that we couldn't have kep' our boy; he'd been comin' fourteen years old this fall, most a grown man, and he'd work right 'longside of ye now the whole time."

"'T was hard to lose him; I do seem to miss little John," said the father sadly. "I expect there was reasons why 't was best. I feel able an' smart to work; my father was a girt strong man, an' a monstrous worker afore me. 'T ain't that; but I was thinkin' by myself what a sight o' company the boy would ha' been. You know, small's he was, how I could trust to leave him anywheres with the team, and how he'd beseech to go with me wherever I was goin'; always right in my tracks I used to tell 'em. Poor little John, for all he was so young he had a great deal o' judgment; he'd ha' made a likely man."

The mother sighed heavily as she sat within the shadow.

"But then there's the little girls, a sight o' help an' company," urged the father eagerly, as if it were wrong to dwell upon sorrow and loss. "Katy, she's most as good as a boy, except that she ain't very rugged. She's a real little farmer, she's helped me a sight this spring; an' you've got Susan Ellen, that makes a complete little housekeeper for ye as far as she's learnt. I don't see but we're better off than most folks, each on us having a work-mate."

"That's so, John," acknowledged Mrs. Hilton wistfully, beginning to rock steadily in her straight, splint-bottomed chair. It was always a good sign when she rocked.

"Where be the little girls so late?" asked their father. " 'T is gettin' long past eight o'clock. I don't know when we've all set up so late, but it's kind of summer-like an' pleasant. Why, where be they gone?"

"I've told ye; only over to Becker's folks," answered the mother. "I don't see myself what keeps 'em so late; they beseeched me after supper till I let them go. They're all in a dazzle with the new teacher; she asked 'em to come over. They say she's unusual smart with 'rithmetic, but she has a kind of gorpen look to me. She's goin' to give Katy some pieces for her doll, but I told Katy she ought to be ashamed wantin' doll pieces, big as she's gettin' to be. I don't know's she ought, though; she ain't but nine this summer."

"Let her take her comfort," said the kind-hearted father. "Them things draws her to the teacher, and makes them acquainted. Katy's shy with new folks, more so 'n Susan Ellen, who's of the business kind. Katy's shy-feelin' and wishful."

"I don't know but she is," agreed the mother slowly. "Ain't it sing'lar how well acquainted you be with that one, and I with Susan Ellen? 'T was always so from the first. I'm doubtful sometimes our Katy ain't one that'll be like to get married—anyways not about here. She lives right with herself, but Susan Ellen ain't nothin' when she's alone, she's always after company; all the boys is waitin' on her a'ready. I ain't afraid but she'll take her pick when the time comes. I expect to see Susan Ellen well settled,—she feels grown up now,—but Katy don't care one mite 'bout none o' them things. She wants to be rovin' out o' doors. I do believe she'd stand an' hark to a bird the whole forenoon."

"Perhaps she'll grow up to be a teacher," suggested John Hilton. "She takes to her book more 'n the other one. I should like one on 'em to be a teacher same's my mother was. They're good girls as anybody's got."

"So they be," said the mother, with unusual gentleness, and the creak of her rocking-chair was heard, regular as the ticking of a clock. The night breeze stirred in the great woods, and the sound of a brook that went falling down the hillside grew louder and louder. Now and then one could hear the plaintive chirp of a bird. The moon glittered with whiteness like a winter moon, and shone upon the low-roofed house until its small window-panes gleamed like silver, and one could almost see the

114

colors of a blooming bush of lilac that grew in a sheltered angle by the kitchen door. There was an incessant sound of frogs in the lowlands.

"Be you sound asleep, John?" asked the wife presently.

"I don't know but what I was a'most," said the tired man, starting a little. "I should laugh if I was to fall sound asleep right here on the step; 't is the bright night, I expect, makes my eyes feel heavy, an' 't is so peaceful. I was up an' dressed a little past four an' out to work. Well, well!" and he laughed sleepily and rubbed his eyes. "Where's the little girls? I'd better step along an' meet 'em."

"I wouldn't just yet; they'll get home all right, but 't is late for 'em certain. I don't want 'em keepin' Mis' Becker's folks up neither. There, le' 's wait a few minutes," urged Mrs. Hilton.

"I've be'n a-thinkin' all day I'd like to give the child'n some kind of a treat," said the father, wide awake now. "I hurried up my work 'cause I had it so in mind. They don't have the opportunities some do, an' I want 'em to know the world, an' not stay right here on the farm like a couple o' bushes."

"They're a sight better off not to be so full o' notions as some is," protested the mother suspiciously.

"Certain," answered the farmer; "but they're good, bright child'n, an' commencin' to take a sight o' notice. I want 'em to have all we can give 'em. I want 'em to see how other folks does things."

"Why, so do I,"—here the rocking-chair stopped ominously,—"but so long 's they're contented"—

"Contented ain't all in this world; hopper-toads may have that quality an' spend all their time a-blinkin'. I don't know's bein' contented is all there is to look for in a child. Ambition 's somethin' to me."

"Now you've got your mind on to some plot or other." (The rocking-chair began to move again.) "Why can't you talk right out?"

"'T ain't nothin' special," answered the good man, a little ruffled; he was never prepared for his wife's mysterious powers of divination. "Well there, you do find things out the master! I only thought perhaps I'd take 'em to-morrow, an' go off somewhere if 't was a good day. I've been promisin' for a good while I'd take 'em to Topham Corners; they've never been there since they was very small."

"I believe you want a good time yourself. You ain't never got over bein' a boy." Mrs. Hilton seemed much amused. "There, go if you want to an' take 'em; they've got their summer hats an' new dresses. I don't know o' nothin' that stands in the way. I should sense it better if there was a circus or anythin' to go to. Why don't you wait an' let the girls pick 'em some strawberries or nice ros'berries, and then they could take an' sell 'em to the stores?"

John Hilton reflected deeply. "I should like to get me some good yellow-turnip seed to plant late. I ain't more 'n satisfied with what I've been gettin' o' late years o' Ira Speed. An' I'm goin' to provide me with a good hoe; mine's gettin' wore out an' all shackly. I can't seem to fix it good."

"Them's excuses," observed Mrs. Hilton, with friendly tolerance. "You just cover up the hoe with somethin', if you get it—I would. Ira Speed's so jealous he'll remember it of you this twenty year, your goin' an' buyin' a new hoe o' anybody but him."

"I've always thought 't was a free country," said John Hilton soberly. "I don't want to vex Ira neither; he favors us all he can in trade. 'T is difficult for him to spare a cent, but he's as honest as daylight."

At this moment there was a sudden sound of young voices, and a pair of young figures came out from the shadow of the woods into the moon-lighted open space. An old cock crowed loudly from his perch in the shed, as if he were a herald of royalty. The little girls were hand in hand, and a brisk young dog capered about them as they came.

"Wa'n't it dark gettin' home through the woods this time o' night?" asked the mother hastily, and not without reproach.

"I don't love to have you gone so late; mother an' me was timid about ye, and you've kep' Mis' Becker's folks up, I expect," said their father regretfully. "I don't want to have it said that my little girls ain't got good manners."

"The teacher had a party," chirped Susan Ellen, the elder of the two children. "Goin' home from school she asked the Grover boys, an' Mary an' Sarah Speed. An' Mis' Becker was real pleasant to us; she passed round some cake, an' handed us sap sugar on one of her best plates, an' we played games an' sung some pieces too. Mis' Becker thought we did real well. I can pick out most of a tune on the cabinet organ; teacher says she'll give me lessons."

"I want to know, dear!" exclaimed John Hilton.

"Yes, an' we played Copenhagen, an' took sides spellin', an' Katy beat everybody spellin' there was there."

Katy had not spoken; she was not so strong as her sister, and while Susan stood a step or two away addressing her eager little audience, Katy had seated herself close to her father on the doorstep. He put his arm around her shoulders, and drew her close to his side, where she stayed.

"Ain't you got nothin' to tell, daughter?" he asked, looking down fondly; and Katy gave a pleased little sigh for answer.

"Tell 'em what's goin' to be the last day o' school, and about our trimmin' the schoolhouse," she said; and Susan Ellen gave the programme in a most spirited fashion.

" 'T will be a great time," said the mother, when she had finished. "I don't see why folks want to go trapesin' off to strange places when such things is happen' right about 'em." But the children did not observe her mysterious air. "Come, you must step yourselves right to bed!"

They all went into the dark, warm house; the bright moon shone upon it steadily all night, and the lilac flowers were shaken by no breath of wind until the early dawn.

The Hiltons always waked early. So did their neighbors, the crows and song-sparrows and robins, the light-footed foxes and the squirrels in the woods. When John Hilton waked, before five o'clock, an hour later than usual because he had sat up late, he opened the house door and came out into the yard, crossing the short green turf hurriedly as if the day were too far spent for any loitering. The magnitude of the plan for taking a whole day of pleasure confronted him seriously, but the weather was fair, and his wife, whose disapproval could not have been set aside, had accepted and even smiled upon the great project. It was inevitable now, that he and the children should go to Topham Corners. Mrs. Hilton had the pleasure of waking them, and telling the news.

In a few minutes they came frisking out to talk over the great plans. The cattle were already fed, and their father was milking. The only sign of high festivity was the wagon pulled out into the yard, with both seats put in as if it were Sunday; but Mr. Hilton still wore his every-day clothes, and Susan Ellen suffered instantly from disappointment.

"Ain't we goin', father?" she asked complainingly; but he nodded and smiled at her, even though the cow, impatient to get to pasture, kept whisking her rough tail across his face. He held his head down and spoke cheerfully, in spite of his vexation.

"Yes, sister, we're goin' certain, an' goin' to have a great time, too." Susan Ellen thought that he seemed like a boy at that delightful moment, and felt new sympathy and pleasure at once. "You go an' help mother about breakfast an' them things; we want to get off quick's we can. You coax mother now, both on ye, an' see if she won't go with us."

"She said she wouldn't be hired to," responded Susan Ellen. "She says it's goin' to be hot, an' she'd laid out to go over an' see how her aunt Tamsen Brooks is this afternoon."

The father gave a little sigh; then he took heart again. The truth was that his wife made light of the contemplated pleasure, and, much as he usually valued her companionship and approval, he was sure that they should have a better time without her. It was impossible, however, not to feel guilty of disloyalty at the thought. Even though she might be completely unconscious of his best ideals, he only loved her and the ideals the more, and bent his energies to satisfying her indefinite expectations. His wife still kept much of that youthful beauty which Susan Ellen seemed likely to reproduce.

An hour later the best wagon was ready, and the great expedition set forth. The little dog sat apart, and barked as if it fell entirely upon him to voice the general excitement. Both seats were in the wagon, but the empty place testified to Mrs. Hilton's unyielding disposition. She had wondered why one broad seat would not do, but John Hilton meekly suggested that the wagon looked better with both. The little girls sat on the back seat dressed alike in their Sunday hats of straw with blue ribbons, and their little plaid shawls pinned neatly about their small shoulders. They wore gray thread gloves, and sat very straight. Susan Ellen was half a head the taller, but otherwise, from behind, they looked much alike. As for their father, he was in his Sunday best,—a plain black coat, and a winter hat of felt, which was heavy and rusty-looking for that warm early summer day. He had it in mind to buy a new straw hat at Topham, so that this with the turnip seed and the hoe made three important reasons for going.

"Remember an' lay off your shawls when you get there, an' carry them over your arms," said the mother, clucking like an excited hen to her chickens. "They'll do to keep the dust off your new dresses goin' an' comin'. An' when you eat your dinners don't get spots on you, an' don't point at folks as you ride by, an' stare, or they'll know you come from the country. An' John, you call into Cousin Ad'line Marlow's an' see how they all be, an' tell her I expect her over certain to stop awhile before hayin'. It always eases her phthisic to git up here on the highland, an' I've got a new notion about doin' over her best-room carpet sence I see her that'll save rippin' one breadth. An' don't come home all wore out; an', John, don't you go an' buy me no kickshaws to fetch home. I ain't a child, an' you ain't got no money to waste. I expect you'll go, like 's not, an' buy you some kind of a foolish boy's hat; do look an' see if it's reasonable good straw, an' won't splinter all off round the edge. An' you mind, John"—

"Yes, yes, hold on!" cried John impatiently; then he cast a last affectionate, reassuring look at her face, flushed with the hurry and responsibility of starting them off in proper shape. "I wish you was goin' too," he said, smiling. "I do so!" Then the old horse started, and they went out at the bars, and began the careful long descent of the hill. The young dog, tethered to the lilac-bush, was frantic with piteous appeals; the little girls piped their eager good-bys again and again, and their father turned many times to look back and wave his hand. As for their mother, she stood alone and watched them out of sight.

There was one place far out on the high-road where she could catch a last glimpse of the wagon, and she waited what seemed a very long time until it appeared and then was lost to sight again behind a low hill. "They're nothin' but a pack o' child'n together," she said aloud; and then felt lonelier than she expected. She even stooped and patted the unresigned little dog as she passed him, going into the house.

The occasion was so much more important than any one had foreseen that both the little girls were speechless. It seemed at first like going to church in new clothes, or to a funeral; they hardly knew how to behave at the beginning of a whole day of pleasure. They made grave bows at such persons of their acquaintance as happened to be straying in the road. Once or twice they stopped before a farmhouse, while their father talked an inconsiderately long time with some one about the crops and the weather, and even dwelt upon town business and the doings of the selectmen, which might be talked of at any time. The explanations that he gave of their excursion seemed quite unnecessary. It was made entirely clear that he had a little business to do at Topham Corners, and thought he had better give the little girls a ride; they had been very steady at school, and he had finished planting, and could take the day as well as not. Soon, however, they all felt as if such an excursion were an every-day affair, and Susan Ellen began to ask eager questions, while Katy silently sat apart enjoying herself as she never had done before. She liked to see the strange houses, and the children who belonged to them; it was delightful to find flowers that she knew growing all along the road, no matter how far she went from home. Each small homestead looked its best and pleasantest, and shared the exquisite beauty that early summer made,—shared the luxury of greenness and floweriness that decked the rural world. There was an early peony or a late lilac in almost every dooryard.

It was seventeen miles to Topham. After a while they seemed very far from home, having left the hills far behind and descended to a great level country with fewer tracts of woodland, and wider fields where the crops were much more forward. The houses were all painted, and the roads were smoother and wider. It had been so pleasant driving along that Katy dreaded going into the strange town when she first caught sight of it, though Susan Ellen kept asking with bold fretfulness if they were not almost there. They counted the steeples of four churches, and their father presently showed them the Topham Academy, where their grandmother once went to school, and told them that perhaps some day they would go there too. Katy's heart gave a strange leap; it was such a tremendous thing to think of, but instantly the suggestion was transformed for her into one of the certainties of life. She looked with solemn awe at the tall belfry, and the long rows of windows in front of the academy, there where it stood high and white among the clustering trees. She hoped that they were going to drive by, but something forbade her taking the responsibility of saying so.

Soon the children found themselves among the crowded village houses. Their father turned to look at them with affectionate solicitude.

"Now sit up straight and appear pretty," he whispered to them. "We're among the best people now, an' I want folks to think well of you."

"I guess we're as good as they be," remarked Susan Ellen, looking at some innocent passers-by with dark suspicion, but Katy tried to sit straight, and folded her hands prettily in her lap, and wished with all her heart to be pleasing for her father's sake. Just then an elderly woman saw the wagon and the sedate party it carried, and smiled so kindly it seemed to Katy as if Topham Corners had welcomed and received them. She smiled back again as if this hospitable person were an old friend, and entirely forgetful that the eyes of all Topham had been upon her.

"There, now we're coming to an elegant house that I want you to see; you'll never forget it," said John Hilton. "It's where Judge Masterson lives, the great lawyer; the handsomest man in the county, everybody says."

"Do you know him, father?" asked Susan Ellen.

"I do," answered John Hilton proudly. "Him and my mother went to school together in their young days, and were always called the two best scholars of their time. The judge called to see her once; he stopped to our house to see her when I was a boy. An' then, some years ago— you've heard me tell how I was on the jury, an' when he heard my name spoken he looked at me sharp, and asked me if I wa'n't the son of Catharine Winn, an' spoke most beautiful of your grandmother, an' how well he remembered their young days together."

"I like to hear about that," said Katy.

"She had it pretty hard, I'm afraid, up on the old farm. She was keepin' school in our district when father married her—that's the main reason I backed 'em down when they wanted to tear the old schoolhouse to pieces," confided John Hilton, turning eagerly. "They all say she lived longer up here on the hill than she could anywhere, but she never had her health. I wa'n't but a boy when she died. Father an' me lived alone afterward till the time your mother come; 't was a good while, too; I wa'n't married so young as some. 'T was lonesome, I tell you; father was plum discouraged losin' of his wife, an' her long sickness an' all set him back, an' we'd work all day on the land an' never say a word. I s'pose 't is bein' so lonesome so early in life that makes me so pleased to have some nice girls growin' up round me now."

There was a tone in her father's voice that drew Katy's heart toward him with new affection. She dimly understood, but Susan Ellen was less interested. They had often heard this story before, but to one child it was always new and to the other old. Susan Ellen was apt to think it tiresome to hear about her grandmother, who, being dead, was hardly worth talking about.

"There's Judge Masterson's place," said their father in an every-day manner, as they turned a corner, and came into full view of the beautiful old white house standing behind its green trees and terraces and lawns. The children had never imagined anything so stately and fine, and even Susan Ellen exclaimed with pleasure. At that moment they saw an old gentleman, who carried himself with great dignity, coming slowly down the wide box-bordered path toward the gate.

"There he is now, there's the judge!" whispered John Hilton excitedly, reigning his horse quickly to the green roadside. "He's goin' down-town to his office; we can wait right here an' see him. I can't expect him to remember me; it's been a good many years. Now you are goin' to see the great Judge Masterson!"

There was a quiver of expectation in their hearts. The judge stopped at his gate, hesitating a moment before he lifted the latch, and glanced up the street at the country wagon with its two prim little girls on the back seat, and the eager man who drove. They seemed to be waiting for something; the old horse was nibbling at the fresh roadside grass. The judge was used to being looked at with interest, and responded now with a smile as he came out to the sidewalk, and unexpectedly turned their way. Then he suddenly lifted his hat with grave politeness, and came directly toward them.

"Good-morning, Mr. Hilton," he said. "I am very glad to see you, sir;" and Mr. Hilton, the little girls' own father, took off his hat with equal courtesy, and bent forward to shake hands.

Susan Ellen cowered and wished herself away, but little Katy sat straighter than ever, with joy in her father's pride and pleasure shining in her pale, flower-like little face.

"These are your daughters, I am sure," said the old gentleman kindly, taking Susan Ellen's limp and reluctant hand; but when he looked at Katy, his face brightened. "How she recalls your mother!" he said with great feeling. "I am glad to see this dear child. You must come to see me with your father, my dear," he added, still looking at her. "Bring both the little girls, and let them run about the old garden; the cherries are just getting ripe," said Judge Masterson hospitably. "Perhaps you will have time to stop this afternoon as you go home?"

"I should call it a great pleasure if you would come and see us again some time. You may be driving our way, sir," said John Hilton.

"Not very often in these days," answered the old judge. "I thank you for the kind invitation. I should like to see the fine view again from your hill westward. Can I serve you in any way while you are in town? Good-by, my little friends!"

Then they parted, but not before Katy, the shy Katy, whose hand the judge still held unconsciously while he spoke, had reached forward as he said good-by, and lifted her face to kiss him. She could not have told why, except that she felt drawn to something in the serious, worn face. For the first time in her life the child had felt the charm of manners; perhaps she owned a kinship between that which made him what he was, and the spark of nobleness and purity in her own simple soul. She turned again and again to look back at him as they drove away.

"Now you have seen one of the first gentlemen in the country," said her father. "It was worth comin' twice as far"—but he did not say any more, nor turn as usual to look in the children's faces.

In the chief business street of Topham a great many country wagons like the Hiltons' were fastened to the posts, and there seemed to our holiday-makers to be a great deal of noise and excitement.

"Now I've got to do my errands, and we can let the horse rest and feed," said John Hilton. "I'll slip his head-stall right off, an' put on his halter. I'm goin' to buy him a real good treat o' oats. First we'll go an' buy me my straw hat; I feel as if this one looked a little past to wear in

Topham. We'll buy the things we want, an' then we'll walk all along the street, so you can look in the windows an' see the han'some things, same's your mother likes to. What was it mother told you about your shawls?"

"To take 'em off an' carry 'em over our arms," piped Susan Ellen, without comment, but in the interest of alighting and finding themselves afoot upon the pavement the shawls were forgotten. The children stood in the doorway of a shop while their father went inside, and they tried to see what the Topham shapes of bonnets were like, as their mother had advised them; but everything was exciting and confusing, and they could arrive at no decision. When Mr. Hilton came out with a hat in his hand to be seen in a better light, Katy whispered that she wished he would buy a shiny one like Judge Masterson's; but her father only smiled and shook his head, and said that they were plain folks, he and Katy. There were dry-goods for sale in the same shop, and a young clerk who was measuring linen kindly pulled off some pretty labels with gilded edges and gay pictures, and gave them to the little girls, to their exceeding joy. He may have had small sisters at home, this friendly lad, for he took pains to find two pretty blue boxes besides, and was rewarded by their beaming gratitude.

It was a famous day; they even became used to seeing so many people pass. The village was full of its morning activity, and Susan Ellen gained a new respect for her father, and an increased sense of her own consequence, because even in Topham several persons knew him and called him familiarly by name. The meeting with an old man who had once been a neighbor seemed to give Mr. Hilton the greatest pleasure. The old man called to them from a house doorway as they were passing, and they all went in. The children seated themselves wearily on the wooden step, but their father shook his old friend eagerly by the hand, and declared that he was delighted to see him so well and enjoying the fine weather.

"Oh, yes," said the old man, in a feeble, quavering voice. "I'm astonishin' well for my age. I don't complain, John, I don't complain."

They talked long together of people whom they had known in the past, and Katy, being a little tired, was glad to rest, and sat still with her hands folded, looking about the front yard. There were some kind of flowers that she had never seen before.

"This is the one that looks like my mother," her father said, and touched Katy's shoulder to remind her to stand up and let herself be seen. "Judge Masterson saw the resemblance; we met him at his gate this morning."

"Yes, she certain does look like your mother, John," said the old man, looking pleasantly at Katy, who found that she liked him better than at first. "She does, certain; the best of young folks is, they remind us of the old ones. 'T is nateral to cling to life, folks say, but for me, I git impatient at times. Most everybody's gone now, an' I want to be goin'. 'T is somethin' before me, an' I want to have it over with. I want to be there 'long 'o the rest 'o the folks. I expect to last quite a while though; I may see ye couple o' times more, John."

John Hilton responded cheerfully, and the children were urged to pick some flowers. The old man awed them with his impatience to be gone. There was such a townful of people about him, and he seemed as lonely as if he were the last survivor of a former world. Until that moment they had felt as if everything were just beginning.

"Now I want to buy somethin' pretty for your mother," said Mr. Hilton, as they went soberly away down the street, the children keeping fast hold of his hands. "By now, the old horse will have eat his dinner and had a good rest, so pretty soon we can jog along home. I'm goin' to take you round by the academy, and the old North Meetinghouse where Dr. Barstow used to preach. Can't you think o' somethin' that your mother'd want?" he asked suddenly, confronted by a man's difficulty of choice.

"She was talkin' about wantin' a new pepper-box, one day; the top of the old one won't stay on," suggested Susan Ellen, with delightful readiness. "Can't we have some candy, father?"

"Yes, ma'am," said John Hilton, smiling and swinging her hand to and fro as they walked. "I feel as if some would be good myself. What's all this?" They were passing a photographer's doorway with its enticing array of portraits. "I do declare!" he exclaimed excitedly, "I'm going to have our pictures taken; 't will please your mother more 'n a little."

This was, perhaps, the greatest triumph of the day, except the delightful meeting with the judge; they sat in a row, with the father in the middle, and there was no doubt as to the excellence of the likeness. The best hats had to be taken off because they cast a shadow, but they were not missed, as their owners had feared. Both Susan Ellen and Katy looked their brightest and best; their eager young faces would forever shine there; the joy of the holiday was mirrored in the little picture. They did not know why their father was so pleased with it; they would not know until age had dowered them with the riches of association and remembrance.

Just at nightfall the Hiltons reached home again, tired out and happy. Katy had climbed over into the front seat beside her father, because that was always her place when they went to church on Sundays. It was a cool evening, there was a fresh sea wind that brought a light mist with it, and the sky was fast growing cloudy. Somehow the children looked different; it seemed to their mother as if they had grown older and taller since they went away in the morning, and as if they belonged to the town now as much as to the country. The greatness of their day's experience had left her far behind; the day had been silent and lonely without them, and she had had their supper ready, and been watching anxiously, ever since five o'clock. As for the children themselves they had little to say at first—they had eaten their luncheon early on the way to Topham. Susan Ellen was

123

childishly cross, but Katy was pathetic and wan. They could hardly wait to show the picture, and their mother was as much pleased as everybody had expected.

"There, what did make you wear your shawls?" she exclaimed a moment afterward, reproachfully. "You ain't been an' wore 'em all day long? I wanted folks to see how pretty your new dresses was, if I did make 'em. Well, well! I wish more 'n ever now I'd gone an' seen to ye!"

"An' here's the pepper-box!" said Katy, in a pleased, unconscious tone.

"That really is what I call beautiful," said Mrs. Hilton, after a long and doubtful look. "Our other one was only tin. I never did look so high as a chiny one with flowers, but I can get us another any time for every day. That's a proper hat, as good as you could have got, John. Where's your new hoe?" she asked as he came toward her from the barn, smiling with satisfaction.

"I declare to Moses if I didn't forget all about it," meekly acknowledged the leader of the great excursion. "That an' my yellow-turnip seed, too; they went clean out o' my head, there was so many other things to think of. But 't ain't no sort o' matter; I can get a hoe just as well to Ira Speed's."

His wife could not help laughing. "You an' the little girls have had a great time. They was full o' wonder to me about everything, and I expect they'll talk about it for a week. I guess we was right about havin' 'em see somethin' more o' the world."

"Yes," answered John Hilton, with humility, "yes, we did have a beautiful day. I didn't expect so much. They looked as nice as anybody, and appeared so modest an' pretty. The little girls will remember it perhaps by an' by. I guess they won't never forget this day they had 'long o' their father."

It was evening again, the frogs were piping in the lower meadows, and in the woods, higher up the great hill, a little owl began to hoot. The sea air, salt and heavy, was blowing in over the country at the end of the hot bright day. A lamp was lighted in the house, the happy children were talking together, and supper was waiting. The father and mother lingered for a moment outside and looked down over the shadowy fields; then they went in, without speaking. The great day was over, and they shut the door.

The Life of Nancy, 1895

DAVID GRAYSON

The Burden of the Valley of Vision

Under the name of David Grayson, Ray Stannard Baker, the famous newspaper correspondent and political commentator, wrote a series of charming essays extolling and explaining the simple life he led when he retired to his native New England.

I came here eight years ago as the renter of this farm, of which soon afterward I became the owner. The time before that I like to forget. The chief impression it left upon my memory, now happily growing indistinct, is of being hurried faster than I could well travel. From the moment, as a boy of seventeen, I first began to pay my own way, my days were ordered by an inscrutable power which drove me hourly to my task. I was rarely allowed to look up or down, but always forward, toward that vague Success which we Americans love to glorify.

My senses, my nerves, even my muscles were continually strained to the utmost of attainment. If I loitered or paused by the wayside, as it seems natural for me to do, I soon heard the sharp crack of the lash. For many years, and I can say it truthfully, I never rested. I neither thought nor reflected. I had no pleasure, even though I pursued it fiercely during the brief respite of vacations. Through many feverish years I did not work: I merely produced.

The only real thing I did was to hurry as though every moment were my last, as though the world, which now seems so rich in everything, held only one prize which might be seized upon before I arrived. Since then I have tried to recall, like one who struggles to restore the visions of a fever, what it was that I ran to attain, or why I should have borne without rebellion such indignities to soul and body. That life seems now, of all illusions, the most distant and unreal. It is like the unguessed eternity before we are born: not of concern compared with that eternity upon which we are now embarked.

All these things happened in cities and among crowds. I like to forget them. They smack of that slavery of the spirit which is so much worse than any mere slavery of the body.

One day—it was in April, I remember, and the soft maples in the city park were just beginning to blossom—I stopped suddenly. I did not intend to stop. I confess in humiliation that it was no courage, no will of my own. I intended to go on toward Success: but Fate stopped me. It was as if I had been thrown violently from a moving planet: all the universe streamed around me and past me. It seemed to me that of all animate creation, I was the only thing that was still or silent. Until I stopped I had not known the pace I ran; and I had a vague sympathy and understanding, never felt before, for those who left the running. I lay prostrate with fever and close to death for weeks and watched the world go by: the dust, the noise, the very colour of haste. The only sharp pang that I suffered was the feeling that I should be broken-hearted and that I was not; that I should care and that I did not. It was as though I had died and escaped all further responsibility. I even watched with dim equanimity my friends racing past me, panting as they ran. Some of them paused an instant to comfort me where I lay, but I could see that their minds were still upon the running and I was glad when they went away. I cannot tell with what weariness their haste oppressed me. As for them, they somehow blamed me for dropping out. I knew. Until we ourselves understand, we accept no excuse from the man who stops. While I felt it all, I was not bitter. I did not seem to care. I said to myself: "This is Unfitness. I survive no longer. So be it."

Thus I lay, and presently I began to hunger and thirst. Desire rose within me: the indescribable longing of the convalescent for the food of recovery. So I lay, questioning wearily what it was that I required. One morning I wakened with a strange, new joy in my soul. It came to me at that moment with indescribable poignancy, the thought of walking barefoot in cool, fresh plow furrows as I had once done when a boy. So vividly the memory came to me—the high airy world as it was at that moment, and the boy I was walking free in the furrows—that the weak tears filled my eyes, the first I had shed in many years. Then I thought of sitting in quiet thickets in old fence corners, the wood behind me rising still, cool, mysterious, and the fields in front stretching away in illimitable pleasantness. I thought of the good smell of cows at milking—you do not know, if you do not know!—I thought of the sights and sounds, the heat and sweat of the hay fields. I thought of a certain brook I knew when a boy that flowed among alders and wild parsnips, where I waded with a three-foot rod for trout. I thought of all these things as a man thinks of his first love. Oh, I craved the soil. I hungered and thirsted for the earth. I was greedy for growing things.

And thus, eight years ago, I came here like one sore-wounded creeping from the field of battle. I remember walking in the sunshine, weak yet, but curiously satisfied. I that was dead lived again. It came to me then with a curious certainty, not since so assuring, that I understood the chief marvel of nature hidden within the Story of the Resurrection, the marvel of plant and seed, father and son, the wonder of the seasons, the miracle of life. I, too, had died: I had lain long in darkness, and now I had risen again upon the sweet earth. And I possessed beyond others a knowledge of a former existence, which I knew, even then, I could never return to.

For a time, in the new life, I was happy to drunkenness—working, eating, sleeping. I was an animal again, let out to run in green pastures. I was glad of the sunrise and the sunset. I was glad at noon. It delighted me when my muscles ached with work and when, after supper, I could not keep my eyes open for sheer weariness. And sometimes I was awakened in the night out of a sound sleep—seemingly by the very silences—and lay in a sort of bodily comfort impossible to describe.

I did not want to feel or to think: I merely wanted to live. In the sun or the rain I wanted to go out and come in, and never again know the pain of the unquiet spirit. I looked forward to an awakening not without dread for we are as helpless before birth as in the presence of death.

But like all birth, it came, at last, suddenly. All that summer I had worked in a sort of animal content. Autumn had now come, late autumn, with coolness in the evening air. I was plowing in my upper field—not then mine in fact—and it was a soft afternoon with the earth turning up moist and fragrant. I had been walking the furrows all day long. I had taken note, as though my life depended upon it, of the occasional stones or roots in my field, I made sure of the adjustment of the harness, I drove with peculiar care to save the horses. With such simple details of the work in hand I had found it my joy to occupy my mind. Up to that moment the most important things in the world had seemed a straight furrow and well-turned corners—to me, then, a profound accomplishment.

I cannot well describe it, save by the analogy of an opening door somewhere within the house of my consciousness. I had been in the dark: I seemed to emerge. I had been bound down: I seemed to leap up—and with a marvellous sudden sense of freedom and joy.

I stopped there in my field and looked up. And it was as if I had never looked up before. I discovered another world. It had been there before, for long and long, but I had never seen nor felt it. All discoveries are made in that way: a man finds the new thing, not in nature but in himself.

It was as though, concerned with plow and harness and furrow, I had never known that the world had height or colour or sweet sounds, or that there was *feeling* in a hillside. I forgot myself, or where I was. I stood a long time motionless. My dominant feeling, if I can at all express it, was of a strange new friendliness, a warmth, as though these hills, this field about me, the woods, had suddenly spoken to me and caressed me. It was as though I had been accepted in membership, as though I was now recognized, after long trial, as belonging here.

Across the town road which separates my farm from my nearest neighbour's, I saw a field, familiar, yet strangely new and unfamiliar, lying up to the setting sun, all red with autumn; above it the incalculable heights of the sky, blue, but not quite clear, owing to the Indian summer haze. I cannot convey the sweetness and softness of that landscape, the airiness of it, the mystery of it, as it came to me at that moment. It was as though, looking at an acquaintance long known, I should discover that I loved him. As I stood there I was conscious of the cool tang of burning leaves and brush heaps, the lazy smoke of which floated down the long valley and found me in my field, and finally I heard, as though the sounds were then made for the first time, all the vague murmurs of the countryside—a cowbell somewhere in the distance, the creak of a wagon, the blurred evening hum of birds, insects, frogs. So much it means for a man to stop and look up from his task. So I stood, and I looked up and down with a glow and a thrill which I cannot now look back upon without some envy and a little amusement at the very grandness and seriousness of it all. And I said aloud to myself:

"I will be as broad as the earth. I will not be limited."

Thus I was born into the present world, and here I continue, not knowing what other world I may yet achieve. I do not know, but I wait in expectancy, keeping my furrows straight and my corners well turned. Since that day in the field, though my fences include no more acres, and I still plow my own fields, my real domain has expanded until I crop wide fields and take the profit of many curious pastures. From my farm I can see most of the world; and if I wait here long enough all people pass this way.

And I look out upon them not in the surroundings which they have chosen for themselves, but from the vantage ground of my familiar world. The symbols which meant so much in cities mean little here. Sometimes it seems to me as though I saw men naked. They come and stand beside my oak, and the oak passes solemn judgment; they tread my furrows and the clods give silent evidence; they touch the green blades of my corn, the corn whispers its sure conclusions. Stern judgments that will be deceived by no symbols!

Thus I have delighted, secretly, in calling myself an unlimited farmer, and I make this confession in answer to the inner and truthful demand of the soul that we are not, after all, the slaves of things, whether corn, or bank-notes, or spindles; that we are not the used, but the users; that life is more than profit and loss. And so I shall expect that while I am talking farm some of you may be thinking dry goods, banking, literature, carpentry, or what-not. But if you can say: I am an unlimited dry goods merchant, I am an unlimited carpenter, I will give you an old-fashioned country hand-shake, strong and warm. We are friends; our orbits coincide.

Adventures in Contentment, 1907

WOODROW WILSON

From *War Message to Congress*

Frank I. Cobb, a New York WORLD *editorial writer, tells of being summoned by the President the night before this message was delivered to Congress, and of finding Wilson alone on a White House porch at 1 A.M., tapping out this, his most eloquent state paper, on a typewriter. The President read what he had written to Cobb and expressed agony at being compelled to take so grave a step.*

I have called the Congress into extraordinary session because there are serious, very serious, choices of policy to be made, and made immediately, which it was neither right nor constitutionally permissible that I should assume the responsibility of making.

On the third of February last I officially laid before you the extraordinary announcement of the Imperial German Government that on and after the first day of February it was its purpose to put aside all restraints of law or of humanity and use its submarines to sink every vessel that sought to approach either the ports of Great Britain and Ireland or the western coasts of Europe or any of the ports controlled by the enemies of Germany within the Mediterranean. . . .

I was for a little while unable to believe that such things would in fact be done by any government that had hitherto subscribed to the humane practices of civilized nations. International law had its origin in the attempt to set up some law which would be respected and observed upon the seas, where no nation had right of dominion and where lay the free highways of the world. By painful stage after stage has that law been built up, with meager enough results, indeed, after all was accomplished that could be accomplished, but always with a clear view, at least, of what the heart and conscience of mankind demanded. This minimum of right the German Government has swept aside under the plea of retaliation and necessity and because it had no weapons which it could use at sea except those which it is impossible to employ as it is employing them without throwing to the winds all scruples of humanity or of respect for the understandings that were supposed to underlie the intercourse of the world. I am not now thinking of the loss of property involved, immense and serious as that is, but only of the wanton and wholesale destruction of the lives of noncombatants, men, women, and children, engaged in pursuits which have always, even in the darkest periods of modern history, been deemed innocent and legitimate. Property can be paid for; the lives of peaceful and innocent people cannot be. The present German submarine warfare against commerce is a warfare against mankind.

It is a war against all nations. American ships have been sunk, American lives taken, in ways which it has stirred us very deeply to learn of, but the ships and people of other neutral and friendly nations have been sunk and overwhelmed in the waters in the same way. There has been no discrimination. The challenge is to all mankind. Each nation must decide for itself how it will meet it. The choice we make for ourselves must be made with a moderation of counsel and a temperateness of judgment befitting our character and our motives as a nation. We must put excited feeling away. Our motive will not be revenge, or the victorious assertion of the physical might of the nation, but only the vindication of right, of human right, of which we are only a single champion. . . .

There is one choice we cannot make, we are incapable of making:—we will not choose the path of submission and suffer the most sacred rights of our nation and our people to be ignored or violated. The wrongs against which we now array ourselves are no common wrongs; they cut to the very roots of human life.

With a profound sense of the solemn and even tragic character of the step I am taking and of the grave responsibilities which it involves, but in unhesitating obedience to what I deem my constitutional duty, I advise that Congress declare the recent course of the Imperial German Government to be in fact nothing less than war against the government and people of the United States; that it formally accept the status of belligerent which has thus been thrust upon it, and that it take immediate steps not only to put the country in a more thorough state of defense but also to exert all its power and employ all its resources to bring the Government of the German Empire to terms and end the war. . . .

While we do these things, these deeply momentous things, let us be very clear, and make very clear to all the world what our motives and our objects are. My own thought has not been driven from its habitual and normal course by the unhappy events of the last two months, and I do not believe that the thought of the nation has been altered or clouded by them. I have exactly the same things in mind now that I had in mind when I addressed the Senate on the twenty-second of January last; the same that I had in mind when I addressed the Congress on the third of February and on the twenty-sixth of February. Our object now, as then, is to vindicate the principles of peace and justice in the life of the world as against selfish and autocratic power and to set up amongst the really free and self-governed peoples of the world such a concert of purpose and of action as will henceforth insure the observance of those principles. Neutrality is no longer feasible or desirable where the peace of the world is involved and the freedom of its peoples, and the menace to that peace and freedom lies in the existence of the autocratic governments backed by organized force which is controlled wholly by their will, not by the will of their people.

We have seen the last of neutrality in such circumstances. We are at the beginning of an age in which it will be insisted that the same standards of conduct and of responsibility for wrong done shall be observed among nations and their governments that are observed among the individual citizens of civilized states.

We have no quarrel with the German people. We have no feeling towards them but one of sympathy and friendship. It was not upon their impulse that their government acted in entering this war. It was not with their previous knowledge or approval. It was a war determined upon as wars used to be determined upon in the old, unhappy days when peoples were nowhere consulted by their rulers and wars were provoked and waged in the interest of dynasties or of little groups of ambitious men who were accustomed to use their fellow-men as pawns or tools. Self-governed nations do not fill their neighbour states with spies or set the course of intrigue to bring about some critical posture of affairs which will give them an opportunity to strike and make conquest. Such designs can be successfully worked out only under cover and where no one has the right to ask questions. Cunningly contrived plans of deception or aggression, carried, it may be, from generation to generation, can be worked out and kept from the light only within the privacy of courts or behind the carefully guarded confidences of a narrow and privileged class. They are happily impossible where public opinion commands and insists upon full information concerning all the nation's affairs.

A steadfast concert for peace can never be maintained except by a partnership of democratic nations. No autocratic government could be trusted to keep faith within it or observe its covenants. It must be a league of honour, a partnership of opinion. Intrigue would eat its vitals away; the plottings of inner circles who could plan what they would and render account to no one would be a corruption seated at its very heart. Only free peoples can hold their purpose and their honour steady to a common end and prefer the interests of mankind to any narrow interest of their own. . . .

One of the things that has served to convince us that the Prussian autocracy was not and could never be our friend is that from the very outset of the present war it has filled our unsuspecting communities and even our offices of government with spies and set criminal intrigues everywhere afoot against our national unity of counsel, our peace within and without, our industries and our commerce. . . .

We are accepting this challenge of hostile purpose because we know that in such a government, following such methods, we can never have a friend; and that in the presence of its organized power, always lying in wait to accomplish we know not what purpose, there can be no assured security for the democratic governments of the world. We are now about to accept gauge of battle with this natural foe to liberty and shall, if necessary, spend the whole force of the nation to check and nullify its preten-

131

sions and its power. We are glad, now that we see the facts with no veil of false pretense about them, to fight thus for the ultimate peace of the world and for the liberation of its peoples, the German peoples included: for the rights of nations great and small and the privilege of men everywhere to choose their way of life and of obedience. The world must be made safe for democracy. Its peace must be planted upon the tested foundations of political liberty. We have no selfish ends to serve. We desire no conquest, no dominion. We seek no indemnities for ourselves, no material compensation for the sacrifices we shall freely make. We are but one of the champions of the rights of mankind. We shall be satisfied when those rights have been made as secure as the faith and the freedom of nations can make them.

Just because we fight without rancour and without selfish object, seeking nothing for ourselves but what we shall wish to share with all free peoples, we shall, I feel confident, conduct our operations as belligerents without passion and ourselves observe with proud punctilio the principles of right and of fair play we profess to be fighting for. . . .

It will be all the easier for us to conduct ourselves as belligerents in a high spirit of right and fairness because we act without animus, not in enmity towards a people or with the desire to bring any injury or disadvantage upon them, but only in armed opposition to an irresponsible government which has thrown aside all considerations of humanity and of right and is running amuck. We are, let me say again, the sincere friends of the German people, and shall desire nothing so much as the early reestablishment of intimate relations of mutual advantage between us,—however hard it may be for them, for the time being, to believe that this is spoken from our hearts. We have borne with their present government through all these bitter months because of that friendship,—exercising a patience and forbearance which would otherwise have been impossible. We shall, happily, still have an opportunity to prove that friendship in our daily attitude and actions towards the millions of men and women of German birth and native sympathy who live among us and share our life, and we shall be proud to prove it toward all who are in fact loyal to their neighbours and to the Government in the hour of test. They are, most of them, as true and loyal Americans as if they had never known any other fealty or allegiance. They will be prompt to stand with us in rebuking and restraining the few who may be of a different mind and purpose. If there should be disloyalty, it will be dealt with with a firm hand of stern repression; but, if it lifts its head at all, it will lift it only here and there and without countenance except from a lawless and malignant few.

It is a distressing and oppressive duty, Gentlemen of the Congress, which I have performed in thus addressing you. There are, it may be, many months of fiery trial and sacrifice ahead of us. It is a fearful thing to lead this great peaceful people into war, into the most terrible and disastrous of all wars, civilization itself seeming to be in the balance. But the right is more precious than peace, and we shall fight for the things which we have always carried nearest our hearts,—for democracy, for the right of those who submit to authority to have a voice in their own governments, for the rights and liberties of small nations, for a universal dominion of right by such a concert of free peoples as shall bring peace and safety to all nations and make the world itself at last free. To such a task we can dedicate our lives and our fortunes, everything that we are and everything that we have, with the pride of those who know that the day has come when America is privileged to spend her blood and her might for the principles that gave her birth and happiness and the peace which she has treasured. God helping her, she can do no other.

Selected Literary Papers and Speeches, 1917

FRANK MOORE COLBY

Some of the Difficulties of Frolicking

Readers of this passage perhaps will share the puzzlement of others as to why so engaging a writer should be so persistently neglected. He was a professor at Amherst, Columbia, Barnard and New York University, and the editor of several encyclopedias.

Frolicking at midnight, a week or so ago, under the roof-tree of the New Amsterdam Theatre, I suddenly realized that I was missing some of the gaiety of the occasion.

Midnight frolicking, I may say in passing, is a technical term, and means simply that, for the most part, I sat perfectly still at a small table, looking from time to time at some young ladies in opera-length tights who stood on a glass platform above me; and that twice I skimmed a little wooden mallet over the floor, and hit the feet of a sleeping youth across the room, and that once I touched a lighted cigarette to a toy balloon—sewn on the parti-colored skirt of a chorus girl—and burst it.

I tried to give to both of these gestures an air of easy abandon, but I think I failed. Several others who were manifestly aiming at abandon seemed to me also to fail. They say it is achieved sometimes—not only here but at several other roof theaters and cabarets—but if so, it does not proceed from any of the habitués; it probably bubbles up from some justice of the Supreme Court who is there, incognito, or from the Governor of a Western state.

The crowd that night had the air of having been there, or in similar places, very often, and (like most "gay" and expensive New York crowds, amid the vivacities and audacities of the white-light region, the glitter, the movement, the dash, dazzle, and all the rest of it) this crowd was exceedingly dull.

Not that it was inappreciative. It showed the usual "gay" crowd's willingness, and likewise its incapacity, for pleasure. Individually its members had the "gay" crowd's usual look. I do not know that I can describe that expression exactly, but in general I should say it was about what a man's face would naturally come to after watching trained dogs ten nights in succession.

Or, take an ardent, hopeful, sensitive stockbroker and place him every evening where he can see eight young women in tights lying on their backs with bells on their toes which sound an octave, and by which, as they alternately wiggle their feet in the air, they play what is almost a tune. In a week he will have the "gay" expression, or what is known, more technically, as the "Broadway pleasure-face." There is nothing pained or peevish about it. It is merely the face of one who has forgotten his day's work and not yet replaced it with any other human interest. You see it often at the theater when the play is just powerful enough to drive away your own thoughts, but unable to put any others in their place. . . .

Some say these places are like Sodom and Gomorrah. But one knew very well that had there been, the other night, some sudden Babylonian extinguishment, it would have taken off many of the simplest, purest, most primitive folk imaginable—hundreds of people almost ascetic for lack of any external inducement to be otherwise.

What excited us most the other night, for example?

Not the dancing, or the waving of bell-ringing legs, or the tight-rope, or the *demi-monde*. Our one real burst of enthusiasm was when we sang, in unison, "Little Brown Jug" and followed it up with "My Old Kentucky Home," along with two banjoists and the rest of the audience. At that moment we let ourselves go quite wildly. Scratch a New Yorker and you get an up-state deacon, probably of unblemished moral character, but at any rate a perfectly pure deacon in taste. Most desperate New York roués are deacons in their bones.

Lulled by these mild reflections I think I may have drowsed off, and it was then that, pulling myself together, I suddenly realized, as I said before, that I was missing some of the gaiety of the occasion. I hope I was not noticeably asleep, for a little incident soon showed with what suspicion sleep was regarded. One of the men exclaimed, suddenly, "Look at the funny drunks," and threw a mallet across the room at two college youths asleep at their little table.

Other mallets followed, and the crowd seemed determined to wake them up, but fortunately their aim was bad, and the mallets didn't disturb them. To be sure, the boys may possibly have been drinking, but even so, in sleeping they were doing only what was natural, reasonable, and appropriate. They were sensible looking young men, and their sleep was entirely decorous; no sprawling or snoring or drooping of jaws. Possessed of strong, natural intelligence, and richly sensuous artistic natures—but cut off by the hazards of New York social life from an appropriate outlet—they may have wandered in here merely because they had been almost everywhere else, and perhaps they were responding to the occasion in the manner which, after serious reflection, they had concluded was what such occasions deserved.

Habit and Repetition, those twin divinities, protect the chastity of New York's roof and cabaret celibates. Multitude, and miscellany, and iteration save a man from many an entanglement. One could become enamored of a single cabaret nymph or perhaps of three of them, but no manly amorous bosom could hold, at the same time, forty. Women singly do a good deal of harm. Woman in bulk are chastening. Great droves of the most enticing beings in the world do not entice. A single pair of graceful legs—if I may speak coarsely—are appealing. Perhaps two pairs, also. But legs conceived merely as railway ties, stretching over the roofs of twenty theaters and hotels, legs regarded as strings of sausages, reaching almost to the Borough of the Bronx, take on a homely and familiar significance.

And passing rapidly from one gay place to another often has a strangely sobering effect. Too many legs together sometimes look like the monuments in Woodlawn Cemetery, as you rush past it in the train.

It is the same way with backs. The first eight or ten backs do, naturally, engage the attention, but the eye that has roamed over four or five acres of backs is as safely at home with them as in a cow-pasture.

Hence the air of fatigue, almost of domesticity, on the faces of the habitually gay. When temptations march monotonously in regiments, one waits for them to pass by.

The Colby Essays, Vol. I, 1926

CHRISTOPHER MORLEY

Housebroken

After Simmons had been married two years he began to feel as though he needed a night off. But he hesitated to mention the fact, for he knew his wife would feel hurt to think that he could dream of an evening spent elsewhere than in their cosy sitting room. However, there were no two ways about it: the old unregenerate male in Simmons yearned for something more exciting than the fireside armchair, the slippers and smoking jacket, and the quiet game of cards. Visions of the old riotous evenings with the boys ran through his mind; a billiard table and the click of balls; the jolly conversations at the club, and glass after glass of that cold amber beer. The large freedom of the city streets at night, the warm saloons on every corner, the barrooms with their pyramids of bottles flashing in the gaslight—these were the things that made a man's life amusing. And here he was cooped up in a little cage in the suburbs like a tame cat!

Thoughts of this kind had agitated Simmons for a long time, and at last he said something to Ethel. He had keyed himself up to meet a sharp retort, some sarcastic comment about his preferring a beer garden to his own home, even an outburst of tears. But to his amazement Ethel took it quite calmly.

"Why, yes, of course, dear," she said. "It'll do you good to have an evening with your friends."

A little taken aback, he asked whether she would rather he didn't go.

"Why, no," she answered. "I shall have a lovely time. I won't be lonely."

This was on Monday. Simmons planned to go out on Friday night, meeting the boys for dinner at the club, and after that they would spend the evening at Boelke's bowling alley. All the week he went about in a glow of anticipation. At the office he spoke in an offhand way of the pleasant evenings a man can have in town, and pitied the prosaic beggars who never stir from the house at night.

On Friday evening he came home hurriedly, staying just long enough to shave and change his collar. Ethel had on a pretty dress and seemed very cheerful. A strange sinking came over him as he saw the familiar room shining with firelight and the shabby armchair.

"Would you rather I stayed at home?" he asked.

"Not a bit," she said, quite as though she meant it. "Diana has a steak in the oven, and I've got a new book to read. I won't wait up for you."

He kissed her and went off.

When he got on the trolley a sudden revulsion struck him. He was tired and wanted to go home. Why on earth spend the evening with a lot of drunken rowdies when he might be at his own hearth watching Ethel's face bent over her sewing? He saw little enough of her anyway.

At the door of the club he halted. Inside, the crowd was laughing, shouting jests, dicing for cocktails. Suddenly he turned and ran.

He cursed himself for a fool, but none the less an irresistible force seemed to draw him home. On the car he sat glum and silent, wondering how all the other men could read their papers so contentedly.

At last he reached the modest little suburb. He hurried along the street and had almost entered his gate when he paused.

Through the half-drawn curtains he could see Ethel sitting comfortably by the lamp. She was reading, and the cat was in her lap. His heart leaped with a great throb. But how could he go in now? It was barely eight o'clock. After all his talk about a man's need of relaxation and masculine comradeship—why, she would never stop laughing! He turned and tiptoed away.

136

That evening was a nightmare for Simmons. Opposite his house was a little suburban park, and thither he took himself. For a long while he sat on a bench cursing. Twice he started for the trolley, and again returned. It was a damp autumn night; little by little the chill pierced his light coat and he sneezed. Up and down the little park he tramped, biting a dead cigar. Once he went as far as the drugstore and bought a box of crackers.

At last—it seemed years—the church chimes struck ten and he saw the lights go out in his house. He forced himself to make twenty-five more trips around the gravel walk and then he could wait no longer. Shivering with weariness and cold, he went home.

He let himself in with his latch key and tiptoed upstairs. He leaned over the bed and Ethel stirred sleepily.

"What time is it, dear?" she murmured. "You're early, aren't you?"

"One o'clock," he lied bravely—and just then the dining-room clock struck half-past ten and supported him.

"Did you have a good time?"

"Bully—perfectly bully," he said. "There's nothing like a night with the boys now and then."

Essays, 1928

CLARENCE DAY

My Father's Religion

> For all his wrath and expostulations, Clarence Day's Father would probably have basked in the fame he has achieved, but he certainly would never have admitted enjoying it. This particular account appears to contain less exaggeration than some of the other chapters about the elder Day.

My father's idea of religion seemed straightforward and simple. He had noticed when he was a boy that there were buildings called churches; he had accepted them as a natural part of the surroundings in which he had been born. He would never have invented such things himself. Nevertheless they were here. As he grew up he regarded them as unquestioningly as he did banks. They were substantial old structures, they were respectable, decent, and venerable. They were frequented by the right sort of people. Well, that was enough.

On the other hand he never allowed churches—or banks—to dictate to him. He gave each the respect that was due to it from his point of view; but he also expected from each of them the respect he felt due to him.

As to creeds he knew nothing about them, and cared nothing either; yet he seemed to know which sect he belonged with. It had to be a sect with the minimum of nonsense about it; no total immersion, no exhorters, no holy confession. He would have been a Unitarian, naturally, if he'd lived in Boston. Since he was a respectable New Yorker, he belonged in the Episcopal Church.

As to living a spiritual life, he never tackled that problem. Some men who accept spiritual beliefs try to live up to them daily; other men, who reject such beliefs try sometimes to smash them. My father would have disagreed with both kinds entirely. He took a more distant attitude. It disgusted him when atheists attacked religion: he thought they were vulgar. But he also objected to have religion make demands upon him—he felt that religion too was vulgar, when it tried to stir up men's feelings. It had its own proper field of activity, and it was all right there, of course; but there was one place religion should let alone, and that was a man's soul. He especially loathed any talk of walking hand in hand with his Saviour. And if he had ever found the Holy Ghost trying to soften his heart, he would have regarded the behavior as distinctly uncalled for, even ungentlemanly.

The only religious leader or prophet I can think of who might have suited my father was Confucius—though even Confucius would have struck him as addled. Confucius was an advocate of peace, and of finding the path; and he enjoined the Golden Rule on his followers long before Christ. My father would not have been his follower in any of these. Finding "the path"? Not even Confucius could have made him see what that meant. He was too busy for that, too hot tempered for peace, and the Golden Rule he regarded as claptrap; how could things work both ways? Whatever he did unto others he was sure was all right, but that didn't mean he would have allowed them to do the same things to him. He saw other men as disorderly troops, and himself as a general; and the Golden Rule was plainly too mushy to apply in such circumstances. He disciplined himself quite as firmly as he tried to discipline others, but it wasn't necessarily by any means the same kind of discipline. There was one saying of Confucius', however, with which he would have agreed: "Respect spiritual things—if there are any—but keep aloof from them." My father would have regarded that principle as thoroughly sound.

When Confucius was asked about the rule to return good for evil, he said: "What then will you return for good? No: return good for good; for evil, return justice." If my father had been asked to return good for evil he would have been even more pithy—his response would have consisted of a hearty and full-throated "Bah!"

If he had been let alone, he would have brought up his sons in this spirit. But my mother's feelings and teachings were different, and this complicated things for us. Like my father, she had accepted religion with-

138

out any doubtings, but she had accepted more of it. She was far more devout. And she loved best the kind of faith that comforted her and sweetened her thoughts. My father didn't object to this at all—it was all right enough—for a woman; but it led to her giving us instructions that battled with his.

They both insisted strongly, for example, on our going to church, but they didn't agree in their reasons. It was the right thing to do, Father said. "But why do we have to go, Father?" "Because I wish to bring you up properly. Men who neglect going to church are a lazy, disreputable lot." A few might be good fellows, he would admit, but they were the exceptions. As a rule, non-churchgoers were not solid, respectable citizens. All respectable citizens owed it to themselves to attend.

My mother put it differently to us. She said we owed it to God. Church to her was a place where you worshiped, and learned to be good. My father never thought of attending for any such reason. In his moral instructions to us he never once mentioned God. What he dwelt on was integrity. My mother once wrote in my plush-covered album, "Fear God and keep His commandments"; but the motto that Father had written on the preceding page, over his bolder signature, was "Do your duty and fear no one." And nobody could tell him his duty—he knew it without that, it seemed. It wasn't written down in any book, certainly not in the Bible, but it was a perfectly definite and indisputable thing nevertheless. It was a code, a tradition. It was to be upright and fearless and honorable and to brush your clothes properly; and in general to do always the right thing in every department of life. The right thing to do for religion was to go to some good church on Sundays.

When Father went to church and sat in his pew, he felt he was doing enough. Any further spiritual work ought to be done by the clergy.

When hymns were sung he sometimes joined in mechanically, for the mere sake of singing; but usually he stood as silent as an eagle among canaries and doves, leaving others to abase themselves in sentiments that he didn't share. The hymns indicated meekness and submission, and dependence on God; but Father was quick to resent an injury, and he had no meekness in him.

> *Jesus lover of my soul,*
> *Let me to thy bosom fly,*
> *While the nearer waters roll,*
> *While the tempest still is nigh.*

How could Father sing that? He had no desire to fly to that bosom.

> *Hide me O my Saviour hide*
> *Till the storm of life be past;*
> *Safe into the haven guide,*
> *Oh receive my soul at last. . . .*

All my trust on thee is stayed;
All my help from thee I bring;
Cover my defenseless head
With the shadow of thy wing.

But Father's head was far from defenseless, and he would have scorned to hide or to ask shelter. As he stood there, looking critically about him, high-spirited, resolute, I could imagine him marching with that same independence through space—a tiny speck masterfully dealing with death and infinity.

When our rector talked of imitating the saints, it seemed drivel to Father. What! imitate persons who gave their whole lives to religion and took only a perfunctory interest in the affairs of this world? Father regarded himself as a more all-round man than the saints. They had neglected nine-tenths of their duties from his point of view—they had no business connections, no families, they hadn't even paid taxes. In a word, saints were freaks. If a freak spent an abnormal amount of time being religious, what of it?

The clergy were a kind of freaks also. A queer lot. Father liked Bishop Greer and a few others, but he hadn't much respect for the rest of them. He thought of most clergymen as any busy man of action thinks of philosophers, or of those scholars who discuss the fourth dimension, which is beyond human knowing. He regarded the self-alleged intimacy of our rector with that fourth dimension most sceptically. He himself neither was nor wished to be intimate with a thing of that sort. But this didn't mean that he doubted the exisence of God. On the contrary, God and Father had somehow contrived to achieve a serene and harmonious relation that the clergy themselves might have envied.

How did Father think God felt towards my mother? Why, about the way he did. God probably knew she had faults, but He saw that she was lovely and good; and in spite of some mistaken ideas that she had about money—He doubtless looked on her most affectionately. Father didn't expect God to regard *him* affectionately—they stood up as man to man —but naturally God loved my mother, as everyone must. At the gate of Heaven, if there was any misunderstanding about his own ticket, Father counted on Mother to get him in. That was her affair.

This idea runs far back, or down, into old human thoughts. "The unbelieving husband is sanctified by the wife." (First Corinthians, vii, 14.) Medical missionaries report that today, in some primitive tribes, a healthy woman will propose to swallow medicine in behalf of her sick husband. This plan seems to her husband quite reasonable. It seemed so—in religion —to Father.

As to his mental picture of God, I suppose that Father was vague, but in a general way, he seemed to envisage a God in his image. A God who had small use for emotionalism and who prized strength and dignity.

A God who probably found the clergy as hard to bear as did Father himself. In short Father and God, as I said, usually saw eye to eye. They seldom met, or even sought a meeting, their spheres were so different; but they had perfect confidence in each other—at least at most moments. The only exceptions were when God seemed to be neglecting His job— Father's confidence in Him was then withdrawn, instantly. But I'll come to this later.

As to the nature of God's sphere, namely Heaven, compared to Father's, the earth, Heaven wasn't nearly so solid and substantial. Father had all the best of it. Life here on earth was trying, but it shouldn't be—it was all right intrinsically—he felt it was only people's damned carelessness that upset things so much. Heaven on the other hand had a more serious and fundamental defect; the whole place was thin and peculiar. It didn't inspire much confidence. Father saw glumly that the time would come when he would have to go there, but he didn't at all relish the prospect. He clung to his own battered realm.

Yet its faults and stupidities weighed on his spirit at times; all the chuckle-headed talk and rascality in business and politics. He was always getting indignant about them, and demanding that they be stamped out; and when he saw them continually spreading everywhere, it was maddening. Nature too, though in general sound and wholesome, had a treacherous streak. He hated and resented decay and failing powers. He hated to see little children or animals suffer. His own aches and pains were an outrage; he faced them with anger. And aside from these treacheries there was a spirit of rebellion in things. He would come in from a walk over his fields—which to me had seemed pleasant—oppressed at the balky disposition of both his fields and his farmer. He would get up from an inspection of his account books with the same irritation; there were always some bonds in his box that had not behaved as they should. And twice a day, regularly, he would have a collision, or bout, with the newspaper: it was hard to see why God had made so many damned fools and democrats.

I would try to persuade him sometimes—in my argumentative years— that it would be better for him to accept the world as it was and adapt himself to it, since he could scarcely expect to make the planet over, and change the whole earth single-handed. Father listened to this talk with suspicion, as to an advocatus diaboli. If he ever was tempted to give in, it was only in his weak moments; a minute later he was again on the warpath, like a materialistic Don Quixote.

There was one kind of depression that afflicted Mother which Father was free from; he never once had any moments of feeling "unworthy." This was a puzzle to Mother, and it made her look at Father with a mixture of awe and annoyance. Other people went to church to be made better, she told him. Why didn't he? He replied in astonishment that he had no need to be better—he was all right as he was. Mother couldn't get over his taking this stand, but she never could get him to see what the matter was with it. It wasn't at all easy for Father to see that he had any faults; and if he did, it didn't even occur to him to ask God to forgive them. He forgave them himself. In his moments of prayer, when he and God tried to commune with each other, it wasn't his own shortcomings that were brought on the carpet, but God's.

He expected a good deal of God, apparently. Not that he wanted God's help, of course; or far less His guidance. No, but it seemed that God—like the rest of us—spoiled Father's plans. Father was always trying to bring this or that good thing to pass, only to find that there were obstacles in the way. These of course roused his wrath. He would call God's attention to such things. They should not have been there. He didn't actually accuse God of gross inefficiency, but when he prayed his tone was loud and angry, like that of a dissatisfied guest in a carelessly managed hotel.

I never saw Father kneel in supplication on such occasions. On the contrary he usually talked with God lying in bed. My room was just above Father's, and he could easily be heard through the floor. On those rare nights when he failed to sleep well the sound of damns would float up—at first deep, tragic and low, then more loud and exasperated. Fragments of thoughts and strong feelings came next or meditations on current bothers. At the peak of these, God would be summoned. I would hear him call "Oh God?" over and over, with a rising inflection, as though he were demanding that God should present Himself instantly, and sit in the fat green chair over in the corner and be duly admonished. Then when Father seemed to feel that God was listening, he would begin to expostulate. He would moan in a discouraged but strong voice: "Oh God, it's too much. Amen. . . . I say it's too damned much. . . . No, no, I can't stand it. Amen." After a pause if he didn't feel better, he would seem to suspect that God might be trying to sneak back into Heaven without doing anything, and I would hear him shout warningly: "Oh God! I *won't* stand it! Amen. Oh damnation! A-a-men." Sometimes he would ferociously bark a few extra Amens, and then, soothed and satisfied, peacefully go back to sleep. And one night in the country, when the caretaker of our house in town telephoned to Father that the rain was pouring in through a hole in the roof I heard so much noise that I got out of bed and looked over the bannisters, and saw Father standing alone in the hall, shaking his fist at the ceiling, and shouting in hot indignation to Heaven, "What next?"

But Father was patient with God after all. If he didn't forgive, he forgot. His wrath didn't last—he had other things to think of—and he was genial at heart. The very next Sunday after an outburst he would be back in church. Not perhaps as a worshiper or a devotee, but at least as a patron.

God and My Father, 1931

ROBERT FROST

The Death of the Hired Man

Mary sat musing on the lamp-flame at the table
Waiting for Warren. When she heard his step,
She ran on tip-toe down the darkened passage
To meet him in the doorway with the news
And put him on his guard. "Silas is back."
She pushed him outward with her through the door
And shut it after her. "Be kind," she said.
She took the market things from Warren's arms
And set them on the porch, then drew him down
To sit beside her on the wooden steps.

"When was I ever anything but kind to him?
But I'll not have the fellow back," he said.
"I told him so last haying, didn't I?
'If he left then,' I said, 'that ended it.'
What good is he? Who else will harbour him
And his age for the little he can do?
What help he is there's no depending on.
Off he goes always when I need him most.
'He thinks he ought to earn a little pay,
Enough at least to buy tobacco with,
So he won't have to beg and be beholden.'
'All right,' I say, 'I can't afford to pay
Any fixed wages, though I wish I could.'
'Someone else can.' 'Then someone else will have to.'
I shouldn't mind his bettering himself
If that was what it was. You can be certain,
When he begins like that, there's someone at him
Trying to coax him off with pocket-money,—
In haying time, when any help is scarce.
In winter he comes back to us. I'm done."

"Sh! not so loud: he'll hear you," Mary said.

"I want him to: he'll have to soon or late."

"He's worn out. He's asleep beside the stove.
When I came up from Rowe's I found him here,
Huddled against the barn-door fast asleep,
A miserable sight, and frightening, too—
You needn't smile—I didn't recognise him—

I wasn't looking for him—and he's changed.
Wait till you see."

          "Where did you say he'd been?"

"He didn't say. I dragged him to the house,
And gave him tea and tried to make him smoke.
I tried to make him talk about his travels.
Nothing would do: he just kept nodding off."

"What did he say? Did he say anything?"

"But little."

          "Anything? Mary, confess
He said he'd come to ditch the meadow for me."

"Warren!"

          "But did he? I just want to know."

"Of course he did. What would you have him say?
Surely you wouldn't grudge the poor old man
Some humble way to save his self-respect.
He added, if you really care to know,
He meant to clear the upper pasture, too.
That sounds like something you have heard before?
Warren, I wish you could have heard the way
He jumbled everything. I stopped to look
Two or three times—he made me feel so queer—
To see if he was talking in his sleep.
He ran on Harold Wilson—you remember—
The boy you had in haying four years since.
He's finished school, and teaching in his college.
Silas declares you'll have to get him back.
He says they two will make a team for work:
Between them they will lay this farm as smooth!
The way he mixed that in with other things.
He thinks young Wilson a likely lad, though daft
On education—you know how they fought
All through July under the blazing sun,
Silas up on the cart to build the load,
Harold along beside to pitch it on."

"Yes, I took care to keep well out of earshot."

"Well, those days trouble Silas like a dream.
You wouldn't think they would. How some things linger!
Harold's young college boy's assurance piqued him.
After so many years he still keeps finding

Good arguments he sees he might have used.
I sympathise. I know just how it feels
To think of the right thing to say too late.
Harold's associated in his mind with Latin.
He asked me what I thought of Harold's saying
He studied Latin like the violin
Because he liked it—that an argument!
He said he couldn't make the boy believe
He could find water with a hazel prong—
Which showed how much good school had ever done him.
He wanted to go over that. But most of all
He thinks if he could have another chance
To teach him how to build a load of hay—"

"I know, that's Silas' one accomplishment.
He bundles every forkful in its place,
And tags and numbers it for future reference,
So he can find and easily dislodge it
In the unloading. Silas does that well.
He takes it out in bunches like big birds' nests.
You never see him standing on the hay
He's trying to lift, straining to lift himself."

"He thinks if he could perhaps teach him that, he'd be
Some good perhaps to someone in the world.
He hates to see a boy the fool of books.
Poor Silas, so concerned for other folk,
And nothing to look backward to with pride,
And nothing to look forward to with hope,
So now and never any different."

Part of a moon was falling down the west,
Dragging the whole sky with it to the hills.
Its light poured softly in her lap. She saw
And spread her apron to it. She put out her hand
Among the harp-like morning-glory strings,
Taut with the dew from garden bed to eaves,
As if she played unheard the tenderness
That wrought on him beside her in the night.
"Warren," she said, "he has come home to die:
You needn't be afraid he'll leave you this time."

"Home," he mocked gently.

          "Yes, what else but home?
It all depends on what you mean by home.
Of course he's nothing to us, any more

Than was the hound that came a stranger to us
Out of the woods, worn out upon the trail."

"Home is the place where, when you have to go there,
They have to take you in."

              "I should have called it
Something you somehow haven't to deserve."

Warren leaned out and took a step or two,
Picked up a little stick, and brought it back
And broke it in his hand and tossed it by.
"Silas has better claim on us, you think,
Than on his brother? Thirteen little miles
As the road winds would bring him to his door.
Silas has walked that far no doubt to-day.
Why didn't he go there? His brother's rich,
A somebody—director in the bank."

"He never told us that."

              "We knew it though."

"I think his brother ought to help, of course,
I'll see to that if there is need. He ought of right
To take him in, and might be willing to—
He may be better than appearances.
But have some pity on Silas. Do you think
If he'd had any pride in claiming kin
Or anything he looked for from his brother,
He'd keep so still about him all this time?"

"I wonder what's between them."

              "I can tell you.
Silas is what he is—we wouldn't mind him—
But just the kind that kinsfolk can't abide.
He never did a thing so very bad.
He don't know why he isn't quite as good
As anyone. He won't be made ashamed
To please his brother, worthless though he is."

"I can't think Si ever hurt anyone."

"No, but he hurt my heart the way he lay
And rolled his old head on that sharp-edged chair-back.
He wouldn't let me put him on the lounge.
You must go in and see what you can do.

I made the bed up for him there to-night.
You'll be surprised at him—how much he's broken.
His working days are done; I'm sure of it."

"I'd not be in a hurry to say that."

"I haven't been. Go, look, see for yourself.
But, Warren, please remember how it is:
He's come to help you ditch the meadow.
He has a plan. You mustn't laugh at him.
He may not speak of it, and then he may.
I'll sit and see if that small sailing cloud
Will hit or miss the moon."

> It hit the moon.
Then there were three there, making a dim row,
The moon, the little silver cloud, and she.

Warren returned—too soon, it seemed to her,
Slipped to her side, caught up her hand and waited.

"Warren?" she questioned.

> "Dead," was all he answered.
>
> *Collected Poems,* 1936

IRWIN EDMAN

Maria Prepares Luncheon for the Priest

> *As a professor of philosophy at Columbia University, Edman was a great teacher and an eminent scholar. With this tale about Maria his cook he shows himself also a man of warmth and understanding.*

A student of philosophy likes to think of himself as rather magnificently homeless, his mind ranging freely in the great spaces between the stars,

> *Voyaging through strange seas of thought alone.*

But a philosopher must live somewhere. I once heard a distinguished thinker say that the greatest philosophers in the nineteenth century all lived in hotels and that they were unmarried. Freedom from family obligations and the cares of a household might well be calculated to liberate the spirit for empyrean flights. But one must eat and sleep, have clean linen (unless like Diogenes one takes to a barrel). A philosopher must have a refuge, and in that respect I am very lucky.

Maria has been keeping house for me for nearly ten years. She has been in various parts of my family for more than twenty, and has known me since I was a college boy visiting my sister, at which time she would force milk upon me—"It'll keep up your strength; it'll keep you from falling in the gutter; it's just like food."

Maria came from Ireland at the age of eighteen, the seventh daughter of the second gardener on an Irish estate, as she told me for the first time the other day. She and her sister were sent to America by their mother. Somebody had said to the latter one day: "Mrs. Powers, why don't you send your daughters to America? There's gold on the streets there."

Maria and her sister came, and since then Maria has been in numerous households, as parlourmaid in a large brownstone house, nursemaid, cook. But since she has come to my apartment, she runs the whole establishment and (she says I am the first adult she has ever had to take care of) she takes very good care of me.

She is not very clear about what my work consists in, but she is convinced that it is very important, especially such of it as I do at home. She frequently tells people over the telephone that I must not be disturbed. "He is concentrating."

She has seen a good many professors at one time or another in the last ten years, and she is rather convinced that "brain work" destroys the nerves. But she found John Dewey, when he came one day in a snow-storm, a fine healthy old gentleman who looked very much like John Flynn, the old farmer in Galway, whom the children loved and feared.

Maria has been in New York over forty years, but her work, her church, and her sister—and occasionally trips downtown to do window-shopping —are all her connexion with it. Except what she reads in the "tragedy" papers, she reads nothing. I know a good deal about her church, for she brings me the parish magazine, tells me how long or how short the sermon was (she prefers the short ones), and I have an indirect connexion with it for I occasionally contribute to St. Anthony's box for the poor via Maria. Maria is a very faithful Catholic. She never misses Mass, she observes most fast days, though the priest says working people need not do so; but she does not overdo religion, she tells me, like some people.

I know a good deal by hearsay about Maria's married, now widowed, sister. But I have to take her on faith in Maria's unimpeachable honesty, for that sister might be like Dickens's Mrs. Harris as far as my direct acquaintance with her is concerned. Via Maria we exchange greetings, we hear about each other's minor ailments and major griefs and joys. Maria's sister's house is the place I know Maria goes to most of the times she goes out. But though I have urged her to have her sister come to visit her and me, Maria always replies that her sister is a homebody and does not like to travel.

Maria's interest in my own social life is proud and constant. She is under the impression that I see only the very best people—"the high ups"—but she is rather careful if I am going out to dinner at what she gathers to be a very grand establishment (indicated by my wearing a dinner jacket) that I make a good tea first. "You never get very much to eat at the wealthy people's," she says.

She is also very eager to protect my own dignity and maintain my own status. "We're having a millionaire to lunch today," I said to Maria once. It happened to be true. "We must have a very good lunch," she said; "those people never get enough to eat; I've worked for millionaires. And besides, he mustn't think you can't afford to eat properly."

Again, a lady of my acquaintance had called up in answer to my inquiry as to whether I should wear a white or black tie, and had left word: "Mr. Edman is to wear a black tie Thursday night." Maria awaited me that evening, arms akimbo, to inform me that she had said in just those words that Dr. Edman knew perfectly well what to wear. But she has a fixed notion that nobody with anything important to say says it over the telephone, and her casualness on that score, especially about names and numbers, is her one imperfection. She is, incidentally, more patient with and attentive to gentlemen than to ladies.

Everybody, quite properly, admires Maria's cooking (especially her carrots, about the cooking of which she has a secret), but she has asked me not to boast about it, as then people will be disappointed and she will be humiliated. The chief cross she has to bear is that the digestion of a brain worker prevents me from letting her give free rein to her art. She saves that for visitors, and the freest rein she ever gave was for Father Ford.

I had been telling Maria for some time that Father Ford—the counsellor to Catholic students at Columbia—was coming to lunch soon. I had never seen any news produce so electric an effect upon her. For Father Ford, it turned out, had once been the parish priest at her sister's church, St. Anne's on Jerome Avenue. And, what was more, she said in all her years of service she had never yet been in a place where they had had a priest to lunch.

Usually Maria takes upon herself the problem of the menu. But, despite the fact that I was often "concentrating" in the next week, she would appear time and again to announce some suggested change in the lunch for Thursday. I finally desperately waived all ability to decide; she was a good Catholic; she should know what priests liked. She was wavering, she said, between grilled chicken and lamb chops with rolled bacon as the principal course.

The day Father Ford was to come to lunch at half-past twelve, I was a little late. I had had a lecture on the Philosophy of Religion from eleven to twelve, and had stopped to argue with a young man named Riley about the origins of Christianity. He was one of Father Ford's protégés, by the way. He had taken the course because Father Ford had told him his faith was not worth very much if it could not stand up against the Department of Philosophy and the Higher Criticism of the Bible.

I came in to find Father Ford seated in that favourite armchair which I have gradually come to realize I can decently use only when I am alone: guests are entitled to its virtues. Father Ford looked very placid and content, and a little amused. I wondered at the amusement.

"I am sorry to be late," I said.

"It's quite all right," he replied; "I have been very well entertained."

We had an excellent and an enormous lunch—grapefruit, timbale of oysters, lamb chops and bacon with three kinds of vegetables, including Maria's specialty—buttered carrots—hearts of lettuce, strawberries in cream—in January—and a cream cake and coffee. There was wine and there was a liqueur; there had been sherry and hors d'oeuvre.

About the middle of lunch Father Ford eyed me curiously.

"Do you always have lunch like this?" he asked. "If so, I must steal Maria away for the Newman House."

"No, Father," I said, "this is an obeisance to the Church. I had nothing to do with the ordering of this lunch, and I assure you when I *am* home to lunch I don't get anything like this."

"God looks after you almost as well as if you were one of the faithful," he said.

Father Ford left and I settled down in the easy chair to recuperate from the enormous meal. I began to look over some mail. Maria appeared at the door. She seemed in a fever of restrained excitement.

"Are you concentrating?" she asked.

"No, Maria, I couldn't, not right after that lunch."

"Do you mind if I talk to you, or shall I be disturbing your brains?" (Her regular gambit.)

"I'm so glad you came late," she said.

I was surprised at that, for if there is one thing about which Maria will not conceal her displeasure it is my being late when a guest is coming. She was once quite angry with me for two whole days because I had gone out to get some cigarettes and guests had come before I had returned.

"You're glad I came home late, Maria? That's odd, and for a priest, too!"

She beamed and could contain herself no longer. Maria doesn't talk much, but once in a while, in cases of special excitement—like the time she saw somebody jump from a ninth-story window just as she was coming home, or the day the Irish elevator boy told her his wife had had twins—the floodgates are let loose. This was obviously a time of special excitement.

"Well, I must tell you," she said. "Father Ford rang the bell. I opened the door. . . . I said: 'How do you do, Father Ford; I'm so glad you've come. I used to see you in my sister's, St. Anne's Church on Jerome Avenue; and everybody was so fond of you, and the mothers and children cried when you went to Columbia.'

" 'But we must go where the Church tells us to,' he said, casting his eyes down.

" 'Yes, I know, Father Ford,' I said, 'but the women and children cried anyway. And would you like to see the apartment?' And he said yes. And I showed him the kitchen. And he said: 'What a lovely sunny kitchen!' And he said: 'Professor Edman is one of the best of the young professors at Columbia.' And I said: 'Yes, I know, and he's so quiet you'd never know he was in the house.' And I showed him the other rooms and the books, and I asked him to sit down and I offered him some sherry, and I told him to make himself quite at home, and I gave him your book on St. Paul. I said you were always thinking about the saints, and I was sure you would end up in the arms of the Church some day, and I am sure you will, too, though everybody's religion is as good as everybody else's, so long as it's his own and he believes it, and is good in his own way. And then you came in, and I'm so glad you came in late, and he did seem to like the lunch. He said so to me when he left."

"Indeed, he did," I said. "And he wants to steal you for the Newman House."

"Oh, he was only fooling, and it'd be too great a nervous strain to be always working for a priest. But I am glad you came in late."

"Maria," I said, "would you like to take the afternoon off and go up to the Bronx and tell all about this to your sister? You really wouldn't get much done this afternoon."

"I surely would," said Maria.

Maria never enjoyed a guest of mine so much, not even the friend of mine, who, she insists, falsely, looks like Rudy Vallee.

At my suggestion Maria came to the consecration of Father Ford's new Church of Corpus Christi near Columbia. Many of us from the university had been invited to attend in academic garb and march in the procession. The Cardinal gave his blessing.

That evening I asked Maria how she liked the ceremonies.

"Very fine," she said, "and you and Professor C—— looked lovely in the procession."

She thought a moment and looked at me.

"You've received a papal blessing," she said, "do you know that?"

"Yes," I said.

"Well, you're holy now," she said, and added as she walked out: "Now be sure to stay that way."

I do not think Maria would mind finding herself in this book, though she will not read it. She never reads books; she says they're all alike, and wonders why I keep "poring over" them. In any case, she cannot mind my writing a little about one of the kindest and most competent persons I have ever known, and one with a great gift for happiness who has made Apartment 9A a wonderful natural basis for ideal flights into the empyrean with all the comforts of home. She's been blessed and by more than a Cardinal. And so have I.

Philosopher's Holiday, 1938

BOB CONSIDINE

Coiled Venom

It is surprising that sports writers produce so many excellent accounts under the pressure of deadlines and surrounded by excited crowds. But only from a highly competent craftsman of Considine's caliber could one expect such superb reporting turned out right at the ringside.

Listen to this, buddy, for it comes from a guy whose palms are still wet, whose throat is still dry, and whose jaw is still agape from the utter shock of watching Joe Louis knock out Max Schmeling.

It was a shocking thing, that knockout—short, sharp, merciless, complete. Louis was like this:

He was a big lean copper spring, tightened and retightened through weeks of training until he was one pregnant package of coiled venom.

Schmeling hit that spring. He hit it with a whistling right-hand punch in the first minute of the fight—and the spring, tormented with tension, suddenly burst with one brazen spang of activity. Hard brown arms, propelling two unerring fists, blurred beneath the hot white candelabra of the ring lights. And Schmeling was in the path of them, a man caught and mangled in the whirring claws of a mad and feverish machine.

The mob, biggest and most prosperous ever to see a fight in a ball yard, knew that here was the end before the thing had really started. It knew, so it stood up and howled one long shriek. People who had paid as much as $100 for their chairs didn't use them—except perhaps to stand on, the better to let the sight burn forever in their memories.

There were four steps to Schmeling's knockout. A few seconds after he landed his only punch of the fight, Louis caught him with a lethal little left hook that drove him into the ropes so that his right arm was hooked over the top strand, like a drunk hanging to a fence. Louis swarmed over him and hit with everything he had—until Referee Donovan pushed him away and counted one.

Schmeling staggered away from the ropes, dazed and sick. He looked drunkenly toward his corner, and before he had turned his head back Louis was on him again, first with a left and then that awe-provoking right that made a crunching sound when it hit the German's jaw. Max fell down, hurt and giddy, for a count of three.

He clawed his way up as if the night air were as thick as black water, and Louis—his nostrils like the mouth of a double-barreled shotgun—took a quiet lead and let him have both barrels.

Max fell almost lightly, bereft of his senses, his fingers touching the canvas like a comical stew-bum doing his morning exercises, knees bent and the tongue lolling in his head.

He got up long enough to be knocked down again, this time with his dark unshaven face pushed in the sharp gravel of the resin.

Louis jumped away lightly, a bright and pleased look in his eyes, and as he did the white towel of surrender which Louis' handlers had refused to use two years ago tonight came sailing into the ring in a soggy mess. It was thrown by Max Machon, oblivious to the fact that fights cannot end this way in New York.

The referee snatched it off the floor and flung it backwards. It hit the ropes and hung there, limp as Schmeling. Donovan counted up to five over Max, sensed the futility of it all, and stopped the fight.

The big crowd began to rustle restlessly toward the exits, many only now accepting Louis as champion of the world. There were no eyes for Schmeling, sprawled on his stool in his corner.

He got up eventually, his dirty gray-and-black robe over his shoulders, and wormed through the happy little crowd that hovered around Louis. And he put his arm around the Negro and smiled. They both smiled and could afford to—for Louis had made around $200,000 a minute and Schmeling $100,000 a minute.

But once he crawled down in the belly of the big stadium, Schmeling realized the implications of his defeat. He, who won the title on a partly phony foul, and beat Louis two years ago with the aid of a crushing punch after the bell had sounded, now said Louis had fouled him. That would read better in Germany, whence earlier in the day had come a cable from Hitler, calling on him to win.

International News Service, June 22, 1938

HEYWOOD BROUN

The Master Workman

In his column for the New York WORLD *Heywood Broun was quick and pointed in his criticism of social conditions and injustices. Because of his sloppy dress and appearance a crony once called him "a one-man slum," but Broun rarely turned in a slovenly column, and perhaps never a trite one. This piece illustrates his originality and the fanciful nature of some of his best work.*

"Could I have a mousetrap, please?" I asked. The old gentleman who was fussing around with a couple of wires and hammer did not put his tools down upon the instant. This gave me a chance to wipe the blood off my face, which had been rather badly cut by the thorns and brambles of the wilderness.

The master workman adjusted his specs and said, "I guess you found it rather heavy going getting here to my little place."

"Yes," I answered. "I must have lost the path. There wasn't any sign of a road at all. I just had to hack my way through."

"Path," chuckled the skilled artist mirthlessly; "there isn't even a cow track."

Naturally I was surprised, and instinctively I quoted from Emerson, or whoever said it, "If a man can make a better mousetrap the world will beat a pathway to his door, even though it lie in the trackless forest"—or words to that effect.

My friend was not amused. "It's stuff and nonsense," he told me. "You're the first customer who's been here in ten years. In fact, I don't want 'em any more. They interfere with my work."

"But," I objected, "that is a mousetrap you're making, isn't it?"

He fondled the model lovingly and answered, "It is, indeed. That's the finest mousetrap in the world. It's the best one I ever made. When I was a young man I couldn't do half so good. They keep getting better. I change the specifications every day. That's what keeps me young. In the beginning I made only a pretty good mousetrap. This one is sheer genius."

"Maybe," I suggested, "it was your lesser mousetraps that the public wanted. Perhaps fifty years ago they beat a pathway to your door."

This time he fairly snorted with petulance. "I told you once already, stranger, that the pathway thing is just a lie. I've been a hermit all my life. Mousetraps don't sell on merit. If you want to sell mousetraps you've got to buy machines to make 'em. You can't pay any attention to the product yourself. To be a tycoon in the mousetrap field you've got to sit outside the tent and beat a drum and think up advertising slogans

154

such as 'The Pied Piper was a sucker; he didn't have a Malcolm. It satisfies everybody but the mouse.' And then you've got to take newspaper advertising and go on the air with a jazz band, a blues singer and two comics. I hate radio and jazz and comics. I like mousetraps. That's why I never sell any."

He took the model on which he was working and placed it on the floor near the window. For the first time I noticed that every strand of wire was of a different color.

"Look," said the old man. "See how the sun plays on it. That might be a rainbow. It's better than a rainbow, because I know more about mixing colors. And look at the shape of it—round as a hill and just as much alive as any river."

"But in a cellar," I protested, "there isn't much sunlight. And maybe the mice don't care about the architectural perfection. It's the cheese they're after."

"Sure," he said. "It's just the same with mice and men. They want the golden stuff which satisfies the belly. My traps are made for the satisfaction of my soul."

This time I proferred money. After such an arduous journey I didn't want to go away empty-handed. But he shook his head.

"My traps are not for sale," he explained. "I make them for posterity. If a man makes a better mousetrap the world will stay away from his door in droves, but they will beat a pathway to his grave. After I'm gone these traps of mine will stand as ornaments on every mantel. I don't want to hurry you, young fellow, but the generations unborn become impatient. I must get on with my work. Tomorrow I may make an even better mousetrap."

When I picked up my hat I found that the felt was full of minute punctures. The brim was riddled.

"Really," I exclaimed, "I had no idea the thorns and brambles were quite as thick as all that in the forest."

This time he laughed in high good humor. "Not brambles or thorns," he said. "Them's mice, stranger. The house is full of 'em. They're my audience. They're the ones that have beat the pathway to my door through the trackless forest. They take things on faith without listening to the radio, and that's why I sit all day and build 'em little palaces."

Collected Edition of Heywood Broun, 1941

ROBERT BENCHLEY

Polyp with a Past

Of all forms of animal life, the polyp is probably the most neglected by fanciers. People seem willing to pay attention to anything, cats, lizards, canaries, or even fish, but simply because the polyp is reserved by nature and not given to showing off or wearing its heart on its sleeve, it is left alone under the sea to slave away at coral-building with never a kind word or a pat on the tentacles from anybody.

It was quite by accident that I was brought face to face with the human side of a polyp. I had been working on a thesis on "Emotional Crisis in Sponge Life," and came upon a polyp formation on a piece of coral in the course of my laboratory work. To say that I was astounded would be putting it mildly. I was surprised.

The difficulty in research work in this field came in isolating a single polyp from the rest in order to study the personal peculiarities of the little organism, for, as is so often the case (even, I fear, with us great big humans sometimes), the individual behaves in an entirely different manner in private from the one he adopts when there is a crowd around. And a polyp, among all creatures, has a minimum of time to himself in which to sit down and think. There is always a crowd of other polyps dropping in on him, urging him to make a fourth in a string of coral beads or just to come out and stick around on a rock for the sake of good-fellowship.

The one which I finally succeeded in isolating was an engaging organism with a provocative manner and a little way of wrinkling up its ectoderm, which put you at once at your ease. There could be no formality about your relations with this polyp five minutes after your first meeting. You were just like one great big family.

Although I have no desire to retail gossip, I think that readers of this treatise ought to be made aware of the fact (if, indeed, they do not already know it) that a polyp is really neither one thing nor another in matters of gender. One day it may be a little boy polyp, another day a little girl, according to its whim or practical considerations of policy. On gray days, when everything seems to be going wrong, it may decide that it will be neither boy nor girl but will just drift. I think that if we big human cousins of the little polyp were to follow the example set by these lowliest of God's creatures in this matter, we all would find ourselves much better off in the end. Am I not right, little polyp?

What was my surprise, then, to discover my little friend one day in a gloomy and morose mood. It refused the peanut-butter which I had brought it and I observed through the microscope that it was shaking with sobs. Lifting it up with a pair of pincers I took it over to the window to let it watch the automobiles go by, a diversion which had, in the past, never failed to amuse. But I could see that it was not interested. A tune from the Victrola fell equally flat, even though I set my little charge on the center of the disc and allowed it to revolve at a dizzy pace, which frolic usually sent it into spasms of excited giggling. Something was wrong. It was under emotional stress of the most racking kind.

I consulted Klunzinger's "Die Korallenthiere des Rothen Meeres" and there found that at an early age the polyp is quite likely to become the victim of a sentimental passion which is directed at its own self.

In other words, my tiny companion was in love with itself, bitterly, desperately, head-over-heels in love.

In an attempt to divert it from this madness, I took it on an extended tour of the Continent, visiting all the old cathedrals and stopping at none but the best hotels. The malady grew worse, instead of better. I thought that perhaps the warm sun of Granada would bring the color back into those pale tentacles, but there the inevitable romance in the soft air was only fuel to the flame, and, in the shadows of the Alhambra, my little polyp gave up the fight and died of a broken heart without ever having declared its love to itself.

I returned to America shortly after not a little chastened by what I had witnessed of Nature's wonders in the realm of passion.

Benchley Beside Himself, 1943

WALTER LIPPMANN

A Remarkable Analysis of Things to Come [1943]

Russia and the United States, placed "on opposite sides of the globe," have always been antagonistic in their political ideology, always suspicious that close contact would be subversive. Yet each has always opposed the dismemberment of the other. Each has always wished the other to be strong. They have never had a collision which made them enemies. Each has regarded the other as a potential friend in the rear of its potential enemies.

May this historical relationship be expected to continue after the destruction of the military power of Germany and Japan? The answer must be, whatever the future may bring, that we are at a decisive turning point in our relations with Russia. . . . Germany will never again be able to make a bid for the mastery of Europe and of the transatlantic region of American security; Japan will never again be able to seek an empire over China and the Indies. . . . Germany and Japan are in the last phase of their last attempt at world empire. . . .

The postwar world is likely to see China industrialized, Russia in Siberia become immensely stronger, and the United States conscious of its military potential. . . .

Russian-American relations will no longer be controlled by the historic fact that each is for the other a potential friend in the rear of its potential enemies. Russia will, on the contrary, be the greatest power in the rear of our indispensable friends, the British, Scandanavian, Dutch, Belgian, and Latin members of the Atlantic Community. In Asia, Russia will be our nearest neighbor across the Northern Pacific and by air over the Polar regions; Russia will be the nearest neighbor of China.

Thus the question in Europe is whether Russia will seek to extend her power westward into Europe in such a way that it threatens the security of the Atlantic states. The question in the Pacific is whether as nearest neighbor by land, sea, and air, the United States and Russia will move towards rivalry or toward a common ground of understanding. The two questions are inseparable because, as the Russian statesmen have often insisted, peace is indivisible. We should, therefore, be lacking in candor and realism if we did not face the fact that the crucial question of the epoch that we are now entering is the relationship between Russia and that Atlantic Community in which Britain and the United States are the leading military powers.

Out of this question there arises America's vital interest in the settlement of European affairs. . . . American, and therefore also British, military power against Russia in Europe would set the stage inexorably for a third World War in Europe and in Asia as well. . . .

The objective test of whether there is to be peace or war will be whether the borderland between Russia and the Atlantic states is settled by consent or by pressure, dictation, and diplomatic violence. This borderland begins with Finland in the North and includes Sweden, and extends through Poland, the Danubian nations, the Balkan nations, to Turkey, and it includes Germany. If in this region the effort to settle territorial boundaries and to decide what governments shall be recognized discloses deep and insoluble conflicts between Russia's conception of her vital interests and that of the Western Allies, then every nation will know that it must be ready and must choose sides in the eventual but unavoidable next war. . . .

We cannot agree to the underlying conception of the Versailles settlement which treated the border region as a military barrier, as the *cordon sanitaire*, between Russia and the rest of Europe. The barrier has no military value. Germany broke through it easily. Russia could break through it easily. . . . The barrier cannot be reconstructed because Russia, emerging from this war the great military power of Europe whereas in 1918 she was prostrate, can erase the barrier by forming an alliance with post-Nazi Germany.

To encourage the nations of Central and Eastern Europe to organize themselves as a barrier against Russia would be to make a commitment that the United States could not carry out. . . .

Does this mean that Poland, the Danubian states, and the Balkan states have no prospect of assured independence and that they are destined inexorably to became satellites of Russia or to be incorporated into the Soviet Union? The question cannot be answered categorically at this time. We may say, I believe, that these states would have no prospect of independence if America and Britain, working with the governments-in-exile, were to attempt to reconstitute them as the outposts of a Western Coalition against Russia. When the war ends, the Russians will almost certainly have an overwhelming preponderance of military force in this region, and it is inconceivable that the Red Army, if it liberates these peoples from the Nazi conquerors, will permit governments operating from London and Washington to organize anti-Russian states on the Russian border. The very attempt to do this, even the suspicion of an attempt, is bound to revive the bitter memories of the Allied intervention of 1919 in the Russian Civil War. Then the question will not be how firmly we can guarantee the independence of these states, but whether Russia will permit them to exist at all as independent states.

U.S. Foreign Policy, 1943

THE SOUTH

WILLIAM BYRD

In the Dismal Swamp

> William Byrd, landed proprietor and Receiver General of the
> Royal Revenues, in 1728 was appointed one of three commission-
> ers to fix the dividing line between Virginia and North Carolina,
> the line running east from the coast through the Dismal Swamp.
> He kept a journal of the experience.

March 25 [1728]. Surely there is no place in the world where the Inhabitants live with less labour than in N. Carolina. It approaches nearer
to the Description of Lubberland than any other, by the great felicity of
the Climate, the easiness of raising Provisions, and the Slothfulness of
the People.

Indian Corn is of so great increase, that a little Pains will Subsist a
very large Family with Bread, and then they may have Meat without
any pains at all, by the Help of the Low Grounds, and great Variety of
Mast that grows on the High-land. The Men, for their Parts, just like
the Indians, impose all the Work upon the poor Women. They make
their Wives rise out of their Beds early in the Morning, at the same time
that they lye and Snore, till the Sun has run one third of his course, and
disperst all the unwholesome Damps. Then, after Stretching and Yawning for half an Hour, they light their Pipes, and under the Protection
of a cloud of Smoak, venture out into the open Air; tho', if it happens to
be never so cold, they quickly return Shivering into the Chimney corner.
When the Weather is mild, they stand leaning with both their arms upon
the corn-field fence, and gravely consider whether they had best go and
take a Small Heat at the Hough: but generally find reasons to put it off
till another time.

Thus they loiter away their Lives, like Solomon's Sluggard, with their Arms across, and at the Winding up of the Year Scarcely have Bread to Eat.

To speak the Truth, tis a thorough Aversion to Labor that makes People file off to N. Carolina, where Plenty and a Warm Sun confirm them in their Disposition to Laziness for their whole Lives.

26 [March]. Since we were like to be confin'd to this place, till the People return'd out of the Dismal, twas agreed that our Chaplain might Safely take a turn to Edenton, to preach the Gospel to the Infidels there, and Christen their Children. He was accompany'd thither by Mr. Little, One of the Carolina Commissioners, who, to shew his regard for the Church, offer'd to treat Him on the Road with a Fricassee of Rum. They fry'd half a Dozen Rashers of very fat Bacon in a Pint of Rum, both which being disht up together, serv'd the Company at once for meat and Drink.

Most of the Rum they get in this Country comes from New England, and is so bad and unwholesome, that it is not improperly call'd "Kill-Devil." It is distill'd there from foreign molosses, which, if Skillfully manag'd, yields near Gallon for Gallon. Their molosses comes from the same country, and has the name of "Long Sugar" in Carolina, I suppose from the Ropiness of it, and Serves all the purposes of Sugar, both in their Eating and Drinking.

When they entertain their Friends bountifully, they fail not to set before them a Capacious Bowl of Bombo, so call'd from the Admiral of that name. This is a compound of Rum and Water in Equal Parts, made palatable with the said long Sugar. As good Humour begins to flow, and the Bowl to Ebb, they take Care to replenish it with Shear Rum, of which there always is a Reserve under the Table. But such Generous doings happen only when the Balsam of life is plenty. . . . Very few in this Country have the Industry to plant Orchards, which, in a Dearth of Rum, might supply them with much better Liquor.

The Truth is, there in one Inconvenience that easily discourages lazy People from making This Improvement: very often, in Autumn, when the Apples begin to ripen, they are visited with Numerous Flights of para-queets, that bite all the Fruit to Pieces in a moment, for the sake of the Kernels. The Havock they make is Sometimes so great, that whole Orchards are laid waste in Spite of all the Noises that can be made, or Mawkins that can be dresst up, to fright 'em away. These Ravenous Birds visit North Carolina only during the Warm Season, and so soon as the Cold begins to come on, retire back towards the Sun. They rarely Venture so far North as Virginia, except in a very hot Summer, when they visit the most Southern Parts of it. They are very Beautiful; but like some other pretty Creatures, are apt to be loud and mischievous.

27 [March]. Betwixt this and Edenton there are many thuckleberry Slashes, which afford a convenient Harbour for Wolves and Foxes. The

first of these wild Beasts is not so large and fierce as they are in other countries more Northerly. He will not attack a Man in the keenest of his Hunger, but run away from him, as from an Animal more mischievous than himself.

The Foxes are much bolder, and will Sometimes not only make a Stand, but likewise assault any one that would balk them of their Prey. The Inhabitants hereabouts take the trouble to dig abundance of Wolf-Pitts, so deep and perpendicular, that when a Wolf is once tempted into them, he can no more Scramble out again, than a Husband who has taken the Leap can Scramble out of Matrimony. . . .

Provisions here are extremely cheap, and extremely good, so that People may live plentifully at a triffleing expense. Nothing is dear but Law, Physick, and Strong Drink, which are all bad in their kind, and the last they get with so much Difficulty, that they are never so guilty of the Sin of Suffering it to Sour upon their Hands. Their Vanity generally lies not so much in having a Handsome Dining-Room, as a Handsome House of Office: in this kind of Structure they are really extravagant.

They are rarely guilty of Flattering or making any Court to their governors, but treat them with all the Excesses of Freedom and Familiarity. They are of Opinion their rulers wou'd be apt to grow insolent, if they grew Rich, and for that reason take care to keep them poorer, and more dependent, if possible, than the Saints in New England used to do their Governors. They have very little coin, so they are forced to carry on their Home-Traffick with Paper-Money. This is the only Cash that will tarry in the Country, and for that reason the Discount goes on increasing between that and real Money, and will do so to the end of the Chapter.

The History of the Dividing Line Betwixt
Virginia and North Carolina, 1841

GEORGE WASHINGTON

To American Troops Before the Battle of Long Island [August 1776]

The time is now near at hand which must probably determine whether Americans are to be freedmen or slaves; whether they are to have any property they can call their own; whether their houses and farms are to be pillaged and destroyed, and themselves consigned to a state of wretchedness from which no human effort will deliver them. The fate of unborn millions will now depend, under God, on the courage and conduct of this army. Our cruel and unrelenting enemy leaves us only the choice of a brave resistance, or the most abject submission. We have, therefore, to resolve to conquer or to die.

Our own, our country's honor, calls upon us for a vigorous and manly exertion; and if we now shamefully fail, we shall become infamous to the whole world. Let us, then, rely on the goodness of our cause, and the aid of the Supreme Being, in Whose hands victory is, to animate and encourage us to great and noble actions. The eyes of all our countrymen are now upon us; and we shall have their blessings and praises; if happily we are the instruments of saving them from the tyranny meditated against them. Let us, therefore, animate and encourage each other, and show the whole world that a freedman contending for liberty on his own ground is superior to any slavish mercenary on earth.

Liberty, property, life and honor, are all at stake. Upon your courage and conduct rest the hopes of our bleeding and insulted country. Our wives, children and parents expect safety from us only; and they have every reason to believe that Heaven will crown with success so just a cause. The enemy will endeavor to intimidate by show and appearance; but re-member they have been repulsed on various occasions by a few brave Americans. Their cause is bad—their men are conscious of it; and, if op-posed with firmness and coolness on their onset, with our advantage of works, and knowledge of the ground, the victory is most assuredly ours. Every good soldier will be silent and attentive, wait for orders, and reserve his fire until he is sure of doing execution.

Speeches of George Washington, 1888

To One Colonel Nichola, Who Proposed a Kingdom with Washington as Its Head

Newburgh, May 22ᵈ '82

Sir,

With a mixture of great surprise and astonishment I have read with attention the Sentiments you have submitted to my perusal.—Be assured, Sir, no occurrence in the course of the War, has given me more painful sensations than your information of there being such ideas existing in the Army as you have expressed, and I must view with abhorrence, and repre-hend with severity—For the present, the communication of them will rest in my own bosom, unless some further agitation of the matter shall make a disclosure necessary.—

I am much at a loss to conceive what part of my conduct could have given encouragement to an address which to me seems so big with the greatest mischiefs that can befall my Country.—If I am not deceived in the knowledge of myself, you could not have found a person to whom your

166

schemes are more disagreeable—at the same time in justice to my own feelings I must add, that no man possesses a more sincere wish to see ample justice done to the Army than I do, and as far as my powers and influence, in a constitution, may extend, they shall be employed to the utmost of my abilities to effect it, should there be any occasion—Let me conjure you then, if you have any regard for your Country—concern for yourself or posterity—or respect for me, to banish these thoughts from your mind, and never communicate, as from yourself, or any one else, a sentiment of the like nature.—

With esteem I am Sir
Yr Most Obed Ser
G. WASHINGTON

Col Nichola,

The World's Great Letters, edited by M. Lincoln Schuster

WILLIAM BARTRAM

An Encounter with Alligators in Florida Swamps

> *This Philadelphia Quaker was first better known in Europe than in his native America. His wildlife studies of the northeastern states, and especially this account of the Florida alligators, excited the interest of Coleridge, Wordsworth, Chateaubriand, and others.*

Being desirous of continuing my travels and observations, higher up the [St. John's] river, and having an invitation from a gentleman who was agent for, and resident at a large plantation, the property of an English gentleman, about sixty miles higher up, I resolved to pursue my researches to that place; and having engaged in my service a young Indian, nephew to the White Captain, he agreed to assist me in working my vessel up as high as a certain bluff, where I was, by agreement, to land him, on the West or Indian shore, whence he designed to go in quest of the camp of the White Trader, his relation.

Provisions and all necessaries being procured, and the morning pleasant, we went on board and stood up the river. We passed for several miles on the left, by islands of high swamp land, exceedingly fertile, their banks for a good distance from the water, much higher than the interior part, and sufficiently so to build upon, and be out of the reach of inundations. They consist of a loose black mould, with a mixture of sand, shells and dissolved vegetables. The opposite Indian coast is a perpendicular bluff, ten or twelve feet high, consisting of a black sandy earth, mixed with a large proportion of shells, chiefly various species of fresh water Cochlea and Mytuli. Near the river, on this high shore, grew Corypha palma, Magnolia grandiflora, Live Oak, Callicarpa, Myrica cerifera, Hybiscus spinifex, and the beautiful evergreen shrub called Wild lime or Tallow nut. This last shrub grows six or eight feet high, many erect stems rising from a root; the leaves are lanciolate and intire, two or three inches in length and one in breadth, of a deep green colour, and polished; at the foot of each leaf grows a stiff, sharp thorn; the flowers are small and in clusters, of a greenish yellow colour, and sweet scented; they are succeeded by a large oval fruit, of the shape and size of an ordinary plumb, of a fine yellow colour when ripe, a soft sweet pulp covers a nut which has a thin shell, enclosing a white kernel somewhat of the consistence and taste of the sweet Almond, but more oily and very much like hard tallow, which induced my father when he first observed it, to call it the Tallow nut.

At the upper end of this bluff is a fine Orange grove. Here my Indian companion requested me to set him on shore, being already tired of rowing under a fervid sun, and having for some time intimated a dislike to his situation. I readily complied with his desire, knowing the impossibility of compelling an Indian against his own inclinations, or even prevailing upon him by reasonable arguments, when labour is in the question; before my vessel reached the shore, he sprang out of her and landed, when uttering a shrill and terrible whoop, he bounded off like a roebuck, and I lost sight of him. I at first apprehended that as he took his gun with him, he intended to hunt for some game and return to me in the evening. The day being excessively hot and sultry, I concluded to take up my quarters here until next morning.

The Indian not returning this morning, I sat sail alone. The coasts on each side had much the same appearance as already described. The Palm trees here seem to be of a different species from the Cabbage tree; their strait trunks are sixty, eighty or ninety feet high, with a beautiful taper of a bright ash colour, until within six or seven feet of the top, where it is a fine green colour, crowned with an orb of rich green plumed leaves: I have measured the stem of these plumes fifteen feet in length, besides the plume, which is nearly of the same length.

The little lake, which is an expansion of the river, now appeared in view; on the East side are extensive marshes, and on the other high forests and Orange groves, and then a bay, lined with vast Cypress swamps, both coasts gradually approaching each other, to the opening of the river again, which is in this place about three hundred yards wide; evening now drawing on, I was anxious to reach some high bank of the river, where I intended to lodge, and agreeably to my wishes, I soon after discovered on the West shore, a little promontory, at the turning of the river, contracting it here to about one hundred and fifty yards in width. This promontory is a peninsula, containing about three acres of high ground, and is one entire

Orange grove, with a few Live Oaks, Magnolias and Palms. Upon doubling the point, I arrived at the landing, which is a circular harbour, at the foot of the bluff, the top of which is about twelve feet high; and back of it is a large Cypress swamp, that spreads each way, the right wing forming the West coast of the little lake, and the left stretching up the river many miles, and encompassing a vast space of low grassy marshes. From this promontory, looking Eastward across the river, we behold a landscape of low country, u[n]paralleled as I think; on the left is the East coast of the little lake, which I had just passed, and from the Orange bluff at the lower end, the high forests begin, and increase in breadth from the shore of the lake, making a circular sweep to the right, and contain many hundred thousand acres of meadow, and this grand sweep of high forests encircles, as I apprehend, at least twenty miles of these green fields, interspersed with hommocks or islets of evergreen trees, where the sovereign Magnolia and lordly Palm stand conspicuous. The islets are high shelly knolls, on the sides of creeks or branches of the river, which wind about and drain off the super-abundant waters that cover these meadows, during the winter season.

The evening was temperately cool and calm. The crocodiles began to roar and appear in uncommon numbers along the shores and in the river. I fixed my camp in an open plain, near the utmost projection of the promontory, under the shelter of a large Live Oak, which stood on the highest part of the ground and but a few yards from my boat. From this open, high situation, I had a free prospect of the river, which was a matter of no trivial consideration to me, having good reason to dread the subtle attacks of the alligators, who were crouding about my harbour. Having collected a good quantity of wood for the purpose of keeping up a light and smoke during the night, I began to think of preparing my supper, when, upon examining my stores, I found but a scanty provision, I thereupon determined, as the most expeditious way of supplying my necessities, to take my bob and try for some trout. About one hundred yards above my harbour, began a cove or bay of the river, out of which opened a large lagoon. The mouth or entrance from the river to it was narrow, but the waters soon after spread and formed a little lake, extending into the marshes, its entrance and shores within I observed to be verged with floating lawns of the Pistia and Nymphea and other aquatic plants; these I knew were excellent haunts for trout.

The verges and islets of the lagoon were elegantly embellished with flowering plants and shrubs; the laughing coots with wings half spread were tripping over the little coves and hiding themselves in the tufts of grass; young broods of the painted summer teal, skimming the still surface of the waters, and following the watchful parent unconscious of danger, were frequently surprised by the voracious trout, and he in turn, as often by the subtle, greedy alligator. Behold him rushing forth from the flags and reeds. His enormous body swells. His plaited tail brandished high, floats upon the lake. The waters like a cataract descend from his opening jaws. Clouds of smoke issue from his dilated nostrils. The earth trembles with his thunder. When immediately from the opposite coast of the lagoon, emerges from the deep his rival champion. They suddenly dart upon each other. The boiling surface of the lake marks their rapid course, and a terrific conflict commences. They now sink to the bottom folded together in horrid wreaths. The water becomes thick and discoloured. Again they rise, their jaws clap together, re-echoing through the deep surrounding forests. Again they sink, when the contest ends at the muddy bottom of the lake, and the vanquished makes a hazardous escape, hiding himself in the muddy turbulent waters and sedge on a distant shore. The proud victor exulting returns to the place of action. The shores and forests resound his dreadful roar, together with the triumphing shouts of the plaited tribes around, witnesses of the horrid combat.

My apprehensions were highly alarmed after being a spectator of so dreadful a battle; it was obvious that every delay would but tend to encrease my dangers and difficulties, as the sun was near setting, and the alligators gathered around my harbour from all quarters; from these considerations I concluded to be expeditious in my trip to the lagoon, in order to take some fish. Not thinking it prudent to take my fusee with me, lest I might lose it overboard in case of a battle, which I had every reason to dread before my return, I therefore furnished myself with a club for my defence, went on board, and penetrating the first line of those which surrounded my harbour, they gave way; but being pursued by several very large ones, I kept strictly on the watch, and paddled with all my might towards the entrance of the lagoon, hoping to be sheltered there from the multitude of my assailants; but ere I had half-way reached the place, I was attacked on all sides, several endeavouring to overset the canoe. My situation now became precarious to the last degree: two very large ones attacked me closely, at the same instant, rushing up with their heads and part of their bodies above the water, roaring terribly and belching floods of water over me. They struck their jaws together so close to my ears, as almost to stun me, and I expected every moment to be dragged out of the boat and instantly devoured, but I applied my weapons so effectually about me, though at random, that I was so successful as to beat them off a little; when, finding that they designed to renew the battle, I made for the shore, as the only means left me for my preservation, for, by keeping close to it, I should have my enemies on one side of me only, whereas I was before surrounded by them, and there was a probability, if pushed to the last extremity, of saving myself, by jumping out of the canoe on shore, as it is easy to outwalk them on land, although comparatively as swift as lightning in the water. I found this last expedient alone could fully answer my expectations, for as soon as I gained the shore they drew off and kept aloof. This was a happy relief, as my confidence was, in some degree, recovered by it. On recollecting myself, I discovered that I had almost reached the entrance of the lagoon, and determined to venture in, if possible to take a few fish and then return to my harbour, while day-light continued; for I could now, with caution and resolution, make my way with safety along shore, and indeed there was no other way to regain my camp, without leaving my boat and making my retreat through the marshes and reeds, which, if I could even effect, would have been in a manner throwing myself away, for then there would have been no hopes of ever recovering my bark, and returning in safety to any settlements of men. I accordingly proceeded and made good my entrance into the lagoon, though not without opposition from the alligators, who formed a line across the entrance, but did not pursue me into it, nor was I molested by any there, though there were some very large ones in a cove at the upper end. I soon caught more trout than I had present occasion for, and the air was too hot and sultry to admit of their being kept for many hours, even though salted or barbecued. I now prepared for my return to camp, which I succeeded in with but little trouble, by keeping close to the shore, yet I was opposed upon re-entering the river out of the lagoon, and pursued near to my landing (though not closely attacked) particularly by an old daring one, about twelve feet in length, who kept close after me, and when I stepped on shore and turned about, in order to draw up my canoe, he rushed up near my feet and lay there for some time, looking me in the face, his head and shoulders out of water; I resolved he should pay for his temerity, and having a heavy load in my fusee, I ran to my camp, and returning with my piece, found him with his foot on the gunwale of the boat, in search of fish, on my coming up he withdrew sullenly and slowly into the water, but soon returned and placed himself in his former position, looking at me and seeming neither fearful or any way disturbed. I soon dispatched him by lodging the contents of my gun in his head, and then proceeded to cleanse and prepare my fish for supper, and accordingly took them out of the boat, laid them down on the sand close to the water, and began to scale them, when, raising my head, I saw before me, through the clear water, the head and shoulders of a very large alligator, moving slowly towards me; I instantly stepped back, when, with a sweep of his tail, he brushed off several of my fish. It was certainly most providential that I looked up at that instant, as the monster would probably, in less than a minute, have seized and dragged me into the river. This incredible boldness of the animal disturbed me greatly, supposing there could now be no reasonable safety for me during the night, but by keeping continually on the watch; I, therefore, as soon as I had prepared the fish, proceeded to secure myself and effects in the best manner I could: in the first place, I hauled my bark upon the shore, almost clear out of the water, to prevent their oversetting or sinking her, after this every moveable was taken out and carried to my camp, which was but a few yards off; then ranging some dry wood in such order as was the most convenient, cleared the ground round about it, that there might be no impediment in my way, in case of an attack in the night, either from the water or the land; for I discovered by this time, that this small isthmus, from its remote situation and fruitfulness, was resorted to by bears and wolves. Having prepared myself in the best manner I could, I charged my gun and proceeded to reconnoitre my camp and the adjacent grounds; when I discovered that the peninsula and grove, at the distance of about two hundred yards from my encampment, on the land side, were invested by a Cypress swamp, covered with water, which below was joined to the shore of the little lake, and above to the marshes surrounding the lagoon, so that I was confined to an islet exceedingly circumscribed, and I found there was no other retreat for me, in case of an attack, but by either ascending one of the large Oaks, or pushing off with my boat.

It was by this time dusk, and the alligators had nearly ceased their roar, when I was again alarmed by a tumultuous noise that seemed to be in my harbour, and therefore engaged my immediate attention. Returning to my camp I found it undisturbed, and then continued on to the extreme point of the promontory, where I saw a scene, new and surprising, which at first threw my senses into such a tumult, that it was some time before I could comprehend what was the matter; however, I soon accounted for the pro-digious assemblage of crocodiles at this place, which exceeded every thing of the kind I had ever heard of.

How shall I express myself so as to convey an adequate idea of it to the reader, and at the same time avoid raising suspicions of my want of veracity. Should I say, that the river (in this place) from shore to shore, and perhaps near half a mile above and below me, appeared to be one solid bank of fish, of various kinds, pushing through this narrow pass of St. Juans into the little lake, on their return down the river, and that the alligators were in such incredible numbers, and so close together from shore to shore, that it would have been easy to have walked across on their heads, had the animals been harmless. What expressions can sufficiently declare the shock-ing scene that for some minutes continued, whilst this mighty army of fish were forcing the pass? During this attempt, thousands, I may say hundreds of thousands of them were caught and swallowed by the devour-ing alligators. I have seen an alligator take up out of the water several great fish at a time, and just squeeze them betwixt his jaws, while the tails of the great trout flapped about his eyes and lips, ere he had swallowed them. The horrid noise of their closing jaws, their plunging amidst the broken banks of fish, and rising with their prey some feet upright above the water, the floods of water and blood rushing out of their mouths, and the clouds of vapour issuing from their wide nostrils, were truly frightful. This scene continued at intervals during the night, as the fish came to the pass. After this sight, shocking and tremendous as it was, I found myself somewhat easier and more reconciled to my situation, being convinced that their ex-traordinary assemblage here, was owing to this annual feast of fish, and that they were so well employed in their own element, that I had little occasion to fear their paying me a visit.

It being now almost night, I returned to my camp, where I had left my fish broiling, and my kettle of rice stewing, and having with me, oil, pepper and salt, and excellent oranges hanging in abundance over my head (a valuable substitute for vinegar) I sat down and regaled myself chearfully; having finished my repast, I re-kindled my fire for light, and whilst I was revising the notes of my past day's journey, I was suddenly roused with a noise behind me toward the main land; I sprang up on my feet, and listening, I distinctly heard some creature wading in the water of the isthmus; I seized my gun and went cautiously from my camp, directing my steps towards the noise; when I had advanced about thirty yards, I halted behind a coppice of Orange trees, and soon perceived two very large bears, which had made their way through the water, and had landed in the grove, about one hundred yards distance from me, and were advancing towards me. I waited until they were within thirty yards of me, they there began to snuff and look towards my camp, I snapped my piece, but it flashed, on which they both turned about and galloped off, plunging through the water and swamp, never halting as I suppose, until they reached fast land, as I could hear them leaping and plunging a long time; they did not presume to return again, nor was I molested by any other creature, except being occasionally awakened by the whooping of owls, screaming of bitterns, or the wood-rats running amongst the leaves.

The wood-rat is a very curious animal, they are not half the size of the domestic rat; of a dark brown or black colour; their tail slender and shorter in proportion, and covered thinly with short hair; they are singular with respect to their ingenuity and great labour in the construction of their habitations, which are conical pyramids about three or four feet high, constructed with dry branches, which they collect with great labour and perseverance, and pile up without any apparent order, yet they are so interwoven with one another, that it would take a bear or wild-cat some time to pull one of these castles to pieces, and allow the animals sufficient time to secure a retreat with their young.

The noise of the crocodiles kept me awake the greater part of the night, but when I arose in the morning, contrary to my expectations, there was perfect peace; very few of them to be seen, and those were asleep on the shore, yet I was not able to suppress my fears and apprehensions of being attacked by them in future; and indeed yesterday's combat with them, notwithstanding I came off in a manner victorious, or at least made a safe retreat, had left sufficient impression on my mind to damp my courage, and it seemed too much for one of my strength, being alone in a very small boat to encounter such collected danger. To pursue my voyage up the river, and be obliged every evening to pass such dangerous defiles, appeared to me as perilous as running the gauntlet betwixt two rows of Indians armed with knives and fire brands; I however resolved to continue my voyage one day longer, if I possibly could with safety, and then return down the river, should I find the like difficulties to oppose. Accordingly I got every thing on board, charged my gun, and set sail cautiously along shore; as I passed by Battle lagoon, I began to tremble and keep a good look out, when suddenly a huge alligator rushed out of the reeds, and with a tremendous roar, came up, and darted as swift as an arrow under my boat, emerging upright on my lea quarter, with open jaws, and belching water and smoke that fell upon me like rain in a hurricane; I laid soundly about his head with my club and beat him off, and after plunging and darting about my boat, he went off on a strait line through the water, seemingly with the rapidity of lightning, and entered the cape of the lagoon; I now employed my time to the very best advantage in paddling close along shore, but could not forbear looking now and then behind me, and presently perceived one of them coming up again; the water of the river hereabouts, was shoal and very clear, the monster came up with the usual roar and menaces, and passed close by the side of my boat, when I could distinctly see a young brood of alligators to the number of one hundred or more, following after her in a long train, they kept close together in a column without straggling off to the one side or the other, the young appeared to be of an equal size, about fifteen inches in length, almost black, with pale yellow transverse waved clouds or blotches, much like rattle snakes in colour. I now lost sight of my enemy again.

Still keeping close along shore; on turning a point or projection of the river bank, at once I beheld a great number of hillocks or small pyramids, resembling hay cocks, ranged like an encampment along the banks, they stood fifteen or twenty yards distant from the water, on a high marsh, about four feet perpendicular above the water; I knew them to be the nests of the crocodile, having had a description of them before, and now expected a furious and general attack, as I saw several large crocodiles swimming abreast of these buildings. These nests being so great a curiosity to me, I was determined at all events immediately to land and examine them. Accordingly I ran my bark on shore at one of their landing places, which was a sort of nick or little dock, from which ascended a sloping path or road up to the edge of the meadow, where their nests were, most of them were deserted, and the great thick whitish egg-shells lay broken and scattered upon the ground round about them.

The nests or hillocks are of the form of an obtuse cone, four feet high and four or five feet in diameter at their bases; they are constructed with mud, grass and herbage: at first they lay a floor of this kind of tempered mortar upon the ground, upon which they deposit a layer of eggs, and upon this a stratum of mortar seven or eight inches in thickness, and then another layer of eggs, and in this manner one stratum upon another, nearly to the top: I believe they commonly lay from one to two hundred eggs in a nest: these are hatched I suppose by the heat of the sun, and perhaps the vegetable substances mixed with the earth, being acted upon by the sun, may cause a small degree of fermentation, and so increase the heat in those hillocks. The ground for several acres about these nests showed evident marks of a continual resort of alligators; the grass was everywhere beaten down, hardly a blade or straw was left standing; whereas, all about, at a distance, it was five or six feet high, and as thick as it could grow together. The female, as I imagine, carefully watches her own nest of eggs until they are all hatched, or perhaps while she is attending her own brood, she takes under her care and protection, as many as she can get at one time, either from her own particular nest or others: but certain it is, that the young are not left to shift for themselves, having had frequent opportunities of seeing the female alligator, leading about the shores her train of young ones, just like a hen does her chickens, and she is equally assiduous and courageous in defending the young, which are under her care, and providing for their subsistence; and when she is basking upon the warm banks, with her brood around her, you may hear the young ones continually whining and barking, like young puppies. I believe but few of the brood live to the years of full growth and magnitude, as the old feed on the young as long as they can make prey of them.

The alligator when full grown is a very large and terrible creature, and of prodigious strength, activity and swiftness in the water. I have seen them twenty feet in length, and some are supposed to be twenty-two or twenty-three feet; their body is as large as that of a horse; their shape exactly resembles that of a lizard, except their tail, which is flat or cuniform, being compressed on each side, and gradually diminishing from the abdomen to the extremity, which, with the whole body is covered with horny plates or squammae, impenetrable when on the body of the live animal, even to a rifle ball, except about their head and just behind their fore-legs or arms, where it is said they are only vulnerable. The head of a full grown one is about three feet, and the mouth opens nearly the same length, the eyes are small in proportion and seem sunk deep in the head, by means of the prominency of the brows; the nostrils are large, inflated and prominent on the top, so that the head in the water, resembles, at a distance, a great chunk of wood floating about. Only the upper jaw moves, which they raise almost perpendicular, so as to form a right angle with the lower one. In the fore part of the upper jaw, on each side, just under the nostrils, are two very large, thick, strong teeth or tusks, not very sharp, but rather the shape of a cone, these are as white as the finest polished ivory, and are not covered by any skin or lips, and always in sight, which gives the creature a frightful appearance; in the lower jaw are holes opposite to these teeth, to receive them; when they clap their jaws together it causes a surprising noise, like that which is made by forcing a heavy plank with violence upon the ground, and may be heard at a great distance.

But what is yet more surprising to a stranger, is the incredible loud and terrifying roar, which they are capable of making, especially in the spring season, their breeding time; it most resembles very heavy distant thunder, not only shaking the air and waters, but causing the earth to tremble; and when hundreds and thousands are roaring at the same time, you can scarcely be persuaded, but that the whole globe is violently and dangerously agitated.

An old champion, who is perhaps absolute sovereign of a little lake or lagoon (when fifty less than himself are obliged to content themselves with swelling and roaring in little coves round about) darts forth from the reedy coverts all at once, on the surface of the waters, in a right line; at first seemingly as swift as lightning, but gradually more slowly until he arrives at the center of the lake, when he stops; he now swells himself by drawing in wind and water through his mouth, which causes a loud sonorous rattling in the throat for near a minute, but it is immediately forced out again through his mouth and nostrils, with a loud noise, brandishing his tail in the air, and the vapour ascending from his nostrils like smoke. At other times, when swollen to an extent ready to burst, his head and tail lifted up, he spins or twirls round on the surface of the water. He acts his part like an Indian chief, when rehearsing his feats of war, and then retiring, the exhibition is continued by others who dare to step forth, and strive to excel each other, to gain the attention of the favorite female.

Having gratified my curiosity at this general breeding place and nursery of crocodiles, I continued my voyage up the river without being greatly disturbed by them.

The Travels, 1791

THOMAS JEFFERSON

"The Unalienable Rights of Man"

This brief letter sums up, as well as any single short piece can, the core of the political philosophy that exercised so profound an influence on the founding of the nation.

. . . You will perceive by these details, that we have not yet so far perfected our constitutions as to venture to make them unchangeable. But still, in their present state, we consider them not otherwise changeable than by the authority of the people, on a special election of representatives for that purpose expressly: they are until then the *lex legum.*

But can they be made unchangeable? Can one generation bind another, and all others, in succession forever? I think not. The Creator has made the earth for the living, not the dead. Rights and powers can only belong to persons, not to things, not to mere matter, unendowed with will. The dead are not even things. The particles of matter which composed their bodies, make part now of the bodies of other animals, vegetables, or min-

176

erals, of a thousand forms. To what then are attached the rights and powers they held while in the form of men? A generation may bind itself as long as its majority is in place, holds all the rights and powers their predecessors once held, and may change their laws and institutions to suit themselves. Nothing then is unchangeable but the inherent and unalienable rights of man.

Letter to John Cartwright, June 5, 1824

CHIEF JUSTICE JOHN MARSHALL

"The Government of All"

> *Jefferson seriously disagreed with Chief Justice Marshall about the function and power of the Supreme Court. Gradually, however, Marshall's view prevailed as the court laid the constitutional basis for the expanding authority of the federal government.*

If any one proposition could command the universal assent of mankind, we might expect it would be this: that the government of the Union, though limited in its powers, is supreme within its sphere of action. This would seem to result necessarily from its nature. It is the government of all; its powers are delegated by all; it represents all, and acts for all. Though any one State may be willing to control its operations, no State is willing to allow others to control them. The nation, on those subjects on which it can act, must necessarily bind its component parts. But this question is not left to mere reason: the people have, in express terms, decided it, by saying, "this Constitution, and the laws of the United States, which shall be made in pursuance thereof," "shall be the supreme law of the land," and by requiring that the members of the State legislatures, and the officers of the executive and judicial departments of the States, shall take the oath of fidelity to it.

The government of the United States, then, though limited in its powers, is supreme; and its laws, when made in pursuance of the Constitution, form the supreme law of the land, "anything in the constitution or laws of any State to the contrary notwithstanding."

M'Culloch v. Maryland, 1819

"A Single Nation"

. . . A constitution is framed for ages to come and is designed to approach immortality as nearly as human institutions can approach it. Its course cannot always be tranquil. It is exposed to storms and tempests, and its

177

framers must be unwise statesmen indeed if they have not provided it, so far as its nature will permit, with the means of self-preservation from the perils it may be destined to encounter.

No government ought to be so defective in its organization as not to contain within itself the means of securing the execution of its own laws against other dangers than those which occur every day. . . .

That the United States form, for many and for most important purposes, a single nation, has not yet been denied. In war we are one people. In making peace we are one people. In all commercial regulations we are one and the same people. In many other respects the American people are one, and the government which is alone capable of controlling and managing their interests in all these respects is the government of the Union. It is their government, and in that character they have no other. America has chosen to be, in many respects, and to many purposes, a nation; and for all these purposes her government is complete; to all these objects it is compctent. The people have declared that in the exercise of all the powers given for these objects it is supreme. It can, then, in effecting these objects, legitimately control all individuals or governments within the American territory. The constitution and laws of a State, so far as they are repugnant to the Constitution and laws of the United States, are absolutely void. These States are constituent parts of the United States. They are members of one great empire—for some purposes sovereign, for some purposes subordinate.

Cohens v. Virginia, 1821

AUGUSTUS B. LONGSTREET

The Horse-Swap

> *Although now remembered only for his sketches of native humor, Longstreet was a successful practicing attorney in Georgia, a member of the legislature, a judge, a Methodist minister and president of four different colleges.*

During the session of the Supreme Court, in the village of ——, about three weeks ago, when a number of people were collected in the principal street of the village, I observed a young man riding up and down the street, as I supposed, in a violent passion. He galloped this way, then that, and then the other; spurred his horse to one group of citizens, then to another;

178

then dashed off at half-speed, as if fleeing from danger; and, suddenly checking his horse, returned first in a pace, then in a trot, and then in a canter. While he was performing these various evolutions, he cursed, swore, whooped, screamed, and tossed himself in every attitude which man could assume on horseback. In short, he *cavorted* most magnanimously (a term which, in our tongue, expresses all that I have described, and a little more), and seemed to be setting all creation at defiance. As I like to see all that is passing, I determined to take a position a little nearer to him, and to ascertain, if possible, what it was that affected him so sensibly. Accordingly, I approached a crowd before which he had stopped for a moment, and examined it with the strictest scrutiny. But I could see nothing in it that seemed to have anything to do with the cavorter. Every man appeared to be in good humour, and all minding their own business. Not one so much as noticed the principal figure. Still he went on. After a semicolon pause, which my appearance seemed to produce (for he eyed me closely as I approached), he fetched a whoop, and swore that "he could out-swap any man alive, woman, or child, that ever walked these hills, or that ever straddled horseflesh since the days of old daddy Adam. Stranger," said he to me, "did you ever see the Yellow Blossom from Jasper?"

"No," said I, "but I have often heard of him."

"I'm the boy," continued he; "perhaps a *leetle*, *jist a leetle*, of the best man at a horse-swap that ever trod shoe leather."

I began to feel my situation a little awkward, when I was relieved by a man somewhat advanced in years, who stepped up and began to survey the Yellow Blossom's horse with much apparent interest. This drew the rider's attention, and he turned the conversation from me to the stranger.

"Well, my old coon," said he, "do you want to swap *hosses?*"

"Why, I don't know," replied the stranger; "I believe I've got a beast I'd trade with you for that one, if you like him."

"Well, fetch up your nag, my old cock; you're jist the lark I wanted to get hold of. I am perhaps a *leetle*, *jist a leetle*, of the best man at a horse-swap that ever stole *cracklins* out of his mammy's fat gourd. Where's your *hoss?*"

"I'll bring him presently; but I want to examine your horse a little."

"Oh! look at him," said the Blossom alighting and hitting him a cut— "look at him! He's the best piece of *hoss*flesh in the thirteen united universal worlds. There's no sort o' mistake in little Bullet. He can pick up miles on his feet, and fling 'em behind him as fast as the next man's *hoss*, I don't care where he comes from. And he can keep at it as long as the sun can shine without resting."

During this harangue, little Bullet looked as if he understood it all, believed it, and was ready at any moment to verify it. He was a horse of goodly countenance, rather expressive of vigilance than fire; though an

179

unnatural appearance of fierceness was thrown into it by the loss of his ears, which had been cropped pretty close to his head. Nature had done but little for Bullet's head and neck; but he managed, in a great measure, to hide the defects by bowing perpetually. He had obviously suffered severely for corn; but if his ribs and hip bones had not disclosed the fact, *he* never would have done it; for he was in all respects as cheerful and happy as if he commanded all the corn-cribs and fodder-stacks in Georgia. His height was about twelve hands; but as his shape partook somewhat that of the giraffe, his haunches stood much lower. They were short, strait, peaked, and concave. Bullet's tail, however, made amends for all his defects. All that the artist could do to beautify it had been done; and all that horse could do to compliment the artist, Bullet did. His tail was nicked in superior style, and exhibited the line of beauty in so many directions, that it could not fail to hit the most fastidious taste in some of them. From the root it dropped into a graceful festoon, then rose in a handsome curve, then resumed its first direction, and then mounted suddenly upward like a cypress knee to a perpendicular of about two and a half inches. The whole had a careless and bewitching inclination to the right. Bullet obviously knew where his beauty lay, and took all occasions to display it to the best advantage. If a stick cracked, or if any one moved suddenly about him, or coughed, or hawked, or spoke a little louder than common, up went Bullet's tail like lightning; and if the *going up* did not please, the *coming down* must of necessity, for it was as different from the other movement as was its direction. The first was a bold and rapid flight upward, usually to an angle of forty-five degrees. In this position he kept his interesting appendage until he satisfied himself that nothing in particular was to be done; when he commenced dropping it by half inches, in second beats, then in triple time, then faster and shorter, and faster and shorter still, until it finally died away imperceptibly into its natural position. If I might compare sights to sounds, I should say its *settling* was more like the note of a locust than anything else in nature.

Either from native sprightliness of disposition, from uncontrollable activity, or from an unconquerable habit of removing flies by the stamping of the feet, Bullet never stood still; but always kept up a gentle fly-scaring movement of his limbs, which was peculiarly interesting.

"I tell you, man," proceeded the Yellow Blossom, "he's the best live hoss that ever trod the grit of Georgia. Bob Smart knows the hoss. Come here, Bob, and mount this hoss, and show Bullet's motions." Here Bullet bristled up, and looked as if he had been hunting for Bob all day long, and had just found him. Bob sprang on his back. "Boo-oo-oo!" said Bob, with a fluttering noise of the lips, and away went Bullet, as if in a quarter race, with all his beauties spread in handsome style.

"Now fetch him back," said Blossom. Bullet turned and came in pretty much as he went out.

"Now trot him by." Bullet reduced his tail to *"customary"*; sidled to the right and left airily, and exhibited at least three varieties of trot in the short space of fifty yards.

"Make him pace!" Bob commenced twitching the bridle and kicking at the same time. These inconsistent movements obviously (and most naturally) disconcerted Bullet; for it was impossible for him to learn, from them, whether he was to proceed or stand still. He started to trot, and was told that wouldn't do. He attempted a canter, and was checked again. He stopped, and was urged to go on. Bullet now rushed into the wide field of experiment, and struck out a gait of his own, that completely turned the tables upon his rider, and certainly deserved a patent. It seemed to have derived its elements from the jig, the minuet, and the cotillion. If it was not a pace, it certainly had *pace* in it, and no man would venture to call it anything else; so it passed off to the satisfaction of the owner.

"Walk him!" Bullet was now at home again, and he walked as if money were staked on him.

The stranger, whose name I afterwards learned was Peter Ketch, having examined Bullet to his heart's content, ordered his son Neddy to go and bring up Kit. Neddy soon appeared upon Kit, a well-formed sorrel of the middle size, and in good order. His *tout ensemble* threw Bullet entirely in the shade, though a glance was sufficient to satisfy any one that Bullet had the decided advantage of him in point of intellect.

"Why, man," said Blossom, "do you bring such a hoss as that to trade for Bullet? Oh, I see, you've no notion of trading."

"Ride him off, Neddy!" said Peter. Kit put off at a handsome lope.

"Trot him back!" Kit came in at a long, sweeping trot, and stopped suddenly at the crowd.

"Well," said Blossom, "let me look at him; maybe he'll do to plough."

"Examine him!" said Peter, taking hold of the bridle close to the mouth; "he's nothing but a tacky. He an't as *pretty* a horse as Bullet, I know; but he'll do. Start 'em together for a hundred and fifty *mile*; and if Kit an't twenty mile ahead of him at the coming out, any man may take Kit for nothing. But he's a monstrous mean horse, gentlemen; any man may see that. He's the scariest horse, too, you ever saw. He won't do to hunt on, no how. Stranger, will you let Neddy have your rifle to shoot off him? Lay the rifle between his ears, Neddy, and shoot at the blaze in that stump. Tell me when his head is high enough."

Ned fired and hit the blaze; and Kit did not move a hair's breadth.

"Neddy, take a couple of sticks, and beat on that hogshead at Kit's tail."

Ned made a tremendous rattling, at which Bullet took fright, broke his bridle, and dashed off in grand style; and would have stopped all further negotiations by going home in disgust, had not a traveller arrested him and brought him back; but Kit did not move.

"I tell you, gentlemen," continued Peter, "he's the scariest horse you ever saw. He an't as gentle as Bullet, but he won't do any harm if you watch him. Shall I put him in a cart, gig, or wagon for you, stranger? He'll cut the same capers there he does here. He's a monstrous mean horse."

During all this time Blossom was examining him with the nicest scrutiny. Having examined his frame and limbs, he now looked at his eyes.

"He's got a curious look out of his eyes," said Blossom.

"Oh yes, sir," said Peter, "just as blind as a bat. Blind horses always have clear eyes. Make a motion at his eyes, if you please, sir."

Blossom did so, and Kit threw up his head rather as if something pricked him under the chin than as if fearing a blow. Blossom repeated the experiment, and Kit jerked back in considerable astonishment.

"Stone blind, you see, gentlemen," proceeded Peter; "but he's just as good to travel of a dark night as if he had eyes."

"Blame my buttons," said Blossom, "if I like them eyes."

"No," said Peter, "nor I neither. I'd rather have 'em made of diamonds; but they'll do—if they don't show as much white as Bullet's."

"Well," said Blossom, "make a pass at me."

"No," said Peter; "you made the banter, now make your pass."

"Well, I'm never afraid to price my hosses. You must give me twenty-five dollars boot."

"Oh, certainly; say fifty, and my saddle and bridle in. Here, Neddy, my son, take away daddy's horse."

"Well," said Blossom, "I've made my pass, now you make yours."

"I'm for short talk in a horse-swap, and therefore always tell a gentleman at once what I mean to do. You must give me ten dollars."

Blossom swore absolutely, roundly, and profanely that he never would give boot.

"Well," said Peter, "I didn't care about trading; but you cut such high shines that I thought I'd like to back you out, and I've done it. Gentlemen, you see I've brought him to a hack."

"Come, old man," said Blossom, "I've been joking with you. I begin to think you do want to trade; therefore, give me five dollars and take Bullet. I'd rather lose ten dollars any time than not make a trade, though I hate to fling away a good hoss."

"Well," said Peter, "I'll be as clever as you are. Just put the five dollars on Bullet's back, and hand him over; it's a trade."

Blossom swore again, as roundly as before, that he would not give boot; and, said he, "Bullet wouldn't hold five dollars on his back, no how. But, as I bantered you, if you say an even swap, here's at you."

"I told you," said Peter, "I'd be as clever as you, therefore, here goes two dollars more, just for trade sake. Give me three dollars, and it's a bargain."

Blossom repeated his former assertion; and here the parties stood for a long time, and the by-standers (for many were now collected) began to taunt both parties. After some time, however, it was pretty unanimously decided that the old man had backed Blossom out.

At length Blossom swore he "never would be backed out for three dollars after bantering a man"; and, accordingly, they closed the trade.

"Now," said Blossom, as he handed Peter the three dollars, "I'm a man that, when he makes a bad trade, makes the most of it until he can make a better. I'm for no rues and after-claps."

"That's just my way," said Peter; "I never goes to law to mend my bargains."

"Ah, you're the kind of boy I love to trade with. Here's your hoss, old man. Take the saddle and bridle off him, and I'll strip yours; but lift up the blanket easy from Bullet's back, for he's a mighty tender-backed hoss."

The old man removed the saddle, but the blanket stuck fast. He attempted to raise it, and Bullet bowed himself, switched his tail, danced a little, and gave signs of biting.

"Don't hurt him, old man," said Blossom, archly; "take it off easy. I am, perhaps, a leetle of the best man at a horse-swap that ever catched a coon."

Peter continued to pull at the blanket more and more roughly, and Bullet became more and more *cavortish*; insomuch that, when the blanket came off, he had reached the *kicking* point in good earnest.

The removal of the blanket disclosed a sore on Bullet's back-bone that seemed to have defied all medical skill. It measured six full inches in length and four in breadth, and had as many features as Bullet had motions. My heart sickened at the sight; and I felt that the brute who had been riding him in that situation deserved the halter.

The prevailing feeling, however, was that of mirth. The laugh became loud and general at the old man's expense, and rustic witticisms were liberally bestowed upon him and his late purchase. These Blossom continued to provoke by various remarks. He asked the old man "if he thought Bullet would let five dollars lie on his back." He declared most seriously that he had owned the horse three months, and had never discovered that he had a sore back, "or he never should have thought of trading him," &c., &c.

The old man bore it all with the most philosophic composure. He evinced no astonishment at his late discovery, and made no replies. But his son Neddy had not disciplined his feelings quite so well. His eyes opened wider and wider from the first to the last pull of the blanket; and, when the whole sore burst upon his view, astonishment and fright seemed to contend for the mastery of his countenance. As the blanket disappeared, he stuck his hands in his breeches pockets, heaved a deep sigh, and lapsed into a profound revery, from which he was only roused by the cuts at his father. He bore them as long as he could; and, when he could contain himself no longer, he began, with a certain wildness of expression which gave a peculiar interest to what he uttered: "His back's mighty bad off; but dod drot my soul if he's put to daddy as bad as he thinks he has, for old Kit's both blind and *deef*, I'll be dod drot if he eint."

"The devil he is," said Blossom.

"Yes, dod drot my soul if he *eint*. You walk him, and see if he *eint*. His eyes don't look like it; but he'd *jist as leve go agin* the house with you, or in a ditch, as any how. Now you go try him." The laugh was now turned on Blossom; and many rushed to test the fidelity of the little boy's report. A few experiments established its truth beyond controversy.

"Neddy," said the old man, "you oughtn't to try and make people discontented with their things. Stranger, don't mind what the little boy says. If you can only get Kit rid of them little failings, you'll find him all sorts of a horse. You are a *leetle* the best man at a horse-swap that ever I got hold of; but don't fool away Kit. Come, Neddy, my son, let's be moving; the stranger seems to be getting snappish."

Georgia Scenes, 1835

JOHN JAMES AUDUBON

The Mocking-Bird

A widely cultivated country gentleman of small means, Audubon spent twenty years on the American frontier studying, drawing and making notes on bird and animal life. But he had to go to England to get his first volume published. American then claimed him as its greatest naturalist.

It is where the great magnolia shoots up its majestic trunk, crowned with evergreen leaves, and decorated with a thousand beautiful flowers that perfume the air around; where the forests and fields are adorned with blossoms of every hue; where the golden orange ornaments the gardens and the groves; where bigonias of various kinds interlace their climbing stems around the white-flowered stuartia, and mounting still higher, cover the summits of the lofty trees around, accompanied with innumerable vines that here and there festoon the dense foliage of a magnificent woods, lending to the vernal breeze a slight portion of the perfume of their clustered flowers; where a genial warmth seldom forsakes the atmosphere; where berries and fruits of all descriptions are met with at every step;—in a word, kind reader, it is where Nature seems to have paused, as she passed over the earth, and opening her stores, to have strewed with unsparing hand the diversified seeds from which have sprung all the beautiful and splendid forms which I should in vain attempt to describe, that the mocking-bird should have fixed his abode, there only that its wondrous song should be heard.

But where is that favoured land? It is in that great continent to whose distant shores Europe has sent forth her adventurous sons, to wrest for themselves a habitation from the wild inhabitants of the forest, and to convert the neglected soil into fields of exuberant fertility. It is, reader, in Louisiana that these bounties of Nature are in the greatest perfection. It is there that you should listen to the love-song of the mocking-bird, as I at this moment do. See how he flies round his mate, with motions as light as those of the butterfly! His tail is widely expanded, he mounts in the air to a small distance, describes a circle, and, again alighting, approaches his beloved one, his eyes gleaming with delight, for she has already promised to be his and his only. His beautiful wings are gently raised, he bows to his love, and again bouncing upwards, opens his bill, and pours forth his melody, full of exultation at the conquest which he has made.

They are not the soft sounds of the flute or the hautboy that I hear, but the sweeter notes of Nature's own music. The mellowness of the song, the varied modulations and gradations, the extent of its compass, the great brilliancy of execution, are unrivalled. There is probably no bird in the world that possesses all the musical qualifications of this king of song, who has derived all from Nature's self. Yes, reader, all!

No sooner has he again alighted near his mate than, as if his breast was about to be rent with delight, he again pours forth his notes with more softness and richness than before. He now soars higher, glancing with a vigilant eye, to assure himself that none has witnessed his bliss. When these love scenes are over, he dances through the air, full of animation and delight, and, as if to convince his lovely mate that to enrich her hopes he has much more love in store, he that moment begins anew, and imitates all the notes which Nature has imparted to the other songsters of the grove.

For a while, each long day and pleasant night are thus spent. A nest is to be prepared, and the choice of a place in which to lay it is to become a matter of mutual consideration. The orange, the fig, the pear-tree of the gardens are inspected; the thick briar patches are also visited. They appear all so well suited for the purpose in view, and so well do the birds know that man is not their most dangerous enemy, that, instead of retiring from him, they at length fix their abode in his vicinity, perhaps in the nearest tree to his window. Dried twigs, leaves, grasses, cotton, flax, and other substances are picked up, carried to a forked branch, and there arranged. Five eggs are deposited in due time, when the male, having little more to do than to sing his mate to repose, attunes his pipe anew. Every now and then he spies an insect on the ground, the taste of which he is sure will please his beloved one. He drops upon it, takes it in his bill, beats it against the earth, and flies to the nest to feed and receive the warm thanks of his devoted female. . . .

In winter, nearly all the mocking-birds approach the farmhouses and plantations, living about the gardens or outhouses. They are then frequently seen on the roofs, and perched on the chimney-tops; yet they always appear full of animation. Whilst searching for food on the ground, their motions are light and elegant, and they frequently open their wings as butterflies do when basking in the sun, moving a step or two, and again throwing out their wings. When the weather is mild, the old males are heard singing with as much spirit as during the spring or summer, while the younger birds are busily engaged in practicing, preparatory to the love season. They seldom resort to the interior of the forest during the day or by night, but usually roost among the foliage of evergreens, in the immediate vicinity of houses in Louisiana, although in the Eastern States they prefer low fir trees.

The flight of the mocking-bird is performed by short jerks of the body and wings, at every one of which a strong twitching motion of the tail is perceived. This motion is still more apparent while the bird is walking, when it opens its tail like a fan and instantly closes it again. . . . When travelling, this flight is only a little prolonged, as the bird goes from tree to tree, or at most across a field, scarcely, if ever, rising higher than the top of the forest. During this migration, it generally resorts to the highest parts of the woods near water-courses, utters its usual mournful note, and roosts in these places. It travels mostly by day. . . .

The musical powers of this bird have often been taken notice of by European naturalists, and persons who find pleasure in listening to the song of different birds whilst in confinement or at large. Some of these persons have described the notes of the Nightingale as occasionally fully equal to those of our bird. I have frequently heard both species, in confinement and in the wild state, and without prejudice have no hesitation in pronouncing the notes of the European philomel equal to those of a soubrette of taste, which, could she study under Mozart, might perhaps in time become very interesting in her way. But to compare her essays to the finished talent of the mocking-bird is, in my opinion, quite absurd.

Ornithological Biographies, 1839

EDGAR ALLAN POE

To Helen

Helen, thy beauty is to me
    Like those Nicean barks of yore,
That gently, o'er a perfumed sea,
    The weary, wayworn wanderer bore
To his own native shore.

On desperate seas long wont to roam,
    Thy hyacinth hair, thy classic face,
Thy Naiad airs, have brought me home
    To the Glory that was Greece
And the grandeur that was Rome.

Lo! in yon brilliant window-niche
How statue-like I see thee stand,
The agate lamp within thy hand!
Ah, Psyche, from the regions which
Are Holy Land!

Poems, 1831

Ligeia

And the will therein lieth, which dieth not. Who knoweth the mysteries of the will, with its vigor? For God is but a great will pervading all things by nature of its intentness. Man doth not yield himself to the angels, nor unto death utterly, save only through the weakness of his feeble will.—Joseph Glanvill

I cannot, for my soul, remember how, when, or even precisely where, I first became acquainted with the lady Ligeia. Long years have since elapsed, and my memory is feeble through much suffering. Or, perhaps, I cannot *now* bring these points to mind, because, in truth, the character of my beloved, her rare learning, her singular yet placid cast of beauty, and the thrilling and enthralling eloquence of her low musical language, made their way into my heart by paces so steadily and stealthily progressive that they have been unnoticed and unknown. Yet I believe I met her first and most frequently in some large, old decaying city near the Rhine. Of her family—I have surely heard her speak. That it is of a remotely ancient date cannot be doubted. Ligeia! Ligeia! Buried in studies of a nature more than all else adapted to deaden impressions of the outward world, it is by that sweet word alone—by Ligeia—that I bring before mine eyes in fancy the image of her who is no more. And now, while I write, a recollection flashes upon me that I have *never known* the paternal name of her who was my friend and my betrothed, and who became the partner of my studies, and finally the wife of my bosom. Was it a playful charge on the part of my Ligeia? or was it a test of my strength of affection, that I should institute no inquiries upon this point? or was it rather a caprice of my own—a wildly romantic offering on the shrine of the most passionate devotion? I but indistinctly recall the fact myself—what wonder that I have utterly forgotten the circumstances which originated or attended it? And, indeed, if ever that spirit which is entitled *Romance*—if ever she, the wan and misty winged *Astophet* of idolatrous Egypt, presided, as they tell, over marriages ill-omened, then most surely she presided over mine.

There is one dear topic, however, on which my memory fails me not. It is the *person* of Ligeia. In stature she was tall, somewhat slender, and, in her latter days, even emaciated. I would in vain attempt to portray the majesty, the quiet ease, of her demeanor, or the incomprehensible lightness and elasticity of her footfall. She came and departed as a shadow. I was never made aware of her entrance into my closed study save by the dear music of her low sweet voice, as she placed her marble hand upon my shoulder. In beauty of face no maiden ever equalled her. It was the radiance of an opium dream—an airy and spirit-lifting vision more wildly divine that the phantasies which hovered about the slumbering souls of the daughters of Delos. Yet her features were not of that regular mould which we have been falsely taught to worship in the classical labors of the heathen. "There is no exquisite beauty," said Bacon, Lord Verulam, speaking truly of all forms and *genera* of beauty, "without some *strangeness* in the proportion." Yet, although I saw that the features of Ligeia were not of a classic regularity—although I perceived that her loveliness was indeed "exquisite," and felt that there was much of "strangeness" pervading it, yet I have tried in vain to detect the irregularity and to trace home my own perception of "the strange." I examined the contours of the lofty and pale forehead—it was faultless—how cold indeed that word when applied to a majesty so divine!—the skin rivaling the purest ivory, the commanding extent and repose, the gentle prominence of the regions above the temples; and then the raven-black, the glossy, the luxuriant and naturally curling tresses, setting forth the full force of the Homeric epithet, "hyacinthe"! I looked at the delicate outlines of the nose—and nowhere but in the graceful medallions of the Hebrews had I beheld a similar perfection. There was the same luxurious smoothness of surface, the same scarcely perceptible tendency to the aquiline, the same harmoniously curved nostrils speaking the free spirit. I regarded the sweet mouth. Here was indeed the triumph of all things heavenly—the magnificent turn of the short upper lip—the soft, voluptuous slumber of the under—the dimples which sported, and the color which spoke—the teeth glancing back, with a brilliancy almost startling, every ray of the holy light which fell upon them in her serene and placid, yet most exultingly radiant of all smiles. I scrutinized the formation of the chin—and here, too, I found the gentleness of breadth, the softness and the majesty, the fullness and the spirituality, of the Greek—the contour which the God Apollo revealed but in a dream, to Cleomenes, the son of the Athenian. And then I peered into the large eyes of Ligeia.

For eyes we have no models in the remotely antique. It might have been, too, that in these eyes of my beloved lay the secret to which Lord Verulam alludes. They were, I must believe, far larger than the ordinary eyes of our own race. They were even fuller than the fullest of the gazelle eyes of the tribe of the valley of Nourjahad. Yet it was only at intervals—in moments of intense excitement—that this peculiarity became more than slightly noticeable in Ligeia. And at such moments was her beauty—in my heated fancy thus it appeared perhaps—the beauty of being either above or apart from the earth—the beauty of the Fabulous Houri of the Turk. The hue of the orbs was the most brilliant of black, and, far over them, hung jetty lashes of great length. The brows, slightly irregular in outline, had the same tint. The "strangeness," however, which I found in the eyes, was of a nature distinct from the formation, or the color, or the brilliancy of the features, and must, after all, be referred to the *expression*. Ah, word of no meaning! behind whose vast latitude of mere sound we intrench our ignorance of so much of the spiritual. The expression of the eyes of Ligeia! How for long hours have I pondered upon it! How have I, through the whole of a midsummer night, struggled to fathom it! What was it—that something more profound than the well of Democritus—which lay far within the pupils of my beloved? What *was* it? I was possessed with a passion to discover. Those eyes! those large, those shining, those divine orbs! they became to me twin stars of Leda, and I to them devoutest of astrologers.

There is no point, among the many incomprehensible anomalies of the science of mind, more thrillingly exciting than the fact—never, I believe, noticed in the schools—that, in our endeavors to recall to memory something long forgotten, we often find ourselves *upon the very verge* of remembrance, without being able, in the end, to remember. And thus how frequently, in my intense scrutiny of Ligeia's eyes, have I felt approaching the full knowledge of their expression—felt it approaching—yet not quite be mine—and so at length entirely depart! And (strange, oh strangest mystery of all!) I found, in the commonest objects of the universe, a circle of analogies to that expression. I mean to say that, subsequently to the period when Ligeia's beauty passed into my spirit, there dwelling as in a shrine, I derived, from many existences in the material world, a sentiment such as I felt always aroused within me by her large and luminous orbs. Yet not the more could I define that sentiment, or analyze, or even steadily view it. I recognized it, let me repeat, sometimes in the survey of a rapidly-growing vine—in the contemplation of a moth, a butterfly, a chrysalis, a stream of running water. I have felt it in the ocean; in the falling of a meteor. I have felt it in the glances of unusually aged people. And there are one or two stars in heaven—(one especially, a star of the sixth magnitude, double and changeable, to be found near the large star in Lyra) in a telescopic scrutiny of which I have been made aware of the feeling. I have been filled with it by certain sounds from stringed instruments, and not unfrequently by passages from books. Among innumerable other instances, I well remember something in a volume of Joseph Glanvill, which (perhaps merely from its quaintness—who shall say?) never failed to inspire me with the sentiment;—"And the will therein lieth, which dieth not. Who knoweth the mysteries of the will, with its vigor? For God is but a great will pervading all things by nature of its intentness. Man doth not yield him to the angels, nor unto death utterly, save only through the weakness of his feeble will."

Length of years, and subsequent reflection, have enabled me to trace, indeed, some remote connection between this passage in the English moralist and a portion of the character of Ligeia. An *intensity* in thought, action, or speech, was possibly, in her, a result, or at least an index of that gigantic volition which, during our long intercourse, failed to give other and more immediate evidence of its existence. Of all the women whom I have ever known, she, the outwardly calm, the ever-placid Ligeia, was the most violently a prey to the tumultuous vultures of stern passion. And of such passion I could form no estimate, save by the miraculous expansion of those eyes which at once so delighted and appalled me—by the almost magical melody, modulation, distinctness, and placidity of her very low voice—and by the fierce energy (rendered doubly effective by contrast with her manner of utterance) of the wild words which she habitually uttered.

I have spoken of the learning of Ligeia: it was immense—such as I have never known in woman. In the classical tongues was she deeply proficient, and as far as my own acquaintance extended in regard to the modern dialects of Europe, I have never known her at fault. Indeed upon any theme of the most admired, because simply the most abstruse of the boasted erudition of the academy, have I *ever* found Ligeia at fault? How singularly—how thrillingly, this one point in the nature of my wife forced itself, at this late period only, upon my attention! I said her knowledge was such as I have never known in woman—but where breathes the man who has traversed, and successfully, *all* the wide areas of moral, physical, and mathematical science: I saw not then what I now clearly perceive, that the acquisitions of Ligeia were gigantic, were astounding; yet I was sufficiently aware of her infinite supremacy to resign myself, with a child-like confidence, to her guidance through the chaotic world of metaphysical investigation at which I was most busily occupied during the earlier years of our marriage. With how vast a triumph—with how vivid a delight—with how much of all that is ethereal in hope—did I *feel*, as she bent over me in studies but little sought—but less known—that delicious vista by slow degrees expanding before me, down whose long, gorgeous, and all untrodden path, I might at length pass onward to the goal of a wisdom too divinely precious not to be forbidden!

How poignant, then, must have been the grief with which, after some years, I beheld my well-grounded expectations take wings to themselves and fly away! Without Ligeia I was but a child groping benighted. Her presence, her readings alone, rendered vividly luminous the many mysteries of the transcendentalism in which we were immersed. Wanting the radiant lustre of her eyes, letters, lambent and golden, grew duller than Saturnian lead. And now those eyes shone less and less frequently upon the pages over which I pored. Ligeia grew ill. The wild-eyes blazed with a too-too glorious effulgence; the pale fingers became of the transparent waxen hue of the grave, and the blue veins upon the lofty forehead swelled and sank impetuously with the tides of the most gentle emotion. I saw that she must die—and I struggled desperately in spirit with the grim Azrael. And the struggles of the passionate wife were, to my astonishment, even more energetic than my own. There had been much in her stern nature to impress me with the belief that, to her, death would have come without its terrors;—but not so. Words are impotent to convey any just idea of the fierceness of the resistance with which she wrestled with the Shadow. I groaned in anguish at the pitiable spectacle. I would have soothed—I would have reasoned; but, in the intensity of her wild desire for life,—for life—*but* for life—solace and reason were alike amid the utmost of folly. Yet not until the last instance, amid the most convulsive writhings of her fierce spirit, was shaken the external placidity of her demeanor. Her voice grew more gentle—grew more low—yet I would not wish to dwell upon the wild meaning of the quietly uttered words. My brain reeled as I hearkened entranced, to a melody more mortal—to assumptions and aspirations which mortality had never before known.

That she loved me I should not have doubted; and I might have been easily aware that, in a bosom such as hers, love would have reigned no ordinary passion. But in death only, was I fully impressed with the strength of her affection. For long hours, detaining my hand, would she pour out before me the overflowing of a heart whose more than passionate devotion amounted to idolatry. How had I deserved to be so blessed by such confessions?—how had I deserved to be so cursed with the removal of my beloved in the hour of her making them? But upon this subject I cannot bear to dilate. Let me say only, that in Ligeia's more than womanly abandonment to a love, alas! all unmerited, all unworthily bestowed, I at length recognized the principle of her longing with so wildly earnest a desire for the life which was now fleeing so rapidly away. It is this wild longing—it is this eager vehemence of desire for life—*but* for life—that I have no power to portray—no utterance capable of expressing.

At high noon of the night in which she departed, beckoning me, peremptorily, to her side, she bade me repeat certain verses composed by herself not many days before. I obeyed her.—They were these:

> *Lo! 'tis a gala night*
> > *Within the lonesome latter years!*
> *An angel throng, bewinged, bedight*
> > *In veils, and drowned in tears,*
> *Sit in a theatre, to see*
> > *A play of hopes and fears,*
> *While the orchestra breathes fitfully*
> > *The music of the spheres.*

> *Mimes, in the form of God on high,*
> > *Mutter and mumble low,*
> *And hither and thither fly—*
> > *Mere puppets they, who come and go*
> *At bidding of vast formless things*
> > *That shift the scenery to and fro,*
> *Flapping from out their Condor wings*
> > *Invisible Woe!*

That motley drama!—oh, be sure
It shall not be forgot!
With its Phantom chased forevermore,
By a crowd that seized it not,
Through a circle that ever returneth in
To the self-same spot,
And much of madness and more of Sin
And Horror the soul of the plot.

But see, amid the mimic rout,
A crawling shape intrude!
A blood-red thing that writhes from out
The scenic solitude!
It writhes!—it writhes!—with mortal pangs
The mimes become its food,
And the seraphs sob at vermin fangs
In human gore imbued.

Out—out are the lights—out all!
And over each quivering form,
The curtain, a funeral pall,
Comes down with the rush of a storm,
And the angels, all pallid and wan,
Uprising, unveiling, affirm
That the play is the tragedy, "Man,"
And its hero the Conqueror Worm.

"O God!" half shrieked Ligeia, leaping to her feet and extending her arms aloft with a spasmodic movement, as I made an end of these lines— "O God! O Divine Father!—shall these things be undeviatingly so?—shall this Conqueror be not once conquered? Are we not part and parcel of Thee? Who—who knoweth the mysteries of the will with its vigor? Man doth not yield him to the angels, *nor unto death utterly* save only through the weakness of his feeble will."

And now, as if exhausted with emotion, she suffered her white arms to fall, and returned solemnly to her bed of death. And as she breathed her last sighs, there came mingled with them a low murmur from her lips. I bent to them my ear and distinguished, again, the concluding words of the passage in Glanvill—"*Man doth not yield him to the angels, nor unto death utterly, save only through the weakness of his feeble will.*"

She died;—and I, crushed into the very dust with sorrow, could no longer endure the lonely desolation of my dwelling in the dim and decaying city by the Rhine. I had no lack of what the world calls wealth. Ligeia had brought me far more, very far more than ordinarily falls to the lot of mortals. After a few months, therefore, of weary and aimless wandering, I purchased, and put in some repair, an abbey, which I shall not name, in one of the wildest and least frequented portions of fair England. The gloomy and dreary grandeur of the building, the almost savage aspect of the domain, the many melancholy and time-honored memories connected with both, had much in unison with the feelings of utter abandonment which had driven me into that remote and unsocial region of the country. Yet although the external abbey, with its verdant decay hanging about it, suffered but little alteration, I gave way, with a child-like perversity, and perchance with a faint hope of alleviating my sorrows, to a display of more than regal magnificence within.—For such follies, even in childhood, I had imbibed a taste and now they came back to me as in the dotage of grief. Alas, I feel how much even of incipient madness might have been discovered in the gorgeous and fantastic draperies, in the solemn carvings of Egypt, in the wild cornices and furniture, in the Bedlam patterns of the carpets of tufted gold! I had become a bounden slave in the trammels of opium, and my labors and my orders had taken a coloring from my dreams. But these absurdities I must not pause to detail. Let me speak only of that one chamber, ever accursed, whither in a moment of mental alienation, I led from the altar as my bride—as the successor of the unforgotten Ligeia—the fair-haired and blue-eyed Lady Rowena Trevanion of Tremaine.

There is no individual portion of the architecture and decoration of that bridal chamber which is not now visibly before me. Where were the souls of the haughty family of the bride, when, through thirst of gold, they permitted to pass the threshold of an apartment so bedecked, a maiden and a daughter so beloved? I have said that I minutely remember the details of the chamber—yet I am sadly forgetful on topics of deep moment—and here there was no system, no keeping, in the fantastic display, to take hold upon the memory. The room lay in a high turret of the castellated abbey, was pentagonal in shape, and of capacious size. Occupying the whole southern face of the pentagon was the sole window—an immense sheet of unbroken glass from Venice—a single pane and tinted of a leaden hue, so that the rays of either the sun or moon, passing through it, fell with a ghastly lustre on the objects within. Over the upper portion of this huge window, extended the trellis-work of an aged vine, which clambered up the massy walls of the turret. The ceiling, of gloomy-looking oak, was excessively lofty, vaulted, and elaborately fretted with the wildest and most grotesque specimens of semi-Gothic, semi-Druidical device. From out the most central recess of this melancholy vaulting, depended, by a single chain of gold with long links, a huge censer of the same metal, Saracenic in pattern, and with many perforations so contrived that there writhed in and out of them, as if endued with a serpent vitality, a continual succession of parti-colored fires.

Some few ottomans and golden candelabra, of Eastern figure, were in various stations about—and there was the couch, too—the bridal couch —of an Indian model, and low, and sculptured of solid ebony, with a pall-like canopy above. In each of the angles of the chamber stood on end a gigantic sarcophagus of black granite, from the tombs of the kings over against Luxor, with their aged lids full of immemorial sculpture. But in draping of the apartment lay, alas the chief phantasy of all. The lofty walls, gigantic in height—even unproportionately so—were hung from summit to foot, in vast folds, with a heavy and massive-looking tapestry—tapestry of a material which was found alike as a carpet on the floor, as a covering for the ottomans and the ebony bed, as a canopy for the bed, and as the gorgeous volutes of the curtains which partially shaded the window. The material was the richest cloth of gold. It was spotted all over, at irregular intervals, with arabesque figures, about a foot in diameter, and wrought upon the cloth in patterns of the most jetty black. But these figures partook of the true character of the arabesque only when regarded from a single point of view. By a contrivance now common, and indeed traceable to a very remote period of antiquity, they were made changeable in aspect. To one entering the room, they bore the appearance of simple monstrosities; but upon a farther advance, this appearance gradually departed; and step by step, as the visitor moved his station in the chamber, he saw himself surrounded by an endless succession of the ghastly forms which belong to the superstition of the Norman, or arise in the guilty slumbers of the monk. The phantasmagoric effect was vastly heightened by the artificial introduction of a strong continual current of wind behind the draperies—giving a hideous and uneasy animation to the whole.

In halls such as these—in a bridal chamber such as this—I passed, with the lady of Tremaine, the unhallowed hours of the first month of our marriage—passed them with but little disquietude. That my wife dreaded the fierce moodiness of my temper—that she shunned me and loved me but little—I could not help perceiving; but it gave me rather pleasure than otherwise. I loathed her with a hatred belonging more to demon than to man. My memory flew back (oh, with what intensity of regret!) to Ligeia, the beloved, the august, the beautiful, the entombed. I revelled in recollections of her purity, of her wisdom, of her lofty, her ethereal nature, of her passionate, her idolatrous love. Now, then, did my spirit fully and freely burn with more than all the fires of her own. In the excitement of my opium dreams (for I was habitually fettered in the shackles of the drug) I would call aloud upon her name, during the silence of the night, or among the sheltered recesses of the glens by day, as if, through the wild eagerness, the solemn passion, the consuming ardor of my longing for the departed, I could restore her to the pathway she had abandoned—ah, *could* it be forever?—upon the earth.

About the commencement of the second month of the marriage, the Lady Rowena was attacked with sudden illness, from which her recovery was slow. The fever which consumed her rendered her nights uneasy; and in her perturbed state of half-slumber, she spoke of sounds, and of motions in and about the chamber of the turret, which I concluded had no origin save in the distemper of her fancy, or perhaps in the phantasmagoric influences of the chamber itself. She became at length convalescent —finally well. Yet but a brief period elapsed, ere a second more violent disorder again threw her upon a bed of suffering; and from this attack her frame, at all times feeble, never altogether recovered. Her illnesses were, after this epoch, of alarming character, and of more alarming recurrence, defying alike the knowledge and the great exertions of her physicians. With the increase of the chronic disease which had thus, apparently, taken too sure hold upon her constitution to be eradicated by human means, I could not fail to observe a similar increase in the nervous irritation of her temperament, and in her excitability by trivial causes of fear. She spoke again, and now more frequently and pertinaciously, of the sounds—of the slight sounds—and of the unusual motions among the tapestries, to which she had formerly alluded.

One night, near the closing in of September, she pressed this distressing subject with more than usual emphasis upon my attention. She had just awakened from an unquiet slumber, and I had been watching, with feelings half of anxiety, half of vague terror, the workings of her emaciated countenance. I sat by the side of her ebony bed, upon one of the ottomans of India. She partly arose, and spoke, in an earnest low whisper, of sounds which she *then* heard, but which I could not hear—and of motions which she *then* saw, but which I could not perceive. The wind was rushing hurriedly behind the tapestries, and I wished to show her (what, let me confess it, I could not *all* believe) that those almost inarticulate breathings, and those very gentle variations of the figures upon the wall, were but the natural effects of that customary rushing of the wind. But a deadly pallor, overspreading her face, had proved to me that my exertions to reassure her would be fruitless. She appeared to be fainting, and no attendants were within call. I remembered where was deposited a decanter of light wine which had been ordered by her physicians, and hastened across the chamber to procure it. But, as I stepped beneath the light of the censer, two circumstances of a startling nature attracted my attention. I had felt that some palpable although invisible object had passed lightly by my person; and I saw that there lay upon the golden carpet, in the very middle of the rich lustre thrown from the censer, a shadow—a faint, indefinite shadow of angelic aspect—such as might be fancied for the shadow of a shade. But I was wild with the excitement of an immoderate dose of opium, and heeded these things but little, nor spoke of them to Rowena. Having found the wine, I recrossed the chamber and poured out a gobletful, which I held to the lips of the fainting lady. She had now partially recovered, however, and took the vessel herself, while I sank upon an ottoman near me, with my eyes fastened upon her person. It was then that I became distinctly aware of a gentle foot-fall upon the carpet, and near the couch; and in a second thereafter, as Rowena was in the act of raising the wine to her lips, I saw, or may have dreamed that I saw, fall within the goblet, as if from some invisible spring in the atmosphere of the room, three or four large drops of a brilliant and ruby colored fluid. If this I saw—not so Rowena. She swallowed the wine unhesitatingly, and I forbore to speak to her of a circumstance which must, after all, I considered, have been but the suggestion of a vivid imagination, rendered morbidly active by the terror of the lady, by the opium, and by the hour.

Yet I cannot conceal it from my own perception that, immediately subsequent to the fall of the ruby-drops, a rapid change for the worse took place in the disorder of my wife; so that, on the third subsequent night, the hands of her menials prepared her for the tomb, and on the fourth, I sat alone, with her shrouded body, in that fantastic chamber which had received her as my bride. Wild visions, opium-engendered, flitted, shadow-like, before me. I gazed with unquiet eye upon the sarcophagi in the angles of the room, upon the varying figures of the drapery, and upon the writh-ing of the parti-colored fires in the censer overhead. My eyes then fell, as I called to mind the circumstances of a former night, to the spot beneath the glare of the censer where I had seen the faint traces of the shadow. It was there, however, no longer; and breathing with greater freedom, I turned my glances to the pallid and rigid figure upon the bed. Then rushed upon me a thousand memories of Ligeia—and then came back upon my heart, with the turbulent violence of a flood, the whole of that unutterable woe with which I had regarded *her* thus enshrouded. The night waned; and still, with a bosom full of bitter thoughts of the one only and supremely beloved, I remained gazing upon the body of Rowena.

It might have been midnight, or perhaps earlier, or later, for I had taken no note of time, when a sob, low, gentle, but very distinct, startled me from my revery.—I *felt* that it came from the bed of ebony—the bed of death. I listened in an agony of superstitious terror—but there was no repetition of the sound. I strained my vision to detect any motion in the corpse—but there was not the slightest perceptible. Yet I could not have been deceived. I *had* heard the noise, however faint, and my soul was awakened within me. I resolutely and perseveringly kept my attention riveted upon the body. Many minutes elapsed before any circumstance occurred tending to throw light upon the mystery. At length it became evident that a slight, a very feeble, and barely noticeable tinge of color had flushed up within the cheeks, and along the sunken small veins of the eyelids. Through a species of unutterable horror and awe, for which the language of mortality has no sufficiently energetic expression, I felt my heart cease to beat, my limbs grow rigid where I sat. Yet a sense of duty finally operated to restore my self-possession. I could no longer doubt that we had been precipitate in our preparations—that Rowena still lived. It was necessary that some immediate exertion be made; yet the turret was altogether apart from the portion of the abbey tenanted by the servants— there were none within call—I had no means of summoning them to my aid without leaving the room for many minutes—and this I could not venture to do. I therefore struggled alone in my endeavors to call back the spirit still hovering. In a short period it was certain, however, that a relapse had taken place; the color disappeared from both eyelid and cheek, leaving a wanness ever more than that of marble; the lips became doubly shrivelled and pinched up in the ghastly expression of death; a repulsive clamminess and coldness overspread rapidly the surface of the body; and all the usual rigorous stiffness immediately supervened. I fell back with a shudder upon the couch from which I had been so startlingly aroused, and again gave myself up to passionate waking visions of Ligeia.

An hour thus elapsed when (could it be possible?) I was a second time aware of some vague sound issuing from the region of the bed. I listened —in extremity of horror. The sound came again—it was a sigh. Rushing to the corpse, I saw—distinctly saw—a tremor upon the lips. In a minute afterward they relaxed, disclosing a bright line of the pearly teeth. Amazement now struggled in my bosom with the profound awe which had hitherto reigned there alone. I felt that my vision grew dim, that my reason wandered; and it was only by a violent effort that I at length succeeded in nerving myself to the task which duty thus once more had pointed out. There was now a partial glow upon the forehead and upon the cheek and throat; a perceptible warmth pervaded the whole frame; there was even a slight pulsation at the heart. The lady *lived*; and with redoubled ardor I betook myself to the task of restoration. I chafed and bathed the temples and the hands, and used every exertion which experience, and no little medical reading, could suggest. But in vain. Suddenly, the color fled, the pulsation ceased, the lips resumed the expression of the dead, and in an instant afterward, the whole body took upon itself the icy chilliness, the livid hue, the intense rigidity, the sunken outline, and all the loathsome peculiarities of that which has been, for many days, a tenant of the tomb.

And again I sunk into visions of Ligeia—and again (what marvel that I shudder while I write?) *again* there reached my ears a low sob from the region of the ebony bed. But why shall I minutely detail the unspeakable horror of that night? Why shall I pause to relate how, time after time, until near the period of the gray dawn, this hideous drama of revivification was repeated; how each terrific relapse was only into a a sterner and apparently more irredeemable death; how each agony wore the aspect of a struggle with some invisible foe; and how each struggle was succeeded by I know not what wild change in the personal appearance of the corpse? Let me hurry to a conclusion.

The greater part of the fearful night had worn away, and she who had been dead, once again stirred—and now more vigorously than hitherto, although arousing from a dissolution more appalling in its utter hopelessness than any. I had long ceased to struggle or to move, and remained sitting rigidly upon the ottoman, a helpless prey to a whirl of violent emotions, of which extreme awe was perhaps the least terrible, the least consuming. The corpse, I repeat, stirred and now more vigorously than before. The hues of life flushed up with unwonted energy into the countenance—the limbs relaxed—and, save that the eyelids were yet pressed heavily together, and that the bandages and draperies of the grave still imparted their charnel character to the figure, I might have dreamed that Rowena had indeed shaken off utterly the fetters of Death. But if this idea was not, even then, altogether adopted, I could at least doubt no longer, when arising from the bed, tottering, with feeble steps, with closed eyes, and with the manner of one bewildered in a dream, the thing that was enshrouded advanced boldly and palpably into the middle of the apartment.

I trembled not—I stirred not—for a crowd of unutterable fancies connected with the air, the stature, the demeanor of the figure, rushing hurriedly through my brain, had paralyzed—had chilled me into stone. I stirred not—but gazed upon the apparition. There was a mad disorder in my thoughts—a tumult unappeasable. Could it, indeed be the *living* Rowena who confronted me? Could it indeed be Rowena *at all*—the fair-haired, the blue-eyed Lady Rowena Trevanion of Tremaine? Why, *why* should I doubt it? The bandage lay heavily about the mouth—but then might it not be the mouth of the breathing Lady of Tremaine? And the cheeks—there were the roses as in her noon of life—yes, these might indeed be the fair cheeks of the living Lady of Tremaine. And the chin, with its dimples, as in health, might it not be hers?—*but had she then grown taller since her malady?* What inexpressible madness seized me with what thought? One bound, and I had reached her feet! Shrinking from my touch, she let fall from her head, unloosened, the ghastly cerements which had confined it, and there streamed forth, into the rushing atmosphere of the chamber, huge masses of long and dishevelled hair; *it was blacker than the raven wings of the midnight!* And now slowly opened *the eyes* of the figure which stood before me. "Here then, at least," I shrieked aloud, "can I never—can I never be mistaken—these are the full, and the black, and the wild eyes—of my lost love—of the lady—of the LADY LIGEIA!"

Tales of the Grotesque and Arabesque, 1846

ROBERT E. LEE

To the Virginia Convention, Accepting Command of the Virginia Forces, April 23, 1861

Mr. President and Gentlemen of the Convention: Deeply impressed with the solemnity of the occasion on which I appear before you, and profoundly grateful for the honor conferred upon me, I accept the position your partiality has assigned me, though I would greatly have preferred your choice should have fallen on one more capable.

Trusting to Almighty God, an approving conscience, and the aid of my fellow-citizens, I will devote myself to the defense and service of my native State, in whose behalf alone would I have ever drawn my sword.

Farewell Order to the Army

Headquarters, Army of Northern Virginia,
April 10, 1865

After four years of arduous service, marked by unsurpassed courage and fortitude, the Army of Northern Virginia has been compelled to yield to overwhelming numbers and resources. I need not tell the survivors of so many hard-fought battles, who have remained steadfast to the last, that I have consented to this result from no distrust of them; but, feeling that valour and devotion could accomplish nothing that could compensate for the loss that would have attended the continuation of the contest, I have determined to avoid the useless sacrifice of those whose past service has endeared them to their countrymen. By the terms of the agreement, officers and men can return to their homes and remain there until exchanged. You will take with you the satisfaction that proceeds from the consciousness of duty faithfully performed; and I earnestly pray that a merciful God will extend to you His blessing and protection. With an increasing admiration of your constancy and devotion to your country, and a grateful remembrance of your kind and generous consideration of myself, I bid you an affectionate farewell.

R. E. LEE, GENERAL.

Accepting the Presidency of Washington College

Powhatan County, August 24, 1865

Gentlemen:—I have delayed for some days replying to your letter of the 5th inst., informing me of my election by the board of trustees to the presidency of Washington College, from a desire to give the subject due consideration. Fully impressed with the responsibilities of the office, I have feared that I should be unable to discharge its duties to the satisfaction of the trustees or to the benefit of the country. The proper education of youth requires not only great ability, but I fear more strength than I now possess, for I do not feel able to undergo the labour of conducting classes in regular courses of instruction. I could not, therefore, undertake more than the general administration and supervision of the institution. There is another subject which has caused me serious reflection, and is, I think, worthy of the consideration of the board. Being excluded from the terms of amnesty in the proclamation of the President of the United States of the 29th of May last, and an object of censure to a portion of the country, I have thought it probable that my occupation of the position of president might draw upon the college a feeling of hostility; and I should, therefore, cause injury to an institution which it would be my highest desire to advance. I think it the duty of every citizen, in the present condition of the country, to do all in his power to aid in the restoration of peace and harmony, and in no way to oppose the policy of the State or general government directed to that object. It is particularly incumbent on those charged with the instruction of the young to set them an example of submission to authority, and I could not consent to be the cause of animadversion upon the college. Should you, however, take a different view, and think that my services in the position tendered to me by the board will be advantageous to the college and country, I will yield to your judgment and accept it; otherwise I must most respectfully decline the office. Begging you to express to the trustees of the college my heartfelt gratitude for the honour conferred upon me, and requesting you to accept my cordial thanks for the kind manner in which you have communicated their decision, I am, gentlemen, with great respect, your most obedient servant.

R. E. LEE.

The Virginia Reader, edited by Rosenberger

AUTHOR UNKNOWN

Lee and the Texans at the Battle of the Wilderness

As we stood upon this hill, Lee excited and in close consultation with Longstreet—our batteries thundering into the Wilderness below, the roar of musketry from the undergrowth below—our men retreating in a disorganized mass, and the Yankees pressing on and within musket shot, almost, of the hill upon which stood our idolized chief, indeed was an exciting time, and the emergency called for *immediate* and *determined* action upon the part of the Confederate General. Lee was equal to the hour. Action must *not* be delayed, for in less than five minutes the enemy would be upon the hill. Longstreet's corps as it then stood in one mingled mass upon the plank road, could not be thrown in, and time must be allowed for it to re-form, and place itself in line of battle. The cannon thundered, musketry rolled, stragglers were fleeing, couriers riding here and there in post-haste, minnies began to sing, the dying and wounded were jolted by the flying ambulances, and filling the road-side, adding to the excitement the terror of death. The "Texas brigade," was in front of Fields' division—while "Humphrey's brigade" of Mississippians led the van of Kershaw's division.

The consultation ended. Gen. Gregg and Gen. Humphrey were ordered to form their brigades in line of battle, which was quickly done, and we found ourselves near the brow of the hill, Gregg on the left—Humphrey on the right. "Gen. Gregg prepare to move," was the order from Gen. L.

About this time, Gen. Lee, with his staff, rode up to Gen. Gregg—"General what brigade is this?" said Lee.

"The Texas brigade," was General G.'s reply.

"I am glad to see it," said Lee. "When you go in there, I wish you to give those men the cold steel—they will stand and fire all day, and never move unless you charge them."

"That is my experience," replied the brave Gregg.

By this time an aide from General Longstreet rode up and repeated the order, "advance your command, Gen. Gregg." And now comes the point upon which the interest of this "o'er true tale" hangs. "*Attention Texas Brigade*" was rung upon the morning air, by Gen. Gregg, "*the eyes of General Lee are upon you, forward, march.*" Scarce had we moved a step, when Gen. Lee, in front of the whole command, raised himself in his stirrups, uncovered his grey hairs, and with an earnest, yet anxious voice, exclaimed above the din and confusion of the hour, "*Texans always move them.*"

201

Reader, for near four years I followed the fortunes of the Virginia army, heard, saw and experienced much that saddened the heart or appealed in one form or another to human passions, but never before in my lifetime or since, did I ever witness such a scene as was enacted when Lee pronounced these words, with the appealing look that he gave. A yell rent the air that must have been heard for miles around, and but few eyes in that old brigade of veterans and heroes of many a bloody field was undimmed by honest, heartfelt tears. Leonard Gee, a courier to Gen. Gregg, and riding by my side, with tears coursing down his cheeks and yells issuing from his throat exclaimed, "I would charge hell itself for that old man." It was not what Gen. Lee said that so infused and excited the men, as his tone and look, which each one of us knew was born of the dangers of the hour.

With yell after yell we moved forward, passed the brow of the hill, and moved down the declivity towards the undergrowth—a distance in all not exceeding 200 yards. After moving over half the ground we all saw that Gen. Lee was following us into battle—care and anxiety upon his countenance—refusing to come back at the request and advice of his staff. If I recollect correctly, the brigade halted when they discovered Gen. Lee's intention, and all eyes were turned upon him. Five and six of his staff would gather around him, seize him, his arms, his horse's reins, but he shook them off and moved forward. Thus did he continue until just before we reached the undergrowth, not, however, until the balls began to fill and whistle through the air. Seeing that we would do all that men could do to retrieve the misfortunes of the hour, accepting the advice of his staff, and hearkening to the protest of his advancing soldiers, he at last turned round and rode back to a position on the hill.

We reached the undergrowth—entered it with a yell, and in less than 100 yards came face to face with the advancing, triumphant, and sanguine foe—confronted only by a few brave souls who could only fire and yield their ground. The enemy were at least five or six to one of us, and death seemed to be our portion. With only 15 or 20 paces separating us, the contest waxed hot and deadlier. We gave a cheer and tried a charge, but with our handful of men our only success was to rush up to them, shoot them down, and shove them back some 10 or 15 yards. For 25 minutes we held them steady—not a foot did they advance, and at the expiration of that time more than half of our brave fellows lay around us dead, dying and wounded, and the few survivors could stand it no longer. By order of Gen. Gregg, whose manly form was seen wherever danger gloried most— I bore the order to the 5th and 1st Texas, to fall back in order.

After retreating some 50 yards, a most deafening yell was borne upon the breeze, and ere we were prepared to realize its cause, Gen. Longstreet's corps came sweeping by us, re-formed, and reinforced by Gen. Anderson's division, and with a valor that stands unrivaled swept everything before them for three long miles—driving, in that long charge, the yankees from four different lines of breastworks that they had thrown up in their rear. The "Battle of the Wilderness" was won—all other fighting by the enemy that day and next was to prevent defeat from terminating in destruction. . . .

The "Texas Brigade" entered the fight 673 strong. We lost in killed and wounded over 450.—Did we or did we not do all that men could? Gen. Gregg entered the fight with at least 12 commissioned and non-commissioned on his staff. Of these, several were killed, some wounded, and only two horses untouched. Gen. G.'s horse was pierced by 5 balls —each creating a mortal wound—though he rode him until we fell back —sent him to the rear where he died.

The Land We Love, V, 1868

HENRY TIMROD

Ode

Sung at memorial exercises for decorating the graves of the Confederate dead at Magnolia Cemetery, Charleston, S.C.

Timrod abandoned law for letters when he became intimate with a group of Charleston writers. During the Civil War he served as a correspondent with the Southern armies and later came to be known as "the Laureate of the Confederacy."

> Sleep sweetly in your humble graves,
>   Sleep, martyrs of a fallen cause;
> Though yet no marble column craves
>   The pilgrim here to pause.
>
> In seeds of laurel in the earth
>   The blossom of your fame is blown,
> And somewhere, waiting for its birth,
>   The shaft is in the stone!
>
> Meanwhile, behalf the tardy years
>   Which keep in trust your storied tombs,
> Behold! your sisters bring their tears,
>   And these memorial blooms.

Small tributes! but your shades will smile
More proudly on these wreaths today,
Than when some cannon-moulded pile
Shall overlook this bay.

Stop, angels, hither from the skies!
There is no holier spot of ground
Than where defeated valor lies,
By mourning beauty crowned!

Poems, 1866

SUSAN DABNEY SMEDES

"Oh, Thou Heroic Old Man"

When Gladstone read the biography of Thomas Dabney, written by his daughter, England's famous Prime Minister pronounced
Dabney "one of the very noblest of human characters."

He was at Burleigh when he heard of General Lee's surrender. On the
day that the news reached him he called his son Thomas to him, and
they rode together to the field where the Negroes were at work. He informed them of the news that had reached him and that they were now
free. His advice was that they should continue to work the crop as they
had been doing. At the end of the year they should receive such compensation for their labor as he thought just.

From this time till January 1, 1866, no apparent change took place
among the Burleigh Negroes. Those who worked in the fields went out
as usual and cultivated and gathered in the crops. In the house they
went about their customary duties. We expected them to go away or to
demand wages or at least to give some sign that they knew they were free.
But, except that they were very quiet and serious and more obedient and
kind than they had ever been known to be for more than a few weeks
at a time of sickness or other affliction, we saw no change in them.

At Christmas such compensation was made for them for their services
as seemed just. Afterward fixed wages were offered and accepted. Thomas
called them up now and told them that as they no longer belonged to him
they must discontinue calling him master.

"Yes, marster," "Yes, marster," was the answer to this. "They seem to
bring in 'master' and say it oftener than they ever did," was his comment
as he related the occurrence to his children. This was true. The name
seemed to grow into a term of endearment. As time went on and under

the changed order of things Negroes whom he had never known became tenants on his plantation, these new people called him master also. This was unprecedented in the South, I think. They were proud of living on his place on account of the good name that he had won for himself as a master. Not infrequently they were heard to express a regret that they had not belonged to him, when they saw the feeling that existed between himself and his former slaves. Sometimes he came to us with a puzzled look to ask who those Negroes were who had just called him "old master" and shaken hands with him.

"I cannot recall their faces," he would say; "surely I never owned them."

Finally the Negroes on the neighboring plantations and wherever he went came to call him "old master." They seemed to take pride in thus claiming a relationship with him, as it were; and he grew accustomed to the voluntary homage.

He had come home to a house denuded of nearly every article of furniture and to a plantation stripped of the means of cultivating any but a small proportion of it. A few mules and one cow comprised the stock. We had brought a few pieces of common furniture from Georgia, and a very few necessary articles were bought. In the course of time some home-made contrivances and comforts relieved the desolate appearance of the rooms, but no attempt was ever made to refurnish the house.

He owned nothing that could be turned into money without great sacrifice but five bales of cotton. There were yet two sons and two daughters to be educated. He decided to get a tutor for them and to receive several other pupils in his house in order to make up the salary. The household was put on an economical footing. The plantation Negroes were hired to work in the fields, and things seemed to promise more prosperous days. So the first year was passed. . . .

His chivalrous nature had always revolted from the sight of a woman doing hard work. He determined to spare his daughters all such labor as he could perform. General Sherman had said that he would like to bring every Southern woman to the washtub. "He shall never bring my daughters to the washtub," Thomas Dabney said. "I will do the washing myself." And he did it for two years. He was in his seventieth year when he began to do it.

This may give some idea of the labors, the privations, the hardships, of those terrible years. The most intimate friends of Thomas, nay, his own children who were not in the daily life at Burleigh, have never known the unprecedented self-denial, carried to the extent of acutest bodily sufferings, which he practised during this time. A curtain must be drawn over this part of the life of my lion-hearted father!

When he grew white and thin and his frightened daughters prepared a special dish for him, he refused to eat the delicacy. It would choke him, he said, to eat better food than they had, and he yielded only to their

205

earnest solicitations. He would have died rather than ask for it. When the living was so coarse and so ill prepared that he could scarcely eat it, he never failed, on rising from the table, to say earnestly and reverently as he stood by his chair, "Thank the Lord for this much."

During a period of eighteen months no light in summer and none but a fire in winter, except in some case of necessity, was seen in the house. He was fourteen years in paying the debts that fell on him in his sixty-ninth year. He lived but three years after the last dollar was paid.

When he was seventy years of age he determined to learn to cultivate a garden. He had never performed manual labor, but he now applied himself to learn to hoe as a means of supplying his family with vegetables. With the labor of those aged hands he made a garden that was the best ordered that we had ever seen at Burleigh. He made his garden, as he did everything that he undertook, in the most painstaking manner, neglecting nothing that could insure success. The beds and rows and walks in that garden were models of exactness and neatness. It was a quarter of a mile from the house and from water, on the top of a long, high hill, and three-quarters of an acre in extent. In a time of drought or if he had set out anything that needed watering, he toiled up that long, precipitous hill with bucket after bucket of water. "I never look at the clouds" had been a saying of his in cultivating his plantation, and he carried it out now. That garden supplied the daily food of his family nearly all the year round. He planted vegetables in such quantities that it was impossible to consume all on the table, and he sold barrels of vegetables of different kinds in New Orleans.

Oftentimes he was so exhausted when he came in to dinner that he could not eat for a while. He had his old bright way of making everyone take an interest in his pursuits—sympathy was as necessary and sweet to him as to a child—and he showed with pride what he had done by his personal labor in gardening and in washing. He placed the clothes on the line as carefully as if they were meant to hang there always, and they must be admired, too! He said, and truly, that he had never seen snowier ones.

Oh, thou heroic old man! Thou hast a right to thy pride in those exact strokes of the hoe and in those superb potatoes, "the best ever seen in the New Orleans market," and in those long lines of snowy drapery! But those to whom thou art showing these things are looking beyond them, at the man! They are gazing reverently and with scarce suppressed tears on the hands that have been in this world for threescore and ten years and are beginning today to support a houseful of children!

At the end of the hard day's work he would say sometimes: "General Sherman has not brought my daughters to the washtub. I could not stand that."

Memorials of a Southern Planter, 1887

HENRY W. GRADY

The New South

The writer of this influential speech was a Georgia journalist, editor and part owner of the Atlanta CONSTITUTION. *Grady was regarded as the leading spokesman of the New South.*

"There was a South of slavery and secession—that South is dead. There is a South of union and freedom—that South, thank God, is living, breathing, growing every hour." These words, delivered from the immortal lips of Benjamin H. Hill, at Tammany Hall, in 1866, true then and truer now, I shall make my text tonight. . . .

I bespeak the utmost stretch of your courtesy tonight. I am not troubled about those from whom I come. You remember the man whose wife sent him to a neighbor with a pitcher of milk, and who, tripping on the top step, fell with such casual interruptions as the landings afforded into the basement, and, while picking himself up, had the pleasure of hearing his wife call out: "John, did you break the pitcher?"

"No, I didn't," said John, "but I'll be dinged if I don't."

So, while those who call me from behind may inspire me with energy, if not with courage, I ask an indulgent hearing from you. I beg that you will bring your full faith in American fairness and frankness to judgment upon what I shall say. There was an old preacher once who told some boys of the Bible lesson he was going to read in the morning. The boys, finding the place, glued together the connecting pages. The next morning he read on the bottom of one page: "When Noah was one hundred and twenty years old he took unto himself a wife who was"—then turning the page—"140 cubits long—40 cubits wide, built of gopher wood —and covered with pitch inside and out." He was naturally puzzled at this. He read it again, verified it, and then said: "My friends, this is the first time I ever met this in the Bible, but I accept this as an evidence of the assertion that we are fearfully and wonderfully made." If I could get you to hold such faith tonight I could proceed cheerfully to the task I otherwise approach with a sense of consecration. . . .

My friends, Dr. Talmage has told you that the typical American has yet to come. Let me tell you that he has already come. Great types, like valuable plants, are slow to flower and fruit. But from the union of these colonists, Puritans and Cavaliers, from the straightening of their purposes and the crossing of their blood, slow perfecting through a century, came he who stands as the first typical American, the first who comprehended within himself all the strength and gentleness, all the majesty and grace of this republic—Abraham Lincoln. He was the sum of Puritan and Cavalier, for in his ardent nature were fused the virtues of both, and in the depths of his great soul the faults of both were lost. He was greater than Puritan, greater than Cavalier, in that he was American, and that in his honest form were first gathered the vast and thrilling forces of his ideal government—charging it with such tremendous meaning and elevating it above human suffering that martyrdom, though infamously aimed, came as a fitting crown to a life consecrated from the cradle to human liberty. Let us, each cherishing the traditions and honoring his fathers, build with reverent hands to the type of this simple but sublime life, in which all types are honored, and in our common glory as Americans there will be plenty and to spare for your forefathers and for mine.

Dr. Talmage has drawn for you, with a master's hand, the picture of your returning armies. He has told you how, in the pomp and circumstance of war, they came back to you, marching with proud and victorious tread, reading their glory in a nation's eyes! Will you bear with me while I tell you of another army that sought its home at the close of the late war—an army that marched home in defeat and not in victory—in pathos and not in splendor, but in glory that equaled yours, and to hearts as loving as ever welcomed heroes home! Let me picture to you the footsore Confederate soldier, as buttoning up in his faded gray jacket the parole which was to bear testimony to his children of his fidelity and faith, he turned his face southward from Appomattox in April, 1865. Think of him as ragged, half-starved, heavy-hearted, enfeebled by want and wounds, having fought to exhaustion, he surrenders his gun, wrings the hands of his comrades in silence, and lifting his tear-stained and pallid face for the last time to the graves that dot old Virginia hills, pulls his gray cap over his brow and begins the slow and painful journey. What does he find—let me ask you who went to your homes eager to find, in the welcome you had justly earned, full payment for four years' sacrifice—what does he find when, having followed the battle-stained cross against overwhelming odds, dreading death not half so much as surrender, he reaches the home he left so prosperous and beautiful? He finds his house in ruins, his farm devastated, his slaves free, his stock killed, his barns empty, his trade destroyed, his money worthless, his social system, feudal in its magnificence, swept away; his people without law or legal status; his comrades slain, and the burdens of others heavy on his shoulders. Crushed by defeat, his very traditions are gone. Without money, credit, employment, material, or training; and beside all this, confronted with the gravest problem that ever met human intelligence—the establishing of a status for the vast body of his liberated slaves.

What does he do—this hero in gray with a heart of gold? Does he sit down in sullenness and despair? Not for a day. Surely God, who has stripped him of his prosperity, inspired him in his adversity. As ruin was never before so overwhelming, never was restoration swifter. The soldier stepped from the trenches into the furrow; horses that had charged Federal guns marched before the plow, and fields that ran red with human blood in April were green with the harvest in June; women reared in luxury cut up their dresses and made breeches for their husbands, and, with a patience and heroism that fit women always as a garment, gave their hands to work. There was little bitterness in all this. Cheerfulness and frankness prevailed. "Bill Arp" struck the key-note when he said: "Well, I killed as many of them as they did of me, and now I'm going to work." [Or] the soldier returning home after defeat and roasting some corn on the roadside, who made the remark to his comrades: "You may leave the South if you want to, but I am going to Sandersville, kiss my wife and raise a crop, and if the Yankees fool with me any more, I'll whip 'em again." I want to say to General Sherman, who is considered an able man in our parts, though some people think he is a kind of careless man about fire, that from the ashes he left us in 1864 we have raised a brave and beautiful city; that somehow or other we have caught the sunshine in the bricks and mortar of our homes, and have builded therein not one ignoble prejudice or memory.

But what is the sum of our work? We have found out that in the summing up the free Negro counts more than he did as a slave. We have planted the schoolhouse on the hilltop and made it free to white and black. We have sowed towns and cities in the place of theories, and put business above politics. We have challenged your spinners in Massachusetts and your iron-makers in Pennsylvania. We have learned that the $400,000,000 annually received from our cotton crop will make us rich when the supplies that make it are home-raised. We have reduced the commercial rate of interest from 24 to 6 per cent, and are floating 4 per cent bonds. We have learned that one northern immigrant is worth fifty foreigners; and have smoothed the path to southward, wiped out the place where Mason and Dixon's line used to be, and hung out [the] latchstring to you and yours. We have reached the point that marks perfect harmony in every household, when the husband confesses that the pies which his wife cooks are as good as those his mother used to bake; and we admit that the sun shines as brightly and the moon as softly as it did before the war. We have established thrift in city and country. We have fallen in love with work. We have restored comfort to homes from which culture and elegance never departed. We have let economy take root and spread among us as rank as the crabgrass which sprung from Sherman's cavalry camps, until we are ready to lay odds on the Georgia Yankee as he manufactures relics of the battlefield in a one-story shanty and squeezes pure olive oil out of his cotton seed, against any down-easter that ever swapped wooden nutmegs for flannel sausages in the valleys of Vermont. Above all, we know that we have achieved in these "piping times of peace" a fuller independence for the South than that which our fathers sought to win in the forum by their eloquence or compel in the field by their swords.

It is a rare privilege, sir, to have had part, however humble, in this work. Never was nobler duty confided to human hands than the uplifting and upbuilding of the prostrate and bleeding South—misguided, perhaps, but beautiful in her suffering, and honest, brave and generous always. In the record of her social, industrial and political illustration we await with confidence the verdict of the world. . . .

The relations of the Southern people with the Negro are close and cordial. We remember with what fidelity for four years he guarded our defenseless women and children, whose husbands and fathers were fighting against his freedom. To his eternal credit be it said that whenever he struck a blow for his own liberty he fought in open battle, and when at last he raised his black and humble hands that the shackles might be struck off, those hands were innocent of wrong against his helpless charges, and worthy to be taken in loving grasp by every man who honors loyalty and devotion. Ruffians have maltreated him, rascals have misled him, philanthropists established a bank for him, but the South, with the North, protests against injustice to this simple and sincere people. To liberty and enfranchisement is as far as law can carry the Negro. The rest must be left to conscience and common sense. It must be left to those among whom his lot is cast, with whom he is indissolubly connected, and whose prosperity depends upon their possessing his intelligent sympathy and confidence. Faith has been kept with him, in spite of calumnious assertions to the contrary by those who assume to speak for us or by frank opponents. Faith will be kept with him in the future, if the South holds her reason and integrity.

But have we kept the faith with you? In the fullest sense, yes. When Lee surrendered—I don't say when Johnson surrendered, because I understand he still alludes to the time when he met General Sherman last as the time he determined to abandon any further prosecution of the struggle—when Lee surrendered, I say, and Johnson quit, the South became, and has since been, loyal to this Union. We fought hard enough to know that we were whipped, and in perfect frankness accept as final the arbitrament of the sword to which we had appealed. The South found her jewel in the toad's head of defeat. The shackles that had held her in narrow limitations fell forever when the shackles of the Negro slave were broken. Under the old regime the Negroes were slaves to the South; the South was a slave to the system. The old plantation, with its simple police regulations and feudal habit, was the only type possible under slavery. Thus was gathered in the hands of a splendid and chivalric oligarchy the substance that should have been diffused among the people, as the rich blood, under certain artificial conditions, is gathered at the heart, filling that with affluent rapture but leaving the body chill and colorless.

The old South rested everything on slavery and agriculture, unconscious that these could neither give nor maintain healthy growth. The new South presents a perfect democracy, the oligarchs leading in the popular movement—a social system compact and closely knitted, less splendid on the surface, but stronger at the core—a hundred farms for every plantation, fifty homes for every palace—and a diversified industry that meets the complex need of this complex age.

The new South is enamored of her new work. Her soul is stirred with the breath of a new life. The light of a grander day is falling fair on her face. She is thrilling with the consciousness of growing power and prosperity. As she stands upright, full-statured and equal among the people of the earth, breathing the keen air and looking out upon the expanded horizon, she understands that her emancipation came because through the inscrutable wisdom of God her honest purpose was crossed, and her brave armies were beaten.

This is said in no spirit of time-serving or apology. The South has nothing for which to apologize. She believes that the late struggle between the States was war and not rebellion; revolution and not conspiracy, and that her convictions were as honest as yours. I should be unjust to the dauntless spirit of the South and to my own convictions if I did not make this plain in this presence. The South has nothing to take back. In my native town of Athens is a monument that crowns its central hill—a plain, white shaft. Deep cut into its shining side is a name dear to me above the names of men—that of a brave and simple man who died in brave and simple faith. Not for all the glories of New England, from Plymouth Rock all the way, would I exchange the heritage he left me in his soldier's death. To the foot of that I shall send my children's children to reverence him who ennobled their name with his heroic blood. But, sir, speaking from the shadow of that memory which I honor as I do nothing else on earth, I say that the cause in which he suffered and for which he gave his life was adjudged by higher and fuller wisdom than his or mine, and I am glad that the omniscient God held the balance of battle in His Almighty hand and that human slavery was swept forever from American soil, the American Union was saved from the wreck of war.

This message, Mr. President, comes to you from consecrated ground. Every foot of soil about the city in which I live is as sacred as a battleground of the republic. Every hill that invests it is hallowed to you by the blood of your brothers who died for your victory, and doubly hallowed to us by the blow of those who died hopeless, but undaunted, in defeat— sacred soil to all of us—rich with memories that make us purer and stronger and better—silent but staunch witnesses in its red desolation of the matchless valor of American hearts and the deathless glory of American arms— speaking an eloquent witness in its white peace and prosperity to the indissoluble union of American States and the imperishable brotherhood of the American people.

Now, what answer has New England to this message? Will she permit the prejudice of war to remain in the hearts of the conquerors, when it has died in the hearts of the conquered? Will she transmit this prejudice to the next generation, that in their hearts which never felt the generous ardor of conflict it may perpetuate itself? Will she withhold, save in strained courtesy, the hand which straight from his soldier's heart Grant offered to Lee at Appomattox? Will she make the vision of a restored and happy people, which gathered above the couch of your dying captain, filling his heart with grace; touching his lips with praise, and glorifying his path to the grave—will she make this vision on which the last sigh of his expiring soul breathed a benediction, a cheat and delusion? If she does, the South, never abject in asking for comradeship, must accept with dignity its refusal; but if she does not refuse to accept in frankness and sincerity this message of good will and friendship, then will the prophecy of Webster, delivered in this very society forty years ago amid tremendous applause, become true, be verified in its fullest sense, when he said: "Standing hand to hand and clasping hands, we should remain united as we have been for sixty years, citizens of the same country, members of the same government, united, all united now and united forever." There have been difficulties, contentions, and controversies, but I tell you that in my judgment,

> Those opened eyes,
> Which like the meteors of a troubled heaven,
> All of one nature, of one substance bred,
> Did lately meet in th' intestine shock,
> Shall now, in mutual well beseeming ranks,
> March all one way.

From an address delivered before the New England Society of New York, December 1886, in *Life of Henry W. Grady* by Joel Chandler Harris

CLAUDE G. BOWERS

The Carpetbaggers

The carpetbaggers have been exposed and castigated many times, but rarely so brilliantly as by journalist, historian and diplomat Bowers.

We may as well make a hurried trip to Tallahassee in Florida and visit a Legislature, now familiar, composed of swindlers, stealing on mileage and dancing ostentatiously on auction blocks. Here again we meet the infamous Littlefield, busy with his railroad steals, and prodigal as need be with his bribery funds. He is interested in the Georgia Railroad and the Tallahassee

Railroad, and legislation is required. No one knows better how to get it. The hotels and boarding houses are filled with shabby strangers, the meanest of the carpetbaggers drinking champagne, and the poorest in possession of the finest of beaver hats. The lordly Littlefield, amiably accessible, keeps his carriage at the hotel door to facilitate responses to eager calls from the Legislature. Night finds bright lights and abundant whiskey in hotel rooms, whence members, won by money, stagger joyously. Having sold a United States Senatorship, these importunate statesmen are now blackmailing the purchasers with threats of exposure, and money is again forthcoming. Negro members, suspecting a sliding scale of bribery to their disadvantage, have caucused and named a "smelling committee" to investigate and exact justice. Even the Northern Radicals are a little embarrassed by their leaders in Florida—M. L. Stearns, who as a Freedmen's Bureau agent, had made free with Government pork and flour, and Harrison Reed, the Governor, who was something of a hypocrite and everything of a scamp. These odious parasites had played, as elsewhere, on the credulity of the blacks for power. Nights found the carpetbaggers campaigning on plantations, kissing the babies, while the old black mammies fervently exclaimed, "I will vote ebery day foh dat man," for "dat man is a good 'publican"; and the carpetbaggers would piously reply, "Jesus Christ was a Republican." "The worst imaginable spectacle that could afflict the eyes of anybody," thought *The Nation* in 1875. That was the year William D. Bloxham, former slave-owner, who voluntarily has built the first Negro school on his plantation, stepped forth to give cohesiveness and courage to the opposition and to revive the spirit of the native whites in a brilliant campaign of denunciation.

Florida was putrid.

Putrid, too, was Alabama, where we may pause a moment at Montgomery, and look in on its Legislature. We have heard of the scenes of the first sessions under reconstruction, with galleries, windows, and seats packed with Negro spectators voting with the members with shouts and hysterical laughter, and with colored members sleeping in their chairs, eating peanuts, and soaked with whiskey, quarreling, fighting, pursuing one another with murderous intent. Well, conditions have not greatly changed. Less festivity, perhaps, more concentration on the main chance; for we are now shown a room set aside where the lobbyists can interview members in seclusion and distribute the bribe money. In the Exchange Hotel we learn that the lobby maintains four rooms for entertainment and business. The carpetbag members, all "loyal men," have their prices. Speaker Harrington boasts he had received seventeen hundred dollars for getting one bill through; a Senator had a fixed price of five hundred dollars for railroad bills; another exacted twice that sum; and a leader got thirty-five thousand dollars for the successful management of a railroad bond issue, most of it sticking to his hands.

Alabama was saturated with corruption.

And even worse was Louisiana. Here, even when the thieves fell out, honest men failed to get their due. New Orleans, the reconstruction capital, is a city of charm, Canal Street with its imposing width and partly grass-grown dais in the center dominating all, the streets in the business section paved with large blocks. Close to the levee on Canal Street looms the Custom-House, important in our story, built of Maine granite, and presided over by Collector Casey, brother-in-law of the President, with a reputation none too good. Somehow through all its miseries the city has managed to preserve something of its Gallic gayety. Young blades still speed their racers over the famous Shell Road, "straight as an arrow, hard as flint, and smooth as a backgammon board," pausing for a cocktail or a sherry cobbler in the shade of fragrant trees at the road-houses. The nights are lively with balls and masquerades, and the gambling-houses are never deserted except on Sunday, when a pensive serenity descends upon the town.

Here in the capital sits Henry Clay Warmoth, ruling with a rod of iron. No ordinary person, this dashing young soldier of fortune who had drifted into town as blithesomely as a Gascon of the fourteenth century ever moved on Paris with his sword. Born in Illinois, he had just begun the practice of law in Missouri, when the war swept him into the army, and at the close, in light-hearted mood, he moved on to New Orleans, where his commanding person, courtly manners, and genius for politics smoothed his path to political preferment. His enemies have said he was penniless when he reached the city; he himself insists he had enough, and had entered at once on a lucrative practice of his profession. In the beginning it was all a lark—caucuses, conferences, were to his liking, and, besides, was not this the land of the plum tree? The Negroes, attracted to the merry young blade, elected him to Congress before the State's Representatives were admitted, and he sallied forth to Washington to be cordially received by the Republican leaders and turned away. But it was ordained of destiny that he should have bigger fish to fry. When the Grand Army of the Republic was organized in Louisiana, he was made Grand Commander, and a few weeks later, at the age of twenty-six, he was elected Governor. His enemies soon were to comment significantly on his capacity to save one hundred thousand dollars a year on his salary of eight thousand dollars and to accumulate a million in four years. But an English tourist, who found him "a young man of spirit and ability," observed that "his wealth, if the wages of corruption, had been so deftly acquired that no one can lay his finger on the spot."

The Legislature we find sitting in Mechanics' Hall is typical of the others we have seen in the land of jubilee. Here, presiding over the House, we find a shrewd, unscrupulous, audacious youth of twenty-six, Carr of Maryland. And such scenes! The lobbies teem with laughing Negroes from the plantations, with whites of the pinch-faced, parasitic type; and Negro women in red turbans peddle cakes and oranges to the very doors of the chambers. Within, some coal-black members, but most of the lighter hue, though Lieutenant-Governor Dunn, presiding over the Senate, is a black. The abysmally ignorant eschew debate, some of the coal-blacks speak incoherently. It is a monkey-house—with guffaws, disgusting interpolations, amendments offered that are too obscene to print, followed by shouts of glee. Bad in the beginning, the travesty grows worse. The vulgarity of the speeches increases; members stagger from the basement bar to their seats. The Speaker in righteous mood sternly forbids the introduction of liquor on the floor. A curious old planter stands in the galleries a moment looking down upon the scene, and with an exclamation, "My God!" he turns and runs, as from a pestilence, into the street. Visitors from the North organize "slumming expeditions" to the Legislature or go as to a zoo. A British member of Parliament, asking if there are any curiosities in the city, is taken forthwith to Mechanics' Hall.

Corruption is inevitable, and members openly charged with bribery are not offended. "I want to know how much the gentleman gets to support this bill," demands one member of another, and it is not an insult. Measures involving millions, many criminal, and having to do with railroads, canals, and levees, are passed without examination, and members vote vast sums into their pockets openly, defiantly. The mileage and *per diem* for members and clerks leapt from a quarter of a million in 1869 to half a million the next year. Careless with the people's money? Preposterous. "What we give to the community," exclaims an outraged member—"What we give to the community is without money and without price. It is so valuable that the price cannot be fixed—there is no standard." "I should like to know," says another, "if there is a good thing, in the name of God, why not let the representatives of the State of Louisiana have a hand in it." When the Appropriations Bill reduces the printing bill to a mere one hundred and forty thousand dollars a tearful plea that legislators "open their hearts" and embrace more newspapers brings an amendment adding sixty thousand dollars.

For in Louisiana, too, the party press is heavily subsidized out of the Treasury. The Board of Printing Commissioners, dominated by the Governor, had been a godsend to Warmoth, who sent his agents to edit papers to which contracts were given, and, as fourth owner of the *New Orleans Republican*, the chief beneficiary, he profited both politically and financially. Through his subsidized press he brought pressure to bear in favor of four measures intended to give him dictatorial power and prolong his reign. The Registration Bill made every parish registration official his minion, and gave them power to accept or reject votes without interference from the courts. Thus he could determine nominations. The Election Bill superseded sheriffs on election day with Warmoth's appointees, forbade the courts to interfere, and authorized him to deny certificates of election to successful candidates if he saw fit; and all this was climaxed by the creation of a returning board composed of members of the machine specified in the bill itself. The Constabulary Bill authorized Warmoth to name a chief constable in each parish who could name a deputy, and these were absolute. And the Militia Bill empowered him to organize and equip as many men as he wished and placed one hundred thousand dollars at his disposal for the purpose.

These four revolutionary measures were the concentrated essence of Radicalism. The people in mass meeting protested violently, speakers denouncing the measures as designed for plunder and the perpetuation of pillage, and attacks on the legislators favoring them were greeted with cries of "Kill them!" and "Lynch them!" But behind the Legislature was Warmoth; behind him his militia and the constables; and behind them Federal bayonets—and the laws went into operation. . . .

Now let us cross over to Arkansas, the barony of the most astute and stern of the carpetbaggers, Powell Clayton, who has just retired as Governor to enter the Senate, but whose work lives after him. No cowardly mediocrity he, but a daring, resourceful, unscrupulous man of vaulting ambition, with a touch of genius. A brave soldier, even when he dismounted and laid the sword aside he remained a cavalry dare-devil. The fighting had taken him into Arkansas, and when the firing ceased he settled on a plantation and remained. From that point of vantage, he cunningly studied the situation, and at the psychological moment he grasped the opportunity. Gathering the Negroes and carpetbaggers behind him, he seized on power. Coldly calculating, unsympathetic to suffering, autocratic, impatient of opposition or restraint, he ruled for three years as an absolute monarch. The argus-eyed Henry Watterson observed him critically. "The distance between him and Washington, his friendliness to the Government, the ease with which his acts could be concealed, made him bold and careless. He knew his game. Clayton's policy was extermination. Nothing could divert him. He is not a milksop, but a man of genius and his field is fruitful." His was the master mind that organized the Republican party in Arkansas, that directed the framing of the constitution, making a despot of the Governor; and he took the governorship. He waved his wand, and a system emerged that destroyed civil liberty, and reduced overwhelming majorities to impotency. This Clayton system reserved the loaves and fishes for the carpetbaggers alone. Adventurers from abroad, including the Governor and two Senators, controlled the executive department, the courts, the Treasury, the military power. Nowhere such concentration of power as in the hands of Clayton. He distributed printing patronage to party papers, exacting as a consideration absolute obedience to his will. In him was lodged the power to award millions in aid to railroads, and he demanded that aid be given. His militia was so tied up with registration as to make it a partisan army. In one campaign he set aside the registration in eleven counties, ten with heavy Democratic majorities, on the ground of "interference with registration." By the waving of his wand, this cavalryman wiped out a Democratic majority of almost three thousand. When the people grumbled, he evoked the sword. His militia was frankly an instrument of party, his followers having demanded an instrument that "would strike early and strike hard." The *Daily Republican* boldly proclaimed that of course the militia was to be armed to enforce the policies of the party. Immediately the Negroes were enlisted and armed—with the approval of Washington. The Republican Congressional Executive Committee was sending assurance that Federal troops were at Clayton's service whenever he declared martial law. The Northern press was being fed with stories of "outrages" in Arkansas. Soon the proclamation of martial law; soon two thousand undisciplined Negroes were preying on the people of ten counties, stealing, arresting, imprisoning, executing, looting houses, and occasionally violating women. Clayton soon was sending the officers lists of men to be arrested, with the comment that many of them could be executed. "It is absolutely necessary that some example be made," he wrote. So infamous did the brutality become that the *Daily Republican* bitterly denounced the proceedings, but when he was disciplined by his removal from Speakership of the House, and deprived of public printing, the editor made a hasty recantation with the inspiring statement that "we'll make Arkansas Republican or a waste howling wilderness." . . .

With a military autocrat as Governor, with terror spread by gun-men from the mountains, and armed Negroes posing as militia, with no recourse to the ballot, the people, oppressed with unbearable taxation, have no recourse to the courts—for these too are packed with the tools of the system. Chief Justice John McClure, a notorious carpetbagger, is boasting of his guilt of bribery, editing the *Daily Republican* from his chambers, and handling the slush funds for the debauchery of the Legislature. . . .

To understand the times, we must bear in mind that distinguished statesmen in Washington, honored with monuments today, were loudly defending the Scotts, the Moseses, Bullocks, Warmoths, Caseys, Ameses, and Claytons; that pious women in Northern villages, shamefully deceived, were praying for the success of these "good men and true." But some were growing weary of the sordid game, and Greeley, in the fall of 1871, was giving warning: "Men and brethren, there is to be a general overhauling of pretensions, a sweeping-out of dark corners, a dragging to light of hidden iniquities the coming winter. If there be those who dread such an ordeal, they may wisely put an ocean between them and the scenes of their misdoings without delay."

The Tragic Era, 1929

SIDNEY LANIER

The Marshes of Glynn

Glooms of the live-oaks, beautiful-braided and woven
With intricate shades of the vines that myriad-cloven
    Clamber the forks of the multiform boughs—
              Emerald twilights—
              Virginal shy lights,
Wrought of the leaves to allure to the whisper of vows,
When lovers pace timidly down through the green colonnades
Of the dim, sweet woods, of the dear dark woods,
    Of the heavenly woods and glades,
That run to the radiant marginal sand-beach within
    The wide sea-marshes of Glynn—
Beautiful glooms, soft dusks in the noonday fire—
Wildwood privacies, closets of lone desire,
Chamber from chamber parted with wavering arras of leaves—
Cells for the passionate pleasure of prayer to the soul that grieves,
Pure with a sense of the passing of saints through the wood,
Cool for the dutiful weighing of ill with good—

O braided dusks of the oak and woven shades of the vine,
While the riotous noonday sun of the June-day long did shine,
Ye held me fast in your heart and I held you fast in mine;
But now when the noon is no more, and riot is rest,
And the sun is a-wait at the ponderous gate of the West,
And the slant, yellow beam down the wood-aisle doth seem
Like a lane into heaven that leads from a dream—
Aye, now, when my soul all day hath drunken the soul of the oak,
And my heart is at ease from men, and the wearisome sound of the stroke
    Of the scythe of time and the trowel of trade is low,
    And belief overmasters doubt, and I know that I know,
    And my spirit is grown to a lordly great compass within,
That the length and the breadth and the sweep of the marshes of Glynn
    Will work me no fear like the fear they have wrought me of yore
When length was fatigue, and when breadth was but bitterness sore,
And when terror and shrinking and dreary unnamable pain
Drew over me out of the merciless miles of the plain—

    Oh, now, unafraid, I am fain to face
      The vast, sweet visage of space.
    To the edge of the wood I am drawn, I am drawn,
Where the gray beach glimmering runs, as a belt of the dawn,

For a mete and a mark
   To the forest-dark—
                         So,
Affable live-oak, leaning low—
Thus—with your favor-soft, with a reverent hand
(Not lightly touching your person, Lord of the land!),
Bending your beauty aside, with a step I stand
   On the firm-packed sand,
      Free
By a world of marsh that borders a world of sea.
Sinuous southward and sinuous northward the shimmering band
   Of the sand-beach fastens the fringe of the marsh to the folds of the
      land.
Inward and outward to northward and southward the beach-lines linger
      and curl
As a silver-wrought garment that clings to and follows the firm, sweet limbs
      of a girl.
   Vanishing, swerving, evermore curving again into sight,
   Softly the sand-beach wavers away to a dim gray looping of light.
   And what if behind me to westward the wall of the woods stands high?
   The world lies east: how ample, the marsh and the sea and the sky!
A league and a league of marsh-grass, waist-high, broad in the blade,
Green, and all of a height, and unflecked with a light or a shade,
Stretch leisurely off, in a pleasant plain,
      To the terminal blue of the main.
Oh, what is abroad in the marsh and the terminal sea?
   Somehow my soul seems suddenly free
   From the weighing of fate and the sad discussion of sin,
By the length and the breadth and the sweep of the marshes of Glynn.

Ye marshes, how candid and simple and nothing-withholding and free
Ye publish yourselves to the sky and offer yourselves to the sea!
Tolerant plains, that suffer the sea and the rains and the sun,
Ye spread and span like the catholic man who hath mightily won
God out of knowledge and good out of infinite pain
And sight out of blindness and purity out of a stain.

As the marsh-hen secretly builds on the watery sod
Behold I will build me a nest on the greatness of God:
I will fly in the greatness of God as the marsh-hen flies
In the freedom that fills all the space 'twixt the marsh and the skies:
By so many roots as the marsh-grass sends in the sod
I will heartily lay me a-hold on the greatness of God:
Oh, like to the greatness of God is the greatness within
The range of the marshes, the liberal marshes of Glynn.

And the sea lends large, as the marsh: lo, out of his plenty the sea
Pours fast: full soon the time of the flood-tide must be:
Look how the grace of the sea doth go
About and about through the intricate channels that flow
                    Here and there,
                         Everywhere,
Till his waters have flooded the uttermost creeks and the low-lying lanes,
And the marsh is meshed with a million veins,
That like as with rosy and silvery essences flow
    In the rose-and-silver evening glow.
                    Farewell, my lord Sun!
The creeks overflow; a thousand rivulets run
'Twixt the roots of the sod; the blades of the marsh-grass stir;
Passeth a hurrying sound of wings that westward whirr;
Passeth, and all is still; and the currents cease to run;
And the sea and the marsh are one.

How still the plains of the waters be!
    The tide is in his ecstasy.
The tide is at his highest height:
    And it is night.
And now from the Vast of the Lord will the waters of sleep
Roll in on the souls of men,
But who will reveal to our waking ken
The forms that swim and the shapes that creep
    Under the waters of sleep?
And I would I could know what swimmeth below when the tide comes in
On the length and the breadth of the marvelous marshes of Glynn.

                                        Poems, 1878

GEORGE WASHINGTON CABLE

Jean-ah Poquelin

> Cable was famous for his stories about New Orleans which were
> based on old city records. By studying the writings of Poe, Dickens
> and Thackeray he learned to convert these Creole legends into
> imaginative stories. Later he antagonized the South by his vehe-
> ment protests against injustices to the Negro.

In the first decade of the present century, when the newly established
American Government was the most hateful thing in Louisiana—when
the Creoles were still kicking at such vile innovations as the trial by jury,

American dances, anti-smuggling laws, and the printing of the Governor's proclamation in English—when the Anglo-American flood that was presently to burst in a crevasse of immigration upon the delta had thus far been felt only as slippery seepage which made the Creole tremble for his footing—there stood, a short distance above what is now Canal Street, and considerably back from the line of villas which fringed the river-bank on Tchoupitoulas Road, an old colonial plantation-house half in ruin.

It stood aloof from civilization, the tracts that had once been its indigo fields given over to their first noxious wildness, and grown up into one of the horridest marshes within a circuit of fifty miles.

The house was of heavy cypress, lifted up on pillars, grim, solid, and spiritless, its massive build a strong reminder of days still earlier, when every man had been his own peace officer and the insurrection of the blacks a daily contingency. Its dark, weather-beaten roof and sides were hoisted up above the jungly plain in a distracted way, like a gigantic ammunition-wagon stuck in the mud and abandoned by some retreating army. Around it was a dense growth of low water willows, with half a hundred sorts of thorny or fetid bushes, savage strangers alike to the "language of flowers" and to the botanist's Greek. They were hung with countless strands of discolored and prickly smilax, and the impassable mud below bristled with *chevaux de frise* of the dwarf palmetto. Two lone forest-trees, dead cypresses, stood in the center of the marsh, dotted with roosting vultures. The shallow strips of water were hid by myriads of aquatic plants, under whose coarse and spiritless flowers, could one have seen it, was a harbor of reptiles, great and small, to make one shudder to the end of his days.

The house was on a slightly raised spot, the levee of a drainage canal. The waters of this canal did not run; they crawled, and were full of big, ravening fish and alligators, that held it against all comers.

Such was the home of old Jean Marie Poquelin, once an opulent indigo planter, standing high in the esteem of his small, proud circle of exclusively male acquaintances in the old city; now a hermit, alike shunned by and shunning all who had ever known him. "The last of his line," said the gossips. His father lies under the floor of the St. Louis Cathedral, with the wife of his youth on one side, and the wife of his old age on the other. Old Jean visits the spot daily. His half-brother—alas! there was a mystery; no one knew what had become of the gentle, young half-brother, more than thirty years his junior, whom once he seemed so fondly to love, but who, seven years ago, had disappeared suddenly, once for all, and left no clew of his fate.

They had seemed to live so happily in each other's love. No father, mother, wife to either, no kindred upon earth. The elder a bold, frank, impetuous, chivalric adventurer; the younger a gentle, studious, book-loving recluse; they lived upon the ancestral estate like mated birds, one always on the wing, the other always in the nest.

There was no trait in Jean Marie Poquelin, said the old gossips, for which he was so well known among his few friends as his apparent fondness for his "little brother." "Jacques said this," and "Jacques said that"; he "would leave this or that, or anything to Jacques," for "Jacques was a scholar," and "Jacques was good," or "wise," or "just," or "farsighted," as the nature of the case required; and "he should ask Jacques as soon as he got home," since Jacques was never elsewhere to be seen.

It was between the roving character of the one brother, and the bookishness of the other, that the estate fell into decay. Jean Marie, generous gentleman, gambled the slaves away one by one, until none was left, man or woman, but one old African mute.

The indigo-fields and vats of Louisiana had been generally abandoned as unremunerative. Certain enterprising men had substituted the culture of sugar; but while the recluse was too apathetic to take so active a course, the other saw larger, and at that time, equally respectable profits, first in smuggling, and later in the African slave-trade. What harm could he see in it? The whole people said it was vitally necessary, and to minister to a vital public necessity,—good enough, certainly, and so he laid up many a doubloon, that made him none the worse in the public regard.

One day old Jean Marie was about to start upon a voyage that was to be longer, much longer, than any that he had yet made. Jacques had begged him hard for many days not to go, but he laughed him off, and finally said, kissing him:

"*Adieu, 'tit frère.*"

"No," said Jacques. "I shall go with you."

They left the old hulk of a house in the sole care of the African mute, and went away to the Guinea coast together.

Two years after, old Poquelin came home without his vessel. He must have arrived at his house by night. No one saw him come. No one saw "his little brother"; rumor whispered that he, too, had returned, but he had never been seen again.

A dark suspicion fell upon the old slave-trader. No matter that the few kept the many reminded of the tenderness that had ever marked his bearing to the missing man. The many shook their heads. "You know he has a quick and fearful temper"; and "why does he cover his loss with mystery?" "Grief would out with the truth."

"But," said the charitable few, "look in his face; see that expression of true humanity." The many did look in his face, and, as he looked in theirs, he read the silent question: "Where is thy brother Abel?" The few were silenced, his former friends died off, and the name of Jean Marie Poquelin became a symbol of witchery, devilish crime, and hideous nursery fictions.

The man and his house were alike shunned. The snipe and duck hunters forsook the marsh, and the woodcutters abandoned the canal. Sometimes the hardier boys who ventured out there snake-shooting heard a slow thumping of oar-locks on the canal. They would look at each other for a moment half in consternation, half in glee, then rush from their sport in wanton haste to assail with their gibes the unoffending, withered old man who, in rusty attire, sat in the stern of a skiff, rowed homeward by his white-headed African mute.

"O Jean-ah Poquelin! O Jean-ah! Jean-ah Poquelin!"

It was not necessary to utter more than that. No hint of wickedness, deformity, or any physical or moral demerit; merely the name and tone of mockery: "Oh, Jean-ah Poquelin!" and while they tumbled one over another in their needless haste to fly, he would rise carefully from his seat, while the aged mute, with downcast face, went on rowing, and rolling up his brown fist and extending it toward the urchins, would pour forth such an unholy broadside of French imprecation and invective as would all but craze them with delight.

Among both blacks and whites the house was the object of a thousand superstitions. Every midnight, they affirmed, the *feu follet* came out of the marsh and ran in and out of the rooms, flashing from window to window. The story of some lads, whose words in ordinary statements were worthless, was generally credited, that the night they camped in the woods, rather than pass the place after dark, they saw, about sunset, every window blood-red, and on each of the four chimneys an owl sitting, which turned his head three times round, and moaned and laughed with a human voice. There was a bottomless well, everybody professed to know, beneath the sill of the big front door under the rotten veranda; whoever set his foot upon that threshold disappeared forever in the depth below.

What wonder the marsh grew as wild as Africa! Take all the Faubourg Ste. Marie, and half the ancient city, you would not find one graceless daredevil reckless enough to pass within a hundred yards of the house after nightfall.

The alien races pouring into old New Orleans began to find the few streets named for the Bourbon princes too strait for them. The wheel of fortune, beginning to whirl, threw them off beyond the ancient corporation lines, and sowed civilization and even trade upon the lands of the Graviers and Girods. Fields became roads, roads streets. Everywhere the leveler was peering through his glass, rodsmen were whacking their way through willow-brakes and rose-hedges, and the sweating Irishmen tossed the blue clay up with their long-handled shovels.

"Ha! that is all very well," quoth the Jean-Baptistes, feeling the reproach of an enterprise that asked neither co-operation nor advice of them, "but wait till they come yonder to Jean Poquelin's marsh; ha! ha! ha!" The supposed predicament so delighted them that they put on a mock terror and whirled about in an assumed stampede, then caught their clasped hands between their knees in excess of mirth, and laughed till the tears ran; for whether the street-makers mired in the marsh, or contrived to cut through old "Jean-ah's" property, either event would be joyful. Meantime a line of tiny rods, with bits of white paper in their split tops, gradually extended its way straight through the haunted ground, and across the canal diagonally.

"We shall fill that ditch," said the men in mud-boots, and brushed close along the chained and padlocked gate of the haunted mansion. Ah, Jean-ah Poquelin, those were not Creole boys, to be stampeded with a little hard swearing.

He went to the Governor. That official scanned the odd figure with no slight interest. Jean Poquelin was of short, broad frame, with a bronzed leonine face. His brow was ample and deeply furrowed. His eye, large and black, was bold and open like that of a war-horse, and his jaws shut together with the firmness of iron. He was dressed in a suit of Attakapas cottonade, and his shirt unbuttoned and thrown back from the throat and bosom, sailor-wise, showed a herculean breast, hard and grizzled. There was no fierceness or defiance in his look, no harsh ungentleness, no symptom of his unlawful life or violent temper; but rather a peaceful and peaceable fearlessness. Across the whole face, not marked in one or another feature, but as it were laid softly upon the countenance like an almost imperceptible veil, was the imprint of some great grief. A careless eye might easily overlook it, but, once seen, there it hung—faint, but unmistakable.

The Governor bowed.

"*Parlez-vous français?*" asked the figure.

"I would rather talk English, if you can do so," said the Governor.

"My name, Jean Poquelin."

"How can I serve you, Mr. Poquelin?"

"My 'ouse is yond'; *dans le marais là-bas.*"

The Governor bowed.

"Dat *marais* billong to me."

"Yes, sir."

"To me; Jean Poquelin; I hown 'im meself."

"Well, sir?"

"He don't billong to you; I get him from me father."

"That is perfectly true, Mr. Poquelin, as far as I am aware."

"You want to make strit pass yond'?"

"I do not know, sir; it is quite probable; but the city will indemnify you for any loss you may suffer—you will get paid, you understand."

"Strit can't pass dare."

"You will have to see the municipal authorities about that, Mr. Poquelin."

A bitter smile came upon the old man's face:

"*Pardon, Monsieur,* you is not *le Gouverneur?*"

"Yes."

"*Mais,* yes. You har' *le Gouverneur*—yes. Veh-well. I come to you. I tell you, strit can't pass at me 'ouse."

"But you will have to see—"

"I come to you. You is *le Gouverneur*. I know not the new laws. I ham a Fr-r-rench-a-man! Fr-rench-a-man have something *aller au contraire*—he come at his *Gouverneur*. I come at you. If me not had been bought from me king like *bossals* in the hold time, ze king gof—France would-a-show *Monsieur le Gouverneur* to take care his men to make strit in right places. *Mais*, I know; we billong to *Monsieur le Président*. I want you do somesin for me, eh?"

"What is it?" asked the patient Governor.

"I want you tell *Monsieur le Président*, strit—can't—pass—at—me—'ouse."

"Have a chair, Mr. Poquelin"; but the old man did not stir. The Governor took a quill and wrote a line to a city official, introducing Mr. Poquelin, and asking for him every possible courtesy. He handed it to him, instructing him where to present it.

"Mr. Poquelin," he said with a conciliatory smile, "tell me, is it your house that our Creole citizens tell such odd stories about?"

The old man glared sternly upon the speaker, and with immovable features said:

"You don't see me trade some Guinea nigga'?"

"Oh, no."

"You don't see me make some smugglin'?"

"No, sir; not at all."

"But, I am Jean Marie Poquelin. I mine me hown bizniss. Dat all right? *Adieu*."

He put his hat on and withdrew. By and by he stood, letter in hand, before the person to whom it was addressed. This person employed an interpreter.

"He says," said the interpreter to the officer, "he come to make you the fair warning how you muz not make the street pas' at his 'ouse."

The officer remarked that "such impudence was refreshing"; but the experienced interpreter translated freely.

"He says: 'Why you don't want?' " said the interpreter.

The old slave-trader answered at some length.

"He says," said the interpreter, again turning to the officer, "the marass is a too unhealth' for peopl' to live."

"But we expect to drain his old marsh; it's not going to be a marsh."

"*Il dit*—" The interpreter explained in French.

The old man answered tersely.

"He says the canal is a private," said the interpreter.

"Oh! *that* old ditch; that's to be filled up. Tell the old man we're going to fix him up nicely."

Translation being duly made, the man in power was amused to see a thundercloud gathering on the old man's face.

"Tell him," he added, "by the time we finish, there'll not be a ghost left in his shanty."

The interpreter began to translate, but—

"*J'comprends, j'comprends,*" said the old man, with an impatient gesture, and burst forth, pouring curses upon the United States, the President, the Territory of Orleans, Congress, the Governor and all his subordinates, striding out of the apartment as he cursed, while the object of his maledictions roared with merriment and rammed the floor with his foot.

"Why, it will make his old place worth ten dollars to one," said the official to the interpreter.

" 'Tis not for de worse of de property," said the interpreter.

"I should guess not," said the other, whittling his chair—"seems to me as if some of these old Creoles would liever live in a crawfish hole than to have a neighbor."

"You know what make old Jean Poquelin make like that? I will tell you. You know—"

The interpreter was rolling a cigarette, and paused to light his tinder; then, as the smoke poured in a thick double stream from his nostrils, he said, in a solemn whisper:

"He is a witch."

"Ho, ho, ho!" laughed the other.

"You don't believe it? What you want to bet?" cried the interpreter, jerking himself half up and thrusting out one arm while he bared it of its coat sleeve with the hand of the other. "What you want to bet?"

"How do you know?" asked the official.

"Dass what I goin' to tell you. You know, one evening I was shooting some *grosbec*. I killed three; but I had trouble to fine them, it was becoming so dark. When I have them I start' to come home; then I got to pas' at Jean Poquelin's house."

"Ho, ho, ho!" laughed the other, throwing his leg over the arm of his chair.

"Wait," said the interpreter. "I come along slow, not making some noises; still, still—"

"And scared," said the smiling one.

"*Mais*, wait. I get all pas' the 'ouse. 'Ah!' I say; 'all right!' Then I see two thing' before! Hah! I get as cold and humide, and shake like leaf. You think it was nothing? There I see, so plain as can be (though it was making nearly dark), I see Jean—Marie—Po-que-lin walkin' right in front, and right there beside of him was something like a man—but not a man— white like paint! I dropp' on the grass from scared—they pass'; so sure as I live 'twas the ghos' of Jacques Poquelin, his brother!"

"Pooh!" said the listener.

"I'll put my han' in the fire," said the interpreter.

"But did you never think," asked the other, "that that might be Jack Poquelin, as you call him, alive and well, and for some cause hid away by his brother?"

226

"But there har' no cause!" said the other, and the entrance of third parties changed the subject.

Some months passed, and the street was opened. A canal was first dug through the marsh, the small one which passed so close to Jean Poquelin's house was filled, and the street, or rather a sunny road, just touched a corner of the old mansion's dooryard. The morass ran dry. Its venomous denizens slipped away through the bulrushes; the cattle roaming freely upon its hardened surface trampled the superabundant undergrowth. The bellowing frogs croaked to westward. Lilies and the flower-de-luce sprang up in the place of reeds; smilax and poison-oak gave way to the purple-plumed ironweed and pink spiderwort; the bindweeds ran everywhere blooming as they ran, and on one of the dead cypresses a giant creeper hung its green burden of foliage and lifted its scarlet trumpets. Sparrows and red-birds flitted through the bushes, and dewberries grew ripe beneath. Over all these came a sweet, dry smell of salubrity which the place had not known since the sediments of the Mississippi first lifted it from the sea.

But its owner did not build. Over the willow-brakes, and down the vista of the open street, bright new houses, some singly, some by ranks, were prying in upon the old man's privacy. They even settled down toward his southern side. First a wood-cutter's hut or two, then a market gardener's shanty, then a painted cottage, and all at once the faubourg had flanked and half surrounded him and his dried-up marsh.

Ah! then the common people began to hate him. "The old tyrant!" "You don't mean an old *tyrant?*" "Well, then, why don't he build when the public need demands it? What does he live in that unneighborly way for?" "The old pirate!" "The old kidnaper!" How easily even the most ultra Louisianians put on the imported virtues of the North when they could be brought to bear against the hermit. "There he goes, with the boys after him! Ah! ha! ha! Jean-ah Poquelin! Ah! Jean-ah! Aha! aha! Jean-ah Marie! Jean-ah Poquelin! The old villain!" How merrily the swarming Américains echo the spirit of persecution! "The old fraud," they say—"pretends to live in a haunted house, does he? We'll tar and feather him some day. Guess we can fix him."

He cannot be rowed home along the old canal now; he walks. He has broken sadly of late, and the street urchins are ever at his heels. It is like the days when they cried: "Go up, thou bald-head," and the old man now and then turns and delivers ineffectual curses.

To the Creoles—to the incoming lower class of superstitious Germans, Irish, Sicilians, and others—he became an omen and embodiment of public and private ill-fortune. Upon him all the vagaries of their superstitions gathered and grew. If a house caught fire, it was imputed to his machinations. Did a woman go off in a fit, he had bewitched her. Did a child stray off for an hour, the mother shivered with the apprehension that Jean Poquelin had offered him to strange gods. The house was the subject of every bad boy's invention who loved to contrive ghostly lies. "As long as that house stands, we shall have bad luck. Do you not see our peas and beans dying, our cabbages and lettuce going to seed, and our gardens turning to dust, while every day you can see it raining in the woods? The rain will never pass old Poquelin's house. He keeps a fetish. He has conjured the whole Faubourg Ste. Marie. And why, the old wretch? Simply because our playful and innocent children call after him as he passes."

A "Building and Improvement Company," which had not yet got its charter, "but was going to," and which had not, indeed, any tangible capital yet, but "was going to have some," joined the "Jean-ah Poquelin" war. The haunted property would be such a capital site for a market-house! They sent a deputation to the old mansion to ask its occupant to sell. The deputation never got beyond the chained gate and a very barren interview with the African mute. The President of the Board was then empowered (for he had studied French in Pennsylvania and was considered qualified) to call and persuade M. Poquelin to subscribe to the company's stock; but—

"Fact is, gentlemen," he said at the next meeting, "it would take us at least twelve months to make Mr. Pokaleen understand the rather original features of our system, and he wouldn't subscribe when we'd done; besides, the only way to see him is to stop him on the street."

There was a great laugh from the Board; they couldn't help it. "Better meet a bear robbed of her whelps," said one.

"You're mistaken as to that," said the President. "I did meet him, and stopped him, and found him quite polite. But I could get no satisfaction from him; the fellow wouldn't talk in French, and when I spoke in English he hoisted his old shoulders up, and gave the same answer to everything I said."

"And that was—?" asked one or two, impatient of the pause.

"That it 'don't worse w'ile.'"

One of the Board said: "Mr. President, this market-house project, as I take it, is not altogether a selfish one; the community is to be benefited by it. We may feel that we are working in the public interest (the Board smiled knowingly), if we employ all possible means to oust this old nuisance from among us. You may know that at the time the street was cut through, this old Poquelin did all he could to prevent it. It was owing to a certain connection which I had with that affair that I heard a ghost story (smiles, followed by a sudden dignified check)—ghost story, which, of course, I am not going to relate; but I *may* say that my profound conviction, arising from a prolonged study of that story, is that this old villain, John Poquelann, has his brother locked up in that old house. Now, if this is so, and we can fix it on him, I merely *suggest* that we can make the matter highly useful. I don't know," he added, beginning to sit down, "but that it is an action we owe to the community—hem!"

"How do you propose to handle the subject?" asked the President.

228

"I was thinking," said the speaker, "that, as a Board of Directors, it would be unadvisable for us to authorize any action involving trespass; but if you, for instance, Mr. President, should, as it were, for mere curiosity, *request* someone, as, for instance, our excellent Secretary, simply as a personal favor, to look into the matter—this is merely a suggestion."

The Secretary smiled sufficiently to be understood that, while he certainly did not consider such preposterous service a part of his duties as secretary, he might, notwithstanding, accede to the President's request; and the Board adjourned.

Little White, as the Secretary was called, was a mild, kind-hearted little man, who, nevertheless, had no fear of anything, unless it was the fear of being unkind.

"I tell you frankly," he privately said to the President, "I go into this purely for reasons of my own."

The next day, a little after nightfall, one might have descried this little man slipping along the rear fence of the Poquelin place, preparatory to vaulting over into the rank, grass-grown yard, and bearing himself altogether more after the manner of a collector of rare chickens than according to the usage of secretaries.

The picture presented to his eye was not calculated to enliven his mind. The old mansion stood out against the western sky, black and silent. One long, lurid pencil-stroke along a sky of slate was all that was left of daylight. No sign of life was apparent; no light at any window, unless it might have been on the side of the house hidden from view. No owls were on the chimney; no dogs were in the yard.

He entered the place, and ventured up behind a small cabin which stood apart from the house. Through one of its many crannies he easily detected the African mute crouched before a flickering pine-knot, his head on his knees, fast asleep.

He concluded to enter the mansion, and, with that view, stood and scanned it. The broad rear steps of the veranda would not serve him; he might meet someone midway. He was measuring, with his eye, the proportions of one of the pillars which supported it, and estimating the practicability of climbing it, when he heard a footstep. Someone dragged a chair out toward the railing, then seemed to change his mind and began to pace the veranda, his footfalls resounding on the dry boards with singular loudness. Little White drew a step backward, got the figure between himself and the sky, and at once recognized the short, broad-shouldered form of old Jean Poquelin.

He sat down upon a billet of wood, and, to escape the stings of a whining cloud of mosquitoes, shrouded his face and neck in his handkerchief, leaving his eyes uncovered.

He had sat there but a moment when he noticed a strange, sickening odor, faint, as if coming from a distance, but loathsome and horrid.

Whence could it come? Not from the cabin; not from the marsh, for it was dry as powder. It was not in the air; it seemed to come from the ground.

Rising up, he noticed, for the first time, a few steps before him a narrow footpath leading toward the house. He glanced down it—ha! right there was someone coming—ghostly white!

Quick as thought, and as noiselessly, he lay down at full length against the cabin. It was bold strategy, and yet, there was no denying it, little White felt that he was frightened. "It is not a ghost," he said to himself. "I know it cannot be a ghost"; but the perspiration burst out at every pore, and the air seemed to thicken with heat. "It is a living man," he said in his thoughts. "I hear his footstep, and I hear old Poquelin's footsteps, too, separately, over on the veranda. I am not discovered; the thing has passed; there is that odor again; what a smell of death! Is it coming back? Yes. It stops at the door of the cabin. Is it peering in at the sleeping mute? It moves away. It is in the path again. Now it is gone." He shuddered. "Now, if I dare venture, the mystery is solved." He rose cautiously, close against the cabin, and peered along the path.

The figure of a man, a presence if not a body—but whether clad in some white stuff or naked the darkness would not allow him to determine—had turned, and now, with a seeming painful gait, moved slowly from him. "Great Heaven! can it be that the dead do walk?" He withdrew again the hands which had gone to his eyes. The dreadful object passed between two pillars and under the house. He listened. There was a faint sound as of feet upon a staircase; then all was still except the measured tread of Jean Poquelin walking on the veranda, and the heavy respirations of the mute slumbering in the cabin.

The little Secretary was about to retreat; but as he looked once more toward the haunted house, a dim light appeared in the crack of a closed window, and presently old Jean Poquelin came, dragging his chair, and sat down close against the shining cranny. He spoke in a low, tender tone in the French tongue, making some inquiry. An answer came from within. Was it the voice of a human? So unnatural was it—so hollow, so discordant, so unearthly—that the stealthy listener shuddered again from head to foot, and when something stirred in some rushes near by—though it may have been nothing more than a rat—and came scuttling through the grass, the little Secretary actually turned and fled. As he left the enclosure he moved with bolder leisure through the bushes; yet now and then he spoke aloud: "Oh, oh! I see, I understand!" and shut his eyes in his hands.

How strange that henceforth little White was the champion of Jean Poquelin! In season and out of season—wherever a word was uttered against him—the Secretary, with a quiet, aggressive force that instantly arrested gossip, demanded upon what authority the statement or conjecture was made; but as he did not condescend to explain his own remarkable attitude, it was not long before the disrelish and suspicion which had followed Jean Poquelin so many years fell also upon him.

It was only the next evening but one after his adventure that he made himself a source of sullen amazement to one hundred and fifty boys, by ordering them to desist from their wanton hallooing. Old Jean Poquelin, standing and shaking his cane, rolling out his long-drawn maledictions, paused and stared, then gave the Secretary a courteous bow and started on. The boys, save one, from pure astonishment, ceased; but a ruffianly little Irish lad, more daring than any had yet been, threw a big hurtling clod, that struck old Poquelin between the shoulders and burst like a shell. The enraged old man wheeled with uplifted staff to give chase to the scampering vagabond; and—he may have tripped, or he may not, but he fell full length. Little White hastened to help him up, but he waved him off with a fierce imprecation and staggering to his feet resumed his way homeward. His lips were reddened with blood.

Little White was on his way to the meeting of the Board. He would have given all he dared spend to have stayed away, for he felt both too fierce and too tremulous to brook the criticisms that were likely to be made.

"I can't help it, gentlemen; I can't help you to make a case against the old man, and I'm not going to."

"We did not expect this disappointment, Mr. White."

"I can't help that, sir. No, sir; you had better not appoint any more investigations. Somebody'll investigate himself into trouble. No, sir; it isn't a threat, it is only my advice, but I warn you that whoever takes the task in hand will rue it to his dying day—which may be hastened, too."

The President expressed himself "surprised."

"I don't care a rush," answered little White, wildly and foolishly. "I don't care a rush if you are, sir. No, my nerves are not disordered; my head's as clear as a bell. No, I'm *not* excited."

A Director remarked that the Secretary looked as though he had waked from a nightmare.

"Well, sir, if you want to know the fact, I have; and if you choose to cultivate old Poquelin's society, you can have one, too."

"White," called a facetious member, but White did not notice. "White," he called again.

"What?" demanded White, with a scowl.

"Did you see the ghost?"

"Yes, sir; I did," cried White, hitting the table, and handing the President a paper which brought the Board to other business.

The story got among the gossips that somebody (they were afraid to say little White) had been to the Poquelin mansion by night and beheld something appalling. The rumor was but a shadow of the truth, magnified and distorted as is the manner of shadows. He had seen skeletons walking, and had barely escaped the clutches of one by making the sign of the cross.

Some madcap boys with an appetite for the horrible plucked up courage to venture through the dried marsh by the cattle-path, and come before the house at a spectral hour when the air was full of bats. Something which they but half saw—half a sight was enough—sent them tearing back through the willow-brakes and acacia bushes to their homes, where they fairly dropped down and cried:

"Was it white?" "No—yes—nearly so—we can't tell—but we saw it." And one could hardly doubt, to look at their ashen faces, that they had, whatever it was.

"If that old rascal lived in the country we come from," said certain Américains, "he'd have been tarred and feathered before now, wouldn't he, Sanders?"

"Well, now, he just would."

"And we'd have rid him on a rail, wouldn't we?"

"That's what I allow."

"Tell you what you *could* do." They were talking to some rollicking Creoles who had assumed an absolute necessity for doing *something*. "What is it you call this thing where an old man marries a young girl, and you come out with horns and—"

"*Charivari?*" asked the Creoles.

"Yes, that's it. Why don't you shivaree him?" Felicitous suggestion.

Little White, with his wife beside him, was sitting on their doorsteps on the sidewalk, as Creole custom had taught them, looking toward the sunset. They had moved into the lately-opened street. The view was not attractive on the score of beauty. The houses were small and scattered, and across the flat commons, spite of the lofty tangle of weeds and bushes, and spite of the thickets of acacia, they needs must see the dismal old Poquelin mansion, tilted awry and shutting out the declining sun. The moon, white and slender, was hanging the tip of its horn over one of the chimneys.

"And you say," said the Secretary, "the old black man has been going by here alone? Patty, suppose old Poquelin should be concocting some mischief; he don't lack provocation; the way that clod hit him the other day was enough to have killed him. Why, Patty, he dropped as quick as *that!* No wonder you haven't seen him. I wonder if they haven't heard something about him up at the drug-store. Suppose I go and see."

"Do," said his wife.

She sat alone for half an hour, watching that sudden going out of the day peculiar to the latitude.

"That moon is ghost enough for one house," she said, as her husband returned. "It has gone right down the chimney."

"Patty," said little White, "the drug-clerk says the boys are going to shivaree old Poquelin tonight. I'm going to try to stop it."

"Why, White," said his wife, "you'd better not. You'll get hurt."

"No, I'll not."

"Yes, you will."

"I'm going to sit out here until they come along. They're compelled to pass right by here."

"Why, White, it may be midnight before they start; you're not going to sit out here till then."

"Yes, I am."

"Well, you're very foolish," said Mrs. White in an undertone, looking anxious, and tapping one of the steps with her foot.

They sat a very long time talking over little family matters.

"What's that?" at last said Mrs. White.

"That's the nine-o'clock gun," said White, and they relapsed into a long-sustained, drowsy silence.

"Patty, you'd better go in and go to bed," said he at last.

"I'm not sleepy."

"Well, you're very foolish," quietly remarked little White, and again silence fell upon them.

"Patty, suppose I walk out to the old house and see if I can find out anything."

"Suppose," said she, "you don't do any such—listen!"

Down the street arose a great hubbub. Dogs and boys were howling and barking; men were laughing, shouting, groaning, and blowing horns, whooping, and clanking cow-bells, whinnying, and howling, and rattling pots and pans.

"They are coming this way," said little White. "You had better go into the house, Patty."

"So had you."

"No. I'm going to see if I can't stop them."

"Why, White!"

"I'll be back in a minute," said White, and went toward the noise.

In a few moments the little Secretary met the mob. The pen hesitates on the word, for there is a respectable difference, measurable only on the scale of the half century, between a mob and a *charivari*. Little White lifted his ineffectual voice. He faced the head of the disorderly column, and cast himself about as if he were made of wood and moved by the jerk of a string. He rushed to one who seemed, from the size and clatter of his tin pan, to be a leader. "*Stop these fellows, Bienvenu, stop them just a minute, till I tell them something.*" Bienvenu turned and brandished his instruments of discord in an imploring way to the crowd. They slackened their pace, two or three hushed their horns and joined the prayer of little White and Bienvenu for silence. The throng halted. The hush was delicious.

"Bienvenu," said little White, "don't shivaree old Poquelin tonight; he's—"

"My fwang," said the swaying Bienvenu, "who tail you I goin' to chahivahi somebody, eh? You sink bickause I make a little playfool wiz zis tin pan zat I am *dhonk*?"

"Oh, no, Bienvenu, old fellow, you're all right. I was afraid you might not know that old Poquelin was sick, you know, but you're not going there, are you?"

"My fwang, I vay soy to tail you zat you ah dhonk as de dev'. I am *shem* of you. I ham ze servan' of ze *publique*. Zese *citoyens* goin' to wickwest Jean Poquelin to give to the Ursuline' two hondred fifty dolla'—"

"*Hé quoi!*" cried a listener, "*cinq cent piastres, oui!*"

"*Oui!*" said Bienvenu, "and if he wiffuse we make him some lit' *musique; ta-ra ta!*" He hoisted a merry hand and foot, then frowning, added: "Old Poquelin got no bizniz dhink s'much w'isky."

"But, gentlemen," said little White, around whom a circle had gathered, "the old man is very sick."

"My faith!" cried a tiny Creole, "we did not make him to be sick. W'en we have say we going make *le charivari*, do you want that we shall tell a lie? My faith! 'sfools!"

"But you can shivaree somebody else," said desperate little White.

"*Oui!*" cried Bienvenu, "*et chahivahi* Jean-ah Poquelin tomo'w!"

"Let us go to Madame Schneider!" cried two or three, and amid huzzas and confused cries, among which was heard a stentorian Celtic call for drinks, the crowd again began to move.

"*Cent piastres pour l'hôpital de charité!*"

"Hurrah!"

"One hondred dolla' for Charity Hospital."

"Hurrah!"

"Whang!" went a tin pan, the crowd yelled, and Pandemonium gaped again. They were off at a right angle.

Nodding, Mrs. White looked at the mantel-clock.

"Well, if it isn't away after midnight."

The hideous noise down street was passing beyond earshot. She raised a sash and listened. For a moment there was silence. Someone came to the door.

"Is that you, White?"

"Yes." He entered. "I succeeded, Patty."

"Did you?" said Patty joyfully.

"Yes. They've gone down to shivaree the old Dutchwoman who married her stepdaughter's sweetheart. They say she has got to pay a hundred dollars to the hospital before they stop."

The couple retired, and Mrs. White slumbered. She was awakened by her husband snapping the lid of his watch.

"What time?" she asked.

"Half-past three. Patty, I haven't slept a wink. Those fellows are out yet. Don't you hear them?"

"Why, White, they're coming this way!"

"I know they are," said White, sliding out of bed and drawing on his clothes, "and they're coming fast. You'd better go away from that window, Patty. My! what a clatter!"

"Here they are," said Mrs. White, but her husband was gone. Two or three hundred men and boys passed the place at a rapid walk straight down the broad, new street, toward the hated house of ghosts. The din was terrific. She saw little White at the head of the rabble brandishing his arms and trying in vain to make himself heard; but they only shook their heads, laughing and hooting the louder, and so passed, bearing him on before them.

Swiftly they pass out from among the houses, away from the dim oil lamps of the street, out into the broad starlit commons, and enter the willowy jungles of the haunted ground. Some hearts fail and their owners lag behind and turn back, suddenly remembering how near morning it is. But the most part push on, tearing the air with their clamor.

Down ahead of them in the long thicket-darkened way there is—singularly enough—a faint, dancing light. It must be very near the old house; it is. It has stopped now. It is a lantern, and is under a well-known sapling which was grown up on the wayside since the canal was filled. Now it swings mysteriously to and fro. A goodly number of the more ghost-fearing give up the sport; but a full hundred move forward at a run, doubling their devilish howling and banging.

Yes, it is a lantern, and there are two persons under the tree. The crowd draws near—drops into a walk; one of the two is the old African mute; he lifts the lantern up so that it shines on the other; the crowd recoils; there is a hush of all clangor, and all at once, with a cry of mingled fright and horror from every throat, the whole throng rushes back, dropping everything, sweeping past little White and hurrying on, never stopping until the jungle is left behind, and then to find that not one in ten has seen the cause of the stampede, and not one of the tenth is certain what it was.

There is one huge fellow among them who looks capable of any villainy. He finds something to mount on, and, in the Creole *patois*, calls a general halt. Bienvenu sinks down, and, vainly trying to recline gracefully, resigns the leadership. The herd gather round the speaker; he assures them that they have been outraged. Their right peaceably to traverse the public streets has been trampled upon. Shall such encroachments be endured? It is now daybreak. Let them go now by the open light of day and force a free passage of the public highway!

A scattering consent was the response, and the crowd, thinned now and drowsy, straggled quietly down toward the old house. Some drifted ahead, others sauntered behind, but everyone, as he again neared the tree, came to a stand-still. Little White sat upon a bank of turf on the opposite side of the way looking very stern and sad. To each new-comer he put the same question:

"Did you come here to go to old Poquelin's?"

"Yes."

"He's dead." And if the shocked hearer started away he would say: "Don't go away."

"Why not?"

"I want you to go to the funeral presently."

If some Louisianian, too loyal to dear France or Spain to understand English, looked bewildered, someone would interpret for him; and presently they went. Little White led the van, the crowd trooping after him down the middle of the way. The gate, that had never been seen before unchained, was open. Stern little White stopped a short distance from it; the rabble stopped behind him. Something was moving out from under the veranda. The many whisperers stretched upward to see. The African mute came very slowly toward the gate, leading by a cord in the nose a small brown bull, which was harnessed to a rude cart. On the flat body of the cart, under a black cloth, were seen the outlines of a long box.

"Hats off, gentlemen," said little White, as the box came in view, and the crowd silently uncovered. "Gentlemen," said little White, "here comes the last remains of Jean Marie Poquelin, a better man, I'm afraid, with all his sins—yes, a better man—a kinder man to his blood—a man of more self-forgetful goodness—than all of you put together will ever dare to be."

There was a profound hush as the vehicle came creaking through the gate; but when it turned away from them toward the forest, those in front started suddenly. There was a backward rush, then all stood still again staring one way; for there, behind the bier, with eyes cast down and labored step, walked the living remains—all that was left—of little Jacques Poquelin, the long-hidden brother—a leper, as white as snow.

Dumb with horror, the cringing crowd gazed upon the walking death. They watched, in silent awe, the slow *cortège* creep down the long, straight road and lessen on the view, until by and by it stopped where a wild, unfrequented path branched off into the undergrowth toward the rear of the ancient city.

"They are going to the *Terre aux Lépreux*," said one in the crowd. The rest watched them in silence.

The little bull was set free; the mute, with the strength of an ape, lifted the long box to his shoulder. For a moment more the mute and the leper stood in sight, while the former adjusted his heavy burden; then, without one backward glance upon the unkind human world, turning their faces toward the ridge in the depths of the swamp known as the Leper's Land, they stepped into the jungle, disappeared, and were never seen again.

Old Creole Days, 1879

JOEL CHANDLER HARRIS

Mr. Rabbit Nibbles Up the Butter

When Harris worked as a printer for a newspaper issued from a Georgia plantation, he heard many folk tales from the slaves. Years later, as an editorial writer for the Atlanta CONSTITUTION, *he began his skillful retelling and embellishment of those stories. Many of them helped dissipate the ill will of extremists in both North and South.*

"De animils en de creeturs," said Uncle Remus, shaking his coffee around in the bottom of his tin-cup, in order to gather up all the sugar, "dey kep' on gittin' mo' en mo' familious wid wunner nudder, twel bimeby, twan't long fo' Brer Rabbit, en Brer Fox, en Brer Possum got ter sorter bunchin' der perwishuns tergedder in de same shanty. Atter w'ile de roof sorter 'gun ter leak, en one day Brer Rabbit, en Brer Fox, en Brer Posssum, 'semble fer ter see ef dey can't kinder patch her up. Dey had a big day's work in front un um, en dey fotch der dinner wid um. Dey lump de vittles up in one pile, en de butter w'at Brer Fox brung, dey goes en puts in de spring-'ouse fer ter keep cool, en den dey went ter wuk, en 'twan't long 'fo' Brer Rabbit stummuck 'gun ter sorter growl en pester 'im. Dat butter er Brer Fox sot heavy on his mine, en his mouf water eve'y time he 'member 'bout it. Present'y he say ter hisse'f dat he bleedzd ter have a nip at dat butter, en den he lay his plans, he did. Fus' news you know, w'ile dey wuz all wukkin' 'long, Brer Rabbit raise his head quick en fling his years forrerd en holler out:

"'Here I is. W'at you want wid me?' en off he put like sump'n wuz atter 'im.

"He sallied 'roun', ole Brer Rabbit did, en atter he make sho dat nobody ain't foller'n un 'im, inter de spring-'ouse he bounces, en dar he stays twel he git a bait er butter. Den he santer on back en go to wuk.

"'Whar you bin?' sez Brer Fox, sezee.

"'I hear my chilluns callin' me,' sez Brer Rabbit, sezee, 'en I hatter go see w'at dey want. My ole 'oman done gone en tuck mighty sick,' sezee.

"Dey wuk on twel bimeby de butter tas'e so good dat ole Brer Rabbit wants some mo'. Den he raise up his head, he did, en holler out:

"'Heyo! Hole on! I'm a comin'! 'en off he put.

"Dis time he stay right smart w'ile, en w'en he git back Brer Fox ax him whar he bin.

"'I been ter see my ole 'oman, en she's a sinkin',' sezee.

"Dreckly Brer Rabbit hear um callin' 'im ag'in en off he goes en dis time, bless yo' soul, he gits de butter out so clean dat he kin see hisse'f in de bottom er de bucket. He scrape it clean en lick it dry, en den he go back ter wuk lookin' mo' samer dan a nigger w'at de patter-rollers bin had holt un.

" 'How's yo' ole 'oman dis time?' sez Brer Fox, sezee.

" 'I'm oblije ter you, Brer Fox,' sez Brer Rabbit, sezee, 'but I'm fear'd she's done gone by now,' en dat sorter make Brer Fox en Brer Possum feel in moanin' wid Brer Rabbit.

"Bimeby, w'en dinner-time come, dey all got out der vittles, but Brer Rabbit keep on lookin' lonesome, en Brer Fox en Brer Possum dey sorter rustle roun' fer ter see ef dey can't make Brer Rabbit feel sorter splimmy."

"What is that, Uncle Remus?" asked the little boy.

"Sorter splimmy-splammy, honey—sorter like he in a crowd—sorter like his ole 'oman aint dead ez she mout be. You know how fokes duz w'en dey gits whar people's a moanin'.''

The little boy didn't know, fortunately for him, and Uncle Remus went on:

"Brer Fox en Brer Possum rustle roun', dey did, gittin' out de vittles, en bimeby Brer Fox, he say, sezee:

" 'Brer Possum, you run down ter de spring en fetch de butter, en I'll sail 'roun' yer en set de table,' sezee.

"Brer Possum, he lope off atter de butter, en dreckly here he come lopin' back wid his years a trimblin' en his tongue a hangin' out. Brer Fox, he holler out:

" 'W'at de matter now, Brer Possum?' sezee.

" 'Yo all better run yer, fokes,' sez Brer Possum, sezee. 'De las' drap er dat butter done gone!'

" 'Whar she gone?' sez Brer Fox, sezee.

" 'Look like she dry up,' sez Brer Possum, sezee.

"Den Brer Rabbit, he look sorter sollum, he did, en he up'n say, sezee:

" 'I speck dat butter melt in somebody mouf,' sezee.

"Den dey went down ter de spring wid Brer Possum, en sho nuff de butter done gone. W'iles dey wuz sputin' over der wunderment, Brer Rabbit say he see tracks all 'roun' dar, en he p'int out dat ef dey'll all go ter sleep, he kin ketch de chap w'at stole de butter. Den dey all lie down en Brer Fox en Brer Possum dey soon drapt off ter sleep, but Brer Rabbit he stay 'wake, en w'en de time come he raise up easy en smear Brer Possum mouf wid de butter on his paws, en den he run off en nibble up de bes' er de dinner w'at dey lef' layin' out, en den he come back en wake up Brer Fox, en show 'im de butter on Brer Possum mouf. Den dey wake up Brer Possum, en tell 'im 'bout it, but c'ose Brer Possum 'ny it ter de las'. Brer Fox, dough, he's a kinder lawyer, en he argafy dis way—dat Brer Possum wuz de fus one at de butter, en de fus one fer ter miss it, en mo'n dat, der hang de signs on his mouf. Brer Possum see dat dey got 'im jammed up in a cornder, en den he up en say dat de way fer ter ketch de man w'at stole de butter is ter b'il' a big bresh-heap en set her afier, en all han's try ter jump over, en de one w'at fall in, den he de chap w'at stole de butter. Brer Rabbit en Brer Fox dey bofe 'gree, dey did, en dey whirl in en b'il' de bresh-heap, en dey b'il' her high en dey b'il' her wide, en den dey totch her off. W'en she got ter blazin' up good, Brer Rabbit, he tuck de fus turn. He sorter step back, en look 'roun' en giggle, en over he went mo' samer dan a bird flyin'. Den come Brer Fox. He got back little fudder, en spit on his han's, en lit out en made de jump, en he come so nigh gittin' in dat de een' er his tail kotch afier. Ain't you never see no fox, honey?" inquired Uncle Remus, in a tone that implied both conciliation and information.

The little boy thought probably he had, but he wouldn't commit himself.

"Well, den," continued the old man, "nex' time you see one un um, you look right close en see ef de een' er his tail ain't w'ite. Hit's des like I tell you. Dey b'ars de skyar er dat bresh-heap down ter dis day. Dey er marked—dat's w'at dey is—dey er marked."

"And what about Brother Possum?" asked the little boy.

"Ole Brer Possum he tuck a runnin' start he did, en he come lumberin' 'long, en he lit—kerblam!—right in de middle er de fier, en dat wuz de las' er ole Brer Possum."

"But, Uncle Remus, Brother Possum didn't really steal the butter after all," said the little boy, who was not at all satisfied with such summary injustice.

"Dat w'at make I say w'at I duz, honey. In dis worril, lots er fokes is gotter suffer fer udder fokes sins. Look like hit's mighty onwrong; but hit's des dat away. Tribbalashun seem like she's a waitin' roun' de cornder fer ter ketch one en all un us, honey."

Uncle Remus: His Songs and Sayings, 1895

JOHN FOX, JR.

The Kentucky Mountain Feud

It is natural that this Kentucky-born novelist should take an interest in the local mountain feuding. He is gently humorous in this understanding portrayal.

About thirty-five years ago two boys were playing marbles in the road along the Cumberland River—down in the Kentucky mountains. One had a patch on the seat of his trousers. The other boy made fun of it, and the boy with the patch went home and told his father. Thirty years of local war was the result. The factions fought on after they had forgotten why they had fought at all. While organized warfare is now over, an occasional fight yet comes over the patch on those trousers and a man or two is killed. A county as big as Rhode Island is still bitterly divided on the subject. In a race for the legislature not long ago, the feud was the sole issue. And, without knowing it, perhaps, a mountaineer carried that patch like a flag to victory, and sat under it at the capital—making laws for the rest of the State.

That is the feud that has stained the highland border of the State with blood, and abroad, has engulfed the reputation of the lowland blue-grass, where there are, of course, no feuds—a fact that sometimes seems to require emphasis, I am sorry to say. Almost every mountain country has, or has had, its feud. On one side is a leader whose authority is rarely questioned. Each leader has his band of retainers. Always he arms them; usually he feeds them; sometimes he houses and clothes them, and sometimes, even, he hires them. In one local war, I remember, four dollars per day were the wages of the fighting man, and the leader on one occasion, while besieging his enemies—in the county court-house—tried to purchase a cannon, and from no other personage than the governor himself.

It is the feud that most sharply differentiates the Kentucky mountaineer from his fellows, and it is extreme isolation that makes possible in this age such a relic of medieval barbarism. For the feud means, of course, ignorance, shiftlessness, incredible lawlessness, a frightful estimate of the value of human life; the horrible custom of ambush, a class of cowardly assassins who can be hired to murder for a gun, a mule, or a gallon of moonshine.

Now these are the blackest shadows in the only picture of Kentucky mountain life that has reached the light of print through the press. There is another side, and it is only fair to show it.

The feud is an inheritance. There were feuds before the war, even on the edge of the blue-grass; there were fierce family fights in the backwoods before and during the Revolution—when the war between Whig and Tory served as a pretext for satisfying personal animosities already existing, and it is not a wild fancy that the Kentucky mountain feud takes root in Scotland. For, while it is hardly possible that the enmities of the Revolution were transmitted to the Civil War, it is quite sure that whatever race-instinct, old-world trait of character, or moral code the backwoodsman may have taken with him into the mountains—it is quite sure that that instinct, that trait of character, that moral code, are living forces in him to-day. The late war was, however, the chief cause of feuds. When it came, the river-bottoms were populated, the clans were formed. There were more slave-holders among them than among other Southern mountaineers. For that reason, the war divided them more evenly against themselves, and set them fighting. When the war stopped elsewhere, it simply kept on with them, because they were more isolated, more evenly divided; because they were a fiercer race, and because the issue had become personal. The little that is going on now goes on for the same reason, for while civilization pressed close enough in 1890 and 1891 to put an end to organized fighting, it is a consistent fact that after the failure of Baring Brothers, and the stoppage of the flow of English capital into the mountains, and the check to railroads and civilization, these feuds slowly started up again. When I left home for the Cuban War, two companies of State militia were on their way to the mountains to put down a feud. On the day of the Las Guasimas fight these feudsmen fought, and they lost precisely as many men killed as the Rough Riders—eight.

Again: while the feud may involve the sympathies of a county, the number of men actually engaged in it are comparatively few. Moreover, the feud is strictly of themselves, and is based primarily on a privilege that the mountaineer, the world over, has most grudgingly surrendered to the law, the privilege of avenging his private wrongs. The non-partisan and the traveller are never molested. Property of the beaten faction is never touched. The women are safe from harm, and I have never heard of one who was subjected to insult. Attend to your own business, side with neither faction in act or word and you are much safer among the Kentucky mountaineers, when a feud is going on, than you are crossing Broadway at Twenty-third Street. As you ride along, a bullet may plough through the road ten yards in front of you. That means for you to halt. A mountaineer will come out of the bushes and ask who you are and where you are going and what your business is. If your answers are satisfactory, you go on unmolested. Asking for a place to stay all night, you may be told, "Go to So and So's house; he'll pertect ye"; and he will, too, at the risk of his own life when you are past the line of suspicion and under his roof.

There are other facts that soften a too harsh judgment of the mountaineer and his feud—harsh as the judgment should be. Personal fealty is the cornerstone of the feud. The mountaineer admits no higher law; he understands no conscience that will violate that tie. You are my friend or my kinsman; your quarrel is my quarrel; whoever strikes you, strikes me. If you are in trouble, I must not testify against you. If you are an officer, you must not arrest me, you must send me word to come into court. If I'm innocent, why, maybe I'll come.

Moreover, the worst have the list of rude virtues already mentioned; and, besides, the mountaineer is never a thief nor a robber, and he will lie about one thing and one thing only, and that is land. He has cleared it, built his cabin from the trees, lived on it and he feels than any means necessary to hold it are justifiable. Lastly, religion is as honestly used to cloak deviltry as it ever was in the Middle Ages.

A feud leader who had about exterminated the opposing faction, and had made a good fortune for a mountaineer while doing it, for he kept his men busy getting out timber when they weren't fighting, said to me, in all seriousness:

"I have triumphed agin my enemies time and time agin. The Lord's on my side, and I gits a better and better Christian ever' year."

A preacher, riding down a ravine, came upon an old mountaineer hiding in the bushes with his rifle.

"What are you doing there, my friend?"

"Ride on, stranger," was the easy answer. "I'm a-waitin' fer Jim Johnson, and with the help of the Lawd I'm goin' to blow his damn head off."

Even the ambush, the hideous feature of the feud, took root in the days of the Revolution, and was borrowed, maybe, from the Indians. Milfort, the Frenchman, who hated the backwoodsman, says Mr. Roosevelt, describes with horror their extreme malevolence and their murderous disposition toward one another. He says that whether a wrong had been done to a man personally or to his family, he would, if necessary, travel a hundred miles and lurk around the forest indefinitely to get a chance to shoot his enemy.

But the Civil War was the chief cause of bloodshed; for there is evidence, indeed, that though feeling between families was strong, bloodshed was rare and the English sense of fairness prevailed, in certain communities at least. Often you shall hear an old mountaineer say: "Folks usen to talk about how fer they could kill a *deer*. Now hit's how fer they can kill a *man*. Why, I have knowed the time when a man would hev been druv outen the county fer drawin' a knife or a pistol, an' if a man was ever killed, hit wus kinder accidental by a Barlow. I reckon folks got used to weepons an' killin' an shootin' from the bresh endurin' the war. But hit's been gettin' wuss ever sence, and now hit's dirk an' Winchester all the time." Even for the ambush there is an explanation.

"Oh, I know all the excuses folks make. Hit's fair for one as 'tis fer t'other. You can't fight a man fa'r and squar who'll shoot you in the back. A pore man can't fight money in the courts. Thar hain't no witnesses in the lorrel but leaves, an' dead men don't hev much to say. I know hit all. Looks like lots o' decent young folks hev got usen to the idee; thar's so much of it goin' on and thar's so much talk about shootin' from the bresh. I do reckon hit's wuss'n stealin' to take a feller critter's life that way."

Blue Grass and Rhododendron, 1901

EDWIN ANDERSON ALDERMAN

The South's Political Contribution to American Life

As educator, lecturer, writer and president at various times of the University of North Carolina, Tulane University, and the University of Virginia, Alderman was a respected and effective spokesman for the South.

Englishmen of the same age of revolutionary feeling, and of the same passion for principle, settled and gave character to Tidewater Virginia. Men called these Englishmen "Cavaliers." They had their religion, though it was primarily adventure and conquest, rather than religion, that haled them over the sea. Following afar off, they even took a hand at persecuting a Quaker or two now and then. They were just as ready as the Puritans to fight for an ideal. As the tide flowed westward, many of them, too, left home for conscience's sake. They knew the same sensation of devotion to a cause, and they had a conception of political liberty just as clear and, perhaps, an even greater genius for political debate and philosophical exposition. I can understand the enthusiasm of a Virginian for these large-statured men of their Tidewater lands, out of whom came our supreme national hero, and a Homeric group of resourceful men, without whose influence it would be difficult to see how this Republic could have ever been born. It is endlessly pleasant to a Southerner to hark back to their manly simplicity, their activity, their disinterested public spirit, their continental grasp, and their wholesome, catholic lovableness.

Long generations afterwards, Robert E. Lee flowered out of the same bud, very like the old stock, only gentler and more able, through virtue and suffering, to evoke the love of millions. Two such men as Washington and Lee in one century is a mighty tribute to the character of the Tidewater stock.

But to understand the composite traits in Southern character, one must forget the Cavalier for a moment, and look into the valleys and hills of Virginia and the Carolinas, into which poured a half-million Scotch-Irishmen in the last years of the eighteenth century. These Scotch-Irishmen were neither Englishmen nor Irish, but just plain Scotch, and here and there, their French prototypes, Huguenots, all of whom were Calvinists, with the Calvinist's fearful intimacy with God, and sureness of opinion and passion for his sort of truth. The Scotch-Irishmen in Virginia and the Puritan in Massachusetts were blood kin in spirit and in their moral point of view. The character of each was formed by his religion. The theory of life of each demanded education. Each held to his form of truth and stood ready, and even counted it a glory, for an opportunity to fight for its prevalence, with a fierce intensity of conviction.

Who that has scrutinized the lives and careers of John C. Calhoun and John Quincy Adams and Patrick Henry and Samuel Adams does not recognize their essential oneness in spirit and in character? If Oliver Cromwell could have chosen his ideal soldier in the Civil War, who doubts that his choice would have fallen upon Stonewall Jackson? The Scotch-Irishmen, under Jefferson, made the Valley of Virginia the fountain of American democracy, as New England had made her stony soil the nursery of free institutions and the nurse of the most alert mass of political intelligence the country ever knew.

Washington, Jefferson, Marshall, Madison, and Henry were the products of plantation and country government. Samuel Adams, John Hancock, John Adams, James Otis, and Joseph Warren were the products of town meetings and of the congregation and free labor. In men, in imperialistic measures, and in great theories of government Virginia excelled. In efficient institutions and diffused intelligence New England excelled.

In the grip of great economic forces these two groups of Englishmen thought deeply and differently about the meaning of liberty. Liberty continued to mean, as it had once meant in both sections, his home and his native State to the man of the South. It came to mean the right of any individual human being and the nation at large to the New Englander. To the Southerner the presence of the African on this soil grew to be more and more an economic fact, a problem of how to handle an alien system of labor. The intellectualism of the New Englander swept his section, in the middle of the nineteenth century, with a storm of enthusiasm for humanity, modifying his religion, his institutions, and his sense of responsibility for others to such an extent that the African, whom he had once held in slavery, became a great moral problem, appealing to his emotions and to his heart. Thus fate driven, these sections came to war, the New Englander fighting for the liberty of the individual wherever seated and the majesty of the idea of union; the Southerner for the liberty of local self-government and the right of Englishmen to determine their affairs, which was the original essence of the American idea of liberty. No war in human history was a sincerer conflict than the American Civil War. It was not a war of conquest or glory. To call it rebellion is to speak ignorantly. To call it treason is to add viciousness to stupidity. It was a war of ideals, of principles, of political conceptions, of loyalty to ancient ideals of English freedom held dearer than life by both sides. Neither abolitionist nor fire-eater brought on this war. It was a "brothers' war," which ought to have been avoided, but which was brought on, as our human nature is constituted, by the operation of economic forces and the clashing of inherited feelings, woven by no will

244

of either side into the life of the Republic. It was settled at last by neither abolitionist nor fire-eater, but by men of the West who had not inherited unbroken political traditions, but simply saw the union of American States as the ark of their salvation, and beheld its flag, as Webster beheld it, "full high advanced, floating over land and sea."

Some great facts were forever settled by the war, but few great principles. A new American ideal of nationality was set up; the curse of slavery was removed, the indestructibility of the Union established, and a great debate in political philosophy was ended with a blow. The value to liberty of the idea of local self-government still remains, as before, the deepest and most vital principle in our national life. The doctrine of States' rights as a necessity of popular government is again engaging the thought of this Republic, because mightier forces than war are vitalizing this old issue under new forms, and those who understand it best and love it dearest and who will fight for it longest are those who live in the States where devotion to it once had power to separate them from a country they had fought to found. There is nothing stranger or more interesting in political history than the recurrence of this best-loved dogma of the South, unconnected with secession and unconfused with slavery, as necessary to Federal union and human freedom. . . . If the struggle is on between the growing power of the Federal Government and the decreasing authority of the States, you can count on the Southerner to be on the side of maintaining the just balance, for no American sees more clearly than he just what is the vital spot in the liberty of a State. He is a learner, albeit a rapid learner, in the art of using the machinery of local self-government to enrich and beautify a State, but he is a past master in the matter of insight into the very core of democratic freedom. . . .

Our present democracy, so long concerned with interpretation of constitutions, now strikes at the very nature of the social order. No democracy has ever been tempted like this one. No democracy has ever been able to organize its forces like this one. No such field of exploitation has ever opened before any democracy, and never before has the current of the world's genius contributed to perfecting machinery for such vast exploitation. No democracy ever dreamed how it would act if fabulous wealth, ever increasing through the agency of co-operation, had gone to its head. . . . We are simply facing a new question in human liberty, a new phase of the ever-expanding content of democracy, how to retain in our system the priceless glory of individual excellence and individual initiative, which is our deepest national instinct, and how to control in the interest of justice the great co-operative forces which the plans of this giant age demand.

> From an address delivered before the New England Society of New York, December 1906, A *Southern Treasury of Life and Literature* edited by Stark Young

WILLIAM FAULKNER

That Evening Sun Go Down

Monday is no different from any other week day in Jefferson now. The streets are paved now, and the telephone and the electric companies are cutting down more and more of the shade trees—the water oaks, the maples and locusts and elms—to make room for iron poles bearing clusters of bloated and ghostly and bloodless grapes, and we have a city laundry which makes the rounds on Monday morning, gathering the bundles of clothes into bright-colored, specially made motor-cars: the soiled wearing of a whole week now flees apparition-like behind alert and irritable electric horns, with a long diminishing noise of rubber and asphalt like a tearing of silk, and even the Negro women who still take in white people's washing after the old custom, fetch and deliver it in automobiles.

But fifteen years ago, on Monday morning the quiet, dusty, shady streets would be full of Negro women with, balanced on their steady turbaned heads, bundles of clothes tied up in sheets, almost as large as cotton bales, carried so without touch of hand between the kitchen door of the white house and the blackened wash-pot beside a cabin door in Negro Hollow.

Nancy would set her bundle on the top of her head, then upon the bundle in turn she would set the black straw sailor hat which she wore Winter and Summer. She was tall, with a high, sad face sunken a little where her teeth were missing. Sometimes we would go a part of the way down the lane and across the pasture with her, to watch the balanced bundle and the hat that never bobbed nor wavered, even when she walked down into the ditch and climbed out again and stooped through the fence. She would go down on her hands and knees and crawl through the gap, her head rigid, up-tilted, the bundle steady as a rock or a balloon, and rise to her feet and go on.

Sometimes the husbands of the washing women would fetch and deliver the clothes, but Jubah never did that for Nancy, even before father told him to stay away from our house, even when Dilsey was sick and Nancy would come to cook for us.

And then about half the time we'd have to go down the lane to Nancy's house and tell her to come on and get breakfast. We would stop at the ditch, because father told us not to have anything to do with Jubah—he was a short black man, with a razor scar down his face—and we would throw rocks at Nancy's house until she came to the door, leaning her head around it without any clothes on.

"What you all mean, chunking my house?" Nancy said. "What you little devils mean?"

"Father says for you to come and get breakfast," Caddy said. "Father says it's over half an hour now, and you've got to come this minute."

"I ain't studying no breakfast," Nancy said. "I going to get my sleep out."

"I bet you're drunk," Jason said. "Father says you're drunk. Are you drunk, Nancy?"

"Who says I is?" Nancy said. "I got to get my sleep out. I ain't studying no breakfast."

So after a while we quit chunking the house and went back home. When she finally came, it was too late for me to go to school. So we thought it was whiskey until that day when they arrested her again and they were taking her to jail and they passed Mr. Stovall. He was the cashier in the bank and a deacon in the Baptist church, and Nancy began to say:

"When you going to pay me, white man? When you going to pay me, white man? It's been three times now since you paid me a cent—" Mr. Stovall knocked her down, but she kept on saying, "When you going to pay me, white man? It's been three times now since—" until Mr. Stovall kicked her in the mouth with his heel and the marshal caught Mr. Stovall back, and Nancy lying in the street, laughing. She turned her head and spat out some blood and teeth and said, "It's been three times now since he paid me a cent."

That was how she lost her teeth, and all that day they told about Nancy and Mr. Stovall, and all that night the ones that passed the jail could hear Nancy singing and yelling. They could see her hands holding to the window bars, and a lot of them stopped along the fence, listening to her and to the jailer trying to make her shut up. She didn't shut up until just before daylight, when the jailer began to hear a bumping and scraping upstairs and he went up there and found Nancy hanging from the window bar. He said that it was cocaine and not whiskey, because no nigger would try to commit suicide unless he was full of cocaine, because a nigger full of cocaine was not a nigger any longer.

The jailer cut her down and revived her; then he beat her, whipped her. She had hung herself with her dress. She had fixed it all right, but when they arrested her she didn't have on anything except a dress and so she didn't have anything to tie her hands with and she couldn't make her hands let go of the window ledge. So the jailer heard the noise and ran up there and found Nancy hanging from the window, stark naked.

When Dilsey was sick in her cabin and Nancy was cooking for us, we could see her apron swelling out; that was before father told Jubah to stay away from the house. Jubah was in the kitchen, sitting behind the stove, with his razor scar on his black face like a piece of dirty string. He said it was a watermelon that Nancy had under her dress. And it was Winter, too.

"Where did you get a watermelon in the Winter?" Caddy said.

"I didn't," Jubah said. "It wasn't me that give it to her. But I can cut it down, same as if it was."

"What makes you want to talk that way before these chillen?" Nancy said. "Whyn't you go on to work? You done et. You want Mr. Jason to catch you hanging around his kitchen, talking that way before these chillen?"

"Talking what way, Nancy?" Caddy said.

"I can't hang around white man's kitchen," Jubah said. "But white man can hang around mine. White man can come in my house, but I can't stop him. When white man want to come in my house, I ain't got no house. I can't stop him, but he can't kick me outen it. He can't do that."

Dilsey was still sick in her cabin. Father told Jubah to stay off our place. Dilsey was still sick. It was a long time. We were in the library after supper.

"Isn't Nancy through yet?" mother said. "It seems to me that she has had plenty of time to have finished the dishes."

"Let Quentin go and see," father said. "Go and see if Nancy is through, Quentin. Tell her she can go on home."

I went to the kitchen. Nancy was through. The dishes were put away and the fire was out. Nancy was sitting in a chair, close to the cold stove. She looked at me.

"Mother wants to know if you are through," I said.

"Yes," Nancy said. She looked at me. "I done finished." She looked at me.

"What is it?" I said. "What is it?"

"I ain't nothing but a nigger," Nancy said. "It ain't none of my fault."

She looked at me, sitting in the chair before the cold stove, the sailor hat on her head. I went back to the library. It was the cold stove and all, when you think of a kitchen being warm and busy and cheerful. And with a cold stove and the dishes all put away, and nobody wanting to eat at that hour.

"Is she through?" mother said.

"Yessum," I said.

"What is she doing?" mother said.

"She's not doing anything. She's through."

"I'll go and see," father said.

"Maybe she's waiting for Jubah to come and take her home," Caddy said.

"Jubah is gone," I said. Nancy told us how one morning she woke up and Jubah was gone.

"He quit me," Nancy said. "Done gone to Memphis, I reckon. Dodging them city po-lice for a while, I reckon."

"And a good riddance," father said. "I hope he stays there."

"Nancy's scaired of the dark," Jason said.

"So are you," Caddy said.

"I'm not," Jason said.

"Scairy cat," Caddy said.

"I'm not," Jason said.

"You, Candace!" mother said. Father came back.

"I am going to walk down the lane with Nancy," he said. "She says Jubah is back."

"Has she seen him?" mother said.

"No. Some Negro sent her word that he was back in town. I won't be long."

"You'll leave me alone, to take Nancy home?" mother said. "Is her safety more precious to you than mine?"

"I won't be long," father said.

"You'll leave these children unprotected, with that Negro about?"

"I'm going, too," Caddy said. "Let me go, father."

"What would he do with them, if he were unfortunate enough to have them?" father said.

"I want to go, too," Jason said.

"Jason!" mother said it. She was speaking to father. You could tell that by the way she said it. Like she believed that all day father had been trying to think of doing the thing that she wouldn't like the most, and that she knew all the time that after a while he would think of it. I stayed quiet, because father and I both knew that mother would want him to make me stay with her, if she just thought of it in time. So father didn't look at me. I was the oldest. I was nine and Caddy was seven and Jason was five.

"Nonsense," father said. "We won't be long."

Nancy had her hat on. We came to the lane. "Jubah always been good to me," Nancy said. "Whenever he had two dollars, one of them was mine." We walked in the lane. "If I can just get through the lane," Nancy said, "I be all right then."

The lane was always dark. "This is where Jason got scared on Hallowe'en," Caddy said.

"I didn't," Jason said.

"Can't Aunt Rachel do anything with him?" father said. Aunt Rachel was old. She lived in a cabin beyond Nancy's, by herself. She had white hair and she smoked a pipe in the door, all day long; she didn't work any more. They said she was Jubah's mother. Sometimes she said she was and sometimes she said she wasn't any kin to Jubah.

"Yes you did," Caddy said. "You were scairder than Frony. You were scairder than T.P. even. Scairder than niggers."

"Can't nobody do nothing with him," Nancy said. "He say I done woke up the devil in him, and ain't but one thing going to lay it again."

"Well, he's gone now," father said. "There's nothing for you to be afraid of now. And if you'd just let white men alone."

"Let what white men alone?" Caddy said. "How let them alone?"

"He ain't gone nowhere," Nancy said. "I can feel him. I can feel him, now, in this lane. He hearing us talk, every word, hid somewhere, waiting. I ain't seen him, and I ain't going to see him again but once more with that razor. That razor on that string down his back, inside his shirt. And then I ain't going to even be surprised."

"I wasn't scaired," Jason said.

"If you'd behave yourself, you'd have kept out of this," father said. "But it's all right now. He's probably in St. Louis now. Probably got another wife by now and forgot all about you."

"If he has, I better not find it out," Nancy said. "I'd stand there and every time he wropped her, I'd cut that arm off. I'd cut his head off and I'd slit her belly and I'd shove—"

"Hush," father said.

"Slit whose belly, Nancy?" Caddy said.

"I wasn't scaired," Jason said. "I'd walk right down this lane by myself."

"Yah," Caddy said. "You wouldn't dare to put your foot in it if we were not with you."

II

Dilsey was still sick, and so we took Nancy home every night until mother said, "How much longer is this going to go on? I to be left alone in this big house while you take home a frightened Negro?"

We fixed a pallet in the kitchen for Nancy. One night we waked up, hearing the sound. It was not singing and it was not crying, coming up the dark stairs. There was a light in mother's room and we heard father going down the hall, down the back stairs, and Caddy and I went into the hall. The floor was cold. Our toes curled away from the floor while we listened to the sound. It was like singing and it wasn't like singing, like the sounds that Negroes make.

Then it stopped and we heard father going down the back stairs, and we went to the head of the stairs. Then the sound began again, in the stairway, not loud, and we could see Nancy's eyes half way up the stairs, against the wall. They looked like cat's eyes do, like a big cat against the wall, watching us. When we came down the steps to where she was she quit making the sound again, and we stood there until father came back up from the kitchen, with his pistol in his hand. He went back down with Nancy and they came back with Nancy's pallet.

We spread the pallet in our room. After the light in mother's room went off, we could see Nancy's eyes again. "Nancy," Caddy whispered, "are you asleep, Nancy?"

Nancy whispered something. It was oh or no, I don't know which. Like nobody had made it, like it came from nowhere and went nowhere, until it was like Nancy was not there at all; that I had looked so hard at her eyes on the stair that they had got printed on my eyelids, like the sun does when you have closed your eyes and there is no sun. "Jesus," Nancy whispered. "Jesus."

"Was it Jubah?" Caddy whispered. "Did he try to come into the kitchen?"

250

"Jesus," Nancy said. Like this: Jeeeeeeeeeeeeeeeeesus, until the sound went out like a match or a candle does.

"Can you see us, Nancy?" Caddy whispered. "Can you see our eyes too?"

"I ain't nothing but a nigger," Nancy said. "God knows. God knows."

"What did you see down there in the kitchen?" Caddy whispered. "What tried to get in?"

"God knows," Nancy said. We could see her eyes. "God knows."

Dilsey got well. She cooked dinner. "You'd better stay in bed a day or two longer," father said.

"What for?" Dilsey said. "If I had been a day later, this place would be to rack and ruin. Get on out of here, now, and let me get my kitchen straight again."

Dilsey cooked supper, too. And that night, just before dark, Nancy came into the kitchen.

"How do you know he's back?" Dilsey said. "You ain't seen him."

"Jubah is a nigger," Jason said.

"I can feel him," Nancy said. "I can feel him laying yonder in the ditch."

"To-night?" Dilsey said. "Is he there to-night?"

"Dilsey's a nigger too," Jason said.

"You try to eat something," Dilsey said.

"I don't want nothing," Nancy said.

"I ain't a nigger," Jason said.

"Drink some coffee," Dilsey said. She poured a cup of coffee for Nancy. "Do you know he's out there to-night? How come you know it's to-night?"

"I know," Nancy said. "He's there, waiting. I know. I done lived with him too long. I know what he fixing to do 'fore he knows it himself."

"Drink some coffee," Dilsey said. Nancy held the cup to her mouth and blew into the cup. Her mouth pursed out like a spreading adder's, like a rubber mouth, like she had blown all the color out of her lips with blowing the coffee.

"I ain't a nigger," Jason said. "Are you a nigger, Nancy?"

"I hell-born, child," Nancy said. "I won't be nothing soon. I going back where I come from soon."

III

She began to drink the coffee. While she was drinking, holding the cup in both hands, she began to make the sound again. She made the sound into the cup and the coffee sploshed out on to her hands and her dress. Her eyes looked at us and she sat there, her elbows on her knees, holding the cup in both hands, looking at us across the wet cup, making the sound.

"Look at Nancy," Jason said. "Nancy can't cook for us now. Dilsey's got well now."

"You hush up," Dilsey said. Nancy held the cup in both hands, looking at us, making the sound, like there were two of them; one looking at us and the other making the sound. "Whyn't you let Mr. Jason telefoam the marshal?" Dilsey said. Nancy stopped then, holding her cup in her long brown hands. She tried to drink some coffee again, but it sploshed out of her cup, on to her hands and her dress, and she put the cup down. Jason watched her.

"I can't swallow it," Nancy said. "I swallows but it won't go down me."

"You go down to the cabin," Dilsey said. "Frony will fix you a pallet and I'll be there soon."

"Won't no nigger stop him," Nancy said.

"I ain't a nigger," Jason said. "Am I, Dilsey?"

"I reckon not," Dilsey said. She looked at Nancy. "I don't reckon so. What you going to do, then?"

Nancy looked at us. Her eyes went fast, like she was afraid there wasn't time to look, without hardly moving at all. She looked at us, at all three of us at one time. "You 'member that night I stayed on you all's room?" she said. She told about how we waked up early the next morning, and played. We had to play quiet, on her pallet, until father woke and it was time for her to go down and get breakfast. "Go and ask your maw to let me stay here to-night," Nancy said. "I won't need no pallet. We can play some more," she said.

Caddy asked mother. Jason went too. "I can't have Negroes sleeping in the house," mother said. Jason cried. He cried until mother said he couldn't have any dessert for three days if he didn't stop. Then Jason said he would stop if Dilsey would make a chocolate cake. Father was there.

"Why don't you do something about it?" mother said. "What do we have officers for?"

"Why is Nancy afraid of Jubah?" Caddy said. "Are you afraid of father, mother?"

"What could they do?" father said. "If Nancy hasn't seen him, how could the officers find him?"

"Then why is she afraid?" mother said.

"She says he is there. She says she knows he is there to-night."

"Yet we pay taxes," mother said. "I must wait here alone in this big house while you take a Negro woman home."

"You know that I am not lying outside with a razor," father said.

"I'll stop if Dilsey will make a chocolate cake," Jason said. Mother told us to go out and father said he didn't know if Jason would get a chocolate cake or not, but he knew what Jason was going to get in about a minute. We went back to the kitchen and told Nancy.

"Father said for you to go home and lock the door, and you'll be all right," Caddy said. "All right from what, Nancy? Is Jubah mad at you?" Nancy was holding the coffee cup in her hands, her elbows on her knees and her hands holding the cup between her knees. She was looking into the cup. "What have you done that made Jubah mad?" Caddy said. Nancy let the cup go. It didn't break on the floor, but the coffee spilled out, and Nancy sat there with her hands making the shape of the cup. She began to make the sound again, not loud. Not singing and not un-singing. We watched her.

"Here," said Dilsey. "You quit that, now. You get a-holt of yourself. You wait here. I going to get Versh to walk home with you." Dilsey went out.

We looked at Nancy. Her shoulders kept shaking, but she had quit making the sound. We watched her. "What's Jubah going to do to you?" Caddy said. "He went away."

Nancy looked at us. "We had fun that night I stayed in you all's room, didn't we?"

"I didn't," Jason said. "I didn't have any fun."

"You were asleep," Caddy said. "You were not there."

"Let's go down to my house and have some more fun," Nancy said.

"Mother won't let us," I said. "It's too late now."

"Don't bother her," Nancy said. "We can tell her in the morning. She won't mind."

"She wouldn't let us," I said.

"Don't ask her now," Nancy said. "Don't bother her now."

"They didn't say we couldn't go," Caddy said.

"We didn't ask," I said.

"If you go, I'll tell," Jason said.

"We'll have fun," Nancy said. "They won't mind just to my house. I been working for you all a long time. They won't mind."

"I'm not afraid to go," Caddy said. "Jason is the one that's afraid. He'll tell."

"I'm not," Jason said.

"Yes, you are," Caddy said. "You'll tell."

"I won't tell," Jason said. "I'm not afraid."

"Jason ain't afraid to go with me," Nancy said. "Is you, Jason?"

"Jason is going to tell," Caddy said. The lane was dark. We passed the pasture gate. "I bet if something was to jump out from behind that gate, Jason would holler."

"I wouldn't," Jason said. We walked down the lane. Nancy was talking loud.

"What are you talking so loud for, Nancy?" Caddy said.

"Who; me?" Nancy said. "Listen at Quentin and Caddy and Jason saying I'm talking loud."

"You talk like there was four of us here," Caddy said. "You talk like father was here too."

"Who; me talking loud, Mr. Jason?" Nancy said.

"Nancy called Jason 'Mister,' " Caddy said.

"Listen how Caddy and Quentin and Jason talk," Nancy said.

"We're not talking loud," Caddy said. "You're the one that's talking like father—"

"Hush," Nancy said; "hush, Mr. Jason."

"Nancy called Jason 'Mister' aguh—"

"Hush," Nancy said. She was talking loud when we crossed the ditch and stooped through the fence where she used to stoop through with the clothes on her head. Then we came to her house. We were going fast then. She opened the door. The smell of the house was like the lamp and the smell of Nancy was like the wick, like they were waiting for one another to smell. She lit the lamp and closed the door and put the bar up. Then she quit talking loud, looking at us.

"What're we going to do?" Caddy said.

"What you all want to do?" Nancy said.

"You said we would have some fun," Caddy said.

There was something about Nancy's house; something you could smell. Jason smelled it, even. "I don't want to stay here," he said. "I want to go home."

"Go home, then," Caddy said.

"I don't want to go by myself," Jason said.

"We're going to have some fun," Nancy said.

"How?" Caddy said.

Nancy stood by the door. She was looking at us, only it was like she had emptied her eyes, like she had quit using them.

"What do you want to do?" she said.

"Tell us a story," Caddy said. "Can you tell a story?"

"Yes," Nancy said.

"Tell it," Caddy said. We looked at Nancy. "You don't know any stories," Caddy said.

"Yes," Nancy said. "Yes, I do."

She came and sat down in a chair before the hearth. There was some fire there; she built it up; it was already hot. You didn't need a fire. She built a good blaze. She told a story. She talked like her eyes looked, like her eyes watching us and her voice talking to us did not belong to her. Like she was living somewhere else, waiting somewhere else. She was outside the house. Her voice was there and the shape of her, the Nancy that could stoop under the fence with the bundle of clothes balanced as though without weight, like a balloon, on her head, was there. But that was all. "And so this here queen come walking up to the ditch, where that bad man was hiding. She was walking up the ditch, and she say, 'If I can just get past this here ditch,' was what she say. . . ."

"What ditch?" Caddy said. "A ditch like that one out there? Why did the queen go into the ditch?"

"To get to her house," Nancy said. She looked at us. "She had to cross that ditch to get home."

"Why did she want to go home?" Caddy said.

Nancy looked at us. She quit talking. She looked at us. Jason's legs stuck straight out of his pants, because he was little. "I don't think that's a good story," he said. "I want to go home."

"Maybe we had better," Caddy said. She got up from the floor. "I bet they are looking for us right now." She went toward the door.

"No," Nancy said. "Don't open it." She got up quick and passed Caddy. She didn't touch the door, the wooden bar.

"Why not?" Caddy said.

"Come back to the lamp," Nancy said. "We'll have fun. You don't have to go."

"We ought to go," Caddy said. "Unless we have a lot of fun." She and Nancy came back to the fire, the lamp.

"I want to go home," Jason said. "I'm going to tell."

"I know another story," Nancy said. She stood close to the lamp. She looked at Caddy, like when your eyes look up at a stick balanced on your nose. She had to look down to see Caddy, but her eyes looked like that, like when you are balancing a stick.

"I won't listen to it," Jason said. "I'll bang on the floor."

"It's a good one," Nancy said. "It's better than the other one."

"What's it about?" Caddy said. Nancy was standing by the lamp. Her hand was on the lamp, against the light, long and brown.

"Your hand is on that hot globe," Caddy said. "Don't it feel hot to your hand?"

Nancy looked at her hand on the lamp chimney. She took her hand away, slow. She stood there, looking at Caddy, wringing her long hand as though it were tied to her wrist with a string.

"Let's do something else," Caddy said.

"I want to go home," Jason said.

"I got some popcorn," Nancy said. She looked at Caddy and then at Jason and then at me and then at Caddy again. "I got some popcorn."

"I don't like popcorn," Jason said. "I'd rather have candy."

Nancy looked at Jason. "You can hold the popper." She was still wringing her hand; it was long and limp and brown.

"All right," Jason said. "I'll stay a while if I can do that. Caddy can't hold it. I'll want to go home, if Caddy holds the popper."

Nancy built up the fire. "Look at Nancy putting her hands in the fire," Caddy said. "What's the matter with you, Nancy?"

"I got popcorn," Nancy said. "I got some." She took the popper from under the bed. It was broken. Jason began to cry.

"We can't have any popcorn," he said.

"We ought to go home, anyway," Caddy said. "Come on, Quentin."

"Wait," Nancy said; "wait; I can fix it. Don't you want to help me fix it?"

"I don't think I want any," Caddy said. "It's too late now."

"You help me, Jason," Nancy said. "Don't you want to help me?"

"No," Jason said. "I want to go home."

"Hush," Nancy said; "hush. Watch. Watch me. I can fix it so Jason can hold it and pop the corn." She got a piece of wire and fixed the popper.

"It won't hold good," Caddy said.

"Yes, it will," Nancy said. "You all watch. You all help me shell the corn."

The corn was under the bed too. We shelled it into the popper and Nancy helped Jason hold the popper over the fire.

"It's not popping," Jason said. "I want to go home."

"You wait," Nancy said. "It'll begin to pop. We'll have fun then." She was sitting close to the fire. The lamp was turned up so high it was beginning to smoke.

"Why don't you turn it down some?" I said.

"It's all right," Nancy said. "I'll clean it. You all wait. The popcorn will start in a minute."

"I don't believe it's going to start," Caddy said. "We ought to go home, anyway. They'll be worried."

"No," Nancy said. "It's going to pop. Dilsey will tell um you all with me. I been working for you all a long time. They won't mind if you at my house. You wait, now. It'll start popping in a minute."

Then Jason got some smoke in his eyes and he began to cry. He dropped the popper into the fire. Nancy got a wet rag and wiped Jason's face, but he didn't stop crying.

"Hush," she said. "Hush." He didn't hush. Caddy took the popper out of the fire.

"It's burned up," she said. "You'll have to get some more popcorn, Nancy."

"Did you put it all in?" Nancy said.

"Yes," Caddy said. Nancy looked at Caddy. Then she took the popper and opened it and poured the blackened popcorn into her apron and began to sort the grains, her hands long and brown, as we sat watching her.

"Haven't you got any more?" Caddy said.

"Yes," Nancy said; "yes. Look. This here ain't burnt. All we need to do is——"

"I want to go home," Jason said. "I'm going to tell."

"Hush," Caddy said. We all listened. Nancy's head was already turned toward the barred door, her eyes filled with red lamplight. "Somebody is coming," Caddy said.

Then Nancy began to make that sound again, not loud, sitting there above the fire, her long hands dangling between her knees; all of a sudden water began to come out on her face in big drops, running down her face, carrying in each one a little turning ball of firelight until it dropped off her chin.

256

"She's not crying," I said.

"I ain't crying," Nancy said. Her eyes were closed. "I ain't crying. Who is it?"

"I don't know," Caddy said. She went to the door and looked out. "We've got to go home now," she said. "Here comes father."

"I'm going to tell," Jason said. "You all made me come."

The water still ran down Nancy's face. She turned in her chair. "Listen. Tell him. Tell him we going to have fun. Tell him I take good care of you all until in the morning. Tell him to let me come home with you all and sleep on the floor. Tell him I won't need no pallet. We'll have fun. You remember last time how we had so much fun?"

"I didn't have any fun," Jason said. "You hurt me. You put smoke in my eyes."

v

Father came in. He looked at us. Nancy did not get up.

"Tell him," she said.

"Caddy made us come down here," Jason said. "I didn't want to."

Father came to the fire. Nancy looked up at him. "Can't you go to Aunt Rachel's and stay?" he said. Nancy looked up at father, her hands between her knees. "He's not here," father said. "I would have seen. There wasn't a soul in sight."

"He in the ditch," Nancy said. "He waiting in the ditch yonder."

"Nonsense," father said. He looked at Nancy. "Do you know he's there?"

"I got the sign," Nancy said.

"What sign?"

"I got it. It was on the table when I come in. It was a hog bone, with blood meat still on it, laying by the lamp. He's out there. When you all walk out that door, I gone."

"Who's gone, Nancy?" Caddy said.

"I'm not a tattletale," Jason said.

"Nonsense," father said.

"He out there," Nancy said. "He looking through that window this minute, waiting for you all to go. Then I gone."

"Nonsense," father said. "Lock up your house and we'll take you on to Aunt Rachel's."

" 'Twon't do no good," Nancy said. She didn't look at father now, but he looked down at her, at her long, limp, moving hands. "Putting it off won't do no good."

"Then what do you want to do?" father said.

"I don't know," Nancy said. "I can't do nothing. Just put it off. And that don't do no good. I reckon it belong to me. I reckon what I going to get ain't no more than mine."

"Get what?" Caddy said. "What's yours?"

"Nothing," father said. "You all must get to bed."

"Caddy made me come," Jason said.

"Go on to Aunt Rachel's," father said.

"It won't do no good," Nancy said. She sat before the fire, her elbows on her knees, her long hands between her knees. "When even your own kitchen wouldn't do no good. When even if I was sleeping on the floor in the room with your own children, and the next morning there I am, and blood all——"

"Hush," father said. "Lock the door and put the lamp out and go to bed."

"I scared of the dark," Nancy said. "I scared for it to happen in the dark."

"You mean you're going to sit right here, with the lamp lighted?" father said. Then Nancy began to make the sound again, sitting before the fire, her long hands between her knees. "Ah, damnation," father said. "Come along, chillen. It's bedtime."

"When you all go, I gone," Nancy said. "I be dead to-morrow. I done have saved up the coffin money with Mr. Lovelady——"

Mr. Lovelady was a short, dirty man who collected the Negro insurance, coming around to the cabins and the kitchens every Saturday morning, to collect fifteen cents. He and his wife lived in the hotel. One morning his wife committed suicide. They had a child, a little girl. After his wife committed suicide Mr. Lovelady and the child went away. After a while Mr. Lovelady came back. We would see him going down the lanes on Saturday morning. He went to the Baptist church.

Father carried Jason on his back. We went out Nancy's door; she was sitting before the fire. "Come and put the bar up," father said. Nancy didn't move. She didn't look at us again. We left her there, sitting before the fire with the door opened, so that it wouldn't happen in the dark.

"What, father?" Caddy said. "Why is Nancy scared of Jubah? What is Jubah going to do to her?"

"Jubah wasn't there," Jason said.

"No," father said. "He's not there. He's gone away."

"Who is that waiting in the ditch?" Caddy said. We looked at the ditch. We came to it, where the path went down into the thick vines and went up again.

These Thirteen, 1931

258

WILLIAM MARCH

The Funeral

When her little niece died, Mrs. Kirby went at once to her brother's house on Madison Street and took charge of things. She had made all the arrangements for the funeral herself; she had even selected the small, satin casket, and she stood, now, receiving late floral offerings and greeting the friends who came to offer their sympathy.

"It's very sad," she kept saying. "I can't believe it, even yet. Only a week ago and she was as well and strong as you or I. She took sick two days after her seventh birthday."

The bell rang again and she turned from her friends and opened the front door. It was then that she saw Reba, the cook's little girl. Reba stood beside the fence, a look of amazement on her scarred, black face. Her nappy hair had been plaited by her mother and tied with thread the Sunday before, but the thread was coming loose and the plaits, unraveled a little now, stood up on her skull like tiny lengths of frayed, black hemp. She was wearing a faded, print dress which the dead child had outgrown; but the dress was too small for Reba, as well, and beneath it her bare legs and a stretch of her lathlike, black thighs were visible.

Mrs. Kirby opened her mouth, as if to speak to the child, but she did not. She merely took the wreath from the delivery boy and went into the parlor where the coffin was. She put the flowers down, and when she came back to the hall, she saw that other friends had come. The new arrivals went at once and stood above the small white casket. They were early, and after whispering together, they seated themselves at the far end of the room and waited for the funeral service to begin.

Mrs. Kirby came onto the porch once more, stopping beside the cypress vines. "Reba," she said, "you can't stand out here staring at people. Go play in the back yard."

"Yassum," said Reba. "Yassum." She moved from the fence regretfully, looking back over her shoulder. At that moment the florist's wagon turned the corner and stopped again, and the delivery boy came up the walk with another design. It was from the schoolchildren of the little girl's class this time. The design was almost as tall as Reba herself, and it showed two gates swinging outward, gates made of dampened moss into which flowers had been stuck. Above the opening gates, and supported by a rod, there floated a stuffed white dove with outspread wings.

"Reba," said Mrs. Kirby patiently. "Reba, don't you hear me talking to you? Go back to the kitchen and stay with your mother."

Reba looked at her imploringly. "Yassum," she said meekly. "Yassum." But it was not possible for her to move from the fence. She turned her neck and her black, bullet-shaped head slowly, following the floral offering up the steps with her eyes and sighing when the door shut away its magnificence. Mrs. Kirby started to speak again, but changed her mind. She went to the kitchen where Cora, the cook, bent over her sink, was scrubbing pots.

"You must tell your little girl to stay away from the fence," she said. "She's standing there staring at everybody who comes in. I've told her to go away, but she won't mind me."

Cora looked up and wiped her lips on her sleeve. "Reba ain't got good sense," she said reproachfully. "You knows that. You knows Reba never did have good sense." She turned ponderously and reached for the thick switch that lay on the shelf above the wood-box. She went into the side yard and stood half-screened by shrubbery. "Come away from that fence, gal!" she whispered fiercely. "Come away from that fence befo' I put another knot on your haid!"

"Yassum," said Reba meekly. "Yassum."

She backed warily away from her mother, making a wide half-circle, but when the clump of cypress trees and small crêpe-myrtles was between them, she turned and ran, throwing her legs out.

"Let me ketch you by that fence agin," said Cora. "Jes' let me hear one mo' word about how you doin'!" She followed her daughter, shaking her switch, but Reba ran into the kitchen, picked up the scouring cloth and began washing the pots still left in the sink.

When the dishes were done, she went onto the back porch and stood beside the steps, remembering once more the remarkable things she had seen that day. She sat down by the window on an upturned scrubbing bucket and began plaiting the strands of an old mop with her black fingers. Then she got up quickly, having forgotten her mother's wrath, and went again to the side yard, but this time she did not go near the gate; instead, she sat in the swing that hung from the limb of a small sycamore tree.

The swing and the tree were partly surrounded by the half-circle of crêpe-myrtles and cypress saplings, and it would be difficult for Mrs. Kirby to see her there. She gripped the two ropes of the swing and propelled herself backward and forward, her head nodding rhythmically to the creaking of the ropes, one bare skinny leg dragging in the dust like a brake.

Between gaps in the shrubbery she caught glimpses of the sidewalk. Many people were coming to the funeral now, and when she twisted sideways and craned her neck she could see them open the gate and walk on tiptoes up the gravel path. At length the minister turned in at the gate, and the funeral service was about to begin. The minister was dressed in black, and he was tall and solemn. His eyes, at once stern and forgiving, looked searchingly at the congregated people before he inclined his head a little, as if he gave his blessing to all alike.

Reba began swinging wildly, her head higher than the limb to which the swing was fastened, her black, outthrust legs agitating the tops of the crêpe-myrtles. It was then she saw, above the tops of the shrubbery, that there was no longer room for visitors inside the house, and that latecomers stood on the porch outside. Beyond the gate, on the sidewalk, the classmates of the dead child waited, their backs pressed against the picket fence.

She swung back and forth furiously and laughed with a strange excitement which she did not understand. Then all at once she became quiet. She brought the swing to a standstill as quickly as she could, trailing one leg in the dust as a brake, and glanced fearfully from Mrs. Kirby to her mother.

Mrs. Kirby said: "You can't hear anything inside except that swing creaking back and forth, and it looks from the windows like a hurricane had hit the tops of those crêpe-myrtle bushes."

"Come away from that swing, gal!" said Cora angrily. "Come away, like I tell you!"

"Yassum," said Reba in her soft, meek voice. "Yassum."

She sidled cautiously away, and when she had the shrubbery between herself and her mother, she began to run. She ran as far as the old carriage-house, but she stopped there, grinning foolishly. "You see, Mrs. Kirby?" said Cora. "You see?"

When Mrs. Kirby had gone, Cora walked toward the carriage-house but she stopped when she was almost there. "What make you pick a day like this to act so crazy?" she asked. "If it wasn't disrespectful to the daid, I'd whup you within an inch of your life." She went back to her work, pretending that she had forgotten about the swing, and a few moments later Reba came trotting up the path.

Cora seized her by the neck when she came in the door. "Now, Miss," she said triumphantly. "I got you now, and I ain't gwiner let you get away from me agin." She shoved her down onto the stool beside the stove and thrust a bowl into her hands. "Here, gal," she said. "Finish shelling them peas." She went into the pantry and began sifting flour on her bread-board. "Say something, Reba," she said. "Keep saying something so I'll know you ain't run off agin."

"I don't know nothing to say."

"Say yassum. Keep saying yassum."

"Yassum," said Reba meekly.

She picked up the bowl and began shelling the peas, thinking once more of the funeral. It was the first time she had seen a funeral for white folks, and she had not imagined that anything could be so magnificent; but there was much that she did not understand, and as her mother walked from pantry to kitchen and back again, she considered these puzzling matters with her slow mind. A week ago the little girl who had died had merely been another child, like any other, but with death she had taken on a strange sort of importance; and people who had hardly known her now crowded the house for the privilege of looking at her;

they wept openly for her; they wore black in her honor; they sent her flowers.

It was then that Mrs. Kirby came into the kitchen and asked Cora if she wanted to see the little girl for the last time. Cora began to cry, wiping her eyes on her skirt. She rolled down her sleeves, put on a clean apron, and followed Mrs. Kirby into the hall; but she stopped in the doorway and spoke warningly: "Keep sitting on that stool until I get back, Reba," she said. "You move one inch off that stool and I'm going to put a knot on your head. See if I don't."

"Yassum," said Reba meekly. "Yassum."

She sat quietly for a time, trying to concentrate on the peas before her, but when somebody began to play on a fiddle, and somebody began to sing a white-folks' hymn which was both sad and comforting, she could hold out no longer. She put down the bowl and twisted her raveling plaits, rolling her black, bullet-shaped head from side to side. Then she got up from the stool and went through the back door. "Yassum," she said pleadingly in the direction her mother had taken. "Yassum."

When she turned the corner of the house, she saw that the hearse and the carriages for people to ride in to the cemetery had come. The hearse was drawn by white horses and they stood, now, shaking out their manes and biting at each other's necks. Reba took in these details quickly and then dropped to her hands and knees, following the line of shrubbery that circled the house. She crawled carefully, and when she reached the parlor window, she stretched her thin neck upward and peered in.

The first thing she saw was the coffin. It was set in the middle of the room. It was pure white and beautiful, and it was piled high with flowers. There were silver handles to the coffin, and streamers of white ribbons hung from its sides. She caught her breath with amazement. She stared with her mouth half-open, her eyes wide with wonder.

The preacher stood beside the casket and comforted the weeping people. Then he turned and spoke to the parents of the dead child: The ways of God are not our ways, and it was not given to mortals to understand them. We could only bear our losses with fortitude, and this mother and this father must comfort themselves in the knowledge that their child was not dead in the real sense of the word, but that she awaited them in heaven.

Reba sighed and shifted her weight. She craned forward a little, and she saw her mother standing against the far wall. Cora's shoulders shook with her grief, and at intervals she lifted her apron and pressed it flat against her streaming eyes. All at once Reba sank back on her haunches, her face cupped in her palms. "Yassum," she said softly, drawing the word out interminably. "Yassum."

The service was over at last and men carried the coffin down the steps and put it into the waiting hearse, piling the flowers around it. Then, when the carriages were filled and the hearse moved away, Reba could remain hidden no longer. She went again to the fence and stared openly, dragging her feet in the dust. The procession was under way now, and as it moved off, the schoolchildren, who had waited so patiently, fell in behind the last carriage and marched solemnly.

The last carriage had disappeared around the corner when Reba felt her head jerked backward and heard her mother's voice. "Now, then!" Cora said. "Now, then, I'll settle with you, Miss!" She shoved her daughter forward until they reached the old carriage-house. Reba fell down and pressed her face into the dust. "Don't whup me," she begged. "I won't do it no more. Don't whup me, please, ma'am." But her mother brought the stick down over her cringing head and shoulders. "You gwiner mind me," she said. "From now on, you gwiner do what I tell you!"

The whipping was over at last and Cora started back to the house, but she stopped in the path. "They'll be back from the graveyard in a little while, and they'll be hongry. I got to get supper going," she said. Then she sighed despairingly and raised her arms outward. "What make you *do* the way you do, Reba?" she asked. "What make you provoke me the way you do?" She rolled down her sleeves. "I ain't a mean woman. Ever'body knows I ain't a mean woman."

"Yassum," said Reba.

"Go wash that blood off'n your haid," said Cora, "and then bring me in some stovewood."

"Yassum," said Reba meekly. "Yassum."

She waited until her mother was in the kitchen and then she stood up, leaning against the door. She unbuttoned her dress and turned her head sideways, examining the bruises on her scarred back. She touched the bleeding place on her head and began to cry again. "Yassum," she said. "Yassum." She sank to the ground once more, her hands, with fingers interlocked, clutched between her thin, black knees. She rocked back and forth and made her foolish, intaken sound. "Yassum!" she said over and over. "Yassum! Yassum! Yassum!"

She got up after a while and carried in the wood for her mother, but when the box was filled, she went again to the side yard and stood at the gate. It was beginning to get dark, and already the cypresses and the crêpe-myrtle bushes cast shadows against the house. Before her, on the gravel walk, were the heads of flowers, fixed by florist's wire to toothpicks, which had fallen from the mossy designs in which they had originally rested. Reba picked up the flowers and stuck them into her tightly plaited, nappy hair, until it looked, after a moment, as if she wore a white wreath on her head.

Afterwards she went to the swing and shoved herself backwards and forwards, thinking once more of the little white girl's funeral. At first it had seemed to her that the funeral could not have been more magnificent, but familiarity with its details made her, now, more critical; and as she swung back and forth, one leg dragging in the dust like a brake, she talked to herself:

"When I have *my* funeral," she said, "I'm gwiner have me a band, too. Gwiner have *all* white horses at my funeral, and folks gwiner send up rockets that night."

Then, slowly, she let the swing come to rest and sat quietly.

Something important had occurred to her and she was motionless for a time, her hands gripping the ropes of the swing. "Why, I can have a funeral, too, if I feel like it," she said in surprise. "Nothing to stop me from having a funeral as good as *anybody*, if I want to."

She swung back and forth slowly, pondering this idea, her toes almost reaching to the edge of the crêpe-myrtle bushes. It seemed to her at that moment that she had found out, unaided, a fact of great importance, a thing which should be known to everybody, but was not. She opened her eyes very wide. She threw back her bullet-shaped head, and made her foolish, intaken sound. The thing she had discovered seemed so simple, so easy to arrange, that she wondered why everybody else didn't think of it too.

"Why, there ain't nothing to having a funeral," she said contemptuously. "I can have a funeral if *I* want to; ever'body can have a funeral if *they* want to." She swung more rapidly, her legs shooting up above the top of the crêpe-myrtles. When she remembered again the words the preacher had spoken as he stood beside the white child's coffin that very afternoon, it did not seem sensible that anybody would want to live in a world as harsh as this one was when they could have, so easily, not only eternal happiness in heaven, but a magnificent funeral as well. She brought the swing to a stop and got up. She took the wooden seat from the swing and stood it carefully against the trunk of the tree.

She hesitated a moment, then, having made up her mind, she climbed the sycamore like a small, excited monkey, anxious to put her plan through before her mother or Mrs. Kirby found out what she was up to and stopped her. She straddled the limb to which the swing was fixed and unfastened the knots in the rope; she wound the rope around the limb until she had shortened it expertly to the length she needed, laughing all the time with pleasure and nodding her head in anticipation of her triumph.

Cora came onto the porch and called, "Reba? Reba, where you at? I want you to go to the meat market for me."

But Reba flattened against the tree. She held her breath while her mother continued to call, seeing again, in her mind's eye, the triumphant details of her approaching funeral. First, there were the white horses and the brass bands. The bands played slow, sad music continuously, and the proud horses, as if conscious of the importance of such an occasion, pawed at the ground and shook out their white, silken manes. Mrs. Kirby was dressed in black silk, and she pressed a lace handkerchief to her eyes. She stood at the front door to take the floral designs, explaining the details of Reba's death to the mayor of the town, the minister of the Baptist church, and the unending stream of lesser people who crowded behind them.

"It's little Reba, this time," said Mrs. Kirby. "Yes, sir, it's little Reba, and we're all so upsot we just don't know *what* to do!" She began to cry again. "Looks like we don't get shut of one funeral in this house till we have another one, now does it?" She bowed her head submissively. "Yassum," she continued, as if answering a particular question, "Reba was a sweet child, and no two ways about it. I tell you *ever*'body gwiner miss Reba, and that's a fact!"

Cora called from the porch: "Reba! Reba! Where you at? You better answer me, gal, if you know what's good for you!" She stood a moment on the steps as if debating a point, then she went toward the old carriage-house, mumbling to herself angrily. When she was out of earshot, Reba spoke: "Yassum," she said in her small, meek voice. "Yassum, I hears you."

She stretched her neck and peered around the trunk of the tree, but when her mother reached the carriage-house and went inside, she bent down and caught up the dangling rope. Then she straddled the limb and inched forward cautiously. She stopped when she reached the middle of the limb and looked about her. She lifted the rope and wrapped it around her throat, tying a knot solidly at the side. "Yassum," she said, drawing the word out interminably. "Yassum."

Cora came away from the carriage-house and stopped beside the canna bed. "I knows you're hiding out someplace," she said. "I knows as well as I'm standing here that you hear every word I'm a-saying." She went back onto the porch and took a drink of water, throwing what was left in the dipper onto the ground with a faint splash.

But Reba sat quietly for a time, her black knees gripping the sycamore limb, looking about her slowly and listening to her mother's voice. At that instant she had a clear picture of Cora weeping over her coffin, just as she had wept over the coffin of the white child. "Reba! Reba, come back to us!" she said over and over, her face twisted with the force of her grief. "Don't leave us here to mourn, sweet little Reba! Don't leave us this a-way, honey!"

Then Reba drew back her head and made her foolish, intaken sound. "Yassum," she said softly. "Yassum." Suddenly she lifted her arms and swayed forward. She unlocked her knees from the limb and fell eagerly, the rope pulling her up and jerking her head sideways. At once she lifted her lathlike arms and tried to grasp the limb above her head, but she could not; then she jerked her body convulsively and made a shrill, strangled noise while the rope spun outward in a circle.

Cora said: "I hear you, Miss. I hear you laughing and acting silly and provoking me!" She shook her shoulders angrily. "All right, stay where you is! You'll get hongry befo' long, and then I'll catch you!" She went inside and rattled the stove-lid, throwing in firewood. A few minutes later she came back to the porch and looked about her again.

"There ain't no way to get away from me, gal," she said. "You'd know that by now if you had any sense." She looked straight at the clump of crêpe-myrtles that screened the swing from the house and raised her voice a little, as if she addressed personally the bundle which hung limp and strangled at the end of the still-vibrating rope. She said: "When I get supper cooked I'm gwiner come look for you; and when I look for you I'm gwiner *find* you; and when I find you I'm gwiner give you a whupping you'll *remember!*"

Some Like Them Short, 1939

EUDORA WELTY

The Whistle

Night fell. The darkness was thin, like some sleazy dress that has been worn and worn for many winters and always lets the cold through to the bones. Then the moon rose. The farm lay quite visible like a sunken stone among the stretches of deep woods in their colorless dead leaf. By a closer and more searching eye than the moon's, the tiny tomato plants belonging to the Mortons might have been seen in their neat rows beside the house—gray and feather-like, appalling in their exposed fragility. The moonlight covered everything, and lay upon the darkest shape of all, the farmhouse where the lamp had just been blown out.

Inside, Jason and Sara Morton were lying between the quilts of a pallet which had been made up close to the fireplace. A fire still fluttered in the grate, making a drowsy sound now and then, and its exhausted light beat up and down the wall, across the rafters, and over the dark pallet where the old people lay, like a bird trying to find its way out of the room.

The long-spaced, tired breathing of Jason was the only noise besides the flutter of the fire. He lay under the quilt in a long shape like a bean, turned on his side to face the barred door. His thin beard hung from his wryly held jaw, his lips moved once in the silence, and in and out he breathed, in and out, slowly and with a sound like a wind among the dead trees— a rattle and a sigh.

Sara lay on her back with her toothless mouth agape, as silent as Jason was noisy. Her eyes seemed opened too wide, the lids strained and limp, like openings which have been stretched shapeless and made useless. She

266

was staring at the dark and indistinguishable places among the rafters. Once a hissing yellow flame stood erect on the old log, and her grey face and carrot-colored hair, flattened on the pallet, were illuminated for a moment, with shadows bright-blue. Then she laid her sleeve across her eyes.

Neither husband nor wife had spoken. They lay trembling with cold, but no more communicative in their misery than a pair of windowshutters beaten by a storm. Sometimes many days, weeks, went by without words. They were fifty years old; their lives were filled with tiredness, with a great lack of necessity to speak, with poverty which may have bound them like a disaster too great for any discussion but left them still separate and undesirous of sympathy. Perhaps, years ago, the long habit of silence may have been started in anger or passion. Who could tell now?

As the fire grew lower and lower, Jason's breathing grew heavy and solemn, and at last he was asleep. Sara's body was as weightless as a strip of cane; there was hardly a shape to the quilt under which she was lying, and sometimes it seemed to her that it was her lack of weight which kept her from ever getting warm. Sara was so tired of the cold! That was all it could do any more—make her tired. Year after year, she felt sure that she would die before the cold was over. Now, according to the almanac, it was spring. But year after year, it was all the same. This was not their farm any longer now; it belonged to Mr. Perkins, but that too was almost forgotten in the sameness of the years. The tomato plants would be set out in their frames, transplanted always too soon, often killed before any start had been made at all. And then some years they would grow tall and full, if the freezes only held off, and then there was a crop.

Like a vain dream, Sara began to have thoughts of the spring and summer. At first she thought only simply—of the colors of green and red, the smell of sun on the ground, of leaves and warm ripening tomatoes. Then, her arms pressing together under the quilt, she began to imagine and remember the town of Verdy in the shipping season. It became a time of almost legendary festivity, a place of pleasure. On the roads everybody was bringing tomatoes to the packing sheds on the railroad at Verdy Station, where Mr. Perkins, the tall gesticulating figure, stood in the very center of everything, buying, directing, waving telegrams, shouting with impatience. Long trains of empty freight cars stood waiting and being filled. There were all the strange people—the younger farmers they never saw at any other time, the harassed storekeepers of Verdy, the packers who had come all the way from Florida, tanned, stockingless, some of them tattooed. The music box was playing in the café across the road, and the old crippled man was back taking pictures for a dime of the young people with their heads together. The men were getting drunk, and a pistol would go off. The children were having a tomato fight and running along beside the railroad track, smeared red and screaming, bumping into their elders. In the sheds the sorters were throwing out onto the rotting ground the hundreds of oversized tomatoes, the irregulars, the overripe. A strong, sickening, sweet smell hung over everything. Some of the packers were resting for only a moment, stretched out, stained with sweat, in the shade, and one was playing a guitar. The girl wrappers from Florida had small brown hands, young, incredibly rapid, red with juice. Their faces were sleepy and flushed; when the men spoke to them, they laughed.

And Jason and Sara would be standing there. How quickly the tomatoes were purchased! They were nodding their heads, and then there was nothing else to do but stand in the burning sun near the shed, watching the tomatoes shoved at once into the breath-taking procedure of sorting, wrapping, loading . . . seeing that it was all over with, that they were out of it now, themselves, of no more use, even to Mr. Perkins, until another year. The packers would walk by and stare at them briefly, burned brown from Florida, where the crops there had driven down the Mississippi prices to almost nothing again. In Florida, perhaps, it did not freeze in spring. Later, in Mr. Perkins' book, a few small debts might be written off, leaving the longstanding debts still there. Sometimes the season lasted six weeks, sometimes only three. It depended on the weather.

Sara, cold, stiff and weightless under the quilt, could think of the pleasures of Verdy and of the ripe tomatoes only in brief snatches, like the flare-up of the little fire. The rest of the time she thought only of cold, of the cold going on before and after. She felt the chill of the here and now, which was not to think at all, but was only a trembling in the dark.

She coughed patiently and turned her head to one side. She peered beneath her arm and saw that the fire had at last gone out and left only a hulk of red log, a still red bent shape, like one of Jason's wool socks thrown into the fireplace. With only this to comfort her, Sara closed her eyes and fell asleep. The husband and wife now lay perfectly still, with Jason's hoarse, slow breathing, like the commotion of some clumsy old bear trying to climb a tree, heard by nobody at all.

Every hour it was getting colder and colder. The moon, intense and white as the snow that never falls in Mississippi, drew lower in the sky, in the long night, and nearer to earth. The farm looked as hard and still as a sea shell, with the little knob of a house surrounded by its curved furrows of tomato plants. Cold like a white pressing hand reached down and lay over the shell.

In Verdy there is a great whistle which is blown when a freeze threatens. It is Mr. Perkins' whistle. Now it sounded out in the clear night, blast after blast. Over the countryside, lights appeared in the windows of the farms, and men and women ran out into the fields and covered up their plants with whatever they had.

Jason Morton was not waked up by the great whistle. On and on he slept, his cavernous breathing like roars coming from a hollow tree. His right hand had been thrown out in his sleep and lay stretched on the cold floor, all its misshapen swollen fingers, with the big veins standing in them, shining in the moonlight which had moved across the room.

Sara felt herself waking. She knew that the whistle was blowing, what it meant—and that it now remained for her to get Jason and go out to the field. A soft laxity, an illusion of warmth, flowed stubbornly down her body and for a few moments she continued to lie still.

Then she was sitting up and seizing her husband by the shoulders, without saying a word, rocking him back and forth. It took all her strength. He coughed and sat up. He said nothing either, and they both listened to the whistle. After a silence, it blew again, a long rising blast.

Sara and Jason got out of bed. They were both fully dressed, except for their shoes, because of the cold. Jason lighted the lantern and Sara gathered the bedclothes over her arm and followed him out.

Everything was white. White in a shadowed pit, abandoned from summer to summer, the old sorghum mill stood like the machine of a dream, with its long prostrate pole, its blunted axis.

Stooping over the little plants, Jason and Sara touched them and touched the earth. For their own knowledge, by their hands, they found everything to be true—the cold, the rightness of the warning, the desperation. Over the sticks set in among the plants, they laid all the quilts, spreading them with a slow ingenuity. Jason took off his coat and laid it over the small tender plants by the side of the house. Then he glanced at Sara, and she reached down and pulled her dress off over her head. Her hair fell down out of its pins and she began at once to tremble violently. The skirt was long and full, and all the rest of the plants were covered by the dress. Then Sara and Jason stood for a moment and stared almost idly at the field and up at the sky.

There was no wind. There was only the intense whiteness of moonlight. Yet its cold sank into them like the teeth of a trap. They bent their shoulders and walked silently back into the house.

The room was not much warmer. They had forgotten to shut the door behind them when they went out. Jason poured kerosene over more kindling and struck a light to it. Squatting, they got near it and sat motionless until it had all burned down. Then Jason, in his underwear and long blue trousers, went out and brought in another load, and the last big cherry log which they had been saving.

The extravagant warmth of the room had sent some kind of agitation over Sara, like her memories of Verdy in the shipping season. She sat huddled in a long brown cotton petticoat with a string run around the waist. Her carrot-colored hair, white at the temples, was hanging loose down to her shoulders, like a child's unbound for a party. She held her knees against her numb, pendulant breasts and stared into the fire, her eyes widening.

On the other side of the hearth, Jason watched the fire burning too.

His thin cracked lips parted, and through his open mouth his breath came quickly, gently, noiselessly, as though he were concealing all his tiredness. He lifted his long arms and held his trembling misshapen hands out to the fire.

Towards morning the kindling was all gone. The cherry log had burned to ashes. Jason and Sara sat in darkness, where their bed had lain, and it was colder than ever.

Sara trembled violently, again pressing her hard knees against her breast. In the return of winter, of the night's cold, something strange, like fright, or dependency, a sensation of complete loss, took possession of her shaking body.

All at once she spoke, without turning her head, but loudly.

"Jason, are you cold over there?"

She heard a silence break the rhythm of his difficult breathing. But only for a moment.

"No," said her husband's uncertain voice.

Then they were silent as before.

A Curtain of Green, 1941

THE MIDWEST

THE MIDWEST

MORGAN NEVILLE

The Last of the Boatmen

Despite myth, legend and exaggerations, Mike Fink was truly, in Davy Crockett's phrase, "a helliferocious fellow"—a sadistic prankster who eventually joined trapping expeditions in the Rockies and finally died in a brawl in Montana.

I embarked a few years since, at Pittsburg, for Cincinnati, on board of a steam boat—more with a view of realising the possibility of a speedy return against the current than in obedience to the call of either business or pleasure. It was a voyage of speculation. I was born on the banks of the Ohio, and the only vessels associated with my early recollections were the canoes of the Indians, which brought to Fort Pitt their annual cargoes of skins and bear's oil. The Flat boat of Kentucky, destined only to float with the current, next appeared; and after many years of interval, the Keel boat of the Ohio, and the Barge of the Mississippi were introduced for the convenience of the infant commerce of the West.

At the period, at which I have dated my trip to Cincinnati, the steam boat had made but few voyages back to Pittsburg. We were generally skeptics as to its practicability. The mind was not prepared for the change that was about to take place in the West. It is now consummated; and we yet look back with astonishment at the result.

The rudest inhabitant of our forests;—the man whose mind is least of all imbued with a relish for the picturesque—who would gaze with vacant stare at the finest painting, listen with apathy to the softest melody, and turn with indifference from a mere display of ingenious mechanism—is struck with the sublime power and self-moving majesty of a steam boat;— lingers on the shore where it passes and follows its rapid, and almost

273

magic course with silent admiration. The steam engine in five years has enabled us to anticipate a state of things, which, in the ordinary course of events, it would have required a century to have produced. The art of printing scarcely surpassed it in its beneficial consequences.

In the old world, the places of the greatest interest to the philosophic traveller are ruins, and monuments, that speak of faded splendour and departed glory. The broken columns of Tadmor—the shapeless ruins of Babylon—are rich in matter for almost endless speculation. Far different is the case in the western regions of America. The stranger views here, with wonder, the rapidity with which cities spring up in forests; and with which barbarism retreats before the approach of art and civilization. The reflection possessing the most intense interest is—not what has been the character of the country, but what shall be her future destiny.

As we coasted along this cheerful scene, one reflection crossed my mind to diminish the pleasure it excited. This was caused by the sight of the ruins of the once splendid mansion of Blennerhasset. I had spent some happy hours here, when it was the favorite residence of taste and hospitality. I had seen it when a lovely and accomplished woman presided —shedding a charm around, which made it as inviting, though not so dangerous, as the island of Calypso;—when its liberal and polished owner made it the resort of every stranger, who had any pretensions to literature or science.—I had beheld it again under more inauspicious circumstances: —when its proprietor, in a moment of visionary speculation, had abandoned this earthly paradise to follow an adventurer—himself the dupe of others. A military banditti held possession, acting "by authority." The embellishments of art and taste disappeared beneath the touch of a band of Vandals: and the beautiful domain which presented the imposing appearance of a palace, and which had cost a fortune in the erection, was changed in one night, into a scene of devastation. The chimneys of the house remained for some years—the insulated monument of the folly of their owner, and pointed out to the stranger the place where once stood the temples of hospitality. Drift wood covered the pleasure grounds; and the massive, cut stone that formed the columns of the gateway was scattered more widely than the fragments of the Egyptian Memnon.

When we left Pittsburg, the season was not far advanced in vegetation. But as we proceeded the change was more rapid than the difference of latitude justified. I had frequently observed this in former voyages: but it never was so striking as on the present occasion. The old mode of traveling in the sluggish flat boat seemed to give time for the change of season; but now a few hours carried us into a different climate. We met spring with all her laughing train of flowers and verdure rapidly advancing from the south. The buck-eye, cottonwood, and maple had already assumed, in this region, the rich livery of summer. The thousand varieties of the floral kingdom spread a gay carpet over the luxuriant bottoms on each side of the river. The thick woods resounded with the notes of the feathered tribe—each striving to outdo his neighbor in noise, if not in melody. We had not yet reached the region of paroquets; but the clear toned whistle of the cardinal was heard in every bush; and the cat-bird was endeavouring, with its usual zeal, to rival the powers of the more gifted mockingbird.

A few hours brought us to one of those stopping points, known by the name of "wooding places." It was situated immediately above Letart's Falls. The boat, obedient to the wheel of the pilot, made a graceful sweep towards the island above the chute and, rounding to, approached the wood pile. As the boat drew near the shore, the escape steam reverberated through the forest and hills like the chafed bellowing of the caged tiger. The root of a tree, concealed beneath the water, prevented the boat from getting sufficiently near the bank, and it became necessary to use the paddles to take a different position.

"Back out! Mannee! and try it again!" exclaimed a voice from the shore. "Throw your pole wide—and brace off!—or you'll run against a snag!"

This was a kind of language long familiar to us on the Ohio. It was a sample of the slang of the Keel boatmen.

The speaker was immediately cheered by a dozen of voices from the deck; and I recognised in him the person of an old acquaintance, familiarly known to me from my boyhood. He was leaning carelessly against a large beech; and, as his left arm negligently pressed a rifle to his side, presented a figure that Salvator would have chosen from a million as a model for his wild and gloomy pencil. His stature was upwards of six feet, his proportions perfectly symmetrical, and exhibiting the evidence of Herculean powers. To a stranger, he would have seemed a complete mulatto. Long exposure to the sun and weather on the lower Ohio and Mississippi had changed his skin; and, but for the fine European cast of his countenance, he might have passed for the principal warrior of some powerful tribe. Although at least fifty years of age, his hair was as black as the wing of the raven. Next to his skin he wore a red flannel shirt, covered by a blue capot, ornamented with white fringe. On his feet were moccasins, and a broad leathern belt, from which hung, suspended in a sheath, a large knife, encircled his waist.

As soon as the steam boat became stationary, the cabin passengers jumped on shore. On ascending the bank, the figure I have just described advanced to offer me his hand.

"How are you, Mike?" said I.

"How goes it?" replied the boatman—grasping my hand with a squeeze, that I can compare to nothing, but that of a blacksmith's vise.

"I am glad to see you, Mannee!"—continued he in his abrupt manner. "I am going to shoot at the tin cup for a quart—off hand—and you must be judge."

I understood Mike at once and, on any other occasion, should have remonstrated, and prevented the daring trial of skill. But I was accompanied by a couple of English tourists, who had scarcely ever been beyond the sound of Bow Bells; and who were traveling post over the United States to make up a book of observation, on our manners and customs. There were, also, among the passengers, a few bloods from Philadelphia and Baltimore, who could conceive of nothing equal to Chestnut or Howard streets; and who expressed great disappointment, at not being able to find terrapins and oysters at every village—marvellously lauding the comforts of Rubicum's. My tramontane pride was aroused; and I resolved to give them an opportunity of seeing a Western Lion—for such Mike undoubtedly was—in all his glory. The philanthropist may start and accuse me of want of humanity. I deny the charge and refer for apology to one of the best understood principles of human nature.

Mike, followed by several of his crew, led the way to a beech grove, some little distance from the landing. I invited my fellow passengers to witness the scene.—On arriving at the spot, a stout, bull-headed boatman, dressed in a hunting shirt but bare-footed—in whom I recognised a younger brother of Mike—drew a line with his toe; and stepping off thirty yards—turned around fronting his brother—took a tin cup, which hung from his belt, and placed it on his head. Although I had seen this feat performed before, I acknowledge I felt uneasy, whilst this silent preparation was going on. But I had not much time for reflection; for this second Albert exclaimed—

"Blaze away, Mike! and let's have the quart."

My *compagnons de voyage*, as soon as they recovered from the first effect of their astonishment, exhibited a disposition to interfere. But Mike, throwing back his left leg, levelled his rifle at the head of his brother. In this horizontal position the weapon remained for some seconds as immovable, as if the arm which held it, was affected by no pulsation.

"Elevate your piece a little lower, Mike! or you will pay the corn," cried the imperturbable brother.

I know not if the advice was obeyed or not; but the sharp crack of the rifle immediately followed, and the cup flew off thirty or forty yards—rendered unfit for future service. There was a cry of admiration from the strangers, who pressed forward to see if the foolhardy boatman was really safe. He remained as immovable, as if he had been a figure hewn out of stone. He had not even winked, when the ball struck the cup within two inches of his skull.

"Mike has won!" I exclaimed; and my decision was the signal which, according to their rules, permitted him of the target to move from his position. No more sensation was exhibited among the boatmen, than if a common wager had been won. The bet being decided, they hurried back to their boat, giving me and my friends an invitation to partake of "the treat." We declined, and took leave of the thoughtless creatures. In a few minutes afterwards, we observed their "Keel" wheeling into the current, —the gigantic form of Mike, bestriding the large steering oar, and the others arranging themselves in their places in front of the cabin, that extended nearly the whole length of the boat, covering merchandize of immense value. As they left the shore, they gave the Indian yell; and broke out into a sort of unconnected chorus—commencing with—

> Hard upon the beech oar!—
> She moves too slow!
> All the way to Shawneetown,
> Long while ago.

In a few minutes the boat "took the chute" of Letart's Falls, and disappeared behind the point, with the rapidity of an Arabian courser.

Our travellers returned to the boat, lost in speculation on the scene, and the beings they had just beheld; and, no doubt, the circumstance has been related a thousand times with all the necessary amplifications of finished tourists.

Mike Fink may be viewed, as the correct representative of a class of men now extinct; but who once possessed as marked a character, as that of the Gypsies of England, or the Lazaroni of Naples. The period of their existence was not more than a third of a century. The character was created by the introduction of trade on the Western waters; and ceased with the successful establishment of the steam boat.

There is something inexplicable in the fact, that there could be men found, for ordinary wages, who would abandon the systematic, but not laborious pursuits of agriculture, to follow a life, of all others, except that of the soldier, distinguished by the greatest exposure and privation. The occupation of a boatman was more calculated to destroy the constitution and to shorten life, than any other business. In ascending the river, it was a continued series of toil, rendered more irksome by the snail like rate, at which they moved. The boat was propelled by poles, against which the shoulder was placed; and the whole strength and skill of the individual were applied in this manner. As the boatmen moved along the running board, with their heads nearly touching the plank on which they walked, the effect produced on the mind of an observer was similar to that on beholding the ox, rocking before an overloaded cart. Their bodies, naked to their waist for the purpose of moving with greater ease, and of enjoying the breeze of the river, were exposed to the burning suns of summer and to the rains of autumn. After a hard day's push, they would take their "fillee," or ration of whiskey, and having swallowed a miserable supper of meat half burnt, and of bread half baked, stretch themselves without covering, on the deck, and slumber till the steersman's call invited them to the morning "fillee." Notwithstanding this, the boatman's life had charms as irresistible as those presented by the splendid illusions of the state. Sons abandoned the comfortable farms of their fathers, and apprentices fled from the service of their masters. There was a captivation in the idea of "going down the river"; and the youthful boatman who had "pushed a Keel" from New Orleans, felt all the pride of a young merchant, after his first voyage to an English sea port. From an exclusive association together, they had formed a kind of slang peculiar to themselves; and from the constant exercise of wit, with "the squatters" on shore, and crews of other boats, they acquired a quickness, and smartness of vulgar retort, that was quite amusing. The frequent battles they were engaged in with the boatmen of different parts of the river, and with the less civilized inhabitants of the lower Ohio, and Mississippi, invested them with that ferocious reputation, which has made them spoken of throughout Europe.

On board of the boats thus navigated, our merchants entrusted valuable cargoes, without insurance, and with no other guarantee than the receipt of the steersman, who possessed no property but his boat; and the confidence so reposed was seldom abused.

Among these men, Mike Fink stood an acknowledged leader for many years. Endowed by nature with those qualities of intellect that give the possessor influence, he would have been a conspicuous member of any society, in which his lot might have been cast. An acute observer of human nature has said—"Opportunity alone makes the hero. Change but their situations, and Caesar would have been but the best wrestler on the green." With a figure cast in a mould that added much of the symmetry of an Apollo to the limbs of a Hercules, he possessed gigantic strength; and accustomed from an early period of life to brave the dangers of a frontier life, his character was noted for the most daring intrepidity. At the court of Charlemagne, he might have been a Roland; with the Crusaders, he would have been the favourite of the Knight of the Lion-heart; and in our revolution, he would have ranked with the Morgans and Putnams of the day. He was the hero of a hundred fights, and the leader in a thousand daring adventures. From Pittsburg to St. Louis and New Orleans, his fame was established. Every farmer on the shore kept on good terms with Mike—otherwise, there was no safety for his property. Wherever he was an enemy, like his great prototype, Rob Roy, he levied the contribution of Black Mail for the use of his boat. Often at night, when his tired companions slept, he would take an excursion of five or six miles, and return before morning, rich in spoil. On the Ohio, he was known among his companions by the appellation of the "Snapping Turtle"; and on the Mississippi, he was called "The Snag."

At the early age of seventeen, Mike's character was displayed, by enlisting himself in a corps of Scouts—a body of irregular rangers, which was employed on the North-western frontiers of Pennsylvania, to watch the Indians, and to give notice of any threatened inroad.

At that time, Pittsburg was on the extreme verge of white population, and the spies, who were constantly employed, generally extended their explorations forty or fifty miles to the west of this post. They went out, singly, lived as did the Indian, and in every respect became perfectly assimilated in habits, taste, and feeling, with the red men of the desert. A kind of border warfare was kept up, and the scout thought it as praiseworthy to bring in the scalp of a Shawnee, as the skin of a panther. He would remain in the woods for weeks together, using parched corn for bread, and depending on his rifle for his meat—and slept at night in perfect comfort, rolled in his blanket.

In this corps, whilst yet a stripling, Mike acquired a reputation for boldness, and cunning, far beyond his companions. A thousand legends illustrate the fearlessness of his character. There was one, which he told himself, with much pride, and which made an indelible impression on my boyish memory. He had been out on the hills of Mahoning, when, to use his own words, "he saw signs of Indians being about."—He had discovered the recent print of the moccasin on the grass, and found drops of fresh blood of a deer on the green bush. He became cautious, skulked for some time in the deepest thickets of hazel and briar; and, for several days, did not discharge his rifle. He subsisted patiently on parched corn and jerk, which he had dried on his first coming into the woods. He gave no alarm to the settlements, because he discovered with perfect certainty that the enemy consisted of a small hunting party, who were receding from the Alleghany.

As he was creeping along one morning, with the stealthy tread of a cat, his eye fell upon a beautiful buck, browsing on the edge of a barren spot, three hundred yards distant. The temptation was too strong for the woodsman, and he resolved to have a shot at every hazard. Re-priming his gun, and picking his flint, he made his approaches in the usual noiseless manner. At the moment he reached the spot, from which he meant to take his aim, he observed a large savage, intent upon the same object, advancing from a direction a little different from his own. Mike shrunk behind a tree, with a quickness of thought, and, keeping his eye fixed on the hunter, waited the result with patience. In a few moments, the Indian halted within fifty paces, and levelled his piece at the deer. In the meanwhile, Mike presented his rifle at the body of the savage; and at the moment the smoke issued from the gun of the latter, the bullet of Fink passed through the red man's breast. He uttered a yell, and fell dead at the same instant with the deer. Mike re-loaded his rifle, and remained in his covert for some minutes, to ascertain whether there were more enemies at hand. He then stepped up to the prostrate savage, and having satisfied himself that life was extinguished, turned his attention to the buck, and took from the carcass those pieces, suited to the process of jerking.

In the meantime, the country was filling up with a white population, and in a few years the red man, with the exception of a few fractions of tribes, gradually receded to the Lakes and beyond the Mississippi. The corps of Scouts was abolished, after having acquired habits, which unfitted them for the pursuits of civilized society. Some incorporated themselves with the Indians; and others, from a strong attachment to their erratic mode of life, joined the boatmen, then just becoming a distinct class. Among these was our hero, Mike Fink, whose talents were soon developed; and for many years, he was as celebrated on the rivers of the West, as he had been in the woods.

I gave to my fellow travellers the substance of the foregoing narrative, as we sat on deck by moonlight and cut swiftly through the magnificent sheet of water between Letart and the Great Kanhawa. It was one of those beautiful nights, which permitted every thing to be seen with sufficient distinctness to avoid danger;—yet created a certain degree of illusion, that gave reins to the imagination. The outline of the river hills lost all its harshness; and the occasional bark of the house dog from the shore, and the distant scream of the solitary loon, gave increased effect to the scene. It was altogether so delightful, that the hours till morning flew swiftly by, whilst our travellers dwelt with rapture on the surrounding scenery, which shifted every moment like the capricious changes of the kaleidoscope—and listening to the tales of border warfare, as they were brought to mind, by passing the places where they happened. The celebrated Hunter's Leap, and the bloody battle of Kanhawa, were not forgotten.

The afternoon of the next day brought us to the beautiful city of Cincinnati, which, in the course of thirty years, has risen from a village of soldiers' huts to a town,—giving promise of future splendour, equal to any on the sea-board.

Some years after the period, at which I have dated my visit to Cincinnati, business called me to New Orleans. On board of the steam boat, on which I had embarked, at Louisville, I recognised, in the person of the pilot, one of those men, who had formerly been a patroon, or Keel boat captain. I entered into conversation with him on the subject of his former associates.

"They are scattered in all directions," said he. "A few, who had capacity, have become pilots of steam boats. Many have joined the trading parties that cross the Rocky mountains; and a few have settled down as farmers."

"What has become," I asked, "of my old acquaintance, Mike Fink?"

"Mike was killed in a skrimmage," replied the pilot. "He had refused several good offers on steam boats. He said he could not bear the hissing of steam, and he wanted room to throw his pole. He went to the Missouri, and about a year since was shooting the tin cup, when he had corned too heavy. He elevated too low, and shot his companion through the head. A friend of the deceased, who was present, suspecting foul play, shot Mike through the heart, before he had time to reload his rifle."

With Mike Fink expired the spirit of the Boatmen.

The Western Souvenir, 1829

ABRAHAM LINCOLN

To the Parents of Colonel Elmer E. Ellsworth

May 25, 1861

My dear Sir and Madam, In the untimely loss of your noble son, our affliction here, is scarcely less than your own. So much of promised usefulness to one's country, and of bright hopes for one's self and friends, have rarely been so suddenly dashed, as in his fall. In size, in years, and in youthful appearance, a boy only, his power to command men, was surpassingly great. This power, combined with a fine intellect, an indomitable energy, and a taste altogether military, constituted in him, as seemed to me, the best natural talent, in that department, I ever knew. And yet he was singularly modest and deferential in social intercourse. My acquaintance with him began less than two years ago; yet through the latter half of the intervening period, it was as intimate as the disparity of our ages, and my engrossing engagements, would permit. To me, he appeared to have no indulgences or pastime; and I never heard him utter a profane, or an intemperate word. What was conclusive of his good heart, he never forgot his parents. The honors he labored for so laudably, and, in the sad end, so gallantly gave his life, he meant for them, no less than for himself.

In the hope that it may be no intrusion upon the sacredness of your sorrow, I have ventured to address you this tribute to the memory of my young friend, and your brave and early fallen child.

May God give you that consolation which is beyond all earthly power. Sincerely your friend in a common affliction—

A. LINCOLN

From Annual Message to Congress, 1862

The dogmas of the quiet past are inadequate to the stormy present. The occasion is piled high with difficulty, and we must rise with the occasion. As our case is new, so we must think anew and act anew. We must disenthrall ourselves, and then we shall save our country.

Fellow-citizens, we cannot escape history. We of this Congress and this administration will be remembered in spite of ourselves. No personal significance or insignificance can spare one or another of us. The fiery trial through which we pass will light us down, in honor or dishonor, to the latest generation. We say we are for the Union. The world will not forget that we say this. We know how to save the Union. The world knows that we know how to save it. We—even we here—hold the power and bear the responsibility. In giving freedom to the slave, we assure freedom to the free—honorable alike in what we give and what we preserve. We shall nobly save or meanly lose the last, best hope of earth. Other means may succeed; this could not fail. The way is plain, peaceful, generous, just—a way which, if followed, the world will forever applaud, and God must forever bless.

Life and Writings of Lincoln, edited by P. Van Doren Stern

FRANK A. HASKELL

"The Crest Is Safe"

> *The author of this classic account of Pickett's charge was a colonel of a Wisconsin regiment at Gettysburg. After the battle he wrote a book-long letter to his brother, giving the story of the battle. Haskell himself was killed a year later at Cold Harbor.*

Half-past two o'clock, an hour and a half since the commencement, and still the cannonade did not in the least abate; but soon thereafter some signs of weariness and a little slacking of fire began to be apparent upon both sides. . . . All things must end, and the great cannonade was no exception to the general law of earth. In the number of guns active at one time, and in the duration and rapidity of their fire, this artillery engagement, up to this time, must stand alone and pre-eminent in this war. It has not been often, or many times, surpassed in the battles of the world. Two hundred and fifty guns, at least, rapidly fired for two mortal hours. . . .

At three o'clock almost precisely, the last shot hummed, and bounded and fell, and the cannonade was over. The purpose of General Lee in all this fire of his guns—we know it now, we did not at the time so well— was to disable our artillery and break up our infantry upon the position of the Second Corps, so as to render them less an impediment to the sweep of his own brigades and divisions over our crest and through our lines. . . . There was a pause between acts, with the curtain down, soon to rise upon the great final act, and catastrophe of Gettysburg. We have passed by the left of the Second Division, coming from the First; when we crossed the crest the enemy was not in sight, and all was still—we walked slowly along in the rear of the troops, by the ridge cut off now from a view of the enemy on his position, and were returning to the spot where we had left our horses. . . . In a moment afterwards we met Captain Wessels and the orderlies who had our horses; they were on foot leading the horses. Captain Wessels was pale, and he said, excited: "General, they say the enemy's infantry is advancing." We sprang into our saddles, a score of bounds brought us upon the all-seeing crest.

To say that men grew pale and held their breath at what we and they there saw would not be true. Might not six thousand men be brave and without shade of fear, and yet, before a hostile eighteen thousand, armed, and not five minutes' march away, turn ashy white? None on that crest now need be told that *the enemy is advancing*. Every eye could see his legions, an overwhelming resistless tide of an ocean of armed men sweeping upon us! Regiment after regiment and brigade after brigade moved from the woods and rapidly take their places in the lines forming the assault. Pickett's proud division, with some additional troops, hold their right; Pettigrew's (Worth's) their left. The first line at short interval is followed by a second, and that a third succeeds; and columns between support the lines. More than half a mile their front extends; more than a thousand yards the dull gray masses deploy, man touching man, rank pressing rank, and line supporting line. The red flags wave, their horsemen gallop up and down; the arms of eighteen thousand men, barrel and bayonet, gleam in the sun, a sloping forest of flashing steel. Right on they move, as with one soul, in perfect order, without impediment of ditch, or wall or stream, over ridge and slope, through orchard and meadow, and cornfield, magnificent, grim, irresistible.

All was orderly and still upon our crest; no noise and no confusion. The men had little need of commands, for the survivors of a dozen battles knew well enough what this array in front portended, and, already in their places, they would be prepared to act when the right time should come. The click of the locks as each man raised the hammer to feel with his fingers that the cap was on the nipple; the sharp jar as a musket touched a stone upon the wall when thrust in aiming over it, and the clicking of the iron axles as the guns were rolled up by hand a little further to the front, were quite all the sounds that could be heard. Cap-boxes were slid around to the front of the body; cartridge boxes opened, officers opened their pistol-holsters. Such preparations, little more was needed. The trefoil flags, colors of the brigades and divisions moved to their places in rear; but along the lines in front the grand old ensign that first waved in battle at Saratoga in 1777, and which these people coming would rob of half its stars, stood up, and the west wind kissed it as the sergeants sloped its lance towards the enemy. I believe that not one above whom it then waved but blessed his God that he was loyal to it, and whose heart did not swell with pride towards it, as the emblem of the Republic before that treason's flaunting rag in front.

General Gibbon rode down the lines, cool and calm, and in an unimpassioned voice he said to the men, "Do not hurry, men, and fire too fast, let them come up close before you fire, and then aim low and steadily." The coolness of their General was reflected in the faces of his men. Five minutes had elapsed since first the enemy have emerged from the woods—no great space of time surely if measured by the usual standard by which men estimate duration, but it was long enough for us to note and weigh some of the elements of mighty moment that surrounded us; the disparity of numbers between the assailants and the assailed; that few as were our numbers we could not be supported and reinforced until support would not be needed or would be too late; that upon the ability of the two trefoil divisions to hold the crest and repel the assault depended not only their own safety or destruction, but also the honor of the Army of the Potomac and defeat or victory at Gettysburg. Should these advancing men pierce our line and become the entering wedge, driven home, that would sever our army asunder, what hope would there be afterwards, and where the blood-earned fruits of yesterday? It was long enough for the Rebel storm to drift across more than half the space that had at first separated it from us. None, or all, of these considerations either depressed or elevated us. They might have done the former, had we been timid; the latter had we been confident and vain. But, we were there waiting, and ready to do our duty—that done, results could not dishonor us.

Our skirmishers open a spattering fire along the front, and, fighting, retire upon the main line—the first drops, the heralds of the storm, sounding on our windows. Then the thunders of our guns, first Arnold's then Cushing's and Woodruff's and the rest, shake and reverberate again through the air, and their sounding shells smite the enemy. . . . All our available guns are now active, and from the fire of shells, as the range grows shorter and shorter, they change to shrapnel, and from shrapnel to canister; but in spite of shells, and shrapnel and canister, without wavering or halt, the hardy lines of the enemy continue to move on. The Rebel guns make no reply to ours, and no charging shout rings out today, as is the Rebel wont; but the courage of these silent men amid our shots seems not to need the stimulus of other noise.

The enemy's right flank sweeps near Stannard's bushy crest, and his concealed Vermonters rake it with a well-delivered fire of musketry. The gray lines do not halt or reply, but withdrawing a little from that extreme, they still move on. And so across all that broad open ground they have come, nearer and nearer, nearly half the way, with our guns bellowing in their faces, until now a hundred yards, no more, divide our ready left from their advancing right. The eager men there are impatient to begin. Let them. First, Harrow's breastworks flame; then Hall's; then Webb's. As if our bullets were the fire coals that touched off their muskets, the enemy in front halts, and his countless level barrels blaze back upon us. The Second Division is struggling in battle. The rattling storm soon spreads to the right, and the blue trefoils are vieing with the white. All along each hostile front, a thousand yards, with narrowest space between, the volleys blaze and roll; as thick the sound as when a summer hailstorm pelts the city roofs; as thick the fire as when the incessant lightning fringes a summer cloud.

When the Rebel infantry had opened fire our batteries soon became silent, and this without their fault, for they were foul by long previous use. They were the targets of the concentrated Rebel bullets, and some of them had expended all their canister. But they were not silent before Rhorty was killed, Woodruff had fallen mortally wounded, and Cushing, firing almost his last canister, had dropped dead among his guns shot through the head by a bullet. The conflict is left to the infantry alone. . . .

The conflict was tremendous, but I had seen no wavering in all our line. Wondering how long the Rebel ranks, deep though they were, could stand our sheltered volleys, I had come near my destination, when—great heaven! were my senses mad? The larger portion of Webb's brigade—my God, it was true—there by the group of trees and the angles of the wall, was breaking from the cover of their works, and, without orders or reason, with no hand lifted to check them, was falling back, a fear-stricken flock of confusion! The fate of Gettysburg hung upon a spider's single thread!

A great magnificent passion came on me at the instant, not one that overpowers and confounds, but one that blanches the face and sublimes every sense and faculty. My sword that had always hung idle by my side, the sign of rank only in every battle, I drew, bright and gleaming, the symbol of command. Was not that a fit occasion, and these fugitives the men on whom to try the temper of the Solinzen steel? All rules and proprieties were forgotten; all considerations of person and danger and safety despised; for, as I met the tide of these rabbits, the damned red flags of the rebellion began to thicken and flaunt along the wall they had just deserted, and one was already waving over one of the guns of the dead Cushing. I ordered these men to "halt," and "face about" and "fire," and they heard my voice and gathered my meaning, and obeyed my commands. On some unpatriotic backs of those not quick of comprehension, the flat of my sabre fell not lightly, and at its touch their love of country returned, and, with a look at me as if I were the destroying angel, as I might have become theirs, they again faced the enemy.

General Webb soon came to my assistance. He was on foot, but he was active, and did all that one could do to repair the breach, or to avert its calamity. The men that had fallen back, facing the enemy, soon regained confidence in themselves, and became steady. This portion of the wall was lost to us, and the enemy had gained the cover of the reverse side, where he now stormed with fire. But Webb's men, with their bodies in part protected by the abruptness of the crest, now sent back in the enemies' faces as fierce a storm. Some scores of venturesome Rebels, that in their first push at the wall had dared to cross at the further angle, and those that had desecrated Cushing's guns, were promptly shot down, and speedy death met him who should raise his body to cross it again.

At this point little could be seen of the enemy, by reason of his cover and the smoke, except the flash of his muskets and his waving flags. These red flags were accumulating at the wall every moment, and they maddened us as the same color does the bull. Webb's men are falling fast, and he is among them to direct and encourage; but, however well they may now do, with that walled enemy in front, with more than a dozen flags to Webb's three, it soon becomes apparent that in not many minutes they will be overpowered, or that there will be none alive for the enemy to overpower. Webb has but three regiments, all small, the 69th, 71st and 72d Pennsylvania—the 106th Pennsylvania, except two companies, is not here today—and he must have speedy assistance, or this crest will be lost.

Oh, where is Gibbon? where is Hancock?—some general—anybody with the power and the will to support that wasting, melting line? No general came, and no succor! . . . As a last resort I resolved to see if Hall and Harrow could not send some of their commands to reinforce Webb. I galloped to the left in the execution of my purpose, and as I attained the rear of Hall's line, from the nature of the ground and the position of the enemy it was easy to discover the reason and the manner of this gathering of Rebel flags in front of Webb.

The enemy, emboldened by his success in gaining our line by the group of trees and the angle of the wall, was concentrating all his right against and was further pressing that point. There was the stress of his assault; there would he drive his fiery wedge to split our line. In front of Harrow's and Hall's Brigades he had been able to advance no nearer than when he first halted to deliver fire, and these commands had not yielded an inch. To effect the concentration before Webb, the enemy would march the regiment on his extreme right of each of his lines by the left flank to the rear of the troops, still halted and facing to the front, and so continuing to draw in his right, when they were all massed in the position desired, he would again face them to the front, and advance to the storming. This was the way he made the wall before Webb's line blaze red with his battle flags, and such was the purpose there of his thick-crowding battalions.

Not a moment must be lost. Colonel Hall I found just in rear of his line, sword in hand, cool, vigilant, noting all that passed and directing the battle of his brigade. The fire was constantly diminishing now in his front, in the manner and by the movement of the enemy that I have mentioned, drifting to the right.

"How is it going?" Colonel Hall asked me, as I rode up.

"Well, but Webb is hotly pressed and must have support, or he will be overpowered. Can you assist him?"

"Yes."

"You cannot be too quick."

"I will move my brigade at once."

"Good."

He gave the order, and in the briefest time I saw five friendly colors hurrying to the aid of the imperilled three; and each color represented true, battle-tried men, that had not turned back from Rebel fire that day nor yesterday, though their ranks were sadly thinned; to Webb's brigade, pressed back as it had been from the wall, the distance was not great from Hall's right. The regiments marched by the right flank. . . . . The movement, as it did, attracting the enemy's fire, and executed in haste, as it must be, was difficult; but in reasonable time, and in order that is serviceable, if not regular, Hall's men are fighting gallantly side by side with Webb's before the all important point.

I did not stop to see all this movement of Hall's, but from him I went at once further to the left, to the 1st brigade. Gen'l Harrow I did not see, but his fighting men would answer my purpose as well. The 19th Me., the 15th Mass., and 32d N.Y. and the shattered old thunderbolt, the 1st Minn.—poor Farrell was dying then upon the ground where he had fallen—all men that I could find I took over to the right at the *double quick.*

As we were moving to, and near the other brigade of the division, from my position on horseback, I could see that the enemy's right, under Hall's fire, was beginning to stagger and to break. "See," I said to the men. "See the *chivalry!* See the gray-backs run!" The men saw, and as they swept to their places by the side of Hall and opened fire, they roared, and this in a manner that said more plainly than words—for the deaf could have seen it in their faces, and the blind could have heard it in their voices— *the crest is safe!*

The whole Division concentrated, and changes of position, and new phases, as well on our part as on that of the enemy, having as indicated occurred, for the purpose of showing the exact present posture of affairs, some further description is necessary. Before the 2d Division the enemy is massed, the main bulk of his force covered by the ground that slopes to his rear, with his front at the stone wall. Between his front and us extends the very apex of the crest. All there are left of the White Trefoil Division —yesterday morning there were three thousand eight hundred, this morning there were less than three thousand—at this moment there are somewhat over two thousand;—twelve regiments in three brigades are below or behind the crest, in such a position that by the exposure of the head and upper part of the body above the crest they can deliver their fire in the enemy's faces along the top of the wall.

By reason of the disorganization incidental in Webb's brigade to his men's having broken and fallen back, as mentioned, in the two other brigades to their rapid and difficult change of position under fire, and in all the divisions in part to severe and continuous battle, formation of companies and regiments in regular ranks is lost; but commands, companies, regiments and brigades are blended and intermixed—an irregular extended mass—men enough, if in order, to form a line of four or five ranks along the whole front of the division. The twelve flags of the regiments wave defiantly at intervals along the front; at the stone wall, at unequal distances from ours of forty, fifty or sixty yards, stream nearly double this number of the battle flags of the enemy.

These changes accomplished on either side, and the concentration complete, although no cessation or abatement in the general din of conflict since the commencement had at any time been appreciable, now it was as if a new battle, deadlier, stormier than before, had sprung from the body of the old—a young Phoenix of combat, whose eyes stream lightning, shaking his arrowy wings over the yet glowing ashes of his progenitor. The jostling, swaying lines on either side boil, and roar, and dash their flamy spray, two hostile billows of a fiery ocean. Thick flashes stream from the wall, thick volleys answer from the crest. No threats or expostulation now, only example and encouragement. All depths of passion are stirred, and all combatives fire, down to their deep foundations. Individuality is drowned in a sea of clamor, and timid men, breathing the breath of the multitude, are brave. The frequent dead and wounded lie where they stagger and fall—there is no humanity for them now, and none can be spared to care for them. The men do not cheer or shout; they growl, and over that uneasy sea, heard with the roar of musketry, sweeps the muttered thunder of a storm of growls. Webb, Hall, Devereux, Mallon, Abbott among the men where all are heroes are doing deeds of note.

Now the loyal wave rolls up as if it would overleap its barrier, the crest. Pistols flash with the muskets. My "Forward to the wall" is answered by the Rebel counter-command, "Steady, men!" and the wave swings back. Again it surges, and again it sinks. These men of Pennsylvania, on the soil of their own homesteads, the first and only to flee the wall, must be the first to storm it. . . . "Sergeant, forward with your color. Let the Rebels see it close to their eyes once before they die." The color sergeant of the 72d Pa., grasping the stump of the severed lance in both his hands, waved the flag above his head and rushed towards the wall. "Will you see your color storm the wall alone?" One man only starts to follow. Almost half way to the wall, down go color bearer and color to the ground—the gallant sergeant is dead. The line springs—the crest of the solid ground with a great roar, heaves forward its maddened load, men, arms, smoke, fire, a fighting mass. It rolls to the wall—flash meets flash, the wall is crossed—a moment ensues of thrusts, yells, blows, shots, and undistinguishable conflict, followed by a shout universal that makes the welkin ring again, and the last and bloodiest fight of the great battle of Gettysburg is ended and won. *The Battle of Gettysburg, 1878*

CARL SANDBURG

Tribute to Lincoln Before Joint Session of Congress

Not often in the story of mankind does a man arrive on earth who is both steel and velvet, who is as hard as rock and soft as drifting fog, who holds in his heart and mind the paradox of terrible storm and peace unspeakable and perfect. Here and there across centuries come reports of men alleged to have these contrasts. And the incomparable Abraham Lincoln, born 150 years ago this day, is an approach if not a perfect realization of this character.

In the time of the April lilacs in the year 1865, on his death, the casket with his body was carried north and west a thousand miles; and the American people wept as never before; bells sobbed, cities wore crepe; people stood in tears and with hats off as the railroad burial car paused in the leading cities of seven states, ending its journey at Springfield, Ill., the home town.

During the four years he was President he at times, especially in the first three months, took to himself the powers of a dictator; he commanded the most powerful armies till then assembled in modern warfare; he enforced conscription of soldiers for the first time in American history; under imperative necessity he abolished the right of habeas corpus; he directed politically and spiritually the wild, massive, turbulent forces let loose in civil war. . . .

In the month the war began he told his secretary, John Hay, "My policy is to have no policy." Three years later in a letter to a Kentucky friend made public, he confessed plainly, "I have been controlled by events." His words at Gettysburg were sacred, yet strange with a color of the familiar: "We cannot consecrate—we cannot hallow—this ground. The brave men, living and dead, who struggled here, have consecrated it, far beyond our poor power to add or detract."

He could have said "the brave Union men." Did he have a purpose in omitting the word "Union"? Was he keeping himself and his utterance clear of the passion that would not be good to look at when the time came for peace and reconciliation? Did he mean to leave an implication that there were brave Union men and brave Confederate men, living and dead, who had struggled there? We do not know, of a certainty.

Was he thinking of the Kentucky father whose two sons died in battle, one in Union blue, the other in Confederate gray, the father inscribing on the stone over their double grave, "God knows which was right"? We do not know. . . .

While the war winds howled he insisted that the Mississippi was one river meant to belong to one country, that railroad connection from coast to coast must be pushed through and the Union Pacific Railroad made a reality. While the luck of war wavered and broke and came again, as generals failed and campaigns were lost, he held enough forces of the North together to raise new armies and supply them, until generals were found who made war as victorious war has always been made, with terror, frightfulness, destruction, and on both sides, North and South, valor and sacrifice past words of man to tell.

In the mixed shame and blame of the immense wrongs of two crashing civilizations, often with nothing to say, he said nothing, slept not at all, and on occasions he was seen to weep in a way that made weeping appropriate, decent, majestic.

As he rode alone on horseback near the soldiers' home on the edge of Washington one night his hat was shot off; a son he loved died as he watched at the bed; his wife was accused of betraying information to the enemy, until denials from him were necessary.

An Indiana man at the White House heard him say, "Voorhees, don't it seem strange to you that I, who could never so much as cut off the head of a chicken, should be elected, or selected, into the midst of all this blood?" . . .

Among the million words in the Lincoln utterance record, he interprets himself with a more keen precision than someone else offering to explain him. His simple opening of the House Divided speech in 1858 serves for today:

"If we could know where we are, and whither we are tending we could better judge what to do, and how to do it."

To his Kentucky friend, Joshua F. Speed, he wrote in 1855:

"Our progress in degeneracy appears to me to be pretty rapid. As a nation we began by declaring that 'all men are created equal, except Negroes.' When the Know-Nothings get control, it will read 'All men are created equal except Negroes and foreigners and Catholics.' When it comes to this, I shall prefer emigrating to some country where they make no pretense of loving liberty."

Infinitely tender was his word from a White House balcony to a crowd on the White House lawn, "I have not willingly planted a thorn in any man's bosom," or to a military governor, "I shall do nothing through malice; what I deal with is too vast for malice."

He wrote for Congress to read on December 1, 1862:

"In times like the present men would utter nothing for which they would not willingly be responsible through time and eternity."

Like an ancient psalmist he warned Congress:

"Fellow citizens, we cannot escape history. We will be remembered in spite of ourselves. No personal significance or insignificance can spare one or another of us. The fiery trial through which we pass will light us down in honor or dishonor to the latest generation."

Wanting Congress to break and forget past traditions his words came keen and flashing. "The dogmas of the quiet past are inadequate for the stormy present. We must think anew, we must act anew, we must disenthrall ourselves." They are the sort of words that actuated the mind and will of the men who created and navigated that marvel of the sea, the *Nautilus*, and her voyage from Pearl Harbor and under the North Pole icecap.

The people of many other countries take Lincoln now for their own. He belongs to them. He stands for decency, honest dealing, plain talk, and funny stories. "Look where he came from—don't he know all us strugglers and wasn't he a kind of tough struggler all his life right up to the finish?" Something like that you can hear in any near-by neighborhood and across the seas.

Millions there are who take him as a personal treasure. He had some-thing they would like to see spread everywhere over the world. Democracy? We can't find words to say exactly what it is, but he had it. In his blood and bones he carried it. In the breath of his speeches and writings it is there. Popular government? Republican institutions? Government where the people have the say-so, one way or another telling their elected leaders what they want? He had the idea. It's there in the lights and shadows of his personality, a mystery that can be lived but never fully spoken in words.

Our good friend the poet and playwright Mark Van Doren tells us:

"To me, Lincoln seems, in some ways, the most interesting man who ever lived. He was gentle, but his gentleness was combined with a terrific toughness, an iron strength."

How did Lincoln say he would like to be remembered? His beloved friend, Representative Owen Lovejoy of Illinois, had died in May of 1864 and friends wrote to Lincoln and he replied that the pressure of duties kept him from joining them in efforts for a marble monument to Lovejoy, the last sentence of his letter saying, "Let him have the marble monument along with the well-assured and more enduring one in the hearts of those who love liberty, unselfishly, for all men."

So perhaps we may say that the well assured and most enduring memorial to Lincoln is invisibly there, today, tomorrow and for a long time yet to come in the hearts of lovers of liberty, men and women who understand that wherever there is freedom there have been those who fought, toiled and sacrificed for it.

February 12, 1959

HORACE WHITE

The Great Chicago Fire

> As editor of the Chicago TRIBUNE at the time of the fire, White wrote this account of his experiences during that holocaust. Later he moved to New York and succeeded the famous Godkin on the EVENING POST.

I had retired to rest, though not to sleep (Sunday, October 8) when the great bell struck the alarm, but fires had been so frequent of late, and had been so speedily extinguished, that I did not deem it worth while to get up and look at it, or even to count the strokes on the bell to learn where it was. The bell paused for fifteen minutes before giving the general alarm, which distinguishes a great fire from a small one. When it sounded the general alarm I rose and looked out. There was a great light to the southwest of my residence, but no greater than I had frequently seen in that quarter, where vast piles of pine lumber have been stored all the time I have lived in Chicago, some eighteen years. But it was not pine lumber that was burning this time. It was a row of wooden tenements in the South Division of the city, in which a few days ago were standing whole rows of the most costly buildings which it has entered into the hearts of architects to conceive. I watched the increasing light for a few moments. Red tongues of light began to shoot upward; my family were all aroused by this time, and I dressed myself for the purpose of going to the "Tribune" office to write something about the catastrophe. Once out upon the street, the magnitude of the fire was suddenly disclosed to me.

The dogs of hell were upon the housetops of La Salle and Wells streets, just south of Adams, bounding from one to another. The fire was moving northward like ocean surf on a sand beach. It had already traveled an eighth of a mile and was far beyond control. A column of flame would shoot up from a burning building, catch the force of the wind, and strike the next one, which in turn would perform the same direful office for its neighbor. It was simply indescribable in its terrible grandeur. Vice and crime had got the first scorching. The district where the fire got its firm foothold was the Alsatia of Chicago. Fleeing before it was a crowd of blear-eyed, drunken and diseased wretches, male and female, half-naked, ghastly, with painted cheeks, cursing and uttering ribald jests as they drifted along.

I went to the "Tribune" office, ascended to the editorial rooms, took the only inflammable thing there, a kerosene lamp, and carried it to the basement, where I emptied the oil into the sewer. This was scarcely done when I perceived the flames breaking out of the roof of the court house, the old nucleus of which, in the center of the edifice, was not constructed of fire-proof material, as the new wings had been. As the flames had leapt a vacant space of nearly two hundred feet to get at this roof, it was evident that most of the business portion of the city must go down, but I did not reflect that the city water works, with their four great pumping engines, were in a straight line with the fire and wind. Nor did I know then that this priceless machinery was covered by a wooden roof. The flames were driving thither with demon precision.

Billows of fire were rolling over the business palaces of the city and swallowing up their contents. Walls were falling so fast that the quaking of the ground under our feet was scarcely noticed, so continuous was the reverberation. Sober men and women were hurrying through the streets from the burning quarter, some with bundles of clothes on their shoulders, others dragging trunks along the sidewalks by means of strings and ropes fastened to the handles, children trudging by their sides or borne in their arms. Now and then a sick man or woman would be observed, half concealed in a mattress doubled up and borne by two men. Droves of horses were in the streets, moving by some sort of guidance to a place of safety. Vehicles of all descriptions were hurrying to and fro, some laden with trunks and bundles, others seeking similar loads and immediately finding them, the drivers making more money in one hour than they were used to see in a week or a month. Everybody in this quarter was hurrying toward the lake shore. All the streets crossing that part of Michigan Avenue which fronts on the lake (on which my own residence stood) were crowded with fugitives, hastening toward the blessed water.

We saw the tall buildings on the opposite sides of the two streets melt down in a few moments without scorching ours. The heat broke the plate-glass windows in the lower stories, but not in the upper ones. After the fire in our neighborhood had spent its force, the editorial and composing rooms did not even smell of smoke. Several of our brave fellows who had been up all night had gone to sleep on the lounges, while others were at the sink washing their faces, supposing that all danger to us had passed. So I supposed, and in this belief went home to breakfast. The smoke to the northward was so dense that we could not see the North Division, where sixty thousand people were flying in mortal terror before the flames. The immense store of Field, Leiter & Co. I observed to be under a shower of water from their own fire-apparatus, and since the First National Bank, a fire-proof building, protected it on one corner, I concluded that the progress of the flames in that direction was stopped, as the "Tribune" building had stopped it where we were. Here, at least, I thought was a saving of twenty millions of property, including the great Central depot and the two grain-elevators adjoining, effected by two or three buildings which had been erected with a view to such an emergency. The post-office and custom-house building (also fire-proof, according to public rumor) had stopped the flames a little farther to the southwest, although the interior of that structure was burning. A straight line drawn northeast from the post-office would nearly touch the "Tribune," First National Bank, Field, Leiter & Co.'s store, and the Illinois Central Railroad land department, another fire-proof building. Everything east of that line seemed perfectly safe. And with this feeling I went home. . . .

There was still a mass of fire to the southwest, in the direction whence it originally came, but as the engines were all down there, and the buildings small and low, I felt sure that the firemen would manage it. As soon as I had swallowed a cup of coffee and communicated to my family the facts that I had gathered, I started out to see the end of the battle. Reaching State Street, I glanced down to Field, Leiter & Co.'s store, and to my surprise noticed that the streams of water which had before been showering it, as though it had been a great artificial fountain, had ceased to run. But I did not conjecture the awful reality, viz., that the great pumping engines had been disabled by a burning roof falling upon them. I thought perhaps the firemen on the store had discontinued their efforts because the danger was over. But why were men carrying out goods from the lower story?

This query was soon answered by a gentleman who asked me if I had heard that the water had stopped! The awful truth was here! The pumping engines were disabled, and though we had at our feet a basin sixty miles wide by three hundred and sixty long, and seven hundred feet deep, all full of clear green water, we could not lift enough to quench a cooking-stove. Still the direction of the wind was such that I thought the remaining fire would not cross State Street, nor reach the residences on Wabash and Michigan avenues and the terrified people on the lake shore. I determined to go down to the black cloud of smoke which was rising away to the southwest, the course of which could not be discovered on account of the height of the intervening buildings, but thought it most prudent to go home again, and tell my wife to get the family wearing-apparel in readiness for moving. I found that she had already done so. I then hurried toward the black cloud, some ten squares distant, and there found the rows of wooden houses on Third and Fourth avenues falling like the ripe wheat before the reaper. At a glance I perceived that all was lost in our part of the city, and I conjectured that the "Tribune" building was doomed too, for I had noticed with consternation that the fire-proof post-office had been completely gutted, notwithstanding it was detached from other buildings. The "Tribune" was fitted into a niche, one side of which consisted of a wholesale stationery store, and the other of McVicker's Theater. But there was now no time to think of property. Life was in danger. The lives of those most dear to me depended upon their getting out of our house, out of our street, through an infernal gorge of horses, wagons, men, women, children, trunks and plunder.

My brother was with me, and we seized the first empty wagon we could find, pinning the horse by the head. A hasty talk with the driver disclosed that we could have his establishment for one load for twenty dollars. I had not expected to get him for less than a hundred, unless we should take him by force, and this was a bad time for a fight. He proved himself a muscular as well as a faithful fellow, and I shall always be glad that I avoided a personal difficulty with him. One peculiarity of the situation was that nobody could get a team without ready money. I had not thought of this when I was revolving in my mind the offer of one hundred dollars, which was more greenbacks than our whole family could have put up if our lives had depended upon the issue. This driver had divined that, as all the banks were burned, a check on the Commercial National would not carry him very far, although it might carry me to a place of safety. All the drivers had divined the same. Every man who had anything to sell perceived the same. "Pay as you go" had become the watchword of the hour. Never was there a community so hastily and so completely emancipated from the evils of the credit system.

With some little difficulty we reached our house, and in less time than we ever set out on a journey before, we dragged seven trunks, four bundles, four valises, two baskets, and one hamper of provisions into the street and piled them on the wagon. The fire was still more than a quarter of a mile distant, and the wind, which was increasing in violence, was driving it not exactly in our direction. The low wooden houses were nearly all gone, and after that the fire must make progress, if at all, against brick and stone. Several churches of massive architecture were between us and harm, and the great Palmer House had not been reached, and might not be if the firemen, who had now got their hose into the lake, could work efficiently in the ever-increasing jam of fugitives.

My wife thought we should have time to take another load; my brother thought so; we all thought so. We had not given due credit either to the savage strength of the fire or the firm pack on Michigan Avenue. Leaving my brother to get the family safely out if I did not return in time, and to pile the most valuable portion of my library into the drawers of bureaus and tables ready for moving, I seized a bird-cage containing a talented green parrot, and mounted the seat with the driver. For one square southward from the corner of Monroe Street we made pretty fair progress. The dust was so thick that we could not see the distance of a whole square ahead. It came, not in clouds, but in a steady storm of sand, the particles impinging against our faces like needle-points. Pretty soon we came to a dead halt. We could move neither forward nor backward, nor sidewise. The gorge had caught fast somewhere. Yet everybody was good-natured and polite. If I should say I didn't hear an oath all the way down Michigan Avenue, there are probably some mule-drivers in Cincinnati who would say it was a lie. But I did not. The only quarrelsome person I saw was a German laborer (a noted exception to his race), who was protesting that he had lost everything, and that he would not get out of the middle of the road although he was on foot. He became obstreperous on this point, and commenced beating the head of my horse with his fist. My driver was preparing to knock him down with the butt-end of the whip, when two men seized the insolent Teuton and dragged him to the water's edge, where it is to be hoped he was ducked.

Presently the jam began to move, and we got on perhaps twenty paces and stuck fast again. By accident we had edged over to the east side of the street, and nothing but a board fence separated us from the lake park, a strip of ground a little wider than the street itself. A benevolent laborer on the park side of the fence pulled a loose post from the ground, and with this for a catapult knocked off the boards and invited us to pass through. It was a hazardous undertaking, as we had to drive diagonally over a raised sidewalk, but we thought it was best to risk it. Our horse mounted and gave us a jerk which nearly threw us off the seat, and sent the provision basket and one bundle of clothing whirling into the dirt. The eatables were irrecoverable. The bundle was rescued, with two or three pounds of butter plastered upon it. We started again, and here our parrot broke out with great rapidity and sharpness of utterance, "Get up, get up, get up, hurry up, hurry up, it's eight o'clock," ending with a shrill whistle. These ejaculations frightened a pair of carriage-horses, close to us, on the other side of the fence, but the jam was so tight they couldn't run.

By getting into the park we succeeded in advancing two squares without impediment, and we might have gone farther had we not come upon an excavation which the public authorities had recently made. This drove us back to the avenue, where another battering-ram made a gap for us at the intersection of Van Buren Street, the north end of Michigan Terrace. Here the gorge seemed impassable. The difficulty proceeded from teams entering Michigan Avenue from cross-streets. Extempore policemen stationed themselves at these crossings and helped, as well as they could, but we were half an hour passing the terrace. From this imposing row of residences the millionaires were dragging their trunks and their bundles, and yet there was no panic, no frenzy, no boisterousness, but only the haste which the situation authorized. There was real danger to life all along this street, but nobody realized it, because the park was ample to hold all the people. None of us asked or thought what would become of those nearest the water if the smoke and cinders should drive the whole crowd down to the shore, or if the vast bazaar of luggage should itself take fire, as some of it afterward did. Fortunately for those in the street, there was a limit to the number of teams available in that quarter of the city. The contributions from the cross-streets grew less; and soon we began to move on a walk without interruption.

At Eldridge Court, I turned into Wabash Avenue, where the crowd was thinner. Arriving at the house of a friend, who was on the windward side of the fire, I tumbled off my load and started back to get another. Halfway down Michigan Avenue, which was now perceptibly easier to move in, I perceived my family on the sidewalk with their arms full of light household effects. My wife told me that the house was already burned, that the flames burst out readymade in the rear hall before she knew that the roof had been scorched, and that one of the servants, who had disobeyed orders in her eagerness to get some article, had got singed, though not burned, in coming out. My wife and my mother and all the rest were begrimed with dirt and smoke, like blackamoors; everybody was. The "bloated aristocrats" all along the streets, who supposed they had lost both home and fortune at one swoop, were a sorry but not despairing congregation. They had saved their lives at all events, and they knew that many of their fellow creatures must have lost theirs. I saw a great many kindly acts done as we moved along. The poor helped the rich, and the rich helped the poor (if anybody could be called rich at such a time), to get on with their loads. I heard of cartmen demanding one hundred and fifty dollars (in hand, of course) for carrying a single load. Very likely it was so, but those cases did not come under my own notice. It did come under my notice that some cartmen worked for whatever the sufferers felt able to pay, and one I knew worked for nothing. It takes all sorts of people to make a great fire.

Presently we heard loud detonations, and a rumor went around that buildings were being blown up with gunpowder. The depot of the Hazard Powder Company was situated at Brighton, seven or eight miles from the nearest point of the fire. At what time the effort was first made to reach this magazine, and bring powder into service, I have not learned, but I know that Col. M. C. Stearns made heroic efforts with his great lime-wagons to haul the explosive material to the proper point.

This is no time to blame anybody, but in truth there was no directing head on the ground. Everybody was asking everybody else to pull down buildings. There were no hooks, no ropes, no axes. I had met General Sheridan on the street in front of the post-office two hours before. He had been trying to save the army records, including his own invaluable papers relating to the war of the rebellion. He told me they were all lost, and then added that "the post-office didn't seem to make a good fire." This was when we supposed the row of fire-proof buildings, already spoken of, had stopped the flames in our quarter. Where was General Sheridan now? everybody asked. Why didn't he do something when everybody else had failed? Presently a rumor went around that Sheridan was handling the gunpowder; then everybody felt relieved. The reverberations of the powder, whoever was handling it, gave us all heart again. Think of a people feeling encouraged because somebody was blowing up houses in the midst of the city, and that a shower of bricks was very likely to come down on their heads!

I had paid and discharged my driver after extorting his solemn promise to come back and move me again if the wind should shift to the north—in which event everybody knew that the whole South Division, for a distance of four miles, must perish. We soon arrived at the house of the kind friend on Wabash Avenue, where our trunks and bundles had been deposited. This was south of the line of fire, but this did not satisfy anybody, since we had all seen how resolutely the flames had gone transversely across the direction of the wind. Then came a story from down the street that Sheridan was going to blow up the Wabash Avenue Methodist Church on the corner of Harrison Street. We observed a general scattering away of people from that neighborhood. I was nearly four squares south of the locality, and thought that the missiles wouldn't come so far. We awaited the explosion, but it did not come. By and by we plucked up courage to go around two or three blocks and see whether the church had fallen down of its own accord.

We perceived that two or three houses in the rear of the edifice had been leveled to the ground, that the church itself was standing, and that the fire was out, in that quarter at least; also that the line of Harrison Street marked the southern limits of the devastation. The wind continued to blow fiercely from the southwest, and has not ceased to this hour (Saturday, October 14). But it was liable to change. If it chopped around to the north, the burning embers would be blown back upon the South Division. If it veered to the east, they would be blown into the West Division, though the river afforded rather better protection there. Then we should have nothing to do but to keep ahead of the flames and get down as fast as possible to the open prairie, and there spend the night houseless and supperless—and what of the morrow? A full hundred thousand of us. And if we were spared, and the West Division were driven out upon their prairie (a hundred and fifty thousand according to the Federal census), how would the multitude be fed? If there could be anything more awful than what we had already gone through, it would be what we would certainly go through if the wind should change; for with the embers of this great fire flying about, and no water to fight them, we knew that there was not gunpowder enough in Illinois to stop the inevitable conflagration. But this was not all.

A well-authenticated rumor came up to the city that the prairie was on fire south of Hyde Park, the largest of the southern suburbs. The grass was as dry as tinder, and so were the leaves in Cottage Grove, a piece of timber several miles square, containing hundreds of residences of the better class, some of them of palatial dimensions. A fire on the prairie, communicating itself to the grove, might cut off the retreat of the one hundred thousand people in the South Division; might invade the South Division itself, and come up under the impulsion of that fierce wind, and where should we all be then? There were three or four bridges leading to the West Division, the only possible avenues of escape; but what were these among so many? And what if the "Commune" should go to work and start incendiary fires while all was yet in confusion? These fiends were improving the daylight by plundering along the street. Before dark the whole male population of the city was organized by spontaneous impulse into a night patrol, with pallid determination to put every incendiary to instant death.

About five o'clock P.M. I applied to a friend on Wabash Avenue for the use of a team to convey my family and chattels to the southern suburbs, about four miles distant, where my brother happened to own a small cottage, which, up to the present time, nobody could be induced to occupy and pay rent for. My friend replied that his work-teams were engaged in hauling water for people to drink. Here was another thing that I had not thought of—a great city with no water to drink. Plenty in the lake, to be sure, but none in the city mains or the connecting pipes. Fortunately the extreme western limits were provided with a number of artesian wells, bored for manufacturing establishments. Then there was the river—the horrible, black, stinking river of a few weeks ago, which has since become clear enough for fish to live in, by reason of the deepening of the canal, which draws to the Mississippi a perpetual flow of pure

298

water from Lake Michigan. With the city pumping-works stopped, the sewers could no longer discharge themselves into the river. So this might be used; and it was. Twenty-four hours had not passed before tens of thousands of people were drinking the water of Chicago River, with no unpleasant taste or effects.

The work-teams of my friend being engaged in hauling water for people who could not get any from the wells or the river or the lake, he placed at my disposal his carriage, horses and coachman, whom he directed to take me and the ladies to any place we desired to reach. While we were talking he hailed another gentleman on the street, who owned a large stevedore wagon, and asked him to convey my trunks, etc. to Cottage Grove Avenue, near Forty-third Street, to which request an immediate and most gracious assent was given. And thus we started again, our hostess pressing a mattress upon us from her store. All the streets leading southward were yet filled with fugitives. Where they all found shelter that night I know not, but every house seemed open to anybody who desired to enter. Arrived at our new home, about dusk, we found in it, as we expected, a cold reception, there being neither stove, nor grate, nor fireplace, nor fuel, nor light therein. But I will not dwell upon these things. We really did not mind them, for when we thought of the thousands of men, women, and tender babes huddled together in Lincoln Park, seven miles to the north of us, with no prospect of food, exposed to rain, if it should come, with no canopy but the driving smoke of their homes, we thought how little we had suffered.

Cincinnati Commercial, 1871

SAMUEL L. CLEMENS

Life on the Mississippi

THE BOYS' AMBITION

When I was a boy, there was but one permanent ambition among my comrades in our village [Hannibal, Mo.] on the west bank of the Mississippi River. That was, to be a steamboatman. We had transient ambitions of other sorts, but they were only transient. When a circus came and went, it left us all burning to become clowns; the first negro minstrel show that ever came to our section left us all suffering to try that kind of life; now and then we had a hope that, if we lived and were good, God would permit us to be pirates. These ambitions faded out, each in its turn; but the ambition to be a steamboatman always remained.

Once a day a cheap, gaudy packet arrived upward from St. Louis, and another downward from Keokuk. Before these events, the day was glorious with expectancy; after them, the day was a dead and empty thing. Not only the boys, but the whole village, felt this. After all these years I can picture that old time to myself now, just as it was then: the white town drowsing in the sunshine of a summer's morning; the streets empty, or pretty nearly so; one or two clerks sitting in front of the Water street stores, with their splint-bottomed chairs titled back against the walls, chins on breasts, hats slouched over their faces, asleep—with shingle-shavings enough around to show what broke them down; a sow and a litter of pigs loafing along the sidewalk, doing a good business in watermelon rinds and seeds; two or three lonely little freight piles scattered about the "levee"; a pile of "skids" on the slope of the stone-paved wharf, and the fragrant town drunkard asleep in the shadow of them; two or three wood flats at the head of the wharf, but nobody to listen to the peaceful lapping of the wavelets against them; the great Mississippi, the majestic, the magnificent Mississippi, rolling its mile-wide tide along, shining in the sun; the dense forest away on the other side; the "point" above the town, and the "point" below, bounding the river-glimpse and turning it into a sort of sea, and withal a very still and brillant and lonely one. Presently a film of dark smoke appears above one of those remote "points"; instantly a negro drayman, famous for his quick eye and prodigious voice, lifts up the cry, "S-t-e-a-m-boat a-comin'!" and the scene changes! The town drunkard stirs, the clerks wake up, a furious clatter of drays follows, every house and store pours out a human contribution, and all in a twinkling the dead town is alive and moving. Drays, carts, men, boys, all go hurrying from many quarters to a common center, the wharf. Assembled there, the people fasten their eyes upon the coming boat as upon a wonder they are seeing for the first time. And the boat *is* rather a handsome sight, too. She is long and sharp and trim and pretty; she has two tall, fancy-topped chimneys, with a gilded device of some kind swung between them; a fanciful pilot-house, all glass and "gingerbread," perched on top of the "texas" deck behind them; the paddle-boxes are gorgeous with a picture or with gilded rays above the boat's name; the boiler deck, the hurricane deck, and the texas deck are fenced and ornamented with clean white railings; there is a flag gallantly flying from the jackstaff; the furnace doors are open and the fires glaring bravely; the upper decks are black with passengers; the captain stands by the big bell, calm, imposing, the envy of all; great volumes of the blackest smoke are rolling and tumbling out of the chimneys— a husbanded grandeur created with a bit of pitch pine just before arriving at a town; the crew are grouped on the forecastle; the broad stage is run far out over the port bow, and an envied deck-hand stands picturesquely on the end of it with a coil of rope in his hand; the pent steam is screaming through the gauge-cocks; the captain lifts his hand, a bell rings, the wheels stop; then they turn back, churning the water to foam, and the steamer is at rest. Then such a scramble as there is to get aboard, and to get ashore, and to take in freight and to discharge freight, all at one and the same time; and such a yelling and cursing as the mates facilitate it all with! Ten minutes later the steamer is under way again, with no flag on the jackstaff and no black smoke issuing from the chimneys. After ten more minutes the town is dead again, and the town drunkard asleep by the skids once more.

My father was a justice of the peace, and I supposed he possessed the power of life and death over all men, and could hang anybody that offended him. This was distinction enough for me as a general thing: but the desire to be a steamboatman kept intruding, nevertheless. I first wanted to be a cabin-boy, so that I could come out with a white apron on and shake a table-cloth over the side, where all my old comrades could see me; later I thought I would rather be the deck-hand who stood on the end of the stage-plank with the coil of rope in his hand, because he was particularly conspicuous. But these were only day-dreams—they were too heavenly to be contemplated as real possibilities. By and by one of our boys went away. He was not heard of for a long time. At last he turned up as apprentice engineer or "striker" on a steamboat. This thing shook the bottom out of all my Sunday-school teachings. That boy had been notoriously worldly, and I just the reverse; yet he was exalted to this eminence, and I left in obscurity and misery. There was nothing generous about this fellow in his greatness. He would always manage to have a rusty bolt to scrub while his boat tarried at our town, and he would sit on the inside guard and scrub it, where we all could see him and envy him and loathe him. And whenever his boat was laid up he would come home and swell around the town in his blackest and greasiest clothes, so that nobody could help remembering that he was a steamboatman; and he used all sorts of steamboat technicalities in his talk, as if he were so used to them that he forgot common people could not understand them. He would speak of the "labboard" side of a horse in an easy, natural way that would make one wish he was dead. And he was always talking about "St. Looy" like an old citizen; he would refer casually to occasions when he was "coming down Fourth street," or when he was "passing by the Planter's House," or when there was a fire and he took a turn on the brakes of "the old Big Missouri"; and then he would go on and lie about how many towns the size of ours were burned down there that day. Two or three of the boys had long been persons of consideration among us because they had been to St. Louis once and had a vague general knowledge of its wonders, but the day of their glory was over now. They lapsed into a humble silence, and learned to disappear when the ruthless "cub"-engineer approached. This fellow had money, too, and hair-oil. Also an ignorant silver watch and a showy brass watch-chain. He wore a leather belt and used no suspenders. If ever a youth was cordially admired and hated by his comrades, this one was. No girl could withstand his charms. He "cut out" every boy in the village. When his boat blew up at last, it diffused a tranquil contentment among us such as we had not known for months. But when he came home the next week, alive, renowned, and appeared in church all battered up and bandaged, a shining hero, stared at and wondered over by everybody, it seemed to us that the partiality of Providence for an undeserving reptile had reached a point where it was open to criticism.

This creature's career could produce but one result, and it speedily followed. Boy after boy managed to get on the river. The minister's son became an engineer. The doctor's and the postmaster's sons became "mud clerks"; the wholesale liquor dealer's son became a barkeeper on a boat; four sons of the chief merchant, and two sons of the county judge, became pilots. Pilot was the grandest position of all. The pilot, even in those days of trivial wages, had a princely salary—from a hundred and fifty to two hundred and fifty dollars a month, and no board to pay. Two months of his wages would pay a preacher's salary for a year. Now some of us were left disconsolate. We could not get on the river—at least our parents would not let us.

So, by and by, I ran away. I said I would never come home again till I was a pilot and could come in glory. But somehow I could not manage it. I went meekly aboard a few of the boats that lay packed together like sardines at the long St. Louis wharf, and humbly inquired for the pilots, but got only a cold shoulder and short words from mates and clerks. I had to make the best of this sort of treatment for the time being, but I had comforting day-dreams of a future when I should be a great and honored pilot, with plenty of money, and could kill some of these mates and clerks and pay for them.

A DARING DEED

The pilot-house was full of pilots, going down to "look at the river." What is called the "upper river" (the two hundred miles between St. Louis and Cairo, where the Ohio comes in) was low; and the Mississippi changes its channel so constantly that the pilots used to always find it necessary to run down to Cairo to take a fresh look, when their boats were to lie in port a week; that is, when the water was at a low stage. A deal of this "looking at the river" was done by poor fellows who seldom had a berth, and whose only hope of getting one lay in their being always freshly posted and therefore ready to drop into the shoes of some reputable pilot, for a single trip, on account of such pilot's sudden illness, or some other necessity. And a good many of them constantly ran up and down inspecting the river, not because they ever really hoped to get a berth, but because (they being guests of the boat) it was cheaper to "look at the river" than stay ashore and pay board. In time these fellows grew dainty in their tastes, and only infested boats that had an established reputation for setting good tables. All visiting pilots were useful, for they were always ready and willing, summer or winter, night or day, to go out in the yawl and help buoy the channel or assist the boat's pilots in any way they could. They were likewise welcomed because all pilots are tireless talkers, when gathered together, and as they talk only about the river they are always understood and are always interesting. Your true pilot cares nothing about anything on earth but the river, and his pride in his occupation surpasses the pride of kings.

We had a fine company of these river inspectors along this trip. There were eight or ten, and there was abundance of room for them in our great pilot-house. Two or three of them wore polished silk hats, elaborate shirt-fronts, diamond breastpins, kid gloves, and patent-leather boots. They were choice in their English, and bore themselves with a dignity proper to men of solid means and prodigious reputation as pilots. The others were more or less loosely clad, and wore upon their heads tall felt cones that were suggestive of the days of the Commonwealth.

I was a cipher in this august company, and felt subdued, not to say torpid. I was not even of sufficient consequence to assist at the wheel when it was necessary to put the tiller hard down in a hurry; the guest that stood nearest did that when occasion required—and this was pretty much all the time, because of the crookedness of the channel and the scant water. I stood in a corner; and the talk I listened to took the hope all out of me. One visitor said to another:

"Jim, how did you run Plum Point, coming up?"

"It was in the night, there, and I ran it the way one of the boys on the *Diana* told me; started out about fifty yards above the wood-pile on the false point, and held on the cabin under Plum Point till I raised the reef —quarter less twain—then straightened up for the middle bar till I got well abreast the old one-limbed cottonwood in the bend, then got my stern on the cottonwood, and head on the low place above the point, and came through a-booming—nine and a half."

"Pretty square crossing, an't it?"

"Yes, but the upper bar's working down fast."

Another pilot spoke up and said:

"I had better water than that, and ran it lower down; started out from the false point—mark twain—raised the second reef abreast the big snag in the bend, and had quarter less twain."

One of the gorgeous ones remarked:

"I don't want to find fault with your leadsmen, but that's a good deal of water for Plum Point, it seems to me."

There was an approving nod all around at this quiet snub dropped on the boaster and "settled" him. And so they went on talk-talk-talking. Meantime, the thing that was running in my mind was, "Now, if my ears hear aright, I have not only to get the names of all the towns and islands and bends, and so on, by heart, but I must even get up a warm personal acquaintanceship with every old snag and one-limbed cottonwood and obscure wood-pile that ornaments the banks of this river for twelve hundred miles; and more than that, I must actually know where these things are in the dark, unless these guests are gifted with eyes that can pierce through two miles of solid blackness. I wish the piloting business was in Jericho and I had never thought of it."

At dusk Mr. Bixby tapped the big bell three times (the signal to land), and the captain emerged from his drawing-room in the forward end of the "texas," and looked up inquiringly. Mr. Bixby said:

"We will lay up here all night, captain."

"Very well, sir."

That was all. The boat came to shore and was tied up for the night. It seemed to me a fine thing that the pilot could do as he pleased, without asking so grand a captain's permission. I took my supper and went immediately to bed, discouraged by my day's observations and experiences. My late voyage's note-booking was but a confusion of meaningless names. It had tangled me all up in a knot every time I had looked at it in the daytime. I now hoped for respite in sleep; but no, it reveled all through my head till sunrise again, a frantic and tireless nightmare.

Next morning I felt pretty rusty and low-spirited. We went booming along, taking a good many chances, for we were anxious to "get out of the river" (as getting out to Cairo was called) before night should overtake us. But Mr. Bixby's partner, the other pilot, presently grounded the boat, and we lost so much time getting her off that it was plain the darkness would overtake us a good long way above the mouth. This was a great misfortune, especially to certain of our visiting pilots, whose boats would have to wait for their return, no matter how long that might be. It sobered the pilot-house talk a good deal. Coming up-stream, pilots did not mind low water or any kind of darkness; nothing stopped them but fog. But down-stream work was different; a boat was too nearly helpless, with a stiff current pushing behind her; so it was not customary to run downstream at night in low water.

There seemed to be one small hope, however: if we could get through the intricate and dangerous Hat Island crossing before night, we could venture the rest, for we would have plainer sailing and better water. But it would be insanity to attempt Hat Island at night. So there was a deal of looking at watches all the rest of the day, and a constant ciphering upon the speed we were making; Hat Island was the eternal subject, sometimes hope was high and sometimes we were delayed in a bad crossing, and down it went again. For hours all hands lay under the burden of this suppressed excitement; it was even communicated to me, and I got to feeling so solicitous about Hat Island, and under such an awful pressure of responsibility, that I wished I might have five minutes on shore to draw a good, full, relieving breath, and start over again. We were standing no regular watches. Each of our pilots ran such portions of the river as he had run when coming up-stream, because of his greater familiarity with it; but both remained in the pilot-house constantly.

An hour before sunset Mr. Bixby took the wheel, and Mr. W. stepped aside. For the next thirty minutes every man held his watch in his hand and was restless, silent, and uneasy. At last somebody said, with a doomful sigh:

"Well, yonder's Hat Island—and we can't make it."

All the watches closed with a snap, everybody sighed and muttered something about its being "too bad, too bad—ah, if we could *only* have got here half an hour sooner!" and the place was thick with the atmosphere of disappointment. Some started to go out, but loitered, hearing no bell-tap to land. The sun dipped behind the horizon, the boat went on. Inquiring looks passed from one guest to another; and one who had his hand on the door-knob and had turned it, waited, then presently took away his hand and let the knob turn back again. We bore steadily down the bend. More looks were exchanged, and nods of surprised admiration—but no words. Insensibly the men drew together behind Mr. Bixby, as the sky darkened and one or two dim stars came out. The dead silence and sense of waiting became oppressive. Mr. Bixby pulled the cord, and two deep, mellow notes from the big bell floated off on the night. Then a pause, and one more note was struck. The watchman's voice followed, from the hurricane-deck:

"Labboard lead, there! Stabboard lead!"

The cries of the leadsmen began to rise out of the distance, and were gruffly repeated by the word-passers on the hurricane-deck.

"M-a-r-k three! M-a-r-k three! Quarter-less-three! Half twain! Quarter twain! M-a-r-k twain! Quarter-less—"

Mr. Bixby pulled two bell-ropes, and was answered by faint jinglings far below in the engine-room, and our speed slackened. The steam began to whistle through the gauge-cocks. The cries of the leadsmen went on— and it is a weird sound, always, in the night. Every pilot in the lot was watching now, with fixed eyes, and talking under his breath. Nobody was calm and easy but Mr. Bixby. He would put his wheel down and stand on a spoke, and as the steamer swung into her (to me) utterly invisible marks—for we seemed to be in the midst of a wide and gloomy sea—he would meet and fasten her there. Out of the murmur of half-audible talk, one caught a coherent sentence now and then—such as:

"There; she's over the first reef all right!"

After a pause, another subdued voice:

"Her stern's coming down just *exactly* right, by *George*!"

"Now she's in the marks; over she goes!"

Somebody else muttered:

"Oh, it was done beautiful—*beautiful*!"

Now the engines were stopped altogether, and we drifted with the current. Not that I could see the boat drift, for I could not, the stars being all gone by this time. This drifting was the dismalest work; it held one's heart still. Presently I discovered a blacker gloom than that which surrounded us. It was the head of the island. We were closing right down upon it. We entered its deeper shadow, and so imminent seemed the peril that I was likely to suffocate; and I had the strongest impulse to do *something*, anything, to save the vessel. But still Mr. Bixby stood by his wheel, silent, intent as a cat, and all the pilots stood shoulder to shoulder at his back.

"She'll not make it!" somebody whispered.

The water grew shoaler and shoaler, by the leadsman's cries, till it was down to:

"Eight-and-a-half! E-i-g-h-t feet! E-i-g-h-t feet! Seven-and—"

Mr. Bixby said warningly through his speaking-tube to the engineer: "Stand by, now!"

"Ay, ay, sir!"

"Seven-and-a-half! Seven feet! *Six*-and—"

We touched bottom! Instantly Mr. Bixby set a lot of bells ringing, shouted through the tube, "*Now*, let her have it—every ounce you've got!" then to his partner, "Put her hard down! snatch her! snatch her!" The boat rasped and ground her way through the sand, hung upon the apex of disaster a single tremendous instant, and then over she went! And such a shout as went up at Mr. Bixby's back never loosened the roof of a pilot-house before!

There was no more trouble after that. Mr. Bixby was a hero that night; and it was some little time, too, before his exploit ceased to be talked about by river-men.

Fully to realize the marvelous precision in laying the great steamer in her marks in that murky waste of water, one should know that not only must she pick her intricate way through snags and blind reefs, and then shave the head of the island so closely as to brush the overhanging foliage with her stern, but at one place she must pass almost within arm's reach of a sunken and invisible wreck that would snatch the hull timbers from under her if she should strike it, and destroy the quarter of a million dollars' worth of steamboat and cargo in five minutes, and maybe a hundred and fifty lives into the bargain.

The last remark I heard that night was a compliment to Mr. Bixby, uttered in soliloquy and with unction by one of our guests. He said:

"By the Shadow of Death, but he's a lightning pilot!"

CONTINUED PERPLEXITIES

I promptly put such a strain on my memory that by and by even the shoal water and the countless crossing-marks began to stay with me. But the result was just the same. I never could more than get one knotty thing learned before another presented itself. Now I had often seen pilots gazing at the water and pretending to read it as if it were a book; but it was a book that told me nothing. A time came at last, however, when Mr. Bixby seemed to think me far enough advanced to bear a lesson on water-reading. So he began:

"Do you see that long, slanting line on the face of the water? Now, that's a reef. Moreover, it's a bluff reef. There is a solid sand-bar under it that is nearly as straight up and down as the side of a house. There is plenty of water close up to it, but mighty little on top of it. If you were to hit it you would knock the boat's brains out. Do you see where the line fringes out at the upper end and begins to fade away?"

"Yes, sir."

"Well, that is a low place; that is the head of the reef. You can climb over there, and not hurt anything. Cross over, now, and follow along closely under the reef—easy water there—not much current."

I followed the reef along till I approached the fringed end. Then Mr. Bixby said: "Now get ready. Wait till I give the word. She won't want to mount the reef; a boat hates shoal water. Stand by—wait—*wait*—keep her well in hand. *Now* cramp her down! Snatch her! snatch her!"

He seized the other side of the wheel and helped to spin it around until it was hard down, and then we held it so. The boat resisted, and refused to answer for a while, and next she came surging to starboard, mounted the reef, and sent a long, angry ridge of water foaming away from her bows.

"Now watch her; watch her like a cat, or she'll get away from you. When she fights strong and the tiller slips a little, in a jerky, greasy sort of way, let up on her a trifle; it is the way she tells you at night that the water is too shoal; but keep edging her up, on the bar now, there is a bar under every point, because the water that comes down around it forms an eddy and allows the sediment to sink. Do you see those fine lines on the face of the water that branch out like the ribs of a fan? Well, those are little reefs; you want to just miss the ends of them, but run them pretty close. Now look out—look out! Don't you crowd that slick, greasy-looking place; there ain't nine feet there; she won't stand it. She begins to smell it; look sharp, I tell you! Oh, blazes, there you go! Stop the starboard wheel! Quick! Ship up to back! Set her back!"

The engine bells jingled and the engines answered promptly, shooting white columns of steam far aloft out of the 'scape-pipes, but it was too late. The boat had "smelt" the bar in good earnest; the foamy ridges that radiated from her bows suddenly disappeared, a great dead swell came rolling forward, and swept ahead of her, she careened far over to larboard, and went tearing away toward the shore as if she were about scared to death. We were a good mile from where we ought to have been when we finally got the upper hand of her again.

During the afternoon watch the next day, Mr. Bixby asked me if I knew how to run the next few miles. I said:

"Go inside the first snag above the point, outside the next one, start out from the lower end of Higgin's woodyard, make a square crossing, and—"

"That's all right. I'll be back before you close up on the next point."

But he wasn't. He was still below when I rounded it and entered upon a piece of the river which I had some misgivings about. I did not know that he was hiding behind a chimney to see how I would perform. I went gaily along, getting prouder and prouder, for he had never left the boat in my sole charge for such a length of time before. I even got to "setting" her and letting the wheel go entirely, while I vaingloriously turned my back and inspected the stern marks and hummed a tune, a sort of easy indifference which I had prodigiously admired in Bixby and other great pilots. Once I inspected rather long, and when I faced to the front again my heart flew into my mouth so suddenly that if I hadn't clapped my teeth together I should have lost it. One of those frightful bluff reefs was stretching its deadly length right across our bows! My head was gone in a moment; I did not know which end I stood on; I gasped and could not get my breath; I spun the wheel down with such rapidity that it wove itself together like a spider's web; the boat answered and turned square away from the reef, but the reef followed her! I fled, but still it followed, still it kept—right across my bows! I never looked to see where I was going, I only fled. The awful crash was imminent. Why didn't that villain come? If I committed the crime of ringing the bell I might get thrown overboard. But better that than kill the boat. So in blind desperation, I started such a rattling "shivaree" down below as never had astounded an engineer in this world before, I fancy. Amidst the frenzy of the bells the engines began to back and fill in a curious way, and my reason forsook its throne—we were about to crash into the woods on the other side of the river. Just then Mr. Bixby stepped calmly into view on the hurricane-deck. My soul went out to him in gratitude. My distress vanished; I would have felt safe on the brink of Niagara with Mr. Bixby on the hurricane-deck. He blandly and sweetly took his toothpick out of his mouth between his fingers, as if it were a cigar—we were just in the act of climbing an overhanging big tree, and the passengers were scudding astern like rats—and lifted up these commands to me ever so gently:

"Stop the starboard! Stop the larboard! Set her back on both!"

The boat hesitated, halted, pressed her nose among the boughs a critical instant, then reluctantly began to back away.

"Stop the larboard! Come ahead on it! Stop the starboard! Come ahead on it! Point her for the bar!"

I sailed away as serenely as a summer's morning. Mr. Bixby came in and said, with mock simplicity:

"When you have a hail, my boy, you ought to tap the big bell three times before you land, so that the engineers can get ready."

I blushed under the sarcasm, and said I hadn't had any hail.

"Ah! Then it was for wood, I suppose. The officer of the watch will tell you when he wants to wood up."

I went on consuming, and said I wasn't after wood.

"Indeed? Why, what could you want over here in the bend, then? Did you ever know of a boat following a bend up-stream at this stage of the river?"

"No, sir—and I wasn't trying to follow it. I was getting away from a bluff reef."

"No, it wasn't a bluff reef; there isn't one within three miles of where you were."

"But I saw it. It was as bluff as that one yonder."

"Just about. Run over it!"

"Do you give it as an order?"

"Yes. Run over it!"

"If I don't, I wish I may die."

"All right; I'm taking the responsibility."

I was just as anxious to kill the boat, now, as I had been to save it before. I impressed my orders upon my memory, to be used at the inquest, and made a straight break for the reef. As it disappeared under our bows I held my breath; but we slid over it like oil.

"Now, don't you see the difference? It wasn't anything but a *wind* reef. The wind does that."

"So I see. But it is exactly like a bluff reef. How am I ever going to tell them apart?"

"I can't tell you. It is an instinct. By and by you will just naturally *know* one from the other, but you never will be able to explain why or how you know them apart."

It turned out to be true. The face of the water, in time, became a wonderful book—a book that was a dead language to the uneducated passenger, but which told its mind to me without reserve, delivering its most cherished secrets as clearly as if it uttered them with a voice. And it was not a book to be read at once and thrown aside, for it had a new story to tell every day. Throughout the long twelve hundred miles there was never a page that was void of interest, never one that you could leave unread without loss, never one that you would want to skip, thinking you could find higher enjoyment in some other thing. There never was so wonderful a book written by man; never one whose interest was so absorbing, so unflagging, so sparklingly renewed with every reperusal. The passenger who could not read it was charmed with a peculiar sort of faint dimple on its surface (on the rare occasions when he did not overlook it altogether); but to the pilot that was an *italicized* passage; indeed, it was more than that, it was a legend of the largest capitals, with a string of shouting exclamation-points at the end of it, for it meant that a wreck or a rock was buried there that could tear the life out of the strongest vessel that ever floated. It is the faintest and simplest expression the water ever makes, and the most hideous to a pilot's eye. In truth, the passenger who could not read this book saw nothing but all manner of pretty pictures in it, painted by the sun and shaded by the clouds, whereas to the trained eye these were not pictures at all, but the grimmest and most dead-earnest of reading-matter.

Now when I had mastered the language of this water, and had come to know every trifling feature that bordered the great river as familiarly as I knew the letters of the alphabet, I had made a valuable acquisition. But I had lost something, too. I had lost something which could never be restored to me while I lived. All the grace, the beauty, the poetry, had gone out of the majestic river! I still kept in mind a certain wonderful sunset which I witnessed when steamboating was new to me. A broad expanse of the river was turned to blood; in the middle distance the red hue brightened into gold, through which a solitary log came floating, black and conspicuous; in one place a long, slanting mark lay sparkling upon the water; in another the surface was broken by boiling, tumbling rings, that were as many-tinted as an opal; where the ruddy flush was faintest, was a smooth spot that was covered with graceful circles and radiating lines, ever so delicately traced; the shore on our left was densely wooded, and the somber shadow that fell from this forest was broken in one place by a long, ruffled trail that shone like silver; and high above the forest wall a clean-stemmed dead tree waved a single leafy bough that glowed like a flame in the unobstructed splendor that was flowing from the sun. There were graceful curves, reflected images, woody heights, soft distances; and over the whole scene, far and near, the dissolving lights drifted steadily, enriching it every passing moment with new marvels of coloring.

I stood like one bewitched. I drank it in, in a speechless rapture. The world was new to me, and I had never seen anything like this at home. But as I have said, a day came when I began to cease from noting the glories and the charms which the moon and the sun and the twilight wrought upon the river's face; another day came when I ceased altogether to note them. Then, if that sunset scene had been repeated, I should have looked upon it without rapture, and should have commented upon it, inwardly, after this fashion: "The sun means that we are going to have wind to-morrow; that floating log means that the river is rising, small thanks to it; that slanting mark on the water refers to a bluff reef which is going to kill somebody's steamboat one of these nights, if it keeps on stretching out like that; those tumbling 'boils' show a dissolving bar and a changing channel there; the lines and circles in the slick water over yonder are a warning that that troublesome place is shoaling up dangerously; that silver streak in the shadow of the forest is the 'break' from a new snag, and he has located himself in the very best place he could have found to fish for steamboats; that tall dead tree, with a single living branch, is not going to last long, and then how is a body ever going to get through this blind place at night without the friendly old landmark?"

No, the romance and beauty were all gone from the river. All the value any feature of it had for me now was the amount of usefulness it could furnish toward compassing the safe piloting of a steamboat. Since those days, I have pitied doctors from my heart. What does the lovely flush in a beauty's cheek mean to a doctor but a "break" that ripples above some deadly disease? Are not all her visible charms sown thick with what are to him the signs and symbols of hidden decay? Does he ever see her beauty at all, or doesn't he simply view her professionally, and comment upon her unwholesome condition all to himself? And doesn't he sometimes wonder whether he has gained most or lost most by learning his trade?

Life on the Mississippi, 1883

EUGENE FIELD

The Tribune Primer

Although Field is best remembered for his sentimental verse, he was a man of varied activities. His poetic accomplishments ranged from translating Horace to writing bawdy verse. The instigator of elaborate and often crude practical jokes, he could also turn out the sardonic humor of these extracts.

THE EDITOR'S HOME

Here is a Castle. It is the Home of an Editor. It has stained Glass Windows and Mahogany stairways. In front of the Castle is a Park. Is it not Sweet? The lady in the Park is the editor's wife. She wears a Costly robe of Velvet trimmed with Gold Lace, and there are Pearls and Rubies in her Hair. The editor sits on the front Stoop smoking an Havana Cigar. His little Children are playing with diamond Marbles on the Tessellated Floor. The editor can afford to Live in Style. He gets Seventy-Five Dollars a month Wages.

THE BAD MAN

Here is a Man who has just Stopped his Paper. What a Miserable looking Creature he is. He looks as if he had been stealing Sheep. How will he Know what is going on, now that he has Stopped his Paper? He will Borrow his Neighbor's Paper. One of these Days he will Break his leg, or be a Candidate for Office, and then the Paper will Say Nothing about it. That will be treating him just Right, will it not, little Children?

THE OYSTER

Here we have an Oyster. It is going to a Church Fair. When it Gets to the Fair, it will Swim around in a big Kettle of Warm Water, A Lady will Stir it with a Spoon, and sell the Warm Water for Forty Cents a pint. Then the Oyster will move on to the next Fair. In this Way, the Oyster will visit all the Church Fairs in Town, and Bring a great many Dollars into the Church Treasury. The Oyster goes a Great Way in a Good Cause.

THE GUN

This is a Gun. Is the Gun loaded? Really, I do not know. Let us Find out. Put the Gun on the table, and you, Susie, blow down one Barrel, while you, Charlie, blow down the other. Bang! Yes, it was loaded. Run quick, Jennie, and pick up Susie's head and Charlie's lower Jaw before the Nasty Blood gets over the New carpet.

THE DEEP WELL

The Well is very Dark and Deep. There is Nice Cool Water in the Well. If you Lean way Over the Side, maybe you will Fall in the Well and down in the Dear Water. We will give you some Candy if you will Try. There is a Sweet Little Birdie in the bottom of the Well. Your Mamma would be Surprised to find you in the Well, would she not?

THE BLIND MAN

The old Man is Blind and cannot See. He holds his Hat in his Hand and there is a Dime in the Hat. Go up quietly and Take the Dime out of the Hat. The Man cannot See you. Next Sunday you can put the Dime in the Sabbath School box and the Teacher will Praise you. Your Papa will put some Money in the Contribution box, too. He will put More in than you do. But his Opportunities for Robbing are better than yours.

THE UNFORTUNATE MOUSIE

Poor little Mouse! He got into the Flour Barrel and Made Himself Dead. The Cook baked him in a Loaf of Bread, and here he lies on the Table cut in two by the Sharp bread Knife. But we will not Eat poor Mouse. We will eat the Bread, but we will Take the Mousie and Put him in the Cistern.

MAMMA'S SCISSORS

These are Mamma's Scissors. They do not Seem to be in good Health. Well, they are a little Aged. They have considerable Work to Do. Mamma uses them to Chop Kindling, cut Stove Pipe, pull Tacks, drive

Nails, cut the children's Hair, punch new Holes in the Calendar, slice Bar soap, pound beef Steak, open tomato Cans, shear the New Foundland dog and cut out her New silk Dress. Why doesn't Papa get Mamma a new Pair of Scissors? You should not Ask such a Naughty question. Papa cannot Afford to play Billiards and Indulge his Extravagant Family in the Luxuries of Life.

THE BOTTLE

This is a Bottle. What is in the Bottle? Very bad Whiskey. It has been Sent to the Local Editor. He did not Buy it. If he had Bought it the Whiskey would have been Poorer than it is. Little children, you Must never drink Bad Whiskey.

THE MUD

The Mud is in the Street. The Lady has on a pair of Red Stockings. She is trying to Cross the Street. Let us all give Three cheers for the Mud.

THE WASP

See the Wasp. He has pretty yellow Stripes around his Body, and a Darning Needle in his Tail. If you Will Pat the Wasp upon the Tail, we will Give you a Nice Picture Book.

THE BUSINESS MANAGER

Here we Have a Business Manager. He is Blowing about the Circulation of the Paper. He is Saying the Paper has Entered upon an Era of Unprecedented Prosperity. In a Minute he will Go up Stairs and Chide the Editor for leaving his Gas Burning while he Went out for a Drink of Water, and he will dock a Reporter Four Dollars because a Subscriber has Licked him and he cannot Work. Little Children, if we Believed Business Managers went to Heaven, we would Give up our Pew in the Church.

THE CONCENTRATED LYE

What a Pretty Can it is. What do you Suppose is in the Can? Open it and see. Goodness me, it is Concentrated Lye! How nice! Are you not Glad? Let us eat it. Taste it and See how Warm it is. If you will Eat it you will not Want anything More to Eat for a Long Time.

Denver *Tribune*, 1882, later in a book, *The Complete Tribune Primer*, 1901

FREDERICK JACKSON TURNER

The Significance of the Frontier
in American History

> Turner, a professor, first at the University of Wisconsin and later
> Harvard, fascinated scholars with his new way of interpreting
> American history. His original premise here was modified by later
> historians.

In a recent bulletin of the Superintendent of the Census for 1890 appear
these significant words: "Up to and including 1880 the country had a
frontier of settlement, but at present the unsettled area has been so
broken into by isolated bodies of settlement that there can hardly be
said to be a frontier line. In the discussion of its extent, its westward
movement, etc., it can not, therefore, any longer have a place in the
census reports." This brief official statement marks the closing of a great
historic movement. Up to our own day American history has been in a
large degree the history of the colonization of the Great West. The
existence of an area of free land, its continued recession, and the advance
of American settlement westward, explain American development.

Behind institutions, behind constitutional forms and modifications, lie
the vital forces that call these organs into life and shape them to meet
changing conditions. The peculiarity of American institutions is the fact
that they have been compelled to adapt themselves to the changes of an
expanding people—to the changes involved in crossing a continent, in
winning a wilderness, and in developing at each area of this progress out
of the primitive economic and political conditions of the frontier into
the complexity of city life. Said Calhoun in 1817, "We are great, and
rapidly—I was about to say fearfully—growing!" So saying, he touched the
distinguishing feature of American life. All peoples show development; the
germ theory of politics has been sufficiently emphasized. In the case of
most nations, however, the development has occurred in a limited area;
and if the nation has expanded, it has met other growing peoples whom
it has conquered. But in the case of the United States we have a different
phenomenon. Limiting our attention to the Atlantic coast, we have the
familiar phenomenon of the evolution of institutions in a limited area,
such as the rise of representative government; the differentiation of simple
colonial governments into complex organs; the progress from primitive
industrial society, without division of labor, up to manufacturing civilization. But we have in addition to this a recurrence of the process of evolution in each western area reached in the process of expansion. Thus
American development has exhibited not merely advance along a single

line, but a return to primitive conditions on a continually advancing frontier line, and a new development for that area. American social development has been continually beginning over again on the frontier. This perennial rebirth, this fluidity of American life, this expansion westward with its new opportunities, its continuous touch with the simplicity of primitive society, furnish the forces dominating American character. The true point of view in the history of this nation is not the Atlantic coast, it is the Great West. Even the slavery struggle . . . occupies its important place in American history because of its relation to westward expansion.

In this advance, the frontier is the outer edge of the wave, the meeting point between savagery and civilization. Much has been written about the frontier from the point of view of border warfare and the chase, but as a field for the serious study of the economist and the historian it has been neglected.

The American frontier is sharply distinguished from the European frontier, a fortified boundary line running through dense populations. The most significant thing about the American frontier is that it lies at the hither edge of free land. In the census reports it is treated as the margin of that settlement which has a density of two or more to the square mile. The term is an elastic one, and for our purposes does not need sharp definition. We shall consider the whole frontier belt, including the Indian country and the outer margin of the "settled area" of the census reports. This paper will make no attempt to treat the subject exhaustively; its aim is simply to call attention to the frontier as a fertile field for investigation, and to suggest some of the problems which arise in connection with it.

In the settlement of America we have to observe how European life entered the continent, and how America modified and developed that life and reacted on Europe. Our early history is the study of European germs developing in an American environment. Too exclusive attention has been paid by institutional students to the Germanic origins, too little to the American factors. The frontier is the line of most rapid and effective Americanization. The wilderness masters the colonist . . . at the frontier the environment is at first too strong for the man. He must accept the conditions which it furnishes, or perish, and so he fits himself into the Indian clearings and follows the Indian trails. Little by little he transforms the wilderness, but the outcome is not the old Europe, not simply the development of Germanic germs. . . . The fact is that here is a new product that is American. At first, the frontier was the Atlantic coast. It was the frontier of Europe in a very real sense. Moving westward, the frontier became more and more American. As successive terminal moraines result from successive glaciations, so each frontier leaves its traces behind it, and when it becomes a settled area the region still partakes of the frontier characteristics. Thus the advance of the frontier has meant a steady movement away from the influence of Europe, a steady growth of independence on American lines. And to study this advance, the men who grow up under these conditions, and the political, economic, and social results of it, is to study the really American part of our history. . . .

The frontier promoted the formation of a composite nationality for the American people. The coast was preponderantly English, but the later tides of continental immigration flowed across to the free lands. This was the case from the early colonial days. The Scotch-Irish and the Palatine Germans, or "Pennsylvania Dutch," furnished the dominant element in the stock of the colonial frontier. With these peoples were also the freed indentured servants, or redemptioners, who at the expiration of their time of service passed to the frontier. . . . Very generally these redemptioners were of non-English stock. In the crucible of the frontier the immigrants were Americanized, liberated, and fused into a mixed race, English in neither nationality nor characteristics. The process has gone on from the early days to our own. Burke and other writers in the middle of the eighteenth century believed that Pennsylvania was "threatened with the danger of being wholly foreign in language, manners and perhaps even inclinations." The German and Scotch-Irish elements in the frontier of the South were only less great. In the middle of the present century the German element in Wisconsin was already so considerable that leading publicists looked to the creation of a German state out of the commonwealth by concentrating their colonization. Such examples teach us to beware of misinterpreting the fact that there is a common English speech in America into a belief that the stock is also English.

In another way the advance of the frontier decreased our dependence on England. The coast, particularly of the South, lacked diversified industries, and was dependent on England for the bulk of its supplies. In the South there was even a dependence on the Northern colonies for articles of food. . . . Before long the frontier created a demand for merchants. As it retreated from the coast it became less and less possible for England to bring her supplies directly to the consumer's wharfs, and carry away staple crops, and staple crops began to give way to diversified agriculture for a time. The effect of this phase of the frontier action upon the northern section is perceived when we realize how the advance of the frontier aroused seaboard cities like Boston, New York, and Baltimore to engage in rivalry for what Washington called "the extensive and valuable trade of a rising empire." . . .

The men of the frontier had closer resemblances to the Middle region than to either of the other sections. Pennsylvania had been the seed-plot of frontier emigration, and, although she passed on her settlers along the Great Valley into the west of Virginia and the Carolinas, yet the industrial society of these Southern frontiersmen was always more like that of the Middle region than like that of the tide water portion of the

316

South, which later came to spread its industrial type throughout the South.

The Middle region, entered by New York harbor, was an open door to all Europe. The tide water part of the South represented typical Englishmen, modified by a warm climate and servile labor, and living in baronial fashion on great plantations; New England stood for a special English movement, Puritanism. The Middle region was less English than the other sections. It had a wide mixture of nationalities, a varied society, the mixed town and county system of local government, a varied economic life, many religious sects. In short, it was a region mediating between New England and the South, and the East and the West. It represented that composite nationality which the contemporary United States exhibits, that juxtaposition of non-English groups, occupying a valley or a little settlement, and presenting reflections of the map of Europe in their variety. It was democratic and non-sectional, if not national; "easy, tolerant, and contented"; rooted strongly in material prosperity. It was typical of the modern United States. It was least sectional, not only because it lay between North and South, but also because with no barriers to shut out its frontiers from its settled region, and with a system of connecting waterways, the Middle region mediated between East and West as well as between North and South. Thus it became the typically American region. Even the New Englander, who was shut out from the frontier by the Middle region, tarrying in New York or Pennsylvania on his westward march, lost the acuteness of his sectionalism on the way. . . .

On the tide of the Father of Waters, North and South met and mingled into a nation. Interstate migration went steadily on—a process of cross-fertilization of ideas and institutions. The fierce struggle of the sections over slavery on the western frontier does not diminish the truth of this statement; it proves the truth of it. Slavery was a sectional trait that would not down, but in the West it could not remain sectional. It was the greatest of frontiersmen who declared: "I believe this Government can not endure permanently half slave and half free. It will become all of one thing or all of the other." Nothing works for nationalism like intercourse within the nation. Mobility of population is death to localism, and the western frontier worked irresistibly in unsettling population. The effect reached back from the frontier and affected profoundly the Atlantic coast and even the Old World.

But the most important effect of the frontier has been in the promotion of democracy here and in Europe. As has been indicated, the frontier is productive of individualism. Complex society is precipitated by the wilderness into a kind of primitive organization based on the family. The tendency is anti-social. It produces antipathy to control, and particularly to any direct control. The tax-gatherer is viewed as a representative of oppression. . . . Frontier conditions prevalent in the colonies are im-

317

portant factors in the explanation of the American Revolution, where individual liberty was sometimes confused with absence of all effective government. The same conditions aid in explaining the difficulty of instituting a strong government in the period of the confederacy. The frontier individualism has from the beginning promoted democracy. . . .

From the conditions of frontier life came intellectual traits of profound importance. The works of travelers along each frontier from colonial days onward describe certain common traits, and these traits have, while softening down, still persisted as survivals in the place of their origin, even when a higher social organization succeeded. The result is that to the frontier the American intellect owes its striking characteristics. That coarseness and strength combined with acuteness and inquisitiveness; that practical, inventive turn of mind, quick to find expedients; that masterful grasp of material things, lacking in the artistic but powerful to effect great ends; that restless, nervous energy; that dominant individualism, working for good and for evil, and withal that buoyancy and exuberance which comes with freedom—these are traits of the frontier, or traits called out elsewhere because of the existence of the frontier. Since the days when the fleet of Columbus sailed into the waters of the New World, America has been another name for opportunity, and the people of the United States have taken their tone from the incessant expansion which has not only been open but has even been forced upon them. He would be a rash prophet who would assert that the expansive character of American life has now entirely ceased. Movement has been its dominant fact, and, unless this training has no effect upon a people, the American energy will continually demand a wider field for its exercise. But never again will such gifts of free land offer themselves. For a moment, at the frontier, the bonds of custom are broken and unrestraint is triumphant. There is no *tabula rasa*. The stubborn American environment is there with its imperious summons to accept its conditions; the inherited ways of doing things are also there; and yet, in spite of environment, and in spite of custom, each frontier did indeed furnish a new field of opportunity, a gate of escape from the bondage of the past; and freshness, and confidence, and scorn of older society, impatience of its restraints and its ideas, and indifference to its lessons, have accompanied the frontier. What the Mediterranean Sea was to the Greeks, breaking the bond of custom, offering new experiences, calling out new institutions and activities, that, and more, the ever retreating frontier has been to the United States directly, and to the nations of Europe more remotely. And now, four centuries from the discovery of America, at the end of a hundred years of life under the Constitution, the frontier has gone, and with its going has closed the first period of American history.

The Significance of the Frontier in American History, 1894

HAMLIN GARLAND

Under the Lion's Paw

During Garland's early life in Wisconsin, Iowa and Dakota he saw at first hand the harsh existence of the farmer. His most successful writing is about these intrepid people of the Midwestern plains.

It was the last of autumn and first day of winter coming together. All day long the plowmen on their prairie farms had moved to and fro on their wide level fields through the falling snow, which melted as it fell, wetting them to the skin—all day, notwithstanding the frequent squalls of snow, the dripping, desolate clouds, and the muck of the furrows, black and tenacious as tar.

Under their dripping harness the horses swung to and fro silently, with that marvelous uncomplaining patience which marks the horse. All day the wild geese, honking wildly as they sprawled sidewise down the wind, seemed to be fleeing from an enemy behind, and with neck out-thrust and wings extended, sailed down the wind, soon lost to sight.

Yet the plowman behind his plow, though the snow lay on his ragged great-coat, and the cold clinging mud rose on his heavy boots, fettering him like gyves, whistled in the very beard of the gale. As day passed, the snow, ceasing to melt, lay along the plowed land, and lodged in the depth of the stubble, till on each slow round the last furrow stood out black and shining as jet between the plowed land and the gray stubble.

When night began to fall, and the geese, flying low, began to alight invisibly in the near cornfield, Stephen Council was still at work "finishing a land." He rode on his sulky-plow when going with the wind, but walked when facing it. Sitting bent and cold but cheery under his slouch hat, he talked encouragingly to his four-in-hand.

"Come round there, boys! Round agin! We got t' finish this land. Come in there, Dan! *Stiddy,* Kate—stiddy! None o' y'r tantrums, Kittie. It's purty tuff, but got a be did. *Tchk! tchk!* Step along, Pete! Don't let Kate git y'r single-tree on the wheel. *Once* more!"

They seemed to know what he meant, and that this was the last round, for they worked with greater vigor than before.

"Once more, boys, an' then sez I oats an' a nice warm stall, an' sleep f'r all."

By the time the last furrow was turned on the land, it was too dark to see the house, and the snow was changing to rain again. The tired and hungry man could see the light from the kitchen shining through the leafless hedge, and he lifted a great shout, "Supper f'r half a dozen!"

319

It was nearly eight o'clock by the time he had finished his chores and started for supper. He was picking his way carefully through the mud, when the tall form of a man loomed up before him with a premonitory cough.

"Waddy ye want?" was the rather startled question of the farmer.

"Well, ye see," began the stranger, in a deprecating tone, "we'd like t' git in f'r the night. We've tried every house f'r the last two miles, but they hadn't any room f'r us. My wife's jest about sick, 'n' the children are cold and hungry——"

"Oh, y' want 'o stay all night, eh?"

"Yes, sir; it 'ud be a great accom——"

"Waal, I don't make it a practice t' turn anybody away hungry, not on sech nights as this. Drive right in. We ain't got much, but sech as it is——"

But the stranger had disappeared. And soon his steaming, weary team, with drooping heads and swinging single-trees, moved past the well to the block beside the path. Council stood at the side of the "schooner" and helped the children out—two little half-sleeping children—and then a small woman with a babe in her arms.

"There ye go!" he shouted, jovially, to the children. "Now we're all right! Run right along to the house there, an' tell Mam' Council you wants sumpthin' t' eat. Right this way, Mis'—keep right off t' the right there. I'll go an' git a lantern. Come," he said to the dazed and silent group at his side.

"Mother," he shouted as he neared the fragrant and warmly-lighted kitchen, "here are some wayfarers an' folks who need sumpthin' t' eat an' a place t' snooze." He ended by pushing them all in.

Mrs. Council, a large, jolly, rather coarse-looking woman, took the children in her arms. "Come right in, you little rabbits. 'Most asleep, hey? Now here's a drink o' milk f'r each o' ye. I'll have s'm tea in a minute. Take off y'r things and set up t' the fire."

While she set the children to drinking milk, Council got out his lantern and went out to the barn to help the stranger about his team, where his loud hearty voice could be heard as it came and went between the haymow and the stalls.

The woman came to light as a small, timid, and discouraged-looking woman, but still pretty, in a thin and sorrowful way.

"Land sakes! An' you've traveled all the way from Clear Lake t'day in this mud! Waal! waal! No wonder you're all tired out. Don't wait f'r the men, Mis'——" She hesitated for the name.

"Haskins."

"Mis' Haskins, set right up to the table an' take a good swig o' tea whilst I make y' s'm toast. It's green tea, an' it's good. I tell Council as I git old I don't seem to enjoy young Hyson n'r Gunpowder. I want the real green tea, jest as it comes off'n the vines. Seems t' have more heart in it some way. Don't s'pose it has. Council says it's all in m' eye."

320

Going on in this easy way, she soon had the children filled with bread and milk and the woman thoroughly at home, eating some toast and sweet-melon pickles, and sipping the tea.

"See the little rats!" she laughed at the children. "They're full as they can stick now, and they want to go to bed. Now, don't git up, Mis' Haskins; set right where you are an' let me look after 'em. I know all about young ones, though I'm all alone now. Jane went an' married last fall. But, as I tell Council, it's lucky we keep our health. Set right there, Mis' Haskins; I won't have you stir a finger."

It was an unmeasured pleasure to sit there in the warm, homely kitchen, the jovial chatter of the housewife driving out and holding at bay the growl of the impotent, cheated wind.

The little woman's eyes filled with tears which fell down upon the sleeping baby in her arms. The world was not so desolate and cold and hopeless, after all.

"Now I hope Council won't stop out there and talk politics all night. He's the greatest man to talk politics an' read the *Tribune*— How old is it?"

She broke off and peered down at the face of the babe.

"Two months 'n five days," said the mother, with a mother's exactness.

"Ye don't say! I want 'o know! The dear little pudzy-wudzy!" she went on, stirring it up in the neighborhood of the ribs with her fat forefinger. "Pooty tough on 'oo to go gallivant'n' 'cross lots this way—"

"Yes, that's so; a man can't lift a mountain," said Council entering the door. "Mother, this is Mr. Haskins, from Kansas. He's been eat up 'n' drove out by grasshoppers."

"Glad t' see yeh!—Pa, empty that wash-basin 'n' give him a chance t' wash."

Haskins was a tall man, with a thin, gloomy face. His hair was a reddish brown, like his coat, and seemed equally faded by the wind and sun. And his sallow face, though hard and set, was pathetic somehow. You would have felt that he had suffered much, by the line of his mouth showing under his thin yellow mustache.

"Hain't Ike got home yet, Sairy?"

"Hain't seen 'im."

"Wa-a-l, set right up, Mr. Haskins; wade right into what we've got; 'tain't much, but we manage to live on it—she gits fat on it," laughed Council, pointing his thumb at his wife.

After supper, while the women put the children to bed, Haskins and Council talked on, seated near the huge cooking-stove, the steam rising from their wet clothing. In the western fashion Council told as much of his own life as he drew from his guest. He asked but few questions, but by and by the story of Haskins's struggles and defeat came out. The story was a terrible one, but he told it quietly, seated with his elbows on his knees, gazing most of the time at the hearth.

"I didn't like the looks of the counrty, anyhow," Haskins said, partly rising and glancing at his wife. "I was ust t' northern Ingyannie, where we have lots o' timber 'n' lots o' rain, 'n' I didn't like the looks o' that dry prairie. What galled me the worst was goin' s' far way acrosst so much fine land layin' all through here vacant."

"And the 'hoppers eat ye four years hand runnin', did they?"

"Eat! They wiped us out. They chawed everything that was green. They jest set around waitin' f'r us to die t' eat us, too. My God! I ust t' dream of 'em sittin' 'round on the bed-post, six feet long, workin' their jaws. They et the fork-handles. They got worse 'n' worse till they jest rolled on one another, piled up like snow in winter. Well, it ain't no use. If I was t' talk all winter I couldn't tell nawthin'. But all the while I couldn't help thinkin' of all that land back here that nobuddy was usin' that I ought o' had stead o' bein' out there in that cussed country."

"Waal, why didn't ye stop an' settle here?" asked Ike, who had come in and was eating his supper.

"Fer the simple reason that you fellers wantid ten 'r fifteen dollars an acre fer the bare land, and I hadn't no money fer that kind o' thing."

"Yes, I do my own work," Mrs. Council was heard to say in the pause which followed. "I'm gettin' purty heavy t' be on m' laigs all day, but we can't afford t' hire, so I keep rackin' around somehow, like a foundered horse. S' lame—I tell Council he can't tell how lame I am, f'r I'm jest as lame in one laig as t' other." And the good soul laughed at the joke on herself as she took a handful of flour and dusted the biscuit-board to keep the dough from sticking.

"Well, I hain't *never* been very strong," said Mrs. Haskins. "Our folks was Canadians an' small-boned, and then since my last child I hain't got up again fairly. I don't like t' complain. Tim has about all he can bear now—but they was days this week when I jest wanted to lay right down an' die."

"Wall, now, I'll tell ye," said Council, from his side of the stove, silencing everybody with his good-natured roar, "I'd go down and *see* Butler, *anyway*, if I was you. I guess he'd let you have his place purty cheap; the farm's all run down. He's been anxious t' let t' somebuddy next year. It 'ud be a good chance fer you. Anyhow, you go to bed and sleep like a babe. I've got some plowing t' do, anyhow, an' we'll see if somethin' can't be done about your case. Ike, you go out, an' see if the horses is all right, an' I'll show the folks t' bed."

When the tired husband and wife were lying under the generous quilts of the spare bed, Haskins listened a moment to the wind in the eaves, and then said, with a slow and solemn tone:

"There are people in this world who are good enough t' be angels an' only haff t' die to *be* angels."

II

Jim Butler was one of these men called in the West "land poor." Early in the history of Rock River he had come into the town and started in the grocery business in a small way, occupying a small building in a mean part of the town. At this period of his life he earned all he got, and was up early and late sorting beans, working over butter, and carting his goods to and from the station. But a change came over him at the end of the second year, when he sold a lot of land for four times what he paid for it. From that time forward he believed in land speculation as the surest way of getting rich. Every cent he could save or spare from his trade he put into land at forced sale, or mortgages on land, which were "just as good as the wheat," he was accustomed to say.

Farm after farm fell into his hands, until he was recognized as one of the leading landowners of the county. His mortgages were scattered all over Cedar County, and as they slowly but surely fell in, he sought usually to retain the former owner as tenant.

He was not ready to foreclose; indeed, he had the name of being one of the "easiest" men in the town. He let the debtor off again and again, extending the time whenever possible.

"I don't want y'r land," he said. "All I'm after is the int'rest on my money—that's all. Now, if y' want 'o stay on the farm, why, I'll give y' a good chance. I can't have the land layin' vacant." And in many cases the owner remained as tenant.

In the meantime he had sold his store; he couldn't spend time in it; he was mainly occupied now with sitting around town on rainy days smoking and "gassin' with the boys," or in riding to and from his farms. In fishing time he fished a good deal. Doc Grimes, Ben Ashley, and Cal Cheatham were his cronies on these fishing excursions or hunting trips for chickens or partridges. In winter they went to northern Wisconsin to shoot deer.

In spite of all these signs of easy life Butler persisted in saying he "hadn't enough money to pay taxes on his land," and was careful to convey the impression that he was poor in spite of his twenty farms. At one time he was said to be worth fifty thousand dollars, but land had been a little slow of sale of late, so that he was not worth so much.

A fine farm, known as the Higley place, had fallen into his hands in the usual way the previous year, and he had not been able to find a tenant for it. Poor Higley, after working himself nearly to death on it in the attempt to lift the mortgage, had gone off to Dakota, leaving the farm and his curse to Butler.

This was the farm which Council advised Haskins to apply for; and the next day Council hitched up his team and drove down town to see Butler.

"You jest let *me* do the talkin'," he said. "We'll find him wearin' out his pants on some salt barrel somew'ers; and if he thought you *wanted* a place he'd sock it to you hot and heavy. You jest keep quiet; I'll fix 'im."

Butler was seated in Ben Ashley's store telling fish yarns, when Council sauntered in casually.

"Hello, But; lyin' agin, hey?"

"Hello, Steve! How goes it?"

"Oh, so-so. Too dang much rain in these days. I thought it was goin' t' freeze up f'r good last night. Tight squeak if I get m' plowin' done. How's farmin' with *you* these days?"

"Bad. Plowin' ain't half done."

"It 'ud be a religious idee f'r you t' go out an' take a hand y'rself."

"I don't haff to," said Butler, with a wink.

"Got anybody on the Higley place?"

"No. Know of anybody?"

"Wall, no; not eggsackly. I've got a relation back t' Michigan who's ben hot an' cold on the idee o' comin' West f'r some time. *Might* come if he could get a good lay-out. What do you talk on the farm?"

"Well, I d' know. I'll rent it on shares or I'll rent it money rent."

"Wall, how much money, say?"

"Well, say ten per cent on the price—two-fifty."

"Wall, that ain't bad. Wait on 'im till 'e thrashes?"

Haskins listened eagerly to his important question, but Council was coolly eating a dried apple which he had speared out of a barrel with his knife. Butler studied him carefully.

"Well, knocks me out of twenty-five dollars interest."

"My relation'll need all he's got t' git his crops in," said Council, in the same indifferent way.

"Well, all right; *say* wait," concluded Butler.

"All right, this is the man. Haskins, this is Mr. Butler—no relation to Ben—the hardest working man in Cedar County."

On the way home, Haskins said: "I ain't much better off. I'd like that farm; it's a good farm, but it's all run down, an' so'm I. I could make a good farm of it if I had half a show. But I can't stock it n'r seed it."

"Wall, now, don't you worry," roared Council in his ear. "We'll pull y' through somehow till next harvest. He's agreed t' hire it plowed, an' you can earn a hundred dollars plowin' an' y' c'n git the seed o' me, an' pay me back when y' can."

Haskins was silent with emotion, but at last he said: "I ain't got nothin' t' live on."

"Now don't you worry 'bout that. You jest make your headquarters at ol' Steve Council's. Mother 'll take a pile o' comfort in havin' y'r wife an' children 'round. Y' see, Jane's married off lately, an' Ike's away a good 'eal, so we'll be darn glad t' have y' stop with us this winter. Nex' spring we'll see if y' can't git a start agin." And he chirruped to the team, which sprang forward with the rumbling, clattering wagon.

"Say, looky here, Council, you can't do this. I never saw——" shouted Haskins in his neighbor's ear.

Council moved about uneasily in his seat and stopped his stammering gratitude by saying, "Hold on, now; don't make such a fuss over a little thing. When I see a man down, an' things all on top of 'm, I jest like t' kick 'em off an' help 'm up. That's the kind of religion I got, an' it's about the *only* kind."

324

They rode the rest of the way home in silence. And when the red light of the lamp shone out into the darkness of the cold and windy night, and he thought of this refuge for his children and wife, Haskins could have put his arm around the neck of his burly companion and squeezed him like a lover. But he contented himself with saying: "Steve Council, you'll git y'r pay f'r this some day!"

"Don't want any pay. My religion ain't run on such business principles."

The wind was growing colder, and the ground was covered with a white frost, as they turned into the gate of the Council farm, and the children came rushing out, shouting, "Papa's come!" They hardly looked like the same children who had sat at the table the night before. Their torpidity under the influence of sunshine and Mother Council had given way to a sort of spasmodic cheerfulness, as insects in winter revive when laid on the hearth.

III

Haskins worked like a fiend, and his wife, like the heroic woman that she was, bore also uncomplainingly the most terrible burdens. They rose early and toiled without intermission till the darkness fell on the plain, then tumbled into bed, every bone and muscle aching with fatigue, to rise with the sun next morning to the same round of the same ferocity of labor.

The eldest boy drove a team all through the spring, plowing and seeding, milked the cows, and did chores innumerable, in most ways taking the place of a man.

An infinitely pathetic but common figure—this boy on the American farm, where there is no law against child labor. To see him in his coarse clothing, his huge boots, and his ragged cap, as he staggered with a pail of water from the well, or trudged in the cold and cheerless dawn out into the frosty field behind his team, gave the city-bred visitor a sharp pang of sympathetic pain. Yet Haskins loved his boy, and would have saved him from this if he could, but he could not.

By June the first year the result of such Herculean toil began to show on the farm. The yard was cleaned up and sown to grass, the garden plowed and planted, and the house mended.

Council had given them four of his cows.

"Take 'em and run 'em on shares. I don't want 'o milk s' many. Ike's away s' much now, Sat'dys an' Sund'ys, I can't stand the bother anyhow."

Other men, seeing the confidence of Council in the newcomer, had sold him tools on time; and as he was really an able farmer, he soon had round him many evidences of his care and thrift. At the advice of Council he had taken the farm for three years, with the privilege of re-renting or buying at the end of the term.

"It's a good bargain, an' y' want 'o nail it," said Council. "If you have any kind ov a crop, you c'n pay y'r debts, an' keep seed an' bread."

325

The new hope which now sprang up in the heart of Haskins and his wife grew great almost as a pain by the time the wide field of wheat began to wave and rustle and swirl in the winds of July. Day after day he would snatch a few moments after supper to go and look at it.

"Have ye seen the wheat t'day, Nettie?" he asked one night as he rose from supper.

"No, Tim, I ain't had time."

"Well, take time now. Let's go look at it."

She threw an old hat on her head—Tommy's hat—and looking almost pretty in her thin sad way went out with her husband to the hedge.

"Ain't it grand, Nettie? Just look at it."

It *was* grand. Level, russet here and there, heavy-headed, wide as a lake, and full of multitudinous whispers and gleams of wealth, it stretched away before the gazers like the fabled field of the cloth of gold.

"Oh, I think—I *hope* we'll have a good crop, Tim; and oh, how good the people have been to us!"

"Yes; I don't know where we'd be t'day if it hadn't been for Council and his wife."

"They're the best people in the world," said the little woman, with a great sob of gratitude.

"We'll be in the field on Monday, sure," said Haskins, gripping the rail on the fence as if already at the work of the harvest.

The harvest came, bounteous, glorious, but the winds came and blew it into tangles, and the rain matted it here and there close to the ground, increasing the work of gathering it threefold.

Oh, how they toiled in those glorious days! Clothing dripping with sweat, arms aching, filled with briers, fingers raw and bleeding, backs broken with the weight of heavy bundles, Haskins and his man toiled on. Tommy drove the harvester, while his father and a hired man bound on the machine. In this way they cut ten acres every day and almost every night after supper, when the hand went to bed, Haskins returned to the field, shocking the bound grain in the light of the moon. Many a night he worked till his anxious wife came out at ten o'clock to call him in to rest and lunch.

At the same time she cooked for the men, took care of the children, washed and ironed, milked the cows at night, made the butter, and sometimes fed the horses and watered them while her husband kept at the shocking.

No slave in the Roman galleys could have toiled so frightfully and lived, for this man thought himself a free man, and that he was working for his wife and babes.

When he sank into his bed with a deep groan of relief, too tired to change his grimy, dripping clothing, he felt that he was getting nearer and nearer to a home of his own, and pushing the wolf a little father from his door.

326

There is no despair so deep as the despair of a homeless man or woman. To roam the roads of the country or the streets of the city, to feel there is no rood of ground on which the feet can rest, to halt weary and hungry outside lighted windows and hear laughter and song within—these are the hungers and rebellions that drive men to crime and women to shame.

It was the memory of this homelessness, and the fear of its coming again, that spurred Timothy Haskins and Nettie, his wife, to such ferocious labor during that first year.

IV

" 'M, yes; 'm' yes; first rate," said Butler, as his eye took in the neat garden, the pig-pen, and the well-filled barn-yard. "You're git'n quite a stock around yeh. Done well, eh?"

Haskins was showing Butler around the place. He had not seen it for a year, having spent the year in Washington and Boston with Ashley, his brother-in-law, who had been elected to Congress.

"Yes, I've laid out a good deal of money during the last three years. I've paid out three hundred dollars f'r fencin'."

"Um-h'm! I see, I see," said Butler while Haskins went on:

"The kitchen there cost two hundred; the barn ain't cost much in money, but I've put a lot o' time on it. I've dug a new well, and I—"

"Yes, yes. I see! You've done well. Stawk worth a thousand dollars," said Butler, picking his teeth with a straw.

"About that," said Haskins, modestly. "We begin to feel 's if we was git'n' a home f'r ourselves; but we've worked hard. I tell you we begin to feel it, Mr. Butler, and we're goin' t' begin to ease up purty soon. We've been kind of plannin' a trip back t' *her* folks after the fall plowin's done."

"*Eggs*-actly!" said Butler, who was evidently thinking of something else. "I suppose you've kind o' calc'lated on stayin' here three years more?"

"Well, yes. Fact is, I think I c'n buy the farm this fall, if you'll give me a reasonable show."

"Um-m! What do you call a reasonable show?"

"Wal, say a quarter down and three years' time."

Butler looked at the huge stacks of wheat, which filled the yard, over which the chickens were fluttering and crawling, catching grasshoppers, and out of which the crickets were singing innumerably. He smiled in a peculiar way as he said, "Oh, I won't be hard on yeh. But what did you expect to pay f'r the place?"

"Why, about what you offered it for before, two thousand five hundred, or *possibly* three thousand dollars," he added quickly, as he saw the owner shake his head.

"This farm is worth five thousand and five hundred dollars," said Butler, in a careless and decided voice.

"*What!*" almost shrieked the astounded Haskins. "What's that? Five thousand? Why, that's double what you offered it for three years ago."

327

"Of course; and it's worth it. It was all run down then; now it's in good shape. You've laid out fifteen hundred dollars in improvements, according to your own story."

"But *you* had nothin' t' do about that. It's my work and my money."

"You bet it was; but it's my land."

"But what's to pay me for all my—"

"Ain't you had the use of 'em?" replied Butler, smiling calmly into his face.

Haskins was like a man struck on the head with a sand-bag; he couldn't think; he stammered as he tried to say: "But—I never 'd git the use—— You'd rob me! More'n that: you agreed—you promised that I could buy or rent at the end of three years at——"

"That's all right. But I didn't say I'd let you carry off the improvements, nor that I'd go on renting the farm at two-fifty. The land is doubled in value, it don't matter how; it don't enter into the question; an' now you can pay me five hundred dollars a year rent, or take it on your own terms at fifty-five hundred, or—git out."

He was turning away when Haskins, the sweat pouring from his face, fronted him, saying again:

"But *you've* done nothing to make it so. You hain't added a cent. I put it all there myself, expectin' to buy. I worked an' sweat to improve it. I was workin' for myself an' babes——"

"Well, why didn't you buy when I offered to sell? What y' kickin' about?"

"I'm kickin' 'bout payin' you twice f'r my own things—my own fences, my own kitchen, my own garden."

Butler laughed. "You're too green t' eat, young feller. *Your* improvements! The law will sing another tune."

"But I trusted your word."

"Never trust anybody, my friend. Besides I didn't promise not to do this thing. Why, man, don't look at me like that. Don't take me for a thief. It's the law. The reg'lar thing. Everybody does it."

"I don't care if they do. It's stealin' jes the same. You take three thousand dollars of my money—the work o' my hands and my wife's." He broke down at this point. He was not a strong man mentally. He could face hardships, ceaseless toil, but he could not face the cold and sneering face of Butler.

"But I don't take it," said Butler coolly. "All you've got to do is to go on jest as you've been a-doin', or give me a thousand dollars down, and a mortgage at ten per cent on the rest."

Haskins sat down blindly on a bundle of oats near by, and with staring eyes and drooping head went over the situation. He was under the lion's paw. He felt a horrible numbness in his heart and limbs. He was hid in a mist, and there was no path out.

Butler walked about, looking at the huge stacks of grain, and pulling now and again a few handfuls out, shelling the heads in his hands and blowing the chaff away. He hummed a little tune as he did so. He had an accommodating air of waiting.

Haskins was in the midst of the terrible toil of the last year. He was walking again in the rain and the mud behind his plow; he felt the dust and dirt of the threshing. The ferocious husking time, with its cutting wind and biting, clinging snows, lay hard upon him. Then he thought of his wife, how she had cheerfully cooked and baked, without holiday and without rest.

"Well, what do you think of it?" inquired the cool, mocking, insinuating voice of Butler.

"I think you're a thief and a liar!" shouted Haskins, leaping up. "A black-hearted houn'!" Butler's smile maddened him; with a sudden leap he caught a fork in his hands, and whirled it in the air. "You'll never rob another man, damn ye!" he grated through his teeth, a look of pitiless ferocity in his accusing eyes.

Butler shrank and quivered, expecting the blow; stood, held hypnotized by the eyes of the man he had a moment before despised—a man transformed into an avenging demon. But in the deadly hush between the lift of the weapon and its fall there came a gush of faint, childish laughter and then across the range of his vision, far away and dim, he saw the sun-bright head of his baby girl, as, with the pretty tottering run of a two-year-old, she moved across the grass of the dooryard. His hands relaxed; the fork fell to the ground; his head lowered.

"Make out y'r deed an' mor'gage, an' git off'n my land, an' don't ye never cross my line agin; if y' do, I'll kill ye."

Butler backed away from the man in wild haste, and climbing into his buggy with trembling limbs, drove off down the road, leaving Haskins seated dumbly on the sunny pile of sheaves, his head sunk into his hands.

Main-Traveled Roads, 1891

FINLEY PETER DUNNE

Mr. Dooley On Reform Candidates

> As a reporter for the Chicago TRIBUNE, Dunne made the acquaint-
> ance of a Dearborn Street bartender named McGarrey who fre-
> quently commented at length on local politics. Dunne turned one
> of these conversations into an article, giving the speaker the name
> of "McNeery," which was later changed to Martin Dooley when
> further articles of this kind became popular with Chicagoans. Be-
> fore long Dooley and his friend Hennessey were enjoying national
> celebrity as the first syndicated newspaper feature.

"That frind iv ye'ers, Dugan, is an intilligent man," said Mr. Dooley. "All
he needs is an index an' a few illusthrations to make him a bicyclopedja iv
useless information."

"Well," said Mr. Hennessy, judiciously, "he ain't no Socrates an' he
ain't no answers-to-questions colum; but he's a good man that goes to
his jooty, an' as handy with a pick as some people are with a cocktail
spoon. What's he been doin' again ye?"

"Nawthin'," said Mr. Dooley, "but he was in here Choosday. 'Did ye
vote?' says I. 'I did,' says he. 'Which wan iv th' distinguished bunko steerers
got ye'er invalu'ble suffrage?' says I. 'I didn't have none with me,' says he,
'but I voted f'r Charter Haitch,' says hc. 'I've been with him in six ilic-
tions,' says he, 'an' he's a good man,' he says. 'D'ye think ye're votin f'r
th' best?' says I. 'Why, man alive,' I says, 'Charter Haitch was assassinated
three years ago,' I says. 'Was he?' says Dugan. 'Ah, well, he's lived that
down be this time. He was a good man,' he says.

"Ye see, that's what thim rayform lads wint up again. If I liked ray-
formers, Hinnissy, an wanted f'r to see thim win out wanst in their lifetime, I'd buy thim each a suit iv chilled steel, ar-rm thim with raypeatin'
rifles, an' take thim east iv State Sthreet an' south iv Jackson Bullyvard.
At prisint th' opinion that pre-vails in th' ranks iv th' gloryous ar-rmy iv
ray-form is that there ain't annything worth seein' in this lar-rge an' com-
modyous desert but th' pest-house an' the bridewell. Me frind Willum J.
O'Brien is no rayformer. But Willum J. undherstands that there's a few
hundherds iv thousands iv people livin' in a part iv th' town that looks
like nawthin' but smoke fr'm th' roof iv th' Onion League Club that have
on'y two pleasures in life, to wur-ruk an' to vote, both iv which they do at
th' uniform rate iv wan dollar an' a half a day. That's why Willum J.
O'Brien is now a sinitor an' will be an aldherman afther next Thursdah,
an' it's why other people are sindin' him flowers.

"This is th' way a rayform candydate is ilicted. Th' boys down town has heerd that things ain't goin' r-right somehow. Franchises is bein' handed out to none iv thim; an' wanst in a while a mimber iv th' club, comin' home a little late an' thryin' to riconcile a pair iv r-round feet with an embroidered sidewalk, meets a sthrong ar-rm boy that pushes in his face an' takes away all his marbles. It begins to be talked that th' time has come f'r good citizens f'r to brace up an' do somethin', an' they agree to nomynate a candydate f'r aldherman. 'Who'll we put up?' says they. 'How's Clarence Doolittle?' says wan. 'He's laid up with a coupon thumb, an' can't r-run.' 'An' how about Arthur Doheny?' 'I swore an oath whin I came out iv colledge I'd niver vote f'r a man that wore a made tie.' 'Well, thin, let's thry Willie Boye.' 'Good,' says th' comity. 'He's jus' th' man f'r our money.' An' Willie Boye, after thinkin' it over, goes to his tailor an' ordhers three dozen pairs iv pants, an' decides f'r to be th' sthandard-bearer iv th' people. Musin' over his fried eyesthers an' asparagus an' his champagne, he bets a polo pony again a box of golf-balls he'll be ilicted unanimous; an' all th' good citizens make a vow f'r to set th' alar-rm clock f'r half-past three on th' afthernoon iv iliction day, so's to be up in time to vote f'r th' riprisintitive iv pure gover'mint.

" 'Tis some time befure they comprehind that there ar-re other candy-dates in th' field. But th' other candydates know it. Th' sthrongest iv thim —his name is Flannigan, an' he's a re-tail dealer in wines an' liquors, an' he lives over his establishment. Flannigan was nomynated enthusyastically at a prim'ry held in his bar-rn; an' befure Willie Boye had picked out pants that wud match th' color iv th' Austhreelyan ballot this here Flannigan had put a man on th' day watch, tol' him to speak gently to anny ray-gistered voter that wint to sleep behind th' sthove, an' was out that night visitin' his frinds. Who was it judged th' cake walk? Flannigan. Who was it carrid th' pall? Flannigan. Who was it sthud up at th' christening? Flannigan. Whose ca-ards did th' grievin' widow, and th' blushin' bride-groom, or th' happy father find in th' hack? Flannigan's. Ye bet ye'er life. Ye see Flannigan wasn't out f'r th' good iv th' community. Flannigan was out f'r Flannigan an' th' stuff.

"Well, iliction day come around; an' all th' imminent friends iv good gover'mint had special wires sthrung into th' club, an' waited f'r th' re-turns. Th' first precin't showed 28 votes f'r Willie Boye to 14 f'r Flanni-gan. 'That's my precin't,' says Willie. 'I wondher who voted thim four-teen?' 'Coachmen,' says Clarence Doolittle. 'There are thirty-five precin'ts in this ward,' says th' leader iv th' rayform iliment. 'At this rate, I'm sure iv 440 meejority. Gossoon,' he says, 'put a keg iv sherry wine on th' ice,' he says. 'Well,' he says, 'at last th' community is relieved fr'm misrule,' he says. 'To-morrah I will start in arrangin' amindmints to th' tariff schedool an' th' ar-bitration threety,' he says. 'We must be up an' doin',' he says. 'Hol' on there,' says wan iv th' comity. 'There must be some mistake in this fr'm th' sixth precin't,' he says. 'Where's the sixth precin't?' says Clarence. 'Over be th' dumps,' says Willie. 'I told me futman to see

331

to that. He lives at th' corner iv Desplaines an Bloo Island Av'noo on
Goose's Island,' he says. 'What does it show?' 'Flannigan, three hunherd
an' eighty-five; Hansen, forty-eight; Schwartz, twinty; O'Malley, sivinteen;
Casey, ten; O'Day, eight; Larsen, five; O'Rourke, three; Mulcahy, two;
Schmitt, two; Moloney, two; Riordon, two; O'Malley, two; Willie Boye,
wan.' 'Gintlemin,' says Willie Boye, arisin' with a stern look in his eyes,
'Th's rascal has bethrayed me. Waither, take the sherry wine off th' ice.
They'se no hope f'r sound financial legislation this year. I'm goin' home.'

  "An', as he goes down th' sthreet, he hears a band play an' sees a
procission headed be a calceem light; an', in a carredge, with his plug hat
in his hand an' his di'mond makin' th' calceem look like a piece iv punk
in a smokehouse, is Flannigan, payin' his first visit this side iv th' thracks."

Mr. Dooley in Peace and War, 1898

STEPHEN CRANE

The Blue Hotel

> *Fear is a recurrent theme in Crane's best fiction. He may very well
> have got the idea for this piece when, in the course of his brief and
> troubled life, he once traveled through Nebraska. Possibly he even
> stayed at a blue hotel.*

The Palace Hotel at Fort Romper was painted a light blue, a shade that
is on the legs of a kind of heron, causing the bird to declare its position
against any background. The Palace Hotel, then, was always screaming
and howling in a way that made the dazzling winter landscape of Ne-
braska seem only a grey swampish hush. It stood alone on the prairie, and
when the snow was falling the town two hundred yards away was not
visible. But when the traveller alighted at the railway station he was
obliged to pass the Palace Hotel before he could come upon the company
of low clapboard houses which composed Fort Romper, and it was not to
be thought that any traveller could pass the Palace Hotel without looking
at it. Pat Scully, the proprietor, had proved himself a master of strategy
when he chose his paints. It is true that on clear days, when the great
transcontinental expresses, long lines of swaying Pullmans, swept through
Fort Romper, passengers were overcome at the sight, and the cult that
knows the brown-reds and the subdivisions of the dark greens of the East
expressed shame, pity, horror, in a laugh. But to the citizens of this prairie
town and to the people who would naturally stop there, Pat Scully had
performed a feat. With this opulence and splendour, these creeds, classes,

egotisms, that streamed through Rompers on the rail day after day, they had no colour in common.

As if the displayed delights of such a blue hotel were not sufficiently enticing, it was Scully's habit to go every morning and evening to meet the leisurely trains that stopped at Romper and work his seductions upon any man that he might see wavering, gripsack in hand. One morning, when a snow-crusted engine dragged its long string of freight cars and its one passenger coach to the station, Scully performed the marvel of catching three men. One was a shaky and quick-eyed Swede, with a great shining cheap valise; one was a tall bronzed cowboy, who was on his way to a ranch near the Dakota line; one was a silent little man from the East, who didn't look it, and didn't announce it. Scully practically made them prisoners. He was so nimble and merry and kindly that each probably felt it would be the height of brutality to try to escape. They trudged off over the creaking board sidewalks in the wake of the eager little Irishman. He wore a heavy fur cap squeezed tightly down on his head. It caused his two red ears to stick out stiffly, as if they were made of tin.

At last, Scully, elaborately, with boisterous hospitality, conducted them through the portals of the blue hotel. The room which they entered was small. It seemed to be merely a proper temple for a stove, which, in the centre, was humming with godlike violence. At various points on its surface the iron had become luminous and glowed yellow from the heat. Beside the stove Scully's son Johnnie was playing High-Five with an old farmer who had whiskers both grey and sandy. They were quarrelling. Frequently the old farmer turned his face toward a box of sawdust—coloured brown from tobacco juice—that was behind the stove, and spat with an air of great impatience and irritation. With a loud flourish of words Scully destroyed the game of cards, and bustled his son upstairs with part of the baggage of the new guests. He himself conducted them to three basins of the coldest water in the world. The cowboy and the Easterner burnished themselves fiery red with this water, until it seemed to be some kind of metal-polish. The Swede, however, merely dipped his fingers gingerly and with trepidation. It was notable that throughout this series of small ceremonies the three travellers were made to feel that Scully was very benevolent. He was conferring great favours upon them. He handed the towel from one to another with an air of philanthropic impulse.

Afterwards they went to the first room, and, sitting about the stove, listened to Scully's officious clamour at his daughters, who were preparing the midday meal. They reflected in the silence of experienced men who tread carefully amid new people. Nevertheless, the old farmer, stationary, invincible in his chair near the warmest part of the stove, turned his face from the sawdust box frequently and addressed a commonplace to the strangers. Usually he was answered in short but adequate sentences by either the cowboy or the Easterner. The Swede said nothing. He seemed to be occupied in making furtive estimates of each man in the room. One might have thought that he had the sense of silly suspicion which comes to guilt. He resembled a badly frightened man.

Later, at dinner, he spoke a little, addressing his conversation entirely to Scully. He volunteered that he had come from New York, where for ten years he had worked as a tailor. These facts seemed to strike Scully as fascinating, and afterwards he volunteered that he had lived at Romper for fourteen years. The Swede asked about the crops and the price of labour. He seemed barely to listen to Scully's extended replies. His eyes continued to rove from man to man.

Finally, with a laugh and a wink, he said that some of these Western communities were very dangerous; and after his statement he straightened his legs under the table, tilted his head, and laughed again, loudly. It was plain that the demonstration had no meaning to the others. They looked at him wondering and in silence.

II

As the men trooped back into the front room, the two little windows presented views of a turmoiling sea of snow. The huge arms of the wind were making attempts—mighty, circular, futile—to embrace the flakes as they sped. A gate-post like a still man with a blanched face stood aghast amid this profligate fury. In a hearty voice Scully announced the presence of a blizzard. The guests of the blue hotel, lighting their pipes, assented with grunts of lazy masculine contentment. No island of the sea could be exempt in the degree of this little room with its humming stove. Johnnie, son of Scully, in a tone which defined his opinion of his ability as a card-player, challenged the old farmer of both grey and sandy whiskers to a game of High-Five. The farmer agreed with a contemptuous and bitter scoff. They sat close to the stove, and squared their knees under a wide board. The cowboy and the Easterner watched the game with interest. The Swede remained near the window, aloof, but with a countenance that showed signs of an inexplicable excitement.

The play of Johnnie and the grey-beard was suddenly ended by another quarrel. The old man arose while casting a look of heated scorn at his adversary. He slowly buttoned his coat, and then stalked with fabulous dignity from the room. In the discreet silence of all the other men the Swede laughed. His laughter rang somehow childish. Men by this time had begun to look at him askance, as if they wished to inquire what ailed him.

A new game was formed jocosely. The cowboy volunteered to become the partner of Johnnie, and they all then turned to ask the Swede to throw in his lot with the little Easterner. He asked some questions about the game, and, learning that it wore many names, and that he had played it when it was under an alias, he accepted the invitation. He strode toward the men nervously, as if he expected to be assaulted. Finally, seated, he

334

gazed from face to face and laughed shrilly. This laugh was so strange that the Easterner looked up quickly, the cowboy sat intent and with his mouth open, and Johnnie paused, holding the cards with still fingers.

Afterward there was a short silence. Then Johnnie said, "Well, let's get at it. Come on now!" They pulled their chairs forward until their knees were bunched under the board. They began to play, and their interest in the game caused the others to forget the manner of the Swede.

The cowboy was a board-whacker. Each time that he held superior cards he whanged them, one by one, with exceeding force, down upon the improvised table, and took the tricks with a glowing air of prowess and pride that sent thrills of indignation into the hearts of his opponents. A game with a board-whacker in it is sure to become intense. The countenances of the Easterner and the Swede were miserable whenever the cowboy thundered down his aces and kings, while Johnnie, his eyes gleaming with joy, chuckled and chuckled.

Because of the absorbing play none considered the strange ways of the Swede. They paid strict heed to the game. Finally, during a lull caused by a new deal the Swede suddenly addressed Johnnie: "I suppose there have been a good many men killed in this room." The jaws of the others dropped and they looked at him.

"What in hell are you talking about?" said Johnnie.

The Swede laughed again his blatant laugh, full of a kind of false courage and defiance. "Oh, you know what I mean all right," he answered.

"I'm a liar if I do!" Johnnie protested. The card was halted, and the men stared at the Swede. Johnnie evidently felt that as the son of the proprietor he should make a direct inquiry. "Now, what might you be drivin' at, mister?" he asked. The Swede winked at him. It was a wink full of cunning. His fingers shook on the edge of the board. "Oh, maybe you think I have been to nowheres. Maybe you think I'm a tenderfoot?"

"I don't know nothin' about you," answered Johnnie, "and I don't give a damn where you've been. All I got to say is that I don't know what you're driving at. There hain't never been nobody killed in this room."

The cowboy, who had been steadily gazing at the Swede, then spoke: "What's wrong with you, mister?"

Apparently it seemed to the Swede that he was formidably menaced. He shivered and turned white near the corners of his mouth. He sent an appealing glance in the direction of the little Easterner. During these moments he did not forget to wear his air of advanced pot-valour. "They say they don't know what I mean," he remarked mockingly to the Easterner.

The latter answered after prolonged and cautious reflection. "I don't understand you," he said, impassively.

The Swede made a movement then which announced that he thought he had encountered treachery from the only quarter where he had expected sympathy, if not help. "Oh, I see you are all against me. I see—"

The cowboy was in a state of deep stupefaction. "Say," he cried, as he tumbled the deck violently down upon the board, "say, what are you gittin' at, hey?"

The Swede sprang up with the celerity of a man escaping from a snake on the floor. "I don't want to fight!" he shouted. "I don't want to fight!"

The cowboy stretched his long legs indolently and deliberately. His hands were in his pockets. He spat into the sawdust-box. "Well, who the hell thought you did?" he inquired.

The Swede backed rapidly toward a corner of the room. His hands were out protectingly in front of his chest, but he was making an obvious struggle to control his fright. "Gentlemen," he quavered. "I suppose I am going to be killed before I can leave this house! I suppose I am going to be killed before I can leave this house!" In his eyes was the dying-swan look. Through the windows could be seen the snow turning blue in the shadow of dusk. The wind tore at the house, and some loose thing beat regularly against the clapboards like a spirit tapping.

A door opened, and Scully himself entered. He paused in surprise as he noted the tragic attitude of the Swede. Then he said, "What's the matter here?"

The Swede answered him swiftly and eagerly: "These men are going to kill me."

"Kill you!" ejaculated Scully. "Kill you! What are you talkin'?"

The Swede made the gesture of a martyr.

Scully wheeled sternly upon his son. "What is this, Johnnie?"

The lad had grown sullen. "Damned if I know," he answered. "I can't make no sense to it." He began to shuffle the cards, fluttering them together with an angry snap. "He says a good many men have been killed in this room, or something like that. And he says he's goin' to be killed here too. I don't know what ails him. He's crazy, I shouldn't wonder."

Scully then looked for explanation to the cowboy, but the cowboy simply shrugged his shoulders.

"Kill you?" said Scully again to the Swede. "Kill you? Man, you're off your nut."

"Oh, I know," burst out the Swede. "I know what will happen. Yes, I'm crazy—yes. Yes, of course, I'm crazy—yes. But I know one thing—" There was a sort of sweat of misery and terror upon his face. "I know I won't get out of here alive."

The cowboy drew a deep breath, as if his mind was passing into the last stages of dissolution. "Well, I'm doggoned," he whispered to himself.

Scully wheeled suddenly and faced his son. "You've been troublin' this man!"

Johnnie's voice was loud with its burden of grievance. "Why, good Gawd, I ain't done nothin' to 'im."

The Swede broke in. "Gentlemen, do not disturb yourselves. I will leave this house. I will go away, because"—he accused them dramatically with his glance—"because I do not want to be killed."

336

Scully was furious with his son. "Will you tell me what is the matter, you young divil? What's the matter, anyhow? Speak out!"

"Blame it!" cried Johnnie in despair, "don't I tell you I don't know? He—he says we want to kill him, and that's all I know. I can't tell what ails him."

The Swede continued to repeat: "Never mind, Mr. Scully; never mind. I will leave this house. I will go away, because I do not wish to be killed. Yes, of course, I am crazy—yes. But I know one thing! I will go away. I will leave this house. Never mind, Mr. Scully; never mind. I will go away."

"You will not go 'way," said Scully. "You will not go 'way until I hear the reason of this business. If anybody has troubled you I will take care of him. This is my house. You are under my roof, and I will not allow any peaceable man to be troubled here." He cast a terrible eye upon Johnnie, the cowboy, and the Easterner.

"Never mind, Mr. Scully; never mind. I will go away. I do not wish to be killed." The Swede moved toward the door which opened upon the stairs. It was evidently his intention to go at once for his baggage.

"No, no," shouted Scully peremptorily; but the white-faced man slid by him and disappeared. "Now," said Scully severely, "what does this mane?"

Johnnie and the cowboy cried together: "Why, we didn't do nothin' to 'im!"

Scully's eyes were cold. "No," he said, "you didn't?"

Johnnie swore a deep oath. "Why, this is the wildest loon I ever see. We didn't do nothin' at all. We were jest sittin' here playin' cards, and he—"

The father suddenly spoke to the Easterner. "Mr. Blanc," he asked, "what has these boys been doin'?"

The Easterner reflected again. "I didn't see anything wrong at all," he said at last, slowly.

Scully began to howl, "But what does it mane?" He stared ferociously at his son. "I have a mind to lather you for this, me boy."

Johnnie was frantic. "Well, what have I done?" he bawled at his father.

III

"I think you are tongue-tied," said Scully to his son, the cowboy, and the Easterner; and at the end of this scornful sentence he left the room.

Upstairs the Swede was swiftly fastening the straps of his great valise. Once his back happened to be half-turned to the door, and, hearing a noise there, he wheeled and sprang up, uttering a loud cry. Scully's wrinkled visage showed grimly in the light of the small lamp he carried. This yellow effulgence, streaming upward, coloured only his prominent features, and left his eyes, for instance, in mysterious shadow. He resembled a murderer.

"Man! man!" he exclaimed, "have you gone daffy?"

"Oh, no! Oh, no!" rejoined the other. "There are people in this world who know pretty nearly as much as you do—understand?"

For a moment they stood gazing at each other. Upon the Swede's deathly pale cheeks were two spots brightly crimson and sharply edged, as if they had been carefully painted. Scully placed the light on the table and sat himself on the edge of the bed. He spoke ruminatively. "By cracky, I never heard of such a thing in my life. It's a complete muddle. I can't, for the soul of me, think how you ever got this idea into your head." Presently he lifted his eyes and asked: "And did you sure think they were going to kill you?"

The Swede scanned the old man as if he wished to see into his mind. "I did," he said at last. He obviously suspected that this answer might precipitate an outbreak. As he pulled on a strap his whole arm shook, the elbow wavering like a bit of paper.

Scully banged his hand impressively on the footboard of the bed. "Why, man, we're goin' to have a line of ilictric street-cars in this town next spring."

"A line of electric street-cars," repeated the Swede, stupidly.

"And," said Scully, "there's a new railroad goin' to be built down from Broken Arm to here. Not to mintion the four churches and the smashin' big brick school-house. Then there's the big factory, too. Why, in two years Romper'll be a met-tro-*pol*-is."

Having finished the preparation of his baggage, the Swede straightened himself. "Mr. Scully," he said, with sudden hardihood, "how much do I owe you?"

"You don't owe me anythin'," said the old man, angrily.

"Yes, I do," retorted the Swede. He took seventy-five cents from his pocket and tendered it to Scully; but the latter snapped his fingers in a disdainful refusal. However, it happened that they both stood gazing in a strange fashion at three silver pieces on the Swede's open palm.

"I'll not take your money," said Scully at last. "Not after what's been goin' on here." Then a plan seemed to strike him. "Here," he cried, picking up his lamp and moving toward the door. "Here! Come with me a minute."

"No," said the Swede, in overwhelming alarm.

"Yes," urged the old man. "Come on! I want you to come and see a picter—just across the hall—in my room."

The Swede must have concluded that his hour was come. His jaw dropped and his teeth showed like a dead man's. He ultimately followed Scully across the corridor, but he had the step of one hung in chains.

Scully flashed his light high on the wall of his own chamber. There was revealed a ridiculous photograph of a little girl. She was leaning against a balustrade of gorgeous decoration, and the formidable bang to her hair was prominent. The figure was as graceful as an upright sled-stake, and, withal, it was of the hue of lead. "There," said Scully, tenderly, "that's the picter of my little girl that died. Her name was Carrie. She had the purtiest hair you ever saw! I was that fond of her, she—"

338

Turning then, he saw that the Swede was not contemplating the picture at all, but, instead, was keeping keen watch on the gloom in the rear.

"Look, man!" cried Scully, heartily. "That's the picter of my little gal that died. Her name was Carrie. And then here's the picter of my oldest boy, Michael. He's a lawyer in Lincoln, and doin' well. I gave that boy a grand eddication and I'm glad for it now. He's a fine boy. Look at 'im now. Ain't he bold as blazes, him there in Lincoln, an honoured an' rispicted gintleman! An honoured and rispicted gintleman," concluded Scully with a flourish. And, so saying, he smote the Swede jovially on the back.

The Swede faintly smiled.

"Now," said the old man, "there's only one more thing." He dropped suddenly to the floor and thrust his head beneath the bed. The Swede could hear his muffled voice. "I'd keep it under me piller if it wasn't for that boy Johnnie. Then there's the old woman— Where is it now? I never put it twice in the same place. Ah, now come out with you!"

Presently he backed clumsily from under the bed, dragging with him an old coat rolled into a bundle. "I've fetched him," he muttered. Kneeling on the floor, he unrolled the coat and extracted from its heart a large yellow-brown whisky-bottle.

His first maneuvre was to hold the bottle up to the light. Reassured, apparently, that nobody had been tampering with it, he thrust it with a generous movement toward the Swede.

The weak-kneed Swede was about to eagerly clutch this element of strength, but he suddenly jerked his hand away and cast a look of horror upon Scully.

"Drink," said the old man affectionately. He had risen to his feet, and now stood facing the Swede.

There was a silence. Then again Scully said: "Drink!"

The Swede laughed wildly. He grabbed the bottle, put it to his mouth; and as his lips curled absurdly around the opening and his throat worked, he kept his glance, burning with hatred, upon the old man's face.

IV

After the departure of Scully the three men, with the cardboard still upon their knees, preserved for a long time an astounded silence. Then Johnnie said: "That's the doddangedest Swede I ever see."

"He ain't no Swede," said the cowboy, scornfully.

"Well, what is he then?" cried Johnnie. "What is he, then?"

"It's my opinion," replied the cowboy deliberately, "he's some kind of a Dutchman." It was a venerable custom of the country to entitle as Swedes all light-haired men who spoke with a heavy tongue. In consequence the idea of the cowboy was not without its daring. "Yes, sir," he repeated. "It's my opinion this feller is some kind of a Dutchman."

"Well, he says he's a Swede, anyhow," muttered Johnnie, sulkily. He turned to the Easterner: "What do you think, Mr. Blanc?"

"Oh, I don't know," replied the Easterner.

"Well, what do you think makes him act that way?" asked the cowboy.

"Why, he's frightened." The Easterner knocked his pipe against a rim of the stove. "He's clear frightened out of his boots."

"What at?" cried Johnnie and the cowboy together.

The Easterner reflected over his answer.

"What at?" cried the others again.

"Oh, I don't know, but it seems to me this man has been reading dime novels, and he thinks he's right out in the middle of it—the shootin' and stabbin' and all."

"But," said the cowboy, deeply scandalized, "this ain't Wyoming, ner none of them places. This is Nebrasker."

"Yes," added Johnnie, "an' why don't he wait till he gits *out West?*"

The travelled Easterner laughed. "It isn't different there even—not in these days. But he thinks he's right in the middle of hell."

Johnnie and the cowboy mused long.

"It's awful funny," remarked Johnnie at last.

"Yes," said the cowboy. "This is a queer game. I hope we don't git snowed in, because then we'd have to stand this here man bein' around with us all the time. That wouldn't be no good."

"I wish pop would throw him out," said Johnnie.

Presently they heard a loud stamping on the stairs, accompanied by ringing jokes in the voice of old Scully, and laughter, evidently from the Swede. The men around the stove stared vacantly at each other. "Gosh!" said the cowboy. The door flew open, and old Scully, flushed and anecdotal, came into the room. He was jabbering at the Swede, who followed him, laughing bravely. It was the entry of two roisterers from a banquet hall.

"Come now," said Scully sharply to the three seated men, "move up and give us a chance at the stove." The cowboy and the Easterner obediently sidled their chairs to make room for the new-comers. Johnnie, however, simply arranged himself in a more indolent attitude, and then remained motionless.

"Come! Git over, there," said Scully.

"Plenty of room on the other side of the stove," said Johnnie.

"Do you think we want to sit in the draught?" roared the father.

But the Swede here interposed with a grandeur of confidence. "No, no. Let the boy sit where he likes," he cried in a bullying voice to the father.

"All right! All right!" said Scully, deferentially. The cowboy and the Easterner exchanged glances of wonder.

The five chairs were formed in a crescent about one side of the stove. The Swede began to talk; he talked arrogantly, profanely, angrily. Johnnie, the cowboy, and the Easterner maintained a morose silence, while old

Scully appeared to be receptive and eager, breaking in constantly with sympathetic ejaculations.

Finally the Swede announced that he was thirsty. He moved in his chair, and said that he would go for a drink of water.

"I'll git it for you," cried Scully at once.

"No," said the Swede, contemptuously. "I'll get it for myself." He arose and stalked with the air of an owner off into the executive parts of the hotel.

As soon as the Swede was out of hearing Scully sprang to his feet and whispered intensely to the others: "Upstairs he thought I was tryin' to poison 'im."

"Say," said Johnnie, "this makes me sick. Why don't you throw 'im out in the snow?"

"Why, he's all right now," declared Scully. "It was only that he was from the East, and he thought this was a tough place. That's all. He's all right now."

The cowboy looked with admiration upon the Easterner. "You were straight," he said. "You were on to that there Dutchman."

"Well," said Johnnie to his father, "he may be all right now, but I don't see it. Other time he was scared, but now he's too fresh."

Scully's speech was always a combination of Irish brogue and idiom, Western twang and idiom, and scraps of curiously formal diction taken from the story-books and newspapers. He now hurled a strange mass of language at the head of his son. "What do I keep? What do I keep? What do I keep?" he demanded, in a voice of thunder. He slapped his knee impressively, to indicate that he himself was going to make reply, and that all should heed. "I keep a hotel," he shouted. "A hotel, do you mind? A guest under my roof has sacred privileges. He is to be intimidated by none. Not one word shall he hear that would prijudice him in favour of goin' away. I'll not have it. There's no place in this here town where they can say they iver took in a guest of mine because he was afraid to stay here." He wheeled suddenly upon the cowboy and the Easterner. "Am I right?"

"Yes, Mr. Scully," said the cowboy, "I think you're right."

"Yes, Mr. Scully," said the Easterner, "I think you're right."

v

At six-o'clock supper, the Swede fizzed like a firewheel. He sometimes seemed on the point of bursting into riotous song, and in all his madness he was encouraged by old Scully. The Easterner was encased in reserve; the cowboy sat in wide-mouthed amazement, forgetting to eat, while Johnnie wrathily demolished great plates of food. The daughters of the house, when they were obliged to replenish the biscuits, approached as warily as Indians, and, having succeeded in their purpose, fled with ill-concealed trepidation. The Swede domineered the whole feast, and he gave it the appearance of a cruel bacchanal. He seemed to have grown suddenly taller; he gazed, brutally disdainful, into every face. His voice rang through the room. Once when he jabbed out harpoon-fashion with his fork to pinion a biscuit, the weapon nearly impaled the hand of the Easterner, which had been stretched quietly out for the same biscuit.

After supper, as the men filed toward the other room, the Swede smote Scully ruthlessly on the shoulder. "Well, old boy, that was a good, square meal." Johnnie looked hopefully at his father; he knew that shoulder was tender from an old fall; and, indeed, it appeared for a moment as if Scully was going to flame out over the matter, but in the end he smiled a sickly smile and remained silent. The others understood from his manner that he was admitting his responsibility for the Swede's new view-point.

Johnnie, however, addressed his parent in an aside. "Why don't you license somebody to kick you downstairs?" Scully scowled darkly by way of reply.

When they were gathered about the stove, the Swede insisted on another game of High-Five. Scully gently deprecated the plan at first, but the Swede turned a wolfish glare upon him. The old man subsided, and the Swede canvassed the others. In his tone there was always a great threat. The cowboy and the Easterner both remarked indifferently that they would play. Scully said that he would presently have to go to meet the 6.58 train, and so the Swede turned menacingly upon Johnnie. For a moment their glances crossed like blades, and then Johnnie smiled and said, "Yes, I'll play."

They formed a square, with the little board on their knees. The Easterner and the Swede were again partners. As the play went on, it was noticeable that the cowboy was not board-whacking as usual. Meanwhile, Scully, near the lamp, had put on his spectacles and, with an appearance curiously like an old priest, was reading a newspaper. In time he went out to meet the 6.58 train, and, despite his precautions, a gust of polar wind whirled into the room as he opened the door. Besides scattering the cards, it chilled the players to the marrow. The Swede cursed frightfully. When Scully returned, his entrance disturbed a cosy and friendly scene. The Swede again cursed. But presently they were once more intent, their heads bent forward and their hands moving swiftly. The Swede had adopted the fashion of board-whacking.

Scully took up his paper and for a long time remained immersed in matters which were extraordinarily remote from him. The lamp burned badly, and once he stopped to adjust the wick. The newspaper, as he turned from page to page, rustled with a slow and comfortable sound. Then suddenly he heard three terrible words: "You are cheatin'!"

Such scenes often prove that there can be little of dramatic import in environment. Any room can present a tragic front; any room can be comic. This little den was now hideous as a torture-chamber. The new faces of the men themselves had changed it upon the instant. The Swede held a huge

342

fist in front of Johnnie's face, while the latter looked steadily over it into the blazing orbs of his accuser. The Easterner had grown pallid; the cowboy's jaw had dropped in that expression of bovine amazement which was one of his important mannerisms. After the three words, the first sound in the room was made by Scully's paper as it floated forgotten to his feet. His spectacles had also fallen from his nose, but by a clutch he had saved them in air. His hand, grasping the spectacles, now remained poised awkwardly and near his shoulder. He stared at the card-players.

Probably the silence was while a second elapsed. Then, if the floor had been suddenly twitched out from under the men they could not have moved quicker. The five had projected themselves headlong toward a common point. It happened that Johnnie, in rising to hurl himself upon the Swede, had stumbled slightly because of his curiously instinctive care for the cards and the board. The loss of the moment allowed time for the arrival of Scully, and also allowed the cowboy time to give the Swede a great push which sent him staggering back. The men found tongue together, and hoarse shouts of rage, appeal, or fear burst from every throat. The cowboy pushed and jostled feverishly at the Swede, and the Easterner and Scully clung wildly to Johnnie; but through the smoky air, above the swaying bodies of the peace-compellers, the eyes of the two warriors ever sought each other in glances of challenge that were at once hot and steely.

Of course the board had been overturned, and now the whole company of cards was scattered over the floor, where the boots of the men trampled the fat and painted kings and queens as they gazed with their silly eyes at the war that was waging above them.

Scully's voice was dominating the yells. "Stop now! Stop, I say! Stop, now—"

Johnnie, as he struggled to burst through the rank formed by Scully and the Easterner, was crying, "Well, he says I cheated! He says I cheated! I won't allow no man to say I cheated! If he says I cheated, he's a —— ——!"

The cowboy was telling the Swede, "Quit, now! Quit, d'ye hear—"

The screams of the Swede never ceased: "He did cheat! I saw him! I saw him—"

As for the Easterner, he was importuning in a voice that was not heeded: "Wait a moment, can't you? Oh, wait a moment. What's the good of a fight over a game of cards? Wait a moment—"

In this tumult no complete sentences were clear. "Cheat"—"Quit"—"He says"—these fragments pierced the uproar and rang out sharply. It was remarkable that, whereas Scully undoubtedly made the most noise, he was the least heard of any of the riotous band.

Then suddenly there was a great cessation. It was as if each man had paused for breath; and although the room was still lighted with the anger of men, it could be seen that there was no danger of immediate conflict, and at once Johnnie, shouldering his way forward, almost succeeded in confronting the Swede. "What did you say I cheated for? What did you say I cheated for? I don't cheat, and I won't let no man say I do!"

The Swede said, "I saw you! I saw you!"

"Well," cried Johnnie, "I'll fight any man what says I cheat!"

"No you won't," said the cowboy. "Not here."

"Ah, be still, can't you?" said Scully, coming between them.

The quiet was sufficient to allow the Easterner's voice to be heard. He was repeating, "Oh, wait a moment, can't you? What's the good of a fight over a game of cards? Wait a moment!"

Johnnie, his red face appearing above his father's shoulder, hailed the Swede again. "Did you say I cheated?"

The Swede showed his teeth. "Yes."

"Then," said Johnnie, "we must fight."

"Yes, fight," roared the Swede. He was like a demoniac. "Yes, fight! I'll show you what kind of a man I am! Maybe you think I can't fight! I'll show you, you skin, you card-sharp! Yes, you cheated! You cheated! You cheated!"

"Well, let's go at it, then, mister," said Johnnie, coolly.

The cowboy's brow was beaded with sweat from his efforts in intercepting all sorts of raids. He turned in despair to Scully. "What are you goin' to do now?"

A change had come over the Celtic visage of the old man. He now seemed all eagerness; his eyes glowed.

"We'll let them fight," he answered, stalwartly. "I can't put up with it any longer. I've stood this damned Swede till I'm sick. We'll let them fight."

VI

The men prepared to go out of doors. The Easterner was so nervous that he had great difficulty in getting his arms into the sleeves of his new leather coat. As the cowboy drew his fur cap down over his ears his hands trembled. In fact, Johnnie and old Scully were the only ones who displayed no agitation. These preliminaries were conducted without words.

Scully threw open the door. "Well, come on," he said. Instantly a terrific wind caused the flame of the lamp to struggle in its wick, while a puff of black smoke sprang up from the chimney-top. The stove was in mid-current of the blast, and its voice swelled to equal the roar of the storm. Some of the scarred and bedabbed cards were caught up from the floor and dashed helplessly against the farther wall. The men lowered their heads and plunged into the tempest as into a sea.

No snow was falling, but great whirls and clouds of flakes, swept up from the ground by the frantic winds, were streaming southward with the speed of bullets. The covered land was blue with the sheen of an unearthly satin, and there was no other hue save where, at the low, black railway station—which seemed incredibly distant—one light gleamed like a tiny jewel. As the men floundered into a thigh-deep drift, it was known that the Swede was bawling out something. Scully went to him, put a hand on his shoulder, and projected an ear. "What's that you say?" he shouted.

"I say," bawled the Swede again, "I won't stand much show against this gang. I know you'll all pitch in on me."

Scully smote him reproachfully on the arm. "Tut, man!" he yelled. The wind tore the words from Scully's lips and scattered them far alee.

"You are all a gang of—" boomed the Swede, but the storm also seized the remainder of this sentence.

Immediately turning their backs upon the wind, the men had swung around a corner to the sheltered side of the hotel. It was the function of the little house to preserve here, amid this great devastation of snow, an irregular V-shape of heavily encrusted grass, which crackled beneath the feet. One could imagine the great drifts piled against the windward side. When the party reached the comparative peace of this spot it was found that the Swede was still bellowing.

"Oh, I know what kind of a thing this is! I know you'll all pitch on me. I can lick you all!"

Scully turned upon him panther-fashion. "You'll not have to whip all of us. You'll have to whip my son Johnnie. An' the man what troubles you durin' that time will have me to dale with."

The arrangements were swiftly made. The two men faced each other, obedient to the harsh commands of Scully, whose face, in the subtly luminous gloom, could be seen set in the austere impersonal lines that are pictured on the countenances of the Roman veterans. The Easterner's teeth were chattering, and he was hopping up and down like a mechanical toy. The cowboy stood rock-like.

The contestants had not stripped of any clothing. Each was in his ordinary attire. Their fists were up, and they eyed each other in a calm that had the elements of leonine cruelty in it.

During this pause, the Easterner's mind, like a film, took lasting impressions of the three men—the iron-nerved master of the ceremony; the Swede, pale, motionless, terrible; and Johnnie, serene yet ferocious, brutish yet heroic. The entire prelude had in it a tragedy greater than the tragedy of action and this aspect was accentuated by the long, mellow cry of the blizzard, as it sped the tumbling and wailing flakes into the black abyss of the south.

"Now!" said Scully.

The two combatants leaped forward and crashed together like bullocks. There was heard the cushioned sound of blows, and of a curse squeezing out from between the tight teeth of one.

As for the spectators, the Easterner's pent-up breath exploded from him with a pop of relief, absolute relief from the tension of the preliminaries. The cowboy bounded into the air with a yowl. Scully was immovable as from supreme amazement and fear at the fury of the fight which he himself had permitted and arranged.

For a time the encounter in the darkness was such a perplexity of flying arms that it presented no more detail than would a swiftly revolving wheel. Occasionally a face, as if illumined by a flash of light, would shine out, ghastly and marked with pink spots. A moment later, the men might have been known as shadows, if it were not for the involuntary utterance of oaths that came from them in whispers.

Suddenly a holocaust of warlike desire caught the cowboy, and he bolted forward with the speed of a broncho. "Go it, Johnnie! Kill him! Kill him!"

Scully confronted him. "Kape back," he said; and by his glance the cowboy could tell that this man was Johnnie's father.

To the Easterner there was a monotony of unchangeable fighting that was an abomination. This confused mingling was eternal to his sense, which was concentrated in a longing for the end, the priceless end. Once the fighters lurched near him, and as he scrambled hastily backward he heard them breathe like men on the rack.

"Kill him, Johnnie! Kill him! Kill him!" The cowboy's face was contorted like one of those agony masks in museums.

"Keep still," said Scully, icily.

Then there was a sudden loud grunt, incomplete, cut short, and Johnnie's body swung away from the Swede and fell with sickening heaviness to the grass. The cowboy was barely in time to prevent the mad Swede from flinging himself upon his prone adversary. "No, you don't," said the cowboy, interposing an arm. "Wait a second."

Scully was at his son's side. "Johnnie! Johnnie! me boy!" His voice had a quality of melancholy tenderness. "Johnnie! Johnnie! Can you go on with it?" He looked anxiously down into the bloody, pulpy face of his son.

There was a moment of silence, and then Johnnie answered in his ordinary voice, "Yes, I—it—yes."

Assisted by his father he struggled to his feet. "Wait a bit now 'til you git your wind," said the old man.

A few paces away the cowboy was lecturing the Swede. "No you don't! Wait a second!"

The Easterner was plucking at Scully's sleeve. "Oh, this is enough," he pleaded. "This is enough! Let it go as it stands. This is enough!"

"Bill," said Scully, "git out of the road." The cowboy stepped aside. "Now." The combatants were actuated by a new caution as they advanced toward collision. They glared at each other, and then the Swede aimed a lightning blow that carried with it his entire weight. Johnnie was evidently half stupid from weakness, but he miraculously dodged, and his fist sent the overbalanced Swede sprawling.

The cowboy, Scully, and the Easterner burst into a cheer that was like a chorus of triumphant soldiery, but before its conclusion the Swede had scuffled agilely to his feet and come in berserk abandon at his foe. There was another perplexity of flying arms, and Johnnie's body again swung away and fell, even as a bundle might fall from a roof. The Swede instantly staggered to a little wind-waved tree and leaned upon it, breathing like an engine, while his savage and flame-lit eyes roamed from face to face as the men bent over Johnnie. There was a splendour of isolation in his situation at this time which the Easterner felt once when, lifting his eyes from the man on the ground, he beheld that mysterious and lonely figure, waiting.

"Are you any good yet, Johnnie?" asked Scully in a broken voice.

The son gasped and opened his eyes languidly. After a moment he answered, "No—I ain't—any good—any—more." Then, from shame and bodily ill, he began to weep, the tears furrowing down through the blood-stains on his face. "He was too—too—too heavy for me."

Scully straightened and addressed the waiting figure. "Stranger," he said, evenly, "it's all up with our side." Then his voice changed into that vibrant huskiness which is commonly the tone of the most simple and deadly announcements. "Johnnie is whipped."

Without replying, the victor moved off on the route to the front door of the hotel.

The cowboy was formulating new and unspellable blasphemies. The Easterner was startled to find that they were out in a wind that seemed to come direct from the shadowed arctic floes. He heard again the wail of the snow as it was flung to its grave in the south. He knew now that all this time the cold had been sinking into him deeper and deeper, and he wondered that he had not perished. He felt indifferent to the condition of the vanquished man.

"Johnnie, can you walk?" asked Scully.

"Did I hurt—hurt him any?" asked the son.

"Can you walk, boy? Can you walk?"

Johnnie's voice was suddenly strong. There was a robust impatience in it. "I asked you whether I hurt him any!"

"Yes, yes, Johnnie," answered the cowboy, consolingly; "he's hurt a good deal."

They raised him from the ground, and as soon as he was on his feet he went tottering off, rebuffing all attempts at assistance. When the party rounded the corner they were fairly blinded by the pelting of the snow. It burned their faces like fire. The cowboy carried Johnnie through the drift to the door. As they entered, some cards again rose from the floor and beat against the wall.

The Easterner rushed to the stove. He was so profoundly chilled that he almost dared to embrace the glowing iron. The Swede was not in the room. Johnnie sank into a chair and, folding his arms on his knees, buried his face in them. Scully, warming one foot and then the other at a rim of the stove, muttered to himself with Celtic mournfulness. The cowboy had removed his fur cap, and with a dazed and rueful air he was running one hand through his tousled locks. From overhead they could hear the creaking of boards, as the Swede tramped here and there in his room.

The sad quiet was broken by the sudden flinging open of a door that led toward the kitchen. It was instantly followed by an inrush of women. They precipitated themselves upon Johnnie amid a chorus of lamentation. Before they carried their prey off to the kitchen, there to be bathed and harangued with that mixture of sympathy and abuse which is a feat of their sex, the mother straightened herself and fixed old Scully with an eye of stern reproach. "Shame be upon you, Patrick Scully!" she cried. "Your own son, too. Shame be upon you!"

"There, now! Be quiet, now!" said the old man, weakly.

"Shame be upon you, Patrick Scully!" The girls, rallying to this slogan, sniffed disdainfully in the direction of those trembling accomplices, the cowboy and the Easterner. Presently they bore Johnnie away, and left the three men to dismal reflection.

VII

"I'd like to fight this here Dutchman myself," said the cowboy, breaking a long silence.

Scully wagged his head sadly. "No, that wouldn't do. It wouldn't be right. It wouldn't be right."

"Well, why wouldn't it?" argued the cowboy. "I don't see no harm in it."

"No," answered Scully, with mournful heroism. "It wouldn't be right. It was Johnnie's fight, and now we mustn't whip the man just because he whipped Johnnie."

"Yes, that's true enough," said the cowboy; "but—he better not get fresh with me, because I couldn't stand no more of it."

"You'll not say a word to him," commanded Scully, and even then they heard the tread of the Swede on the stairs. His entrance was made theatric. He swept the door back with a bang and swaggered to the middle of the room. No one looked at him. "Well," he cried, insolently, at Scully, "I s'pose you'll tell me now how much I owe you?"

The old man remained stolid. "You don't owe me nothin'."

"Huh!" said the Swede, "huh! Don't owe 'im nothin'."

The cowboy addressed the Swede. "Stranger, I don't see how you come to be so gay around here."

Old Scully was instantly alert. "Stop!" he shouted, holding his hand forth, fingers upward. "Bill, you shut up!"

The cowboy spat carelessly into the sawdust-box. "I didn't say a word, did I?" he asked.

"Mr. Scully," called the Swede, "how much do I owe you?" It was seen that he was attired for departure, and that he had his valise in his hand.

348

"You don't owe me nothin'," repeated Scully in the same imperturbable way.

"Huh!" said the Swede. "I guess you're right. I guess if it was any way at all, you'd owe me somethin'. That's what I guess." He turned to the cowboy. " 'Kill him! Kill him! Kill him!' " he mimicked, and then guffawed victoriously. " 'Kill him!' " He was convulsed with ironical humour.

But he might have been jeering the dead. The three men were immovable and silent, staring with glassy eyes at the stove.

The Swede opened the door and passed into the storm, giving one derisive glance backward at the still group.

As soon as the door was closed, Scully and the cowboy leaped to their feet and began to curse. They trampled to and fro, waving their arms and smashing into the air with their fists. "Oh, but that was a hard minute!" wailed Scully. "That was a hard minute! Him there leerin' and scoffin'! One bang at his nose was worth forty dollars to me that minute! How did you stand it, Bill?"

"How did I stand it?" cried the cowboy in quivering voice. "How did I stand it? Oh!"

The old man burst into sudden brogue. "I'd loike to take that Swade," he wailed, "and hould 'im down on a shtone flure and bate 'im to a jelly wid a shtick!"

The cowboy groaned in sympathy. "I'd like to git him by the neck and ha-ammer him"—he brought his hand down on a chair with a noise like a pistol-shot—"hammer that there Dutchman until he couldn't tell himself from a dead coyote!"

"I'd bate 'im until he—"

"I'd show *him* some things—"

And then together they raised a yearning, fanatic cry—"Oh-o-oh! if we only could—"

"Yes!"

"Yes!"

"And then I'd—"

"O-o-oh!"

VIII

The Swede, tightly gripping his valise, tacked across the face of the storm as if he carried sails. He was following a line of little naked, gasping trees which, he knew, must mark the way of the road. His face, fresh from the pounding of Johnnie's fists, felt more pleasure than pain in the wind and the driving snow. A number of square shapes loomed upon him finally, and he knew them as the houses of the main body of the town. He found a street and made travel along it, leaning heavily upon the wind whenever, at a corner, a terrific blast caught him.

He might have been in a deserted village. We picture the world as thick with conquering and elate humanity, but here, with the bugles of the tempest pealing, it was hard to imagine a peopled earth. One viewed the existence of man then as a marvel, and conceded a glamour of wonder to these lice which were caused to cling to a whirling, fire-smitten, ice-locked, disease-stricken, space-lost bulb. The conceit of man was explained by this storm to be the very engine of life. One was a coxcomb not to die in it. However, the Swede found a saloon.

In front of it an indomitable red light was burning, and the snowflakes were made blood-colour as they flew through the circumscribed territory of the lamp's shining. The Swede pushed open the door of the saloon and entered. A sanded expanse was before him, and at the end of it four men sat about a table drinking. Down one side of the room extended a radiant bar, and its guardian was leaning upon his elbows listening to the talk of the men at the table. The Swede dropped his valise upon the floor and, smiling fraternally upon the barkeeper, said, "Gimmie some whisky, will you?" The man placed a bottle, a whisky-glass and a glass of ice-thick water upon the bar. The Swede poured himself an abnormal portion of whisky and drank it in three gulps. "Pretty bad night," remarked the bartender, indifferently. He was making the pretension of blindness which is usually a distinction of his class; but it could have been seen that he was furtively studying the half-erased blood-stains on the face of the Swede. "Bad night," he said again.

"Oh, it's good enough for me," replied the Swede, hardily, as he poured himself some more whisky. The barkeep took his coin and maneuvered it through its reception by the highly nickelled cash-machine. A bell rang; a card labelled "20 cts." had appeared.

"No," continued the Swede, "this isn't too bad weather. It's good enough for me."

"So," murmured the barkeep languidly.

The copious drams made the Swede's eyes swim, and he breathed a trifle heavier. "Yes, I like this weather. I like it. It suits me." It was apparently his design to impart a deep significance to these words.

"So?" murmured the bartender again. He turned to gaze dreamily at the scroll-like birds and bird-like scrolls which had been drawn with soap upon the mirrors in back of the bar.

"Well, I guess I'll take another drink," said the Swede presently. "Have something?"

"No, thanks; I'm not drinkin'," answered the bartender. Afterwards he asked, "How did you hurt your face?"

The Swede immediately began to boast loudly. "Why, in a fight. I thumped the soul out of a man down there at Scully's hotel."

The interest of the four men at the table was at last aroused.

"Who was it?" said one.

"Johnnie Scully," blustered the Swede. "Son of the man what runs it. He will be pretty near dead for some weeks, I can tell you. I made a nice

350

thing of him, I did. He couldn't get up. They carried him in the house. Have a drink?"

Instantly the men in some subtle way encased themselves in reserve. "No, thanks," said one. The group was of curious formation. Two were prominent local business men; one was the district attorney; and one was a professional gambler of the kind known as "square." But a scrutiny of the group would not have enabled an observer to pick the gambler from the men of more reputable pursuits. He was, in fact, a man so delicate in manner, when among people of fair class, and so judicious in his choice of victims, that in the strictly masculine part of the town's life he had come to be explicity trusted and admired. People called him a thorough-bred. The fear and contempt with which his craft was regarded were un-doubtedly the reason why his quiet dignity shone conspicuous above the quiet dignity of men who might be merely hatters, or grocery clerks. Be-yond an occasional unwary traveller who came by rail, this gambler was supposed to prey solely upon reckless and senile farmers, who, when flush with good crops, drove into town in all the pride and confidence of an absolutely invulnerable stupidity. Hearing at times in circuitous fashion of the despoilment of such a farmer, the important men of Romper invariably laughed in contempt of the victim, and if they thought of the wolf at all, it was with a kind of pride at the knowledge that he would never dare think of attacking their wisdom and courage. Besides, it was popular that this gambler had a real wife and two real children in a neat cottage in the suburb, where he led an exemplary home life; and when any one even suggested a discrepancy in his character, the crowd im-mediately vociferated descriptions of this virtuous family circle. Then men who led exemplary home lives, all subsided in a bunch, remarking that there was nothing more to be said.

However, when a restriction was placed upon him—as, for instance, when a strong clique of members of the new Pollywog Club refused to permit him, even as a spectator, to appear in the rooms of the organization —the candour and gentleness with which he accepted the judgment dis-armed many of his foes and made his friends more desperately partisan. He invariably distinguished between himself and a respectable Romper man so quickly and frankly that his manner actually appeared to be a continual broadcast compliment.

And one must not forget to declare the fundamental fact of his entire position in Romper. It is irrefutable that in all affairs outside his business, in all matters that occur eternally and commonly between man and man, this thieving card-player was so generous, so just, so moral, that, in a contest, he could have put to flight the consciences of nine tenths of the citizens of Romper.

And so it happened that he was seated in this saloon with the two prominent local merchants and the district attorney.

The Swede continued to drink raw whisky, meanwhile babbling at the barkeep and trying to induce him to indulge in potations. "Come on. Have a drink. Come on. What—no? Well, have a little one. By gawd, I've whipped a man to-night, and I want to celebrate. I whipped him good, too. Gentlemen," the Swede cried to the men at the table, "have a drink?"

"Ssh!" said the barkeeper.

The group at the table, although furtively attentive, had been pretending to be deep in talk, but now a man lifted his eyes toward the Swede and said, shortly. "Thanks. We don't want any more."

At this reply the Swede ruffled out his chest like a rooster. "Well," he exploded, "it seems I can't get anybody to drink with me in this town. Seems so, don't it? Well!"

"Ssh!" said the barkeeper.

"Say," snarled the Swede, "don't you try to shut me up. I won't have it. I'm a gentleman, and I want people to drink with me. And I want 'em to drink with me now. Now—do you understand?" He rapped the bar with his knuckles.

Years of experience had calloused the bartender. He merely grew sulky. "I hear you," he answered.

"Well," cried the Swede, "listen hard then. See those men over there? Well, they're going to drink with me, and don't you forget it. Now you watch."

"Hi!" yelled the barkeeper, "this won't do!"

"Why won't it?" demanded the Swede. He stalked over to the table, and by chance laid his hand upon the shoulder of the gambler. "How about this?" he asked wrathfully. "I asked you to drink with me."

The gambler simply twisted his head and spoke over his shoulder. "My friend, I don't know you."

"Oh, hell!" answered the Swede, "come and have a drink."

"Now, my boy," advised the gambler, kindly, "take your hand off my shoulder and go 'way and mind your own business." He was a little, slim man, and it seemed strange to hear him use this tone of heroic patronage to the burly Swede. The other men at the table said nothing.

"What! You won't drink with me, you little dude? I'll make you, then! I'll make you!" The Swede had grasped the gambler frenziedly at the throat, and was dragging him from his chair. The other men sprang up. The barkeeper dashed around the corner of his bar. There was a great tumult, and then was seen a long blade in the hand of the gambler. It shot forward, and a human body, this citadel of virtue, wisdom, power, was pierced as easily as if it had been a melon. The Swede fell with a cry of supreme astonishment.

The prominent merchants and the district attorney must have at once tumbled out of the place backward. The bartender found himself hanging limply to the arm of a chair and gazing into the eyes of a murderer.

"Henry," said the latter, as he wiped his knife on one of the towels that hung beneath the bar rail, "you tell 'em where to find me. I'll be home, waiting for 'em." Then he vanished. A moment afterward the barkeeper was in the street dinning through the storm for help and, moreover, companionship.

The corpse of the Swede, alone in the saloon, had its eyes fixed upon a dreadful legend that dwelt atop of the cash-machine: "This registers the amount of your purchase."

IX

Months later, the cowboy was frying pork over the stove of a little ranch near the Dakota line, when there was a quick thud of hoofs outside, and presently the Easterner entered with the letters and the papers.

"Well," said the Easterner at once, "the chap that killed the Swede has got three years. Wasn't much, was it?"

"He has? Three years?" The cowboy poised his pan of pork, while he ruminated upon the news. "Three years. That ain't much."

"No. It was a light sentence," replied the Easterner as he unbuckled his spurs. "Seems there was a good deal of sympathy for him in Romper."

"If the bartender had been any good," observed the cowboy, thoughtfully, "he would have gone in and cracked that there Dutchman on the head with a bottle in the beginnin' of it and stopped all this here murderin'."

"Yes, a thousand things might have happened," said the Easterner, tartly.

The cowboy returned his pan of pork to the fire, but his philosophy continued. "It's funny, ain't it? If he hadn't said Johnnie was cheatin' he'd be alive this minute. He was an awful fool. Game played for fun, too. Not for money. I believe he was crazy."

"I feel sorry for that gambler," said the Easterner.

"Oh, so do I," said the cowboy. "He don't deserve none of it for killin' who he did."

"The Swede might not have been killed if everything had been square."

"Might not have been killed?" exclaimed the cowboy. "Everythin' square? Why, when he said that Johnnie was cheatin' and acted like such a jackass? And then in the saloon he fairly walked up to git hurt?" With these arguments the cowboy browbeat the Easterner and reduced him to rage.

"You're a fool!" cried the Easterner, viciously. "You're a bigger jackass than the Swede by a million majority. Now let me tell you one thing. Let me tell you something. Listen! Johnnie *was* cheating!"

"Johnnie," said the cowboy, blankly. There was a minute of silence, and then he said, robustly, "Why, no. The game was only for fun."

"Fun or not," said the Easterner, "Johnnie was cheating. I saw him. I know it. I saw him. And I refused to stand up and be a man. I let the Swede fight it out alone. And you—you were simply puffing around the place and wanting to fight. And then old Scully himself! We are all in it!

This poor gambler isn't even a noun. He is kind of an adverb. Every sin is the result of a collaboration. We, five of us, have collaborated in the murder of this Swede. Usually there are from a dozen to forty women really involved in every murder, but in this case it seems to be only five men—you, I, Johnnie, old Scully; and that fool of an unfortunate gambler came merely as a culmination, the apex of a human movement, and gets all the punishment."

The cowboy, injured and rebellious, cried out blindly into this fog of mysterious theory: "Well, I didn't do anythin', did I?"

The Monster and Other Stories, 1899

GEORGE ADE

The New York Man Who Went Visiting

> *Ade, the Indiana country boy in the big city of Chicago, became a well-known satirist four years after he graduated from college. He especially enjoyed deflating the pompous, but always with the good nature of the* Fables *that led to his first fame.*

A New York man went to visit a Cousin in the Far West.

The name of the Town was Fostoria, Ohio.

When he came into Town he had his Watch-Chain on the outside of his Coat, and his Pink Spats were the first ever seen in Fostoria.

"Have you a Manicure Parlor in this Beastly Hole?" asked the New York Man, as they walked up from the Train.

"What's that?" asked the Cousin, stepping on his own Feet.

"Great Heavens!" exclaimed the New York Man, and was silent for several Moments.

At Dinner he called for Artichokes, and when told that there were none, he said, "Oh, very well," in a Tone of Chastened Resignation.

After Dinner he took the Family into the Parlor, and told the Members how much they would Enjoy going to Weber and Fields'. Seeing a Book on the Table, he sauntered up to It and said, "Ah, one of Dick Davis' Things." Later in the Evening he visited the only Club House in Town. The Local Editor of the Evening Paper was playing Pin-Pool with the Superintendent of the Trolley Line. When the New York Man came into the Room, they began to Tremble and fell down on their Shots.

The Manager of the Hub and Spoke Factory then asked the New York Man to have a Drink. The New York Man wondered if a Small Bottle was already cold. They said Yes, but it was a Lie. The Boy had to go out for it.

354

He found One that had been in the Window of the Turf Exchange since the Grand Opening, the Year after Natural Gas was discovered. The New York Man drank it, remarking that it was hardly as Dry as he usually got it at Martin's.

The Club Members looked at Him and said Nothing. They thought he meant Bradley-Martin's.

Next Day the New York Man was Interviewed by the Local Editor. He said the West had a Great Future. In the Evening he attended the Annual Dinner of the Bicycle Club, and went Home early because the Man sitting next to him put Ice in his Claret.

In due time he returned to New York, and Fostoria took off its White Shirt.

Some Weeks after that, the Cousin of the New York Man had an Opportunity to visit the Metropolis. He rode on an Extra Ticket with a Stockman who was shipping three Car-loads of Horses, and got a Free Ticket for every Car-load.

When the Cousin arrived at New York he went to the address, and found the New York Man at Dinner.

There was a Sheaf of Celery on the Table.

Opposite the New York Man sat a Chiropodist who drank.

At his right was a Large Woman in a Flowered Wrapper—she had been Weeping.

At his left was a Snake-Charmer from Huber's Museum.

The New York Man asked the Cousin to wait Outside, and then explained that he was stopping there Temporarily. That Evening they went to Proctor's, and stood during the Performance.

Moral: *A New York Man never begins to Cut Ice until he is west of Rahway.*

The Fable of the Parents Who Tinkered with the Offspring

A Married Couple possessed two Boys named Joseph and Clarence. Joseph was much the older. His Parents brought him up on a Plan of their Own. They would not permit him to play with other Boys for fear that he would soil himself, and learn to be Rude and Boisterous.

So they kept Him in the House, and his Mother read to him about Little Rollo, who never lied or cheated, and who grew up to be a Bank President. She seemed to think that a Bank President was above Reproach.

Little Joseph was kept away from the Public Schools, and had to Play Games in the Garret with two Spindly Little Girls. He learned Tatting and the Herring-Bone Stitch. When he was Ten Years of age he could play Chop-Sticks on the Piano; his Ears were Translucent, and his Front Teeth showed like those of a Gray Squirrel.

The other Boys used to make Faces at him over the Back Fence and call him "Sis."

In Due Time he went College, where he proved to be a Lobster. The Boys held him under the Pump the first Night. When he walked across the Campus, they would whistle, "I Don't Want to Play in Your Yard." He began to drink Manhattan Cocktails, and he smoked Hemp Cigarettes until he was Dotty. One Day he ran away with a Girl who waited on the Table at his Boarding House, and his Parents Cast him Off. At Present he has charge of the Cloak Room at a Dairy Lunch.

Seeing that the Home Training Experiment had been a Failure in the case of Joseph, the Parents decided to give Clarence a large Measure of Liberty, that he might become Accquainted with the Snares and Temptations of the World while he was Young, and thus be Prepared to side-step the Pitfalls when he was older. They sent him to the Public Schools; they allowed him to roam at large with other Kids, and stay out at Nights; they kept Liquor on the Sideboard.

Clarence stood in with the Toughest Push in Town, and thus became acquainted with the Snares and Temptations of the World. He learned to Chew Tobacco and Spit through his Teeth, shoot Craps and Rush the Can.

When his Father suggested that he enter some Business House, and become a Credit to the Family, he growled like a Boston Terrier, and told his Father to go Chase Himself.

At present, he is working the Shells with a Circus.

Moral: *It all depends.*

Fables in Slang, 1899

WILLA CATHER

The Sculptor's Funeral

A group of the townspeople stood on the station siding of a little Kansas town, awaiting the coming of the night train, which was already twenty minutes overdue. The snow had fallen thick over everything; in the pale starlight the line of bluffs across the wide, white meadows south of the town made soft, smoke-coloured curves against the clear sky. The men on the siding stood first on one foot and then on the other, their hands thrust deep into their trousers' pockets, their overcoats open, their shoulders screwed up with the cold; and they glanced from time to time towards the southeast, where the railroad track wound along the river shore. They conversed in low tones and moved about restlessly, seeming

356

uncertain as to what was expected of them. There was but one of the company who looked as if he knew exactly why he was there, and he kept conspicuously apart; walking to the far end of the platform, returning to the station door, then pacing up the track again, his chin sunk in the high collar of his overcoat, his burly shoulders drooping forward, his gait heavy and dogged. Presently he was approached by a tall, spare, grizzled man clad in a faded Grand Army suit, who shuffled out from the group and advanced with a certain deference, craning his neck forward until his back made the angle of a jack-knife three-quarters open.

"I reckon she's a-goin' to be pretty late again tonight, Jim," he remarked in a squeaky falsetto. "S'pose it's the snow?"

"I don't know," responded the other man with a shade of annoyance, speaking from out an astonishing cataract of red beard that grew fiercely and thickly in all directions.

The spare man shifted the quill toothpick he was chewing to the other side of his mouth. "It ain't likely that anybody from the East will come with the corpse, I s'pose," he went on reflectively.

"I don't know," responded the other, more curtly than before.

"It's too bad he didn't belong to some lodge or other. I like an order funeral myself. They seem more appropriate for people of some reputa-tion," the spare man continued, with an ingratiating concession in his shrill voice, as he carefully placed his toothpick in his vest pocket. He always carried the flag at the G.A.R. funerals in the town.

The heavy man turned on his heel, without replying, and walked up the siding. The spare man rejoined the uneasy group. "Jim's ez full ez a tick, ez ushel," he commented commiseratingly.

Just then a distant whistle sounded, and there was a shuffling of feet on the platform. A number of lanky boys, of all ages, appeared as sud-denly and slimily as eels wakened by the crack of thunder; some came from the waiting-room, where they had been warming themselves by the red stove, or half asleep on the slat benches; others uncoiled themselves from baggage trucks or slid out of express wagons. Two clambered down from the driver's seat of a hearse that stood backed up against the siding. They straightened their stooping shoulders and lifted their heads, and a flash of momentary animation kindled their dull eyes at that cold, vibrant scream, the world-wide call for men. It stirred them like the note of a trumpet; just as it had often stirred the man who was coming home tonight, in his boyhood.

The night express shot, red as a rocket, from out the eastward marsh lands and wound along the river shore under the long lines of shivering poplars that sentinelled the meadows, the escaping steam hanging in grey masses against the pale sky and blotting out the Milky Way. In a moment the red glare from the headlight streamed up the snow-covered track before the siding and glittered on the wet, black rails. The burly man with the dishevelled red beard walked swiftly up the platform toward the approaching train, uncovering his head as he went. The group of men behind him hesitated, glanced questioningly at one another, and awkwardly followed his example. The train stopped, and the crowd shuffled up to the express car just as the door was thrown open, the man in the G.A.R. suit thrusting his head forward with curiosity. The express messenger appeared in the doorway, accompanied by a young man in a long ulster and travelling cap.

"Are Mr. Merrick's friends here?" inquired the young man.

The group on the platform swayed uneasily. Philip Phelps, the banker, responded with dignity: "We have come to take charge of the body. Mr. Merrick's father is very feeble and can't be about."

"Send the agent out here," growled the express messenger, "and tell the operator to lend a hand."

The coffin was got out of its rough-box and down on the snowy platform. The townspeople drew back enough to make room for it and then formed a close semicircle about it, looking curiously at the palm leaf which lay across the black cover. No one said anything. The baggage man stood by his truck, waiting to get at the trunks. The engine panted heavily, and the fireman dodged in and out among the wheels with his yellow torch and long oil-can, snapping the spindle boxes. The young Bostonian, one of the dead sculptor's pupils who had come with the body, looked about him helplessly. He turned to the banker, the only one of that black, uneasy, stoop-shouldered group who seemed enough of an individual to be addressed.

"None of Mr. Merrick's brothers are here?" he asked uncertainly.

The man with the red beard for the first time stepped up and joined the others. "No, they have not come yet; the family is scattered. The body will be taken directly to the house." He stooped and took hold of one of the handles of the coffin.

"Take the long hill road up, Thompson, it will be easier on the horses," called the liveryman as the undertaker snapped the door of the hearse and prepared to mount to the driver's seat.

Laird, the red-bearded lawyer, turned again to the stranger. "We didn't know whether there would be anyone with him or not," he explained. "It's a long walk, so you'd better go up in the hack." He pointed to a single battered conveyance, but the young man replied stiffly: "Thank you, but I think I will go up with the hearse. If you don't object," turning to the undertaker, "I'll ride with you."

They clambered up over the wheels and drove off in the starlight up the long, white hill toward the town. The lamps in the still village were shining from under the low, snow-burdened roofs; and beyond, on every side, the plains reached out into emptiness, peaceful and wide as the soft sky itself, and wrapped in a tangible, white silence.

When the hearse backed up to a wooden sidewalk before a naked, weather-beaten frame house, the same composite, ill-defined group that had stood upon the station siding was huddled about the gate. The front yard was an icy-swamp, and a couple of warped planks, extending from the sidewalk to the door, made a sort of rickety footbridge. The gate hung upon one hinge, and was opened wide with difficulty. Steavens, the young stranger, noticed that something black was tied to the knob of the front door.

The grating sound made by the casket, as it was drawn from the hearse, was answered by a scream from the house; the front door was wrenched open, and a tall, corpulent woman rushed out bareheaded into the snow and flung herself upon the coffin, shrieking, "My boy, my boy! And this is how you have come home to me!"

As Steavens turned away and closed his eyes with a shudder of unutterable repulsion, another woman, also tall, but flat and angular, dressed entirely in black, darted out of the house and caught Mrs. Merrick by the shoulders, crying sharply: "Come, come, mother; you musn't go on like this!" Her tone changed to one of obsequious solemnity as she turned to the banker: "The parlour is ready, Mr. Phelps."

The bearers carried the coffin along the narrow boards, while the undertaker ran ahead with the coffin-rests. They bore it into a large, unheated room that smelled of dampness and disuse and furniture polish, and set it down under a hanging lamp ornamented with jingling glass prisms and before a "Rogers group" of John Alden and Priscilla, wreathed with smilax. Henry Steavens stared about him with the sickening conviction that there had been a mistake, and that he had somehow arrived at the wrong destination. He looked at the clover-green Brussels, the fat plush upholstery, among the hand-painted china placques and panels and vases, for some mark of identification,—for something that might once conceivably have belonged to Harvey Merrick. It was not until he recognized his friend in the crayon portrait of a little boy in kilts and curls, hanging over the piano, that he felt willing to let any of these people approach the coffin.

"Take the lid off, Mr. Thompson; let me see my boy's face," wailed the elder woman between her sobs. This time Steavens looked fearfully, almost beseechingly into her face, red and swollen under its masses of strong, black, shiny hair. He flushed, dropped his eyes, and then, almost incredulously, looked again. There was a kind of power about her face—a kind of brutal handsomeness, even; but it was scarred and furrowed by violence, and so coloured and coarsened by fiercer passions that grief seemed never to have laid a gentle finger there. The long nose was distended and knobbed at the end, and there were deep lines on either side of it; her heavy, black brows almost met across her forehead, her teeth were large and square, and set far apart—teeth that could tear. She filled the room; the men were obliterated, seemed tossed about like twigs in an angry water, and even Steavens felt himself being drawn into the whirlpool.

The daughter—the tall, raw-boned woman in crêpe, with a mourning comb in her hair which curiously lengthened her long face—sat stiffly upon the sofa, her hands, conspicuous for their large knuckles, folded in her lap, her mouth and eyes drawn down, solemnly awaiting the opening of the coffin. Near the door stood a mulatto woman, evidently a servant in the house, with a timid bearing and an emaciated face pitifully sad and gentle. She was weeping silently, the corner of her calico apron lifted to her eyes, occasionally suppressing a long, quivering sob. Steavens walked over and stood beside her.

Feeble steps were heard on the stairs, and an old man, tall and frail, odorous of pipe smoke, with shaggy unkept grey hair and a dingy beard, tobacco stained about the mouth, entered uncertainly. He went slowly up to the coffin and stood rolling a blue cotton handkerchief between his hands, seeming so pained and embarrassed by his wife's orgy of grief that he had no consciousness of anything else.

"There, there, Annie, dear, don't take on so," he quavered timidly, putting out a shaking hand and awkwardly patting her elbow. She turned and sank upon his shoulder with such violence that he tottered a little. He did not even glance toward the coffin, but continued to look at her with a dull, frightened, appealing expression, as a spaniel looks at the whip. His sunken cheeks slowly reddened and burned with miserable shame. When his wife rushed from the room, her daughter strode after her with set lips. The servant stole up to the coffin, bent over it for a moment, and then slipped away to the kitchen, leaving Steavens, the lawyer, and the father to themselves. The old man stood looking down at his dead son's face. The sculptor's splendid head seemed even more noble in its rigid stillness than in life. The dark hair had crept down upon the wide forehead; the face seemed strangely long, but in it there was not that repose we expect to find in the faces of the dead. The brows were so drawn that there were two deep lines above the beaked nose, and the chin was thrust forward defiantly. It was as though the strain of life had been so sharp and bitter that death could not at once relax the tension and smooth the countenance into perfect peace—as though he were still guarding something precious, which might even yet be wrested from him.

The old man's lips were working under his stained beard. He turned to the lawyer with timid deference: "Phelps and the rest are comin' back to set up with Harve, ain't they?" he asked. "Thank 'ee, Jim, thank 'ee." He brushed the hair back gently from his son's forehead. "He was a good boy, Jim; always a good boy. He was ez gentle ez a child and the kindest of 'em all—only we didn't none of us ever onderstand him." The tears trickled slowly down his beard and dropped upon the sculptor's coat.

"Martin, Martin! Oh! Martin! come here," his wife wailed from the top of the stairs. The old man started timorously: "Yes, Annie, I'm coming." He turned away, hesitated, stood for a moment in miserable indecision;

then reached back and patted the dead man's hair softly, and stumbled from the room.

"Poor old man, I didn't think he had any tears left. Seems as if his eyes would have gone dry long ago. At his age nothing cuts very deep," remarked the lawyer.

Something in his tone made Steavens glance up. While the mother had been in the room, the young man had scarcely seen any one else; but now, from the moment he first glanced into Jim Laird's florid face and blood-shot eyes, he knew that he had found what he had been heartsick at not finding before—the feeling, the understanding, that must exist in some one, even here.

The man was red as his beard, with features swollen and blurred by dissipation, and a hot, blazing blue eye. His face was strained—that of a man who is controlling himself with difficulty—and he kept plucking at his beard with a sort of fierce resentment. Steavens, sitting by the window, watched him turn down the glaring lamp, still its jangling pendants with an angry gesture, and then stand with his hands locked behind him, staring down into the master's face. He could not help wondering what link there had been between the porcelain vessel and so sorry a lump of potter's clay.

From the kitchen an uproar was sounding; when the dining-room door opened, the import of it was clear. The mother was abusing the maid for having forgotten to make the dressing for the chicken salad which had been prepared for the watchers. Steavens had never heard anything in the least like it; it was injured, emotional, dramatic abuse, unique and masterly in its excruciating cruelty, as violent and unrestrained as had been her grief of twenty minutes before. With a shudder of disgust the lawyer went into the dining-room and closed the door into the kitchen.

"Poor Roxy's getting it now," he remarked when he came back. "The Merricks took her out of the poor-house years ago; and if her loyalty would let her, I guess the poor old thing could tell tales that would curdle your blood. She's the mulatto woman who was standing in here a while ago, with her apron to her eyes. The old woman is a fury; there never was anybody like her. She made Harvey's life a hell for him when he lived at home; he was so sick ashamed of it. I never could see how he kept himself so sweet."

"He was wonderful," said Steavens slowly, "wonderful; but until to-night I have never known how wonderful."

"That is the eternal wonder of it, anyway; that it can come even from such a dung heap as this," the lawyer cried, with a sweeping gesture which seemed to indicate much more than the four walls within which they stood.

"I think I'll see whether I can get a little air. The room is so close that I am beginning to feel rather faint," murmured Steavens, struggling with one of the windows. The sash was stuck, however, and would not yield, so he sat down dejectedly and began pulling at his collar. The lawyer came over, loosened the sash with one blow of his red fist and sent the window up a few inches. Steavens thanked him, but the nausea which had been gradually climbing into his throat for the last half hour left him with but one desire—a desperate feeling that he must get away from this place with what was left of Harvey Merrick. Oh, he comprehended well enough now the quiet bitterness of the smile that he had seen so often on his master's lips!

Once when Merrick returned from a visit home, he brought with him a singularly feeling and suggestive bas-relief of a thin, faded old woman, sitting and sewing something pinned to her knee; while a full-lipped, full-blooded little urchin, his trousers held up by a single gallows, stood beside her, impatiently twitching her gown to call her attention to a butterfly he had caught. Steavens, impressed by the tender and delicate modelling of the thin, tired face, had asked him if it were his mother. He remembered the dull flush that had burned up in the sculptor's face.

The lawyer was sitting in a rocking-chair beside the coffin, his head thrown back, and his eyes closed. Steavens looked at him earnestly, puzzled at the line of the chin, and wondering why a man should conceal a feature of such distinction under that disfiguring shock of beard. Suddenly, as though he felt the young sculptor's keen glance, Jim Laird opened his eyes.

"Was he always a good deal of an oyster?" he asked abruptly. "He was terribly shy as a boy."

"Yes, he was an oyster, since you put it so," rejoined Steavens. "Although he could be very fond of people, he always gave one the impression of being detached. He disliked violent emotion; he was reflective, and rather distrustful of himself—except, of course, as regarded his work. He was sure enough there. He distrusted men pretty thoroughly and women even more, yet somehow without believing ill of them. He was determined, indeed, to believe the best; but he seemed afraid to investigate."

"A burnt dog dreads the fire," said the lawyer grimly, and closed his eyes.

Steavens went on and on, reconstructing that whole miserable boyhood. All this raw, biting ugliness had been the portion of the man whose mind was to become an exhaustless gallery of beautiful impressions—so sensitive that the mere shadow of a poplar leaf flickering against a sunny wall would be etched and held there for ever. Surely, if ever a man had the magic word in his finger tips, it was Merrick. Whatever he touched, he revealed its holiest secret; liberated it from enchantment and restored it to its pristine loveliness. Upon whatever he had come in contact with, he had left a beautiful record of the experience—a sort of ethereal signature; a scent, a sound, a colour that was his own.

Steavens understood now the real tragedy of his master's life; neither

362

love nor wine, as many had conjectured; but a blow which had fallen earlier and cut deeper than anything else could have done—a shame not his, and yet so unescapably his, to hide in his heart from his very boyhood. And without—the frontier warfare; the yearning of a boy, cast ashore upon a desert of newness and ugliness and sordidness, for all that is chastened and old, and noble with traditions.

At eleven o'clock the tall, flat woman in black announced that the watchers were arriving, and asked them to "step into the dining-room." As Steavens rose, the lawyer said dryly: "You go on—it'll be a good experience for you. I'm not equal to that crowd tonight; I've had twenty years of them."

As Steavens closed the door after him he glanced back at the lawyer, sitting by the coffin in the dim light, with his chin resting on his hand.

The same misty group that had stood before the door of the express car shuffled into the dining-room. In the light of the kerosene lamp they separated and became individuals. The minister, a pale, feeble-looking man with white hair and blond chin-whiskers, took his seat beside a small side table and placed his Bible upon it. The Grand Army man sat down behind the stove and tilted his chair back comfortably against the wall, fishing his quill toothpick from his waistcoat pocket. The two bankers, Phelps and Elder, sat off in a corner behind the dinner-table, where they could finish their discussion of the new usury law and its effect on chattel security loans. The real estate agent, an old man with a smiling, hypocritical face, soon joined them. The coal and lumber dealer and the cattle shipper sat on opposite sides of the hard coal-burner, their feet on the nickel-work. Steavens took a book from his pocket and began to read. The talk around him ranged through various topics of local interest while the house was quieting down. When it was clear that the members of the family were in bed, the Grand Army man hitched his shoulders and, untangling his long legs, caught his heels on the rounds of his chair.

"S'pose there'll be a will, Phelps?" he queried in his weak falsetto.

The banker laughed disagreeably, and began trimming his nails with a pearl-handled pocket-knife.

"There'll scarcely be any need for one, will there?" he queried in his turn.

The restless Grand Army man shifted his position again, getting his knees still nearer his chin. "Why, the ole man says Harve's done right well lately," he chirped.

The other banker spoke up. "I reckon he means by that Harve ain't asked him to mortgage any more farms lately, so as he could go on with his education."

"Seems like my mind don't reach back to a time when Harve wasn't bein' edycated," tittered the Grand Army man.

There was a general chuckle. The minister took out his handkerchief and blew his nose sonorously. Banker Phelps closed his knife with a snap.

"It's too bad the old man's sons didn't turn out better," he remarked with reflective authority. "They never hung together. He spent money enough on Harve to stock a dozen cattle-farms, and he might as well have poured it into Sand Creek. If Harve had stayed at home and helped nurse what little they had, and gone into stock on the old man's bottom farm, they might all have been well fixed. But the old man had to trust everything to tenants and was cheated right and left."

"Harve never could have handled stock none," interposed the cattle-man. "He hadn't it in him to be sharp. Do you remember when he bought Sander's mules for eight-year olds, when everybody in town knew that Sander's father-in-law give 'em to his wife for a wedding present eighteen years before, an' they was full-grown mules then?"

The company laughed discreetly, and the Grand Army man rubbed his knees with a spasm of childish delight.

"Harve never was much account for anything practical, and he shore was never fond of work," began the coal and lumber dealer. "I mind the last time he was home; the day he left, when the old man was out to the barn helpin' his hand hitch up to take Harve to the train, and Cal Moots was patchin' up the fence; Harve, he come out on the step and sings out, in his ladylike voice: Cal Moots, Cal Moots! please come cord my trunk!'"

"That's Harve for you," approved the Grand Army man. "I kin hear him howlin' yet, when he was a big feller in long pants and his mother used to whale him with a rawhide in the barn for lettin' the cows git foundered in the cornfield when he was drivin' 'em home from pasture. He killed a cow of mine that-away onct—a pure Jersey and the best milker I had, an' the ole man had to put up for her. Harve, he was watchin' the sun set acrost the marshes when the anamile got away."

"Where the old man made his mistake was in sending the boy East to school," said Phelps, stroking his goatee and speaking in a deliberate, judicial tone. "There was where he got his head full of nonsense. What Harve needed, of all people, was a course in some first-class Kansas City business college."

The letters were swimming before Steavens's eyes. Was it possible that these men did not understand, that the palm on the coffin meant nothing to them? The very name of their town would have remained for ever buried in the postal guide had it not been now and again mentioned in the world in connection with Harvey Merrick's. He remembered what his master had said to him on the day of his death, after the congestion of both lungs had shut off any probability of recovery, and the sculptor had asked his pupil to send his body home. "It's not a pleasant place to be lying while the world is moving and doing and bettering," he had said with a feeble smile, "but it rather seems as though we ought to go back to the place we came from, in the end. The townspeople will come in for a look at me; and after they have had their say, I shan't have much to fear from the judgment of God!"

The cattleman took up the comment. "Forty's young for a Merrick to cash in; they usually hang on pretty well. Probably he helped it along with whisky."

"His mother's people were not long lived, and Harvey never had a robust constitution," said the minister mildly. He would have liked to say more. He had been the boy's Sunday-school teacher, and had been fond of him; but he felt that he was not in a position to speak. His own sons had turned out badly, and it was not a year since one of them had made his last trip home in the express car, shot in a gambling-house in the Black Hills.

"Nevertheless, there is no disputin' that Harve frequently looked upon the wine when it was red, also variegated, and it shore made an oncommon fool of him," moralized the cattleman.

Just then the door leading into the parlour rattled loudly and every one started involuntarily, looking relieved when only Jim Laird came out. The Grand Army man ducked his head when he saw the spark in his blue, blood-shot eye. They were all afraid of Jim; he was a drunkard, but he could twist the law to suit his client's needs as no other man in all western Kansas could do, and there were many who tried. The lawyer closed the door behind him, leaned back against it and folded his arms, cocking his head a little to one side. When he assumed this attitude in the court-room, ears were always pricked up, as it usually foretold a flood of withering sarcasm.

"I've been with you gentlemen before," he began in a dry, even tone, "when you've sat by the coffins of boys born and raised in this town; and, if I remember rightly, you were never any too well satisfied when you checked them up. What's the matter, anyhow? Why is it that reputable young men are as scarce as millionaires in Sand City? It might almost seem to a stranger that there was some way something the matter with your progressive town. Why did Reuben Sayer, the brightest young lawyer you ever turned out, after he had come home from the university as straight as a die, take to drinking and forge a check and shoot himself? Why did Bill Merrit's son die of the shakes in a saloon in Omaha? Why was Mr. Thomas's son, here, shot in a gambling-house? Why did young Adams burn his mill to beat the insurance companies and go to the pen?"

The lawyer paused and unfolded his arms, laying one clenched fist quietly on the table. "I'll tell you why. Because you drummed nothing but money and knavery into their ears from the time they wore knickerbockers; because you carped away at them as you've been carping here tonight, holding our friends Phelps and Elder up to them for their models, as our grandfathers held up George Washington and John Adams. But the boys were young, and raw at the business you put them to, and how could they match coppers with such artists as Phelps and Elder? You wanted them to be successful rascals; they were only unsuccessful ones—that's all the difference. There was only one boy ever raised in this borderland between ruffianism and civilization who didn't come to grief, and you hated Harvey Merrick more for winning out than you hated all the other boys who got under the wheels. Lord, Lord, how you did hate him! Phelps, here, is fond of saying that he could buy and sell us all out any time he's a mind to; but he knew Harve wouldn't have given a tinker's damn for his bank and all his cattlefarms put together; and a lack of appreciation, that way, goes hard with Phelps.

"Old Nimrod thinks Harve drank too much; and this from such as Nimrod and me!

"Brother Elder says Harve was too free with the old man's money—fell short in filial consideration, maybe. Well, we can all remember the very tone in which brother Elder swore his own father was a liar, in the county court; and we all know that the old man came out of that partnership with his son as bare as a sheared lamb. But maybe I'm getting personal, and I'd better be driving ahead at what I want to say."

The lawyer paused a moment, squared his heavy shoulders, and went on: "Harvey Merrick and I went to school together, back East. We were dead in earnest, and we wanted you all to be proud of us some day. We meant to be great men. Even I, and I haven't lost my sense of humour, gentlemen, I meant to be a great man. I came back here to practise, and I found you didn't in the least want me to be a great man. You wanted me to be a shrewd lawyer—oh, yes! Our veteran here wanted me to get him an increase of pension, because he had dyspepsia; Phelps wanted a new county survey that would put the widow Wilson's little bottom farm inside his south line; Elder wanted to lend money at 5 per cent a month, and get it collected; and Stark here wanted to wheedle old women up in Vermont into investing their annuities in real-estate mortgages that are not worth the paper they are written on. Oh, you needed me hard enough, and you'll go on needing me!

"Well, I came back here and became the damned shyster you wanted me to be. You pretended to have some sort of respect for me; and yet you'll stand up and throw mud at Harvey Merrick, whose soul you couldn't dirty and whose hands you couldn't tie. Oh, you're a discriminating lot of Christians! There have been times when the sight of Harvey's name in some Eastern paper made me hang my head like a whipped dog; and, again, times when I liked to think of him off there in the world, away from all this hog-wallow, climbing the big, clean up-grade he'd set for himself.

"And we? Now that we've fought and lied and sweated and stolen, and hated as only the disappointed strugglers in a bitter, dead little Western town know how to do, what have we got to show for it? Harvey Merrick wouldn't have given one sunset over your marshes for all you've got put together, and you know it. It's not for me to say why, in the inscrutable wisdom of God, a genius should ever have been called from this place of hatred and bitter waters; but I want this Boston man to know that the drivel he's been hearing here tonight is the only tribute a truly great man could have from such a lot of sick, side-tracked, burnt-dog, land-poor sharks as the here-present financiers of Sand City—upon which town may God have mercy!"

The lawyer thrust out his hand to Steavens as he passed him, caught up his overcoat in the hall, and had left the house before the Grand Army man had had time to lift his ducked head and crane his long neck about at his fellows.

Next day Jim Laird was drunk and unable to attend the funeral services. Steavens called twice at his office, but was compelled to start East without seeing him. He had a presentiment that he would hear from him again, and left his address on the lawyer's table; but if Laird found it, he never acknowledged it. The thing in him that Harvey Merrick had loved must have gone under ground with Harvey Merrick's coffin; for it never spoke again, and Jim got the cold he died of crossing the Colorado mountains to defend one of Phelps's sons who had got into trouble out there by cutting government timber.

Youth and the Bright Medusa, 1920

WILLIAM ALLEN WHITE

A Farewell to a Fellow-Editor

"The Sage of Emporia, Kansas" was a much-loved man and the best-known small-town editor in the country.

Editor Phillips, late editor, owner and publisher of the Emporia *Daily and Weekly Democrat,* has left for parts unknown, probably to the horror and consternation of the parts, and certainly for the general betterment of this community. Far be it from this paper to say aught that would cast an unwarranted aspersion upon an earnest though unfortunate gentleman. It is not the purpose of the *Gazette* to be sensational nor to exaggerate interesting facts. But as a matter of news and stated in the precise terms of scientific description, without coloring the statement by loose vernacular, the simple, homely truth demands that it be said of Phillips that he was, is and will be while he lives on this easy old earth, the most picturesque, unique, original, shameless, deliberate, conscienceless, malicious and indefatigable dead beat that ever pressed the sidewalk of Commercial street with his velvety feline feet. It is but just to him to add that he was not a harsh or irascible man. He did not exact tribute with either club or buzz saw. He had the soft, self-deprecatory, insinuating voice of a cooing dove; and he glided into his machinations with the gentle, noiseless, hypnotic sinuosity of a rubber-tired rattlesnake. He was as bland as a sunrise and as deadly as a pestilence.

Not only did he have the face to charge for a total circulation of 150 copies, advertising rates that would make reputable editors blush whose papers circulated by the thousand; but Editor Phillips actually got those rates. Earth was a wilderness of suckers for him. He put the marks of his easy touch all over the town and when advertisers were coy he cut their advertisements from other papers, charged up the account, waited till the store keeper was out and traded out the amount of his account and twice as much besides. Rebuffs and insults rebounded from him without denting his pachyderm complacency, nor rubbing the creamed and mantled waters of stagnant moral sense.

Poor old Phillips, he has left us. We may never look upon his like again —thank Heaven—until the sulphurous blazes of perdition illuminate the job lot in the deepest part of the seventh pit.

Emporia *Gazette*, 1889

"To an Anxious Friend"

You tell me that law is above freedom of utterance. And I reply that you can have no wise laws nor free enforcement of wise laws unless there is free expression of the wisdom of the people—and, alas, their folly with it. But if there is freedom, folly will die of its own poison, and the wisdom will survive. That is the history of the race. It is proof of man's kinship with God. You say that freedom is not for time of stress, and I reply with the sad truth that only in time of stress is freedom of utterance in danger. No one questions it in calm days, because it is not needed. And the reverse is true also; only when free utterance is suppressed is it needed, and when it is needed, it is most vital to justice.

Peace is good. But if you are interested in peace through force and without free discussion—that is to say, free utterance decently and in order—your interest in justice is slight. And peace without justice is tyranny, no matter how you may sugar-coat it with expedience. This state today is in no more danger from suppression than from violence, because, in the end, suppression leads to violence. Whoever pleads for justice helps to keep the peace; and whoever tramples on the plea for justice temperately made in the name of peace only outrages peace and kills something fine in the heart of man which God put there when we got our manhood. When that is killed, brute meets brute on each side of the line.

So, dear friend, put fear out of your heart. This nation will survive, this state will prosper, the orderly business of life will go forward if only men can speak in whatever way given them to utter what their hearts hold—by voice, by posted card, by letter, or by press. Reason has never failed men. Only force and repression has made the wrecks in the world.

Emporia *Gazette*, July 27, 1922

SINCLAIR LEWIS

Mr. Babbitt Begins His Day

I

The towers of Zenith aspired above the morning mist; austere towers of steel and cement and limestone, sturdy as cliffs and delicate as silver rods. They were neither citadels nor churches, but frankly and beautifully office-buildings.

The mist took pity on the fretted structures of earlier generations: the Post Office with its shingle-tortured mansard, the red brick minarets of hulking old houses, factories with stingy and sooted windows, wooden tenements colored like mud. The city was full of such grotesqueries, but the clean towers were thrusting them from the business center, and on the farther hills were shining new houses, homes—they seemed—for laughter and tranquillity.

Over a concrete bridge fled a limousine of long sleek hood and noiseless engine. These people in evening clothes were returning from an all-night rehearsal of a Little Theatre play, an artistic adventure considerably illuminated by champagne. Below the bridge curved a railroad, a maze of green and crimson lights. The New York Flyer boomed past, and twenty lines of polished steel leaped into the glare.

In one of the skyscrapers the wires of the Associated Press were closing down. The telegraph operators wearily raised their celluloid eyeshades after a night of talking with Paris and Peking. Through the building crawled the scrubwomen, yawning, their old shoes slapping. The dawn mist spun away. Cues of men with lunch-boxes clumped toward the immensity of new factories, sheets of glass and hollow tile, glittering shops where five thousand men worked beneath one roof, pouring out the honest wares that would be sold up the Euphrates and across the veldt. The whistles rolled out in greeting a chorus cheerful as the April dawn; the song of labor in a city built—it seemed—for giants.

II

There was nothing of the giant in the aspect of the man who was beginning to awaken on the sleeping-porch of a Dutch colonial house in that residential district of Zenith known as Floral Heights.

His name was George F. Babbitt. He was forty-six years old now, in April, 1920, and he made nothing in particular, neither butter nor shoes nor poetry, but he was nimble in the calling of selling houses for more than people could afford to pay.

His large head was pink, his brown hair thin and dry. His face was babyish in slumber, despite his wrinkles and the red spectacle-dents on the slopes of his nose. He was not fat but he was exceedingly well fed; his cheeks were pads, and the unroughened hand which lay helpless upon the khaki-colored blanket was slightly puffy. He seemed prosperous, extremely married and unromantic; and altogether unromantic appeared this sleeping-porch, which looked on one sizable elm, two respectable grass-plots, a cement driveway, and a corrugated iron garage. Yet Babbitt was again dreaming of the fairy child, a dream more romantic than scarlet pagodas by a silver sea.

For years the fairy child had come to him. Where others saw but Georgie Babbitt, she discerned gallant youth. She waited for him, in the darkness beyond mysterious groves. When at last he could slip away from the crowded house he darted to her. His wife, his clamoring friends, sought to follow, but he escaped, the girl fleet beside him, and they crouched together on a shadowy hillside. She was so slim, so white, so eager! She cried that he was gay and valiant, that she would wait for him, that they would sail—

Rumble and bang of the milk-truck.

Babbitt moaned, turned over, struggled back toward his dream. He could see only her face now, beyond misty waters. The furnace-man slammed the basement door. A dog barked in the next yard. As Babbitt sank blissfully into a dim warm tide, the paper-carrier went by whistling, and the rolled-up *Advocate* thumped the front door. Babbit roused, his stomach constricted with alarm. As he relaxed, he was pierced by the familiar and irritating rattle of some one cranking a Ford: snap-ah-ah, snap-ah-ah, snap-ah-ah. Himself a pious motorist, Babbitt cranked with the unseen driver, with him waited through taut hours for the roar of the starting engine, with him agonized as the roar ceased and again began the infernal patient snap-ah-ah—a round, flat sound, a shivering cold-morning sound, a sound infuriating and inescapable. Not till the rising voice of the motor told him that the Ford was moving was he released from the panting tension. He glanced once at his favorite tree, elm twigs against the gold patina of sky, and fumbled for sleep as for a drug. He who had been a boy very credulous of life was no longer greatly interested in the possible and improbable adventures of each new day.

He escaped from reality till the alarm-clock rang, at seven-twenty.

III

It was the best of nationally advertised and quantitatively produced alarm-clocks, with all modern attachments, including cathedral chime, intermittent alarm, and a phosphorescent dial. Babbitt was proud of being awakened by such a rich device. Socially it was almost as creditable as buying expensive cord tires.

He sulkily admitted now that there was no more escape, but he lay and detested the grind of the real-estate business, and disliked his family, and disliked himself for disliking them. The evening before, he had played poker at Vergil Gunch's till midnight, and after such holidays he was irritable before breakfast. It may have been the tremendous home-brewed beer of the prohibition-era and the cigars to which that beer enticed him; it may have been resentment of return from this fine, bold man-world to a restricted region of wives and stenographers, and of suggestions not to smoke so much.

From the bedroom beside the sleeping-porch, his wife's detestably cheerful "Time to get up, Georgie boy," and the itchy sound, the brisk and scratchy sound, of combing hairs out of a stiff brush.

He grunted; he dragged his thick legs, in faded baby-blue pajamas, from under the khaki blanket; he sat on the edge of the cot, running his fingers through his wild hair, while his plump feet mechanically felt for his slippers. He looked regretfully at the blanket—forever a suggestion to him of freedom and heroism. He had bought it for a camping trip which had never come off. It symbolized gorgeous loafing, gorgeous cursing, virile flannel shirts.

He creaked to his feet, groaning at the waves of pain which passed behind his eyeballs. Though he waited for their scorching recurrence, he looked blurrily out at the yard. It delighted him, as always; it was the neat yard of a successful business man of Zenith, that is, it was perfection, and made him also perfect. He regarded the corrugated iron garage. For the three-hundred-and-sixty-fifth time in a year he reflected, "No class to that tin shack. Have to build me a frame garage. But by golly it's the only thing on the place that isn't up-to-date!" While he stared he thought of a community garage for his acreage development, Glen Oriole. He stopped puffing and jiggling. His arms were akimbo. His petulant, sleep-swollen face was set in harder lines. He suddenly seemed capable, an official, a man to contrive, to direct, to get things done.

On the vigor of his idea he was carried down the hard, clean, unused-looking hall into the bathroom.

Though the house was not large it had, like all houses on Floral Heights, an altogether royal bathroom of porcelain and glazed tile and metal sleek as silver. The towel-rack was a rod of clear glass set in nickel. The tub was long enough for a Prussian Guard, and above the set bowl was a sensational exhibit of tooth-brush holder, shaving-brush holder, soap-dish, sponge-dish, and medicine-cabinet, so glittering and so ingenious that they resembled an electrical instrument board. But the Babbitt whose God was Modern Appliances was not pleased. The air of the bathroom was thick with the smell of a heathen toothpaste. "Verona been at it again! 'Stead of sticking to Lilidol, like I've re-peat-ed-ly asked her, she's gone and gotten some confounded stinkum stuff that makes you sick!"

The bath-mat was wrinkled and the floor was wet. (His daughter Verona eccentrically took baths in the morning, now and then.) He slipped on the mat, and slid against the tub. He said "Damn!" Furiously he snatched up his tube of shaving-cream, furiously he lathered, with a belligerent slapping of the unctuous brush, furiously he raked his plump cheeks with a safety-razor. It pulled. The blade was dull. He said, "Damn—oh—oh—damn it!"

He hunted through the medicine-cabinet for a packet of new razor-blades (reflecting, as invariably, "Be cheaper to buy one of these dinguses and strop your own blades") and when he discovered the packet, behind the round box of bicarbonate of soda, he thought ill of his wife for putting it there and very well of himself for not saying "Damn." But he did say it, immediately afterward, when with wet and soap-slippery fingers he tried to remove the horrible little envelope and crisp clinging oiled paper from the new blade.

Then there was the problem, oft-pondered, never solved, of what to do with the old blade, which might imperil the fingers of his young. As usual, he tossed it on top of the medicine-cabinet, with a mental note that some day he must remove the fifty or sixty other blades that were also temporarily piled up there. He finished his shaving in a growing testiness increased by his spinning headache and by the emptiness of his stomach. When he was done, his round face smooth and streamy and his eyes stinging from soapy water, he reached for a towel. The family towels were wet, wet and clammy and vile, all of them wet, he found, as he blindly snatched them—his own face-towel, his wife's, Verona's, Ted's, Tinka's, and the lone bath-towel with the huge welt of initial. Then George F. Babbitt did a dismaying thing. He wiped his face on the guest-towel! It was a pansy-embroidered trifle which always hung there to indicate that the Babbitts were in the best Floral Heights society. No one had ever used it. No guest had ever dared to. Guests secretively took a corner of the nearest regular towel.

He was raging, "By golly, here they go and use up all the towels, every doggone one of 'em, and they use 'em and get 'em all wet and sopping, and never put out a dry one for me—of course, I'm the goat!—and then I want one and—I'm the only person in the doggone house that's got the slightest doggone bit of consideration for other people and thoughtfulness and consider there may be others that may want to use the doggone bath-room after me and consider—"

He was pitching the chill abominations into the bath-tub, pleased by the vindictiveness of that desolate flapping sound; and in the midst his wife serenely trotted in, observed serenely, "Why Georgie dear, what are you doing? Are you going to wash out the towels? Why, you needn't wash out the towels. Oh, Georgie, you didn't go and use the guest-towel, did you?"

It is not recorded that he was able to answer.

For the first time in weeks he was sufficiently roused by his wife to look at her.

IV

Myra Babbitt—Mrs. George F. Babbitt—was definitely mature. She had creases from the corners of her mouth to the bottom of her chin, and her plump neck bagged. But the thing that marked her as having passed the line was that she no longer had reticences before her husband, and no longer worried about not having reticences. She was in a petticoat now, and corsets which bulged, and unaware of being seen in bulgy corsets. She had become so dully habituated to married life that in her full matronliness she was as sexless as an anemic nun. She was a good woman, a kind woman, a diligent woman, but no one, save perhaps Tinka her ten-year old, was at all interested in her or entirely aware that she was alive.

After a rather thorough discussion of all the domestic and social aspects of towels she apologized to Babbitt for his having an alcoholic headache; and he recovered enough to endure the search for a B.V.D. undershirt which had, he pointed out, malevolently been concealed among his clean pajamas.

He was fairly amiable in the conference on the brown suit.

"What do you think, Myra?" He pawed at the clothes hunched on a chair in their bedroom, while she moved about mysteriously adjusting and patting her petticoat and, to his jaundiced eye, never seeming to get on with her dressing. "How about it? Shall I wear the brown suit another day?"

"Well, it looks awfully nice on you."

"I know, but gosh, it needs pressing."

"That's so. Perhaps it does."

"It certainly could stand being pressed, all right."

"Yes, perhaps it wouldn't hurt it to be pressed."

"But, gee, the coat doesn't need pressing. No sense in having the whole darn suit pressed, when the coat doesn't need it."

"That's so."

"But the pants certainly need it, all right. Look at them—look at those wrinkles—the pants certainly do need pressing."

"That's so. Oh, Georgie, why couldn't you wear the brown coat with the blue trousers we were wondering what we'd do with them?"

"Good Lord! Did you ever in all my life know me to wear the coat of one suit and the pants of another? What do you think I am? A busted bookkeeper?"

"Well, why don't you put on the dark gray suit today, and stop in at the tailor and leave the brown trousers?"

"Well, they certainly need— Now where the devil is that gray suit? Oh, yes, here we are."

He was able to get through the other crises of dressing with comparative resoluteness and calm.

His first adornment was the sleeveless dimity B.V.D. undershirt, in which he resembled a small boy humorlessly wearing a cheesecloth tabard at a civic pageant. He never put on B.V.D.'s without thanking the God of Progress that he didn't wear tight, long, old-fashioned undergarments, like his father-in-law and partner, Henry Thompson. His second embellishment was combing and slicking back his hair. It gave him a tremendous forehead, arching up two inches beyond the former hair-line. But most wonder-working of all was the donning of his spectacles.

There is character in spectacles—the pretentious tortoise-shell, the meek pince-nez of the school teacher, the twisted silver-framed glasses of the old villager. Babbitt's spectacles had huge, circular, frameless lenses of the very best glass; the ear-pieces were thin bars of gold. In them he was the modern business man; one who gave orders to clerks and drove a car and played occasional golf and was scholarly in regard to Salesmanship. His head suddenly appeared not babyish but weighty, and you noted his heavy, blunt nose, his straight mouth and thick, long upper lip, his chin overfleshy but strong; with respect you beheld him put on the rest of his uniform as a Solid Citizen.

The gray suit was well cut, well made, and completely undistinguished. It was a standard suit. White piping on the V of the vest added a flavor of law and learning. His shoes were black laced boots, good boots, honest boots, standard boots, extraordinarily uninteresting boots. The only frivolity was in his purple knitted scarf. With considerable comment on the matter to Mrs. Babbitt (who, acrobatically fastening the back of her blouse to her skirt with a safety-pin, did not hear a word he said), he chose between the purple scarf and a tapestry effect with stringless brown harps among blown palms, and into it he thrust a snakehead pin with opal eyes.

A sensational event was changing from the brown suit to the gray the contents of his pockets. He was earnest about these objects. They were of eternal importance, like baseball or the Republican Party. They included a fountain pen and a silver pencil (always lacking a supply of new leads) which belonged in the righthand upper vest pocket. Without them he would have felt naked. On his watch-chain were a gold penknife, silver cigar-cutter, seven keys (the use of two of which he had forgotten), and incidentally a good watch. Depending from the chain was a large, yellowish elk's-tooth—proclamation of his membership in the Brotherly and Protective Order of Elks. Most significant of all was his loose-leaf pocket note-book, that modern and efficient note-book which contained the addresses of people whom he had forgotten, prudent memoranda of postal money-orders which had reached their destinations months ago, stamps which had lost their mucilage, clippings of verses by T. Cholmondeley Frink and of the newspaper editorials from which Babbitt got his opinions and his polysyllables, notes to be sure and do things which he did not intend to do, and one curious inscription—D.S.S.D.M.Y.P.D.F.

But he had no cigarette-case. No one had ever happened to give him one, so he hadn't the habit, and people who carried cigarette-cases he regarded as effeminate.

Last, he stuck in his lapel the Boosters' Club button. With the conciseness of great art the button displayed two words: "Boosters—Pep!" It made Babbitt feel loyal and important. It associated him with Good Fellows, with men who were nice and human, and important in business circles. It was his V.C., his Legion of Honor ribbon, his Phi Beta Kappa key.

With the subtleties of dressing ran other complex worries. "I feel kind of punk this morning," he said. "I think I had too much dinner last evening. You oughtn't to serve those heavy banana fritters."

"But you asked me to have some."

"I know, but— I tell you, when a fellow gets past forty he has to look after his digestion. There's a lot of fellows that don't take proper care of themselves. I tell you at forty a man's a fool or his doctor— I mean, his own doctor. Folks don't give enough attention to this matter of dieting. Now I think— Course a man ought to have a good meal after the day's work, but it would be a good thing for both of us if we took lighter lunches."

"But Georgie, here at home I always do have a light lunch."

"Mean to imply I make a hog of myself, eating down-town? Yes, sure! You'd have a swell time if you had to eat the truck that new steward hands out to us at the Athletic Club! But I certainly do feel out of sorts, this morning. Funny, got a pain down here on the left side—but no, that wouldn't be appendicitis, would it? Last night, when I was driving over to Verg Gunch's, I felt a pain in my stomach, too. Right here it was— kind of a sharp shooting pain. I— Where'd that dime go to? Why don't you serve more prunes at breakfast? Of course I eat an apple every evening—an apple a day keeps the doctor away—but still, you ought to have more prunes, and not all these fancy doodads."

"The last time I had prunes you didn't eat them."

"Well, I didn't feel like eating 'em, I suppose. Matter of fact, I think I did eat some of 'em. Anyway—I tell you it's mighty important too—I was saying to Verg Gunch, just last evening, most people don't take sufficient care of their diges—"

"Shall we have the Gunches for our dinner, next week?"

"Why sure; you bet."

"Now see here, George: I want you to put on your nice dinner-jacket that evening."

"Rats! The rest of 'em won't want to dress."

"Of course they will. You remember when you didn't dress for the Littlefields' supper-party, and all the rest did, and how embarrassed you were."

"Embarrassed, hell! I wasn't embarrassed. Everybody knows I can put on as expensive a Tux. as anybody else, and I should worry if I don't happen to have it on sometimes. All a darn nuisance, anyway. All right for a woman, that stays around the house all the time, but when a fellow's worked like the dickens all day, he doesn't want to go and hustle his head off getting into the soup-and-fish for a lot of folks that he's seen in just reg'lar ordinary clothes that same day."

"You know you enjoy being seen in one. The other evening you ad-

mitted you were glad I'd insisted on your dressing. You said you felt a
lot better for it. And oh, Georgie, I do wish you wouldn't say 'Tux.' It's
'dinner-jacket.' "

"Rats, what's the odds?"

"Well, it's what all the nice folks say. Suppose Lucile McKelvey heard
you calling it a 'Tux.' "

"Well, that's all right now! Lucile McKelvey can't pull anything on
me! Her folks are common as mud, even if her husband and her dad are
millionaires! I suppose you're trying to rub in your *exalted* social position!
Well, let me tell you that your revered paternal ancestor, Henry T., doesn't
even call it a 'Tux.'! He calls it a 'bobtail jacket for a ringtail monkey,'
and you couldn't get him into one unless you chloroformed him!"

"Now, don't be horrid, George."

"Well, I don't want to be horrid, but Lord! you're getting as fussy as
Verona. Ever since she got out of college she's been too rambunctious to
live with—doesn't know what she wants—well, I know what she wants!—
all she wants is to marry a millionaire, and live in Europe, and hold some
preacher's hand, and simultaneously at the same time stay right here in
Zenith and be some blooming kind of socialist agitator or boss charity-
worker or some damn thing! Lord, and Ted is just as bad! He wants to
go to college, and he doesn't want to go to college. Only one of the three
that knows her own mind is Tinka. Simply can't understand how I ever
came to have a pair of shillyshallying children like Rone and Ted. I
may not be any Rockefeller or James J. Shakespeare, but I certainly do
know my own mind, and I do keep right on plugging along in the office
and— Do you know the latest? Far as I can figure out, Ted's new bee is
he'd like to be a movie actor and— And here I've told him a hundred
times, if he'll go to college and law-school and make good, I'll set him
up in business and— Verona's just exactly as bad. Doesn't know what she
wants. Well, well, come on! Aren't you ready yet? The girl rang the bell
three minutes ago."

v

Before he followed his wife, Babbitt stood at the westernmost window
of their room. This residential settlement, Floral Heights, was on a rise;
and though the center of the city was three miles away—Zenith had between three and four hundred thousand inhabitants now—he could see
the top of the Second National Tower, an Indiana limestone building of
thirty-five stories.

Its shining walls rose against the April sky to a simple cornice like a
streak of white fire. Integrity was in the tower, and decision. It bore its
strength lightly as a tall soldier. As Babbitt stared, the nervousness was
soothed from his face, his slack chin lifted in reverence. All he articulated
was "That's one lovely sight!" but he was inspired by the rhythm of the
city; his love of it renewed. He beheld the tower as a temple-spire of the

376

religion of business, a faith passionate, exalted, surpassing common men;
and as he clumped down to breakfast he whistled the ballad "Oh, by gee,
by gosh, by jingo" as though it were a hymn melancholy and noble.

Babbitt, 1922

CARL SANDBURG

The People, Yes

> The people will live on.
> The learning and blundering people will live on.
>   They will be tricked and sold and again sold
> And go back to the nourishing earth for rootholds,
>   The people so peculiar in renewal and comeback,
>   You can't laugh off their capacity to take it.
> The mammoth rests between his cyclonic dramas.
>
> The people so often sleepy, weary, enigmatic,
> is a vast huddle with many units saying:
>   "I earn my living.
>   I make enough to get by
>   and it takes all my time.
>   If I had more time
>   I could do more for myself
>   and maybe for others.
>   I could read and study
>   and talk things over
>   and find out about things.
>   It takes time.
>   I wish I had the time."
>
> The people is a tragic and comic two-face:
> hero and hoodlum: phantom and gorilla twist-
> ing to moan with a gargoyle mouth: "They
> buy and sell me . . . it's a game . . .
> sometime I'll break loose . . ."
>
>   Once having marched
> Over the margins of animal necessity,
> Over the grim line of sheer subsistence
>   Then man came
> To the deeper rituals of his bones,

377

To the lights lighter than any bones,
To the time for thinking things over,
To the dance, the song, the story,
Or the hours given over to dreaming,
      Once having so marched.

Between the finite limitations of the five senses
and the endless yearnings of man for the beyond
the people hold to the humdrum bidding of work and food
while reaching out when it comes their way
for lights beyond the prison of the five senses,
for keepsakes lasting beyond any hunger or death.
      This reaching is alive.
The panderers and liars have violated and smutted it.
      Yet this reaching is alive yet
      for lights and keepsakes.

            The people know the salt of the sea
            and the strength of the winds
            lashing the corners of the earth.
            The people take the earth
            as a tomb of rest and a cradle of hope.
            Who else speaks for the Family of Man?
            They are in tune and step
            with constellations of universal law.

      The people is a polychrome,
      a spectrum and a prism
      hold in a moving monolith,
      a console organ of changing themes,
      a clavilux of color poems
      wherein the sea offers fog
      and the fog moves off in rain
      and the labrador sunset shortens
      to a nocturne of clear stars
      serene over shot spray
      of northern lights.

      The steel mill sky is alive.
      The fire breaks white and zigzag
      shot on a gun-metal gloaming.
      Man is a long time coming.
      Man will yet win.
      Brother may yet line up with brother:

This old anvil laughs at many broken hammers.
      There are men who can't be bought.

The fireborn are at home in fire.
The stars make no noise.
You can't hinder the wind from blowing.
Time is a great teacher.
Who can live without hope?

In the darkness with a great bundle of grief
the people march.
In the night, and overhead a shovel of stars for
keeps, the people march:
"Where to? what next?"
The People, Yes, 1936

JOHN DOS PASSOS

Tin Lizzie

"Mr. Ford the automobileer," the featurewriter wrote in 1900,
*"Mr. Ford the automobileer began by giving his steed three or four
sharp jerks with the lever at the righthand side of the seat; that is, he
pulled the lever up and down sharply in order, as he said, to mix air with
gasoline and drive the charge into the exploding cylinder. . . . Mr. Ford
slipped a small electric switch handle and there followed a puff, puff,
puff. . . . The puffing of the machine assumed a higher key. She was
flying along about eight miles an hour. The ruts in the road were deep,
but the machine certainly went with a dreamlike smoothness. There was
none of the bumping common even to a streetcar. . . . By this time the
boulevard had been reached, and the automobileer, letting a lever fall
a little, let her out. Whiz! She picked up speed with infinite rapidity. As she
ran on there was a clattering behind, the new noise of the automobile."*
For twenty years or more,
ever since he'd left his father's farm when he was sixteen to get a job
in a Detroit machineshop, Henry Ford had been nuts about machinery.
First it was watches, then he designed a steamtractor, then he built a
horseless carriage with an engine adapted from the Otto gasengine he'd
read about in *The World of Science*, then a mechanical buggy with a one-
cylinder fourcycle motor, that would run forward but not back;
at last, in ninetyeight, he felt he was far enough along to risk throwing
up his job with the Detroit Edison Company, where he'd worked his way
up from night fireman to chief engineer, to put all his time into working
on a new gasoline engine,
(in the late eighties he'd met Edison at a meeting of electriclight

379

employees in Atlantic City. He'd gone up to Edison after Edison had delivered an address and asked him if he thought gasoline was practical as a motor fuel. Edison had said yes. If Edison said it, it was true. Edison was the great admiration of Henry Ford's life);

and in driving his mechanical buggy, sitting there at the lever jauntily dressed in a tightbuttoned jacket and a high collar and a derby hat, back and forth over the level illpaved streets of Detroit,

scaring the big brewery horses and the skinny trotting horses and the sleekrumped pacers with the motor's loud explosions,

looking for men scatterbrained enough to invest money in a factory for building automobiles.

He was the eldest son of an Irish immigrant who during the Civil War had married the daughter of a prosperous Pennsylvania Dutch farmer and settled down to farming near Dearborn in Wayne County, Michigan;

like plenty of other Americans, young Henry grew up hating the endless sogging through the mud about the chores, the hauling and pitching manure, the kerosene lamps to clean, the irk and sweat and solitude of the farm.

He was a slender, active youngster, a good skater, clever with his hands; what he liked was to tend the machinery and let the others do the heavy work. His mother had told him not to drink, smoke, gamble or go into debt, and he never did.

When he was in his early twenties his father tried to get him back from Detroit, where he was working as mechanic and repairman for the Drydock Engine Company that built the engines for steamboats, by giving him forty acres of land.

Young Henry built himself an uptodate square white dwellinghouse with a false mansard roof and married and settled down on the farm,

but he let the hired men do the farming;

he bought himself a buzzsaw and rented a stationary engine and cut the timber off the woodlots.

He was a thrifty young man who never drank or smoked or gambled or coveted his neighbor's wife, but he couldn't stand living on the farm.

He moved to Detroit, and in the brick barn behind his house tinkered for years in his spare time with a mechanical buggy that would be light enough to run over the clayey wagonroads of Wayne County, Michigan.

By 1900 he had a practicable car to promote.

He was forty years old before the Ford Motor Company was started and production began to move.

Speed was the first thing the early automobile manufacturers went after. Races advertised the makes of cars.

Henry Ford himself hung up several records at the track at Grosse Pointe and on the ice on Lake St. Clair. In his 999 he did the mile in thirtynine and fourfifths seconds.

But it had always been his custom to hire others to do the heavy work. The speed he was busy with was speed in production, the record records in efficient output. He hired Barney Oldfield, a stunt bicyclerider from Salt Lake City, to do the racing for him.

Henry Ford had ideas about other things than the designing of motors, carburetors, magnetos, jigs and fixtures, punches and dies; he had ideas about sales,

that the big money was in economical quantity production, quick turnover, cheap interchangeable easily-replaced standardized parts;

it wasn't until 1909, after years of arguing with his partners, that Ford put out the first Model T.

Henry Ford was right.

That season he sold more than ten thousand tin lizzies, ten years later he was selling almost a million a year.

In these years the Taylor Plan was stirring up plant-managers and manufacturers all over the country. Efficiency was the word. The same ingenuity that went into improving the performance of a machine could go into improving the performance of the workmen producing the machine.

In 1913 they established the assemblyline at Ford's. That season the profits were something like twentyfive million dollars, but they had trouble keeping the men on the job, machinists didn't seem to like it at Ford's.

Henry Ford had ideas about other things than production.

He was the largest automobile manufacturer in the world; he paid high wages; maybe if the steady workers thought they were getting a cut (a very small cut) in the profits, it would give trained men an inducement to stick to their jobs,

wellpaid workers might save enough money to buy a tin lizzie; the first day Ford's announced that cleancut properlymarried American workers who wanted jobs had a chance to make five bucks a day (of course it turned out that there were strings to it; always there were strings to it)

such an enormous crowd waited outside the Highland Park plant

all through the zero January night

that there was a riot when the gates were opened; cops broke heads, jobhunters threw bricks; property, Henry Ford's own property, was destroyed. The company dicks had to turn on the firehose to beat back the crowd.

The American Plan; automotive prosperity seeping down from above; it turned out there were strings to it.

But that five dollars a day

paid to good, clean American workmen

who didn't drink or smoke cigarettes or read or think,

and who didn't commit adultery

and whose wives didn't take in boarders,

made America once more the Yukon of the sweated workers of the world;

made all the tin lizzies and the automotive age, and incidentally,

made Henry Ford the automobileer, the admirer of Edison, the birdlover,

the great American of his time.

But Henry Ford had ideas about other things besides assemblylines and the livinghabits of his employees. He was full of ideas. Instead of going to the city to make his fortune, here was a country boy who'd made his fortune by bringing the city out to the farm. The precepts he'd learned out of McGuffey's Reader, his mother's prejudices and preconceptions, he had preserved clean and unworn as freshprinted bills in the safe in a bank.

He wanted people to know about his ideas, so he bought the *Dearborn Independent* and started a campaign against cigarettesmoking.

When war broke out in Europe, he had ideas about that too. (Suspicion of armymen and soldiering were part of the midwest farm tradition, like thrift, stickativeness, temperance and sharp practice in money matters.) Any intelligent American mechanic could see that if the Europeans hadn't been a lot of ignorant underpaid foreigners who drank, smoked, were loose about women and wasteful in their methods of production, the war could never have happened.

When Rosika Schwimmer broke through the stockade of secretaries and servicemen who surrounded Henry Ford and suggested to him that he could stop the war,

he said sure they'd hire a ship and go over and get the boys out of the trenches by Christmas.

He hired a steamboat, the *Oscar II*, and filled it up with pacifists and socialworkers,

to go over to explain to the princelings of Europe

that what they were doing was vicious and silly.

It wasn't his fault that Poor Richard's commonsense no longer rules the world and that most of the pacifists were nuts,

goofy with headlines.

When William Jennings Bryan went over to Hoboken to see him off, somebody handed William Jennings Bryan a squirrel in a cage; William Jennings Bryan made a speech with the squirrel under his arm. Henry Ford threw American Beauty roses to the crowd. The band played *I Didn't Raise My Boy to Be a Soldier*. Practical jokers let loose more squirrels. An eloping couple was married by a platoon of ministers in the saloon, and Mr. Zero, the flophouse humanitarian, who reached the dock too late to sail,

dove into the North River and swam after the boat.

The *Oscar II* was described as a floating Chautauqua; Henry Ford said it felt like a middlewestern village, but by the time they reached Christiansand in Norway, the reporters had kidded him so that he had gotten cold feet and gone to bed. The world was too crazy outside of Wayne County, Michigan. Mrs. Ford and the management sent an Episcopal dean after him who brought him home under wraps,
and the pacifists had to speechify without him.

Two years later Ford's was manufacturing munitions, Eagle boats; Henry Ford was planning oneman tanks, and oneman submarines like the one tried out in the Revolutionary War. He announced to the press that he'd turn over his war profits to the government, but there's no record that he ever did.

One thing he brought back from his trip
was the Protocols of the Elders of Zion.
He started a campaign to enlighten the world in the *Dearborn Independent*; the Jews were why the world wasn't like Wayne County, Michigan, in the old horse and buggy days;
the Jews had started the war, Bolshevism, Darwinism, Marxism, Nietzsche, short skirts and lipstick. They were behind Wall Street and the international bankers, and the whiteslave traffic and the movies and the Supreme Court and ragtime and the illegal liquor business.
Henry Ford denounced the Jews and ran for senator and sued the *Chicago Tribune* for libel,
and was the laughingstock of the kept metropolitan press;
but when the metropolitan bankers tried to horn in on his business
he thoroughly outsmarted them.

In 1918 he had borrowed on notes to buy out his minority stockholders for the picayune sum of seventy-five million dollars.
In February, 1920, he needed cash to pay off some of these notes that were coming due. A banker is supposed to have called on him and offered him every facility if the bankers' representative could be made a member of the board of directors. Henry Ford handed the banker his hat,
and went about raising the money in his own way:
he shipped every car and part he had in his plant to his dealers and demanded immediate cash payment. Let the other fellow do the borrowing had always been a cardinal principle. He shut down production and canceled all orders from the supplyfirms. Many dealers were ruined, many supplyfirms failed, but when he reopened his plant,
he owned it absolutely,
the way a man owns an unmortgaged farm with the taxes paid up.
In 1922 there started the Ford boom for President (high wages, waterpower, industry scattered to the small towns) that was skillfully pricked behind the scenes by another crackerbarrel philosopher,

Calvin Coolidge;

but in 1922 Henry Ford sold one million three hundred and thirty-two thousand tin lizzies; he was the richest man in the world.

Good roads had followed the narrow ruts made in the mud by the Model T. The great automotive boom was on. At Ford's production was improving all the time; less waste, more spotters, strawbosses, stool pigeons (fifteen minutes for lunch, three minutes to go to the toilet, the Taylorized speedup everywhere, reach under, adjust washer, screw bolt down, shove in cotterpin, reachunder adjustwasher, screwdown bolt, reachunderadjustscrewdownreachunderadjust until every ounce of life was sucked off into production and at night the workmen went home grey shaking husks).

Ford owned every detail of the process from the ore in the hills until the car rolled off the end of the assemblyline under its own power, the plants were rationalized to the last tenthousandth of an inch as measured by the Johansen scale;

in 1926 the production cycle was reduced to eightyone hours from the ore in the mine to the finished salable car proceeding under its own power,

but the Model T was obsolete.

New Era prosperity and the American Plan
(there were strings to it, always there were strings to it)
had killed Tin Lizzie.
Ford's was just one of many automobile plants.
When the stockmarket bubble burst,
Mr. Ford the crackerbarrel philosopher said jubliantly,
"I told you so.
Serves you right for gambling and getting in debt.
The country is sound."
But when the country on cracked shoes, in frayed trousers, belts tightened over hollow bellies,
idle hands cracked and chapped with the cold of that coldest March day of 1932,
started marching from Detroit to Dearborn, asking for work and the American Plan, all they could think of at Ford's was machineguns.
The country was sound, but they mowed the marchers down.
They shot four of them dead.
Henry Ford as an old man
is a passionate antiquarian,
(lives besieged on his father's farm embedded in an estate of thousands of millionaire acres, protected by an army of servicemen, secretaries, secret agents, dicks under orders of an English exprizefighter,
always afraid of the feet in the broken shoes on the roads, afraid the gangs will kidnap his grandchildren,

that a crank will shoot him,
that Change and the idle hands out of work will break through the
gates and the high fences;
protected by a private army against
the new America of starved children and hollow bellies and cracked
shoes stamping on souplines,
that has swallowed up the old thrifty farmlands
of Wayne County, Michigan,
as if they had never been).
Henry Ford as an old man
is a passionate antiquarian.

He rebuilt his father's farmhouse and put it back exactly in the state
he remembered it in as a boy. He built a village of museums for buggies,
sleighs, coaches, old plows, waterwheels, obsolete models of motorcars. He
scoured the country for fiddlers to play old-fashioned squaredances.

Even old taverns he bought and put back into their original shape, as
well as Thomas Edison's early laboratories.

When he bought the Wayside Inn near Sudbury, Massachusetts, he had
the new highway where the newmodel cars roared and slithered and
hissed oilily past (*the new noise of the automobile*),
moved away from the door,
put back the old bad road,
so that everything might be
the way it used to be,
in the days of horses and buggies.

U.S.A., 1930

GEORGE WELLER

Emergency at Sea

During World War II an unusual and dramatic operation took place aboard a submarine, submerged in the Pacific. One of the crew had been struck with an acute attack of appendicitis. There was no doctor available and the operation was performed by a pharmacist's mate. Weller of the Chicago DAILY NEWS *won a Pulitzer Prize with this account.*

Somewhere in Australia— "They are giving him ether now," was what
they said back in the aft torpedo rooms.

"He's gone under, and they're ready to cut him open," the crew whispered, sitting on their pipe bunks cramped between torpedoes.

385

One man went forward and put his arm quietly around the shoulder of another man who was handling the bow diving planes.

"Keep her steady, Jake," he said. "They've just made the first cut. They're feeling around for it now."

"They" were a little group of anxious-faced men with their arms thrust into reversed white pajama coats. Gauze bandages hid all their expressions except the tensity in their eyes.

"It" was an acute appendix inside Dean Rector of Chautauqua, Kansas. The stabbing pains had become unendurable the day before, which was Rector's first birthday at sea. He was nineteen years old.

The big depth gauge that looks like a factory clock and stands beside the "Christmas tree" of red and green gauges regulating the flooding chambers showed where they were. They were below the surface. And above them were enemy waters crossed and recrossed by whirring propellers of Japanese destroyers and transports.

The nearest naval surgeon competent to operate on the nineteen-year-old seaman was thousands of miles and many days away. There was just one way to prevent the appendix from bursting, and that was for the crew to operate upon their shipmate themselves.

And that's what they did; they operated upon him. It was probably one of the largest operations in number of participants that ever occurred.

"He says he's ready to take his chance," the gobs whispered from bulkhead to bulkhead.

"That guy's regular"—the word traveled from bow planes to propeller and back again.

They "kept her steady."

The chief surgeon was a twenty-three-year-old pharmacist's mate wearing a blue blouse with white-taped collar and squashy white duck cap. His name was Wheeler B. Lipes. He came from Newcastle near Roanoke, Virginia, and had taken the Navy hospital course in San Diego, thereafter serving three years in the naval hospital at Philadelphia, where his wife lives.

Lipes' specialty as laboratory technician was in operating a machine that registers heartbeats. He was classified as an electrocardiographer. But he had seen Navy doctors take out one or two appendixes and thought he could do it. Under the sea, he was given his first chance to operate.

There was difficulty about the ether. When below the surface the pressure inside a boat is above the atmospheric pressure. More ether is absorbed under pressure. The submariners did not know how long their operation would last.

They did not know how long it would take to find the appendix. They did not know whether there would be enough ether to keep the patient under throughout the operation.

They didn't want the patient waking up before they were finished.

They decided to operate on the table in the officers' wardroom. In the newest and roomiest American submarine the wardroom is approximately the size of a Pullman-car drawing room. It is flanked by bench seats attached to the wall, and a table occupies the whole room—you enter with knees already crooked to sit down. The only way anyone can be upright in the wardrooms is by kneeling.

The operating room was just long enough so that the patient's head and feet reached the two ends without hanging over.

First they got out a medical book and read up on the appendix, while Rector, his face pale with pain, lay in the narrow bunk. It was probably the most democratic surgical operation ever performed. Everybody from box-plane man to the cook in the galley knew his role.

The cook provided the ether mask. It was an inverted tea strainer. They covered it with gauze.

The twenty-three-year-old "surgeon" had, as his staff of fellow "physicians," all men his senior in age and rank. His anesthetist was Communications Officer Lieutenant Franz Hoskins of Tacoma, Washington.

Before they carried Rector to the wardroom, the submarine Captain, Lieutenant Commander W. B. Ferrall of Pittsburgh, asked Lipes as the "surgeon" to have a talk with the patient.

"Look, Dean, I never did anything like this before," Lipes said. "You don't have much chance to pull through anyhow. What do you say?"

"I know just how it is, Doc."

It was the first time in his life that anybody had called Lipes "Doc." But there was in him, added to the steadiness that goes with a submariner's profession, a new calmness.

The operating staff adjusted gauze masks while members of the engine-room crew pulled tight their reversed pajama coats over their extended arms. The tools were laid out. They were far from perfect or complete for a major operation. The scalpel had no handle.

But submariners are used to "rigging" things. The medicine chest had plenty of hemostats, which are small pincers used for closing blood vessels. The machinist "rigged" a handle for the scalpel from a hemostat.

When you are going to have an operation, you must have some kind of antiseptic agent. Rummaging in the medicine chest, they found sulfanilamide tablets and ground them to powder. One thing was lacking: there was no means of holding open the wound after the incision had been made. Surgical tools used for this are called "muscular retractors." What would they use for retractors? There was nothing in the medicine chest that gave the answer, so they went as usual to the cook's galley.

In the galley they found tablespoons made of Monel metal. They bent these at right angles and had their retractors.

Sterilizers? They went to one of the greasy copper-colored torpedoes waiting beside the tubes. They milked alcohol from the torpedo mechanism and used it as well as boiling water.

The light in the wardroom seemed insufficient; operating rooms always have big lamps. So they brought one of the big floods used for night loadings and rigged it inside the wardroom's sloping ceiling.

The moment for the operation had come. Rector, very pale and stripped, stretched himself out on the wardroom table under the glare of the lamps.

Rubber gloves dipped in torpedo alcohol were drawn upon the youthful "Doc's" hands. The fingers were too long. The rubber ends dribbled limply over.

"You look like Mickey Mouse, Doc," said one onlooker.

Lipes grinned behind the gauze.

Rector on the wardroom table wet his lips, glancing a side look at the tea-strainer ether mask.

With his superior officers as his subordinates, Lipes looked into their eyes, nodded, and Hoskins put the tea mask down over Rector's face. No words were spoken; Hoskins already knew from the book that he should watch Rector's eye pupils dilate.

The twenty-three-year-old surgeon, following the ancient hand rule, put his little finger on Rector's subsiding umbilicus, his thumb on the point of the hipbone, and, by dropping his index finger straight down, found the point where he intended to cut. At his side stood Lieutenant Norvell Ward of Indian Head, Maryland, who was his assistant surgeon.

"I chose him for his coolness and dependability," said the Doc afterward of his superior officer. "He acted as my third and fourth hands."

Lieutenant Ward's job was to place tablespoons in Rector's side as Lipes cut through successive layers of muscles.

Engineering Officer Lieutenant S. Manning of Cheraw, South Carolina, took the job which in a normal operating room is known as "circulating nurse." His job was to see that packets of sterile dressings kept coming and that the torpedo alcohol and boiling water arrived regularly from the galley.

They had what is called an "instrument passer" in Chief Yeoman H. F. Wieg of Sheldon, North Dakota, whose job was to keep the tablespoons coming and coming clean. Submarine Skipper Ferrall too had his part. They made him "recorder." It was his job to keep count of the sponges that went into Rector. A double count of the tablespoons used as retractors was kept: one by the Skipper and one by the cook, who was himself passing them out from the galley.

It took Lipes in his flap-finger rubber gloves nearly twenty minutes to find the appendix.

"I have tried one side of the caecum," he whispered after the first minutes. "Now, I'm trying the other."

Whispered bulletins seeped back into the engine room and the crews' quarters.

"The Doc has tried one side of something and now is trying the other side."

388

After more search, Lipes finally whispered, "I think I've got it. It's curled way into the blind gut."

Lipes was using the classical McBurney's incision. Now was the time when his shipmate's life was completely in his hands.

"Two more spoons." They passed the word to Lieutenant Ward.

"Two spoons at 14.45 hours [2:45 P.M.]," wrote Skipper Ferrall on his note pad.

"More flashlights. And another battle lantern," demanded Lipes.

The patient's face, lathered with white petrolatum, began to grimace.

"Give him more ether," ordered the Doc.

Hoskins looked doubtfully at the original five pounds of ether now shrunk to hardly three quarters of one can, but once again the tea strainer was soaked in ether. The fumes mounted up, thickening the wardroom air and making the operating staff giddy.

"Want those blowers speeded up?" the Captain asked the Doc.

The blowers began to whir louder.

Suddenly came the moment when the Doc reached out his hand, pointing toward the needle threaded with twenty-day chromic catgut.

One by one the sponges came out. One by one the tablespoons bent into right angles were withdrawn and returned to the galley. At the end it was the Skipper who nudged Lipes and pointed to the tally of bent tablespoons. One was missing. Lipes reached into the incision for the last time and withdrew the wishboned spoon and closed the incision.

They even had the tool ready to cut off the thread. It was a pair of fingernail scissors, well scalded in water and torpedo juice.

At that moment the last can of ether went dry. They lifted up Rector and carried him into the bunk of Lieutenant Charles K. Miller of Williamsport, Pennsylvania. Lieutenant Miller alone had had control of the ship as diving officer during the operation.

It was half an hour after the last tablespoon had been withdrawn that Rector opened his eyes. His first words were, "I'm still in there pitching."

By that time the sweat-drenched officers were hanging up their pajamas to dry. It had taken the amateurs about two and a half hours for an operation ordinarily requiring forty-five minutes.

"It wasn't one of those 'snappy valve' appendixes," murmured Lipes apologetically as he felt the first handclasps upon his shoulders.

Within a few hours, the bow and stern planesmen, who, under Lieutenant Miller's direction, had kept the submarine from varying more than half a degree vertically in 150 minutes below the stormy sea, came around to receive Rector's winks of thanks. Rector's only remark was, "Gee, I wish Earl was here to see this job." His brother Earl, a seaman on the Navy submarine tender *Pigeon*, is among the list of missing at Corregidor, probably captured.

Chicago *Daily News*, December 14, 1942

ERNIE PYLE

The Death of Captain Waskow

Because Pyle could so easily put himself in a G.I.'s shoes, think and feel like him, he became the forces' favorite correspondent during World War II. His human interest reports from the fighting fronts were the most widely syndicated dispatches of any correspondent.

At the Front Lines in Italy, Jan. 10 [1944] (by Wireless)— In this war I have known a lot of officers who were loved and respected by the soldiers under them. But never have I crossed the trail of any man as beloved as Capt. Henry T. Waskow of Belton, Texas.

Capt. Waskow was a company commander in the 36th Division. He was very young, only in his middle twenties, but he carried in him a sincerity and gentleness that made people want to be guided by him.

"After my own father, he comes next," a sergeant told me.

"He always looked after us," a soldier said. "He'd go to bat for us every time."

"I've never known him to do anything unkind," another one said.

I was at the foot of the mule trail the night they brought Capt. Waskow down. The moon was nearly full, and you could see far up the trail, and even part way across the valley. Soldiers made shadows as they walked.

Dead men had been coming down the mountain all evening lashed onto the backs of mules. They came lying belly down across the wooden packsaddles, their heads hanging down on the left side of the mules, their stiffened legs sticking awkwardly from the other side, bobbing up and down as the mule walked.

The Italian mule skinners were afraid to walk beside the dead men, so Americans had to lead the mules down that night. Even the Americans were reluctant to unlash and lift off the bodies when they go to the bottom, so an officer had to do it himself and ask others to help.

The first one came early in the morning. They slid him down from the mule, and stood him on his feet for a moment. In the half light he might have been merely a sick man standing there leaning on the other. Then they laid him on the ground in the shadow of the stone wall alongside the road.

I don't know who the first one was. You feel small in the presence of dead men and you don't ask silly questions.

We left him there beside the road, that first one, and we all went back into the cowshed and sat on watercans or lay on the straw, waiting for the next batch of mules.

390

Somebody said the dead soldier had been dead for four days, and then nobody said anything more about him. We talked for an hour or more; the dead man lay all alone, outside in the shadow of the wall.

Then a soldier came into the cowshed and said there were some more bodies outside. We went out into the road. Four mules stood there in the moonlight, in the road where the trail came down off the mountain. The soldiers who led them stood there waiting.

"This one is Capt. Waskow," one of them said quickly.

Two men unlashed his body from the mule and lifted it off and laid it in the shadow beside the stone wall. Other men took the other bodies off. Finally there were five lying end to end in a long row. You don't cover up dead men in the combat zone. They just lie there in the shadows until somebody else comes after them.

The uncertain mules moved off to their olive groves. The men in the road seemed reluctant to leave. They stood around, and gradually I could sense them moving, one by one, close to Capt. Waskow's body. Not so much to look, I think, as to say something in finality to him and to themselves. I stood close by and I could hear.

One soldier came and looked down, and he said out loud:

"God damn it!"

That's all he said, and then he walked away.

Another one came, and he said, "God damn it to hell, anyway!" He looked down for a few last moments and then turned and left.

Another man came. I think he was an officer. It was hard to tell officers from men in the dim light, for everybody was grimy and dirty. The man looked down into the dead captain's face and then spoke directly to him, as though he were alive:

"I'm sorry, old man."

Then a soldier came in and stood beside the officer and bent over, and he too spoke to his dead captain, not in a whisper but awfully tenderly, and he said:

"I sure am sorry, sir."

Then the first man squatted down, and he reached down and took the captain's hand, and he sat there for a full five minutes holding the dead hand in his own and looking intently into the dead face. And he never uttered a sound all the time he sat there.

Finally he put the hand down. He reached up and gently straightened the points of the captain's shirt collar, and then he sort of rearranged the tattered edges of his uniform around the wound, and then he got up and walked away down the road in the moonlight, all alone.

The rest of us went back into the cowshed, leaving the five dead men lying in a line end to end in the shadow of the low stone wall. We lay down on the straw in the cowshed, and pretty soon we were all asleep.

Brave Men, 1944

JESSAMYN WEST

Reverdy

I never see asters without remembering her—never the haze of their pink and lavender blossoming as summer dies, but her name is in my heart: Reverdy, Reverdy.

I never say her name—not to anyone. When people ask about her, as they do occasionally even now, I say "she" and "her." "She is still gone." "We do not hear from her." "Yes, she was very beautiful," I say. But not her name.

Not Reverdy. That is buried deep, deep in my heart. Where the blood is warmest and thickest. . . . Where it has a sound to me like bells, or water running, or the doves whose voices in the evening wind are like smoke among the madronas and eucalypti.

I have longed all these years to tell her how it was the night she left. You may scarcely believe it, but it is worse to have a good thing that is not true believed about you, than a bad. To be thanked for an act you meant as harmful: Every year those words sharpen until at last they cut like knives.

You mustn't think she was like me. She wasn't in the least. Not inside nor out. She had dark hair like a cloud. Yes, really. It wasn't curly but it didn't hang straight. It billowed out. And her face—oh, you mustn't think it was anything like mine. She had hazel eyes and a pointed chin. And you've seen lots of people, haven't you, with very live, animated faces and dead eyes? It was just the other way with Reverdy. Her face was always quiet, but her eyes were so alive they glowed. Oh, she was the most beautiful, most alive, and most loving girl in the world, and she was my sister.

I cannot bear for people to say we were alike; she was really good, and I was just a show-off.

Mother—she was better later, and gentler, but then she was bad, cruel, and suspicious with Reverdy. Everybody loved Reverdy. Not just the boys. But Mother couldn't see that. She always acted as if Reverdy were boy-crazy, as if Reverdy tried to entice the boys to her. But it wasn't true. Reverdy never lifted a finger to a boy, though they were about her all the time from the day she was ten. Bringing her May baskets, or Valentines, or their ponies to ride.

And the big, tough boys liked her, too. When she was twelve and thirteen, big eighteen-year-olds would come over and sit on the steps and smoke and talk to Reverdy. They never said anything out of the way. I know because most of the time I was with them. Reverdy didn't care. She never wanted to be alone with them. Reverdy would listen to them until she got tired; then she'd say, "Good-bye for now." She'd always say,

"Good-bye for now,"—and then she'd go out and play, maybe run, sheep, run with the little kids my age. And the little kids would all shout when Reverdy came out to play with them, and if the game had been about to die, it would come to life again. If some of the kids had gone home they'd yell "Hey, Johnnie," or "Hey, Mary," or whoever it was, "Reverdy's going to play," and then everyone would come back, and in a minute or two the game would be better than ever.

I used to be awfully proud of being her sister. I don't know what I would have done without her. I was a terribly plain little frump: I wore glasses and had freckles, and if I hadn't been Reverdy's sister I'd have had to sit and play jacks by myself until Joe came along. But boys would try to get Reverdy's attention by doing things for me. They'd say to her, "Does your sister want to ride on my handle bars?" And Reverdy would say, all glowing, happier than if she'd been asked, "Do you, Sister?" Of course I did, and then when the boy came back *she'd* ride with him just to thank him.

I don't know why people—why the boys liked her so. Of course, she was beautiful, but I think it was more that she was so much—well, whatever she was at the moment, she never pretended. She talked with people when she wanted to, and when she got tired of them, she didn't stay on pretending, but said, "Good-bye for now," and left.

But Mother would never believe she wasn't boy-crazy and I would hear her talking to Reverdy about girls who got in trouble, and how she'd rather see a daughter of hers in her grave. I didn't know what she was talking about, but it would make my face burn and scalp tingle just to hear her. She wouldn't talk sorrowfully or lovingly to Reverdy, but with hate. It wasn't Reverdy she hated, but you couldn't tell that, looking at her. She would bend over Reverdy and shake her finger and there would be long ugly lines from her nose to her mouth, and her eyebrows would be drawn down until you could see the bony ridges they were supposed to cover, all bare and hard. It used to make me tremble to see her. Then Reverdy would get mad. I don't think she knew half the time what Mother was talking about either—only that Mother was full of hate and suspicion. She'd wait until Mother had finished; then she'd go to the foothills for a walk—even if it was dark—and stay for a long time. And then Mother would think she was out with some boy again.

I remember one time my mother came to me and said, "Clare, I want you to tiptoe out to the arbor and see what's going on there. Reverdy's out there with Sam Foss and I haven't heard a sound out of them for an hour or more."

The arbor was a kind of little bower covered with honeysuckle. There was only a tiny little door, and the honeysuckle strands hung so thick over it the arbor was a kind of dark, sweet-smelling cave. Reverdy and I used to play house there. I knew I ought to say I wouldn't go spying on Reverdy, but I wanted to please Mother; so I went creeping out toward the arbor, holding my breath, walking on my toes. I didn't know then—but I've found out since—you can't do a thing without becoming that thing. When I started out to look for Reverdy I was her little sister, loving her. But creeping that way, holding my breath, spying, I became a spy. My hands got heavy and hot and my mouth dry, and I wanted to see her doing—whatever it was—Mother was fearful of.

And then when I got to the arbor and peeped in, I saw that Chummie, our ten-year-old brother, was there with them, and they were all practicing sign language. Deaf-and-dumb language was the rage with kids that summer, and there was that big Sam Foss sitting cross-legged, practicing sign language so hard he was sweating. They had oranges rolled until they were soft, and straws stuck in them to suck the juice out.

That's all they were doing. Practicing deaf-and-dumb language, and sucking oranges that way, playing they were bottles of pop. I guess they'd taken a vow not to talk, because nobody said a word. Even when Reverdy saw me peeping in she didn't say anything, but just spelled out, "Hello, Sister." But my hands felt so hot and swollen I couldn't spell a thing, and I just stood there and stared until I heard Mother call me to her, where she was standing strained and waiting on the back steps.

"They're playing sign-language with Chummie," I told her.

"Is Chummie with them?" she asked and her face relaxed and had a sort of shamed look on it, I thought.

I went in the house and put on the old dress I went swimming in, and floated around in the irrigation canal until supper was over and so I wouldn't have to sit and look across the table at Reverdy.

Things like that were always happening. I loved Reverdy more than anybody, and I hated Mother sometimes for spying and suspecting and lecturing. But I wanted people to love me. And especially you want your mother to love you—isn't that true? And no one loved me—the way Reverdy was loved. I wasn't beautiful and spontaneous; I had to work hard and do good deeds to be loved. I couldn't be free the way Reverdy was. I was always thinking of the effect I was making. I couldn't say, "Good-bye for now," and let people go to hell if they didn't like me. I was afraid they'd never come back . . . and I'd be left . . . alone. But Reverdy didn't care. She liked being alone, and that's the reason people loved her, I guess.

One evening in October, when it was almost dark, I was coming home from the library, coasting across lots in the hot dry Santa Ana that had been blowing all day. Cool weather had already come, and then three days of this hot wind. Dust everywhere. Under your eyelids, between your fingers, in your mouth. When we went to school in the morning the first thing we'd do would be to write our names in the dust on our desks. I had on a skirt full of pleats that evening, and I pulled the pleats out wide so the skirt made a sort of sail and the wind almost pushed me along. I watched the tumbleweeds blowing, and listened to the wind in the clump of eucalypti by the barn, and felt miserable and gritty. Then

I saw Reverdy walking up and down the driveway by the house and I felt suddenly glad. Reverdy loved the wind, even Santa Anas, and she was always out walking or running when the wind blew, if she didn't have any work to do. She liked to carry a scarf in her hand and hold it up in the wind so she could feel it tug and snap. When I saw Reverdy I forgot how dusty and hot the wind was and remembered only how alive it was and how Reverdy loved it. I ran toward her, but she didn't wave or say a word, and when she reached the end of the driveway she turned her back on me and started walking toward the barn.

Before I had a chance to say a word to her, Mother came to the door and called to me to come in and not talk to Reverdy. As soon as I heard her voice before I could see her face, I knew there was some trouble— some trouble with Reverdy—and I knew what kind of trouble, too. I went in the house and shut the door. The sound of Reverdy's footsteps on the pepper leaves in the driveway outside stopped and Mother put her head out of the window and said, "You're to keep walking, Reverdy, and not stop. Understand? I want to hear footsteps and I want them to be brisk." Then she closed the window, though it was hard to do so against the wind.

I stood with my face to the window and looked out into the dusty, windy dark where I could just see Reverdy in her white dress walking up and down, never stopping, her head bent, not paying any attention to the wind she loved. It made me feel sick to see her walking up and down there in the dusty dark like a homeless dog, while we were snug inside.

But Mother came over to the window and took the curtain out of my hand and put it back over the glass. Then she put her arm around my shoulders and pressed me close to her and said, "Mother's own dear girl who has never given her a moment's trouble."

That wasn't true. Mother had plenty of fault to find with me usually, but it was sweet to have her speak lovingly to me, to be cherished and appreciated. Maybe you can't understand that, maybe your family was always loving, maybe you were always dear little daughter, or maybe, a big golden wonder-boy. But not me and not my mother. So try to understand how it was with me, then, and how happy it made me to have Mother put her arms about me. Yes, I thought, I'm Mother's comfort. And I forgot I couldn't make a boy look at me if I wanted to and blamed Reverdy for not being able to steer clear of them the way I did. She just hasn't any consideration for any of us, I decided. Oh, I battened on Reverdy's downfall all right.

Then Father and Chummie came in and Mother took Father away to the kitchen and talked to him there in a fast, breathless voice. I couldn't hear what she was saying, but I knew what she was talking about, of course. Chummie and I sat there in the dark. He whirled first one way and then another on the piano stool.

"What's Reverdy doing walking up and down outside there?" he asked.

"She's done something bad again," I told him.

Mother's voice got higher and higher, and Chummie said he'd have to go feed his rabbits, and I was left alone in the dark listening to her, and to Reverdy's footsteps on the pepper leaves. I decided to light the lights, but when I did—we had acetylene lights—the blue-white glare was so terrible I couldn't stand it. Not to sit alone in all that light and look at the dusty room and listen to the dry sound of the wind in the palms outside, and see Reverdy's books on the library table where she'd put them when she got home from school, with a big bunch of wilted asters laid across them. Reverdy always kept her room filled with flowers, and if she couldn't get flowers, she'd have leaves or grasses.

No, I couldn't stand that; so I turned out the lights and sat in the dark and listened to Reverdy's steps, not fast or light now, but heavy and slow. . . . And I sat there and thought I was Mother's comfort, not causing her trouble like Reverdy.

Pretty soon I heard Mother and Father go outside, and then their voices beneath the window. Father was good, and he was for reason, but with Mother he lost his reason. He was just like me, I guess. He wanted Mother to love him, and because he did he would go out and say to Reverdy the things Mother wanted him to say.

Chummie came back from feeding his rabbits and sat with me in the dark room. Then I got the idea of a way to show Mother how much I was her comfort and mainstay, her darling younger daughter, dutiful and harmonious as hell. Mother wanted me and Chummie to be musical; she'd given up with Reverdy, but Chummie and I had taken lessons for years. Usually we kicked and howled at having to play; so, I thought, if we play now it will show Mother how thoughtful and reliable we are. It will cheer her up while she's out there in the wind talking to that bad Reverdy. Yes, she will think, I have one fine, dependable daughter, anyway.

So I said to Chummie, "Let's play something for Mother." So he got out his violin, and we played that piece I've ever afterwards hated. Over and over again, just as sweet as we could make it. Oh, I felt smug as hell as I played. I sat there on the piano stool with feet just so, and my hands just so, and played carefully, every note saying, "Mother's comfort. Mother's comfort. Played by her good, fine, reliable daughter."

We could hear Mother's high voice outside the window and Reverdy's low murmur now and then. Chummie finally got tired of playing—the music wasn't saying anything to him—and went out to the kitchen to get something to eat. I went too, but the minute I took a bite I knew I wasn't hungry, and Chummie and I went to bed. I lay in bed a long time waiting to hear Mother and Reverdy come in, but there wasn't any sound but the wind.

I was asleep when Reverdy did come in. She sat down on the side of my bed, and it was just her sitting there that finally awakened me. Then, when I was awake she picked up my hand and began to press my finger tips one by one, and spoke in the sweetest, kindest voice. You'd never have thought to hear her that she had just spent four or five hours the way she did.

She said, "I'll never forget your playing for me, Sister. Never. Never. It was kind and beautiful of you. Just when I thought I was all alone I heard you telling me not to be sad." Then she leaned over and kissed me and said, "Good night, now. I've put some asters in water for you. They're a little wilted but I think they'll be all right by morning. Go to sleep, now, I'll never forget, Clare."

If I could only have told her—if I could only have told her then. If I could have said to her, "I was playing for Mother, Reverdy. I guess I was jealous of your always having the limelight. I wanted to be first for once." If I could only have said, "I love you more than anything, Reverdy, but I have a mean soul," she would have put her cheek to mine and said, "Oh, Clare, what a thing to say."

But I couldn't do it and next morning she was gone. And there on the table by my bed were the asters she had left for me, grown fresh over night.

New Mexico Quarterly, Spring, 1943

HAL BOYLE

"Dear Mom"

Boyle moved from copy boy with the Associated Press at Kansas City, Missouri, to posts of increasing responsibility in St. Louis and New York. During World War II he became widely known as a war correspondent, winning a Pulitzer Prize.

There is an engaging warmth to this open letter to his mother, Mrs. P. E. Boyle.

Dear Mom,

You are one of the world's hardest gals to please on Mother's Day.

The ordinary presents are no good at all. You don't want jewelry. If your children buy you flowers or candy, you say, "It's just a waste of money." They can't give you money with any sense of satisfaction because they know you won't spend it on yourself. You'll just put it away in an old sock for your grandchildren.

"Oh, don't give me anything—Mother's Day is just a bunch of nonsense," you say. Your happiest Mother's Days have been the ones on which you spent five hours turning your face cherry red over a cookstove fixing a family feast—in the years when the whole family could be there to enjoy it.

What could one who was away do to please you except to call you long-distance and tell you he missed you and wished he was home? It is hard to give anything to a woman who has spent her life in giving to others.

The only thing I have to offer you is the one thing you never asked for—appreciation.

Why do I love you? Let me count the reasons—just a few:

I love you because you are my mother, not only of my body but of my spirit's hunger.

I love you because when I deserved and needed a switching I got it—not later, but right then when I knew I had done wrong, felt guilty, and recognized I should be punished.

I love you because you never let tomorrow's sun rise on yesterday's anger.

I love you because you played no favorites among your children. Your only favorite child (this is still true) was the one that most needed your understanding help at the time.

I love you because when the cat had too many kittens you couldn't bear to have them drowned. (With five kids yourself you could understand the mother cat's problem.)

I love you because, although you had only a third-grade education, you never ceased reading and learning and widening the horizon of your own mind. And from your mind my mind caught fire.

I love you because you always watered and fed my adolescent dreams.

I love you because, when Dad died nearly 19 years ago, you refused to turn into a self-pitying widow. Time has mellowed you. It cannot shrivel or defeat you.

I love you because, now that your children have grown, you refuse to try to run their lives. You merely say mildly "learn to sit loosely in the saddle of life."

I love you because, although you and I have always felt free to talk to each other about anything, from the whims of God to the frailties of man, I feel I really know less about you than almost anyone I know at all. You have always held a mystery to me, you always will. The more you love people, the more you realize there is a part of them you cannot ever know.

Finally, I love you because I know that when you read this you will be embarrassed and say, "Now, why did he have to do that? Can't he think of something more important to write about than that?"

Well, not today, Mom.

Respectfully,
Your long son,
HAROLD

New York *World-Telegram and Sun*, May 12, 1956

THE WEST

FRANCIS PARKMAN

A Visit with Indians of the Sioux Tribe, in Wyoming

*When Boston-born Parkman became interested in history while
studying law at Harvard, he and a college friend, Quincy Adams
Shaw, set out to see the West. His great book was the result of
those two years of adventure and hardship.*

Such a narrative as this is hardly the place for portraying the mental features of the Indians. The same picture, slightly changed in shade and
coloring, would serve with very few exceptions for all the tribes that lie
north of the Mexican territories. But with this striking similarity in their
modes of thought, the tribes of the lake and ocean shores, of the forests
and of the plains, differ greatly in their manner of life.

Having been domesticated for several weeks among one of the wildest
of the wild hordes that roam over the remote prairies, I had extraordinary
opportunities of observing them, and I flatter myself that a faithful picture
of the scenes that passed daily before my eyes may not be devoid of interest and value. These men were thorough savages. Neither their manners nor their ideas were in the slightest degree modified by contact with
civilization. They knew nothing of the power and real character of the
white men, and their children would scream in terror at the sight of me.
Their religion, their superstitions, and their prejudices were the same
that had been handed down to them from immemorial time. They fought
with the same weapons that their fathers fought with and wore the same
rude garments of skins.

Great changes are at hand in that region. With the stream of emigration to Oregon and California, the buffalo will dwindle away, and the
large wandering communities who depend on them for support must be

broken and scattered. The Indians will soon be corrupted by the example of the whites, abased by whisky, and overawed by military posts; so that within a few years the traveler may pass in tolerable security through their country. Its danger and its charm will have disappeared together.

As soon as Raymond and I discovered the village from the gap in the hills, we were seen in our turn; keen eyes were constantly on the watch. As we rode down upon the plain the side of the village nearest us was darkened with a crowd of naked figures gathering around the lodges. Several men came forward to meet us. I could distinguish among them the green blanket of the Frenchman Reynal. When we came up the ceremony of shaking hands had to be gone through with in due form, and then all were eager to know what had become of the rest of my party. I satisfied them on this point, and we all moved forward together toward the village.

"You've missed it," said Reynal; "if you'd been here day before yesterday, you'd have found the whole prairie over yonder black with buffalo as far as you could see. There were no cows, though; nothing but bulls. We made a 'surround' every day till yesterday. See the village there; don't that look like good living?"

In fact I could see, even at that distance, that long cords were stretched from lodge to lodge, over which the meat, cut by the squaws into thin sheets, was hanging to dry in the sun. I noticed too that the village was somewhat smaller than when I had last seen it, and I asked Reynal the cause. He said that old Le Borgne had felt too weak to pass over the mountains, and so had remained behind with all his relations, including Mahto-Tatonka and his brothers. The Whirlwind too had been unwilling to come so far, because, as Reynal said, he was afraid. Only half a dozen lodges had adhered to him, the main body of the village setting their chief's authority at naught, and taking the course most agreeable to their inclinations.

"What chiefs are there in the village now?" said I.

"Well," said Reynal, "there's old Red-Water, and the Eagle-Feather, and the Big Crow, and the Mad Wolf and the Panther, and the White Shield, and—what's his name?—the half-breed Cheyenne."

By this time we were close to the village, and I observed that while the greater part of the lodges were very large and neat in their appearance, there was at one side a cluster of squalid, miserable huts. I looked toward them, and made some remark about their wretched appearance. But I was touching upon delicate ground.

"My squaw's relations live in those lodges," said Reynal very warmly, "and there isn't a better set in the whole village."

"Are there any chiefs among them?" asked I.

"Chiefs?" said Reynal; "yes, plenty!"

"What are their names?" I inquired.

"Their names? Why, there's the Arrow-Head. If he isn't a chief he ought to be one. And there's the Hail-Storm. He's nothing but a boy, to be sure; but he's bound to be a chief one of these days!"

Just then we passed between two of the lodges, and entered the great area of the village. Superb naked figures stood silently gazing on us.

"Where's the Bad Wound's lodge?" said I to Reynal.

"There, you've missed it again! The Bad Wound is away with the Whirlwind. If you could have found him here, and gone to live in his lodge, he would have treated you better than any man in the village. But there's the Big Crow's lodge yonder, next to old Red-Water's. He's a good Indian for the whites, and I advise you to go and live with him."

"Are there many squaws and children in his lodge?" said I.

"No; only one squaw and two or three children. He keeps the rest in a separate lodge by themselves."

So, still followed by a crowd of Indians, Raymond and I rode up to the entrance of the Big Crow's lodge. A squaw came out immediately and took our horses. I put aside the leather nap that covered the low opening, and stooping, entered the Big Crow's dwelling. There I could see the chief in the dim light, seated at one side, on a pile of buffalo robes. He greeted me with a guttural "How, cola!" I requested Reynal to tell him that Raymond and I were come to live with him. The Big Crow gave another low exclamation. If the reader thinks that we were intruding somewhat cavalierly, I beg him to observe that every Indian in the village would have deemed himself honored that white men should give such preference to his hospitality.

The squaw spread a buffalo robe for us in the guest's place at the head of the lodge. Our saddles were brought in, and scarcely were we seated upon them before the place was thronged with Indians, who came crowding in to see us. The Big Crow produced his pipe and filled it with the mixture of tobacco and *shongsasha*, or red willow bark. Round and round it passed, and a lively conversation went forward. Meanwhile a squaw placed before the two guests a wooden bowl of boiled buffalo meat, but unhappily this was not the only banquet destined to be inflicted on us. Rapidly, one after another, boys and young squaws thrust their heads in at the opening, to invite us to various feasts in different parts of the village. For half an hour or more we were actively engaged in passing from lodge to lodge, tasting in each of the bowl of meat set before us, and inhaling a whiff or two from our entertainer's pipe. A thunderstorm that had been threatening for some time now began in good earnest. We crossed over to Reynal's lodge, though it hardly deserved this name, for it consisted only of a few old buffalo robes, supported on poles, and was quite open on one side. Here we sat down, and the Indians gathered round us.

"What is it," said I, "that makes the thunder?"

"It's my belief," said Reynal, "that it is a big stone rolling over the sky."

"Very likely," I replied; "but I want to know what the Indians think about it."

So he interpreted my question, which seemed to produce some doubt and debate. There was evidently a difference of opinion. At last old Mene-Seela, or Red-Water, who sat by himself at one side, looked up with his withered face, and said he had always known what the thunder was. It was a great black bird; and once he had seen it, in a dream, swooping down from the Black Hills, with its loud roaring wings; and when it flapped them over a lake, they struck lightning from the water.

"The thunder is bad," said another old man, who sat muffled in his buffalo robe; "he killed my brother last summer."

Reynal, at my request, asked for an explanation; but the old man remained doggedly silent, and would not look up. Some time after I learned how the accident occurred. The man who was killed belonged to an association which, among other mystic functions, claimed the exclusive power and privilege of fighting the thunder. Whenever a storm which they wished to avert was threatening, the thunder-fighters would take their bows and arrows, their guns, their magic drum, and a sort of whistle, made out of the wingbone of the war eagle. Thus equipped, they would run out and fire at the rising cloud, whooping, yelling, whistling, and beating their drum, to frighten it down again. One afternoon a heavy black cloud was coming up, and they repaired to the top of a hill, where they brought all their magic artillery into play against it. But the undaunted thunder, refusing to be terrified, kept moving straight onward, and darted out in a bright flash which struck one of the party dead, as he was in the very act of shaking his long iron-pointed lance against it. The rest scattered and ran yelling in an ecstasy of superstitious terror back to their lodges.

The lodge of my host Kongra-Tonga, or the Big Crow, presented a picturesque spectacle that evening. A score or more of Indians were seated around in a circle, their dark naked forms just visible by the dull light of the smoldering fire in the center, the pipe glowing brightly in the gloom as it passed from hand to hand round the lodge. Then a squaw would drop a piece of buffalo-fat on the dull embers. Instantly a bright glancing flame would leap up, darting its clear light to the very apex of the tall conical structure, where the tops of the slender poles that supported its covering of leather were gathered together. It gilded the features of the Indians, as with animated gestures they sat around it, telling their endless stories of war and hunting. It displayed rude garments of skins that hung around the lodge; the bow, quiver, and lance suspended over the resting-place of the chief, and the rifles and powder-horns of the two white guests. For a moment all would be bright as day; then the flames would die away, and fitful flashes from the embers would illumine the lodge, and then leave it in darkness. Then all the light would wholly fade, and the lodge and all within it be involved again in obscurity.

As I left the lodge next morning, I was saluted by howling and yelling from all around the village, and half its canine population rushed forth to the attack. Being as cowardly as they were clamorous, they kept jumping around me at the distance of a few yards, only one little cur, about ten inches long, having spirit enough to make a direct assault. He dashed valiantly at the leather tassel which in the Dakota fashion was trailing behind the heel of my moccasin, and kept his hold, growling and snarling all the while, though every step I made almost jerked him over on his back. As I knew that the eyes of the whole village were on the watch to see if I showed any sign of apprehension, I walked forward without looking to the right or left, surrounded wherever I went by this magic circle of dogs. When I came to Reynal's lodge I sat down by it, on which the dogs dispersed growling to their respective quarters. Only one large white one remained, who kept running about before me and showing his teeth. I called him, but he only growled the more. I looked at him well. He was fat and sleek; just such a dog as I wanted. "My friend," thought I, "you shall pay for this! I will have you eaten this very morning!"

I intended that day to give the Indians a feast, by way of conveying a favorable impression of my character and dignity; and a white dog is the dish which the customs of the Dakota prescribe for all occasions of formality and importance. I consulted Reynal; he soon discovered that an old woman in the next lodge was owner of the white dog. I took a gaudy cotton handkerchief, and laying it on the ground, arranged some vermilion, beads, and other trinkets upon it. Then the old squaw was summoned. I pointed to the dog and to the handkerchief. She gave a scream of delight, snatched up the prize, and vanished with it into her lodge. For a few more trifles I engaged the services of two other squaws, each of whom took the white dog by one of his paws, and led him away behind the lodges, while he kept looking up at them with a face of innocent surprise. Having killed him they threw him into a fire to singe; then chopped him up and put him into two large kettles to boil. Meanwhile I told Raymond to fry in buffalo-fat what little flour we had left, and also to make a kettle of tea as an additional item of the repast.

The Big Crow's squaw was set briskly at work sweeping out the lodge for the approaching festivity. I confided to my host himself the task of inviting the guests, thinking that I mighty thereby shift from my own shoulders the odium of fancied neglect and oversight.

When feasting is in question, one hour of the day serves an Indian as well as another. My entertainment came off about eleven o'clock. At that hour, Reynal and Raymond walked across the area of the village, to the admiration of the inhabitants, carrying the two kettles of dogmeat slung on a pole between them. These they placed in the center of the lodge, and then went back for the bread and the tea. Meanwhile I had put on a pair of brilliant moccasins, and substituted for my old buckskin frock a coat which I had brought with me in view of such public occasions. I also made careful use of the razor, an operation which no man will neglect who desires to gain the good opinion of Indians. Thus attired, I seated myself between Reynal and Raymond at the head of the lodge. Only a few minutes elapsed before all the guests had come in and were seated on the ground, wedged together in a close circle around the lodge. Each brought with him a wooden bowl to hold his share of the repast. When all were assembled, two of the officials called "soldiers" by the white men, came forward with ladles made of the horn of the Rocky Mountain sheep, and began to distribute the feast, always assigning a double share to the old men and chiefs. The dog vanished with astonishing celerity, and each guest turned his dish bottom upward to show that all was gone. Then the bread was distributed in its turn, and finally the tea. As the soldiers poured it out into the same wooden bowls that had served for the substantial part of the meal, I thought it had a particularly curious and uninviting color.

"Oh!" said Reynal, "there was not tea enough, so I stirred some soot in the kettle, to make it look strong."

Fortunately an Indian's palate is not very discriminating. The tea was well sweetened, and that was all they cared for.

Now the former part of the entertainment being concluded, the time for speech-making was come. The Big Crow produced a flat piece of wood on which he cut up tobacco and *shongsasha*, and mixed them in due proportions. The pipes were filled and passed from hand to hand around the company. Then I began my speech, each sentence being interpreted by Reynal as I went on, and echoed by the whole audience with the usual exclamations of assent and approval. As nearly as I can recollect, it was as follows:

I had come, I told them, from a country far distant, that at the rate they travel, they could not reach it in a year.

"How howô!"

"There the Meneaska were more numerous than the blades of grass on the prairie. The squaws were far more beautiful than any they had ever seen, and all the men were brave warriors."

"How! how! how!"

Here I was assailed by sharp twinges of conscience, for I fancied I could perceive a fragrance of perfumery in the air, and a vision rose before me of white kid gloves and silken mustaches with the mild and gentle countenances of numerous fair-haired young men. But I recovered myself and began again.

"While I was living in the Meneaska lodges, I had heard of the Ogallalla, how great and brave a nation they were, how they loved the whites, and how well they could hunt the buffalo and strike their enemies. I resolved to come and see if all I heard was true."

"How! how! how! how!"

"As I had come on horseback through the mountains, I had been able to bring them only a very few presents."

"How!"

"But I had enough tobacco to give them all a small piece. They might

406

smoke it, and see how much better it was than the tobacco which they got from the traders."

"How! how! how!"

"I had plenty of powder, lead, knives, and tobacco at Fort Laramie. These I was anxious to give them, and if any of them should come to the fort before I went away, I would make them handsome presents."

"How! howô how! how!"

Raymond then cut up and distributed among them two or three pounds of tobacco, and old Mene-Seela began to make a reply. It was quite long, but the following was the pith of it:

"He had always loved the whites. They were the wisest people on earth. He believed they could do everything, and he was always glad when any of them came to live in the Ogallalla lodges. It was true I had not made them many presents, but the reason of it was plain. It was clear that I liked them, or I never should have come so far to find their village."

Several other speeches of similar import followed, and then this more serious matter being disposed of, there was an interval of smoking, laughing, and conversation; but old Mene-Seela suddenly interrupted it with a loud voice:

"Now is a good time," he said, "when all the old men and chiefs are here together, to decide what the people shall do. We came over the mountain to make our lodges for next year. Our old ones are good for nothing; they are rotten and worn out. But we have been disappointed. We have killed buffalo bulls enough, but we have found no herds of cows, and the skins of bulls are too thick and heavy for our squaws to make lodges of. There must be plenty of cows about the Medicine-Bow Mountain. We ought to go there. To be sure it is farther westward than we have ever been before, and perhaps the Snakes will attack us, for those hunting-grounds belong to them. But we must have new lodges at any rate; our old ones will not serve for another year. We ought not to be afraid of the Snakes. Our warriors are brave, and they are all ready for war. Besides, we have three white men with their rifles to help us."

I could not help thinking that the old man relied a little too much on the aid of allies, one of whom was a coward, another a blockhead, and the third an invalid. This speech produced a good deal of debate. As Reynal did not interpret what was said, I could only judge of the meaning by the features and gestures of the speakers. At the end of it, however, the greater number seemed to have fallen in with Mene-Seela's opinion. A short silence followed, and then the old man struck up a discordant chant, which I was told was a song of thanks for the entertainment I had given them.

"Now," said he, "let us go and give the white men a chance to breathe."

So the company all dispersed into the open air, and for some time the old chief was walking around the village, singing his song in praise of the feast, after the usual custom of the nation.

The Oregon Trail, 1849

WALTER COLTON

The Gold Fever Reaches Monterey

This Vermont-born Congregationalist minister was a teacher and a journalist before his duties as a United States Navy chaplain sent him to California. There he established that state's first newspaper and sent word back east of the discovery of gold.

Monday, May 29 [1848].—Our town [Monterey] was startled out of its quiet dreams today by the announcement that gold had been discovered on the American Fork. Then men wondered and talked, and the women too; but neither believed. . . .

Monday, June 5.—Another report reached us this morning from the American Fork. The rumor ran that several workmen, while excavating for a millrace, had thrown up little shining scales of a yellow ore that proved to be gold; that an old Sonorarian who had spent his life in gold mines pronounced it the genuine thing. Still the public incredulity remained, save here and there a glimmer of faith, like the flash of a firefly at night.

Tuesday, June 6.—I determined to put an end to the suspense and dispatched a messenger this morning to the American Fork. He will have to ride, going and returning, some four hundred miles, but his report will be reliable. We shall then know whether this gold is a fact or a fiction—a tangible reality on the earth or a fanciful treasure at the base of some rainbow, retreating over hill and waterfall, to lure pursuit and disappoint hope.

Monday, June 12.—A straggler came in today from the American Fork, bringing a piece of yellow ore weighing an ounce. The young dashed the dirt from their eyes, and the old from their spectacles. One brought a spyglass, another an iron ladle; some wanted to melt it, others to hammer it, and a few were satisfied with smelling it. All were full of tests, and many who could not be gratified in making their experiments declared it a humbug. One lady sent me a huge gold ring in the hope of reaching the truth by comparison, while a gentleman placed the specimen on the top of his gold-headed cane and held it up, challenging the sharpest eyes to detect a difference. But doubts still hovered on the minds of the great mass. They could not conceive that such a treasure could have lain there so long undiscovered. The idea seemed to convict them of stupidity.

Tuesday, June 20.—My messenger, sent to the mines, has returned with specimens of the gold; he dismounted in a sea of upturned faces. As he drew forth the yellow lumps from his pockets and passed them around among the eager crowd, the doubts, which had lingered till now, fled. All admitted they were gold except one old man who still persisted they were some Yankee invention, got up to reconcile the people to the change of flag. The excitement produced was intense, and many were soon busy in their hasty preparations for a departure to the mines. The family who had kept house for me caught the moving infection. Husband and wife were both packing up; the blacksmith dropped his hammer, the carpenter his plane, the mason his trowel, the farmer his sickle, the baker his loaf, and the tapster his bottle. All were off for the mines, some on horses, some on carts, and some on crutches; and one went in a litter. An American woman who had recently established a boardinghouse here pulled up stakes and was off before her lodgers had even time to pay their bills. Debtors ran, of course. I have only a community of women left and a gang of prisoners, with here and there a soldier who will give his captain the slip at the first chance. I don't blame the fellow a whit; seven dollars a month, while others are making two or three hundred a day! That is too much for human nature to stand.

Saturday, July 15.—The gold fever has reached every servant in Monterey; none are to be trusted in their engagement beyond a week, and as for compulsion, it is like attempting to drive fish into a net with the ocean before them. General Mason, Lieutenant Lanman, and myself form a mess; we have a house and all the table furniture and culinary apparatus requisite, but our servants have run, one after another, till we are almost in despair; even Sambo, who we thought would stick by from laziness, if no other cause, ran last night; and this morning, for the fortieth time, we had to take to the kitchen and cook our own breakfast. A general of the United States Army, the commander of a man-of-war, and the alcalde of Monterey, in a smoking kitchen, grinding coffee, toasting a herring, and peeling onions! These gold mines are going to upset all the domestic arrangements of society, turning the head to the tail, and the tail to the head. Well, it is an ill wind that blows nobody any good; the nabobs have had their time, and now comes that of the "niggers." We shall all live just as long and be quite as fit to die.

Tuesday, July 18.—Another bag of gold from the mines and another spasm in the community. It was brought down by a sailor from Yuba River and contains a hundred and thirty-six ounces. It is the most beautiful gold that has appeared in the market; it looks like the yellow scales of the dolphin passing through his rainbow hues at death. My carpenters, at work on the schoolhouse, on seeing it, threw down their saws and planes, shouldered their picks, and are off for the Yuba. Three seamen ran from the *Warren*, forfeiting their four years' pay; and a whole platoon of soldiers from the fort left only their colors behind. One old woman declared she would never again break an egg or kill a chicken without examining yolk and gizzard.

Saturday, August 12.—My man Bob, who is of Irish extraction and who had been in the mines about two months, returned to Monterey four weeks since, bringing with him over two thousand dollars as the proceeds of his labor. Bob, while in my employ, required me to pay him every Saturday night in gold which he put into a little leather bag and sewed into the lining of his coat after taking out just twelve and a half cents, his weekly allowance for tobacco. But now he took rooms and began to branch out; he had the best horses, the richest viands, and the choicest wines in the place. He never drank himself, but it filled him with delight to brim the sparkling goblet for others. I met Bob today and asked him how he got on. "Oh, very well," he replied, "but I am off again for the mines." "How is that, Bob? You brought down with you over two thousand dollars; I hope you have not spent all that; you used to be very saving; twelve and a half cents a week for tobacco, and the rest you sewed into the lining of your coat." "Oh, yes," replied Bob, "and I have got *that* money yet; I worked hard for it, and the devil can't get it away; but the two thousand dollars came aisily by good luck, and has gone as aisily as it came." Now Bob's story is only one of a thousand like it in California and has a deeper philosophy in it than meets the eye. Multitudes here are none the richer for the mines. He who can shake chestnuts from an exhaustless tree won't stickle about the quantity he roasts.

Thursday, August 16.—Four citizens of Monterey are just in from the gold mines on Feather River, where they worked in company with three others. They employed about thirty wild Indians who are attached to the ranch owned by one of the party. They worked precisely seven weeks and three days and have divided seventy-six thousand eight hundred and forty-four dollars, nearly eleven thousand dollars to each. Make a dot there, and let me introduce a man, well known to me, who has worked on the Yuba River sixty-four days and brought back as the result of his individual labor five thousand three hundred and fifty-six dollars. Make a dot there, and let me introduce another townsman who has worked on the North Fork fifty-seven days and brought back four thousand five hundred and thirty-four dollars. Make a dot there, and let me introduce a boy, fourteen years of age, who has worked on the Mokelumne fifty-four days and brought back three thousand four hundred and sixty-seven dollars. Make another dot there, and let me introduce a woman, of Sonorarian birth, who has worked in the dry diggings forty-six days and brought back two thousand one hundred and twenty-five dollars. Is not this enough to make a man throw down his ledger and shoulder a pick? But the deposits which yielded these harvests were now opened for the first time; they were the accumulation of ages; only the footprints of the elk and wild savage had passed over them. Their slumber was broken for the first time by the sturdy arms of the American emigrant.

Tuesday, August 28.—The gold mines have upset all social and domestic arrangements in Monterey; the master has become his own servant, and the servant his own lord. The millionaire is obliged to groom his own horse and roll his wheelbarrow, and the hidalgo—in whose veins flows the blood of all the Cortes—to clean his own boots! Here is Lady L——, who has lived here seventeen years, the pride and ornament of the place, with a broomstick in her jeweled hand! And here is Lady B——, with her daughter—all the way from old Virginia, where they graced society with their varied accomplishments—now floating between the parlor and kitchen, and as much at home in the one as the other! And here is Lady S——, whose cattle are on a thousand hills, lifting, like Rachel of old, her bucket of water from the deep well! And here is Lady M L——, whose honeymoon is still full of soft seraphic light, unhouseling a potato and hunting the hen that laid the last egg. And here am I, who have been a man of some note in my day, loafing on the hospitality of the good citizens and grateful for a meal though in an Indian's wigwam. Why, is not this enough to make one wish the gold mines were in the earth's flaming center from which they sprung? Out on this yellow dust! it is worse than the cinders which buried Pompeii, for there high and low shared the same fate!

Three Years in California, 1852

BAYARD TAYLOR

A Day in El Dorado

Poet, traveler, novelist Taylor, the most famous staff man on America's greatest newspaper of the period, the New York TRIBUNE, *spent five zestful months in the West reporting the new life that surged through the region as a result of the discovery of gold.*

A better idea of San Francisco in the beginning of September, 1849, cannot be given than by the description of a single day. Supposing the visitor to have been long enough in the place to sleep on a hard plank and in spite of the attack of innumerable fleas, he will be awakened at daylight by the noises of building, with which the hills are all alive. The air is temperate, and the invariable morning fog is just beginning to gather. By sunrise, which gleams hazily over the Coast Mountains across the bay, the whole populace is up and at work. The wooden buildings unlock their doors; the canvas houses and tents throw back their front curtains; the lighters on the water are warped out from ship to ship; carts and porters are busy along the beach; and only the gaming tables, thronged all night by the votaries of chance, are idle and deserted. The temperature is so fresh as to inspire an active habit of body, and even without the stimulus of trade and speculation there would be few sluggards at this season.

411

By nine o'clock the town is in the full flow of business. The streets running down to the water and Montgomery Street, which fronts the bay, are crowded with people, all in hurried motion. The variety of characters and costumes is remarkable. Our own countrymen seem to lose their local peculiarities in such a crowd, and it is by chance epithets rather than by manner that the New Yorker is distinguished from the Kentuckian, the Carolinian from the down-Easter, the Virginian from the Texan. The German and Frenchman are more easily recognized. Peruvians and Chileans go by in their brown ponchos, and the sober Chinese, cool and impassive in the midst of excitement, look out of the oblique corners of their long eyes at the bustle, but are never tempted to venture from their own line of business. The eastern side of the plaza in front of the Parker House and a canvas hell called the El Dorado are the general rendezvous of business and amusement—combining exchange, park, club room, and promenade all in one. There everybody not constantly employed in one spot may be seen at some time of the day.

The day advances. The mist which after sunrise hung low and heavy for an hour or two has risen above the hills, and there will be two hours of pleasant sunshine before the wind sets in from the sea. The crowd in the streets is now wholly alive. Men dart hither and thither as if possessed with a never-resting spirit. You speak to an acquaintance—a merchant, perhaps. He utters a few hurried words of greeting, while his eyes send keen glances on all sides of you; suddenly he catches sight of somebody in the crowd; he is off and in the next five minutes has bought up half a cargo, sold a town lot at treble the sum he gave, and taken a share in some new and imposing speculation. It is impossible to witness this excess and dissipation of business without feeling something of its influence. The very air is pregnant with the magnetism of bold, spirited, unwearied action, and he who but ventures into the outer circle of the whirlpool is spinning, ere he has time for thought, in its dizzy vortex.

About twelve o'clock a wind begins to blow from the northwest, sweeping with most violence through a gap between the hills, opening toward the Golden Gate. The bells and gongs begin to sound for dinner, and these two causes tend to lessen the crowd in the streets for an hour or two. Two o'clock is the usual dinnertime for business men, but some of the old and successful merchants have adopted the fashionable hour of five. Where shall we dine today? The restaurants display their signs invitingly on all sides; we have choice of the United States, Tortoni's, the Alhambra, and many other equally classic resorts, but Delmonico's, like its distinguished original in New York, has the highest prices and the greatest variety of dishes. We enter a little door at the end of the building, ascend a dark, narrow flight of steps, and find ourselves in a long, low room, with ceiling and walls of white muslin and a floor covered with oilcloth.

There are about twenty tables disposed in two rows, all of them so well filled that we have some difficulty in finding places. Taking up the written bill of fare, we find that, with but a moderate appetite, the dinner will cost us five dollars, if we are at all epicurean in our tastes. There are cries of "Steward!" from all parts of the room—the word waiter is not considered sufficiently respectful, seeing that the waiter may have been a lawyer or merchant's clerk a few months before. The dishes look very small as they are placed on the table, but they are skillfully cooked and very palatable to men that have ridden in from the diggings. The appetite one acquires in California is something remarkable. For two months after my arrival, my sensations were like those of a famished wolf.

The afternoon is less noisy and active than the forenoon. Merchants keep within doors, and the gambling rooms are crowded with persons who step in to escape the wind and dust. The sky takes a cold gray cast, and the hills over the bay are barely visible in the dense, dusty air.

The only objects left for us to visit are the gaming tables, whose day has just fairly dawned. We need not wander far in search of one. Denison's Exchange, the Parker House, and El Dorado stand side by side, across the way are the Verandah and Aguila de Oro, higher up the plaza the St. Charles and Bella Union, while dozens of second-rate establishments are scattered through the less-frequented streets. The greatest crowd is about the El Dorado; we find it difficult to effect an entrance. There are about eight tables in the room, all of which are thronged; copper-hued Kanakas, Mexicans rolled in their serapes, and Peruvians thrust through their ponchos stand shoulder to shoulder with the brown and bearded American miners. The stakes are generally small, though when the bettor gets into a streak of luck, as it is called, they are allowed to double until all is lost or the bank breaks. Along the end of the room is a spacious bar supplied with all kinds of bad liquors, and in a sort of gallery suspended under the ceiling a female violinist tasks her talent and strength of muscle to minister to the excitement of play.

There are other places where gaming is carried on privately and to a more ruinous extent—rooms in the rear of the Parker House, in the City Hotel and other places, frequented only by the initiated. Here the stakes are almost unlimited, the players being men of wealth and apparent respectability. Frequently in the absorbing interest of some desperate game the night goes by unheeded and morning breaks upon haggard faces and reckless hearts. Here are lost, in a few turns of a card or rolls of a ball, the product of fortunate ventures by sea or months of racking labor on land.

El Dorado, 1850

BRET HARTE

The Luck of Roaring Camp

There was commotion in Roaring Camp. It could not have been a fight, for in 1850 that was not novel enough to have called together the entire settlement. The ditches and claims were not only deserted, but "Tuttle's grocery" had contributed its gamblers, who, it will be remembered, calmly continued their game the day that French Pete and Kanaka Joe shot each other to death over the bar in the front room. The whole camp was collected before a rude cabin on the outer edge of the clearing. Conversation was carried on in a low tone, but the name of a woman was frequently repeated. It was a name familiar enough in the camp,—"Cherokee Sal."

Perhaps the less said of her the better. She was a coarse, and it is to be feared, a very sinful woman. But at that time she was the only woman in Roaring Camp, and was just then lying in sore extremity, when she most needed the ministration of her own sex. Dissolute, abandoned, and irreclaimable, she was yet suffering a martyrdom hard enough to bear even when veiled by sympathizing womanhood, but now terrible in her loneliness. The primal curse had come to her in that original isolation which must have made the punishment of the first transgression so dreadful. It was, perhaps, part of the expiation of her sin, that, at a moment when she most lacked her sex's intuitive tenderness and care, she met only the half-contemptuous faces of her masculine associates. Yet a few of the spectators were, I think, touched by her sufferings. Sandy Tipton thought it was "rough on Sal," and in the contemplation of her condition, for a moment rose superior to the fact that he had an ace and two bowers in his sleeve.

It will be seen, also, that the situation was novel. Deaths were by no means uncommon in Roaring Camp, but a birth was a new thing. People had been dismissed from the camp effectively, finally, and with no possibility of return; but this was the first time that anybody had been introduced *ab initio*. Hence the excitement.

"You go in there, Stumpy," said a prominent citizen known as "Kentuck," addressing one of the loungers. "Go in there, and see what you kin do. You've had experience in them things."

Perhaps there was a fitness in the selection. Stumpy, in other climes, had been the putative head of two families; in fact, it was owing to some legal informality in these proceedings that Roaring Camp—a city of refuge —was indebted to his company. The crowd approved the choice, and Stumpy was wise enough to bow to the majority. The door closed upon the extempore surgeon and midwife, and Roaring Camp sat down outside, smoked its pipe, and awaited the issue.

The assemblage numbered about a hundred men. One or two of these were actual fugitives from justice, some were criminal, and all were reckless. Physically, they exhibited no indication of their past lives and character. The greatest scamp had a Raphael face, with a profusion of blond hair; Oakhurst, a gambler, had the melancholy air and intellectual abstraction of a Hamlet; the coolest and most courageous man was scarcely over five feet in height, with a soft voice and an embarrassed, timid manner. The term "roughs" applied to them was a distinction rather than a definition. Perhaps in the minor details of fingers, toes, ears, etc., the camp may have been deficient, but these slight omissions did not detract from their aggregate force. The strongest man had but three fingers on his right hand; the best shot had but one eye.

Such was the physical aspect of the men that were dispersed around the cabin. The camp lay in a triangular valley, between two hills and a river. The only outlet was a steep trail over the summit of a hill that faced the cabin, now illuminated by the rising moon. The suffering woman might have seen it from the rude bunk whereon she lay,—seen it winding like a silver thread until it was lost in the stars above.

A fire of withered pine boughs added sociability to the gathering. By degrees the natural levity of Roaring Camp returned. Bets were freely offered and taken regarding the result. Three to five that "Sal would get through with it"; even, that the child would survive; side bets as to the sex and complexion of the coming stranger. In the midst of an excited discussion an exclamation came from those nearest the door, and the camp stopped to listen. Above the swaying and moaning of the pines, the swift rush of the river, and the crackling of the fire hose a sharp, querulous cry— a cry unlike anything heard before in the camp. The pines stopped moaning, the river ceased to rush, and the fire to crackle. It seemed as if Nature had stopped to listen too.

The camp rose to its feet as one man! It was proposed to explode a barrel of gun-powder, but, in consideration of the situation of the mother, better counsels prevailed, and only a few revolvers were discharged; for, whether owing to the rude surgery of the camp, or some other reason, Cherokee Sal was sinking fast. Within an hour she had climbed, as it were, that rugged road that led to the stars, and so passed out of Roaring Camp, its sin and shame forever. I do not think that the announcement disturbed them much, except in speculation as to the fate of the child. "Can he live now?" was asked of Stumpy. The answer was doubtful. The only other being of Cherokee Sal's sex and maternal condition in the settlement was an ass. There was some conjecture as to fitness, but the experiment was tried. It was less problematical than the ancient treatment of Romulus and Remus, and apparently as successful.

When these details were completed, which exhausted another hour, the door was opened, and the anxious crowd, who had already formed themselves into a queue, entered in single file. Beside the low bunk or shelf, on which the figure of the mother was starkly outlined below the blankets, stood a pine table. On this a candle-box was placed, and within it, swathed in staring red flannel, lay the last arrival at Roaring Camp. Beside the candle-box was placed a hat. Its use was soon indicated. "Gentlemen," said Stumpy, with a singular mixture of authority and *ex officio* complacency—"Gentlemen will please pass in at the front door, round the table, and out at the back door. Them as wishes to contribute anything toward the orphan will find a hat handy." The first man entered with his hat on; he uncovered, however, as he looked about him, and so, unconsciously, set an example to the next. In such communities good and bad actions are catching. As the procession filed in, comments were audible,—criticisms addressed, perhaps, rather to Stumpy, in the character of showman,— "Is that him?" "Mighty small specimen"; "Hasn't more'n got the color"; "Ain't bigger nor a derringer." The contributions were as characteristic: A silver tobacco box; a doubloon; a navy revolver, silver mounted; a gold specimen; a very beautifully embroidered lady's handkerchief (from Oakhurst the gambler); a diamond breastpin, a diamond ring (suggested by the pin, with the remark from the giver that he "saw that pin and went two diamonds better"); a slung shot; a Bible (contributor not detected); a golden spur; a silver teaspoon (the initials, I regret to say, were not the giver's); a pair of surgeon's shears; a lancet; a Bank of England note for £5; and about $200 in loose gold and silver coin. During these proceedings Stumpy maintained a silence as impassive as the dead on his left—a gravity as inscrutable as that of the newly-born on his right. Only one incident occurred to break the monotony of the curious procession. As Kentuck bent over the candle-box half curiously, the child turned, and, in a spasm of pain, caught at his groping finger, and held it fast for a moment. Kentuck looked foolish and embarrassed. Something like a blush tried to assert itself in his weather-beaten cheek. "The d—d little cuss!" he said, as he extricated his finger, with, perhaps, more tenderness and care than he might have been deemed capable of showing. He held that finger a little apart from its fellows as he went out, and examined it curiously. The examination provoked the same original remark in regard to the child. In fact, he seemed to enjoy repeating it. "He rastled with my finger," he remarked to Tipton, holding up the member, "the d—d little cuss!"

It was four o'clock before the camp sought repose. A light burnt in the cabin where the watchers sat, for Stumpy did not go to bed that night. Nor did Kentuck. He drank quite freely and related with great gusto his experience, invariably ending with his characteristic condemnation of the newcomer. It seemed to relieve him of any unjust implication of sentiment, and Kentuck had the weaknesses of the nobler sex. When everybody else had gone to bed, he walked down to the river, and whistled reflectingly. Then he walked up the gulch, past the cabin, still whistling with demonstrative unconcern. At a large redwood tree he paused and retraced his steps, and again passed the cabin. Halfway down to the river's bank he again paused, and then returned and knocked at the door. It was opened by Stumpy. "How goes it?" said Kentuck, looking past Stumpy toward the candle-box. "All serene," replied Stumpy. "Anything up?" "Nothing." There was a pause—an embarrassing one—Stumpy still holding the door. Then Kentuck had recourse to his finger, which he held up to Stumpy. "Rastled with it,—the d—d little cuss," he said, and retired.

The next day Cherokee Sal had such rude sepulture as Roaring Camp afforded. After her body had been committed to the hillside, there was a formal meeting of the camp to discuss what should be done with her infant. A resolution to adopt it was unanimous and enthusiastic. But an animated discussion in regard to the manner and feasibility of providing for its wants at once sprung up. It was remarkable that the argument partook of none of those fierce personalities with which discussions were usually conducted at Roaring Camp. Tipton proposed that they should send the child to Red Dog—a distance of forty miles—where female attention could be procured. But the unlucky suggestion met with fierce and unanimous opposition. It was evident that no plan which entailed parting from their new acquisition would for a moment be entertained. "Besides," said Tom Ryder, "them fellows at Red Dog would swap it, and ring in somebody else on us." A disbelief in the honesty of other camps prevailed at Roaring Camp as in other places.

The introduction of a female nurse in the camp also met with objection. It was argued that no decent woman could be prevailed to accept Roaring Camp as her home, and the speaker urged that "they didn't want any more of the other kind." This unkind allusion to the defunct mother, harsh as it may seem, was the first spasm of propriety—the first symptom of the camp's regeneration. Stumpy advanced nothing. Perhaps he felt a certain delicacy interfering with the selection of a possible successor in office. But when questioned, he averred stoutly that he and "Jinny"—the mammal before alluded to—could manage to rear the child. There was something original, independent, and heroic about the plan that pleased the camp. Stumpy was retained. Certain articles were sent for to Sacramento. "Mind," said the treasurer, as he pressed a bag of gold-dust into the expressman's hand, "the best that can be got—lace, you know, and filigree-work and frills,—d—n the cost!"

Strange to say, the child thrived. Perhaps the invigorating climate of the mountain camp was compensation for maternal deficiencies. Nature took the foundling to her broader breast. In that rare atmosphere of the Sierra foothills—that air pungent with balsamic odor, that ethereal cordial, at once bracing and exhilarating, he may have found food and nourishment, or a subtle chemistry that transmuted ass's milk to lime and phosphorus. Stumpy inclined to the belief that it was the latter and good nursing.

"Me and that ass," he would say, "has been father and mother to him! Don't you," he would add, apostrophizing the helpless bundle before him, "never go back on us."

By the time he was a month old, the necessity of giving him a name became apparent. He had generally been known as "the Kid," "Stumpy's boy," "the Cayote" (an allusion to his vocal powers) and even by Kentuck's endearing diminutive of "the d—d little cuss." But these were felt to be vague and unsatisfactory, and were at last dismissed under another influence. Gamblers and adventurers are generally superstitious, and Oakhurst one day declared that the baby had brought "the luck" to Roaring Camp. It was certain that of late they had been successful. "Luck" was the name agreed upon, with the prefix of Tommy for greater convenience. No allusion was made to the mother, and the father was unknown. "It's better," said the philosophical Oakhurst, "to take a fresh deal all around. Call him Luck, and start him fair." A day was accordingly set apart for the christening. What was meant by this ceremony the reader may imagine, who has already gathered some idea of the reckless irreverence of Roaring Camp. The master of ceremonies was one "Boston," a noted wag, and the occasion seemed to promise the greatest facetiousness. This ingenious satirist had spent two days in preparing a burlesque of the church service, with pointed local allusions. The choir was properly trained, and Sandy Tipton was to stand godfather. But after the procession had marched to the grove with music and banners, and the child had been deposited before a mock altar, Stumpy stepped before the expectant crowd. "It ain't my style to spoil fun, boys," said the little man, stoutly, eyeing the faces around him, "but it strikes me that this thing ain't exactly on the squar. It's playing it pretty low down on this yer baby to ring in fun on him that he ain't goin' to understand. And ef there's going to be any godfathers around, I'd like to see who's got any better rights than me." A silence followed Stumpy's speech. To the credit of all humorists be it said that the first man to acknowledge its justice was the satirist, thus stopped of his fun. "But," said Stumpy, quickly, following up his advantage, "we're here for a christening, and we'll have it. I proclaim you Thomas Luck, according to the laws of the United States and the State of California, so help me God." It was the first time that the name of the Deity had been uttered otherwise but profanely in the camp. The form of christening was perhaps even more ludicrous than the satirist had conceived; but strangely enough, nobody saw it and nobody laughed. "Tommy" was christened as seriously as he would have been under a Christian roof, and cried and was comforted in as orthodox fashion.

And so the work of regeneration began in Roaring Camp. Almost imperceptibly a change came over the settlement. The cabin assigned to "Tommy Luck"—or "The Luck," as he was more frequently called—first showed signs of improvement. It was kept scrupulously clean and whitewashed. Then it was boarded, clothed and papered. The rosewood cradle

—packed eighty miles by mule—had, in Stumpy's way of putting it, "sorter killed the rest of the furniture." So the rehabilitation of the cabin became a necessity. The men who were in the habit of lounging at Stumpy's to see "how The Luck got on" seemed to appreciate the change, and, in self-defense, the rival establishment of "Tuttle's grocery" bestirred itself, and imported a carpet and mirrors. The reflections of the latter on the appearance of Roaring Camp tended to produce stricter habits of personal cleanliness. Again Stumpy imposed a kind of quarantine upon those who aspired to the honor and privilege of holding "The Luck." It was a cruel mortification to Kentuck—who, in the carelessness of a large nature and the habits of frontier life, had begun to regard all garments as a second cuticle, which, like a snake's, only sloughed off through decay— to be debarred this privilege from certain prudential reasons. Yet such was the subtle influence of innovation that he thereafter appeared regularly every afternoon in a clean shirt, and face still shining from his ablutions. Nor were moral and social sanitary laws neglected. "Tommy" who was supposed to spend his whole existence in a persistent attempt to repose, must not be disturbed by noise. The shouting and yelling which had gained the camp its infelicitous title was not permitted within hearing distance of Stumpy's. The men conversed in whispers, or smoked with Indian gravity. Profanity was tacitly given up in these sacred precincts, and throughout the camp a popular form of expletive, known as "D—n the luck!" and "Curse the luck!" was abandoned, as having a new personal bearing. Vocal music was not interdicted, being supposed to have a soothing, tranquilizing quality, and one song, sung by "Man-o'-War Jack," an English sailor from Her Majesty's Australian colonies, was quite popular as a lullaby. It was a lugubrious recital of the exploits of "the *Arethusa*, Seventy-four," in a muffled minor, ending with a prolonged dying fall at the burden of each verse, "On b-o-o-o-ard of the *Arethusa*." It was a fine sight to see Jack holding The Luck, rocking from side to side as if with the motion of a ship, and crooning forth this naval ditty. Either through the peculiar rocking of Jack or the length of his song—it contained ninety stanzas, and was continued with conscientious deliberation to the bitter end—the lullaby generally had the desired effect. At such times the men would lie at full length under the trees, in the soft summer twilight, smoking their pipes and drinking in the melodious utterances. An indistinct idea that this was pastoral happiness pervaded the camp. "This 'ere kind o' think," said the Cockney Simmons, meditatively reclining on his elbow, "is 'evingly." It reminded him of Greenwich.

On the long summer days The Luck was usually carried to the gulch, from whence the golden store of Roaring Camp was taken. There, on a blanket spread over pine boughs, he would lie while the men were working in the ditches below. Latterly, there was a rude attempt to decorate this bower with flowers and sweet-smelling shrubs, and generally some one would bring him a cluster of wild honey-suckles, azaleas, or the painted blossoms of Las Mariposas. The men had suddenly awakened to the fact that there were beauty and significance in these trifles, which they had so long trodden carelessly beneath their feet. A flake of glittering mica, a fragment of variegated quartz, a bright pebble from the bed of the creek, became beautiful to eyes thus cleared and strengthened, and were invariably put aside for "The Luck." It was wonderful how many treasures the woods and hillsides yielded that "would do for Tommy." Surrounded by playthings such as never child out of fairyland had before, it is to be hoped that Tommy was content. He appeared to be serenely happy, albeit there was an infantine gravity about him, a contemplative light in his round gray eyes, that sometimes worried Stumpy. He was always tractable and quiet, and it is recorded that once, having crept beyond his "corral"— a hedge of tessellated pine boughs, which surrounded his bed—he dropped over the bank on his head in the soft earth, and remained with his mottled legs in the air in that position for at least five minutes with unflinching gravity. He was extricated without a murmur. I hesitate to record the many other instances of his sagacity, which rest, unfortunately, upon the statements of prejudiced friends. Some of them were not without a tinge of superstition. "I crep' up the bank just now," said Kentuck one day, in a breathless state of excitement, "and dern my skin if he wasn't a talking to a jaybird as was a-sittin on his lap. There they was, just as free and sociable as anything you please, a-jawin at each other just like two cherrybums." Howbeit, whether creeping over the pine boughs or lying lazily on his back, blinking at the leaves above him, to him the birds sang, the squirrels chattered, and the flowers bloomed. Nature was his nurse and playfellow. For him she would let slip between the leaves golden shafts of sunlight that fell just within his grasp; she would send wandering breezes to visit him with the balm of bay and resinous gums; to him the tall redwoods nodded familiarly and sleepily, the bumblebees buzzed, and the rooks cawed a slumbrous accompaniment.

Such was the golden summer of Roaring Camp. They were "flush times"—and the Luck was with them. The claims had yielded enormously. The camp was jealous of its privileges and looked suspiciously on strangers. No encouragement was given to immigration, and, to make their seclusion more perfect, the land on either side of the mountain wall that surrounded the camp they duly pre-empted. This, and a reputation for singular proficiency with the revolver, kept the reserve of Roaring Camp inviolate. The expressman—their only connecting link with the surrounding world— sometimes told wonderful stories of the camp. He would say, "They've a street up there in 'Roaring,' that would lay over any street up there in Red Dog. They've got vines and flowers round their houses, and they wash themselves twice a day. But they're mighty rough on strangers, and they worship an Ingin baby."

With the prosperity of the camp came a desire for further improvement. It was proposed to build a hotel in the following spring, and to invite one or two decent families to reside there for the sake of "The Luck," who might perhaps profit by female companionship. The sacrifice that this concession to the sex cost these men, who were fiercely skeptical in regard to its general virtue and usefulness, can only be accounted for by their affection for Tommy. A few still held out. But the resolve could not be carried into effect for three months, and the minority meekly yielded in the hope that something might turn up to prevent it. And it did.

The winter of '51 will long be remembered in the foothills. The snow lay deep on the Sierras, and every mountain creek became a river, and every river a lake. Each gorge and gulch was transformed into a tumultuous watercourse that descended the hillsides, tearing down giant trees and scattering its drift and debris along the plain. Red Dog had been twice under water, and Roaring Camp had been forewarned. "Water put the gold in them gulches," said Stumpy; "it's been here once and it will be here again!" And that night the North Fork suddenly leaped over its banks, and swept up the triangular valley of Roaring Camp.

In the confusion of rushing water, crashing trees, and crackling timber, and the darkness which seemed to flow with the water and blot out the fair valley, but little could be done to collect the scattered camp. When the morning broke, the cabin of Stumpy nearest the river-bank was gone. Higher up the gulch they found the body of its unlucky owner, but the pride—the hope—the joy—the Luck—of Roaring Camp had disappeared. They were returning with sad hearts, when a shout from the bank recalled them.

It was a relief-boat from down the river. They had picked up, they said, a man and an infant, nearly exhausted, about two miles below. Did anybody know them, and did they belong here?

It needed but a glance to show them Kentuck lying there, cruelly crushed and bruised, but still holding the Luck of Roaring Camp in his arms. As they bent over the strangely assorted pair, they saw that the child was cold and pulseless. "He is dead," said one. Kentuck opened his eyes. "Dead?" he repeated feebly. "Yes, my man, and you are dying, too." A smile lit in the eyes of the expiring Kentuck. "Dying!" he repeated, "he's a-taking me with him—tell the boys I've got the Luck with me now"; and the strong man, clinging to the frail babe, as a drowning man is said to cling to a straw, drifted away into the shadowy river that flows forever to the unknown sea.

The Luck of Roaring Camp and Other Sketches, 1870

BILL NYE

A Hearty Endorsement

Edgar Wilson Nye (Bill Nye), while editor of the DAILY BOOMER-
ANG *of Laramie City, Wyoming, was appointed postmaster. His
letter to the Postmaster General, acknowledging the appoinment,
follows.*

Office of *Daily Boomerang*,
Laramie City, Wy.
August 9, 1882

My Dear General:

I have received by telegraph the news of my nomination by the President and my confirmation by the Senate, as postmaster at Laramie, and wish to extend my thanks for the same.

I have ordered an entirely new set of boxes and post office outfit, including new corrugated cuspidors for the lady clerks.

I look upon the appointment, myself, as a great triumph of eternal truth over error and wrong. It is one of the epochs, I may say, in the Nation's onward march toward political purity and perfection. I do not know when I have noticed any stride in the affairs of state which so thoroughly impressed me with its wisdom.

Now that we are co-workers in the same department, I trust that you will not feel shy or backward in consulting me at any time relative to matters concerning post office affairs. Be perfectly frank with me, and feel perfectly free to just bring anything of that kind right to me. Do not feel reluctant because I may at times appear haughty and indifferent, cold or reserved. Perhaps you do not think I know the difference between a general delivery window and a three-m quad, but that is a mistake. My general information is far beyond my years.

With profoundest regard, and a hearty endorsement of the policy of the President and the Senate, whatever it may be,

I remain, sincerely yours,

BILL NYE, P.M.

Gen. Frank Hatton, Washington, D. C.

Encore.

HUBERT HOWE BANCROFT

Joaquin Murieta: The Terror of the Stanislaus

> This Bancroft of San Francisco, who is not to be confused with
> the Massachusetts George Bancroft, gathered one of the greatest
> collections of historical documents ever assembled by one man
> and, with a corps of able assistants, he produced some thirty-nine
> volumes of history.

The unsettled condition of society in California, the abundance of money,
the amount of travel, mostly by treasure-laden miners, on the lonely roads
of the mountains and plains, the herds of fine horses grazing everywhere
within easy reach of the robber, and finally, the soft and genial climate of
the country, rendered possible, developed, and conduced to the prosperity
of the guild of the highwaymen, who had for their field of operations a
territory quite as extensive, and as rich in booty and stirring hazard, as
was the Spanish Main to the dreaded buccaneers, self-styled the Brotherhood of the Coast.

. . . I will now proceed to relate some of the exploits of him who de-
servedly stood head and shoulders over all other knights of the road in
California, if not, indeed, superior to the most famous leaders of highwaymen recorded in the annals of other countries.

Joaquin Murieta, the terror of the Stanislaus, has a history, which,
though crimson with murder, abounds in dramatic interest. He was a
Mexican of good blood . . . , born in the department of Sonora, and
received an ordinary education in the schools of his native country. In
his youth he is said to have been mild, affectionate, and genial in disposition, the pet of the maestro, and a favorite among his fellows of the play-
ground. Yet, while acknowledging the pulpy sweetness of his boyhood, it
is safe to presume that there was a dash of bandit blood in the veins of
Joaquin, which was eventually to fire his heart with the madness for an
outlaw life. As Joaquin and his Rosita reached the new El Dorado, the
first flash of the great gold fever was then spreading over its wild ranges.
In the memorable spring of 1850 we find him engaged as an honest miner
among the Stanislaus placers, where he had a rich claim, and was fast
amassing a competency, when, one evening, a party of some half dozen
American desperadoes swaggered into his little cabin where with Rosita he
was resting after a hard day's work.

"You don't know, I suppose, that greasers are not allowed to take gold
from American ground," began the leader insolently.

"If you mean that I have no right to my claim, in obtaining which I have conformed to all the laws of the district, I certainly did not know it," answered Joaquin with quiet dignity.

"Well, you may know it now. And you have got to go; so vamoose, git, and that instanter, and take that trumpery with you," jerking his thumb toward Rosita. "The women if anything are worse than the men."

Joaquin stepped forward with clinched hand, while the hot blood mantled his face: "I will leave these parts if such be your wish, but speak one word against that woman, and though you were ten times an American, you shall rue it."

Scarcely were these words uttered when another of the party reached over and struck Joaquin a severe blow in the face. The latter sprang for his bowie-knife, which he had thrown upon the bed on returning from his work, when Rosita, instinct with the danger such rashness threatened, threw herself before him, and seizing him in her arms, frantically held him. For the intruders to thrust aside the woman and strike the unarmed man senseless was the work of a moment. When Joaquin awoke to consciousness, it was to find Rosita prostrate, her face buried in her clothes, sobbing hysterically. Then he knew the worst.

Fleeing from his outraged home on the Stanislaus, Joaquin and his devoted companion sought refuge on a modest little rancho, hid away in the rugged seclusion of the Calaveras mountains. His dream of peace was soon broken, however, by the sudden apparition of two bearded missionaries, whose monosyllabic warning, "Git!" threw down his hopes and household gods once more into the dust. The hapless twain were driven out from the shadows of Calaveras, and once more became fugitives in the land. We next find Joaquin working as a miner at Murphy Diggings; but luck was against him in the placers, and he finally assumed the gay and remunerative occupation of monte-dealer, a department of industry at the time deemed respectable, even for Americans, not a few of them being thorough adepts in the art of "lay-outs," and both swift and relentless in catching their customers "in the door."

The new vocation was well suited to the suave young Sonorense, and fortune for a while seemed to befriend him, the uncoined gold of the miners rolling into his ever thickening purse. But his pathway was destined to blush with redder hues than rosy fortune wears. While riding into town on a horse that he had borrowed from a half-brother of his who lived on a rancho nearby, he was accosted by an American claiming the animal to have been stolen from him. Murieta pleaded that it was not his, but borrowed. This, however, availed him not. Indeed, it seems that the claim was a well-founded one, and Murieta was charged with the theft, the penalty whereof was death. A half-drunken crowd soon gathered around, and Murieta's protestations of innocence, and offers of money for a respite until witnesses could be forthcoming to prove the truth of his statement, were disregarded. He was pulled down from the saddle, and amid cries of "Kill the thief! Hang the greaser!" they hurriedly carried him to the rancho of his brother, whom they summarily launched into eternity from the branch of a neighboring tree. Joaquin was stripped, bound to the same tree, and flogged. While the heavy lash was lacerating his back, a demoniac expression appeared upon his face; he looked around and stamped the features of each of his persecutors on the tablets of his memory. When the executioners had finished their work, they departed, leaving him with his dead. It was then that Joaquin Murieta registered his oath of vengeance which he so relentlessly kept, rarely sparing even the innocent. From that hour he was the implacable foe of every American, and even of every being that bore the resemblance of a gringo. Lucifer had him now for his own.

Words have been put in Murieta's lips to the effect that he had at one time felt a great admiration for Americans and their institutions; and only after experiencing unjust persecution and brutality at their hands, had the scales fallen from his eyes, and a deadly hatred seized him. To avenge the wrongs inflicted on himself and his countrymen, who were constantly kicked, and cuffed, and robbed, was now the purpose of his life. To kill, destroy, marking his swift trail with blood, was now his dream; for every stripe that had been laid upon his yet unhealed back ten Yankee lives should be forfeited, and these ruffianly Anglo-Saxons be made to understand that the free citizens of the sister republic had not wholly sunk their origin, nor lost their manhood. Letting all this pass, however, the fact stands that not long after the infliction of the flogging, an American was found dead near Murphy Diggings, literally hacked to pieces with a knife. The body turned out to be that of one of those who had flogged Joaquin, and hanged his brother. Suspicion was not long at fault reaching the author of the bloody act. Other murders followed in swift succession, robbing being one of the incidents of each case. It then began to be whispered that the young victim of Yankee brutality was wreaking his vengeance. Joaquin's bloody deeds were in everybody's mind, and his name became a terror.

Within a few months the dashing boy was at the head of an organized band of highwaymen, which ravaged the country in every direction. This band consisted sometimes of twenty, and at other times of as many as eighty. The boy leader gave proof every day of possessing a peculiar genius controlling the most accomplished scoundrels that had ever congregated in Christendom. He was their master; his word was their law, and woe betide him who dared to disobey, while to break faith with a fellow-robber was quick death. A member of the band, perforated by four bullets, was captured in February, 1853, at Los Muertos, near Los Angeles, brought to San Andreas, tried, and hanged by the people. He was but an humble member of the profession, and when he saw that death was certain, he was induced to talk a little. He said that no member of the fraternity was much respected who had not killed his man, and each ranked in importance according to the number that he had slain. This was something as it is in the army. Every member was bound under most solemn oaths, first, to obey his superiors. Disobedience was punished with death. There was hardly one chance in a hundred that a traitor could escape; for it was the duty and pleasure of the betrayed whose lives were jeopardized by the treachery to hunt and slay the informer. It was well understood by all, even the stupidest of them, that good faith unto one another, union and discipline, were essential as well to their personal safety as to pecuniary success.

This completeness of organization, coupled with the awful power wielded by the leader, enabled the band during nearly three years to carry on its operations, and its boyish chief to flit between towns and country, flipping his fingers in the face of the police and people, while throughout the length and breadth of the California valley, from Shasta to Tulare, and along the coast line of missions the country was wailing its dead and ringing with rewards. The modus operandi to accomplish the purposes of the organization was as follows: Each subaltern was restricted to certain limits beyond which he dare not step. He had to be at all times ready to receive an order from any captain or lieutenant of the band. His eyes and ears were to be always open, and his mouth closed; passing events were to be narrowly observed, such as the yield of the various mining claims, the drift of the gold dust, where a company kept their money, or certain Chinamen had hidden theirs. It was, moreover, his duty to shelter and protect any of the brotherhood needing his assistance; to warn them of danger, and provide horses and aid to escape; and generally, to assist them in all their undertakings.

Joaquin was always splendidly mounted; in fact much of his success depended on his horses. It was the special business of a certain portion of the brotherhood to keep the company well supplied with the best horses in the country. There were, also, members living in towns, and among the peaceable inhabitants, pursuing honest occupations, who were spies, and kept the officers of the band advised of matters they were desirous of knowing.

To relate the hundreds of incidents in which Joaquin and his chief captains and lieutenants personally displayed their skill and courage would occupy more space than I can devote to the matter. I will, however, narrate some of the most daring deeds of the young leader.

In 1851 while sojourning in a secluded part of San José, he attended a fandango, where he became involved in a fracas, for which he was arrested and fined $12 by the magistrate. Being in charge of Deputy Sheriff Clark, who was not aware of his being the robber chief, he invited the latter to go with him to his house for the money. Clark had become obnoxious to Murieta for his vigorous pursuit of the band. On reaching an unfrequented place the robber suddenly turned upon the officer, and with a smile said, "Accept the compliments of Joaquin," and drove his jeweled poignard to the hilt in his breast. In the autumn of the same year Murieta and his band were at the Sonoran camp near Marysville, where they committed a number of robberies, and five murders, every one of the murdered men bearing on his neck the fatal mark of the flying noose. All had been lassoed, and dragged at the saddle bow by the lariat. In the wild region west of the white pyramid of Shasta, the band roamed many months engaged in horse-stealing, with now and then a murder. Once while two of the band were galloping near the town of Hamilton, an elk rushed past them hotly pursued by a beautiful girl mounted on a fine steed. She hurled her lasso at the animal and secured it, only to find herself in turn held fast by the lariats of the two banditti. Her terror was distracting. She implored them not to harm her, but little did they care for her entreaties. There was only one voice on earth which they would heed, and that came unexpectedly as if from another world. "Restore that girl to her horse instantly." It was Joaquin who spoke.

One evening not long afterward, Joaquin was sitting at a monte table in a small town on the Feather River, when an American boastfully offered to bet $500 that he would kill the scoundrel Joaquin the first time he met him. Carried away by one of his dare-devil impulses, Joaquin sprang upon the table, and thrusting his pistol in the man's face cried, "I take the bet; Joaquin is before you"; then tossing the corner of his serape over his shoulder, he jumped down, strode out of the room, mounted his horse and rode away with some of his henchmen at his heels.

In the spring of 1852 Murieta drove 300 stolen horses through Southern California into Sonora. On his return after a few weeks, he was quartered at the Arroyo de Cantua, situated between the Coast Range and the Tulare Lake. It is possible that it was just previous to this that they sojourned for a while in Los Angeles and vicinity. Riding with some of his men toward San Luis Gonzaga, and his purse being light, Murieta, after the manner of Robin Hood, resolved to rob the first man that came along. The victim happened to be a young fellow named Albert Ruddle, who was driving a wagon loaded with groceries. Joaquin requested the loan of what money he had, promising to return it at an early opportunity. Ruddle made a movement as if to draw a weapon. He was told to keep quiet or he would be killed, but as he persisted, Joaquin with a muttered imprecation, slashed him across the neck with his knife, almost severing the head from the body. After rifling the dead man's pockets, the robbers rode off.

While in Los Angeles for a few days, he heard that Deputy Sheriff Wilson of Santa Barbara was on his trail, with the avowed intention of taking him dead or alive. He got up a sham fight between two Indians in front of the hotel where Wilson was staying. The latter came out to see the fight, when Joaquin rode swiftly to him, and hissing his own terrible name in his ear, drove a bullet through his head and drove away.

Riding one day alone toward the town of Los Hornitos, the chief met young Joe Lake, a playmate of his boyhood. In the course of their conversation Joaquin revealed his present mode of living, and said, "Joe, you are the only American whose good opinion I crave. Believe me my friend, I was driven to this by hellish wrongs." "Why don't you leave the country, and abandon your criminal life?" answered Joe. "Too late, Joe, I must die now as I live, pistol in hand. Do not betray me; do not divulge having met me here. If you do, I shall be very sorry," significantly tapping the stock of his revolver. Lake deemed it his duty to apprise the authorities of Murieta's presence, and the usual persecution began. The next morning a portly ranchero came up to Lake, and saying, "You betrayed me, Joe!" plunged a knife into his breast, and rode away unharmed.

One evening, Joaquin rode into a camp where about 25 miners were at supper, and sitting sideways on his horse entered into conversation with them. It so happened that a man who knew him by sight soon after came from the creek, and on seeing him called out, "That is Joaquin; why, in the name of God, don't you kill him?" Putting spurs to his horse with one bound he cleared the camp and dashed down the canyon. Finding his way blocked there he returned toward the camp, to avail himself of a narrow coyote trail around the brow of a precipice that overhung the awful depths of the canyon below. A shower of bullets greeted his reappearance, but none touched him, as he dashed up and along the dizzy path, waving his dagger and shouting defiance.

In the early part of March, 1853, Joaquin, unattended, visited a large Mexican camp on Burns creek, about twenty miles from the town of Mariposa. He presented the appearance of a dashing cavalier, with plumed sombrero, gold laced cloak, and gaily caparisoned steed, as he slowly rode down the principal thoroughfare of the camp, tinkling his spurs to the measures of some lively fandango, and was the cynosure of many admiring glances from the eyes of the señoritas. Passing in front of a saloon he called for a drink, and was just lifting it to his lips, when an American, one of two who were standing together and had recognized him, drew his revolver and fired a shot that cut the plume of the brigand's hat. The drink was never taken, but Joaquin, after having wounded one of the Americans in the arm and the other in the abdomen, galloped away without a scratch.

Later in the same month, Murieta and three or four of his men robbed a Chinese camp at Rich gulch, not far from San Andreas, of about $10,000, leaving three dead and five wounded. The next morning they entered another Chinese camp at the foot of the mountains, gashed the throats of three of the Chinamen, mortally wounded five others, and carried off some $3,000 in gold. They next visited several other Chinese camps, all of which they desolated, the cries of their victims being heard at long distances. Finding themselves pursued by a party of Americans, they calmly continued their devastation, until the pursuers were within half a mile of them, when they mounted their steeds, and rode away with the speed of the wind.

On one occasion, Murieta riding leisurely in disguise through Stockton saw the hand-bills offering $1,000 for his capture. Taking from his pocket a pencil, he wrote on the margin beneath one of them, "I will give $5,000. Joaquin," and quietly rode away.

One night a cattle-dealer, whose name was Cocariouris, was camping with one companion on the San Joaquin, when they were visited by several Mexicans, splendidly mounted and gaily attired, who asked for supper and a place to sleep. Their occupation being quite evident, they were treated with much politeness, and their requests promptly complied with. In the morning the robber was cordially greeted by the cattle-dealer:

"And how does Señor Joaquin this morning?"

"You know me, then," replied the robber.

"I knew you the moment I saw you," said Cocariouris.

"And why did you not kill me last night when I slept, and secure the reward?" demanded Joaquin.

"I do not like to kill men; I do not care for the reward," replied the host. "Besides, you never injured me; you asked for food; if every man deserving to be hanged went supperless, there would be an empty chair at more tables than mine."

"True," replied Joaquin, meditatively, "and I will see that you lose nothing by your broad philosophy."

Cocariouris was often on the road with large herds of stock, not one head of which was ever, to his knowledge, touched by any of Murieta's band.

The audacity of this chief, united to his celerity of movement, at a time when the country had no communication by railway or telegraph, enabled him and his men to effect the most remarkable escapes, as we have seen. He would show himself now here, now there, like an impish apparition which vanished at the approach of danger.

In February, 1853, Joaquin and his band swept through Calaveras, robbing and slaughtering as they went. Again was a reward of $1,000 offered by the governor for his capture. The people of Mokelumne Hill and elsewhere were indignant at the smallness of the amount, when they themselves had spent many thousands in their fruitless attempts. The scourge continued, and gloom overspread the foothills.

One evening in April, 1853, shortly before Joaquin's death, three men rode up to the house of a rancho on the Salinas plains and demanded refreshments for themselves and their horses, which were readily and politely served. After supper they informed their host that they were from the upper country on their way to Sonora to buy cattle. Their spokesman being asked if they had seen or heard of the famous Joaquin, he replied, "I am that Joaquin, and no man shall take me alive." He then gave his oft-repeated narrative of the wrongs which had been inflicted on him and his. In the morning, after paying for the night's lodging and refreshments, Joaquin and his companions departed southward, as he had said, but only went as far as the region of San Luis Obispo and Santa Barbara, and the cattle they took they seldom paid for. Murieta's movements were now

429

very closely watched, and it was thought that his destination was Lower California.

I have merely referred to a few of the doings of this famous band of marauders, or a portion of it under the immediate direction of Murieta in person. But it should be borne in mind that the excellently organized fraternity was often divided and, under his several lieutenants, Garcia, Claudio, Ruiz, and others, bore the terror of their chief's name simultaneously in widely different directions. Their operations became so repeated and destructive, extending meanwhile over such a great extent of country, that no community felt safe.

At last, the people throughout the state were aroused to the importance of suppressing this overwhelming evil. For three years this bloody work had been going on—a long time in that rushing epoch—and it was a reflection on the manhood of California that the robbers should go so long uncaught. At length, on the 17th of May, 1853, the legislature of California passed an act authorizing Harry Love to bring his mountaineer's experience, bravery, and tested nerve into action, with a well-organized and equipped body of twenty mounted rangers, to hunt the marauders down. Love was soon in the field, and lost no time in getting upon the track of the brigands.

Poor Joaquin! Love encompassed him without and within. For his girl, Antonia la Molinera, who went about with him dressed in men's clothes, proved false, having run away with a traitorous member of the band, Pancho Daniel. Murieta swore he would kill both of them; and Antonia when she heard of it, and knowing him so well, and realizing that her life was not safe for a moment as long as he was at liberty, resolved to betray him into the hands of justice.

Murieta sent first Vergara to kill her, but Vergara proved false, and let the girl live, abandoning the banditti, and going to work on the rancho of Palos Verdes, which was later Wilmington. Murieta sent another member of his band to bring back Vergara, but a few days thereafter the messenger was found murdered in the street in Los Angeles. Likewise, others of Joaquin's girls were giving him trouble. Thus discord was in the camp, men proving traitorous and women false, which shows that the life of a robber is not always a happy one.

Stealthily enough Harry Love, with his fierce eyes and flowing hair, followed upon the trail of Joaquin, spying upon him by night, and keeping under close cover by day, thirsting for the blood-money, thirsting both for the blood and the money, eager to slay the slayer and rob the robber.

Thus the toils which must inevitably sooner or later end such a career were closing round Joaquin. In the latter part of July, with eight of his rangers, Love came upon a party of Mexicans in camp near the Tejon pass. Six of them were seated round a small fire, where preparations for breakfast were going forward, while the seventh, he of the slender figure, and graceful limbs, and large black eyes, and long black hair, a perfect Apollo, richly dressed, blooming in the pride of health and manly beauty, was washing down a superb bay horse, at a little distance from the fire, with some water which he held in a pan. Joaquin was unknown to the rangers, who dashed into the camp before they were discovered, and succeeded in cutting the robbers off from their horses. Captain Love rode up to the one standing by his horse, and enquired whither they were going.

"To Los Angeles," the chief replied.

Turning to one of the others, the captain put the same question when an entirely different answer was returned. Joaquin bit his lip and spoke angrily, "I command here; address yourself to me." He then moved a few steps toward the fire, around which lay the saddles, blankets, and arms of the party. He was ordered to stop, and when he did not heed, Love cocked his revolver upon him and told him to stand or he would shoot. The chief tossed his hair back scornfully while his eyes blazed with the lightnings of his wrath, and stepping backward, he stood again by the side of his handsome steed, his jeweled hand resting lightly on its mane. Three-Fingered Jack stood a little distance away, fully armed and waiting for his chief. At this critical moment Lieutenant Byrnes, with whom Joaquin was well acquainted, moved up, and Joaquin, realizing that the game was up, called out to his followers to save themselves the best they could, and threw himself upon the back of his charger without saddle or bridle, and sped down the mountain like a tempest. He leaped his horse over a precipice, when he fell, but was on his feet again in a moment and, re-mounting, the daring rider dashed on. Close at his heels came the rangers, firing as they rode, and soon the gallant steed, struck in the side, fell to the earth, and Joaquin ran on afoot. Three balls had pierced his body, when he turned with a lifted hand toward his pursuers, and called out: "It is enough; the work is done,"—reeled, fell upon his right arm, and, sinking slowly down before his pursuers, gave up the ghost without a groan.

Three-Fingered Jack, cornered, fought like a tiger, but the end was at hand. And so with others of the company. Claudio had fallen some time before. The bandits, now left without an efficient leader, and admonished by the swift and sorrowful fate of Joaquin, broke up the organization, and stole away from the theatre of their crimes. For purposes of identification, the head of Joaquin, and the mutilated hand of Three-Fingered Jack, were severed from the bodies, and, preserved in spirits, were brought to San Francisco in August, 1853, by Black and Nuttall, two of Harry Love's rangers. The head was placed on exhibition, as the following notice, which appeared in the papers of the city on the 18th of August, and for several days following, will show: "Joaquin's Head! is to be seen at King's, corner of Halleck and Sansome streets. Admission one dollar." Then followed certificates of persons who had known Joaquin, as to the identity of the head. No money was recovered, though one of the prisoners declared that Jack had thrown away a heavy purse of gold during the chase. It is probable that others did the same, as the heavy operations of the band must have kept them well supplied with dust and coin. The growth, after death, of the hair on the head of Joaquin, and the fingernails of Jack's hand, caused quite a sensation among those not accustomed to such phenomena.

The number of murders committed by Joaquin and his men during the comparatively brief period in which they were abroad is truly astonishing. They were particularly hard on the Chinamen, literally strewing the highways with their carcasses, like slaughtered pigs, and robbing them at every turn. Several renegade Americans were among the robbers who won the respect of the bandit chief by deeds as bloody and heartless as ever stained the annals of human wrong.

Claudio . . . met his fate some time before the tragic scene at the Tejon pass. In the early part of 1853, attended by six of his men, Claudio was ravaging the country between Salinas and Monterey, robbing and slaying with a reckless hand. One Cocks, a justice of the peace at Salinas, and, withal a fearless man, summoned a party of eight and started in pursuit of the brigands. On the Salinas river, near Cooper's crossing, stood the adobe cabin of a man named Balder, whose reputation was very bad. Cocks and his party surrounded this house at night, and there, as they expected, found the robbers. A watch dog gave the alarm; but the Americans had already dismounted, and taking off their spurs, rushed in close to the walls. There was but one thing to do, for Claudio was not the kind of villain tamely to die in a kennel; bidding his men to follow, he threw the door open, and boldly led the way into the darkness, firing as he went. Unfortunately for the bandit he ran into the arms of Squire Cocks, who, being a powerful and determined man, held him with a grip of steel, until the robber dropping his revolver, exclaimed, *"Estoy dado, señor; no tengo armas."* "I surrender, sir; I have no arms." The lie was scarcely spoken when something was seen to glitter in the hand of Claudio. It was a murderous dirk which he had drawn from his legging; but a bullet from the pistol of an American stretched him lifeless before he could use it. With a single exception the brigands were all shot dead in the fight that ensued; the one making his escape being wounded, and was captured next day. He was sent to San Quentin for a term of years and afterward hanged.

Works of Bancroft, Vol. XXXIV, 1888

AMBROSE BIERCE

The Man and the Snake

"Bitter Bierce," the witty journalist, short-story writer and literary dictator of San Francisco, was also morbidly concerned with the gruesome and the supernatural. At the age of seventy-one he went off to Mexico and was never heard from again. He seemed to vanish into thin air just as his characters were so apt to do.

It is of veritabyll report, and attested of so many that there be nowe of wyse and learned none to gaynsaye it, that ye serpente hys eye hath a magnetick propertie that whosoe falleth into its svasion is drawn forwards in despyte of his wille and perisheth miserabyll by ye creature hys byte.

    Stretched at ease upon a sofa, in gown and slippers, Harker Brayton smiled as he read the foregoing in old Morryster's *Marvels of Science*. "The only marvel in the matter," he said to himself, "is that the wise and learned in Morryster's day should have believed such nonsense as is rejected by most of even the ignorant in ours."

A train of reflection followed and he unconsciously lowered his book without altering the direction of his eyes. As soon as the volume had gone below the line of sight, something in an obscure corner of the room recalled his attention to his surroundings. What he saw, in the shadow under his bed, was two small points of light, apparently about an inch apart. They might have been reflections of the gas jet above him, in metal nail heads; he gave them but little thought and resumed his reading. A moment later something impelled him to lower the book again and seek for what he saw before. The points of light were still there. They seemed to have become brighter, shining with a greenish lustre. He thought, too, that they might have moved a trifle—were somewhat nearer. They were still too much in shadow, however, to reveal their nature and origin to an indolent attention, and again he resumed his reading. Suddenly something in the text suggested a thought that made him start and drop the book to the side of the sofa. Brayton, half-risen, was staring intently into the obscurity beneath the bed, where the points of light shone with, it seemed to him, an added fire. His attention was now fully aroused, his gaze eager and imperative. It disclosed, almost directly under the foot rail of the bed, the coils of a large serpent—the points of light were its eyes! Its horrible head, thrust flatly forth from the innermost coil and resting upon the outermost, was directed straight toward him, the definition of the wide, brutal jaw and the idiot-like forehead serving to show the direction of its malevolent gaze. The eyes were no longer merely luminous points; they looked into his own with a meaning, a malign significance.

Harker Brayton, a bachelor of thirty-five, a scholar, idler and something of an athlete, rich, popular and of sound health, had returned to San Francisco from all manner of remote and unfamiliar countries. His tastes, always a trifle luxurious, had taken on an added exuberance from long privation; and the resources of even the Castle Hotel being inadequate to their perfect gratification, he had gladly accepted the hospitality of his friend, Dr. Druring, the distinguished scientist. Dr. Druring's house, a large, old-fashioned one in what is now an obscure quarter of the city, had an outer and visible aspect of proud reserve, and appeared to have developed some of the eccentricities which come of isolation. One of these was a "wing," a combination of laboratory, menagerie and museum. It was here that the doctor indulged the scientific side of his nature in the study of such forms of animal life as engaged his interest and comforted his taste —which ran to such "dragons of the prime" as toads and snakes. He loved nature's vulgarians, and described himself as the Zola of zoölogy. His wife and daughters not having the advantage to share his enlightened curiosity regarding the works and ways of our ill-starred fellow-creatures, were excluded from what he called the Snakery.

Architecturally the Snakery had a severe simplicity befitting the humble circumstances of its occupants, many of whom, indeed, could not safely have been intrusted with the liberty that is necessary to the full enjoyment of luxury, for they had the troublesome peculiarity of being alive. In their own apartments, however, they were under as little personal restraint as was compatible with their protection from the baneful habit of swallowing one another; and, as Brayton had thoughtfully been apprised, it was more than a tradition that some of them had at divers times been found in parts of the premises where it would have embarrassed them to explain their presence. Despite the Snakery and its uncanny associations— to which, indeed, he gave little attention—Brayton found life at the Druring mansion very much to his mind.

Beyond a smart shock of surprise and a shudder of mere loathing Mr. Brayton was not greatly affected. His first thought was to ring the call-bell and bring a servant; but although the bell cord dangled within easy reach he made no movement toward it; it had occurred to his mind that the act might subject him to the suspicion of fear, which he certainly did not feel.

The reptile was of a species with which Brayton was unfamiliar. Its length he could only conjecture; the body at the largest visible part seemed about as thick as his forearm. In what way was it dangerous, if in any way? Was it venomous? Was it a constrictor?

If not dangerous, the creature was at least offensive. Even the barbarous taste of our time and country, which had loaded the walls of the room with pictures, the floor with furniture and the furniture with bric-a-brac, had not quite fitted the place for this bit of the savage life of the jungle.

Besides—insupportable thought!—the exhalations of its breath mingled with the atmosphere which he himself was breathing.

Brayton rose to his feet and prepared to back softly away from the snake, without disturbing it if possible, and through the door. He knew that he could walk backward without error. Should the monster follow, the taste which had plastered the walls with paintings had consistently supplied a rack of murderous Oriental weapons from which he could snatch one to suit the occasion.

Brayton lifted his right foot free of the floor to step backward. He was steadying himself with his right hand upon the back of a chair, his foot suspended.

"Nonsense!" he said aloud; "I am not so great a coward as to fear to seem to myself afraid."

He lifted the foot a little higher, and thrust it sharply to the floor— an inch in front of the other! He could not think how that occurred. A trial with the left foot had the same result; it was again in advance of the right. The hand upon the chair back was grasping it; the arm was straight, reaching somewhat backward. One might have said that he was reluctant to lose his hold. The snake's malignant head was still thrust forth from the inner coil as before, the neck level. It had not moved, but its eyes were now electric sparks.

The man had an ashy pallor. Again he took a step forward, and another, partly dragging the chair, which when finally released fell upon the floor with a crash. The man groaned; the snake made neither sound nor motion, but its eyes were two dazzling suns. They gave off enlarging rings of rich and vivid colors; they seemed to approach his very face, and anon were an immeasurable distance away. He heard, somewhere, the continuous throbbing of a great drum, with desultory bursts of distant music, inconceivably sweet.

The music became by insensible degrees the distant roll of a retreating thunder-storm. A landscape, glittering with sun and rain, stretched before him, arched with a vivid rainbow framing in its giant curve a hundred visible cities. In the middle distance a vast serpent, wearing a crown, reared its head out of its voluminous convolutions and looked at him with his dead mother's eyes. Suddenly this enchanting landscape seemed to rise swiftly upward like the drop scene at a theatre, and vanished in a blank. Something struck him a hard blow upon the face and breast. He had fallen to the floor; the blood ran from his broken nose and his bruised lips. For a time he was dazed and stunned, and lay with closed eyes, his face against the floor. In a few moments he had recovered, and then knew that this fall, by withdrawing his eyes, had broken the spell that held him. He felt that now, by keeping his gaze averted, he would be able to retreat. But the thought of the serpent within a few feet of his head, yet unseen—perhaps in the very act of springing upon him

435

and throwing its coils about his throat—was too horrible! He lifted his head, stared again.

The snake had not moved.

Now ensued a fearful scene. The man, prone upon the floor, within a yard of his enemy, raised the upper part of his body upon his elbows, his head thrown back, his legs extended to their full length. His face was white between its stains of blood; his eyes were strained open to their uttermost expansion. There was froth upon his lips; it dropped off in flakes. Strong convulsions ran through his body, making almost serpentine undulations. He bent himself at the waist, shifting his legs from side to side. Every movement left him a little nearer to the snake. He thrust his hands forward to brace himself back, yet constantly advanced upon his elbows.

Dr. Druring and his wife sat in the library. The scientist was in rare good humor.

"I have just obtained by exchange with another collector," he said, "a splendid specimen of the *ophiophagus*."

"And what may that be?" the lady inquired with a somewhat languid interest.

"Why, bless my soul, what profound ignorance! My dear, a man who ascertains after marriage that his wife does not know Greek is entitled to a divorce. The *ophiophagus* is a snake that eats other snakes."

"I hope it will eat all yours," she said, absently. "How does it get the other snakes? By charming them, I suppose."

"That is just like you, dear," said the doctor. "You know how irritating to me is any allusion to that vulgar superstition about a snake's power of fascination."

The conversation was interrupted by a mighty cry, which rang through the silent house like the voice of a demon shouting in a tomb! Again and yet again it sounded, with terrible distinctness. They sprang to their feet, the man confused, the lady pale and speechless with fright. Almost before the echoes of the last cry had died away the doctor was out of the room, springing up the stairs two steps at a time. In the corridor in front of Brayton's chamber he met some servants who had come from the upper floor. Together they rushed at the door without knocking. It was unfastened and gave way. Brayton lay upon his stomach on the floor, dead. His head and arms were partly concealed under the foot rail of the bed. They pulled the body away, turning it upon the back. The face was daubed with blood and froth, the eyes were wide open, staring—a dreadful sight!

"Died in a fit," said the scientist, bending his knee and placing his hand upon the heart. While in that position he chanced to look under the bed. "Good God!" he added, "how did this thing get in here?"

He reached under the bed, pulled out the snake and flung it, still coiled, to the center of the room, whence with a harsh, shuffling sound it slid across the polished floor till stopped by the wall, where it lay without motion. It was a stuffed snake; its eyes were two shoe buttons.

In the Midst of Life, 1891

FRANK NORRIS

The Strike

Norris was the sometime Bohemian son of an affluent father. He traveled widely, lived adventurously on occasion, dabbled with art and various forms of writing. Finally he settled down to naturalistic writing, emphasizing the harsher, more violent aspects of the physical world.

[In the earlier part of this novel McTeague had murdered his wife, fled eastward from San Francisco and drifted about until he teamed up with Cribbens.]

A new life began for McTeague. After breakfast the "pardners" separated, going in opposite directions along the slope of the range, examining rocks, picking and chipping at ledges and bowlders, looking for signs, prospecting. McTeague went up into the little cañons where the streams had cut through the bed rock, searching for veins of quartz, breaking out this quartz when he had found it, pulverizing and panning it. Cribbens hunted for "contacts," closely examining country rocks and outcrops, continually on the lookout for spots where sedimentary and igneous rock came together.

One day, after a week of prospecting, they met unexpectedly on the slope of an arroyo. It was late in the afternoon. "Hello, pardner," exclaimed Cribbens as he came down to where McTeague was bending over his pan. "What luck?"

The dentist emptied his pan and straightened up. "Nothing, nothing. You struck anything?"

"Not a trace. Guess we might as well be moving towards camp." They returned together, Cribbens telling the dentist of a group of antelope he had seen.

"We might lay off tomorrow, an' see if we can plug a couple of them fellers. Antelope steak would go pretty well after beans an' bacon an' coffee week in an' week out."

437

McTeague was answering, when Cribbens interrupted him with an exclamation of profound disgust. "I thought we were the first to prospect along in here, an' now look at that. Don't it make you sick?"

He pointed out evidences of an abandoned prospector's camp just before them—charred ashes, empty tin cans, one or two gold-miner's pans, and a broken pick. "Don't that make you sick?" muttered Cribbens, sucking his mustache furiously. "To think of us mushheads going over ground that's been covered already! Say, pardner, we'll dig out of here tomorrow. I've been thinking, anyhow, we'd better move to the south; that water of ours is pretty low."

"Yes, yes, I guess so," assented the dentist. "There ain't no gold here."

"Yes, there is," protested Cribbens doggedly; "there's gold all through these hills, if we could only strike it. I tell you what, pardner, I got a place in mind where I'll bet no one ain't prospected—least not very many. There don't very many care to try an' get to it. It's over on the other side of Death Valley. It's called Gold Mountain, an' there's only one mine been located there, an' it's paying like a nitrate bed. There ain't many people in that country, because it's all hell to get into. First place, you got to cross Death Valley and strike the Armagosa Range fur off to the south. Well, no one ain't stuck on crossing the Valley, not if they can help it. But we could work down the Panamint some hundred or so miles, maybe two hundred, an' fetch around by the Armagosa River, way to the south'erd. We could prospect on the way. But I guess the Armagosa'd be dried up at this season. Anyhow," he concluded, "we'll move camp to the south tomorrow. We got to get new feed an' water for the horses. We'll see if we can knock over a couple of antelope tomorrow, and then we'll scoot."

"I ain't got a gun," said the dentist; "not even a revolver. I—"

"Wait a second," said Cribbens, pausing in his scramble down the side of one of the smaller gulches. "Here's some slate here; I ain't seen no slate around here yet. Let's see where it goes to."

McTeague followed him along the side of the gulch. Cribbens went on ahead, muttering to himself from time to time:

"Runs right along here, even enough, and here's water too. Didn't know this stream was here; pretty near dry, though. Here's the slate again. See where it runs, pardner?"

"Look at it up there ahead," said McTeague. "It runs right up over the back of this hill."

"That's right," asserted Cribbens. "Hi!" he shouted suddenly, "*here's a 'contact,'* and here it is again, and there, and yonder. Oh, *look* at it, will you? That's granodiorite on slate. Couldn't want it any more distinct than that. *God!* if we could only find the quartz between the two now."

"Well, there it is," exclaimed McTeague. "Look on ahead there; ain't that quartz?"

"You're shouting right out loud," vociferated Cribbens, looking where

438

McTeague was pointing. His face went suddenly pale. He turned to the dentist, his eyes wide.

"By God, pardner," he exclaimed, breathlessly, "By God—" he broke off abruptly.

"That's what you been looking for, ain't it?" asked the dentist.

"*Looking* for! *Looking* for!" Cribbens checked himself. "That's *slate* all right, and that's granodiorite. *I* know"—he bent down and examined the rock—"and here's the quartz between 'em; there can't be no mistake about that. Gi' me that hammer," he cried, excitedly. "Come on, git to work. Jab into the quartz with your pick; git out some chunks of it." Cribbens went down on his hands and knees, attacking the quartz vein furiously. The dentist followed his example, swinging his pick with enormous force, splintering the rocks at every stroke. Cribbens was talking to himself in his excitement.

"Got you *this* time, you son of a gun! By God! I guess we got you *this* time, at last. Looks like it, anyhow. *Get* a move on, pardner. There ain't anybody 'round, is there? Hey?" Without looking, he drew his revolver and threw it to the dentist. "Take the gun an' look around, pardner. If you see any son of a gun *anywhere, plug* him. This yere's *our* claim. I guess we got it *this* tide, pardner. Come on." He gathered up the chunks of quartz he had broken out, and put them in his hat and started towards their camp. The two went along with great strides, hurrying as fast as they could over the uneven ground.

"I don' know," exclaimed Cribbens, breathlessly, "I don' want to say too much. Maybe we're fooled. Lord, that damn camp's a long ways off. Oh, I ain't goin' to fool along this way. Come on, pardner." He broke into a run. McTeague followed at a lumbering gallop. Over the scorched, parched ground, stumbling and tripping over sage-brush and sharp-pointed rocks, under the palpitating heat of the desert sun, they ran and scrambled, carrying the quartz lumps in their hats.

"See any '*color*' in it, pardner?" gasped Cribbens. "I can't, can you? 'Twouldn't be visible nohow, I guess. Hurry up. Lord, we ain't ever going to get to that camp."

Finally they arrived. Cribbens dumped the quartz fragments into a pan.

"You pestle her, pardner, an' I'll fix the scales." McTeague ground the lumps to fine dust in the iron mortar while Cribbens set up the tiny scales and got out the "spoons" from their outfit.

"That's fine enough," Cribbens exclaimed, impatiently. "Now we'll spoon her. Gi' me the water."

Cribbens scooped up a spoonful of the fine white powder and began to spoon it carefully. The two were on their hands and knees upon the ground, their heads close together, still panting with excitement and the exertion of their run.

"Can't do it," exclaimed Cribbens, sitting back on his heels, "hand shakes so. *You* take it, pardner. Careful, now."

439

McTeague took the horn spoon and began rocking it gently in his huge fingers, sluicing the water over the edge a little at a time, each movement washing away a little more of the powdered quartz. The two watched it with the intensest eagerness.

"Don't see it yet; don't see it yet," whispered Cribbens, chewing his mustache. "*Leetle* faster, pardner. That's the ticket. Careful, steady, now; leetle more, leetle more. Don't see color yet, do you?"

The quartz sediment dwindled by degrees as McTeague spooned it steadily. Then at last a thin streak of a foreign substance began to show just along the edge. It was yellow.

Neither spoke. Cribbens dug his nails into the sand, and ground his mustache between his teeth. The yellow streak broadened as the quartz sediment washed away. Cribbens whispered:

"We got it, pardner. That's gold."

McTeague washed the last of the white quartz dust away, and let the water trickle after it. A pinch of gold, fine as flour, was left in the bottom of the spoon.

"There you are," he said. The two looked at each other. Then Cribbens rose into the air with a great leap and a yell that could have been heard for half a mile.

"Yee-e-ow! We *got* it, we struck it. Pardner, we got it. Out of sight. We're millionaires." He snatched up his revolver and fired it with inconceivable rapidity. "*Put* it there, old man," he shouted, gripping McTeague's palm.

"That's gold, all right," muttered McTeague, studying the contents of the spoon.

"You bet your great-grandma's Cochin-China Chessy cat it's gold," shouted Cribbens. "Here, now, we got a lot to do. We got to stake her out an' put up the location notice. We'll take our full acreage, you bet. You—we haven't weighed this yet. Where's the scales?" He weighed the pinch of gold with shaking hands. "Two grains," he cried. "That'll run five dollars to the ton. Rich, it's rich; it's the richest kind of pay, pardner. We're millionaires. Why don't you say something? Why don't you get excited? Why don't you run around an' *do* something?"

"Huh!" said McTeague, rolling his eyes. "Huh! *I* know, I know, we've struck it pretty rich."

"Come on," exclaimed Cribbens, jumping up again. "We'll stake her out an' put up the location notice. Lord, suppose anyone should have come on her while we've been away." He reloaded his revolver deliberately. "We'll drop *him* all right, if there's anyone fooling round there; I'll tell you those right now. Bring the rifle, pardner, an' if you see anyone, *plug* him, an' ask him what he wants afterward."

They hurried back to where they had made their discovery.

"To think," exclaimed Cribbens, as he drove the first stake, "to think those other mushheads had their camp within gunshot of her and never located her. Guess they didn't know the meaning of a 'contact.' Oh, I knew I was solid on 'contacts.'"

They staked out their claim, and Cribbens put up the notice of location. It was dark before they were through. Cribbens broke off some more chunks of quartz in the vein.

"I'll spoon this too, just for the fun of it, when I get home," he explained, as they tramped back to the camp.

"Well," said the dentist, "we got the laugh on those cowboys."

"Have we?" shouted Cribbens. "*Have* we? Just wait and see the rush for this place when we tell 'em about it down in Keeler. Say, what'll we call her?"

"I don' know, I don' know."

"We might call her the 'Last Chance.' 'Twas our last chance, wasn't it? We'd 'a' gone antelope shooting tomorrow, and the next day we'd 'a'— say, what you stopping for?" he added, interrupting himself. "What's up?"

The dentist had paused abruptly on the crest of a cañon. Cribbens, looking back, saw him standing motionless in his tracks.

"What's up?" asked Cribbens a second time.

McTeague slowly turned his head and looked over one shoulder, then over the other. Suddenly he wheeled sharply about, cocking the Winchester and tossing it to his shoulder.

Cribbens ran back to his side, whipping out his revolver.

"What is it?" he cried. "See anybody?" He peered on ahead through the gathering twilight.

"No, no."

"Hear anything?"

"No, didn't hear anything."

"What is it then? What's up?"

"I don' know, I don' know," muttered the dentist, lowering the rifle. "There was something."

"What?"

"Something—didn't you notice?"

"Notice what?"

"I don' know. Something—something or other."

"Who? What? Notice what? What did you see?"

The dentist let down the hammer of the rifle.

"I guess it wasn't anything," he said rather foolishly.

"What d'you think you saw—anybody on the claim?"

"I didn't see anything. I didn't hear anything either. I had an idea, that's all; came all of a sudden, like that. Something, I don' know what."

"I guess you just imagined something. There ain't anybody within twenty miles of us, I guess."

"Yes, I guess so, just imagined it, that's the word."

441

Half an hour later they had the fire going. McTeague was frying strips of bacon over the coals, and Cribbens was still chattering and exclaiming over their great strike. All at once McTeague put down the frying-pan.

"What's that?" he growled.

"Hey? What's what?" exclaimed Cribbens, getting up.

"Didn't you notice something?"

"Where?"

"Off there." The dentist made a vague gesture toward the eastern horizon. "Didn't you hear something—I mean see something—I mean—"

"What's the matter with you, pardner?"

"Nothing. I guess I just imagined it."

But it was not imagination. Until midnight the partners lay broad awake, rolled in their blankets under the open sky, talking and discussing and making plans. At last Cribbens rolled over on his side and slept. The dentist could not sleep.

What! It was warning him again, that strange sixth sense, that obscure brute instinct. It was aroused again and clamoring to be obeyed. Here, in these desolate barren hills, twenty miles from the nearest human being, it stirred and woke and rowelled him to be moving on. It had goaded him to flight from the Big Dipper mine, and he had obeyed. But now it was different; now he had suddenly become rich; he had lighted on a treasure—a treasure far more valuable than the Big Dipper mine itself. How was he to leave that? He could not move on now. He turned about in his blankets. No, he would not move on. Perhaps it was his fancy, after all. He saw nothing, heard nothing. The emptiness of primeval desolation stretched from him leagues and leagues upon either hand. The gigantic silence of the night lay close over everything, like a muffling Titanic palm. Of what was he suspicious? In that treeless waste an object could be seen at half a day's journey distant. In that vast silence the click of a pebble was as audible as a pistol-shot. And yet there was nothing, nothing.

The dentist settled himself in his blankets and tried to sleep. In five minutes he was sitting up, staring into the blue-gray shimmer of the moonlight, straining his ears, watching and listening intently. Nothing was in sight. The browned and broken flanks of the Panamint hills lay quiet and familiar under the moon. The burro moved its head with a clinking of its bell; and McTeague's mule, dozing on three legs, changed its weight to another foot, with a long breath. Everything fell silent again.

"What is it?" muttered the dentist. "If I could only see something, hear something."

He threw off the blankets, and, rising, climbed to the summit of the nearest hill and looked back in the direction in which he and Cribbens had travelled a fortnight before. For half an hour he waited, watching and listening in vain. But as he returned to camp, and prepared to roll his blankets about him, the strange impulse rose in him again abruptly never so strong, never so insistent. It seemed as though he were bitted

442

and ridden; as if some unseen hand were turning him toward the east; some unseen heel spurring him to precipitate and instant flight.

Flight from what? "No," he muttered under his breath. "Go now and leave the claim, and leave a fortune! What a fool I'd be, when I can't see anything or hear anything. To leave a fortune! No, I won't. No, by God!" He drew Cribbens's Winchester toward him and slipped a cartridge into the magazine.

"No," he growled. "Whatever happens, I'm going to stay. If anybody comes—" He depressed the lever of the rifle, and sent the cartridge clashing into the breech.

"I ain't going to sleep," he muttered under his mustache. "I can't sleep; I'll watch." He rose a second time, clambered to the nearest hilltop and sat down, drawing the blanket around him, and laying the Winchester across his knees. The hours passed. The dentist sat on the hilltop a motionless, crouching figure, inky black against the pale blur of the sky. By and by the edge of the eastern horizon began to grow blacker and more distinct in outline. The dawn was coming. Once more McTeague felt the mysterious intuition of approaching danger; an unseen hand seemed reining his head eastward; a spur was in his flanks that seemed to urge him to hurry, hurry, hurry. The influence grew stronger with every moment. The dentist set his great jaws together and held his ground.

"No," he growled between his set teeth. "No, I'll stay." He made a long circuit around the camp, even going as far as the first stake of the new claim, his Winchester cocked, his ears pricked, his eyes alert. There was nothing; yet as plainly as though it were shouted at the very nape of his neck he felt an enemy. It was not fear. McTeague was not afraid.

"If I could only *see* something—somebody," he muttered, as he held the cocked rifle ready, "I—I'd show him."

He returned to camp. Cribbens was snoring. The burro had come down to the stream for its morning drink. The mule was awake and browsing. McTeague stood irresolutely by the cold ashes of the camp-fire, looking from side to side with all the suspicion and wariness of a tracked stag. Stronger and stronger grew the strange impulse. It seemed to him that on the next instant he *must* perforce wheel sharply eastward and rush away headlong in a clumsy, lumbering gallop. He fought against it with all the ferocious obstinacy of his simple brute nature.

"Go, and leave the mine? Go and leave a million dollars? No, *no*, I won't go. No, I'll stay. Ah," he exclaimed, under his breath, with a shake of his huge head, like an exasperated and harassed brute, "ah, show yourself, will you?" He brought the rifle to his shoulder and covered point after point along the range of hills to the west. "Come on, show yourself. Come on a little, all of you. I ain't afraid of you; but don't skulk this way. You ain't going to drive me away from my mine. I'm going to *stay*."

An hour passed. Then two. The stars winked out, and the dawn whitened. The air became warmer. The whole east, clean of clouds, flamed opalescent from horizon to zenith, crimson at the base, where the earth blackened against it; at the top fading from pink to pale yellow, to green, to light blue, to the turquoise iridescence of the desert sky. The long, thin shadows of the early hours drew backward like receding serpents, then suddenly the sun looked over the shoulder of the world, and it was day.

At that moment McTeague was already eight miles away from the camp, going steadily eastward.

McTeague, 1899

OWEN WISTER

"When You Call Me That, Smile*"*

A gently reared Pennsylvanian, Wister traveled in the West as a young man. His Western novel, The Virginian, *surprised experts with its vigor and authenticity. It has pleased millions who have read or seen it either on the stage or on the screen.*

I left that company growing confidential over their leering stories, and I sought the saloon. It was very quiet and orderly. Beer in quart bottles at a dollar I had never met before; but saving its price, I found no complaint to make of it. Through folding doors I passed from the bar proper with its bottles and elk head back to the hall with its various tables. I saw a man sliding cards from a case, and across the table from him another man laying counters down. Near by was a second dealer pulling cards from the bottom of a pack, and opposite him a solemn old rustic piling and changing coins upon the cards which lay already exposed.

But now I heard a voice that drew my eyes to the far corner of the room.

"Why didn't you stay in Arizona?"

Harmless looking words as I write them down here. Yet at the sound of them I noticed the eyes of the others directed to that corner. What answer was given to them I did not hear, nor did I see who spoke. Then came another remark.

"Well, Arizona's no place for amatures."

This time the two card dealers that I stood near began to give a part of their attention to the group that sat in the corner. There was in me a desire to leave this room. So far my hours at Medicine Bow had seemed to glide beneath a sunshine of merriment, of easy-going jocularity. This was suddenly gone, like the wind changing to north in the middle of a warm day. But I stayed, being ashamed to go.

444

Five or six players sat over in the corner at a round table where counters were piled. Their eyes were close upon their cards, and one seemed to be dealing a card at a time to each, with pauses and betting between. Steve was there and the Virginian; the others were new faces.

"No place for amatures," repeated the voice; and now I saw that it was the dealer's. There was in his countenance the same ugliness that his words conveyed.

"Who's that talkin'?" said one of the men near me, in a low voice.

"Trampas."

"What's he?"

"Cow-puncher, bronco-buster, tin-horn, most anything."

"Who's he talkin' at?"

"Think it's the black-headed guy he's talkin' at."

"That ain't supposed to be safe, is it?"

"Guess we're all goin' to find out in a few minutes."

"Been trouble between 'em?"

"They've not met before. Trampas don't enjoy losin' to a stranger."

"Fello's from Arizona, yu' say?"

"No. Virginia. He's recently back from havin' a look at Arizona. Went down there last year for a change. Works for the Sunk Creek Outfit." And then the dealer lowered his voice still further and said something in the other man's ear, causing him to grin. After which both of them looked at me.

There had been silence over in the corner; but now the man Trampas spoke again.

"*And* ten," said he, sliding out some chips from before him. Very strange it was to hear him, how he contrived to make those words a personal taunt. The Virginian was looking at his cards. He might have been deaf.

"*And* twenty," said the next player, easily.

The next threw his cards down.

It was now the Virginian's turn to bet, or leave the game, and he did not speak at once.

Therefore Trampas spoke. "Your bet, you son-of-a—"

The Virginian's pistol came out, and his hand lay on the table, holding it unaimed. And with a voice as gentle as ever, the voice that sounded like a caress, but drawling a very little more than usual, so that there was almost a space between each word, he issued his orders to the man Trampas:—

"When you call me that, *smile.*" And he looked at Trampas across the table.

Yes, the voice was gentle. But in my ears it seemed as if somewhere the bell of death was ringing; and silence, like a stroke, fell on the large room. All men present, as if by some magnetic current, had become aware of this crisis. In my ignorance, and total stoppage of my thoughts, I

445

stood stock-still, and noticed various people crouching, or shifting their positions.

"Sit quiet," said the dealer, scornfully to the man near me. "Can't you see he don't want to push trouble? He has handed Trampas the choice to back down or draw steel."

Then with equal suddenness and ease, the room came out of its strangeness. Voices and cards, the click of chips, the puff of tobacco, glasses lifted to drink,—this level of smooth relaxation hinted no more plainly of what lay beneath than does the surface tell of the depth of the sea.

The Virginian, 1902

MARY AUSTIN

Nurslings of the Sky

A midwesterner by birth, Mary Austin's real love was for the Southwest and California. Her interest in primitive Indian life and her closeness to nature are evident in all her writings.

Choose a hill country for storms. There all the business of the weather is carried on above your horizon and loses its terror in familiarity. When you come to think about it, the disastrous storms are on the levels, sea or sand or plains. There you get only a hint of what is about to happen, the fume of the gods rising from their meeting place under the rim of the world; and when it breaks upon you there is no stay nor shelter. The terrible mewings and mouthings of a Kansas wind have the added terror of viewlessness. You are lapped in them like uprooted grass; suspect them of a personal grudge. But the storms in hill countries have other business. They scoop watercourses, manure the pines, twist them to a finer fibre, fit the firs to be masts and spars, and, if you keep reasonably out of the track of their affairs, do you no harm.

They have habits to be learned, appointed paths, seasons, and warnings, and they leave you in no doubt about their performances. One who builds his house on a water scar or the rubble of a steep slope must take chances. So they did in Overtown who built in the wash of Argus water, and at Kearsarge at the foot of a steep, treeless swale. After twenty years Argus water rose in the wash against the frail houses, and the piled snows of Kearsarge slid down at a thunder peal over the cabins and camp, but you could conceive that it was the fault of neither the water nor the snow.

446

Of the high Sierras choose the neighborhood of the splintered peaks about the Kern and King's river divide for storm study, or the short wide-mouthed canyons opening eastward on high valleys. Days when the hollows are steeped in a warm, winey flood the clouds come walking on the floor of heaven, flat and pearly white above. They gather flockwise, moving on the level currents that roll about the peaks, lock hands and settle with the cooler air, drawing a veil about those places where they do their work. If their meeting or parting takes place at sunrise or sunset, as it often does, one gets the splendor of the apocalypse. There will be cloud pillars miles high, snow-capped, glorified, and preserving an orderly perspective before the unbarred door of the sun, or perhaps mere ghosts of clouds that dance to some pied piper of an unfelt wind. But be it day or night, once they have settled to their work, one sees from the valley only the blank wall of their tents stretched along the ranges. To get the real effect of a mountain storm you must be inside.

One who goes often into a hill country learns not to say: What if it should rain? It always does rain somewhere among the peaks: the unusual thing is that one should escape it. You might suppose that if you took any account of plant contrivances to save their pollen powder against showers. Note how many there are deep-throated and bell-flowered like the pentstemons, how many have nodding pedicels as the columbine, how many grow in copse shelters and grow there only. There is keen delight in the quick showers of summer canyons, with the added comfort, born of experience, of knowing that no harm comes of a wetting at high altitudes. The day is warm; a white cloud spies over the canyon wall, slips up behind the ridge to cross it by some windy pass, obscures your sun. Next you hear the rain drum on the broad-leaved hellebore, and beat down the mimulus beside the brook. You shelter on the lee of some strong pine with shut-winged butterflies and merry, fiddling creatures of the wood. Runnels of rain water from the glacierslips swirl through the pine needles into rivulets; the streams froth and rise in their banks. The sky is white with cloud; the sky is gray with rain; the sky is clear. The summer shower leaves no wake.

Such as these follow each other by day for weeks in August weather. Sometimes they chill suddenly into wet snow that packs about the lake gardens clear to the blossom frills, and melts away harmlessly. Sometimes one has the good fortune from a heather-grown headland to watch a rain-cloud forming in mid-air. Out over meadow or lake region begins a little darling of the sky—no cloud, no wind, just a smokiness such as spirits materialize from in witch stories.

It rays out and draws to it some floating films from secret canyons. Rain begins, "slow dropping veil of thinnest lawn"; a wind comes up and drives the formless thing across a meadow, or a dull lake pitted by the glancing drops, dissolving as it drives. Such rains relieve like tears.

The same season brings the rains that have work to do, ploughing

447

storms that alter the face of things. These come with thunder and the play of live fire along the rocks. They come with great winds that try the pines for their work upon the seas and strike out the unfit. They shake down avalanches of splinters from sky-line pinnacles and raise up sudden floods like battle fronts in the canyons against towns, trees, and boulders. They would be kind if they could, but have more important matters. Such storms, called cloudbursts by the country folk, are not rain, rather the spillings of Thor's cup, jarred by the Thunderer. After such a one the water that comes up in the village hydrants miles away is white with forced bubbles from the wind-tormented streams.

All that storms do to the face of the earth you may read in the geographies, but not what they do to our contemporaries. I remember one night of thunderous rain made unendurably mournful by the house-less cry of a cougar whose lair, and perhaps his family, had been buried under a slide of broken boulders on the slope of Kearsarge. We had heard the heavy detonation of the slide about the hour of the alpenglow, a pale rosy interval in a darkling air, and judged he must have come from hunting to the ruined cliff and paced the night out before it, crying a very human woe. I remember, too, in that same season of storms, a lake made milky white for days, and crowded out of its bed by clay washed into it by a fury of rain, with the trout floating in it belly up, stunned by the shock of the sudden flood. But there were trout enough for what was left of the lake next year and the beginning of a meadow about its upper rim. What taxed me most in the wreck of one of my favorite canyons by cloudburst was to see a bobcat mother mouthing her drowned kittens in the ruined lair built in the wash, far above the limit of accustomed waters, but not far enough for the unexpected. After a time you get the point of view of gods about these things to save you from being too pitiful.

The great snows that come at the beginning of winter, before there is yet any snow except the perpetual high banks, are best worth while to watch. These come often before the late bloomers are gone and while the migratory birds are still in the piney woods. Down in the valley you see little but the flocking of blackbirds in the streets, or the low flight of mallards over the tulares, and the gathering of clouds behind Williamson. First there is a waiting stillness in the wood; the pine-trees creak although there is no wind, the sky glowers, the firs rock by the water borders. The noise of the creek rises insistently and falls off a full note like a child abashed by sudden silence in the room. This changing of the stream-tone following tardily the changes of the sun on melting snows is most meaningful to wood notes. After it runs a little trumpeter wind to cry the wild creatures to their holes. Sometimes the warning hangs in the air for days with increasing stillness. Only Clark's crow and the strident jays make light of it; only they can afford to. The cattle get down to the foothills and ground inhabiting creatures make fast their

448

doors. It grows chill, blind clouds fumble in the canyons, there will be a roll of thunder, perhaps, or a flurry of rain, but mostly the snow is borne in the air with quietness and the sense of strong white pinions softly stirred. It increases, is wet and clogging, and makes a white night of midday.

There is seldom any wind with first snows, more often rain, but later, when there is already a smooth foot or two over all the slopes, the drifts begin. The late snows are fine and dry, mere ice granules at the wind's will. Keen mornings after a storm they are blown out in wreaths and banners from the high ridges sifting into the canyons.

Once in a year or so we have a "big snow." The cloud tents are widened out to shut in the valley and an outlying range or two and are drawn tight against the sun. Such a storm begins warm, with a dry white mist that fills and fills between the ridges, and the air is thick with formless groaning. Now for days you get no hint of the neighboring ridges until the snows begin to lighten and some shouldering peak lifts through a rent. Mornings after the heavy snows are steely blue, two-edged with cold, divinely fresh and still, and these are times to go up to the pine borders. There you may find floundering in the unstable drifts "tainted wethers" of the wild sheep, faint from age and hunger; easy prey. Even the deer make slow going in the thick fresh snow, and once we found a wolverine going blind and feeble in the white glare.

No tree takes the snow stress with such ease as the silver fir. The star-whorled, fan-spread branches droop under the soft wreaths—droop and press flatly to the trunk; presently the point of overloading is reached, there is a soft sough and muffled droppings, the boughs recover, and the weighting goes on until the drifts have reached the midmost whorls and covered up the branches. When the snows are particularly wet and heavy they spread over the young firs in green-ribbed tents wherein harbor winter-loving birds.

All storms of desert hills, except wind storms, are impotent. East and west of the Sierras they rise in nearly parallel ranges, desertward, and no rain breaks over them, except from some far-strayed cloud or roving wind from the California Gulf, and these only in winter. In summer the sky travails with thunderings and the flare of sheet lightnings to win a few blistering big drops, and once in a lifetime the chance of a torrent. But you have not known what force resides in the mindless things until you have known a desert wind. One expects it at the turn of the two seasons, wet and dry, with electrified tense nerves. Along the edge of the mesa where it drops off to the valley, dust devils begin to rise white and steady, fanning out at the top like the genii out of the Fisherman's bottle. One supposes the Indians might have learned the use of smoke signals from these dust pillars as they learn most things direct from the tutelage of the earth. The air begins to move fluently, blowing hot and cold between the ranges. Far south rises a murk of sand against the sky; it grows, the wind shakes itself, and has a smell of earth. The cloud of small dust takes on the color of gold and shuts out the neighborhood, the push of the wind is unsparing. Only man of all folk is foolish enough to stir abroad in it. But being in a house is really much worse; no relief from the dust, and a great fear of the creaking timbers. There is no looking ahead in such a wind, and the bite of the small sharp sand on exposed skin is keener than any insect sting. One might sleep, for the lapping of the wind wears one to the point of exhaustion very soon, but there is dread, in open sand stretches sometimes justified, of being blown over by the drift. It is hot, dry, fretful work, but by going along the ground with the wind behind, one may come upon strange things in its tumultuous privacy. I like these truces of wind and heat that the desert makes, otherwise I do not know how I should come by so many acquaintances with furtive folk. I like to see hawks sitting daunted in shallow holes, not daring to spread a feather, and doves in a row by the prickle bushes, and shut-eyed cattle, turned tail to the wind in a patient doze. I like the smother of sand among the dunes, and finding small coiled snakes in open places, but I never like to come in a wind upon the silly sheep. The wind robs them of what wit they had, and they seem never to have learned the self-induced hypnotic stupor with which most wild things endure weather stress. I have never heard that the desert winds brought harm to any other than the wandering shepherds and their flocks. Once below Pastaria, Little Pete showed me bones sticking out of the sand where a flock of two hundred had been smothered in a bygone wind. In many places the four-foot posts of a cattle fence had been buried by the wind-blown dunes.

It is enough occupation, when no storm is brewing, to watch the cloud currents and the chambers of the sky. From Kearsarge, say, you look over Inyo and find pink soft cloud masses asleep on the level desert air; south of you hurries a white troop late to some gathering of their kind at the back of Oppapago; nosing the foot of Waban, a woolly mist creeps south. In the clean, smooth paths of the middle sky and highest up in air, drift, unshepherded, small flocks ranging contrarily. You will find the proper names of these things in the reports of the Weather Bureau —cirrus, cumulus, and the like—and charts that will teach by study when to sow and take up crops. It is astonishing the trouble men will be at to find out when to plant potatoes, and gloze over the eternal meanings of the skies. You have to beat out for yourself many mornings on the windy headlands the sense of the fact that you get the same rainbow in the cloud drift over Waban and the spray of your garden hose. And not necessarily then do you live up to it.

The Land of Little Rain, 1903

KIRKE L. SIMPSON

The Unknown Soldier

Simpson's prize-winning account of the Unknown Soldier's burial became so famous that the Associated Press was obliged to put it into pamphlet form for distribution throughout the country.

Washington, Nov. 9, 1921.—(By the Associated Press)—A plain soldier, unknown but weighted with honors as perhaps no American before him because he died for the flag in France, lay tonight in a place where only martyred Presidents Lincoln, Garfield and McKinley have slept in death.

He kept lonely vigil lying in state under the vast, shadowy dome of the Capitol. Only the motionless figures of the five armed comrades, one at the head and one facing inward at each corner of the bier, kept watch with him.

But far above, towering from the great bulk of the dome, the brooding figure of Freedom watched too, as though it said "well done" to the servant faithful unto death, asleep there in the vast, dim chamber below.

America's unknown dead is home from France at last, and the nation has no honor too great for him. In him, it pays its unstinted tribute of pride and glory to all those sleeping in the far soil of France. It was their home-coming today; their day of days in the heart of the nation and they must have known it for the heart beat of a nation defies the laws of space, even of eternity.

Sodden skies and a gray, creeping chilling rain all through the day seemed to mark the mourning of this American soil and air at the bier of this unknown hero. But no jot of the full meed of honor was denied the dead on that account. From the highest officials of this democratic government to the last soldier or marine or bluejacket, rain and cold meant nothing beside the desire to do honor to the dead.

The ceremonies were brief today. They began when the far boom of saluting cannon down the river signalled the coming of the great gray cruiser *Olympia*. The fog of rain hid her slow approach up the Potomac, but fort by fort, post by post, the guns took up the tale of honors for the dead as she passed.

Slowly the ship swung into her dock. Along her rails stood her crew in long lines of dark blue, rigid at attention and with a solemn expression uncommon to the young faces beneath the jaunty sailor hats. Astern, under the long, gray muzzle of a gun that once echoed its way into history more than twenty years ago in Manila Bay, lay the flag-draped casket. Above a tented awning held off the dripping rain, the inner side

451

of the canvas lined with great American flags to make a canopy for the sleeper below. At attention stood five sailors and marines as guards of honor for the dead at each corner and the head of his bier.

Below on the cobbled stretch of the old dock at Washington Navy Yard, a regiment of cavalry waited, sabers at "present," and the black-draped gun caisson with its six black horses to carry the casket to the Capitol. The troopers formed in line facing toward the ship as she swung broadside to her place and the gangway was lifted to her quarterdeck. To their right a mounted band stilled its restless horses.

On the ship, the trim files of her marine guard stood at attention. Rear-Admiral Lloyd H. Chandler, to whom had fallen the duty of escorting this dead private soldier over the Atlantic from France, was garbed in the full, formal naval dress as were officers of his staff.

Just as the ship's bell clanged out the quick, double strokes of "eight bells" the sailors' four o'clock and the hour set for arrival, the bugles rang again and the crew again lined the rails far above the dock. The marine guard filed down the gangway to face the troopers across the dock, the ship's band came down and formed beyond the marines. On deck at the gangway head, four sides-boys took their place on each side facing toward each other, the boatswain waiting behind them to pipe a dead comrade over the side with the honors accorded only to full Admirals of the fleet.

Cars bearing Secretaries Weeks and Denby, Assistant Secretary Wain-wright, General Pershing, Major General Harbord, Admiral Coontz and Major General Lejeune, the Marine Commandant, and their aides rolled up, with Secretary Weeks on the right next to the gangway and Secretary Denby next, then General Pershing and Admiral Coontz; these highest officers of the Army and Navy formed in line facing down the open space between the troops and marines.

On deck the bugles called attention. A group of petty officers stepped forward to raise the casket. A forward gun crashed to the first drumming roll of the minute guns of sorrow. The *Olympia's* band sounded the opening chords of Chopin's "Funeral March" and to the slow half-step and carried high on the shoulders of his Navy and Marine Corps comrades, the Unknown was tenderly lifted down the steep pitch to the dock.

Admiral Chandler and his aides came behind, cocked hats off in the cold rain and held across their breasts. Below the Cabinet members also stood bareheaded in the rain, the Army and Navy officers at salute.

Just as the casket passed out through the rails, overside the plank, the wail of the bo'sun's pipe sounded shrilling the last salute of the sea to the dead. It sounded oddly against the background of the dirge and as the sound of the pipe died away, the gun forward barked again the passing of another minute.

Step by step the bearers labored down the plank, sanded against the slippery murk of the rain, to the cobbled dock floor below. Again the

452

pipe above wailed as they stepped ashore at last and the Unknown was again on American soil.

Slowly the flag-draped casket moved down between the line of troops and marines and under the eyes of the bluejackets standing rigidly at the ship's rails high above. As they came abreast of the ship's band, the dirge was stilled, a marine bugler sounded four flourishes of salute to a general officer. Then the stirring, lifting strains of "The Star Spangled Banner" rang out to the gray sky, the nation's own hymn of freedom.

Again the slow march to the waiting gun carriage was taken up; again the wail of the "Funeral March," cut through with the crash of the gun above, sounded. The caisson waited in a space between the second and third squadrons of the full strength of the Third Cavalry from Fort Myer and beside it stood the eight body bearers of the Army headed by Sergeant Woodfill, hero of heroes among Americans who fought in France.

The soldiers took over the burden at the gun carriage and then could be seen a withered handful of flowers, the only decoration on the flag-wrapped casket. They were the blooms with which this casket was chosen from others there in France before the long journey home began. Through it all they have lain there above the breast of the dead, yellowing with each passing day. They will go with the Unknown to his last sleep in the stone crypt at Arlington.

As the casket was strapped in place, an order rang out and the cavalry band swung off to the left, playing "Onward, Christian Soldiers." Behind them, sabers, cap brims and sodden colors dripping with rain, came the troopers four abreast, troop after troop. Then the caisson, the following squadron, Secretaries Weeks and Denby riding together in a closed car, General Pershing and Admiral Coontz, and behind these the other officers and officials.

The horses swung away at a slow trot. Ahead the winding road to the old gateway was lined on either side with marines at "present arms" and behind them, row after row, were packed the thousands of just plain American citizens who had braved cold and rain for hours to stand bareheaded as the body of this honored fellow countryman was carried by.

Out through the gateway the cortege clattered to find other crowds lining the way under the daylight of a fading autumn day. It moved quickly on through the streets, ringing to the melody of the band and the drumming of the horses' shoes on the wet pavement. On it went, to swing at last into the great plaza before the Capitol and there troopers again drew up in line, facing the massive building with sabers at "present" as the casket was lifted down and carried up the wide stairway to be placed on the catafalque in the dim rotunda. The two Secretaries, bareheaded, followed and behind them the officers and others.

There were few in the great hall. The only lights were those high among the pillars above the sculptured walls and the last fading gleams of day through the high windows. The waiting guard, which would stand through the long night about the bier, stood at "present arms" as the casket was carried in and set in place on the high, black-draped structure on which the body of McKinley was last to repose in state.

There was a pause then until the ring of a command out on the plaza, the flurry of drawn steel as the sabers of the cavalry leaped out again to "present" announcing that President and Mrs. Harding had arrived. The last rites of the day were at hand.

As the President and Mrs. Harding came into the dim chamber, brilliant lights leaped up to make possible a picturing of the scene for all America to see. The cameras clicked. There was no other sound. About the bier the guard stood with rifle butts grounded.

Mrs. Harding stepped forward, a wide white ribbon in her hand. She had stitched it herself and stepping up on the base of the catafalque she laid it across the casket, a slash of white across the rain-sodden flag with its withered cluster of French flowers. As Mrs. Harding stepped down, the President took her place and to the ribbon pinned a silver shield of the United States, set with forty-eight golden stars. It is symbolic of the heart of the nation that goes with this soldier to his tomb.

Then a great wreath of crimson roses was handed to Mr. Harding and he laid it softly on the casket near the head and gave place to Vice-President Coolidge and Speaker Gillett who moved forward together to lay the tribute of Congress, a wreath of pink roses and snapdragons, in place. Chief Justice Taft moved forward from the opposite side, bearing the floral tribute of the Supreme Court, a wreath of chrysanthemums and carnations.

Secretary Weeks laid the Army's token of remembrance, a wreath of white roses, against the casket at the head and Secretary Denby placed the Navy's offering, chrysanthemums and roses, set on an easel, at the foot of the bier. Over and to one side, against the wall, were placed the great masses of pink blossoms that were warmed to life by the sun of France to be carried all the long way on the *Olympia*.

Then General Pershing stepped forward to place his own tribute and that of the American Expeditionary Force on this unknown, gallant comrade's coffin. It was a wreath of giant pink chrysanthemums and as he placed it, the officer paused a moment, then stepped back a pace or two and, drawing his figure to its full height, lifted his hand to cap brim in rigid salute to the dead.

The only spectators of these simple rites were the few clustered in the doorways of the great chamber. The bright lights blazed for a few moments as the President and Mrs. Harding went out to receive again formal honors from the troops waiting below. Then the Unknown was

454

left alone with his motionless guard of honor that was changed at frequent intervals through the night, alone with his head eastward toward distant France and at his feet through a far window and the end of a pillared corridor the twinkling lights of Washington.

On either side of the doorway through which he might have gazed stand the statues of Lincoln and Grant, as though they also kept vigil. And as the lights were switched off and the great building was wrapped in the gloom of night, the dim twilight of the few scattered hidden electrics let the shadows fall over the bier and fill the vast cavern of the dome above with a mystery and a peace that will not be broken until daylight streams again through those high windows.

Washington, Nov. 11, 1921.—(By the Associated Press)—Under the wide and starry skies of his own home-land America's unknown dead from France sleeps tonight, a soldier home from the wars.

Alone, he lies in the narrow cell of stone that guards his body; but his soul has entered into the spirit that is America. Wherever liberty is held close in men's hearts, the honor and the glory and the pledge of high endeavor poured out over this nameless one of fame, will be told and sung by Americans for all time.

Scrolled across the marble arch of the memorial raised to American soldier and sailor dead, everywhere, which stands like a monument behind his tomb, runs this legend: "We here highly resolve that these dead shall not have died in vain."

The words were spoken by the martyred Lincoln over the dead at Gettysburg. And today, with voice strong with determination and ringing with deep emotion, another President echoed that high resolve over the coffin of the soldier who died for the flag in France.

Great men in the world's affairs heard that high purpose reiterated by the man who stands at the head of the American people. Tomorrow they will gather in the city that stands almost in the shadow of the new American shrine of liberty dedicated today. They will talk of peace; of the curbing of the havoc of war.

They will speak of the war in France, that robbed this soldier of life and name and brought death to comrades of all nations by the hundreds of thousands. And in their ears when they meet must ring President Harding's declaration today beside that flag-wrapped, honor-laden bier:

"There must be, there shall be, the commanding voice of a conscious civilization against armed warfare."

Far across the seas, other unknown dead, hallowed in memory by their countrymen, as this American soldier is enshrined in the heart of America, sleep their last. He, in whose veins ran the blood of British forebears, lies beneath a great stone in ancient Westminster Abbey; he of France, beneath the Arc de Triomphe, and he of Italy under the altar of the Fatherland in Rome.

And it seemed today that they, too, must be here among the Potomac hills to greet an American comrade come to join their glorious company, to testify their approval of the high words of hope spoken by America's President. All day long the nation poured out its heart in pride and glory for the nameless American. Before the first crash of the minute gun roared its knell for the dead from the shadow of Washington Monument, the people who claim him as their own were trooping out to do him honor. They lined the long road from the Capitol to the hillside where he sleeps tonight; they flowed like a tide over the slopes about his burial place; they choked the bridges that lead across the river to the fields of the brave, in which he is the last comer.

As he was carried past through the banks of humanity that lined Pennsylvania Avenue a solemn, reverent hush held the living walls. Yet there was not so much of sorrow as of high pride in it all, a pride beyond the reach of shouting and the clamor that marks less sacred moments in life.

Out there in the broad avenue was a simple soldier, dead for honor of the flag. He was nameless. No man knew what part in the great life of the nation he had filled when last he passed over his home soil. But in France he had died as Americans always have been ready to die, for the flag and what it means. They read the message of the pageant clear, these silent thousands along the way. They stood in almost holy awe to take their own part in what was theirs, the glory of the American people, honored here in the honors showered on America's nameless son from France.

Soldiers, sailors and marines—all played their part in the thrilling spectacle as the cortege rolled along. And just behind the casket, with its faded French flowers on the draped flag, walked the President, the chosen leader of a hundred million, in whose name he was chief mourner at his bier. Beside him strode the man under whom the fallen hero had lived and died in France, General Pershing, wearing only the single medal of Victory that every American soldier might wear as his only decoration.

Then, row on row, came the men who lead the nation today or have guided its destinies before. They were all there, walking proudly with age and frailties of the flesh forgotten. Judges, Senators, Representatives, highest officers of every military arm of government and a trudging little group of the nation's most valorous sons, the Medal of Honor men. Some were gray and bent and drooping with old wounds; some trim and erect as the day they won their way to fame. All walked gladly in this nameless comrade's last parade.

Behind these came the carriage in which rode Woodrow Wilson, also stricken down by infirmities as he served in the highest place of the nation, just as the humble private riding in such state ahead had gone down before a shell or bullet. For that dead man's sake, the former President had put aside his dread of seeming to parade his physical weakness and risked health, perhaps life, to appear among the mourners for the fallen.

There was handclapping and a cheer here and there for the man in the carriage, a tribute to the spirit that brought him to honor the nation's nameless hero, whose commander-in-chief he had been.

After President Harding and most of the high dignitaries of the Government had turned aside at the White House, the procession, headed by its solid blocks of soldiery and the battalions of sailor comrades, moved on with Pershing, now flanked by Secretaries Weeks and Denby, for the long road to the tomb. It marched on, always between the human borders of the way of victory the nation had made for itself of the great avenue; on over the old bridge that spans the Potomac, on up the long hill to Fort Myer, and at last to the great cemetery beyond, where soldier and sailor folk sleep by the thousands. There the lumbering guns of the artillery swung aside, the cavalry drew their horses out of the long line and left to the foot soldiers and the sailors and marines the last stage of the journey.

Ahead, the white marble of the amphitheater gleamed through the trees. It stands crowning the slope of the hills that sweep upward from the river and just across was Washington, its clustered buildings and monuments to great dead who have gone before, a moving picture in the autumn breeze.

People in thousands were moving about the great circle of the amphitheater. The great ones to whom places had been given in the sacred inclosure and the plain folk who trudged the long way just to glimpse the pageant from afar were finding their places. Everywhere within the pillared inclosure bright uniforms of foreign soldiers appeared. They were laden with the jeweled order of rank to honor an American private soldier, great in the majesty of his sacrifices, in the tribute his honors paid to all Americans who died.

Down below the platform placed for the casket, in a stone vault, lay wreaths and garlands brought from England's King and guarded by British soldiers. To them came the British Ambassador in the full uniform of his rank to bid them keep these tributes from overseas safe against that hour.

Above the platform gathered men whose names ring through history —Briand, Foch, Beatty, Balfour, Jacques, Diaz and others—in a brilliant array of place and power. They were followed by others, Baron Kato from Japan, the Italian statesmen and officers, by the notables from all countries gathered here for tomorrow's conference and by some of the older figures in American life too old to walk beside the approaching funeral train.

Down around the circling pillars the marbled box filled with distinguished men and women, with a cluster of shattered men from army hospitals accompanied by uniformed nurses. A surpliced choir took its place to wait the dead.

Faint and distant, the silvery strains of a military band stole into the big white bowl of the amphitheater. The slow cadences and mourning notes of a funeral march grew clearer amid the roll and mutter of the muffled drums.

At the arch where the choir waited the heroic dead, comrades lifted his casket down and, followed by the Generals and the Admirals, who had walked beside him from the Capitol, he was carried to the place of honor. Ahead moved the white-robed singers, chanting solemnly. Carefully, the casket was placed above the banked flowers and the Marine Band played sacred melodies until the moment the President and Mrs. Harding stepped to their places beside the casket; then the crashing, triumphant chords of "The Star-Spangled Banner" swept the gathering to its feet again.

A prayer, carried out over the crowd by amplifiers so that no word was missed, took a moment or two, then the sharp, clear call of the bugle rang "Attention!" and for two minutes the nation stood at pause for the dead, just at high noon. No sound broke the quiet as all stood with bowed heads. It was much as though a mighty hand had checked the world in full course. Then the band sounded and in a mighty chorus rolled up the words of "America" from the hosts within and without the great open hall of valor.

President Harding stepped forward beside the coffin to say for America the thing that today was nearest to the nation's heart, that sacrifices such as this nameless man, fallen in battle, might perhaps be made unnecessary down through the coming years. Every word that President Harding spoke reached every person through the amplifiers and reached other thousands upon thousands in New York and San Francisco.

Mr. Harding showed strong emotion as his lips formed the last words of the address. He paused, then with raised hand and head bowed, went on in the measured, rolling period of the Lord's Prayer. The response that came back to him from the thousands he faced, from the other thousands out over the slopes beyond, perhaps from still other thousands away near the Pacific, or close packed in the heart of the nation's greatest city, arose like a chant. The marble arches hummed with the solemn sound.

Then the foreign officers who stand highest among the soldiers or sailors of their flags came one by one to the bier to place gold and jeweled emblems for the brave above the breast of the sleeper. Already, as the great prayer ended, the President had set the American seal of admiration for the valiant, the nation's love for brave deeds and the courage that defies death, upon the casket.

Side by side he laid the Medal of Honor and the Distinguished Service

458

Cross. And below, set in place with reverent hands, grew the long line of foreign honors, the Victoria Cross, never before laid on the breast of any but those who had served the British flag; all the highest honors of France and Belgium and Italy and Rumania and Czecho-Slovakia and Poland.

To General Jacques of Belgium it remained to add his own touch to these honors. He tore from the breast of his own tunic the Medal of Valor pinned there by the Belgian King, tore it with a sweeping gesture, and tenderly bestowed it on the unknown American warrior.

Through the religious services that followed, and prayers, the swelling crowd sat motionless until it rose to join in the old, consoling "Rock of Ages," and the last rite for the dead was at hand. Lifted by his hero bearers from the stage, the Unknown was carried in his flag-wrapped, simple coffin out to the wide sweep of the terrace. The bearers laid the sleeper down above the crypt on which had been placed a little of the soil of France. The dust his blood helped redeem from alien hands will mingle with his dust as time marches by.

The simple words of the burial ritual were said by Bishop Brent, flowers from war mothers of America and England were laid in place.

For the Indians of America, Chief Plenty Coos came to call upon the Great Spirit of the Red Men, with gesture and chant and tribal tongue that the dead should not have died in vain, that war might end, peace be purchased by such blood as this. Upon the casket he laid the coup stick of his tribal office and the feathered war bonnet from his own head. Then the casket, with its weight of honors, was lowered into the crypt.

A rocking blast of gunfire rang from the woods. The glittering circle of bayonets stiffened to a salute to the dead. Again the guns shouted their message of honor and farewell. Again they boomed out; a loyal comrade was being laid to his last, long rest.

High and clear and true in the echoes of the guns, a bugle lifted the old, old notes of taps, the lullaby for the living soldier, in death his requiem. Long ago some forgotten soldier poet caught its meaning clear and set it down that soldiers everywhere might know its message as they sing to rest:

> *Fades the light:*
> *And afar*
> *Goeth day, cometh night,*
> *And a star,*
> *Leadeth all, speedeth all,*
> *To their rest.*

The guns roared out again in the national salute. He was home, The Unknown, to sleep forever among his own.

Associated Press, 1921

459

OLIVER LA FARGE

Laughing Boy Comes Back to T'o Tlakai with a Wife

The Pulitzer Prize was awarded to Oliver La Farge for his novel about a young Navajo silversmith, Laughing Boy. However, Mr. La Farge's interest in the Indians of the Southwest goes well beyond writing fiction about them. In addition to being a noted anthropologist he has concerned himself with their problems and fought consistently for justice on their behalf.

Laughing Boy had been half-afraid lest, like Friend of the Eagles, or Reared in a Mountain, he would find that his own people seemed dirty and smelled badly when he returned to them. Secretly, even a little shame-facedly, he considered the life that he was living perhaps not so far removed from that of ordinary Earth People as the Eagles' home in the sky, or the mother-of-pearl and turquoise dwellings of the Divine Ones, but still something apart, like the magic country at the end of Old Age River. He had waited somewhat anxiously for his first impression, and found that his home was delightfully as he had imagined it. Everything was the same; it seemed a miracle. That which had been intimate and dear was so still, only now nothing was taken for granted, but every commonest detail leapt to him with new vividness.

There were constant little surges of delight in his heart over trivial, minor things—a shadow across a cliff, the bend of a cottonwood, the sheep coming in at evening, their silly, solemn faces all about the hogahn—why should they have changed? A man does not realize that he has changed himself, or only partially recognizes it, thinking that the world about him is different; a familiar dish has become no longer enjoyable, a fundamental aphorism no longer true; it is a surprise, then, when his eyes and ears report unchanged, familiar impressions. So the wonderful sameness of things, the unfailing way in which expectation was fulfilled, were proofs of something beautiful in the order of the world. It was glorious to pick up the threads of talk where he had dropped them, discussing the old, well-worn subjects casually and in detail, as though they were still inlaid in his life, with just a little seasoning of the attitude of one who has been farther and seen more.

One could see that his family had expected some outlandishness. Now they were puzzled; some disappointed, and some pleased to see how normal and Navajo were Laughing Boy and his wife. Her blankets spoke for them with many tongues, and the solid evidence of their prosperity, all Navajo, nothing bizarre or American, but good honest silver, turquoise, coral—"hard goods"—and handsome Indian ponies.

He watched Slim Girl, seeing the shutters closed behind her eyes, correct, sure, in hand, doing just the perfect thing. He was swept by constantly recurring waves of pleasure in her, and felt, as he sometimes did, a faint fear of that detached self-command. Slowly they were being forced to accept her as really belonging to the People. It pleased his dramatic instinct, as well as the strong sense of privacy he had concerning their relationship, to play up, being very normal, and letting no look or gesture suggest that they two came from a land of enchantment.

Knowing her well, he could see that she was at high tension, and secretly watchful. He had no idea that that strain, that painful vigilance, was above all for himself.

When he was alone with his father, he showed him the silver-mounted bridle and some of his other jewelry. Two Bows turned over the harness, feeling the surface with his finger-tips.

"I have nothing more to teach you—that is well done." He tapped the check-strap. "I should not have thought of using that design that way."

From Two Bows, such praise made it hard to keep a quiet, modest face.

Jesting Squaw's Son came back in the late afternoon. They drifted off together, with arms over each other's shoulders, until they came back to rest under the scrub oaks behind the peach trees. They discussed this and that, vaguely, trailing off into silence, playing with twigs and pebbles, running their fingers through the sand, occupying their hands. At length Laughing Boy looked at his friend and spoke:

"I do not talk to those people. Some of them have their minds made up, some of them will not understand. I do not think you will know what I am talking about, but you understand me. I want you to know.

"I have been down Old Age River in the log, with sheet-lightning and rainbows and soft rain, and the gods on either side to guide me. The Eagles have put lightning snakes and sunbeams and rainbows under me; they have carried me through the hole in the sky. I have been through the little crack in the rocks with Red God and seen the homes of the Butterflies and the Mountain Sheep and the Divine Ones. I have heard the Four Singers on the Four Mountains. I mean that woman.

"It sounds like insane talk. It is not. It is not just because I am in love. It is not what I feel when I am near her, what happens to my blood when she touches me, I know about that. I have thought about that. It is what goes on there. It is all sorts of things, but you would have to live there to see it.

"I know the kind of things my uncle says. It is not true. We are not acting out here, we are pretending. We have masks on, so they will not see our real faces. You have seen her blankets and my hard goods. Those are true. Those are just part of it."

Jesting Squaw's Son answered: "I have seen the blankets and the hard goods, they sing. I am happy about you."

He felt better after that, he cared that his friend should know, and, in contradistinction to the others, telling him did not lessen the rare quality of the thing described. He returned to the hogahns feeling better able to act his part.

He found the evening meal most enjoyable as he watched the good ways and mannerisms of his family. Among them he could make out a growing perplexity. What had that old man told them to expect? A word slipped from his brother to his younger uncle gave him the clue, filling his heart with glee. When he got a chance he whispered to Slim Girl,

"What my uncle said—they expected you to have no manners. They were waiting for you to act like an American, and give them something to talk about."

He lolled back on the sheepskins, laughing inside himself. A smile shadowed the corners of his wife's mouth.

Laughing Boy, 1929

WILLIAM SAROYAN

The Daring Young Man on the Flying Trapeze

I. SLEEP

Horizontally wakeful amid universal widths, practicing laughter and mirth, satire, the end of all, of Rome and yes of Babylon, clenched teeth, remembrance, much warmth volcanic, the streets of Paris, the plains of Jericho, much gliding as of reptile in abstraction, a gallery of watercolors, the sea and the fish with eyes, symphony, a table in the corner of the Eiffel Tower, jazz at the opera house, alarm clock and the tap-dancing of doom, conversation with a tree, the river Nile, Cadillac coupé to Kansas, the roar of Dostoyevsky, and the dark sun.

This earth, the face of one who lived, the form without the weight, weeping upon snow, white music, the magnified flower twice the size of the universe, black clouds, the caged panther staring, deathless space, Mr. Eliot with rolled sleeves baking bread, Flaubert and Guy de Maupassant, a wordless rhyme of early meaning, Finlandia, mathematics highly polished and slick as a green onion to the teeth, Jerusalem, the path to paradox.

The deep song of man, the sly whisper of someone unseen but vaguely known, hurricane in the cornfield, a game of chess, hush the queen, the king, Karl Franz, black Titanic, Mr. Chaplin weeping, Stalin, Hitler, a multitude of Jews, tomorow is Monday, no dancing in the streets.

O swift moment of life: it is ended, the earth is again now.

II. WAKEFULNESS

He (the living) dressed and shaved, grinning at himself in the mirror. Very unhandsome, he said; where is my tie? (He had but one.) Coffee and a gray sky, Pacific Ocean fog, the drone of a passing streetcar, people going to the city, time again, the day, prose and poetry. He moved swiftly down the stairs to the street and began to walk, thinking suddenly, *It is only in sleep that we may know that we live. There only, in that living death, do we meet ourselves and the far earth, God and the saints, the names of our fathers, the substance of remote moments; it is there that the centuries merge in the moment, that the vast becomes the tiny, tangible atom of eternity.*

He walked into the day as alertly as might be, making a definite noise with his heels, perceiving with his eyes the superficial truth of streets and structures, the trivial truth of reality. Helplessly his mind sang, *He flies through the air with the greatest of ease; the daring young man on the flying trapeze;* then laughed with all the might of his being. It was really a splendid morning: gray, cold, and cheerless, a morning for inward vigor; ah, Edgar Guest, he said, how I long for your music.

In the gutter he saw a coin which proved to be a penny dated 1923, and placing it in the palm of his hand he examined it closely, remembering that year and thinking of Lincoln whose profile was stamped upon the coin. There was almost nothing a man could do with a penny. I will purchase a motorcar, he thought. I will dress myself in the fashion of a fop, visit the hotel strumpets, drink and dine, and then return to the quiet. Or I will drop the coin into a slot and weigh myself.

It was good to be poor, and the Communists—but it was dreadful to be hungry. What appetites they had, how fond they were of food! Empty stomachs. He remembered how greatly he needed food. Every meal was bread and coffee and cigarettes, and now he had no more bread. Coffee without bread could never honestly serve as supper, and there were no weeds in the park that could be cooked as spinach is cooked.

If the truth were known, he was half starved, and yet there was still no end of books he ought to read before he died. He remembered the young Italian in a Brooklyn hospital, a small sick clerk named Mollica, who had said desperately, I would like to see California once before I die. And he thought earnestly, I ought at least to read Hamlet once again; or perhaps Huckleberry Finn.

It was then that he became thoroughly awake: at the thought of dying. Now wakefulness was a state in the nature of a sustained shock. A young man could perish rather unostentatiously, he thought; and already he was very nearly starved. Water and prose were fine, they filled much inorganic space, but they were inadequate. If there were only some work he might do for money, some trivial labor in the name of commerce. If they would only allow him to sit at a desk all day and add trade figures, subtract and multiply and divide, then perhaps he would not die. He would buy food, all sorts of it: untasted delicacies from Norway, Italy, and France; all manner of beef, lamb, fish, cheese; grapes, figs, pears, apples, melons, which he would worship when he had satisfied his hunger. He would place a bunch of red grapes on a dish beside two black figs, a large yellow pear, and a green apple. He would hold a cut melon to his nostrils for hours. He would buy great brown loaves of French bread, vegetables of all sorts, meat; he would buy life.

From a hill he saw the city standing majestically in the east, great towers, dense with his kind, and there he was suddenly outside of it all, almost definitely certain that he should never gain admittance, almost positive that somehow he had ventured upon the wrong earth, or perhaps into the wrong age, and now a young man of twenty-two was to be permanently ejected from it. This thought was not saddening. He said to himself, sometime soon I must write *An Application for Permission To Live*. He accepted the thought of dying without pity for himself or for man, believing that he would at least sleep another night. His rent for another day was paid; there was yet another tomorrow. And after that he might go where other homeless men went. He might even visit the Salvation Army—sing to God and Jesus (unlover of my soul), be saved, eat and sleep. But he knew that he would not. His life was a private life. He did not wish to destroy this fact. Any other alternative would be better.

Through the air on the flying trapeze, his mind hummed. Amusing it was, astoundingly funny. A trapeze to God, or to nothing, a flying trapeze to some sort of eternity; he prayed objectively for the strength to make the flight with grace.

I have one cent, he said. It is an American coin. In the evening I shall polish it until it glows like a sun and I shall study the words.

He was now walking in the city itself, among living men. There were one or two places to go. He saw his reflection in the plate-glass windows of stores and was disappointed with his appearance. He seemed not all as strong as he felt; he seemed, in fact, a trifle infirm in every part of his body, in his neck, his shoulders, arms, trunk, and knees. This will never do, he said, and with an effort he assembled all his disjointed parts and became tensely, artificially alert and solid.

He passed numerous restaurants with magnificent discipline, refusing even to glance into them, and at last reached a building, which he entered. He rose in an elevator to the seventh floor, moved down a hall, and, opening a door, walked into the office of an employment agency. Already there were two dozen young men in the place; he found a corner where he stood waiting his turn to be interviewed. At length he was granted this great privilege and was questioned by a thin, scatter-brained miss of fifty.

Now tell me, she said; what can you do?

He was embarrassed. I can write, he said pathetically.

You mean your penmanship is good? Is that it? said the elderly maiden.

Well, yes, he replied. But I mean that I can write.

Write what? said the miss, almost with anger.

Prose, he said simply.

There was a pause. At last the lady said:

Can you use a typewriter?

Of course, said the young man.

All right, went on the miss, we have your address; we will get in touch with you. There is nothing this morning, nothing at all.

It was much the same at the other agency, except that he was questioned by a conceited young man who closely resembled a pig. From the agencies he went to the large department stores: there was a good deal of pomposity, some humiliation on his part, and finally the report that work was not available. He did not feel displeased, and strangely did not even feel that he was personally involved in all the foolishness. He was a living young man who was in need of money with which to go on being one, and there was no way of getting it except by working for it; and there was no work. It was purely an abstract problem which he wished for the last time to attempt to solve. Now he was pleased that the matter was closed.

He began to perceive the definiteness of the course of his life. Except for moments, it had been largely artless, but now at the last minute he was determined that there should be as little imprecision as possible.

He passed countless stores and restaurants on his way to the Y. M. C. A., where he helped himself to paper and ink and began to compose his *Application*. For an hour he worked on this document, then suddenly, owing to the bad air in the place and to hunger, he became faint. He seemed to be swimming away from himself with great strokes, and hurriedly left the building. In the Civic Center Park, across from the Public Library Building, he drank almost a quart of water and felt himself refreshed. An old man was standing in the center of the brick boulevard surrounded by sea gulls, pigeons, and robins. He was taking handfuls of bread crumbs from a large paper sack and tossing them to the birds with a gallant gesture.

Dimly he felt impelled to ask the old man for a portion of the crumbs, but he did not allow the thought even nearly to reach consciousness; he entered the Public Library and for an hour read Proust, then, feeling himself to be swimming away again, he rushed outdoors. He drank more water at the fountain in the park and began the long walk to his room.

I'll go and sleep some more, he said; there is nothing else to do. He knew now that he was much too tired and weak to deceive himself about being all right, and yet his mind seemed somehow still lithe and alert. It, as if it were a separate entity, persisted in articulating impertinent pleasantries about his very real physical suffering. He reached his room early in the afternoon and immediately prepared coffee on the small gas range. There was no milk in the can and the half pound of sugar he had purchased a week before was all gone; he drank a cup of the hot black fluid, sitting on his bed and smiling.

From the Y. M. C. A. he had stolen a dozen sheets of letter paper upon which he had hoped to complete his document, but now the very notion of writing was unpleasant to him. There was nothing to say. He began to polish the penny he had found in the morning, and this absurd act somehow afforded him great enjoyment. No American coin can be made to shine so brilliantly as a penny. How many pennies would he need to go on living? Wasn't there something more he might sell? He looked about the bare room. No. His watch was gone; also his books. All those fine books; nine of them for eighty-five cents. He felt ill and ashamed for having parted with his books. His best suit he had sold for two dollars, but that was all right. He didn't mind at all about clothes. But the books. That was different. It made him very angry to think that there was no respect for men who wrote.

He placed the shining penny on the table, looking upon it with the delight of a miser. How prettily it smiles, he said. Without reading them he looked at the words, *E Pluribus Unum One Cent United States of America*, and turning the penny over, he saw Lincoln and the words, *In God We Trust Liberty* 1923. How beautiful it is, he said.

He became drowsy and felt a ghastly illness coming over his blood, a feeling of nausea and disintegration. Bewildered, he stood beside his bed, thinking that there *is nothing to do but sleep*. Already he felt himself making great strides through the fluid of the earth, swimming away to the beginning. He fell face down upon the bed, saying, I ought first at least to give the coin to some child. A child could buy any number of things with a penny.

Then swiftly, neatly, with the grace of the young man on the trapeze, he was gone from his body. For an eternal moment he was all things at once: the bird, the fish, the rodent, the reptile, and man. An ocean of print undulated endlessly and darkly before him. The city burned. The herded crowd rioted. The earth circled away, and knowing that he did so, he turned his lost face to the empty sky and became dreamless, unalive, perfect.

The Daring Young Man on the Flying Trapeze, 1934

JOHN STEINBECK

Two for a Cent

Along 66 the hamburger stands—Al & Susy's Place—Carl's Lunch—Joe & Minnie—Will's Eats. Board-and-bat shacks. Two gasoline pumps in front, a screen door, a long bar, stools, and a foot rail. Near the door three slot machines, showing through glass the wealth in nickels three bars will bring. And beside them, the nickel phonograph with records piled up like pies, ready to swing out to the turntable and play dance music, "Ti-pi-ti-pi-tin," "Thanks for the Memory," Bing Crosby, Benny Goodman. At one end of the counter a covered case; candy cough drops, caffeine sulphate called sleepless No-Doze; candy, cigarettes, razor blades, aspirin, Bromo-Seltzer, Alka-Seltzer. The walls decorated with posters, bathing girls, blondes with big breasts and slender hips and waxen faces, in white bathing suits, and holding a bottle of Coca-Cola and smiling— see what you get with a Coca-Cola. Long bar, and salts, peppers, mustard pots, and paper napkins. Beer taps behind the counter, and in back the coffee urns, shiny and steaming, with glass gauges showing the coffee level. And pies in wire cages and oranges in pyramids of four. And little piles of Post Toasties, corn flakes, stacked up in designs.

The signs on cards, picked out with shining mica: Pies Like Mother Used to Make. Credit Makes Enemies, Let's Be Friends. Ladies May Smoke But Be Careful Where You Lay Your Butts. Eat Here and Keep Your Wife for a Pet.

Down at one end the cooking plates, pots of stew, potatoes, pot roast, roast beef, gray roast pork waiting to be sliced.

Minnie or Susy or Mae, middle-aging behind the counter, hair curled and rouge and powder on a sweating face. Taking orders in a soft low voice, calling them to the cook with a screech like a peacock. Mopping the counter with circular strokes, polishing the big shining coffee urns. The cook is Joe or Carl or Al, hot in a white coat and apron, beady sweat on white forehead, below the white cook's cap; moody, rarely speaking, looking up for a moment at each new entry. Wiping the griddle, slapping down the hamburger. He repeats Mae's orders gently, scrapes the griddle, wipes it down with burlap. Moody and silent.

Mae is the contact, smiling, irritated, near to outbreak; smiling while her eyes look on past—unless for truck drivers. There's the backbone of the joint. Where the trucks stop, that's where the customers come. Can't fool truck drivers, they know. They bring the custom. They know. Give 'em a stale cup a coffee, an' they're off the joint. Treat 'em right an' they come back. Mae really smiles with all her might at truck drivers. She bridles a little, fixes her back hair so that her breasts will lift with her raised arms, passes the time of day and indicates great things, great times,

467

great jokes. Al never speaks. He is no contact. Sometimes he smiles a little at a joke, but he never laughs. Sometimes he looks up at the vivaciousness in Mae's voice, and then he scrapes the griddle with a spatula, scrapes the grease into an iron trough around the plate. He presses down a hissing hamburger with his spatula. He lays the split buns on the plate to toast and heat. He gathers up stray onions from the plate and heaps them on the meat and presses them in with the spatula. He puts half the bun on top of the meat, paints the other half with melted butter, with thin pickle relish. Holding the bun on the meat, he slips the spatula under the thin pad of meat, flips it over, lays the buttered half on top, and drops the hamburger on a small plate. Quarter of a dill pickle, two black olives beside the sandwich. Al skims the plate down the counter like a quoit. And he scrapes his griddle with the spatula and looks moodily at the stew kettle.

Cars whisking by on 66. License plates. Mass., Tenn., R.I., N.Y., Vt., Ohio. Going west. Fine cars, cruising at sixty-five.

There goes one of them Cords. Looks like a coffin on wheels.

But, Jesus, how they travel!

See that La Salle? Me for that. I ain't a hog. I go for a La Salle.

'F ya goin' big, what's a matter with a Cad'? Jus' a little bigger, little faster.

I'd take a Zephyr myself. You ain't ridin' no fortune, but you got class an' speed. Give me a Zephyr.

Well, sir, you may get a laugh outa this—I'll take a Buick-Puick. That's good enough.

But, hell, that costs in the Zephyr class an' it ain't got the sap.

I don' care. I don' want nothin' to do with nothin' of Henry Ford's. I don' like 'im. Never did. Got a brother worked in the plant. Oughta hear him tell.

Well, a Zephyr got sap.

The big cars on the highway. . . . The big car cruising along at sixty.

I want a cold drink.

Well, there's something up ahead. Want to stop?

Do you think it would be clean?

Clean as you're going to find in this God-forsaken country.

Well, maybe the bottled soda will be all right.

The great car squeals and pulls to a stop. The fat worried man helps his wife out.

Mae looks at and past them as they enter. Al looks up from his griddle, and down again. Mae knows. They'll drink a five-cent soda and crab that it ain't cold enough. The woman will use six paper napkins and drop them on the floor. The man will choke and try to put the blame on Mae. The woman will sniff as though she smelled rotting meat and they will go out again and tell forever afterward that the people in the West are sullen.

468

Truck drivers. That's the stuff.

Here's a big transport comin'. Hope they stop; take away the taste of them ——. When I worked in that hotel in Albuquerque, Al, the way they steal—ever' darn thing. An' the bigger the car they got, the more they steal—towels, silver, soap dishes. I can't figger it.

And Al, morosely, Where ya think they get them big cars and stuff? Born with 'em? You won't never have nothin'.

The transport truck, a driver and relief. How 'bout stoppin' for a cup a Java? I know this dump.

How's the schedule?

Oh, we're ahead!

Pull up, then. They's a ol' war horse in here that's a kick. Good Java, too.

The truck pulls up. Two men in khaki riding trousers, boots, short jackets, and shiny-visored military caps. Screen door—slam.

H'ya, Mae?

Well, if it ain't Big Bill the Rat! When'd you get back on this run?

Week ago.

The other man puts a nickel in the phonograph, watches the disk slip free and the turntable rise up under it. Bing Crosby's voice—golden. "Thanks for the memory, of sunburn at the shore— You might have been a headache, but you never were a bore—" And the truck driver sings for Mae's ears, you might have been a haddock but you never was a whore—

Mae laughs. Who's ya frien', Bill? New on this run, ain't he?

The other puts a nickel in the slot machine, wins four slugs, and puts them back. Walks to the counter.

Well, what's it gonna be?

Oh, cup a Java. Kinda pie ya got?

Banana cream, pineapple cream, chocolate cream—an' apple.

Make it apple. Wait—Kind is that big thick one?

Mae lifts it out and sniffs it. Banana cream.

Cut off a hunk; make it a big hunk.

Man at the slot machine says, Two all around.

Two it is. . . .

Al, slicing onions carefully on a board, looks up and smiles, and then looks down again. Truck drivers, that's the stuff. Gonna leave a quarter each for Mae. Fifteen cents for pie an' coffee an' a dime for Mae. . . .

Sitting together on the stools, spoons sticking up out of the coffee mugs. Passing the time of day. And Al, rubbing down his griddle, listening but making no comment. Bing Crosby's voice stops. The turntable drops down and the record swings into its place in the pile. The purple light goes off. The nickel, which has caused all this mechanism to work, has caused Crosby to sing and an orchestra to play—this nickel drops from between the contact points into the box where the profits go. This nickel, unlike most money, has actually done a job of work, has been physically responsible for a reaction.

Steam spurts from the valve of the coffee urn. The compressor of the ice machine chugs softly for a time and then stops. The electric fan in the corner waves its head slowly back and forth, sweeping the room with a warm breeze. On the highway, on 66, the cars whiz by.

They was a Massachusetts car stopped a while ago, said Mae.

Big Bill grasped his cup around the top so that the spoon stuck up between his first and second fingers. He drew in a snort of air with the coffee, to cool it. "You ought to be out on 66. Cars from all over the country. All headin' west. Never seen so many before. Sure some honeys on the road."

"We seen a wreck this mornin'," his companion said. "Big car. Big Cad', a special job and a honey, low, cream-color, special job. Hit a truck. Folded the radiator right back into the driver. Must a been doin' ninety. Steerin' wheel went right on through the guy an' lef' him a-wigglin' like a frog on a hook. Peach of a car. A honey. You can have her for peanuts now. Drivin' alone, the guy was."

Al looked up from his work. "Hurt the truck?"

"Oh, Jesus Christ! Wasn't a truck. One of them cut-down cars full a stoves an' pans an' mattresses an' kids an' chickens. Goin' west, you know. This guy come by us doin' ninety—r'ared up on two wheels just to pass us, an' a car's comin' so he cuts in an' whangs this here truck. Drove like he's blin' drunk. Jesus, the air was full a bed clothes an' chickens an' kids. Killed one kid. Never seen such a mess. We pulled up. Ol' man that's drivin' the truck, he jus' stan's there lookin' at the dead kid. Can't get a word out of 'im. Jus' rum-dumb. God Almighty, the road is full a them families goin' west. Never seen so many. Gets worse all a time. Wonder where the hell they all come from?"

"Wonder where they all go to," said Mae. "Come here for gas sometimes, but they don't hardly never buy nothin' else. People say they steal. We ain't got nothin' layin' around. They never stole nothin' from us."

Big Bill, munching his pie, looked up the road through the screened window. "Better tie your stuff down. I think you got some of 'em comin' now."

A 1926 Nash sedan pulled wearily off the highway. The back seat was piled nearly to the ceiling with sacks, with pots and pans, and on the very top, right up against the ceiling, two boys rode. On the top of the car, a mattress and a folded tent; tent poles tied along the running board. The car pulled up to the gas pumps. A dark-haired, hatchet-faced man got slowly out. And the two boys slid down from the load and hit the ground.

Mae walked around the counter and stood in the door. The man was dressed in gray wool trousers and a blue shirt, dark blue with sweat on the back and under the arms. The boys in overalls and nothing else, ragged patched overalls. Their hair was light, and it stood up evenly all

470

over their heads, for it had been roached. Their faces were streaked with dust. They went directly to the mud puddle under the hose and dug their toes into the mud.

The man asked, "Can we git some water, ma'am?"

A look of annoyance crossed Mae's face. "Sure, go ahead." She said softly over her shoulder, "I'll keep my eye on the hose." She watched while the man slowly unscrewed the radiator cap and ran the hose in.

A woman in the car, a flaxen-haired woman, said, "See if you can't git it here."

The man turned off the hose and screwed on the cap again. The little boys took the hose from him and they upended it and drank thirstily. The man took off his dark, stained hat and stood with a curious humility in front of the screen. "Could you see your way to sell us a loaf of bread, ma'am?"

Mae said, "This ain't a grocery store. We got bread to make san'widges."

"I know, ma'am." His humility was insistent. "We need bread and there ain't nothin' for quite a piece, they say."

" 'F we sell bread we gonna run out." Mae's tone was faltering.

"We're hungry," the man said.

"Why'n't you buy a san'widge? We got nice san'widges, hamburgs."

"We'd sure admire to do that, ma'am. But we can't. We got to make a dime do all of us." And he said embarrassedly, "We ain't got but a little."

Mae said, "You can't get no loaf a bread for a dime. We only got fifteen-cent loafs."

From behind her Al growled, "God Almighty, Mae, give 'em bread."

"We'll run out 'fore the bread truck comes."

"Run out, then, goddamn it," said Al. And he looked sullenly down at the potato salad he was mixing.

Mae shrugged her plump shoulders and looked to the truck drivers to show them what she was up against.

She held the screen door open and the man came in, bringing a smell of sweat with him. The boys edged in behind him and they went immediately to the candy case and stared in—not with craving or with hope or even with desire, but just with a kind of wonder that such things could be. They were alike in size and their faces were alike. One scratched his dusty ankle with the toe nails of his other foot. The other whispered some soft message and then they straightened their arms so that their clenched fists in the overall pockets showed through the thin blue cloth.

Mae opened a drawer and took out a long waxpaper-wrapped loaf. "This here is a fifteen-cent loaf."

The man put his hat back on his head. He answered with inflexibile humility, "Won't you—can't you see your way to cut off ten cents' worth?"

Al said snarlingly, "Goddamn it, Mae. Give 'em the loaf."

The man turned toward Al. "No, we want ta buy ten cents' worth of it. We got it figgered awful close, mister, to get to California."

Mae said resignedly, "You can have this for ten cents."

"That'd be robbin' you, ma'am."

"Go ahead—Al says to take it." She pushed the waxpapered loaf across the counter. The man took a deep leather pouch from his rear pocket, untied the strings, and spread it open. It was heavy with silver and with greasy bills.

"May soun' funny to be so tight," he apologized. "We got a thousan' miles to go, an' we don't know if we'll make it." He dug in the pouch with a forefinger, located a dime, and pinched in for it. When he put it down on the counter he had a penny with it. He was about to drop the penny back into the pouch when his eye fell on the boys frozen before the candy counter. He moved slowly down to them. He pointed in the case at big long sticks of striped peppermint. "Is them penny candy, ma'am?"

Mae moved down and looked in. "Which ones?"

"There, them stripy ones."

The little boys raised their eyes to her face and they stopped breathing; their mouths were partly open, their half-naked bodies were rigid.

"Oh—them. Well, no—them's two for a penny."

"Well, gimme two then, ma'am." He placed the copper cent carefully on the counter. The boys expelled their breath softly. Mae held the big sticks out.

"Take 'em," said the man.

They reached timidly, each took a stick, and they held them down at their sides and did not look at them. But they looked at each other, and their mouth corners smiled rigidly with embarrassment.

"Thank you, ma'am." The man picked up the bread and went out the door, and the little boys marched stiffly behind him, the red-striped sticks held tightly against their legs. They leaped like chipmunks over the front seat and onto the top of the load, and they burrowed back out of sight like chipmunks.

The man got in and started his car, and with a roaring motor and a cloud of blue oily smoke the ancient Nash climbed up on the highway and went on its way to the west.

From inside the restaurant the truck drivers and Mae and Al stared after them.

Big Bill wheeled back. "Them wasn't two-for-a-cent candy," he said.

"What's that to you?" Mae said fiercely.

"Them was a nickel apiece candy," said Bill.

"We got to get goin'," said the other man. "We're droppin' time." They reached in their pockets. Bill put a coin on the counter and the other man looked at it and reached again and put down a coin. They swung around and walked to the door.

"So long," said Bill.

Mae called, "Hey! Wait a minute. You got change."

"You go to hell," said Bill, and the screen door slammed.

Mae watched them get into the great truck, watched it lumber off in low gear, and heard the shift up the whining gears to cruising ratio. "Al ——" she said softly.

He looked up from the hamburger he was patting thin and stacking between waxed papers. "What ya want?"

"Look there." She pointed at the coins beside the cups—two half-dollars. Al walked near and looked, and then he went back to his work.

"Truck drivers," Mae said reverently. . . .

Flies struck the screen with little bumps and droned away. The compressor chugged for a time and then stopped. On 66 the traffic whizzed by, trucks and fine streamlined cars and jalopies; and they went by with a vicious whiz. Mae took down the plates and scraped the pie crusts into a bucket. She found her damp cloth and wiped the counter with circular sweeps. And her eyes were on the highway, where life whizzed by.

Al wiped his hands on his apron. He looked at a paper pinned to the wall over the griddle. Three lines of marks in columns on the paper. Al counted the longest line. He walked along the counter to the cash register, rang "No Sale," and took out a handful of nickels.

"What ya doin'?" Mae asked.

"Number three's ready to pay off," said Al. He went to the third slot machine and played his nickels in, and on the fifth spin of the wheels the three bars came up and the jack pot dumped out into the cup. Al gathered up the big handful of coins and went back of the counter. He dropped them in the drawer and slammed the cash register. Then he went back to his place and crossed out the line of dots. "Number three gets more play'n the others," he said. "Maybe I ought to shift 'em around." He lifted a lid and stirred the slowly simmering stew.

"I wonder what they'll do in California?" said Mae.

"Who?"

"Them folks that was just in."

"Christ knows," said Al.

"S'pose they'll get work?"

"How the hell would I know?" said Al.

She stared eastward along the highway. "Here comes a transport, double. Wonder if they stop? Hope they do." And as the huge truck came heavily down from the highway and parked, Mae seized her cloth and wiped the whole length of the counter. And she took a few swipes at the gleaming coffee urn too, and turned up the bottle-gas under the urn. Al brought out a handful of little turnips and started to peel them. Mae's face was gay when the door opened and the two uniformed truck drivers entered.

"Hi, sister!"

"I won't be a sister to no man," said Mae. They laughed and Mae laughed. "What'll it be, boys?"

"Oh, a cup a Java. What kinda pie ya got?"

"Pineapple cream an' banana cream an' chocolate cream an' apple."

The Grapes of Wrath, 1939

J. FRANK DOBIE

Old Blue

Professor Dobie is the outstanding folklorist of the Southwest, an engaging writer, and a forthright man of wide interests, interesting observations and stimulating opinions.

Always in any group of animals, whether men or beasts, certain individuals emerge. The emergers on the trail were mostly lead steers. Trail men talked about them as they talked about cutting horses back home or sure-footed night horses in last night's run. Now and then a steer became so distinguished that his owner would not let him go with the cattle he led but would keep him for leading others. Old Blue, sometimes called Blue the Bell Ox, was known from the Pecos to the Arkansas, in Colorado as well as in Texas. He knew the trail to Dodge City better than hundreds of cowboys who galloped up its Front Street.

Blue was calved down on the Nueces River, near the Texas coast, in the spring of 1870. His mother may have been wild, but, judging by Blue's nature, she was never "snaky." He was four years old before anybody took sufficient notice of him to give him a name, which came from the color the vaqueros call *moro*, or "mulberry."

At the age of three he was put in a herd of other brush cattle bound for New Mexico. Its route was over the Goodnight-Loving Trail. Above Horsehead Crossing on the Pecos, the Apache Indians swooped down one night, stampeded the cattle, and got away with six hundred. In a sharp brush next day six or seven warriors paid for these cattle with their lives, and there was one more cowboy grave on the lone prairie. The remainder of the herd, something over 1,500 head, went on ten days farther and were sold to John Chisum at his Bosque Redondo ranch. That fall the Apaches were fierce, and one morning a hand found Blue with an arrow in his rump. It was cut out and the wound healed rapidly. Blue had learned the smell of Indians.

The next spring Charlie Goodnight bought Blue in a "string" of five

474

thousand steers from John Chisum, cut them into two herds, and trailed them on northward to the Arkansas River above Pueblo, Colorado. Blue went in the first herd. He was a mature beef now, four years old. He had seen a lot of the world and from the day the herd trailed out he asserted his natural leadership. Every morning he took his place at the point and there he held it. Powerful, sober and steady, he understood the least motion of the point men, and in guiding the herd showed himself worth a dozen extra hands. The cowboys all noted him. One youngster from Oxford named Hughes, son of the author of *Tom Brown's School Days*, wanted to call him Sir Walter Raleigh, but Blue was the name that stuck.

Instead of sending Blue on up to feed Indians at an agency in Wyoming, as he sent so many steers, Goodnight kept him on his Colorado range. Cattle thieves were bad, and, one morning while trailing a little bunch of cattle through the snow, Blue's owner discovered him and a dozen other steers in a picket corral snugly hidden in the middle of a thicket. Near by was a pile of hides. Blue had escaped having his shucked off, and for reasons that a certain cottonwood limb was drawn into—or drawn from—this particular gang of cow thieves never butchered another animal on the Arkansas.

Goodnight had one of his hands break Blue to the yoke. A man driving an ox wagon to California wanted to buy him, but he was not for sale. The Goodnight herd moved down on the Canadian River to winter.

In the summer of '76 the restless Goodnight decided to pull up stakes in Colorado and return to Texas. So Blue led the herd that stocked the first ranch in the vast Texas Panhandle of the Staked Plains. There were 1,600 head of cattle in that first herd, and as they filed down the bluffs, rising nearly a thousand feet above the floor of the Palo Duro Canyon, they must have smelled buffalo. The disassembled wagon and its freight were carried down on mules. Below the pass the canyon opens out ten miles wide, the bluffs on either side making a natural fence. Out of this enclosure Goodnight and his men routed ten thousand buffaloes. Then they blocked up the few trails that led from the plains into the mighty Palo Duro cut, and rode line daily to keep the buffaloes out. The cattle wintered "in clover." Goodnight found a Scotchman, Adair by name, with money. Within ten years their JA brand was showing on the sides of 75,000 cattle and the JA range embraced a million acres of land up and down the waters of the Palo Duro. Meanwhile, other outfits had stocked the whole plains country—and Blue had become the outstanding animal in it.

The outlet for the Palo Duro was Dodge City, two hundred and fifty miles north. It was October 26, 1878, that a herd of 1,000 JA steers headed in that direction to trample down the grass over a route thenceforth known as the Palo Duro-Dodge City Trail. Old Blue was in front.

This trip was different from any other he had made. It was customary to bell the mare leading a horse herd. Away back in the sixties some young men belled an old cow to lead a thousand head of maverick yearlings they had caught on the forks of the Llano River—and after a maverick got used to that bell, he would, if cut off, make haste to get to it. But when Blue's owner decided to bell the leader of a trail herd of steers, he was making an innovation. The leaders were often the wildest old steers of the herd and could never have been managed as Blue was.

His bell was brand new, with green stain and red label fresh upon the brass. The collar was clean and shiny and had the wholesome smell of fresh leather. When Blue got that collar around his neck and heard the ling-ling-ling of his bell, he was as proud as a ranch boy stepping out in his first pair of red-topped boots.

The steers soon learned to follow the sound of Blue's bell. Attached to it was a little strap for tying up the clapper. Before the herd was to be bedded down for the night or halted for grazing during the day, one of the cowboys would pitch a rope over Blue's horns, walk up to him and strap the clapper into silence.

After leading a thousand steers all day, Blue believed in exercising the privileges of individuality. He considered himself always as apart from the masses. He would walk right into camp among the pots and pans and eat pieces of bread, meat, dried apples—anything the cook would give him or the boys could steal from the cook. He became a great pet. Often he was hobbled and left to graze with the saddle horses. Sometimes he was staked out at the end of a long rope. He preferred to bed down away from his inferiors—and he had no peer.

The trail work followed a well-established routine. When it was time to travel after the early morning's grazing, Blue nosed out toward one of the point men to have his bell clapper loosened. Then he would give a toss of the head and a switch of the tail, often throwing in a low chuckling bellow to emphasize his pleasure, and stride north. Some waddie with the voice of a bugle horn would sing-song out the old Texas call, "Ho, cattle, ho, ho, ho, ho," and the big steers would soon be strung into line. Blue must have known the North Star, he coursed so unswervingly. He was always "raring to go," and, unless checked, he was apt to walk too fast.

One evening up in the Indian Nation, just beyond Beaver Creek, Blue came near walking right into an unfenced squatter's field, but the point man veered him around it. The squatter came out of his dugout to sell some of the pumpkins he had grown. The JA foreman bought a few and then ordered his men to bed down "away over yonder."

"No, no," pled the squatter, "bed nigh here. I need cow chips for fuel." Blue was just one among many manufacturers of "prairie coal."

When this pioneer herd from the Palo Duro reached the Cimarron River, they found it on a rampage, but Blue shouldered straight into the waters, and after him strung the thousand JA's. After all were across, six of the cowboys swam back to the south bank. Four of them hitched their ropes to the tongue of the chuck wagon; two of them, one on either side hitched ropes to the stays on the bed. Thus pulling and guying the wagon, they helped the cook's team bring it across. It was time to camp, and Old Blue had worked around the herd and was at the bank to meet them when they emerged.

At the Arkansas River, just south of Dodge City, a cold wind was blowing and the north was black. December was at hand. "Every man saddle and tie up," the foreman ordered. "We'll have hell before daylight." About midnight a storm of sleet and snow hit the herd. Every hand went to it. The steers wanted to drift, but the boys held them like a solid wall.

At daylight there was a yell: "Untie Old Blue's clapper and take the river." The water was frozen out from the bank, but plunging into the icy current, the big steers "made the riffle." When they reached the north bank, they felt like running, and harder and faster they crowded Old Blue. Two thousand horns clacked and four thousand feet roared. The frozen ground fairly shook. But if Blue was gentle, he had the speed of a race horse. Still at the lead of his herd, he headed straight for the twenty-foot gate that opened into the big shipping pens. With one bunch of cowboys to cut, another to count, and a third to run the cattle up the chute into the cars, they were loaded long before noon and on their way to Chicago—all but Old Blue.

He had proved himself far too valuable to be sold for steaks. He stayed with the *remuda* and ate hay while the cowboys warmed their stomachs at a bar and their feet on the floor of a dance hall. After a day and a night of celebration, they had spent themselves empty and were ready to leave. So at Wright & Beverley's store next morning the wagon was loaded with chuck and sacks of shelled corn. The grains in those sacks were colored red, white and blue, and on the road home Blue learned to eat corn; in fact, he loved it, and the colored grains seemed to add to his spirits.

The weather was freezing cold, and as the outfit headed southward, men and horses alike felt like making time. Blue was ready to travel also. He had the stride of seven-league boots and could walk up with any horse. Sometimes the thirty-miles-a-day clip made him trot, but he never tired or lagged. Down on Wolf Creek one night a hungry band of Kiowas rode into camp and, pointing at the big steer, demanded "wohaw" (beef), but Chief Lone Wolf and all his warriors could not have taken Blue away from those Palo Duro cowpunchers.

After this trip up the trail as bell ox, Blue's occupation for life was settled, but besides leading herds to Dodge City, he was put to various uses. When the chuck wagon was out in the spring and summer, Blue would generally follow it, taking choice food the boys would hand him. If an outlaw steer was roped in the cedar brakes and had to be led in, he was necked to Old Blue, the pair was turned loose, and, straight as a crow flies, the bell ox would bring him to camp.

If a wild herd of cattle was to be penned, Blue was put with them to show the way in. Wild cattle upon approaching a pen often circle and try to break away; but the wild ones could not break ahead of Blue, and his course was right into the gate. Upon entering a pen, range cattle will rush for the opposite side, pushing, hooking, milling. Blue never got into such jams. As soon as he had brought the lead cattle inside the pen, he would step aside and impatiently wait beside the gate until the last animal entered; then he would bolt out.

Once John Taylor and another cowboy took him up on the Canadian River to bring back a pair of young buffaloes. They necked the two to him, both on one side, and, of course, they were contrariness personified. "Old Blue was the maddest steer a man ever saw." He shook his head and bellowed, worked around until he had one of the green buffaloes on each side of himself, and then struck a course. When he wanted to go to water with them, he went; when he wanted to stop and graze, he grazed. He knew every camping place on the route, and when he got to one would stop, whether the men with him wanted to stop or not, and he would not move until his free will motivated him. He tamed the buffaloes thoroughly and in good time brought them into the Palo Duro, where they were turned loose to help make the famous Goodnight herd.

For eight years Old Blue kept at his occupation of leading herds. Some years he went up to Dodge City twice. The horns and legs of the steers he led were growing shorter and shorter, and often the cowboys had to shoe the fine, big short-horns that the JA's were coming to raise, but never once did Blue limp. His hoofs were as hard and bright as polished steel. All told, ten thousand head or more of the JA cattle followed Blue and his bell into the shipping pens of the "Cowboy Capital."

The older he grew, the more philosophical be became. It sometimes made a Spanish cow horse almost laugh, they say, to see him step aside in a night stampede and go to bawling. No slipping of horns, knocking down of hips and running until his tongue lolled out and his rump was chafed green from entrail-emptying for him. "To step aside is human," and Blue was mighty human when a stampede started. If the boys could get the stampeders to milling, Old Blue's bawl had a powerful effect in quieting them. At the head of a herd he never "buggered" when a jack rabbit suddenly jumped up from under a sagebush at his nose, or something like that happened, and thus day and night he was a steadying influence.

When he was twenty years old, he died. For a long time his horns remained in the office of JA headquarters, over the door leading into the vault. They may be seen today in the fine little museum maintained by the Panhandle-Plains Historical Society and the West Texas Teachers College at Canyon. Like his trail-breaking owner, Old Blue of the Texas Longhorns belongs to history.

The Longhorns, 1941

478

WALTER VAN TILBURG CLARK

The Buck in the Hills

> *Mr. Clark first became prominent on the literary scene when his novel* The Ox-Bow Incident *was acclaimed the finest fictional interpretation of the struggle for justice on the American frontier— a theme hacked to pieces by lesser writers.*

I left the peak about two o'clock, drank the very cold shale-tasting water coming from under last winter's snow in the notch, went on down, and then south through the marshy meadow, already in shadow from the col, the grass yellowing and the sod stiffening from the fall nights, so that I could walk straight across and feel only the first solidity and then a slight give which didn't spring back. It was strange in the meadows, walking in the shadow, but with the sky still bright blue, as in the middle of the afternoon, and the sunlight, when I stopped to look back at the peak, just beginning to look late. It was chilly in the shadow, too, but I didn't hurry. The peak was sacred to me, the climb was pilgrimage, and five years is a long time. I had been very happy all day, climbing with the sun on my neck and shoulders, and I was very lonely and happy now. I took my time, and looked at everything, and remembered a lot, and would have yodeled sometimes, but the quiet was better.

I climbed over the big rock barrier, which a million winters had cracked into terraces, saw the dry, shriveled clumps of leaves and single dead stems in the cracks, and remembered times I had come up in the summer, which is spring at that height, and seen it pouring with green, like cascades, and lighted by flowers. I remembered the dark girl who knew all the flowers, and who, when I bet her she couldn't find more than thirty kinds, found more than fifty, and remembered how we had eaten our pocket lunch dry, in a niche on the east side of the peak, out of the strong wind we could hear among the rocks and more heavily in the notch below. We couldn't see it then, but the image was new in our minds of the big basin to the west, with its rolling of dark-green to pale-blue heavily timbered hills, and the wide, dark-blue flat of Tahoe, rough with wind and jointed exactly into all the bays and coves, and the little lakes at different heights around it, also fitted like single pieces into a relief puzzle. In front of us, way down, squared with fields and pencilled by the straight roads, was the chain of ranching valleys, and then the lesser, burned mountains rolling to the east, and in the far northeast just a sky-colored sliver of Pyramid Lake showing through the last pass. I remembered that the clouds that day had gone all around the horizon in a narrow band, flat underneath, all at exactly the same level, with clear

479

sky between them and the mountains, and with their tops standing up in little, firm bosses and domes, and not a single cloud in the field of sky above them, so that we sat high up in the center of a great circle of distant cloud. This seemed to mean something, and gave our thoughts, and the big arch of the world we looked at, a different quality that made us uneasy but happy, too, the way I was now.

I went on through the sparse trees and the rocks over two ridges, and could see from them, and from the little valley between, the rock castle at the end of the high col to the west, where I had eaten at noon another time, when I was alone, and then stayed for two hours to watch a hawk using the wind over the hollow to the west, feeling myself lift splendidly when he swooped up towards me on the current of the col, and then balanced and turned above.

I was feeling like that when I got back to the little grassy lake where I'd left my pack. The pack was still there all right, under the bench nailed between two of the three trees on the hump at the farther side. Beyond the three trees, which were stunted and twisted by wind, I could see the wall of the col, very dark now, with a thin gold sky above it. Besides the bench, there was a pine-bough bed and a rock fireplace in the shelter of the trees. I hadn't made them, just found them there, but in the dusk the place gave me the hawk lift again. I had the night here alone, and another day in the mountains. That was a lot. And I had already stacked my firewood; brought it down that morning from the east slope.

I went around to the camp side and stood looking at the lake, thinking about swimming before I made a fire and ate. It was cold, and the water would be cold too. The lake was really just a pool of snow water, with no outlet, and no regular inflow, shallow enough so the dead grasses showed up through the edges. But I like that kind of clean, cold feeling, and it had been warm climbing in the middle of the day. I peeled off, and stood liking the cold on my body, and the frozen, pebbly earth under my feet, and then, when I went nearer the edge, the wiry grass. It was very still in the valley, and the water reflected, exactly and without break, the mountains and the last of that thin, yellow light. I got that lift again. This time I would take it out. I ran splashing till I was thigh-deep, and then rolled under. The water was even colder than I had expected, and hardened my whole body at once. For a minute or two I swam rapidly in circles in the small center that was deep enough. Then I was all right, and could roll easily, and even float looking up. The first stars were showing above the ridge in the east. I let go a couple of bars of high, operatic sounding something. It came back at me from under the col, sounding much better, sweet and clear and high. God, I was happy. This was the way I liked it, alone, and clean cold, and a lot of time ahead. I rolled over to dive and start one more fast turn, when I heard a yodel that wasn't an echo.

480

I stood up, feeling the cold rim of the water around my chest, and even in the dusk could see the shape of the man coming over the hump and down towards the lake. When he was part way down, I could tell by the walk, a little pigeon-toed and easy, giving at the knees all the time, that it was Tom Williams. He had his pack on, and his rifle over one shoulder, with a thumb in the sling, the way Tom always carried it. The remainder of ecstasy went out of me. I'd rather have Tom than almost anyone I know for outside company, but I didn't want anybody now. And Tom meant Chet McKenny, and I didn't want Chet now or any other time. Chet was a big-boned, tall Scotchman, probably ten years older than either Tom or me, with grey in his stiff hair. He had a kind of stubborn originality that wouldn't use a joke somebody else had told, but he couldn't make a good one; so he was laughing all the time over bad jokes of his own. But that wasn't what I disliked, though it got tiresome. What I didn't like about McKenny was deeper than stupidity. You saw it when you saw that his eyes were still watching you when he laughed; you were always on guard against McKenny.

The three of us had come up in Tom's car, and they'd left me at the summit meadows. They were going on over to the flat to start a deer hunt. I was supposed to have today and tomorrow and then be back out at the meadows by sunset to wait for them.

Tom came down to where I'd dropped my clothes, and unslung his rifle and pack and put them down.

"Cold?" he asked. He didn't have to speak loudly.

"Plenty," I said.

I kept looking for Chet to come over the rise too.

Tom peeled off and came in, but slowly, and then just lying out and letting himself sink under. He came up slowly, too, as if the water weren't cold at all, and just stood there, not even rubbing himself. There was something wrong.

"Where's Chet?" I asked. It would even be pleasant, with a fire after supper, to have Tom to talk to, if he was alone.

"That bastard," Tom said. Then he let himself down into the water again, and came up a few feet farther off, his thin, blond hair streaming down and the springy, blond mat on his big chest holding a few drops.

"He won't be here, anyway," he said; "so you don't have to worry."

He began to swim hard, and I took another turn, to get the blood stirring again. Then we walked up out of the water. Tom didn't say anything more, and I didn't either. I knew it would come. Tom doesn't often talk much, except about engines, but this was different. It was working in him, hard. He went up to his pack, and I could see the muscles in his heavy white shoulders working while he hunted in it. He got out a towel and threw it to me. Then he went back down to the water, and I saw he had a cake of soap in his hand. But he didn't bathe. I stood there wiping off and watching him, and he just bent over in the shallows and washed his hands. He washed them hard, three or four times, rinsing them between. That was queer for Tom. He was an auto mechanic, ran a little shop of his own, and he'd long ago given up hoping to have his hands really clean. Often on trips like this he'd go two or three days without washing them at all.

He still didn't say anything, though, when he came up; just took the towel from me and began to wipe himself slowly.

It felt good to be in the warm flannel shirt and cords again, and shod heavily. Maybe that's even the best feeling, the cold that makes you feel thin and single, with no waste matter, but beginning to get warm. I lit a cigarette with stiff fingers, and saw against the match flame how dark it was getting. The cigarette tasted very good too. I was all set to be happy again, if Tom was right.

Tom didn't talk while he was dressing, or while we went up to the camp, or while he was cooking and watching the coffee and I was putting some new boughs and the sleeping bags on the bed. The bed was a good one, wide enough for three, and in a pit a foot deep. I went down to the lake to get two cans of beer out of the water. They're a lot of weight to carry in a pack, and I'd thought maybe I was pampering myself when I'd put them in, one for each evening. Now I was glad I'd brought them. When I came back up with them, Tom was just letting the things cook, and standing away from the fire, looking at the stars over the valley and in the little lake.

"This is a swell place," he said in an easier voice. "Gee, I haven't been in here for years. I'd forgot what a swell place it was."

Then I knew it was going to be all right, once he got around to telling me, and I had to sing a little while I put the beers between roots and took the eggs and beans off the fire; not loudly, but just about like the crackling of the fire.

When he came back and sat down on the bench, the light on his face with its fine mouth and big, broken nose and blue eyes, and its hard weather lines, he looked at me because I was singing, and I could see he was still thinking, but not feeling the same way about it.

When we'd started to eat, I asked, "How did the hunting go?"

"Don't you worry," Tom said. "I didn't get anything. I didn't even get a shot. I didn't see a thing."

He looked closed up again, as he had when he came into the water. He finished his beans, staring into the fire. Then he said suddenly, "That McKenny is a first-rate bastard."

"What's he done now?" I asked.

Tom looked right at me for a moment, as if he'd start, but then he said, "Oh, hell, let it go."

He got up and went down to the edge of the lake slowly, and after a moment I saw his match flare, and then, every now and then, the fire point of his cigarette moving.

482

I'd never seen Tom let anything eat on him like that before. He made up his mind very hard about what was wrong and what was right, especially about people, but he did it carefully, and he was usually gentle about it, even afterwards. It was the first time I'd heard him speak out like that. Whatever happened, it must have been pretty bad.

Well, I was sure now that McKenny wasn't coming. I stopped thinking about it, put more wood on the fire, and lay on my back where the light wouldn't be in my eyes. Then I could see the silhouette of the col, where it walled out the stars, and the big peak glimmering in the starlight in the north. The size of the place, and the cold quiet, came back to me, and I was happy again.

I'd forgotten about Chet when Tom came back up and sat down on the bench. He stared at the ground for a moment. Then he looked across at me.

"You always thought so, didn't you?"

"Thought what?"

"That Chet McKenny was a first-rate bastard?"

I didn't like to say so.

"All right," Tom said. "I guess he is, at that."

He didn't say anything more; so I sat up.

"Have a beer?"

"No, thanks."

I had to get him started.

"Did Chet get anything?" I asked.

Tom looked at me hard.

"Yeah, he got one, all right, a good big buck, better than two-twenty, I'd guess. Ten points." He looked down.

Then he looked up again, and said suddenly, and loudly for that place, "You know what that bastard did? He—" but stopped.

"He what?"

"No," Tom said. "I'll tell you the way it was. Maybe I'm wrong.

"I worked down south, towards the lake meadows. I didn't see a thing all day; not even a doe; not even a fresh track or droppings. I figured it had been worked over and got disgusted and went back to the flat in the afternoon to get some sleep. I was washing up at the brook, and when I stood up and turned around, there was this big buck, a mule, on the edge of the trees across the flat. Even from there I could tell he was a big one, and I cussed, because there was my rifle up against a tree thirty yards from me, and the buck had spotted me. You know, his head was up and right at me, and those big ears up too. He was trying the wind. I figured if I moved he'd be back in those trees before I could take a step. So I held it. After a while he let his head down, way low, and began to go along the edge of the flat towards the pass. Then I saw there was something the matter with him. He wasn't using his left front leg; just bucking along on the other one, in little jumps. He was tired out, too, stopping every few jumps and taking the wind again, and then letting his head drop that way, like he couldn't hold it up. I figured somebody'd made a bad shot. I started for the gun. He saw me then, but he was so far gone he didn't even care, just kept hopping and resting. Then I didn't know whether I wanted him or not. Only I might as well, if his leg was really busted.

"I was standing there on the edge of the flat, wondering, when I heard this yell. It was Mac, coming down through the trees. He yelled at me to head the buck off. Your lousy shot then, I thought.

"When I went right out at the buck, it tried to hurry. I yelled at Mac did he want me to finish it, and he yelled at me hell no, it was his buck. The buck stood there with his head up when we yelled; he didn't try to do anything.

"I don't know. It made me mad. But it was Mac's buck. I started to work around so as not to hurry it any more than I had to. Mac was working along in the timber to get right above him. When I got around in front, we worked in closer, and then the buck saw us both, and just stopped and stood there. He was shivering all over, and didn't have any fight left in him. I could see now that he'd been hit in the leg, right up against the body. The blood was mostly dried on black, but there was a little fresh blood coming out all the time too. The bad leg was all banged up from being dragged on things, too, and he was soaked with sweat on the hindquarters and under the throat, and making cotton at the muzzle."

Tom stopped.

Then he said, "It's funny the way they look at you like that. I don't know. There wasn't anything, no fight, no panic, no hope, no nothing. He just looked at you. But you couldn't move. They got such big eyes. I don't know."

Tom kicked at a stone with his boot.

"Well, anyway, I couldn't move. But Mac could. He came up close behind. He had his cap on the back of his head and he was grinning. He said wasn't it a nice one. Ten points, he said.

"When he talked, the buck got going again, that same way. It was headed across the meadow towards the camp. I got ready to finish it, but Mac yelled at me to mind my own damn business and let it go or he'd damn well lather hell out of me. You know the way he does, grinning, but mad as the devil. I asked him what he thought he was doing, but he said that was his business, and to mind my own.

"The buck was going so slow you could pass it walking; had to wait on it. And it stopped two or three times. Mac could have killed it a long time before it got to the flat; I was sure of that. I began to think he wanted to take it in alive, or something. But it wasn't that."

Tom stopped talking and sat there.

"No?" I said.

"No," Tom said. "When the buck stopped near where we'd had the fire, Mac said that was good enough, like he was pleased, and unslung his rifle and took mine, too, and stood them up against a tree. Then he told me to hold the buck's head."

After a moment Tom went on again.

"I don't know why I did it. I just did. I never felt that way before. I guess I thought he was going to operate, as near as I thought anything. He just said to hold it, and I did, like I was in a daze. The buck kind of backed a little, and then, when I had hold of his antlers, he stood still; didn't make a move. Holding onto the antlers, I could feel him shivering all over, you know, like putting your hand on a telephone pole. Mac had his skinning knife out.

" 'Hold his head up,' he said.

"He was kind of leaning over and looking at the bullet hole when he said it, and I did.

"Then all of a sudden he leaned down on the buck's neck with one hand, and slit its throat wide open with the knife in the other. Leaning on it that way, he put all his weight on the buck's one leg, and the buck fell over front, and I didn't get out of the way fast enough. It knocked me onto my knees, too, and the blood came out all over my hands and arms. It kept coming, in big spurts; there was an awful lot of it. I don't know."

Tom got out a cigarette and lit it. I didn't have anything to say. The story made a difference, though, as if it were a lot darker all at once, and we were farther away from other people than before, and there were things alive in the rocks, watching us. I noticed there was a wind coming up too, but didn't think about it, just heard it in the trees as if it had been going all the time.

"It's funny," Tom said. "When the buck got pushed down, it stretched way out; you know. Its muzzle was right in my face, and it blew. It made a little spray of blood, but it had a sweet smelling breath, you know, like a cow's. And then all that blood came out, hot."

Finally, he asked me, "You know what Mac said?"

"No."

"Well, he laughed like hell when the buck pushed me over, and then he said, 'I never take more than one shot,' and then he laughed again.

"I was mad enough, I guess. I told him it was a hell of a shot, and he said two inches to the right would of killed him, and pointed at the hole, and laughed again and said hell, it was perfect. The bullet had busted the joint all to pieces. There were splinters sticking out where they'd worked through."

I was looking at Tom now.

"You mean he meant to?" I asked.

"That's right," Tom said. "He thought he was real clever. He boasted about it. Said he'd spotted the buck way up in that little meadow under the castle rocks; what's its name? The buck was on the north edge of the meadow, and up wind of him, what wind there was. He said he figured it all out, that it was eight miles back to camp, and the buck was a big one. He couldn't see carrying it all that way, so he just laid down there on the edge of the timber, to make his shot good, and waited till the buck was broadside to him, and then busted that foreleg. Said he'd never made a better shot, that it was a hundred and fifty yards if it was an inch, and uphill. He was set up about that shot."

"Well," I said letting out my breath.

"Yes," Tom said.

"He told me all about how he drove it, too," he said angrily. "How it kept trying to run at first, and falling over so he had to laugh, and then how it tried to turn on him, but couldn't stand it when he got close, and what a hell of a time he had driving it out of a couple of manzanita thickets where it tried to hole up. Then he figured that if he stayed off it, it would keep going steadier, and it did.

"So, I guess you were right," Tom said, making it a question.

"I didn't think he was that bad," I said. "You have to keep it up a long time to do a thing like that."

"He was still going strong," Tom said. "Only excited and talking a lot. "Like I am now," he added.

I didn't want to ask. I figured anything he'd done wasn't enough. But I still looked at Tom.

"No," he said. "You don't have to worry. I didn't touch him.

"I don't know," he said doubtfully. "I wanted you to know the way it was, first."

"He had it coming to him," I said. But I was scared, so I nearly laughed when Tom told me.

"I told him if he'd been saving himself so careful, he could damned well carry his buck home, and I left him there."

"I'd like to have seen his face," I said.

"I didn't even look at him," Tom said. "I just put my things into the car and got out.

"He knew better than to say anything, too."

"Well," I said finally, "I wouldn't say you were too hard on him."

"No," Tom said. "But he'll try to bring that buck out."

"Sure," I agreed, "he wouldn't let it go if it was killing him."

Tom heeled his cigarette out carefully and said, "You wouldn't care to go up the mountain again tomorrow, would you?"

"Sure I would," I told him. "Now *you* quit worrying. He had it coming to him."

Tom said he was going to take another swim, and we undressed by the fire, and went down together, and came back up wet. I felt very cold then, and the wind was stronger. But we piled more wood onto the fire, so it threw shadows of the three trees way up the hump, and when we'd dried off it felt so good we didn't get dressed, but just put on our shorts and stayed close to the fire.

"I'll have that beer now," Tom said. He was cheerful.

In the morning the wind was down, but it was snowing. We couldn't even see the mountain. I felt worse about the buck than I had when Tom told me, and kept thinking about it. We packed up and went back down trail, single file and not talking. Snow makes a hush that's even harder to talk in than the clear silence. There was something listening behind each tree and rock we passed, and something waiting among the taller trees down slope, blue through the falling snow. They wouldn't stop us, but they didn't like us, either. The snow was their ally.

The Watchful Gods, 1943